MicroC/OS-II

The Real-Time Kernel

Second Edition

Jean J. Labrosse

CMP **Books**

San Francisco, CA • New York, NY • Lawrence, KS

Published by CMP Books
an imprint of CMP Media LLC
Main office: 600 Harrison Street, San Francisco, CA 94107 USA
Tel: 415-947-6615; fax: 415-947-6015
Editorial office: 1601 West 23rd Street, Suite 200, Lawrence, KS 66046 USA
www.cmpbooks.com
email: books@cmp.com

Acquisition editor:	Robert Ward
Managing editor:	Michelle O'Neal
Copyeditor:	Catherine Janzen
Production and layout:	Justin Fulmer and Michelle O'Neal
Cover art design:	Robert Ward

Distributed in the U.S. by:
Publishers Group West
1700 Fourth Street
Berkeley, California 94710
1-800-788-3123

Distributed in Canada by:
Jaguar Book Group
100 Armstrong Avenue
Georgetown, Ontario M6K 3E7 Canada
905-877-4483

For individual orders and for information on special discounts for quantity orders, please contact:
CMP Books Distribution Center, 6600 Silacci Way, Gilroy, CA 95020
Tel: 1-800-500-6875 or 408-848-3854; fax: 408-848-5784
email: cmp@rushorder.com; Web: www.cmpbooks.com

Printed in the United States of America
06 07 08 09 10 2002 12 11 10 9 8 7

ISBN-13: 978-1-57820-103-7   ISBN-10: 1-57820-103-9

CMP**Books**

To my loving and caring wife, Manon, and to our two lovely children, James and Sabrina.

Table of Contents

Preface

Ten years ago (1992), I wrote my first book called, *μC/OS, The Real-Time Kernel*. Towards the end of 1998, it was replaced by *MicroC/OS-II, The Real-Time Kernel*. The word *Micro* now replaces the Greek letter *μ* on the book cover because bookstores didn't know how to file μC/OS properly. However, for all intents and purposes, MicroC/OS and μC/OS are synonymous, and, in this book, I mostly use μC/OS-II. This is the second edition of μC/OS-II but, in a way, the third edition of the μC/OS series.

Meets the Requirements of Safety-Critical Systems

In July of 2000, μC/OS-II was certified in an avionics product by the Federal Aviation Administration (FAA) for use in commercial aircraft by meeting the demanding requirements of the RTCA DO-178B standard for software used in avionics equipment. In order to meet the requirements of this standard, it must be possible to demonstrate through documentation and testing that the software is both robust and safe. This issue is particularly important for an operating system as it demonstrates that it has the proven quality to be usable in any application. Every feature, function, and line of code of μC/OS-II has been examined and tested to demonstrate that it is safe and robust enough to be used in safety-critical systems where human life is on the line.

What's New in this Edition?

This book has been completely revised since the first edition of *MicroC/OS-II, The Real-Time Kernel*.

More Chapters

The previous edition contained 12 chapters while this edition has 18. I decided to break the old Chapter 6 (Intertask Communications & Synchronization) into six chapters. I now dedicate a whole chapter to event control blocks (ECBs), one for semaphores, one for mutual exclusion semaphores, one for event flags, one for message mailboxes, and finally, one for message queues.

The previous edition contained a port for the Intel 80x86 family of processors, but this port only handled context switching of integer registers. I added a chapter that describes a port that also saves and restores floating-point registers, which are common to the 80486 and Pentium processors.

I also added a chapter that describes the services I use from a PC.

Finally, I added two appendices: Coding Conventions and a μC/OS-II Quick Reference.

Removed Chapters

I decided to remove the chapter on porting μC/OS to μC/OS-II because very few people are still using μC/OS because μC/OS-II offers so much more.

I also removed the appendix on HPLISTC because most good code editors allow you to neatly print source listings.

Removed Code Listings

I decided to remove the code listings that were found in Appendices A, B, and C. I have three reasons for removing the listings. First, this edition contains over 150 pages of new material. If I were to leave the listings in the appendices, this book would exceed 750 pages and would be a monster to carry around (it's already big as it is). The second reason is that the code comes on the companion CD, and it's better to refer to the code using a computer anyway. Also, the code is already described in the book, so the appendices were a duplication of the code. Finally, like any piece of software, μC/OS-II is subject to changes and upgrades. Because of this, the listings in the appendices become obsolete over time and thus have little value.

Additional Services

The code for μC/OS-II is basically the same as the previous edition, except for the addition of new services. The previous edition contained the following services:

- Time management
- Binary and counting semaphores
- Message mailboxes
- Message queues
- Fixed-sized memory block manager

This new edition adds:

- Mutual exclusion semaphores (mutexes)
- Event flags

More Examples

In some of the chapters, I added examples on how you can use the services described.

New Structure

I rearranged the structure of the book to make it much more usable. I found that the way the code was described was cumbersome, and I decided to completely redo it. You should notice that when I reference a specific element in a figure, I use the letter *F* followed by the figure number. The number in parenthese following the figure number represents a specific element in the figure to which I am trying to bring your attention. **F1.2(3)** thus means "please look at the item numbered "**3**" in **F**igure **1.2**. I used this scheme in the previous edition, but this time I decided to place these reference markers in the margin instead of burying them in the text. I find that it's a lot easier to follow the code or figure using this scheme and I hope you do too.

µC/OS-II Goals

My most important goal is to demystify real-time kernel internals. By understanding how a kernel works, you are in a better position to determine whether you need a kernel for your own products. Most of the concepts presented in this book are applicable to a large number of commercial kernels. My next most important goal is to provide you with a quality product that you can potentially use in your own products. µC/OS-II is not freeware nor is it open source code. If you use µC/OS-II in a commercial product, you need to license its use (see Appendix B, "Licensing Policy for µC/OS-II").

Intended Audience

This book is intended for embedded system programmers, consultants, and students interested in real-time operating systems. µC/OS-II is a high performance, deterministic, real-time kernel and can be (and has been) used in commercial embedded products.

Instead of writing your own kernel, you should consider µC/OS-II. You will find, as I did, that writing a kernel is not as easy as it first looks.

I'm assuming that you know C and have a minimum knowledge of assembly language. You should also understand microprocessor architectures.

What You Need to Use µC/OS-II

The code supplied with this book assumes that you are using an IBM-PC/AT or compatible (80386 minimum) computer running under DOS 4.x or higher. The code was compiled with the Borland C++ v4.51. You should have about 10 MB of free disk space on your hard drive. I actually compiled and executed the sample code provided in this book on a 300 MHz Pentium II computer running Microsoft's Windows 2000. I have successfully compiled and run the code on Windows 95, 98, and NT-based machines.

To use µC/OS-II on a different target processor (other than a PC), you need to either port µC/OS-II to that processor yourself or obtain such a port from the official µC/OS-II Web site at http://www.uCOS-II.com.. You also need appropriate software development tools, such as an ANSI C compiler, an assembler, linker/locator, and some way of debugging your application.

The µC/OS Story

Many years ago, I designed a product based on an Intel 80C188 at Dynalco Controls, and I needed a real-time kernel. I had been using a well-known kernel (I'll call it kernel A) in my work for a previous employer, but it was too expensive for the application I was designing. I found a lower-cost kernel ($1,000 at the time) (I'll call it kernel B) and started the design. I spent about two months trying to get a couple of very simple tasks to run. I was calling the vendor almost on a daily basis for help to make it work. The vendor claimed that kernel B was written in C (the language); however, I had to initialize every single object using assembly language code. Although the vendor was very patient, I decided that I had had enough. The product was falling behind schedule, and I really didn't want to spend my time debugging this low-cost kernel. It turns out that I was one of the vendor's first customers, and the kernel really was not fully tested and debugged.

To get back on track, I decided to go back and use kernel A. The cost was about $5,000 for five development seats, and I had to pay a per-usage fee of about $200 for each unit that was shipped. This was a lot of money at the time, but it bought some peace of mind. I got the kernel up and running in about two days. Three months into the project, one of my engineers discovered what looked like a bug in the kernel. I sent the code to the vendor, and, sure enough, the bug was confirmed as being in the kernel. The vendor provided a 90-day warranty but that had expired, so, in order to get support, I had to pay an additional $500 per year for maintenance. I argued with the salesperson for a few months that they should fix the bug because I was actually doing them a favor. They wouldn't budge. Finally, I gave in and bought the maintenance contract, and the vendor fixed the bug six months later. Yes, six months later! I was furious and, most importantly, late delivering the product. In all, it took close to a year to get the product to work reliably with kernel A. I must admit, however, that I have had no problems with it since.

As this was going on, I naively thought that it couldn't be that difficult to write a kernel. All it needs to do is save and restore processor registers. That's when I decided to write my own kernel (part time, nights and weekends). It took me about a year to get the kernel to work as well, and, in some ways better, than kernel A. I didn't want to start a company and sell it because there were already about 50 kernels out there, so why have another one?

Then I thought of writing a paper for a magazine. First, I went to *C User's Journal* (CUJ) because the kernel was written in C. I had heard CUJ was offering $100 per published page when other magazines were only paying $75 per page. My paper had 70 or so pages, so that would be nice compensation for all the time I spent working on my kernel. Unfortunately, the article was rejected for two reasons. First, the article was too long, and the magazine didn't want to publish a series. Second, they didn't want "another kernel article."

I decided to turn to *Embedded Systems Programming* (ESP) magazine because my kernel was designed for embedded systems. I contacted the editor of ESP (Mr. Tyler Sperry) and told him that I had a kernel I wanted to publish in his magazine. I got the same response from Tyler that I did from CUJ: "Not another kernel article?" I told him that this kernel was different — it was preemptive, it was comparable to many commercial kernels, and the source code could be posted on the ESP BBS (bulletin board system). I was calling Tyler two or three times a week, basically begging him to publish my article. He finally gave in, probably because he was tired of my calls. My article was edited down from 70 pages to about 30 pages and was published in two consecutive months (May and June 1992). The article was probably the most popular article in 1992. ESP had over 500 downloads of the code from the BBS in the first month. Tyler might have feared for his life because kernel vendors were upset that he published a kernel in his magazine. I guess that these vendors must have recognized the quality and capabilities of μC/OS (called μCOS then). The article was really the first that exposed the internal workings of a real-time kernel, so some of the secrets were out.

About the time the article came out in ESP, I got a call from Dr. Bernard (Berney) Williams at CMP Books, CMP Media LLC (publisher of CUJ), six months after the initial contact with CUJ. He left a message with my wife and told her that he was interested in the article. I called him back and said, "Don't you think you are a little bit late with this? The article is being published in ESP." Berney said, "No, No, you don't understand. Because the article is so long, I want to make a book out of it." Initially, Berney simply wanted to publish what I had (as is), so the book would only have 80 pages or so. I told him that if I was going to write a book, I wanted to do it right. I then spent about six months adding content to what is now known as the first edition. In all, the book was published at about 250 pages. I changed the name from µCOS to µC/OS because ESP readers had been calling it "mucus," which didn't sound very healthy. Come to think of it, maybe it was a kernel vendor that first came up with the name. Anyway, *µC/OS, The Real-Time Kernel* was born. Sales were somewhat slow to start. Berney and I had projected about 4,000 to 5,000 copies would be sold in the life of the book, but at the rate it was selling, I thought we'd be lucky if it sold 2,000 copies. Berney insisted that these things take time to get known, so he continued advertising in CUJ for about a year.

A month or so before the book came out, I went to my first Embedded Systems Conference (ESC) in Santa Clara, California (September 1992). I met Tyler Sperry for the first time, and I showed him a copy of the first draft of my book. He very quickly glanced at it and asked if I would like to speak at the next Embedded Systems Conference in Atlanta. Not knowing any better, I said I would and asked him what I should talk about. He suggested "Using Small Real-Time Kernels." On the trip back from California, I was thinking, "What did I get myself into? I've never spoken in front of a bunch of people before. What if I make a fool of myself? What if what I speak about is common knowledge? People pay good money to attend this conference." For the next six months, I prepared my lecture. At the conference, I had more than 70 attendees. In the first twenty minutes, I must have lost one pound of sweat. After my lecture, about 15 people or so came up to me to say that they were very pleased with the lecture and liked my book. I was invited back to the conference but could not attend the one in Santa Clara that year (1993) because my wife was due to have our second child, Sabrina. I was able to attend the next conference in Boston (1994), and I have been a regular speaker at ESC ever since. For the past several years, I've been on the conference Advisory Committee. I now do at least three lectures at every conference and each has attendance between 100 and 300 people. My lectures are almost always ranked among the top 10% at the conference.

To date, well over 25,000 copies of my µC/OS and µC/OS-II books have been sold around the world. I have received and answered thousands of e-mails from over 44 countries. I still try to answer every single one. I believe that if you take the time to write me, I owe you a response. In 1995, *µC/OS, The Real-Time Kernel* was translated into Japanese and published in Japan in a magazine called *Interface*. In 2001, µC/OS-II was translated into Chinese. A Korean translation came out in early 2002. A Japanese translation of µC/OS-II is in the works and should be available in 2002.

µC/OS and µC/OS-II have been ported to over 40 different processor architectures, and the number of ports is increasing. You should consult the µC/OS-II Web site at `http://www.uCOS-II.com` to see if the processor you intend to use is available.

In 1994, I decided to write a second book: *Embedded Systems Building Blocks, Complete and Ready-to-Use Modules in C* (ESBB). A second edition of ESBB was published in 2000. For some reason, ESBB has not been as popular as µC/OS, although it contains a lot of valuable information not found anywhere else. I always thought that it would be an ideal book for people just starting in the embedded world.

In 1998, I opened the official µC/OS Web site `http://www.uCOS-II.com`. I intend this site to contain ports, application notes, links, answers to frequently asked questions (FAQs), upgrades for µC/OS-II, and more. All I need is time!

In 2001, I started a news group to allow users to share information and their experiences with µC/OS-II.

Back in 1992, I never imagined that writing an article would change my life as it has. I met a lot of very interesting people and made a number of good friends in the process.

Thanks for choosing this book, and I hope you enjoy it!

Acknowledgments

First and foremost, I would like to thank my wife for her support, encouragement, understanding, and especially patience. Once again, I underestimated the amount of work for this edition — it was supposed to take just a few weeks and be out by January 2002. I would also like to thank my children, James (age 11) and Sabrina (age 8), for putting up with the long hours I had to spend in front of the computer.

A very special thanks to Mr. Gino Vannelli for creating such wonderful music. As far as I'm concerned, Gino redefines the word "perfection." Thanks, Gino, for being with me (in music) for almost 30 years.

I would also like to thank all the fine people at CMP Books for their help in making this book a reality and for putting up with my insistence on having things done my way.

Finally, I would like to thank all the people who have purchased my *μC/OS*, *μC/OS-II*, and *Embedded Systems Building Blocks* books over the years.

Introduction

This book describes the design and implementation of μC/OS-II (pronounced "Micro C O S 2"), which stands for *Micro-Controller Operating System, Version 2*.

μC/OS-II is a completely portable, ROMable, scalable, preemptive, real-time, multitasking kernel. μC/OS-II is written in ANSI C and contains a small portion of assembly language code to adapt it to different processor architectures. To date, μC/OS-II has been ported to over 40 different processor architectures, ranging from 8- to 64-bit CPUs.

μC/OS-II is based on *μC/OS, The Real-Time Kernel* that was first published in 1992. Thousands of people around the world are using μC/OS and μC/OS-II in all kinds of applications, such as cameras, avionics, high-end audio equipment, medical instruments, musical instruments, engine controls, network adapters, highway telephone call boxes, ATM machines, industrial robots, and more. Numerous colleges and universities have also used μC/OS and μC/OS-II to teach students about real-time systems.

μC/OS-II is upward compatible with μC/OS v1.11 (the last released version of μC/OS) but provides many improvements. If you currently have an application that runs with μC/OS, it should run virtually unchanged with μC/OS-II. All of the services (i.e., function calls) provided by μC/OS have been preserved. You may, however, have to change include files and product build files to point to the new filenames.

The companion CD for this book contains all the source code for μC/OS-II and ports for the Intel 80x86 processor running in *real mode* and for the *large model*. The code was developed and executed on a PC running Microsoft Windows 2000 but should work just as well on Windows 95, 98, Me, NT, and XP. Examples run in a DOS-compatible box under these environments. Development was done using the Borland International C/C++ compiler v4.51. Although μC/OS-II was developed and tested on a PC, μC/OS-II was actually targeted for embedded systems and can be ported easily to many different processor architectures.

μC/OS-II Features

Source Code   As I mentioned previously, the companion CD contains all the source code for μC/OS-II (about 5,500 lines). I went to a lot of effort to provide you with a high-quality product. You might not agree with some of the style constructs that I use, but you should agree that the code is both clean and very consistent. Many commercial real-time kernels are provided in source form. I challenge you to find any such code that is as neat, consistent, well commented, and well organized as μC/OS-II. Also, I believe that simply giving you the source code is not enough. You need to know how the code works and how the different pieces fit together. This book provides that type of information. The organization of a real-time kernel is not always apparent when staring at many source files and thousands of lines of code.

Portable   Most of µC/OS-II is written in highly portable ANSI C, with target microprocessor-specific code written in assembly language. Assembly language is kept to a minimum to make µC/OS-II easy to port to other processors. Like µC/OS, µC/OS-II can be ported to a large number of microprocessors, as long as the microprocessor provides a stack pointer and the CPU registers can be pushed onto and popped from the stack. Also, the C compiler should provide either in-line assembly or language extensions that allow you to enable and disable interrupts from C. µC/OS-II can run on most 8-, 16-, 32-, or even 64-bit microprocessors or microcontrollers and digital signal processors (DSP).

All the ports that currently exist for µC/OS can be converted to µC/OS-II in about an hour. Also, because µC/OS-II is upward compatible with µC/OS, your µC/OS applications should run on µC/OS-II with few or no changes. Check for the availability of ports on the µC/OS-II Web site at www.uCOS-II.com.

ROMable   µC/OS-II was designed for embedded applications, which means that if you have the proper tool chain (i.e., C compiler, assembler, and linker/locator), you can actually embed µC/OS-II as part of a product.

Scalable   I designed µC/OS-II so that you can use only the services you need in your application, which means that a product can use just a few µC/OS-II services, while another product can benefit from the full set of features. Scalability allows you to reduce the amount of memory (both RAM and ROM) needed by µC/OS-II on a per-product basis. Scalability is accomplished with the use of conditional compilation. Simply specify (through #define constants) which features you need for your application or product. I did everything I could to reduce both the code and data space required by µC/OS-II.

Preemptive   µC/OS-II is a fully preemptive real-time kernel, which means that µC/OS-II always runs the highest priority task that is ready. Most commercial kernels are preemptive, and µC/OS-II is comparable in performance with many of them.

Multitasking   µC/OS-II can manage up to 64 tasks; however, I recommend that you reserve eight of these tasks for µC/OS-II, leaving your application up to 56 tasks. Each task has a unique priority assigned to it, which means that µC/OS-II cannot do round-robin scheduling. There are thus 64 priority levels.

Deterministic   Execution times for most of µC/OS-II functions and services are deterministic, which means that you can always know how much time µC/OS-II will take to execute a function or a service. Except for OSTimeTick() and some of the event flag services, execution times of µC/OS-II services do not depend on the number of tasks running in your application.

Task Stacks   Each task requires its own stack; however, µC/OS-II allows each task to have a different stack size, which allows you to reduce the amount of RAM needed in your application. With µC/OS-II's stack-checking feature, you can determine exactly how much stack space each task actually requires.

Services   µC/OS-II provides a number of system services, such as semaphores, mutual exclusion semaphores, event flags, message mailboxes, message queues, fixed-sized memory partitions, task management, time management functions, and more.

Interrupt Management   Interrupts can suspend the execution of a task. If a higher priority task is awakened as a result of the interrupt, the highest priority task runs as soon as all nested interrupts complete. Interrupts can be nested up to 255 levels deep.

Robust and Reliable   µC/OS-II is based on µC/OS, which has been used in hundreds of commercial applications since 1992. µC/OS-II uses the same core and most of the same functions as µC/OS, yet offers many more features. Also, in July of 2000, µC/OS-II was certified in an avionics product by the Federal Aviation Administration (FAA) for use in commercial aircraft by meeting the demanding requirements of the RTCA DO-178B standard for software used in avionics equipment. In order to meet the requirements of this standard, it must be possible to demonstrate through documentation and testing that the software is both robust and safe. This issue is particularly important for an operating system as it demonstates that it has the proven quality to be usable in any application. Every feature, function, and line of code of µC/OS-II has been examined and tested to demonstrate that it is safe and robust enough to be used in safety-critical systems where human life is on the line.

Figures, Listings, and Tables

You will notice that when I reference a specific element in a figure, I use the letter "F" followed by the figure number. The number in parenthesis following the figure number represents a specific element in the figure that I am trying to bring your attention to. **F1.2(3)** thus means "please look at the item numbered "**3**" in **Figure 1.2**".

Chapter Contents

Figure I.1 shows the layout and the flow of this book. I thought this diagram would be useful to understand the relationship between the chapters. Chapter 2 is a standalone chapter and doesn't depend on any other chapter. As a minimum, I recommend that you read the Preface, the Introduction, Chapter 1 and Chapter 3. Then with the knowledge you will have gained about µC/OS-II, you ought to be able to start using µC/OS-II and thus move to Chapters 16 and 17 to understand what features are available. If you want to further your understanding of µC/OS-II, you can proceed with Chapters 4, 5, and 6. After you understand Chapter 6, you can either jump to the synchronization or communication services.

Chapter 1, Getting Started with µC/OS-II   This chapter is designed to allow you to experiment with µC/OS-II immediately. In fact, I assume you know little about µC/OS-II and multitasking; concepts are introduced as needed. This chapter has been completely re-written from the previous edition.

Chapter 2, Real-time Systems Concepts   Here, I introduce you to some real-time systems concepts, such as foreground/background systems, critical sections, resources, multitasking, context switching, scheduling, reentrancy, task priorities, mutual exclusion, semaphores, intertask communications, interrupts, and more.

Chapter 3, Kernel Structure   This chapter introduces you to µC/OS-II and its internal structure. You will learn about tasks, task states, and task control blocks; how µC/OS-II implements a ready list, task scheduling, and the idle task; how to determine CPU usage; how µC/OS-II handles interrupts; how to initialize and start µC/OS-II; and more.

Figure I.1   Book layout and flow.

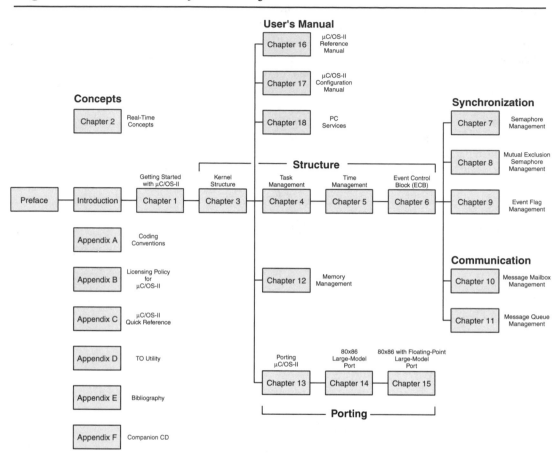

Chapter 4, Task Management   This chapter describes µC/OS-II services that create a task, delete a task, check the size of a task's stack, change a task's priority, suspend and resume a task, and get information about a task.

Chapter 5, Time Management   This chapter describes how µC/OS-II can suspend a task's execution until some user-specified time expires, how such a task can be resumed, and how to get and set the current value of a 32-bit tick counter.

Chapter 6, Event Control Blocks   This chapter describes a data structure that is used by most of the kernel objects to do synchronization and communication. This data structure allows tasks and Interrupt Service Routines (ISR) to communicate with one another and share resources. This chapter is a prerequisite to Chapters 7 through 11.

Chapter 7, Semaphore Management   A semaphore is a kernel object that your tasks needs to acquire in order to gain exclusive access to shared resources. This chapter describes how semaphores are implemented in µC/OS-II.

Chapter 8, Mutual Exclusion Semaphores   A mutual exclusion semaphores (mutex) is a binary semaphore that allows you to gain exclusive access to a resource. The mutex reduces priority inversion issues by automatically changing a task's priority if needed. This chapter describes how (mutex) are implemented in µC/OS-II. Mutexes are new services in this edition.

Chapter 9, Event Flag Management   Event flags are bits for which a task can wait. A task can wait for one or more of these bits to be set or cleared. This chapter shows how event flags are implemented and describes the services that are available to your application. Event flags are new services in this edition.

Chapter 10, Message Mailbox Management   A message mailbox allows your tasks to send messages to one another. This chapter shows how these services are implemented.

Chapter 11, Message Queue Management   A message queue is like a message mailbox, except that it allows multiple messages to be sent to one or more tasks. This chapter shows how message queues are implemented.

Chapter 12, Memory Management   This chapter describes the µC/OS-II dynamic memory allocation feature using fixed-sized memory blocks.

Chapter 13, Porting µC/OS-II   This chapter describes in general terms what needs to be done to adapt µC/OS-II to different processor architectures. This chapter has been completely rewritten from the previous edition.

Chapter 14, 80x86 Port Real Mode, Large Model with Emulated Floating-Point Support   This chapter describes how µC/OS-II was ported to the Intel/AMD 80x86 processor architecture running in real mode and for the large-memory model.

Chapter 15, 80x86 Port Real Mode, Large Model with Hardware Floating-Point Support   This chapter is an extension of the previous one, except that it shows how you can add the floating-point registers of the 80486, 5x86, and Pentium processors to the context switch. This chapter is new to this edition.

Chapter 16, µC/OS-II Reference Manual   This chapter describes each of the functions (i.e., services) provided by µC/OS-II from an application developer's standpoint. Each function contains a brief description, its prototype, the name of the file where the function is found, a description of the function arguments and the return value, special notes, and examples. Many new services have been added in this edition (mutexes and event flags), and these have been added in this chapter.

Chapter 17, µC/OS-II Configuration Manual   This chapter describes each of the #define constants used to configure µC/OS-II for your application. Configuring µC/OS-II allows you to use only the services required by your application. This gives you the flexibility to reduce the µC/OS-II memory footprint (code and data space). This new edition contains more than three times as many configuration options to allow you to reduce the amount of code and data space needed by µC/OS-II.

Chapter 18, PC Services   The examples of Chapter 1 assume the use of a IBM/PC compatible computer. This new chapter shows how I encapsulated some of the services available from a PC.

Appendix A, C Coding Conventions   This appendix shows the coding conventions that I used in this book and in my everyday activities.

Appendix B, Licensing Policy for µC/OS-II   This appendix describes the licensing policy for distributing µC/OS-II in source and object form.

Appendix C, µC/OS-II Quick Reference   This appendix provides a quick reference to µC/OS-II's services.

Appendix D, TO Utility   TO is a DOS utility that allows you to navigate between DOS directories without having to type long CD path commands.

Appendix E, Bibliography   This appendix provides a bibliography of reference material that you might find useful if you are interested in getting further information about embedded real-time systems.

Appendix F, Companion CD   This appendix tells you how to install µC/OS-II and describes what's on the companion CD.

µC/OS-II Web Site

To provide better support to you, I created the µC/OS-II Web site (http://www.uCOS-II.com). You can obtain information about

- news on µC/OS and µC/OS-II,
- upgrades,
- bug fixes,
- availability of ports,
- answers to frequently asked questions (FAQs),
- application notes,
- books,
- classes,
- links to other Web sites, and more.

Getting Started with µC/OS-II

This chapter provides four examples on how to use µC/OS-II. I decided to include this chapter early in the book so you could start using µC/OS-II as soon as possible. In fact, I assume you know little about µC/OS-II and multitasking; concepts are introduced as needed.

The sample code was compiled using the Borland C/C++ compiler v4.51, and options were selected to generate code for an Intel/AMD 80186 processor (large-memory model). The code was actually run and tested on a 300MHz Intel Pentium II PC, running in a DOS window using Microsoft Windows 2000. For all intents and purposes, a Pentium can be viewed as a superfast 80186 processor. The Borland C/C++ v4.51 (called the *Borland Turbo C++ 4.5*) is available from www.Borland.com, and I was assured by Borland that readers would still be able to purchase this compiler for a number of years to come.

I chose a PC as my target system for a number of reasons. First and foremost, it's a lot easier to test code on a PC than on any other embedded environment (i.e., evaluation board or emulator): there are no EPROMs or Flash to burn and no downloads to EPROM emulators, or CPU emulators. You simply compile, link, and run. Second, the 80186 object code (real mode, large model) generated using the Borland C/C++ compiler is compatible with all 80x86 derivative processors from Intel, AMD, and others.

1.00 Installing µC/OS-II

This book includes a companion CD, and you should refer to Appendix F for instruction on how to install the source of µC/OS-II and executables of the examples on your computer. The installation assumes that you are installing the software on a Windows 95, 98, Me, NT, 2000, or XP computer.

1.01　Example #1

Example #1 demonstrates basic multitasking capabilities of μC/OS-II. Ten tasks display a number between 0 and 9 at random locations on the screen. Each task displays only one of the number. In other words, one task displays 0 at random locations, another task displays 1, and so on.

The code for Example #1 is found in the `\SOFTWARE\uCOS-II\EX1_x86L\BC45` directory of the installation drive (the default is C:). You can open a DOS window (called Command Prompt in Microsoft Windows 2000) and type

```
CD \SOFTWARE\uCOS-II\Ex1_x86L\BC45\TEST
```

The CD command allows you to change directory and, in this case, go to the `TEST` directory of Example #1. The `TEST` directory contains four files: `MAKETEST.BAT`, `TEST.EXE`, `TEST.LNK`, and `TEST.MAK`. To execute Example #1, simply type `TEST` at the command line prompt. The DOS window runs the `TEST.EXE` program.

After about one second, you should see the DOS window randomly fill up with numbers between 0 and 9, as shown in Figure 1.1.

Figure 1.1　Example #1 running in a DOS window.

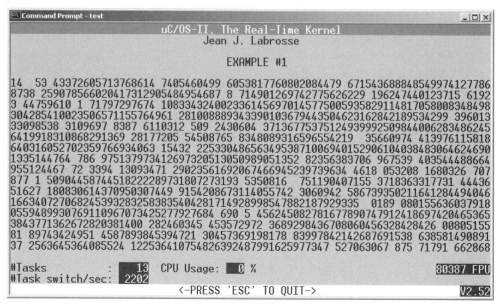

Example #1 consists of 13 tasks, as displayed in the lower left of Figure 1.1. μC/OS-II creates two internal tasks: the idle task and a task that determines CPU usage. The code in Example #1 creates the other 11 tasks.

The source code for Example #1 is found in `TEST.C`, in the `SOURCE` directory. You can get there from the `TEST` directory by typing

```
CD  ..\SOURCE
```

Portions of `TEST.C` are shown in Listing 1.1. You can examine the actual code using your favorite code editor.

Example #1   3

Listing 1.1   Example #1, TEST.C.

```
#include   "includes.h"                                              (1)


#define      TASK_STK_SIZE          512                              (2)
#define      N_TASKS                 10



OS_STK       TaskStk[N_TASKS][TASK_STK_SIZE];                        (3)
OS_STK       TaskStartStk[TASK_STK_SIZE];                            (4)
char         TaskData[N_TASKS];                                      (5)
OS_EVENT     *RandomSem;                                             (6)
```

Note: To describe listings and figures, I place a reference in the margin. The reference corresponds to an element of the listing or figure to which I want to bring your attention. For example, L1.1(1) means: "please refer to Listing 1.1 and locate the item (1)." This notation also applies to figures and thus F3.1(2) means: "please look at Figure 3.1 and examine item (2)."

L1.1(1)   First, you notice that there is only a single #include statement. That's because I like to place all my header files in a master header file called INCLUDES.H. Each source file always references this single include file, and thus I never need to worry about determining which headers I need; they all get included via INCLUDES.H. You can use your code editor to view the contents of INCLUDES.H, which is also found in the SOURCE directory.

μC/OS-II is a multitasking kernel and allows you to have up to 63 application tasks. μC/OS-II decides when to switch from one task to an other, based on information you provide to μC/OS-II. One of the items you must tell μC/OS-II is the priority of your tasks. Changing between tasks is called a *context switch.*

I will return to Listing 1.1 later as needed. Like most C programs, we need a main(), as shown in Listing 1.2.

Listing 1.2   Example #1, TEST.C, main().

```
void  main (void)
{
    PC_DispClrScr(DISP_FGND_WHITE + DISP_BGND_BLACK);               (1)


    OSInit();                                                      (2)


    PC_DOSSaveReturn();                                            (3)
    PC_VectSet(uCOS, OSCtxSw);                                     (4)


    RandomSem   = OSSemCreate(1);                                  (5)
```

Listing 1.2   Example #1, TEST.C, main(). (Continued)

```
OSTaskCreate(TaskStart, (void *)0, &TaskStartStk[TASK_STK_SIZE - 1], 0); (6)

    OSStart();                                                           (7)
}
```

L1.2(1)   main() starts by clearing the screen to ensure that no characters are left over from the previous DOS session. The function PC_DispClrScr() is found in a file called PC.C (see Chapter 18, "PC Services" for details). PC.C contains functions that provide services if you are running in a DOS environment (or a window under the Microsoft Windows 95, 98, Me, NT, 2000, or XP operating systems). The PC_ prefix allows you to easily determine the name of the file from which the function comes; in this case, PC.C. You should note that I specified white letters on a black background. Because the screen will be cleared, I simply could have specified a black background and not specified a foreground. If I did this, and you decided to return to the DOS prompt, you would not see anything on the screen! It's always better to specify a visible foreground just for this reason.

L1.2(2)   A requirement of μC/OS-II is that you call OSInit() before you invoke any of its other services. OSInit() creates two tasks: an idle task, which executes when no other task is ready to run, and a statistic task, which computes CPU usage.

L1.2(3)   The current DOS environment is saved by calling PC_DOSSaveReturn(), which allows you to return to DOS as if you had never started μC/OS-II. You can refer to Chapter 18, "PC Services" for a description of what PC_DOSSaveReturn() does.

L1.2(4)   main() calls PC_VectSet() (see Chapter 18, "PC Services") to install the μC/OS-II context-switch handler. Task-level context switching is done by μC/OS-II by issuing an 80x86 INT instruction to this vector location. I decided to use vector 0x80 (i.e., 128) because it's not used by either DOS or the BIOS.

L1.2(5)   A binary semaphore is created to guard access to the random-number generator function provided by the Borland C/C++ library. A semaphore is an object provided by the kernel to prevent multiple tasks from accessing the same resource (in this case a function) at the same time. I decided to use a semaphore because I didn't know whether or not the random-generator function was reentrant; I assumed it was not. By initializing the semaphore to 1, I'm telling μC/OS-II to allow only one task to access the random-generator function at any given time. A semaphore must be created before it can be used, which is done by calling OSSemCreate() and specifying its initial value. OSSemCreate() returns a handle [see Listing 1.1(6)] to the semaphore, which must be used to reference this particular semaphore.

L1.2(6)   Before starting multitasking, you have to create at least one task. For this example, I called this task TaskStart(). You create a task because you want to tell μC/OS-II to manage the task. The OSTaskCreate() function receives four arguments. The first argument is a pointer to the task's address, in this case TaskStart(). The second argument is a pointer to data that you want to pass to the task when it first starts. In this case, there is nothing to pass, and thus I passed a NULL pointer. It could, however, have been anything. I'll discuss the use of this argument in Example #4. The third argument is the task's top-of-stack (TOS). With μC/OS-II, as with most preemptive kernels, each task requires its own stack space. Each task in μC/OS-II can have a different size, but, for simplicity, I made them all the same. On the 80x86 CPU, the stack grows downwards, and thus we must pass the highest, most valid TOS

Example #1   5

1

address to OSTaskCreate(). In this case, the stack is called TaskStartStk[] and is allocated at compile time. A stack must be declared having a type OS_STK [see Listing 1.1(4)]. The size of the stack is declared in Listing 1.1(2). For the 80x86, an OS_STK is a 16-bit value, and thus the size of the stack is 1024 bytes. Finally, we must specify the priority of the task being created. The lower the priority number, the higher the priority (i.e., its importance).

As previously mentioned, μC/OS-II allows you to create up to 63 tasks. However, each task must have a unique priority number between 0 and 62. You're the one that actually decides what priority to give your tasks, based on your application requirements. Priority level 0 is the highest priority.

L1.2(7)   OSStart() is then called to start multitasking and give control to μC/OS-II. It is very important that you create at least one task before calling OSStart(). Failure to do this action will certainly make your application crash. In fact, you might always want to create only one task if you are planning on using the CPU usage statistic task.

OSStart()'s job is to determine which, of all the tasks created, is the most important one (highest priority) and start executing this task. In our case, μC/OS-II created two low priority tasks: the idle task and the statistic task. main() created TaskStart() with a priority of 0. As I mentioned, priority 0 is the highest priority, and thus OSStart() starts executing TaskStart().

You should note that OSStart() doesn't return to main(). However, if you call PC_DOSReturn(), multitasking is halted, and your application returns to DOS (but not main()). In an embedded system, there is no need for an equivalent function to PC_DOSReturn() because you would most likely not be returning to anything!

As I mentioned in the previous section, OSStart() selects TaskStart() as the most important task to run first. TaskStart() is shown in Listing 1.3.

Listing 1.3   *Example #1, TEST.C, TaskStart().*

```
void  TaskStart (void *pdata)
{
#if OS_CRITICAL_METHOD == 3
    OS_CPU_SR  cpu_sr;
#endif
    char       s[100];
    INT16S     key;


    pdata = pdata;                                              (1)

    TaskStartDispInit();                                       (2)

    OS_ENTER_CRITICAL();                                       (3)
    PC_VectSet(0x08, OSTickISR);                               (4)
    PC_SetTickRate(OS_TICKS_PER_SEC);                          (5)
    OS_EXIT_CRITICAL();                                        (6)
```

Listing 1.3   Example #1, TEST.C, TaskStart(). (Continued)

```
    OSStatInit();                                               (7)

    TaskStartCreateTasks();                                     (8)

    for (;;) {                                                  (9)
        TaskStartDisp();                                       (10)

        if (PC_GetKey(&key) == TRUE) {                         (11)
            if (key == 0x1B) {                                 (12)
                PC_DOSReturn();                                (13)
            }
        }

        OSCtxSwCtr = 0;                                        (14)
        OSTimeDlyHMSM(0, 0, 1, 0);                             (15)
    }
}
```

L1.3(1)   `TaskStart()` begins by setting `pdata` to itself. I do this because some compilers complain (error or warning) if `pdata` is not referenced. In other words, I fake the usage of `pdata`! `pdata` is a pointer passed to your task when the task is created. The second argument passed in `OSTaskCreate()` is none other than the argument `pdata` of a task [see L1.2(6)]. Because I passed a `NULL` pointer [again see L1.2(6)], I am not passing anything to `TaskStart()`.

L1.3(2)   `TaskStart()` then calls `TaskStartDispInit()` to initialize the display, as shown in Figure 1.2. `TaskStartDispInit()` makes 25 consecutive calls to `PC_DispStr()` (see Chapter 18, "PC Services") to fill the 25 lines of text of a typical DOS window.

L1.3(3)   `TaskStart()` then invokes the macro `OS_ENTER_CRITICAL()`. `OS_ENTER_CRITICAL()` is basically a processor-specific macro, and it's used to disable interrupts (see Chapter 13, Porting µC/OS-II).

L1.3(4)   µC/OS-II, like all kernels, requires a time source to keep track of delays and timeouts. In real mode, the PC offers such a time source, which occurs every 54.925ms (18.20648Hz) and is called a tick. `PC_VectSet()` allows us to replace the address where the PC goes to service the DOS tick with one that is used by µC/OS-II. However, µC/OS-II still calls the DOS tick handler every 54.925ms. This technique is called *chaining* and is set up by `PC_DOSSaveReturn()` (see Chapter 18, "PC Services").

L1.3(5)   We then change the tick rate from 18.2Hz to 200Hz. I selected 200Hz because it's almost an exact multiple of 18.2Hz (i.e., 11 times faster). I never quite understood why IBM selected 18.2Hz instead of 20Hz as the tick rate on the original PC. Instead of setting up the 82C54 timer to divide the timer input frequency by 59,659 to obtain a nice 20Hz, it appears that they left the 16-bit timer to overflow every 65,536 pulses! Changing the tick rate is handled by another PC service called `PC_SetTickRate()`, which is passed the desired tick rate (`OS_TICKS_PER_SEC` is set to 200 in `OS_CPU.H`).

Example #1   7

L1.3(6)   We then invoke the macro OS_EXIT_CRITICAL(). OS_EXIT_CRITICAL() is a processor-specific macro and is used to reenable interrupts (see Chapter 13, "Porting μC/OS-II"). OS_ENTER_CRITICAL() and OS_EXIT_CRITICAL() must be used in pairs.

L1.3(7)   OSStatInit() is called to determine the speed of your CPU (see Chapter 3, "Getting Started with μC/OS-II"). This function allows μC/OS-II to know what percentage of the CPU is actually being used by all the tasks.

L1.3(8)   TaskStart() then calls TaskStartCreateTasks() to let μC/OS-II manage more tasks. Specifically, we are adding N_TASKS identical tasks [see Listing 1.1(2)]. TaskStartCreateTasks() is shown in Listing 1.4.

Figure 1.2   *Initialization of the display by* TaskStartDispInit( ).

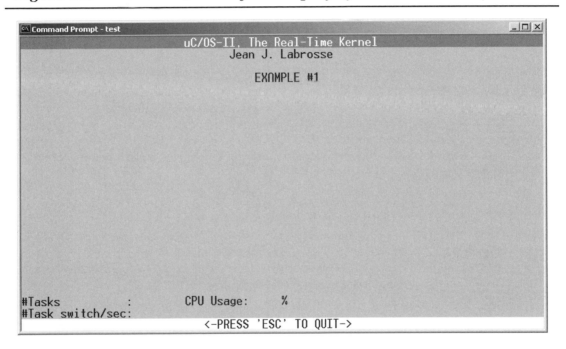

Listing 1.4   *Example #1,* TEST.C, TaskStartCreateTasks( ).

```
static  void  TaskStartCreateTasks (void)
{
    INT8U  i;


    for (i = 0; i < N_TASKS; i++) {
        TaskData[i] = '0' + i;                                    (1)
        OSTaskCreate(Task,                                        (2)
                  (void *)&TaskData[i],                           (3)
```

Listing 1.4   Example #1, TEST.C, TaskStartCreateTasks(). (Continued)

```
        &TaskStk[i][TASK_STK_SIZE - 1],              (4)
        i + 1);                                      (5)
    }
}
```

L1.4(1)   An array is initialized to contain the ASCII characters 0 to 9 [see also Listing 1.1(5)].

L1.4(2)   The loop initializes N_TASKS identical tasks called Task(). Task() is responsible for placing an ASCII character at a random location on the screen. In fact, each instance of Task() places a different character.

L1.4(3)   Each of these task receive a pointer to the array of ASCII characters. Each task in fact receives a pointer to a different character.

L1.4(4)   Again, each task requires its own stack space [see Listing 1.1(3)].

L1.4(5)   With μC/OS-II, each task must have a unique priority. Because priority number 0 is already used by TaskStart(), I decided to create tasks with priorities 1 through 10.

Ⅰ As each task is created, μC/OS-II determines whether the created task is more important than the creator. If the created task had a higher priority, then μC/OS-II would immediately run the created task. However, because TaskStart() has the highest priority (priority 0), none of the created tasks execute just yet.

We can now resume discussion of Listing 1.3.

L1.3(9)   With μC/OS-II, each task must be an infinite loop.

L1.3(10)   TaskStartDisp() is called to display information at the bottom of the DOS window (see Figure 1.1). Specifically, TaskStartDisp() prints the number of tasks created, the current CPU usage in percentage, the number of context switches, the version of μC/OS-II, and, finally, whether your processor has a floating-point unit (FPU) or not.

L1.3(11)   TaskStart() then checks to see if you pressed a key by calling PC_GetKey().

L1.3(12)

L1.3(13)   TaskStart() determines whether you pressed the Esc key on your keyboard and, if so, calls PC_DOSReturn() to exit this example and return to the DOS prompt. You can find out how this action is done by referring to Chapter 18, "PC Services."

L1.3(14)   If you didn't press the Esc key, the global variable OSCtxSwCtr (the context-switch counter) is cleared so that we can display the number of context switches in one second.

L1.3(15)   Finally, TaskStart() is suspended (does not run) for one complete second by calling OSTimeDlyHMSM(). The HMSM stands for hours, minutes, seconds, and milliseconds and corresponds to the arguments passed to OSTimeDlyHMSM(). Because TaskStart() is suspended for one second, μC/OS-II starts executing the next most important task, in this case Task() at priority 1. You should note that without OSTimeDlyHMSM() (or other similar functions), TaskStart() would be a true infinite loop, and other tasks would never get a chance to run.

The code for Task() is shown in Listing 1.5.

L1.5(1)   As I previously mentioned, a μC/OS-II task is typically an infinite loop.

Example #1 9

1

Listing 1.5 *Example #1,* `TEST.C,` `Task().`

```
void  Task (void *pdata)
{
    INT8U  x;
    INT8U  y;
    INT8U  err;

    for (;;) {                                                          (1)
        OSSemPend(RandomSem, 0, &err);                                  (2)
        x = random(80);                                                (3)
        y = random(16);                                                (4)
        OSSemPost(RandomSem);                                          (5)

        PC_DispChar(x, y + 5, *(char *)pdata, DISP_FGND_LIGHT_GRAY);   (6)
        OSTimeDly(1);                                                   (7)
    }
}
```

L1.5(2) The task starts by acquiring the semaphore, which guards access to the Borland compiler random-number-generator function. To call the semaphore, call `OSSemPend()` and pass it the handle [see L1.1(6)] of the semaphore, which was created to guard access to the random-number-generator function. The second argument of `OSSemPend()` is used to specify a time-out. A value of 0 means that this task will wait forever for the semaphore. Because the semaphore was initialized with a count of one and no other task has requested the semaphore, `Task()` is allowed to continue execution. If the semaphore was owned by another task, µC/OS-II would have suspended this task and executed the next most important task.

L1.5(3) The random-number-generator function is called and a value between 0 and 79 (inclusively) is returned. This value happens to be the x-coordinate where we want to display the character 0 (for this task) on the screen.

L1.5(4) Again, the random-number-generator is called, and returns a number between 0 and 15 (inclusively). This value is used to determine the y-coordinate of the character to display.

L1.5(5) The semaphore is released by calling `OSSemPost()`. Here we simply need to specify the semaphore handle.

L1.5(6) We can now display the character that was passed to `Task()` when `Task()` was created. For the first instance of `Task()`, the character is 0, and is the last instance, it's 9. I added an offset of five lines from the top so that I don't overwrite the header at the top of the display (see Figure 1.1).

L1.5(7) Finally, `Task()` calls `OSTimeDly()` to tell µC/OS-II that it's done executing and to give other tasks a chance to run. The value of 1 means that I want this task to delay for one clock tick, or 5ms because the tick rate is 200Hz. When `OSTimeDly()` is called, µC/OS-II suspends the calling function and executes the next most important task. In this case, it is another instance of `Task()`, which displays 1. This process goes on for all instances of `Task()`, and thus that's why Figure 1.1 looks the way it does.

If you have the Borland C/C++ v4.5x compiler installed in the C:\BC45 directory, you can experiment with TEST.C. After modifying TEST.C, you can type MAKETEST from the command prompt of the TEST directory to build a new TEST.EXE. If you don't have the Borland C/C++ v4.5x compiler or you have it installed in a different directory, you can make the appropriate changes to TEST.MAK, INCLUDES.H, and TEST.LNK.

The SOURCE directory contains four files: INCLUDES.H, OS_CFG.H, TEST.C, and TEST.LNK. OS_CFG.H is used to determine μC/OS-II configuration options. TEST.LNK is the linker-command file for the Borland linker, TLINK.

1.02   *Example #2*

Example #2 demonstrates the stack-checking feature of μC/OS-II. The amount of stack space used by each task is displayed along with the amount of free stack space. Also, Example #2 shows the execution time of the stack-checking function OSTaskStkChk() because it depends on the size of each stack. It turns out that a heavily used stack requires less processing time.

The code for Example #2 is found in the \SOFTWARE\uCOS-II\EX2_x86L\BC45 directory. You can open a DOS window and type

```
CD  \SOFTWARE\uCOS-II\Ex2_x86L\BC45\TEST
```

To execute Example #2, type TEST at the command prompt. The DOS window runs the TEST.EXE program.

After about one second, you should see the screen shown in Figure 1.3.

Example #2 consists of nine tasks, as displayed in the lower left of Figure 1.3. Of those nine tasks, μC/OS-II creates two internal tasks: the idle task and a task that determines CPU usage. Example #2 creates the other seven tasks.

Example #2 shows you how you can display task statistics beyond the number of tasks created, the number of context switches, and the CPU usage. Specifically, Example #2 shows you how you can find out how much stack space each task is actually using and how much execution time it takes to determine the size of each task stack.

Example #2 makes use of the extended task-create function (OSTaskCreateExt()) and the μC/OS-II stack-checking feature [OSTaskStkChk()]. Stack checking is useful when you don't actually know ahead of time how much stack space you need to allocate for each task. In this case, you allocate much more stack space than you think you need and let μC/OS-II tell you exactly how much stack space is actually used. You obviously need to run the application long enough and under your worst case conditions to get valid numbers. Your final stack size should accommodate system expansion, so make sure you allocate between 10–25% more. In safety-critical applications, however, you might even want to consider 100% more! What you get from stack checking is a ballpark figure; you are not looking for an exact stack usage.

The μC/OS-II stack-checking function fills the stack of a task with zeros when the task is created. You accomplish this by telling OSTaskCreateExt() that you want to clear the stack upon task creation and that you want to check the stack (i.e., by setting the OS_TASK_OPT_STK_CLR and OS_TASK_OPT_STK_CHK for the opt argument). If you intend to create and delete tasks, you should set these options so that a new stack is cleared every time the task is created. You should note that having OSTaskCreateExt() clear the stack increases execution overhead, which obviously depends on the stack size.

μC/OS-II scans the stack, starting at the bottom until it finds a nonzero entry. As the stack is scanned, μC/OS-II increments a counter that indicates how many entries are free.

The source code for Example #2 is found in TEST.C, in the SOURCE directory. To get there from the TEST directory, type

```
CD  ..\SOURCE
```

Example #2 11

Portions of TEST.C are shown in Listing 1.6. You can examine the actual code using your favorite code editor.

Figure 1.3 *Example #2 running in a DOS window.*

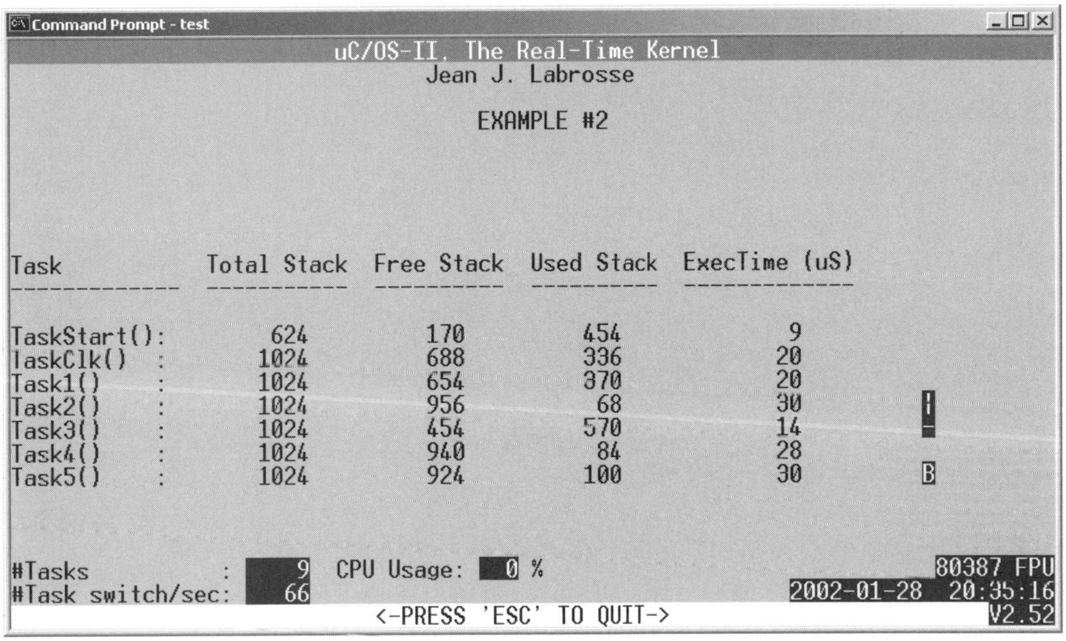

Listing 1.6 *Example #2, TEST.C.*

```
#include "includes.h"                                          (1)

#define        TASK_STK_SIZE      512                          (2)

#define        TASK_START_ID      0                            (3)
#define        TASK_CLK_ID        1
#define        TASK_1_ID          2
#define        TASK_2_ID          3
#define        TASK_3_ID          4
#define        TASK_4_ID          5
#define        TASK_5_ID          6


#define        TASK_START_PRIO    10                           (4)
#define        TASK_CLK_PRIO      11
#define        TASK_1_PRIO        12
#define        TASK_2_PRIO        13
#define        TASK_3_PRIO        14
```

Listing 1.6   Example #2, TEST.C. (Continued)

```
#define        TASK_4_PRIO        15
#define        TASK_5_PRIO        16


OS_STK         TaskStartStk[TASK_STK_SIZE];                          (5)
OS_STK         TaskClkStk[TASK_STK_SIZE];
OS_STK         Task1Stk[TASK_STK_SIZE];
OS_STK         Task2Stk[TASK_STK_SIZE];
OS_STK         Task3Stk[TASK_STK_SIZE];
OS_STK         Task4Stk[TASK_STK_SIZE];
OS_STK         Task5Stk[TASK_STK_SIZE];


OS_EVENT       *AckMbox;                                             (6)
OS_EVENT       *TxMbox;
```

Based on what you learned in Example #1, you should recognize:

L1.6(1)   INCLUDES.H as the master include file.

L1.6(2)   The size of each task's stack (TASK_STK_SIZE). Again, I made all stack sizes the same for simplicity, but, with µC/OS-II, the stack size for each task can be different.

L1.6(5)   The storage for the task stacks.

main() for Example #2 is shown in Listing 1.7 and looks very similar to the main() of Example #1. I only describe the differences.

Listing 1.7   Example #2, TEST.C, main().

```
void main (void)
{
    OS_STK *ptos;
    OS_STK *pbos;
    INT32U  size;

    PC_DispClrScr(DISP_FGND_WHITE);

    OSInit();

    PC_DOSSaveReturn();
    PC_VectSet(uCOS, OSCtxSw);

    PC_ElapsedInit();                                                (1)

    ptos         = &TaskStartStk[TASK_STK_SIZE - 1];                 (2)
```

Example #2   13

Listing 1.7   *Example #2, TEST.C, main( ). (Continued)*

```
    pbos         = &TaskStartStk[0];
    size         = TASK_STK_SIZE;
    OSTaskStkInit_FPE_x86(&ptos, &pbos, &size);                             (3)
    OSTaskCreateExt(TaskStart,                                             (4)
                (void *)0,
                ptos,                                                      (5)
                TASK_START_PRIO,                                           (6)
                TASK_START_ID,                                            (7)
                pbos,                                                      (8)
                size,                                                      (9)
                (void *)0,                                                (10)
                OS_TASK_OPT_STK_CHK | OS_TASK_OPT_STK_CLR);               (11)


    OSStart();
}
```

L1.7(1)   `main( )` calls `PC_ElapsedInit( )` to initialize the elapsed-time-measurement function that is used to measure the execution time of `OSTaskStkChk( )`. This function basically measures the execution time (i.e., overhead) of two functions: `PC_ElapsedStart( )` and `PC_Elapsed-Stop( )`. By measuring this time, we can determine fairly precisely how long it takes to execute code that's wrapped between these two calls.

L1.7(2)

L1.7(3)   `TaskStart( )` in Example #2 is invoking the floating-point emulation library instead of making use of the floating-point unit (FPU), which is present on 80486 and higher-end PCs. The Borland compiler defaults to use its emulation library if an FPU is not detected. In other words, if you were to run `TEST.EXE` on a DOS-based machine equiped with an Intel 80386EX (without an 80387 coprocessor), then the floating-point unit would be emulated. The emulation library is unfortunately non-reentrant, and we have to trick it in order to allow multiple tasks to do floating-point math. For now, let me just say that we have to modify the task stack to accommodate the floating-point emulation library. This modification is accomplished by calling `OSTaskStkInit_FPE_x86( )` (see Chapter 14, "80x86 Port"). You should notice from Figure 1.3 that the stack size reported for `TaskStart( )` is 624 instead of 1024. That's because `OSTaskStkInit_FPE_x86( )` reserves the difference for the floating-point emulation library.

L1.7(4)   Instead of calling `OSTaskCreate( )` to create `TaskStart( )`, we must call `OSTaskCreateExt( )` [the extended version of `OSTaskCreate( )`] because we modified the stack and also because we want to check the stack size at run time (described later).

L1.7(5)   `OSTaskStkInit_FPE_x86( )` modifies the top-of-stack pointer, so we must pass the new pointer to `OSTaskCreateExt( )`.

L1.7(6)   Instead of passing a hard-coded priority (as I did in Example #1), I created a #define symbol [see L1.6(4)].

L1.7(7)   OSTaskCreateExt() requires that you pass a task identifier (ID). The actual value can be anything because this field is not actually used by µC/OS-II at this time.

L1.7(8)   OSTaskStkInit_FPE_x86() modifies the bottom-of-stack pointer, so we must pass the new pointer to OSTaskCreateExt().

L1.7(9)   OSTaskStkInit_FPE_x86() also modifies the size of the stack, so we must pass the new size to OSTaskCreateExt().

L1.7(10)   One of OSTaskCreateExt()'s arguments is a task-control-block (TCB) extension pointer. This argument is not used in Example #2, so we simply pass a NULL pointer.

L1.7(11)   Finally, the last argument to OSTaskCreateExt() is a set of options (i.e., bits) that tell OSTaskCreateExt() that we are doing stack-size checking and that we want to clear the stack when the task is created.

TaskStart() is similar to the one described in Example #1 and is shown in Listing 1.8. Again, I only describe the differences.

Listing 1.8   Example #2, *TEST.C, TaskStart( ).*

```
void  TaskStart (void *pdata)
{
#if OS_CRITICAL_METHOD == 3
    OS_CPU_SR   cpu_sr;
#endif
    INT16S      key;


    pdata = pdata;


    TaskStartDispInit();                                        (1)


    OS_ENTER_CRITICAL();
    PC_VectSet(0x08, OSTickISR);
    PC_SetTickRate(OS_TICKS_PER_SEC);
    OS_EXIT_CRITICAL();


    OSStatInit();


    AckMbox = OSMboxCreate((void *)0);                          (2)
    TxMbox  = OSMboxCreate((void *)0);


    TaskStartCreateTasks();                                     (3)


    for (;;) {
        TaskStartDisp();


        if (PC_GetKey(&key)) {
```

Example #2   15

Listing 1.8   *Example #2,* TEST.C, TaskStart(). *(Continued)*

```
        if (key == 0x1B) {
            PC_DOSReturn();
        }
    }


    OSCtxSwCtr = 0;
    OSTimeDly(OS_TICKS_PER_SEC);                                    (4)
    }
}
```

L1.8(1)   Although the function call is identical, TaskStartDispInit() initializes the display, as shown in Figure 1.4.

Figure 1.4   *Initialization of the display by* TaskStartDispInit().

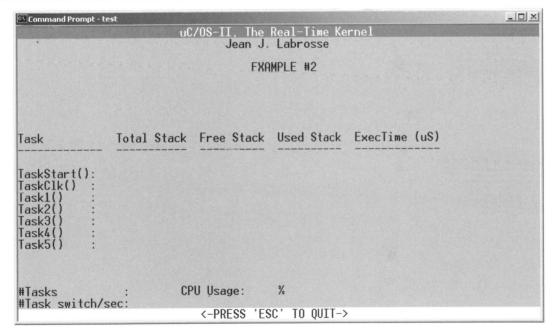

L1.8(2)   μC/OS-II allows you to have tasks or ISRs send messages to other tasks. In Example #2, I have Task 4 send a message to Task 5, and Task 5 will respond back to Task 4 with an acknowledgment message (described later). For this purpose, we need to create two kernel objects that are called *mailboxes.* A mailbox allows a task or an ISR to send a pointer to another task. The mailbox only has room for a single pointer. What the pointer points to is application specific, and, of course both the sender and the receiver need to agree about the contents of the message.

L1.8(3)   TaskStartCreateTasks() creates six tasks using OSTaskCreateExt(). These tasks are not doing floating-point operations, and thus there is no need to call OSTaskStkInit_FPE_x86() to modify the stacks. However, I am doing stack checking on these tasks, so I call OSTaskCreateExt() with the proper options set.

L1.8(4)   In Example #1, I called `OSTimeDlyHMSM()` to delay `TaskStart()` for one second. I decided to use `OSTimeDly(OS_TICKS_PER_SEC)` to show you that you can use either method. However, `OSTimeDly()` is slightly faster than `OSTimeDlyHMSM()`.

The code for `Task1()` is shown in Listing 1.9. `Task1()` checks the size of the stack for each of the seven application tasks (the six tasks created by `TaskStart()` and `TaskStart()` itself).

Listing 1.9   Example #2, TEST.C, Task1().

```
void  Task1 (void *pdata)
{
    INT8U      err;
    OS_STK_DATA data;
    INT16U     time;
    INT8U      i;
    char       s[80];


    pdata = pdata;
    for (;;) {
        for (i = 0; i < 7; i++) {
            PC_ElapsedStart();                                      (1)
            err  = OSTaskStkChk(TASK_START_PRIO + i, &data);        (2)
            time = PC_ElapsedStop();                                (3)
            if (err == OS_NO_ERR) {
                sprintf(s, "%4ld        %4ld        %4ld        %6d",  (4)
                        data.OSFree + data.OSUsed,
                        data.OSFree,
                        data.OSUsed,
                        time);
                PC_DispStr(19, 12 + i, s, DISP_FGND_YELLOW);        (5)
            }
        }
        OSTimeDlyHMSM(0, 0, 0, 100);                                (6)
    }
}
```

L1.9(1)

L1.9(3)   The execution time of `OSTaskStkChk()` is measured by wrapping `OSTaskStkChk()` with calls to `PC_ElapsedStart()` and `PC_ElapsedStop()`. `PC_ElapsedStop()` returns the time difference in microseconds.

L1.9(2)   `OSTaskStkChk()` is a service provided by µC/OS-II to allow your code to determine the actual stack usage of a task. You call `OSTaskStkChk()` by passing it the task priority of the task you want to check. The second argument to the function is a pointer to a data structure

Example #2 **17**

1

that holds information about the task's stack. Specifically, OS_STK_DATA contains the number of bytes used and the number of bytes free. OSTaskStkChk() returns an error code that indicates whether the call was successful. It would not be successful if I had passed the priority number of a task that didn't exist.

L1.9(4)

L1.9(5) The information retrieved by OSTaskStkChk() is formatted into a string and displayed.

L1.9(6) I decided to execute this task 10 times per second, but, in an actual product or application, you would most likely run stack checking every few seconds or so. In other words, it would make no sense to consume valuable CPU-processing time to determine worst-case stack growth.

The code for Task2() and Task3() is shown in Listing 1.10. Both of these tasks display a spinning wheel. The two tasks are almost identical. Task3() allocates and initializes a dummy array of 500 bytes. I wanted to consume stack space to show you that OSTaskStkChk() would report that Task3() has 502 bytes less than Task2() on its stack (500 bytes for the array and two bytes for the 16-bit integer). Task2()'s wheel spins clockwise at five rotations per second, and Task3()'s wheel spins counterclockwise at 2.5 rotations per second. Task4() and Task5() are shown in Listing 1.11.

Note: If you run Example #2 in a window under Microsoft Windows 95, 98, Me, NT, 2000, or XP, the rotation might not appear as quick. Simply press and hold the Alt key and then press the Enter key on your keyboard to make the DOS window use the whole screen. You can go back to window mode by repeating the operation.

Listing 1.10   Example #2, *TEST.C, Task2() and Task3().*

```c
void  Task2 (void *data)
{
    data = data;
    for (;;) {
        PC_DispChar(70, 15, '|',  DISP_FGND_WHITE + DISP_BGND_RED);
        OSTimeDly(10);
        PC_DispChar(70, 15, '/',  DISP_FGND_WHITE + DISP_BGND_RED);
        OSTimeDly(10);
        PC_DispChar(70, 15, '-',  DISP_FGND_WHITE + DISP_BGND_RED);
        OSTimeDly(10);
        PC_DispChar(70, 15, '\\', DISP_FGND_WHITE + DISP_BGND_RED);
        OSTimeDly(10);
    }
}
```

Listing 1.10   *Example #2, TEST.C, Task2() and Task3(). (Continued)*

```
void  Task3 (void *data)
{
    char    dummy[500];
    INT16U  i;

    data = data;
    for (i = 0; i < 499; i++) {
        dummy[i] = '?';
    }
    for (;;) {
        PC_DispChar(70, 16, '|',  DISP_FGND_WHITE + DISP_BGND_BLUE);
        OSTimeDly(20);
        PC_DispChar(70, 16, '\\', DISP_FGND_WHITE + DISP_BGND_BLUE);
        OSTimeDly(20);
        PC_DispChar(70, 16, '-',  DISP_FGND_WHITE + DISP_BGND_BLUE);
        OSTimeDly(20);
        PC_DispChar(70, 16, '/',  DISP_FGND_WHITE + DISP_BGND_BLUE);
        OSTimeDly(20);
    }
}
```

Listing 1.11   *Example #2, TEST.C, Task4() and Task5().*

```
void  Task4 (void *data)
{
    char   txmsg;
    INT8U  err;

    data  = data;
    txmsg = 'A';
    for (;;) {
        OSMboxPost(TxMbox, (void *)&txmsg);                     (1)
        OSMboxPend(AckMbox, 0, &err);                           (2)
        txmsg++;                                                (3)
        if (txmsg == 'Z') {
            txmsg = 'A';
        }
    }
```

Example #2   19

Listing 1.11   Example #2, TEST.C, Task4() and Task5(). (Continued)

```
}
void  Task5 (void *data)
{
    char  *rxmsg;
    INT8U  err;


    data = data;
    for (;;) {
        rxmsg = (char *)OSMboxPend(TxMbox, 0, &err);                    (4)
        PC_DispChar(70, 18, *rxmsg, DISP_FGND_YELLOW + DISP_BGND_RED);  (5)
        OSTimeDlyHMSM(0, 0, 1, 0);                                     (6)
        OSMboxPost(AckMbox, (void *)1);                                (7)
    }
}
```

L1.11(1)   Task4() sends a message (an ASCII character) to Task5() by posting the message to the TxMbox.

L1.11(2)   Task4() then waits for an acknowledgment from Task5() by waiting on the AckMbox. The second argument to the OSMboxPend() call specifies a timeout, and I specified to wait forever because I passed a value of 0. By specifying a non-zero value, Task4() would have given up waiting after the specified timeout. The timeout is specified as an integral number of clock ticks.

L1.11(3)   The message is changed when Task5() acknowledges the previous message.

L1.11(4)   When Task5() starts execution, it immediately waits (forever) for a message to arrive through the mailbox TxMbox.

L1.11(5)   When the message arrives, Task5() displays it on the screen.

L1.11(6)

L1.11(7)   Task5() then waits for one second before acknowledging Task4(). I decided to wait for one second so that you could see it change on the screen. In fact, there must either be a delay in Task5() or one in Task4(), otherwise all lower priority tasks would not be allowed to run!

Finally, the code for `TaskClk()` is shown in Listing 1.12. This task executes every second, simply obtains the current date and time from a PC service called `PC_GetDateTime()` (see Chapter 18, "PC Services"), and displays it on the screen.

Listing 1.12   Example #2, *TEST.C*, *TaskClk()*.

```
void  TaskClk (void *data)
{
    char s[40];


    data = data;
    for (;;) {
        PC_GetDateTime(s);
        PC_DispStr(60, 23, s, DISP_FGND_BLUE + DISP_BGND_CYAN);
        OSTimeDly(OS_TICKS_PER_SEC);
    }
}
```

If you have the Borland C/C++ v4.5x compiler installed in the `C:\BC45` directory, you can experiment with `TEST.C`. After modifying `TEST.C`, you can type `MAKETEST` from the command prompt of the `TEST` directory to build a new `TEST.EXE`. If you don't have the Borland C/C++ v4.5x compiler or you have it installed in a different directory, you can make changes to `TEST.MAK`, `INCLUDES.H`, and `TEST.LNK` accordingly.

The `SOURCE` directory contains four files: `INCLUDES.H`, `OS_CFG.H`, `TEST.C`, and `TEST.LNK`. `OS_CFG.H` is used to determine µC/OS-II configuration options. `TEST.LNK` is the linker-command file for the Borland linker, `TLINK`.

1.03   Example #3

Example #3 shows how you can extend the functionality of µC/OS-II. Specifically, Example #3 uses the TCB extension capability of `OSTaskCreateExt()`, the user-defined context-switch hook [`OSTaskSwHook()`], the user-defined statistic-task hook [`OSTaskStatHook()`], and message queues. In this example, you should see how easy it is to determine how many times a task executes and how much time a task takes to execute. The execution time can be used to determine the CPU usage of a task relative to the other tasks.

The code for Example #3 is found in the `\SOFTWARE\uCOS-II\EX3_x86L\BC45` directory. You can open a DOS window and type

```
CD  \SOFTWARE\uCOS-II\Ex3_x86L\BC45\TEST
```

As usual, to execute Example #3, type `TEST` at the command prompt. The DOS window runs the `TEST.EXE` program.

After about one second, you should see the screen shown in Figure 1.5. I let `TEST.EXE` run for a couple of seconds before I captured the screen shot. Seven tasks are shown along with how many times they executed (*Counter* column), the execution time of each task in microseconds

Example #3   21

(*Exec.Time(uS)* column), the total execution time since I started (*Tot.Exec.Time(uS)* column), and finally, the percentage of execution time of each task relative to the other tasks (*%Tot.* column).

Example #3 consists of nine tasks, as displayed in the lower left of Figure 1.5. Of those nine tasks, μC/OS-II creates two internal tasks: the idle task and a task that determines CPU usage. Example #3 creates the other seven tasks.

Figure 1.5   *Example #3 running in a DOS window.*

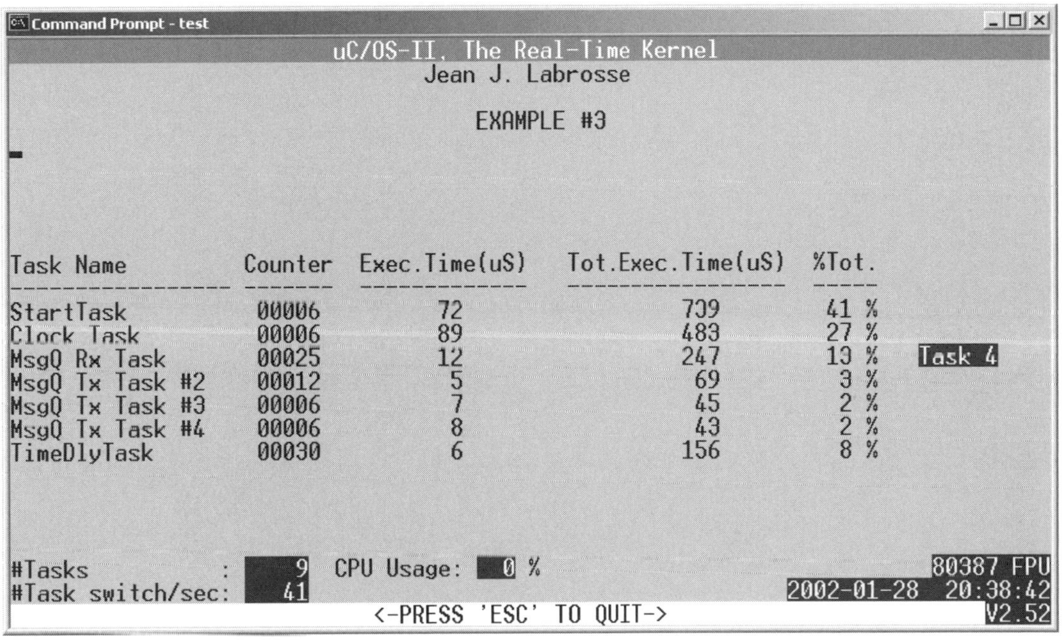

Portions of TEST.C are shown in Listing 1.13. You can examine the actual code using your favorite code editor.

Listing 1.13   *Example #3, TEST.C.*

```
#include   "includes.h"


#define       TASK_STK_SIZE      512


#define       TASK_START_ID      0
#define       TASK_CLK_ID        1
#define       TASK_1_ID          2
#define       TASK_2_ID          3
#define       TASK_3_ID          4
#define       TASK_4_ID          5
#define       TASK_5_ID          6
```

Listing 1.13   Example #3, *TEST.C. (Continued)*

```
#define           TASK_START_PRIO    10
#define           TASK_CLK_PRIO      11
#define           TASK_1_PRIO        12
#define           TASK_2_PRIO        13
#define           TASK_3_PRIO        14
#define           TASK_4_PRIO        15
#define           TASK_5_PRIO        16


#define           MSG_QUEUE_SIZE     20


typedef struct {                                                        (1)
    char    TaskName[30];
    INT16U  TaskCtr;
    INT16U  TaskExecTime;
    INT32U  TaskTotExecTime;
} TASK_USER_DATA;


OS_STK          TaskStartStk[TASK_STK_SIZE];
OS_STK          TaskClkStk[TASK_STK_SIZE];
OS_STK          Task1Stk[TASK_STK_SIZE];
OS_STK          Task2Stk[TASK_STK_SIZE];
OS_STK          Task3Stk[TASK_STK_SIZE];
OS_STK          Task4Stk[TASK_STK_SIZE];
OS_STK          Task5Stk[TASK_STK_SIZE];


TASK_USER_DATA  TaskUserData[7];                                        (2)


OS_EVENT        *MsgQueue;                                              (3)
void            *MsgQueueTbl[20];
```

L1.13(1)   A data structure is created to hold additional information about a task. Specifically, the data structure allows you to add a name to a task (µC/OS-II doesn't directly provide this feature), keep track of how many times a task has executed, how long a task takes to execute, and finally the total time a task has executed.

L1.13(2)   An array of the TASK_USER_DATA structure is allocated to hold information about each task created (except the idle and statistic tasks).

L1.13(3)   µC/OS-II provides another message-passing mechanism called a *message queue*. A message queue is like a mailbox except that instead of being able to send a single pointer, a queue can hold more than one message (i.e., pointers). A message queue thus allows your tasks or ISRs to send messages to other tasks. What each of the pointers point to is application specific, and, of course, both the sender and the receiver need to agree about the contents of the

Example #3   23

messages. Two elements are needed to create a message queue: an OS_EVENT structure and an array of pointers. The depth of the queue is determined by the number of pointers allocated in the pointer array. In this case, the message queue contains 20 entries.

main() is shown in Listing 1.14. Once more, only the new features are described.

Listing 1.14   Example #3, TEST.C, main().

```
void  main (void)
{
    PC_DispClrScr(DISP_BGND_BLACK);

    OSInit();

    PC_DOSSaveReturn();

    PC_VectSet(uCOS, OSCtxSw);

    PC_ElapsedInit();

    strcpy(TaskUserData[TASK_START_ID].TaskName, "StartTask");        (1)
    OSTaskCreateExt(TaskStart,
                    (void *)0,
                    &TaskStartStk[TASK_STK_SIZE - 1],
                    TASK_START_PRIO,
                    TASK_START_ID,
                    &TaskStartStk[0],
                    TASK_STK_SIZE,
                    &TaskUserData[TASK_START_ID],                     (2)
                    0);
    OSStart();
}
```

L1.14(1)   Before a task is created, we assign a name to the task using the ANSI C library function strcpy(). The name is stored in the data structure [see L1.13(1)] assigned to the task.

L1.14(2)   TaskStart() is created using OSTaskCreateExt() and passed a pointer to its user data structure. The TCB of each task in µC/OS-II can store a pointer to a user-provided data structure (see Chapter 3, "Kernel Structure" for details). This feature allows you to extend the functionality of µC/OS-II, as you will see shortly.

The code for TaskStart() is shown in Listing 1.15.

Listing 1.15   Example #3, TEST. C, TaskStart().

```
void  TaskStart (void *pdata)
{
#if OS_CRITICAL_METHOD == 3
    OS_CPU_SR  cpu_sr;
#endif
    INT16S      key;


    pdata = pdata;

    TaskStartDispInit();

    OS_ENTER_CRITICAL();
    PC_VectSet(0x08, OSTickISR);
    PC_SetTickRate(OS_TICKS_PER_SEC);
    OS_EXIT_CRITICAL();

    OSStatInit();

    MsgQueue = OSQCreate(&MsgQueueTbl[0], MSG_QUEUE_SIZE);                    (1)

    TaskStartCreateTasks();                                                  (2)

    for (;;) {
        TaskStartDisp();

        if (PC_GetKey(&key)) {
            if (key == 0x1B) {
                PC_DOSReturn();
            }
        }

        OSCtxSwCtr = 0;
        OSTimeDly(OS_TICKS_PER_SEC);
    }
}
```

Example #3   25

L1.15(1)   Not much has been added except the creation of the message queue that is used by Task1(), Task2(), Task3(), and Task4().

L1.15(2)   As with Example #2, TaskStartCreateTasks() create six tasks. The difference is that each task is assigned an entry in the TaskUserData[] array. As each task is created, it's assigned a name just as I did when I created TaskStart() [see L1.14(1)].

As soon as TaskStart() calls OSTimeDly(OS_TICKS_PER_SEC), μC/OS-II locates the next highest priority task that's ready to run, which is Task1(). Listing 1.16 shows the code for Task1(), Task2(), Task3(), and Task4() because I discuss them next.

Listing 1.16   *Example #3, TEST.C, Task1() through Task4().*

```
void  Task1 (void *pdata)
{
    char  *msg;
    INT8U  err;



    pdata = pdata;
    for (;;) {
        msg = (char *)OSQPend(MsgQueue, 0, &err);                    (1)
        PC_DispStr(70, 13, msg, DISP_FGND_YELLOW + DISP_BGND_BLUE);  (2)
        OSTimeDlyHMSM(0, 0, 0, 100);                                 (3)
    }
}


void  Task2 (void *pdata)
{
    char  msg[20];



    pdata = pdata;
    strcpy(&msg[0], "Task 2");
    for (;;) {
        OSQPost(MsgQueue, (void *)&msg[0]);                          (4)
        OSTimeDlyHMSM(0, 0, 0, 500);                                 (5)
    }
}
```

Listing 1.16   Example #3, `TEST.C`, `Task1()` through `Task4()`. *(Continued)*

```
void  Task3 (void *pdata)
{
    char  msg[20];


    pdata = pdata;
    strcpy(&msg[0], "Task 3");
    for (;;) {
        OSQPost(MsgQueue, (void *)&msg[0]);                          (6)
        OSTimeDlyHMSM(0, 0, 0, 500);
    }
}


void  Task4 (void *pdata)
{
    char  msg[20];


    pdata = pdata;
    strcpy(&msg[0], "Task 4");
    for (;;) {
        OSQPost(MsgQueue, (void *)&msg[0]);                          (7)
        OSTimeDlyHMSM(0, 0, 0, 500);
    }
}
```

L1.16(1)   `Task1()` waits forever for a message to arrive through a message queue.

L1.16(2)   When a message arrives, it is displayed on the screen.

L1.16(3)   The task is delayed for 100ms to allow you to see the message received.

L1.16(4)   `Task2()` sends the message "Task 2" to `Task1()` through the message queue.

L1.16(5)   `Task2()` waits for half a second before sending another message.

L1.16(6)

L1.16(7)   `Task3()` and `Task4()` send their messages and also wait half a second between messages.

Another task, `Task5()` (not shown) does nothing useful except delay itself for 1/10 of a second. Note that all µC/OS-II tasks must call a service provided by µC/OS-II to wait either for time to expire or for an event to occur. If this action is not done, the task prevents all lower priority tasks from running.

Finally, `TaskClk()` (also not shown) displays the current date and time once a second.

Events happen behind the scenes that are not apparent just by looking at the tasks in `TEST.C`. µC/OS-II is provided in source form, and it's quite easy to add functionality to µC/OS-II through special

Example #3 27

functions called *hooks*. As of v2.52, nine hook functions exist, and the prototypes for these functions are shown in Listing 1.17.

Listing 1.17   *µC/OS-II's hooks.*

```
void  OSInitHookBegin(void);
void  OSInitHookEnd(void);
void  OSTaskCreateHook(OS_TCB *ptcb);
void  OSTaskDelHook(OS_TCB *ptcb);
void  OSTaskIdleHook(void);
void  OSTaskStatHook(void);
void  OSTaskSwHook(void);
void  OSTCBInitHook(OS_TCB *ptcb);
void  OSTimeTickHook(void);
```

The hook functions are normally found in a file called OS_CPU_C.C and are generally written by the person who does the port for the processor you intend to use. However, if you set a configuration constant called OS_CPU_HOOKS_EN to 0, you can declare the hook functions in a different file. OS_CPU_HOOKS_EN is one of many configuration constants found in the header file OS_CFG.H. Every project that uses µC/OS-II needs its own version of OS_CFG.H because you might want to configure µC/OS-II differently for each projet. Each example provided in this book contains its own OS_CFG.H in the SOURCE directory.

In Example #3, I set OS_CPU_HOOKS_EN to 0 and redefined the functionality of the hook functions in TEST.C. As shown in Listing 1.18, seven of the nine hooks don't actually do anything and thus don't contain any code.

Listing 1.18   *Example #3,* TEST.C, *empty hook functions.*

```
void  OSInitHookBegin (void)
{
}

void  OSInitHookEnd (void)
{
}

void  OSTaskCreateHook (OS_TCB *ptcb)
{
    ptcb = ptcb;
}

void  OSTaskDelHook (OS_TCB *ptcb)
{
    ptcb = ptcb;
}
```

Listing 1.18   Example #3, TEST.C, empty hook functions. (Continued)

```c
void  OSTaskIdleHook (void)
{
}


void  OSTCBInitHook (OS_TCB *ptcb)
{
    ptcb = ptcb;
}


void  OSTimeTickHook (void)
{
}
```

The code for OSTaskSwHook() is shown in Listing 1.19 and allows us to measure the execution time of each task, keeps track of how often each task executes, and accumulates total execution times of each task. OSTaskSwHook() is called when μC/OS-II switches from a low priority task to a higher priority task.

Listing 1.19   The task switch hook, OSTaskSwHook().

```c
void  OSTaskSwHook (void)
{
    INT16U           time;
    TASK_USER_DATA  *puser;


    time  = PC_ElapsedStop();                           (1)
    PC_ElapsedStart();                                  (2)
    puser = OSTCBCur->OSTCBExtPtr;                      (3)
    if (puser != (TASK_USER_DATA *)0) {                (4)
        puser->TaskCtr++;                              (5)
        puser->TaskExecTime    = time;                 (6)
        puser->TaskTotExecTime += time;                (7)
    }
}
```

L1.19(1) A timer on the PC obtains the execution time of the task being switched out through PC_ElapsedStop().

Example #3   29

1

L1.19(2) It is assumed that the timer was started by calling `PC_ElapsedStart()` when the task was switched in. The first context switch probably reads an incorrect value, but this is not really critical.

L1.19(3) When `OSTaskSwHook()` is called, the global pointer `OSTCBCur` points to the TCB of the current task, while `OSTCBHighRdy` points to the TCB of the new task. In this case, however, we don't use `OSTCBHighRdy`. `OSTaskSwHook()` retrieves the pointer to the TCB extension that was passed in `OSTaskCreateExt()`.

L1.19(4) We then check to make sure we don't de-reference a `NULL` pointer. In fact, some of the tasks in this example do not contain a TCB extension pointer: the idle and the statistic tasks.

L1.19(5) We increment a counter that indicates how many times the task has executed. This counter is useful to determine if a particular task is running.

L1.19(6) The measured execution time (in microseconds) is stored in the TCB extension.

L1.19(7) The total execution time (in microseconds) of the task is also stored in the TCB extension. This element allows you to determine the percent of time each task takes with respect to other tasks in an application (discussed shortly).

When enabled (see `OS_TASK_STAT_EN` in `OS_CFG.H`), the statistic task `OSTaskStat()` calls the user-definable function `OSTaskStatHook()` that is shown in Listing 1.20. `OSTaskStatHook()` is called every second.

Listing 1.20   *The statistic task hook,* `OSTaskStatHook()`.

```
void  OSTaskStatHook (void)
{
    char    s[80];
    INT8U   i;
    INT32U  total;
    INT8U   pct;


    total = 0L;
    for (i = 0; i < 7; i++) {
        total += TaskUserData[i].TaskTotExecTime;          (1)
        DispTaskStat(i);                                   (2)
    }
```

Listing 1.20   *The statistic task hook,*
OSTaskStatHook( ). (Continued)

```
    if (total > 0) {
        for (i = 0; i < 7; i++) {
            pct = 100 * TaskUserData[i].TaskTotExecTime / total;          (3)
            sprintf(s, "%3d %%", pct);
            PC_DispStr(62,                                                 (4)
                       i + 11,
                       s,
                       DISP_FGND_BLACK + DISP_BGND_LIGHT_GRAY);
        }
    }
    if (total > 1000000000L) {
        for (i = 0; i < 7; i++) {
            TaskUserData[i].TaskTotExecTime = 0L;
        }
    }
}
```

L1.20(1)   The total execution time of all the tasks (except the statistic task) is computed.

L1.20(2)   Individual statistics are displayed at the proper location on the screen by `DispTaskStat()`, which takes care of converting the values into ASCII. In addition, `DispTaskStat()` also displays the name of each task.

L1.20(3)

L1.20(4)   The percent execution time is computed for each task and displayed.

If you have the Borland C/C++ v4.5x compiler installed in the `C:\BC45` directory, you can experiment with `TEST.C`. After modifying `TEST.C`, you can type `MAKETEST` from the command prompt of the `TEST` directory to build a new `TEST.EXE`. If you don't have the Borland C/C++ v4.5x compiler or your have it installed in a different directory, you can make changes to `TEST.MAK`, `INCLUDES.H`, and `TEST.LNK` accordingly.

The `SOURCE` directory contains four files: `INCLUDES.H`, `OS_CFG.H`, `TEST.C`, and `TEST.LNK`. `OS_CFG.H` is used to determine µC/OS-II configuration options. `TEST.LNK` is the linker-command file for the Borland linker, `TLINK`.

Example #4   31

1.04   *Example #4*

μC/OS-II is written entirely in C and requires some processor-specific code to adapt it to different processors. This processor-specific code is called a *port*. This book comes with two ports for the Intel 80x86 family of processors: Ix86L (see Chapter 14) and Ix86L-FP (see Chapter 15). Ix86L is used with 80x86 processors that are not fortunate enough to have an FPU, and Ix86L is used in all the examples so far. You should note that Ix86L still runs on 80x86 processors that do have an FPU. Ix86L-FP allows your applications to use the floating-point hardware capabilities of higher-end 80x86 compatible processors. Example #4 uses Ix86L-FP.

In this example, I created 10 identical tasks, each running 200 times per second. Each task computes the sine and cosine of an angle (in degrees). The angle being computed by each task is offset by 36 degrees (360 degrees divided by 10 tasks) from each other. Every time the task executes, it increments the angle to compute by 0.01 degree.

The code for Example #4 is found in the \SOFTWARE\uCOS-II\EX4_x86L.FP\BC45 directory. You can open a DOS window and type

```
CD  \SOFTWARE\uCOS-II\Ex4_x86L.FP\BC45\TEST
```

As usual, to execute Example #4, simply type TEST at the command line prompt. The DOS window runs the TEST.EXE program.

After about two seconds, you should see the screen shown in Figure 1.6. I let TEST.EXE run for a few seconds before I captured the screen shot.

Example #4 consists of 13 tasks, as displayed in the lower left of Figure 1.6. Of those 13 tasks, μC/OS-II creates two internal tasks: the idle task and a task that determines CPU usage. Example #4 creates the other 11 tasks.

Figure 1.6   *Example #4 running in a DOS window.*

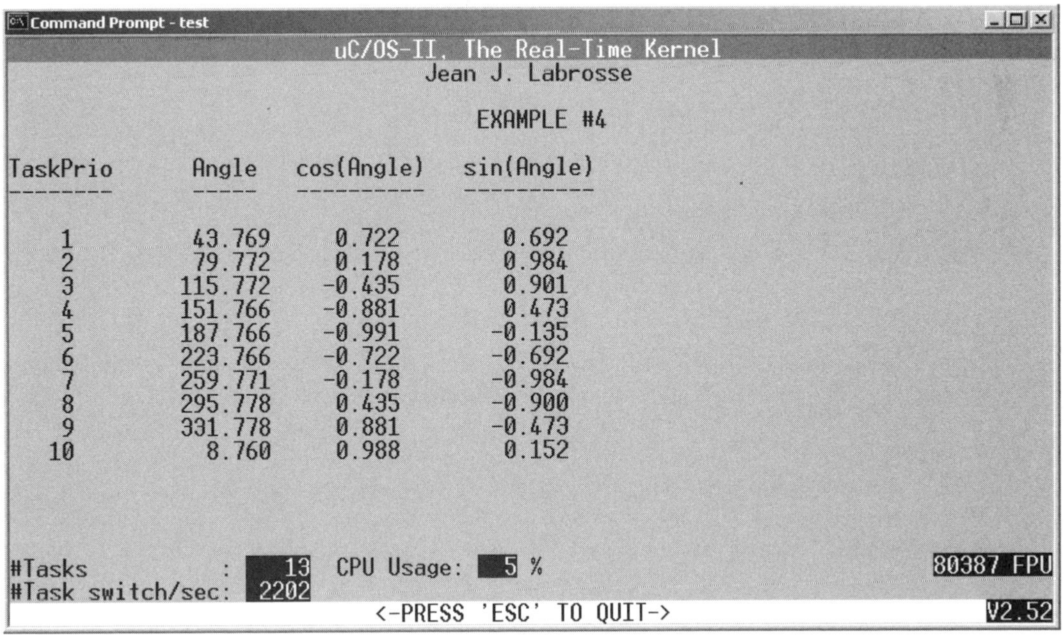

TaskPrio	Angle	cos(Angle)	sin(Angle)
1	43.769	0.722	0.692
2	79.772	0.178	0.984
3	115.772	-0.435	0.901
4	151.766	-0.881	0.473
5	187.766	-0.991	-0.135
6	223.766	-0.722	-0.692
7	259.771	-0.178	-0.984
8	295.778	0.435	-0.900
9	331.778	0.881	-0.473
10	8.760	0.988	0.152

uC/OS-II, The Real-Time Kernel
Jean J. Labrosse

EXAMPLE #4

#Tasks : 13 CPU Usage: 5 % 80387 FPU
#Task switch/sec: 2202
<-PRESS 'ESC' TO QUIT-> V2.52

By now, you should be able to find your way around TEST.C. Example #4 doesn't introduce too many new concepts. However, there are a few subtleties done behind the scene, which I describe after discussing a few items in TEST.C. Listing 1.21 shows the code to create the 10 identical application tasks.

Listing 1.21   Example #4, TEST.C, TaskStartCreateTasks().

```
static  void  TaskStartCreateTasks (void)
{
    INT8U  i;
    INT8U  prio;


    for (i = 0; i < N_TASKS; i++) {
        prio       = i + 1;                                          (1)
        TaskData[i] = prio;                                          (2)
        OSTaskCreateExt(Task,
                   (void *)&TaskData[i],                             (3)
                   &TaskStk[i][TASK_STK_SIZE - 1],
                   prio,
                   0,
                   &TaskStk[i][0],
                   TASK_STK_SIZE,
                   (void *)0,
                   OS_TASK_OPT_SAVE_FP);                             (4)
    }
}
```

L1.21(1)   Because µC/OS-II doesn't allow multiple tasks at the same priority, I offset the priority of the identical tasks by 1 because task priority #0 is assigned to TaskStart().

L1.21(2)   The task priority of each task is placed in an array.

L1.21(3)   µC/OS-II allows you to pass an argument to a task when the task is first started. This argument is a pointer, and I generally call it pdata (pointer to data). The task priority saved in the array is actually passed as the task argument, pdata.

L1.21(4)   Each of the tasks are doing floating-point calculations, and we want to tell the port (see Chapter 15) to save the floating-point registers during a context switch.

Example #4   33

Listing 1.22 shows the actual task code.

Listing 1.22   Example #4, TEST.C, Task().

```c
void  Task (void *pdata)
{
    FP32    x;
    FP32    y;
    FP32    angle;
    FP32    radians;
    char    s[81];
    INT8U   ypos;


    ypos  = *(INT8U *)pdata + 7;
    angle = (FP32)(*(INT8U *)pdata) * (FP32)36.0;                           (1)
    for (;;) {
        radians = (FP32)2.0 * (FP32)3.141592 * angle / (FP32)360.0;         (2)
        x       = cos(radians);
        y       = sin(radians);
        sprintf(s, "  %2d       %8.3f %8.3f      %8.3f",
                *(INT8U *)pdata, angle, x, y);
        PC_DispStr(0, ypos, s, DISP_FGND_BLACK + DISP_BGND_LIGHT_GRAY);
        if (angle >= (FP32)360.0) {
            angle  =    (FP32)0.0;
        } else {
            angle += (FP32)0.01;
        }
        OSTimeDly(1);                                                       (3)
    }
}
```

L1.22(1)   The argument `pdata` points to an 8-bit integer containing the task priority. To make each task calculate different angles (not that it really matters), I decided to offset each task by 36 degrees.

L1.22(2)   `sin()` and `cos()` assumes radians instead of degrees, and thus the conversion.

L1.22(3)   Each task is delayed by one clock tick (i.e., 50ms), and thus each task executes 200 times per second.

Except for specifying `OS_TASK_OPT_SAVE_FP` in `TaskStartCreateTasks()`, you couldn't tell from `TEST.C` that we are using a different port from the other examples. In fact, it might be a good idea to always specify the option `OS_TASK_OPT_SAVE_FP` when you create a task [using `OSTaskCreateExt()`], and, if the port supports floating-point hardware, µC/OS-II can take the necessary steps to save and retrieve the floating-point registers during a context switch. That's, in fact, one of the beauties of µC/OS-II: portability of your applications across different processors.

In order to use a different port (at least for the 80x86), you only need to change the following files:

INCLUDES.H (in the SOURCE directory):
>   Instead of including:
>
>   \software\ucos-ii\ix86l\bc45\os_cpu.h
>
>   you simply need to point to a different directory:
>
>   \software\ucos-ii\ix86l-fp\bc45\os_cpu.h

TEST.LNK (in the SOURCE directory):
>   The linker-command file includes the floating-point emulation library in the non-floating-point version:
>
>   C:\BC45\LIB\EMU.LIB

and the hardware floating-point library needs to be referenced for the code that makes use of the FPU:

>   C:\BC45\LIB\FP87.LIB

TEST.MAK (in the TEST directory):
>   The directory of the port is changed from:
>
>   PORT=\SOFTWARE\uCOS-II\Ix86L\BC45
>
>   to:
>
>   PORT=\SOFTWARE\uCOS-II\Ix86L-FP\BC45

The compiler flags in the macro C_FLAGS include -f287 for the floating-point version of the code and omits it in the non-floating-point version.

Real-time Systems Concepts

Real-time systems are characterized by the severe consequences that result if logical as well as timing correctness properties of the system are not met. Two types of real-time systems exist: *soft* and *hard*. In a soft real-time system, tasks are performed by the system as fast as possible, but the tasks don't have to finish by specific times. In hard real-time systems, tasks have to be performed not only correctly but on time. Most real-time systems have a combination of soft and hard requirements. Real-time applications cover a wide range, but most real-time systems are *embedded*. An embedded system is a computer built into a system and not seen by the user as being a computer. The following list shows a few examples of embedded systems.

Process control
 Food processing
 Chemical plants
Automotive
 Engine controls
 Antilock braking systems
Office automation
 FAX machines
 Copiers
Computer peripherals
 Printers
 Terminals
 Scanners
 Modems

Communication
 Switches
 Routers
Robots
Aerospace
 Flight management systems
 Weapons systems
 Jet engine controls
Domestic
 Microwave ovens
 Dishwashers
 Washing machines
 Thermostats

Real-time software applications are typically more difficult to design than non-real-time applications. This chapter describes real-time concepts.

2.00   *Foreground/Background Systems*

Small systems of low complexity are generally designed as shown in Figure 2.1. These systems are called *foreground/background systems* or *super-loops*. An application consists of an infinite loop that calls modules (i.e., functions) to perform the desired operations (background). Interrupt service routines (ISRs) handle asynchronous events (foreground). Foreground is also called *interrupt level*; background is called *task level*. Critical operations must be performed by the ISRs to ensure that they are dealt with in a timely fashion. Because of this, ISRs have a tendency to take longer than they should. Also, information for a background module that an ISR makes available is not processed until the background routine gets its turn to execute, which is called the *task-level response*. The worst case task-level response time depends on how long the background loop takes to execute. Because the execution time of typical code is not constant, the time for successive passes through a portion of the loop is nondeterministic. Furthermore, if a code change is made, the timing of the loop is affected.

Figure 2.1   *Foreground/background systems.*

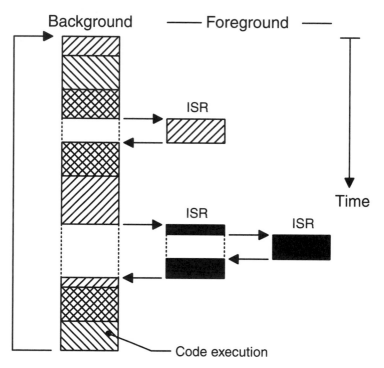

Most high-volume microcontroller-based applications (e.g., microwave ovens, telephones, toys, and so on) are designed as foreground/background systems. Also, in microcontroller-based applications, it might be better (from a power consumption point of view) to halt the processor and perform all of the processing in ISRs.

2.01 Critical Sections of Code

A critical section of code, also called a *critical region*, is code that needs to be treated indivisibly. After the section of code starts executing, it must not be interrupted. To ensure that execution is not interrupted, interrupts are typically disabled before the critical code is executed and enabled when the critical code is finished (see also Section 2.03, "Shared Resources").

2.02 Resources

A resource is any entity used by a task. A resource can thus be an I/O device, such as a printer, a keyboard, a display, a variable, a structure, or an array.

2.03 Shared Resources

A shared resource is a resource that can be used by more than one task. Each task should gain exclusive access to the shared resource to prevent data corruption. This process is called *mutual exclusion*, and techniques to ensure mutual exclusion are discussed in Section 2.18, "Mutual Exclusion".

2.04 Multitasking

Multitasking is the process of scheduling and switching the central processing unit (CPU) between several tasks; a single CPU switches its attention between several sequential tasks. Multitasking is like foreground/background with multiple backgrounds. Multitasking maximizes the use of the CPU and also provides for modular construction of applications. One of the most important aspects of multitasking is that it allows the application programmer to manage complexity inherent in real-time applications. Application programs are typically easier to design and maintain if multitasking is used.

2.05 Tasks

A task, also called a *thread*, is a simple program that thinks it has the CPU all to itself. The design process for a real-time application involves splitting the work to be done into tasks responsible for a portion of the problem. Each task is assigned a priority, its own set of CPU registers, and its own stack area (as shown in Figure 2.2).

Each task typically is an infinite loop that can be in any one of five states: *dormant*, *ready*, *running*, *waiting* (for an event), or *ISR* (interrupted) (Figure 2.3). The dormant state corresponds to a task that resides in memory but has not been made available to the multitasking kernel. A task is ready when it can execute but its priority is less than the currently running task. A task is running when it has control of the CPU. A task is waiting when it requires the occurrence of an event (for example, waiting for an I/O operation to complete, a shared resource to be available, a timing pulse to occur, or time to expire). Finally, a task is in the ISR state when an interrupt has occurred and the CPU is in the process of servicing the interrupt. Figure 2.3 also shows the functions provided by µC/OS-II to make a task move from one state to another.

Figure 2.2   *Multiple tasks.*

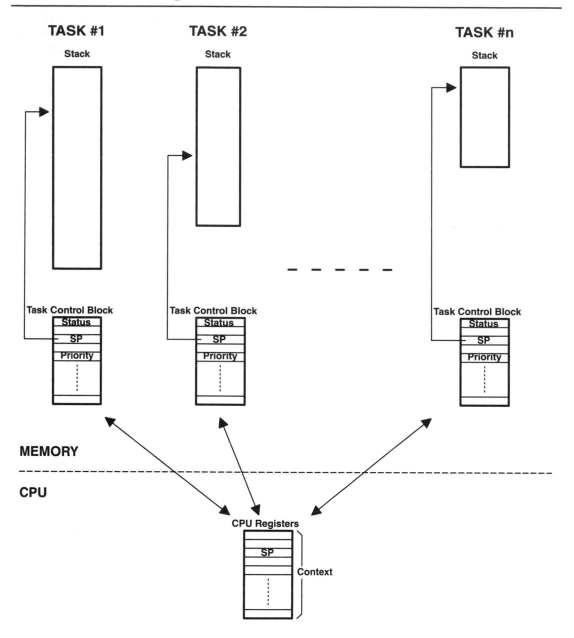

Figure 2.3 **Task states.**

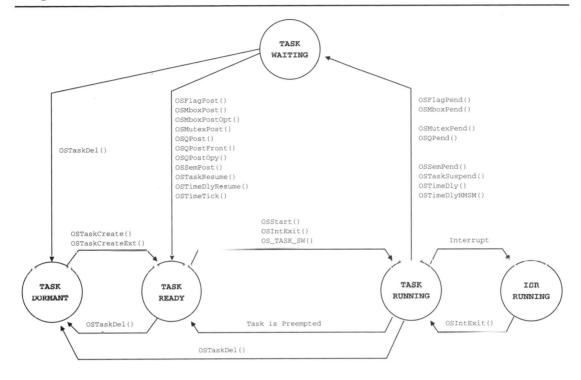

2.06 Context Switches (or Task Switches)

When a multitasking kernel decides to run a different task, it saves the current task's *context* (CPU registers) in the current task's context storage area — its stack (Figure 2.2). After this operation is performed, the new task's context is restored from its storage area and then resumes execution of the new task's code. This process is called a *context switch* or a *task switch*. Context switching adds overhead to the application. The more registers a CPU has, the higher the overhead. The time required to perform a context switch is determined by how many registers have to be saved and restored by the CPU. Performance of a real-time kernel should not be judged by how many context switches the kernel is capable of doing per second.

2.07 Kernels

The kernel is the part of a multitasking system responsible for management of tasks (i.e., for managing the CPU's time) and communication between tasks. The fundamental service provided by the kernel is context switching. The use of a real-time kernel generally simplifies the design of systems by allowing the application to be divided into multiple tasks that the kernel manages.

A kernel adds overhead to your system because the services provided by the kernel require execution time. The amount of overhead depends on how often you invoke these services. In a well-designed application, a kernel uses between 2 and 5% of CPU time. Because a kernel is software that gets added to your application, it requires extra ROM (code space) and additional RAM (data space) for the kernel data structures, and each task requires its own stack space, which eats up RAM quickly.

Single-chip microcontrollers are generally not able to run a real-time kernel because they have very little RAM. A kernel allows you to make better use of your CPU by providing indispensable services, such as semaphore management, mailboxes, queues, and time delays. After you design a system using a real-time kernel, you will not want to go back to a foreground/background system.

2.08   Schedulers

The scheduler, also called the *dispatcher*, is the part of the kernel responsible for determining which task runs next. Most real-time kernels are priority based. Each task is assigned a priority based on its importance. The priority for each task is application specific. In a priority-based kernel, control of the CPU is always given to the highest priority task ready to run. When the highest priority task gets the CPU, however, is determined by the type of kernel used. Two types of priority-based kernels exist: *non-preemptive* and *preemptive*.

2.09   Non-Preemptive Kernels

Non-preemptive kernels require that each task does something to explicitly give up control of the CPU. To maintain the illusion of concurrency, this process must be done frequently. Non-preemptive scheduling is also called *cooperative multitasking*; tasks cooperate with each other to share the CPU. Asynchronous events are still handled by ISRs. An ISR can make a higher priority task ready to run, but the ISR always returns to the interrupted task. The new higher priority task gains control of the CPU only when the current task gives up the CPU.

One of the advantages of a non-preemptive kernel is that interrupt latency is typically low (see Section 2.26, "Interrupt Latency"). At the task level, non-preemptive kernels can also use non-reentrant functions (Section 2.11, "Reentrant Functions"). Non-reentrant functions can be used by each task without fear of corruption by another task. This is because each task can run to completion before it relinquishes the CPU. However, non-reentrant functions should not be allowed to give up control of the CPU.

Task-level response using a non-preemptive kernel can be much lower than with foreground/background systems because task-level response is now given by the time of the longest task.

Another advantage of non-preemptive kernels is the lesser need to guard shared data through the use of semaphores. Each task owns the CPU, and you don't have to fear that a task will be preempted. This rule is not absolute, and, in some instances, semaphores should still be used. Shared I/O devices can still require the use of mutual exclusion semaphores; for example, a task might still need exclusive access to a printer.

The execution profile of a non-preemptive kernel is shown in Figure 2.4 and described as follows.

Figure 2.4   Non-preemptive kernel.

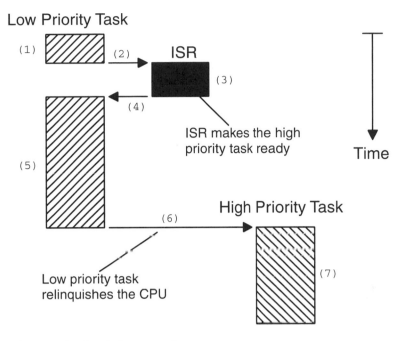

F2.4(1)   A task is executing but is interrupted.

F2.4(2)   If interrupts are enabled, the CPU vectors (jumps) to the ISR.

F2.4(3).   The ISR handles the event and makes a higher priority task ready to run.

F2.4(4)   Upon completion of the ISR, a *Return From Interrupt* instruction is executed, and the CPU returns to the interrupted task.

F2.4(5)   The task code resumes at the instruction following the interrupted instruction.

F2.4(6)   When the task code completes, it calls a service that the kernel provides to relinquish the CPU to another task.

F2.4(7)   The kernel sees that a higher priority task has been made ready to run (it doesn't necessarily know that it was from an ISR nor does it care), and thus the kernel performs a context switch so that it can run (i.e., execute) the higher priority task to handle the event that the ISR signaled.

The most important drawback of a non-preemptive kernel is responsiveness. A higher priority task that has been made ready to run might have to wait a long time to run because the current task must give up the CPU when it is ready to do so. As with background execution in foreground/background systems, task-level response time in a non-preemptive kernel is nondeterministic; you never really know when the highest priority task will get control of the CPU. It is up to your application to relinquish control of the CPU.

To summarize, a non-preemptive kernel allows each task to run until it voluntarily gives up control of the CPU. An interrupt preempts a task. Upon completion of the ISR, the ISR returns to the interrupted task. Task-level response is much better than with a foreground/background system but is still nondeterministic. Very few commercial kernels are non-preemptive.

2.10   Preemptive Kernels

A preemptive kernel is used when system responsiveness is important; therefore, μC/OS-II and most commercial real-time kernels are preemptive. The highest priority task ready to run is always given control of the CPU. When a task makes a higher priority task ready to run, the current task is preempted (suspended), and the higher priority task is immediately given control of the CPU. If an ISR makes a higher priority task ready, when the ISR completes, the interrupted task is suspended, and the new higher priority task is resumed.

The execution profile of a preemptive kernel is shown in Figure 2.5 and described as follows.

Figure 2.5   Preemptive kernel.

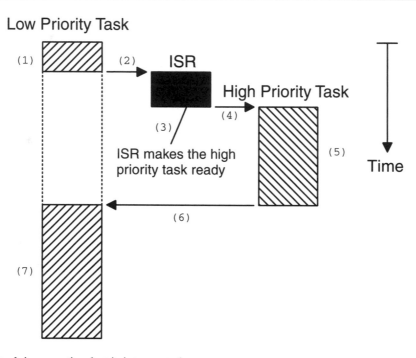

F2.5(1)   A task is executing but is interrupted.

F2.5(2)   If interrupts are enabled, the CPU vectors (jumps) to the ISR.

F2.5(3)   The ISR handles the event and makes a higher priority task ready to run. Upon completion of the ISR, a service provided by the kernel is invoked (i.e., a function that the kernel provides is called).

F2.5(4)

F2.5(5)   This function knows that a more important task has been made ready to run, and thus, instead of returning to the interrupted task, the kernel performs a context switch and executes the code of the more important task. When the more important task is done, another function that the kernel provides is called to put the task to sleep waiting for the event (i.e., the ISR) to occur.

F2.5(6)

F2.5(7)   The kernel then sees that a lower priority task needs to execute, and another context switch is done to resume execution of the interrupted task.

With a preemptive kernel, execution of the highest priority task is deterministic; you can determine when it will get control of the CPU. Task-level response time is thus minimized by using a preemptive kernel.

Application code using a preemptive kernel should not use non-reentrant functions unless exclusive access to these functions is ensured through the use of mutual exclusion semaphores, because both a low and a high priority task can use a common function. Corruption of data can occur if the higher priority task preempts a lower priority task that is using the function.

To summarize, a preemptive kernel always executes the highest priority task that is ready to run. An interrupt preempts a task. Upon completion of an ISR, the kernel resumes execution of the highest priority task ready to run (not "necessarily" the interrupted task). Task-level response is optimum and deterministic. µC/OS-II is a preemptive kernel.

2.11 *Reentrant Functions*

A *reentrant function* can be used by more than one task without fear of data corruption. A reentrant function can be interrupted at any time and resumed at a later time without loss of data. Reentrant functions either use local variables (i.e., CPU registers or variables on the stack) or protect data when global variables are used. An example of a reentrant function is shown in Listing 2.1.

Listing 2.1   *Reentrant function.*

```
void strcpy(char *dest, char *src)
{
    while (*dest++ = *src++) {
        ;
    }
    *dest = NUL;
}
```

Because copies of the arguments to strcpy() are placed on the task's stack, strcpy() can be invoked by multiple tasks without fear that the tasks will corrupt each other's pointers.

An example of a non-reentrant function is shown in Listing 2.2. swap() is a simple function that swaps the contents of its two arguments. For the sake of discussion, I assume that you are using a preemptive kernel, that interrupts are enabled, and that Temp is declared as a global integer:

Listing 2.2   *Non-reentrant function.*

```
int Temp;

void swap(int *x, int *y)
{
    Temp = *x;
    *x   = *y;
    *y   = Temp;
}
```

The programmer intended to make swap() usable by any task. Figure 2.6 shows what could happen if a low-priority task is interrupted while swap() is executing.

Figure 2.6   Non-reentrant function.

LOW PRIORITY TASK   **HIGH PRIORITY TASK**

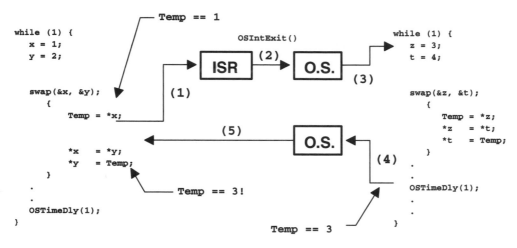

F2.6(1)   When swap() is interrupted Temp contains 1.

F2.6(2)

F2.6(3)   The ISR makes the higher priority task ready to run, so at the completion of the ISR, the kernel (assuming μC/OS-II) is invoked to switch to this task. The high priority task sets Temp to 3 and swaps the contents of its variables correctly (i.e., z is 4 and t is 3).

F2.6(4)   The high priority task eventually relinquishes control to the low priority task by calling a kernel service to delay itself for one clock tick (Section 2.32, "Clock Tick").

F2.6(5)   The lower priority task is thus resumed. Note that at this point, Temp is still set to 3! When the low priority task resumes execution, the task sets y to 3 instead of 1.

Note that this example is simple, so it is obvious how to make the code reentrant. You can make swap() reentrant with one of the following techniques:

- Declare Temp local to swap().
- Disable interrupts before the operation and enable them afterwards.
- Use a semaphore (Section 2.18, "Mutual Exclusion").
- Other situations are not as easy to solve. An error caused by a non-reentrant function might not show up in your application during the testing phase; it will most likely occur after the product has been delivered! If you are new to multitasking, you need to be careful when using non-reentrant functions.

If the interrupt occurs either before or after swap(), the x and y values for both tasks are correct.

2.12 Round-Robin Scheduling

When two or more tasks have the same priority, the kernel allows one task to run for a predetermined amount of time, called a *quantum*, and then selects another task. This process is called *round-robin scheduling or time slicing*. The kernel gives control to the next task in line if

- the current task has no work to do during its time slice or
- the current task completes before the end of its time slice or
- the time slice ends.

µC/OS-II does not currently support round-robin scheduling. Each task must have a unique priority in your application.

2.13 Task Priorities

A priority is assigned to each task. The more important the task, the higher the priority given to it. With most kernels, you are generally responsible for deciding what priority each task gets.

2.14 Static Priorities

Task priorities are *static* when the priority of each task does not change during the application's execution. Each task is thus given a fixed priority at compile time. All the tasks and their timing constraints are known at compile time in a system where priorities are static.

2.15 Dynamic Priorities

Task priorities are *dynamic* if the priority of tasks can be changed during the application's execution; each task can change its priority at run time. This is a desirable feature to have in a real-time kernel to avoid priority inversions. µC/OS-II provides this feature.

2.16 Priority Inversions

Priority inversion is a problem in real-time systems and occurs mostly when you use a real-time kernel. Figure 2.7 illustrates a priority inversion scenario. Task 1 has a higher priority than Task 2, which in turn has a higher priority than Task 3.

Figure 2.7   Priority inversion problem.

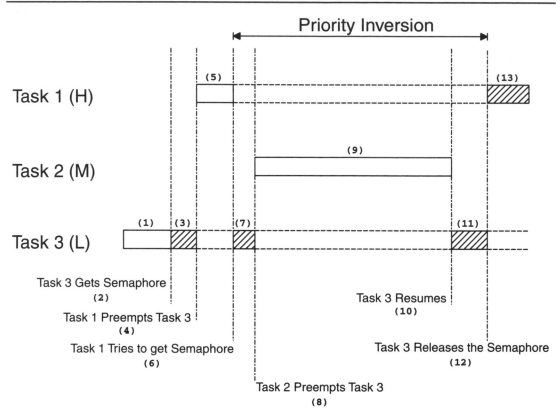

F2.7(1)   Task 1 and Task 2 are both waiting for an event to occurs and Task 3 is executing.

F2.7(2)   At some point, Task 3 acquires a semaphore (see Section 2.18.04, "Semaphores"), which the task needs before it can access a shared resource.

F2.7(3)   Task 3 performs some operations on the acquired resource.

F2.7(4)   The event for which Task 1 was waiting occurs, and thus the kernel suspends Task 3 and starts executing Task 1 because Task 1 has a higher priority.

F2.7(5)

F2.7(6)   Task 1 executes for a while until it also wants to access the resource (i.e., it attempts to get the semaphore that Task 3 owns). Because Task 3 owns the resource, Task 1 is placed in a list of tasks waiting for the kernel to free the semaphore.

F2.7(7)

F2.7(8)   Task 3 resumes and continues execution until it is preempted by Task 2 because the event for which Task 2 was waiting occurred.

F2.7(9)

F2.7(10)   Task 2 handles the event for which it was waiting, and, when it's done, the kernel relinquishes the CPU back to Task 3.

F2.7(11)

F2.7(12) Task 3 finishes working with the resource and releases the semaphore. At this point, the kernel knows that a higher priority task is waiting for the semaphore and performs a context switch to resume Task 1.

F2.7(13) At this point, Task 1 has the semaphore and can access the shared resource.

2

The priority of Task 1 has been virtually reduced to that of Task 3 because Task 1 was waiting for the resource that Task 3 owned. The situation was aggravated when Task 2 preempted Task 3, which further delayed the execution of Task 1.

You can correct this situation by raising the priority of Task 3, just for the time it takes to access the resource, and then restoring the original priority level when the task is finished. The priority of Task 3 should be raised up to or above the highest priority of the other tasks competing for the resource. A multitasking kernel should allow task priorities to change dynamically to help prevent priority inversions. However, it takes some time to change a task's priority. What if Task 3 had completed access of the resource before it was preempted by Task 1 and then by Task 2? Had you raised the priority of Task 3 before accessing the resource and then lowered it when done, you would have wasted valuable CPU time. What is really needed to avoid priority inversion is a kernel that changes the priority of a task automatically, which is called *priority inheritance*. μC/OS-II provides this feature (see Chapter 8, "Mutual Exclusion Semaphores").

Figure 2.8 illustrates what happens when a kernel supports priority inheritance.

Figure 2.8   *Kernel that supports priority inheritance.*

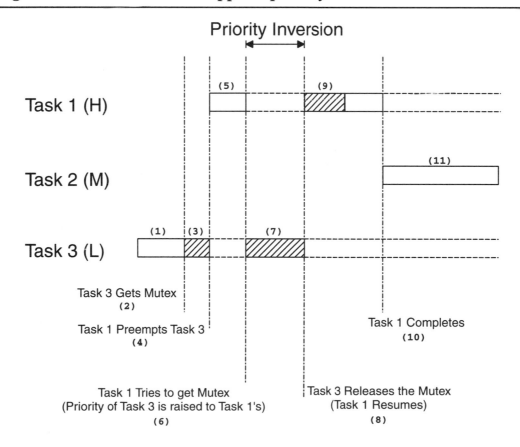

F2.8(1)

F2.8(2)   As with the previous example, Task 3 is running but, this time, acquires a mutual exclusion semaphore (also called a mutex) to access a shared resource.

F2.8(3)

F2.8(4)   Task 3 accesses the resource and then is preempted by Task 1.

F2.8(5)

F2.8(6)   Task 1 executes and tries to obtain the mutex. The kernel sees that Task 3 has the mutex and knows that Task 3 has a lower priority than Task 1. In this case, the kernel raises the priority of Task 3 to the same level as Task 1.

F2.8(7)   The kernel places Task 1 in the mutex wait list and then resumes execution of Task 3 so that this task can continue with the resource.

F2.8(8)   When Task 3 is done with the resource, it releases the mutex. At this point, the kernel reduces the priority of Task 3 to its original value and looks in the mutex waiting list to see if a task is waiting for the mutex. The kernel sees that Task 1 is waiting and gives it the mutex.

F2.8(9)   Task 1 is now free to access the resource.

F2.8(10)

F2.8(11) When Task 1 is done executing, the medium priority task (i.e., Task 2) gets the CPU. Note that Task 2 could have been ready to run any time between F2.8(3) and F2.8(10) without affecting the outcome. Some level of priority inversion cannot be avoided but far less is present than in the previous scenario.

2.17   Assigning Task Priorities

Assigning task priorities is not a trivial undertaking because of the complex nature of real-time systems. In most systems, not all tasks are considered critical. Noncritical tasks should obviously be given low priorities. Most real-time systems have a combination of soft and hard requirements. In a soft real-time system, tasks are performed as quickly as possible, but they don't have to finish by specific times. In hard real-time systems, tasks have to be performed not only correctly but on time.

An interesting technique called *rate monotonic scheduling* (RMS) has been established to assign task priorities based on how often tasks execute. Simply put, tasks with the highest rate of execution are given the highest priority (Figure 2.9).

RMS makes a number of assumptions:

- All tasks are periodic (they occur at regular intervals).

- Tasks do not synchronize with one another, share resources, or exchange data.

- The CPU must always execute the highest priority task that is ready to run. In other words, preemptive scheduling must be used.

Given a set of *n* tasks that are assigned RMS priorities, the basic RMS theorem states that all task hard real-time deadlines are always met if the inequality in Equation [2.1] is verified.

[2.1]
$$\sum_i \frac{E_i}{T_i} \le n(2^{1/n} - 1)$$

Where E_i corresponds to the maximum execution time of task i and T_i corresponds to the execution period of task i. In other words, E_i / T_i corresponds to the fraction of CPU time required to execute task i. Table 2.1 (page 50) shows the value for size $n(2^{1/n} - 1)$ based on the number of tasks. The upper bound for an infinite number of tasks is given by ln(2), or 0.693, which means that to meet all hard real-time deadlines based on RMS, CPU use of all time-critical tasks should be less than 70 percent! Note that you can still have non-time-critical tasks in a system and thus use 100 percent of the CPU's time. Using 100 percent of your CPU's time is not a desirable goal because it does not allow for code changes and added features. As a rule of thumb, you should always design a system to use less than 60 to 70 percent of your CPU.

RMS says that the highest rate task has the highest priority. In some cases, the highest rate task might not be the most important task. Your application dictates how you need to assign priorities. However, RMS is an interesting starting point.

Figure 2.9   Assigning task priorities based on task execution rate.

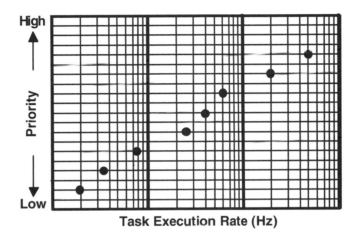

2.18 Mutual Exclusion

The easiest way for tasks to communicate with each other is through shared data structures. This process is especially easy when all tasks exist in a single address space and can reference elements, such as global variables, pointers, buffers, linked lists, and ring buffers. Although sharing data simplifies the exchange of information, you must ensure that each task has exclusive access to the data to avoid contention and data corruption. The most common methods of obtaining exclusive access to shared resources are

- disabling interrupts,
- performing test-and-set operations,
- disabling scheduling, and
- using semaphores.

Table 2.1　　**Allowable CPU use based on number of tasks.**

Number of Tasks	$n(2^{1/n} - 1)$
1	1.000
2	0.828
3	0.779
4	0.756
5	0.743
.	.
.	.
.	.
–	0.693

2.18.01　Disabling and Enabling Interrupts

The easiest and fastest way to gain exclusive access to a shared resource is by disabling and enabling interrupts, as shown in the pseudocode in Listing 2.3.

Listing 2.3　　*Disabling and enabling interrupts.*

```
Disable interrupts;
Access the resource (read/write from/to variables);
Reenable interrupts;
```

µC/OS-II uses this technique (as do most, if not all, kernels) to access internal variables and data structures. In fact, µC/OS-II provides two macros that allow you to disable and then enable interrupts from your C code: OS_ENTER_CRITICAL() and OS_EXIT_CRITICAL(), respectively [see Section 3.00, "Critical Sections, OS_ENTER_CRITICAL() and OS_EXIT_CRITICAL()"]. You always need to use these macros in tandem, as shown in Listing 2.4.

Listing 2.4　　*Using µC/OS-II macros to disable and enable interrupts.*

```
void Function (void)
{
    OS_ENTER_CRITICAL();
    .
    .     /* You can access shared data in here */
    .
    OS_EXIT_CRITICAL();
}
```

You must be careful, however, not to disable interrupts for too long. Doing so affects the response of your system to interrupts, which is known as *interrupt latency*. You should consider this method when you are changing or copying a few variables. Also, this method is the only way that a task can share variables or data structures with an ISR. In all cases, you should keep interrupts disabled for as little time as possible.

If you use a kernel, you are basically allowed to disable interrupts for as much time as the kernel does without affecting interrupt latency. Obviously, you need to know how long the kernel will disable interrupts. Any good kernel vendor should provide you with this information. After all, if they sell a real-time kernel, time is important!

2.18.02   Test-and-Set Operations

If you are not using a kernel, two functions could agree that to access a resource, they must check a global variable and if the variable is 0, the function has access to the resource. To prevent the other function from accessing the resource, however, the first function that gets the resource sets the variable to 1, which is called a *test-and-set* (or TAS) operation. Either the TAS operation must be performed indivisibly (by the processor), or you must disable interrupts when doing the TAS on the variable, as shown in Listing 2.5.

Listing 2.5   *Using test-and-set to access a resource.*

```
Disable interrupts;
if ('Access Variable' is 0) {
    Set variable to 1;
    Reenable interrupts;
    Access the resource;
    Disable interrupts;
    Set the 'Access Variable' back to 0;
    Reenable interrupts;
} else {
    Reenable interrupts;
    /* You don't have access to the resource, try back later; */
}
```

Some processors actually implement a TAS operation in hardware (e.g., the 68000 family of processors have the TAS instruction).

2.18.03   Disabling and Enabling the Scheduler

If your task is not sharing variables or data structures with an ISR, you can disable and enable scheduling (see Section 3.07, "Locking and Unlocking the Scheduler"), as shown in Listing 2.6 (using μC/OS-II as an example). In this case, two or more tasks can share data without the possibility of contention. You should note that while the scheduler is locked, interrupts are enabled, and, if an interrupt occurs while in the critical section, the ISR is executed immediately. At the end of the ISR, the kernel always returns to the interrupted task, even if the ISR has made a higher priority task ready to run. Because the ISR returns to the interrupted task, the behavior of the kernel is very similar to that of a non-preemptive kernel (at least, while the scheduler is locked). The scheduler is invoked when

`OSSchedUnlock()` is called to see if a higher priority task has been made ready to run by the task or an ISR. A context switch results if a higher priority task is ready to run. Although this method works well, you should avoid disabling the scheduler because it defeats the purpose of having a kernel in the first place. The next method should be chosen instead.

Listing 2.6   *Accessing shared data by disabling and enabling scheduling.*

```
void Function (void)
{
    OSSchedLock();
    .
    .    /* You can access shared data in here (interrupts are recognized) */
    .
    OSSchedUnlock();
}
```

2.18.04   *Semaphores*

The semaphore was invented by Edgser Dijkstra in the mid-1960s. It is a protocol mechanism offered by most multitasking kernels. Semaphores are used to

- control access to a shared resource (mutual exclusion),
- signal the occurrence of an event, and
- allow two tasks to synchronize their activities.

A semaphore is a key that your code acquires in order to continue execution. If the semaphore is already in use, the requesting task is suspended until the semaphore is released by its current owner. In other words, the requesting task says: "Give me the key. If someone else is using it, I am willing to wait for it!" Two types of semaphores exist: *binary* semaphores and *counting* semaphores. As its name implies, a binary semaphore can only take two values: 0 or 1. A counting semaphore allows values between 0 and 255, 65,535, or 4,294,967,295, depending on whether the semaphore mechanism is implemented using 8, 16, or 32 bits, respectively. The actual size depends on the kernel used. Along with the semaphore's value, the kernel also needs to keep track of tasks waiting for the semaphore's availability.

Generally, only three operations can be performed on a semaphore: `INITIALIZE` (also called `CREATE`), `WAIT` (also called `PEND`), and `SIGNAL` (also called `POST`). The initial value of the semaphore must be provided when the semaphore is initialized. The waiting list of tasks is always initially empty.

A task desiring the semaphore performs a `WAIT` operation. If the semaphore is available (the semaphore value is greater than 0), the semaphore value is decremented, and the task continues execution. If the semaphore's value is 0, the task performing a `WAIT` on the semaphore is placed in a waiting list. Most kernels allow you to specify a timeout; if the semaphore is not available within a certain amount of time, the requesting task is made ready to run, and an error code (indicating that a timeout has occurred) is returned to the caller.

A task releases a semaphore by performing a `SIGNAL` operation. If no task is waiting for the semaphore, the semaphore value is simply incremented. If any task is waiting for the semaphore, however, one of the tasks is made ready to run, and the semaphore value is not incremented; the "key" is given to one of the tasks waiting for it. Depending on the kernel, the task that receives the semaphore is either

2

- the highest priority task waiting for the semaphore or
- the first task that requested the semaphore (First In First Out, or FIFO).

Some kernels have an option that allows you to choose either method when the semaphore is initialized. µC/OS-II only supports the first method. If the readied task has a higher priority than the current task (the task releasing the semaphore), a context switch occurs (with a preemptive kernel), and the higher priority task resumes execution; the current task is suspended until it again becomes the highest priority task ready to run.

Listing 2.7 shows how you can share data using a semaphore (in µC/OS-II). Any task needing access to the same shared data calls OSSemPend(), and, when the task is done with the data, the task calls OSSemPost(). Both of these functions are described later. You should note that a semaphore is an object that needs to be initialized before it's used; for mutual exclusion, a semaphore is initialized to a value of 1. Using a semaphore to access shared data doesn't affect interrupt latency. If an ISR or the current task makes a higher priority task ready to run while accessing shared data, the higher priority task executes immediately.

Listing 2.7   *Accessing shared data by obtaining a semaphore.*

```
OS_EVENT *SharedDataSem;


void Function (void)
{
    INT8U err;

    OSSemPend(SharedDataSem, 0, &err);
    .
    .    /* You can access shared data in here (interrupts are recognized) */
    .
    OSSemPost(SharedDataSem);
}
```

Semaphores are especially useful when tasks share I/O devices. Imagine what would happen if two tasks were allowed to send characters to a printer at the same time. The printer would contain interleaved data from each task. For instance, the printout from Task 1 printing "I am Task 1!" and Task 2 printing "I am Task 2!" could result in:

I Ia amm T Tasask k1 !2!

In this case, use a semaphore and initialize it to 1 (i.e., a binary semaphore). The rule is simple: to access the printer, each task first must obtain the resource's semaphore. Figure 2.10 shows tasks competing for a semaphore to gain exclusive access to the printer. Note that the semaphore is represented symbolically by a key, indicating that each task must obtain this key to use the printer.

Figure 2.10 *Using a semaphore to get permission to access a printer.*

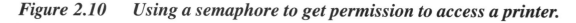

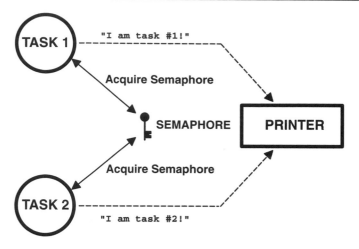

The above example implies that each task must know about the existence of the semaphore in order to access the resource. In some situations, it is better to encapsulate the semaphore. Each task would thus not know that it is actually acquiring a semaphore when accessing the resource. For example, an RS-232C port is used by multiple tasks to send commands and receive responses from a device connected at the other end (Figure 2.11).

The function `CommSendCmd()` is called with three arguments: the ASCII string containing the command, a pointer to the response string from the device, and, finally, a timeout in case the device doesn't respond within a certain amount of time. The pseudocode for this function is shown in Listing 2.8.

Listing 2.8 *Encapsulating a semaphore.*

```
INT8U CommSendCmd(char *cmd, char *response, INT16U timeout)
{
    Acquire port's semaphore;
    Send command to device;
    Wait for response (with timeout);
    if (timed out) {
        Release semaphore;
        return (error code);
    } else {
        Release semaphore;
        return (no error);
    }
}
```

Each task that needs to send a command to the device has to call this function. The semaphore is assumed to be initialized to 1 (i.e., available) by the communication driver initialization routine. The first task that calls `CommSendCmd()` acquires the semaphore, proceeds to send the command, and waits for a response. If another task attempts to send a command while the port is busy, this second task is suspended until the semaphore is released. The second task appears simply to have made a call to a normal function that does not return until the function has performed its duty. When the semaphore is released by the first task, the second task acquires the semaphore and is allowed to use the RS-232C port.

Figure 2.11   Hiding a semaphore from tasks.

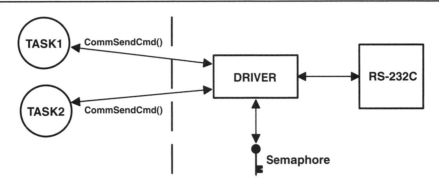

A counting semaphore is used when a resource can be used by more than one task at the same time. For example, a counting semaphore is used in the management of a buffer pool, as shown in Figure 2.12. Assume that the buffer pool initially contains 10 buffers. A task obtains a buffer from the buffer manager by calling BufReq(). When the buffer is no longer needed, the task returns the buffer to the buffer manager by calling BufRel(). The pseudocode for these functions is shown in Listing 2.9.

Listing 2.9   Buffer management using a semaphore.

```
BUF *BufReq(void)
{
    BUF *ptr;

    Acquire a semaphore;
    Disable interrupts;
    ptr         = BufFreeList;
    BufFreeList = ptr->BufNext;
    Enable interrupts;
    return (ptr);
}
```

Listing 2.9   *Buffer management using a semaphore. (Continued)*

```
void BufRel(BUF *ptr)
{
    Disable interrupts;
    ptr->BufNext = BufFreeList;
    BufFreeList  = ptr;
    Enable interrupts;
    Release semaphore;
}
```

Figure 2.12   *Using a counting semaphore.*

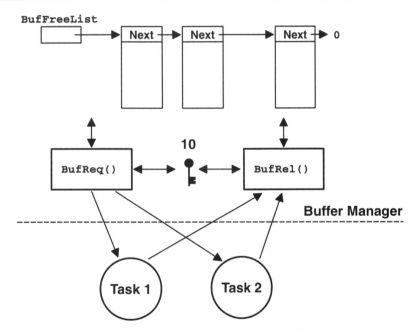

The buffer manager satisfies the first 10 buffer requests because 10 keys exist. When all semaphores are used, a task requesting a buffer is suspended until a semaphore becomes available. Interrupts are disabled to gain exclusive access to the linked list (this operation is very quick). When a task is finished with the buffer it acquired, the task calls BufRel() to return the buffer to the buffer manager; the buffer is inserted into the linked list before the semaphore is released. By encapsulating the interface to the buffer manager in BufReq() and BufRel(), the caller doesn't need to be concerned with the actual implementation details.

Semaphores are often overused. The use of a semaphore to access a simple shared variable is overkill in most situations. The overhead involved in acquiring and releasing the semaphore can consume valuable time. You can do the job just as efficiently by disabling and enabling interrupts (see Section 2.18.01, "Disabling and Enabling Interrupts"). Suppose that two tasks are sharing a 32-bit integer variable. The first task increments the variable while the other task clears it. If you consider how long a processor takes to perform either operation, you should realize that you do not need a semaphore to gain exclusive access to the variable. Each task simply needs to disable interrupts before performing its operation on the variable and enable interrupts when the operation is complete. A semaphore should be used, however, if the variable is a floating-point variable and the microprocessor doesn't support floating point in the hardware. In this case, the processing time involved in processing the floating-point variable could affect interrupt latency if you had disabled interrupts.

2.19 Deadlock (or Deadly Embrace)

A *deadlock*, also called a *deadly embrace*, is a situation in which two tasks are each unknowingly waiting for resources held by the other. Assume Task T1 has exclusive access to Resource R1 and Task T2 has exclusive access to Resource R2. If T1 needs exclusive access to R2 and T2 needs exclusive access to R1, neither task can continue. They are deadlocked. The simplest way to avoid a deadlock is for tasks to

- acquire all resources before proceeding,
- acquire the resources in the same order, and
- release the resources in the reverse order.

Most kernels allow you to specify a timeout when acquiring a semaphore. This feature allows a deadlock to be broken. If the semaphore is not available within a certain amount of time, the task requesting the resource resumes execution. Some form of error code must be returned to the task to notify it that a timeout occurred. A return error code prevents the task from thinking it has obtained the resource. Deadlocks generally occur in large multitasking systems, not in embedded systems (at least they better not!).

2.20 Synchronization

A task can be synchronized with an ISR (or another task when no data is being exchanged) by using a semaphore, as shown in Figure 2.13. Note that, in this case, the semaphore is drawn as a flag to indicate that it is used to signal the occurrence of an event (rather than to ensure mutual exclusion, in which case it would be drawn as a key). When used as a synchronization mechanism, the semaphore is initialized to 0. Using a semaphore for this type of synchronization is called a *unilateral rendezvous*. For example, a task can initiate an I/O operation and then wait for the semaphore. When the I/O operation is complete, an ISR (or another task) signals the semaphore, and the task is resumed.

Figure 2.13   Synchronizing tasks and ISRs.

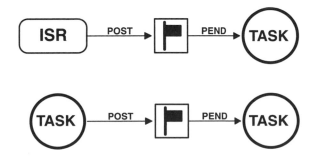

If the kernel supports counting semaphores, the semaphore accumulates events that have not yet been processed. Note that more than one task can be waiting for an event to occur. In this case, the kernel signals the occurrence of the event either to

- the highest priority task waiting for the event to occur or
- the first task waiting for the event.

Depending on the application, more than one ISR or task can signal the occurrence of the event.

Two tasks can synchronize their activities by using two semaphores, as shown in Figure 2.14, which is called a *bilateral rendezvous*. A bilateral rendezvous is similar to a unilateral rendezvous, except both tasks must synchronize with one another before proceeding. A bilateral rendezvous cannot be performed between a task and an ISR because an ISR cannot wait on a semaphore. For example, two tasks are executing, as shown in Listing 2.10.

Figure 2.14   Tasks synchronizing their activities.

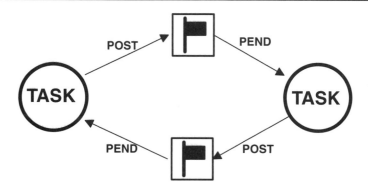

Listing 2.10   Bilateral rendezvous.

```
Task1()
{
    for (;;) {
        Perform operation;
        Signal task #2;                              (1)
        Wait for signal from task #2;                (2)
        Continue operation;
    }
}


Task2()
{
    for (;;) {
        Perform operation;
        Signal task #1;                              (3)
        Wait for signal from task #1;                (4)
        Continue operation;
    }
}
```

L2.10(1)

L2.10(2)   When the first task reaches a certain point, it signals the second task and then waits for a return signal.

L2.10(3)

L2.10(4)   Similarly, when the second task reaches a certain point, it signals the first task and waits for a return signal. At this point, both tasks are synchronized with each other.

2.21   Event Flags

Event flags are used when a task needs to synchronize with the occurrence of multiple events. The task can be synchronized when any of the events have occurred, which is called *disjunctive synchronization* (logical OR). A task can also be synchronized when all events have occurred, which is called *conjunctive synchronization* (logical AND). Disjunctive and conjunctive synchronization are shown in Figure 2.15.

Figure 2.15   Disjunctive and conjunctive synchronization.

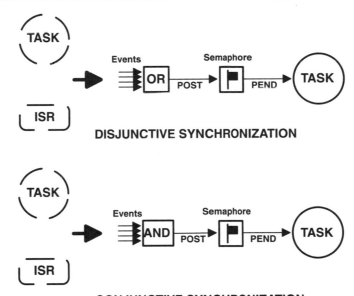

Common events can be used to signal multiple tasks, as shown in Figure 2.16. Events are typically grouped. Depending on the kernel, a group consists of 8, 16, or 32 events, each represented by a bit. (mostly 32 bits, though). Tasks and ISRs can set or clear any event in a group. A task is resumed when all the events it requires are satisfied. The evaluation of which task will be resumed is performed when a new set of events occurs (i.e., during a SET operation).

Kernels, like µC/OS-II, which support event flags offer services to SET event flags, CLEAR event flags, and WAIT for event flags (conjunctively or disjunctively).

2.22 Intertask Communication

It is sometimes necessary for a task or an ISR to communicate information to another task. This information transfer is called *intertask communication*. Information can be communicated between tasks in two ways: through global data or by sending messages.

When using global variables, each task or ISR must ensure that it has exclusive access to the variables. If an ISR is involved, the only way to ensure exclusive access to the common variables is to disable interrupts. If two tasks are sharing data, each can gain exclusive access to the variables either by disabling and enabling interrupts or with the use of a semaphore (as we have seen). Note that a task can only communicate information to an ISR by using global variables. A task is not aware when a global variable is changed by an ISR, unless the ISR signals the task by using a semaphore or unless the task polls the contents of the variable periodically. To correct this situation, you should consider using either a *message mailbox* or a *message queue*.

Figure 2.16 Event flags.

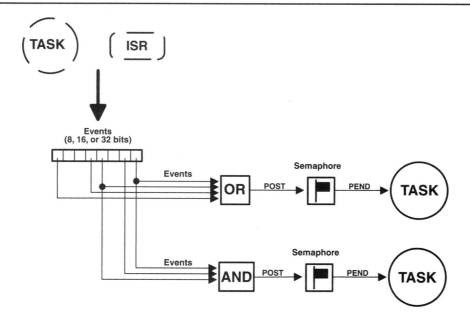

2.23 Message Mailboxes

Messages can be sent to a task through kernel services. A *message mailbox*, also called a *message exchange*, is typically a pointer-size variable. Through a service provided by the kernel, a task or an ISR can deposit a message (the pointer) into this mailbox. Similarly, one or more tasks can receive messages through a service provided by the kernel. Both the sender and receiving task agree on what the pointer is actually pointing to.

A waiting list is associated with each mailbox in case more than one task wants to receive messages through the mailbox. A task desiring a message from an empty mailbox is suspended and placed on the waiting list until a message is received. Typically, the kernel allows the task waiting for a message to specify a timeout. If a message is not received before the timeout expires, the requesting task is made ready to run, and an error code (indicating that a timeout has occurred) is returned to it. When a message is deposited into the mailbox, either the highest priority task waiting for the message is given the message (*priority-based*), or the first task to request a message is given the message (*First-In First-Out*, or FIFO). μC/OS-II only supports the first mechanism – give the message to the highest priority task waiting. Figure 2.17 shows a task depositing a message into a mailbox. Note that the mailbox is represented by an I-beam and the timeout is represented by an hourglass. The number next to the hourglass represents the number of clock ticks (Section 2.32, "Clock Tick") the task will wait for a message to arrive.

2

Figure 2.17   Message mailbox.

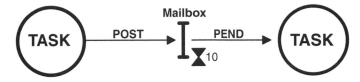

Kernels typically provide the following mailbox services.

- Initialize the contents of a mailbox. The mailbox initially might or might not contain a message.
- Deposit a message into the mailbox (POST).
- Wait for a message to be deposited into the mailbox (PEND).
- Get a message from a mailbox, if one is present, but do not suspend the caller if the mailbox is empty (ACCEPT). If the mailbox contains a message, the message is extracted from the mailbox.

Message mailboxes can also simulate binary semaphores. A message in the mailbox indicates that the resource is available, and an empty mailbox indicates that the resource is already in use by another task.

2.24   Message Queues

A *message queue* is used to send one or more messages to a task. A message queue is basically an array of mailboxes. Through a service provided by the kernel, a task or an ISR can deposit a message (the pointer) into a message queue. Similarly, one or more tasks can receive messages through a service provided by the kernel. Both the sender and receiving task or tasks have to agree as to what the pointer is actually pointing to. Generally, the first message inserted in the queue is the first message extracted from the queue (FIFO). In addition, to extract messages in a FIFO fashion, μC/OS-II allows a task to get messages Last-In-First-Out (LIFO).

As with the mailbox, a waiting list is associated with each message queue, in case more than one task is to receive messages through the queue. A task desiring a message from an empty queue is suspended and placed on the waiting list until a message is received. Typically, the kernel allows the task waiting for a message to specify a timeout. If a message is not received before the timeout expires, the requesting task is made ready to run, and an error code (indicating a timeout has occurred) is returned to it. When a message is deposited into the queue, either the highest priority task, or the first task to wait for the message is given the message. μC/OS-II only supports the first mechanism – give the message to the highest priority task waiting. Figure 2.18 shows an ISR depositing a message into a queue. Note that the queue is represented graphically by a double I-beam. The "10" indicates the number of messages that can accumulate in the queue. A "0" next to the hourglass indicates that the task will wait forever for a message to arrive.

Figure 2.18   Message queue.

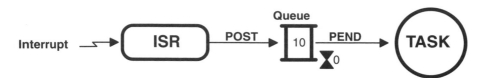

Kernels typically provide these message queue services:

- Initialize the queue. The queue is always assumed to be empty after initialization.
- Deposit a message into the queue (POST).
- Wait for a message to be deposited into the queue (PEND).
- Get a message from a queue, if one is present, but do not suspend the caller if the queue is empty (ACCEPT). If the queue contains a message, the message is extracted from the queue.

2.25   Interrupts

An *interrupt* is a hardware mechanism used to inform the CPU that an asynchronous event has occurred. When an interrupt is recognized, the CPU saves part (or all) of its context (i.e., registers) and jumps to a special subroutine, called an *interrupt service routine* (ISR). The ISR processes the event, and, upon completion of the ISR, the program returns to

- the background for a foreground/background system,
- the interrupted task for a non-preemptive kernel, or
- the highest priority task ready to run for a preemptive kernel.

Interrupts allow a microprocessor to process events when they occur, which prevents the microprocessor from continuously *polling* (looking at) an event to see if it has occurred. Microprocessors allow interrupts to be ignored and recognized through the use of two special instructions: *disable interrupts* and *enable interrupts*, respectively. In a real-time environment, interrupts should be disabled as little as possible. Disabling interrupts affects interrupt latency (see Section 2.26, "Interrupt Latency") and can cause interrupts to be missed. Processors generally allow interrupts to be *nested*, which means that while servicing an interrupt, the processor recognizes and services other (more importantly) interrupts, as shown in Figure 2.19.

2.26   Interrupt Latency

Probably the most important specification of a real-time kernel is the amount of time interrupts are disabled. All real-time systems disable interrupts to manipulate critical sections of code and reenable interrupts when the critical sections have been executed. The longer interrupts are disabled, the higher the *interrupt latency*. Interrupt latency is given by Equation [2.2].

[2.2]   Maximum amount of time interrupts are disabled
                  + Time to start executing the first instruction in the ISR

Figure 2.19   Interrupt nesting.

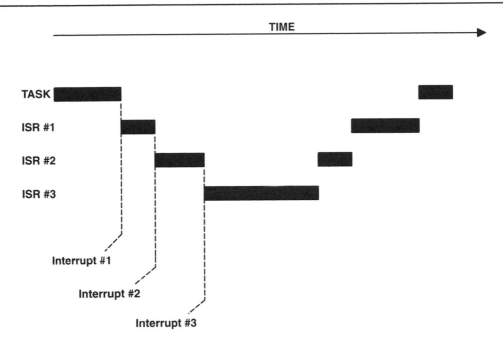

2.27   Interrupt Response

Interrupt response is defined as the time between the reception of the interrupt and the start of the user code that handles the interrupt. The interrupt response time accounts for all of the overhead involved in handling an interrupt. Typically, the processor's context (CPU registers) is saved on the stack before the user code is executed.

For a foreground/background system, the user ISR code is executed immediately after saving the processor's context. The response time is given by Equation [2.3].

[2.3]   Interrupt latency + Time to save the CPU's context

For a non-preemptive kernel, the user ISR code is executed immediately after the processor's context is saved. The response time to an interrupt for a non-preemptive kernel is given by Equation [2.4].

[2.4]   Interrupt latency + Time to save the CPU's context

For a preemptive kernel, a special function provided by the kernel needs to be called to notify the kernel that an ISR is starting. This function allows the kernel to keep track of interrupt nesting. The reason this function is needed is explained in Section 2.28, "Interrupt Recovery". For µC/OS-II, this function is called OSIntEnter(). The response time to an interrupt for a preemptive kernel is given by Equation [2.5].

[2.5]   Interrupt latency
                     + Time to save the CPU's context
                     + Execution time of the kernel ISR entry function

A system's worst case interrupt response time is its only response. Your system might respond to interrupts in 50µs 99 percent of the time, but, if it responds to interrupts in 250µs the other 1 percent, you must assume a 250µs interrupt response time.

2.28   Interrupt Recovery

Interrupt recovery is defined as the time required for the processor to return to the interrupted code or to a higher priority task, in the case of a preemptive kernel. Interrupt recovery in a foreground/background system simply involves restoring the processor's context and returning to the interrupted task. Interrupt recovery is given by Equation [2.6].

[2.6]   Time to restore the CPU's context
               + Time to execute the return from interrupt instruction

As with a foreground/background system, interrupt recovery with a non-preemptive kernel (Equation [2.7]) simply involves restoring the processor's context and returning to the interrupted task.

[2.7]   Time to restore the CPU's context
               + Time to execute the return from interrupt instruction

For a preemptive kernel, interrupt recovery is more complex. Typically, a function provided by the kernel is called at the end of the ISR. For µC/OS-II, this function is called `OSIntExit()` and allows the kernel to determine if all interrupts have nested. If they have nested (i.e., a return from interrupt would return to task-level code), the kernel determines if a higher priority task has been made ready to run as a result of the ISR. If a higher priority task is ready to run as a result of the ISR, this task is resumed. Note that, in this case, the interrupted task resumes only when it again becomes the highest priority task ready to run. For a preemptive kernel, interrupt recovery is given by Equation [2.8].

[2.8]   Time to determine if a higher priority task is ready
               + Time to restore the CPU's context of the highest priority task
               + Time to execute the return from interrupt instruction

2.29   Interrupt Latency, Response, and Recovery

Figure 2.20 through 2.22 show the interrupt latency, response, and recovery for a foreground/background system, a non-preemptive kernel, and a preemptive kernel, respectively.

You should note that for a preemptive kernel, the exit function decides to return either to the interrupted task [F2.22(A)] or to a higher priority task that the ISR has made ready to run [F2.22(B)]. In the later case, the execution time is slightly longer because the kernel has to perform a context switch. I made the difference in execution time somewhat to scale, assuming µC/OS-II.

Figure 2.20 Interrupt latency, response, and recovery (foreground/background).

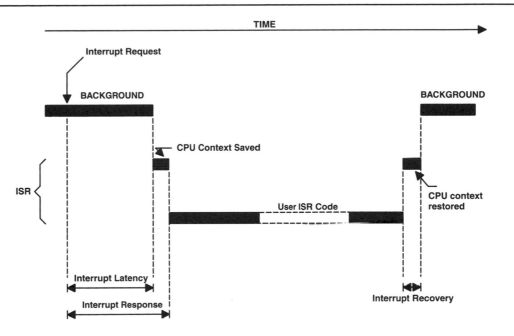

Figure 2.21 Interrupt latency, response, and recovery (non-preemptive kernel).

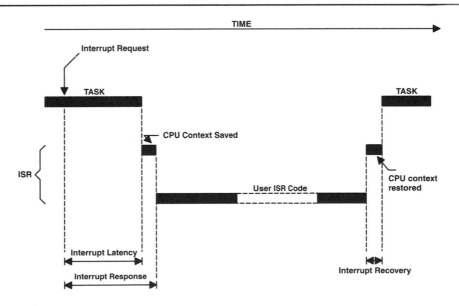

Figure 2.22 ***Interrupt latency, response, and recovery (preemptive kernel).***

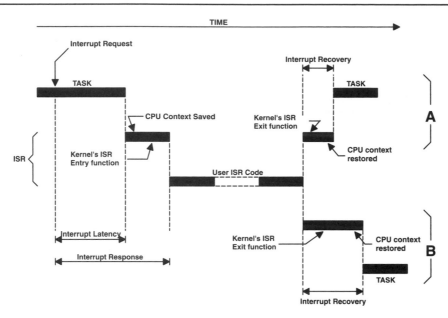

2.30 ISR Processing Time

Although ISRs should be as short as possible, no absolute limits on the amount of time exist for an ISR. One cannot say that an ISR must always be less than 100µs, 500µs, or 1ms. If the ISR code is the most important code that needs to run at any given time, it could be as long as it needs to be. In most cases, however, the ISR should recognize the interrupt, obtain data or a status from the interrupting device, and signal a task to perform the actual processing. You should also consider whether the overhead involved in signaling a task is more than the processing of the interrupt. Signaling a task from an ISR (i.e., through a semaphore, a mailbox, or a queue) requires some processing time. If processing your interrupt requires less than the time required to signal a task, you should consider processing the interrupt in the ISR itself and possibly enabling interrupts to allow higher priority interrupts to be recognized and serviced.

2.31 Nonmaskable Interrupts

Sometimes, an interrupt must be serviced as quickly as possible and cannot afford to have the latency imposed by a kernel. In these situations, you might be able to use the *nonmaskable interrupt* (NMI) provided on most microprocessors. Because the NMI cannot be disabled, interrupt latency, response, and recovery are minimal. The NMI is generally reserved for drastic measures, such as saving important information during a power down. If, however, your application doesn't have this requirement, you could use the NMI to service your most time-critical ISR. The following equations show how to determine the interrupt latency [2.9], response [2.10], and recovery [2.11], respectively, of an NMI.

[2.9]   Interrupt Latency = Time to execute longest instruction
                              + Time to start executing the NMI ISR

[2.10]   Interrupt Response = Interrupt latency
                               + Time to save the CPU's context

[2.11]   Interrupt Recovery = Time to restore the CPU's context
                               + Time to execute the return from interrupt instruction

I have used the NMI in an application to respond to an interrupt that could occur every 150μs. The processing time of the ISR took from 80 to 125μs, and the kernel I used had an interrupt response of about 45μs. As you can see, if I had used maskable interrupts, the ISR could have been late by 20μs (125μs + 45μs > 150μs).

When you are servicing an NMI, you cannot use kernel services to signal a task because NMIs cannot be disabled to access critical sections of code. However, you can still pass parameters to and from the NMI. Parameters passed must be global variables, and the size of these variables must be read or written indivisibly; that is, not as separate byte read or write instructions.

NMIs can be disabled by adding external circuitry, as shown in Figure 2.23. Assuming that both the interrupt and the NMI are positive-going signals, a simple AND gate is inserted between the interrupt source and the processor's NMI input. Interrupts are disabled by writing a 0 to an output port. You wouldn't want to disable interrupts to use kernel services, but you could use this feature to pass parameters (i.e., larger variables) to and from the ISR and a task.

Figure 2.23   Disabling nonmaskable interrupts.

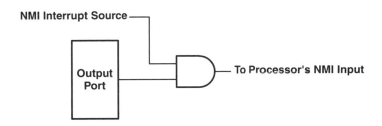

Now, suppose that the NMI service routine needs to signal a task every 40 times it executes. If the NMI occurs every 150μs, a signal would be required every 6ms (40 × 150μs). From a NMI ISR, you cannot use the kernel to signal the task, but you can use the scheme shown in Figure 2.24. In this case, the NMI service routine generates a hardware interrupt through an output port (i.e., brings an output high). Because the NMI service routine typically has the highest priority and interrupt nesting is typically not allowed while servicing the NMI ISR, the interrupt is not recognized until the end of the NMI service routine. At the completion of the NMI service routine, the processor is interrupted to service this hardware interrupt. This ISR clears the interrupt source (i.e., brings the port output low) and posts to a semaphore that wakes up the task. As long as the task services the semaphore well within 6ms, your deadline is met.

Figure 2.24   Signaling a task from a nonmaskable interrupt.

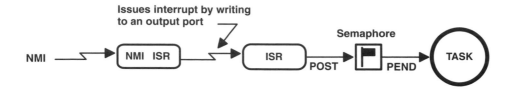

2.32   Clock Tick

A *clock tick* is a special interrupt that occurs periodically. This interrupt can be viewed as the system's heartbeat. The time between interrupts is application specific and is generally between 10 and 200ms. The clock tick interrupt allows a kernel to delay tasks for an integral number of clock ticks and to provide timeouts when tasks are waiting for events to occur. The faster the tick rate, the higher the overhead imposed on the system.

All kernels allow tasks to be delayed for a certain number of clock ticks. The resolution of delayed tasks is one clock tick; however, this does not mean that its accuracy is one clock tick.

Figure 2.25 through 2.27 are timing diagrams that show a task delaying itself for one clock tick. The shaded areas indicate the execution time for each operation performed. Note that the time for each operation varies to reflect typical processing, which would include loops and conditional statements (i.e., if/else, switch, and ?:). The processing time of the tick ISR has been exaggerated to show that it too is subject to varying execution times.

Case 1 (Figure 2.25) shows a situation where higher priority tasks and ISRs execute prior to the task, which needs to delay for one tick. As you can see, the task attempts to delay for 20ms but because of its priority, actually executes at varying intervals. The variables execution time causes the execution of the task to jitter.

Figure 2.25   Delaying a task for one tick (Case 1).

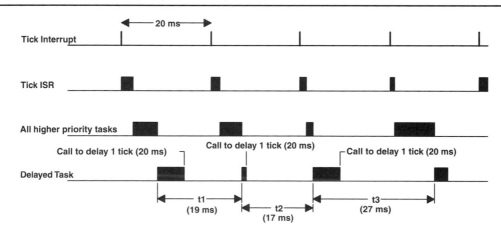

Case 2 (Figure 2.26) shows a situation where the execution times of all higher priority tasks and ISRs are slightly less than one tick. If the task delays itself just before a clock tick, the task executes again almost immediately! Because of this, if you need to delay a task at least one clock tick, you must specify one extra tick. In other words, if you need to delay a task for at least five ticks, you must specify six ticks!

2

Figure 2.26   Delaying a task for one tick (Case 2).

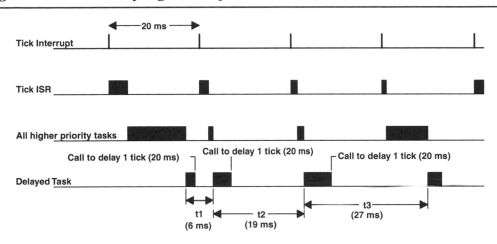

Case 3 (Figure 2.27) shows a situation in which the execution times of all higher priority tasks and ISRs extend beyond one clock tick. In this case, the task that tries to delay for one tick actually executes two ticks later and misses its deadline. Missing the deadline might be acceptable in some applications, but in most cases it isn't.

Figure 2.27   Delaying a task for one tick (Case 3).

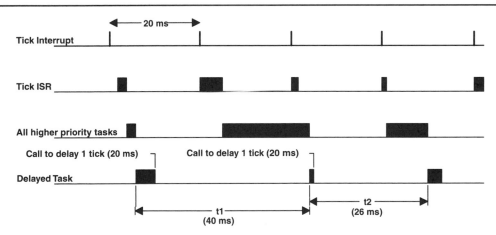

These situations exist with all real-time kernels. They are related to CPU processing load and possibly incorrect system design. Here are some possible solutions to these problems:

- Increase the clock rate of your microprocessor.
- Increase the time between tick interrupts.

- Rearrange task priorities.
- Avoid using floating-point math (if you must, use single precision).
- Get a compiler that performs better code optimization.
- Write time-critical code in assembly language.
- If possible, upgrade to a faster microprocessor in the same family — that is, 8086 to 80186, 68000 to 68020, etc.

Regardless of what you do, jitter will always occur.

2.33   *Memory Requirements*

If you are designing a foreground/background system, the amount of memory required depends solely on your application code. With a multitasking kernel, things are quite different. To begin with, a kernel requires extra code space (ROM). The size of the kernel depends on many factors. Depending on the features provided by the kernel, you can expect anywhere from 1 to 100K bytes. A minimal kernel for an 8-bit CPU that provides only scheduling, context switching, semaphore management, delays, and timeouts should require about 1 to 3K bytes of code space. The total code space is given by Equation [2.12].

[2.12]   Application code size + Kernel code size

Because each task runs independently of the others, it must be provided with its own stack area (RAM). As a designer, you must determine the stack requirement of each task as closely as possible (which is sometimes a difficult undertaking). The stack size must not only account for the task requirements (local variables, function calls, etc.), it must also account for maximum interrupt nesting (saved registers, local storage in ISRs, etc.). Depending on the target processor and the kernel used, a separate stack can be used to handle all interrupt-level code, which is a desirable feature because the stack requirement for each task can be substantially reduced. Another desirable feature is the ability to specify the stack size of each task on an individual basis (μC/OS-II permits this behavior). Conversely, some kernels require that all task stacks be the same size. All kernels require extra RAM to maintain internal variables, data structures, queues, etc. The total RAM required if the kernel does not support a separate interrupt stack is given by Equation [2.13].

[2.13]   Application code requirements
                + Data space (i.e., RAM) needed by the kernel itself
                + SUM(task stacks + MAX(ISR nesting))

If the kernel supports a separate stack for interrupts, the total RAM required is given by Equation [2.14].

[2.14]   Application code requirements
                + Data space (i.e., RAM) needed by the kernel
                + SUM(task stacks)
                + MAX(ISR nesting)

Unless you have large amounts of RAM with which to work, you need to be careful how you use the stack space. To reduce the amount of RAM needed in an application, you must be careful how you use each task's stack for

- large arrays and structures declared locally to functions and ISRs,
- function (i.e., subroutine) nesting,

- interrupt nesting,
- library functions stack usage, and
- function calls with many arguments.

To summarize, a multitasking system requires more code space (ROM) and data space (RAM) than a foreground/background system. The amount of extra ROM depends only on the size of the kernel, and the amount of RAM mostly depends on the number of tasks in your system.

2.34 Advantages and Disadvantages of Real-Time Kernels

A real-time kernel, also called a *Real-Time Operating System* (RTOS), allows real-time applications to be designed and expanded easily; functions can be added without requiring major changes to the software. In fact, if you add low priority tasks to your system, the responsiveness of your system to high priority tasks is almost not affected! The use of an RTOS simplifies the design process by splitting the application code into separate tasks. With a preemptive RTOS, all time-critical events are handled as quickly and as efficiently as possible. An RTOS allows you to make better use of your resources by providing you with valuable services, such as semaphores, mailboxes, queues, time delays, and timeouts.

You should consider using a real-time kernel if your application can afford the extra requirements: extra cost of the kernel, more ROM/RAM, and 2 to 4 percent additional CPU overhead.

The one factor I haven't mentioned so far is the cost associated with the use of a real-time kernel. In some applications, cost is everything and would preclude you from even considering an RTOS.

Currently about 150+ RTOS vendors exist. Products are available for 8-, 16-, 32-, and even 64-bit microprocessors. Some of these packages are complete operating systems and include not only the real-time kernel but also an input/output manager, windowing systems (display), a file system, networking, language interface libraries, debuggers, and cross-platform compilers. The development cost to use an RTOS varies from 70 USD (US Dollars) to well over 30,000 USD. The RTOS vendor might also require *royalties* on a per-target-system basis. Royalties are like buying a chip from the RTOS vendor that you include with each unit sold. The RTOS vendors call this *silicon software*. The royalty fee varies between 5 USD to more than 500 USD per unit. µC/OS-II is not free software and needs to be licensed for commercial use (see Appendix B, "Licensing Policy for µC/OS-II"). Like any other software package these days, you also need to consider the maintenance cost, which can set you back another 15% of the development cost of the RTOS per year!

2.35 Real-Time Systems Summary

Table 2.2 summarizes the three types of real-time systems: foreground/background, non-preemptive kernel, and preemptive kernel.

Table 2.2   Real-time systems summary.

	Foreground/ Background	Non-Preemptive Kernel	Preemptive Kernel

Interrupt latency (Time)	MAX(Longest instruction,
	    User int. disable)
	+ Vector to ISR
		MAX(Longest instruction,
		    User int. disable,
		    Kernel int. disable)
		+ Vector to ISR
			MAX(Longest instruction,
			    User int. disable,
			    Kernel int. disable)
			+ Vector to ISR

Interrupt response (Time)	Int. latency + Save CPU's context	Int. latency + Save CPU's context	Interrupt latency + Save CPU's context + Kernel ISR entry function

Interrupt recovery (Time)	Restore background's
	    context
	+ Return from int.
		Restore task's context
		+ Return from int.
			Find highest priority task
			+ Restore highest priority
			    task's context
			+ Return from interrupt

Task response (Time)	Background	Longest task + Find highest priority task + Context switch	Find highest priority task + Context switch
ROM size	Application code	Application code + Kernel code	Application code + Kernel code

RAM size	Application RAM	Application RAM
		+ Kernel RAM
		+ SUM(Task stacks
		    + MAX(ISR stack))
			Application RAM
			+ Kernel RAM
			+ SUM(Task stacks
			    + MAX(ISR stack))

Services available?	Application code must provide	Yes	Yes

3

Kernel Structure

This chapter describes some of the structural aspects of µC/OS-II. You will learn

- how µC/OS-II handles access to critical sections of code,
- what a task is
- how µC/OS-II knows about your tasks,
- how tasks are scheduled,
- how µC/OS-II determines the percent CPU your application is using,
- how to write interrupt service routines (ISR),
- what a clock tick is, how µC/OS-II handles them,
- how to initialize µC/OS-II, and
- how to start multitasking.

This chapter also describes the application services listed in Table 3.1. The code for OSSchedLock() and OSSchedUnlock() can be disabled by setting OS_SCHED_LOCK_EN to 0 in OS_CFG.H, as shown in Table 3.1. You should note that the other services cannot be compiled out because they are an integral part of the core services offered by µC/OS-II.

Table 3.1   Core services configuration constants in `OS_CFG.H`.

µC/OS-II Core Service	*Enabled when set to 1 in* `OS_CFG.H`
`OS_ENTER_CRITICAL()`	
`OS_EXIT_CRITICAL()`	
`OSInit()`	
`OSStart()`	
`OSIntEnter()`	
`OSIntExit()`	
`OSSchedLock()`	`OS_SCHED_LOCK_EN`
`OSSchedUnlock()`	`OS_SCHED_LOCK_EN`
`OSVersion()`	

Figure 3.1 shows the µC/OS-II architecture and its relationship with the hardware. When you use µC/OS-II in an application, you are responsible for providing the **application software** and the **µC/OS-II configuration** sections. This book and CD contain all the source code for the **processor-independent code** section, as well as the **processor-specific code** section for the Intel 80x86, real mode, large model. If you intend to use µC/OS-II on a different processor, you need to either obtain a copy of a port for the processor you intend to use or write one yourself if the desired processor port is not available. Check the official µC/OS-II Web site at `www.uCOS-II.com` for a list of available ports.

3.00 Critical Sections, `OS_ENTER_CRITICAL()` and `OS_EXIT_CRITICAL()`

µC/OS-II, like all real-time kernels, needs to disable interrupts in order to access critical sections of code and to reenable interrupts when done. Being able to disable interrupts allows µC/OS-II to protect critical code from being entered simultaneously from either multiple tasks or ISRs. The interrupt disable time is one of the most important specifications that a real-time kernel vendor can provide because it affects the responsiveness of your system to real-time events. µC/OS-II tries to keep the interrupt disable time to a minimum, but with µC/OS-II, interrupt disable time is largely dependent on the processor architecture and the quality of the code generated by the compiler.

Processors generally provide instructions to disable/enable interrupts, and your C compiler must have a mechanism to perform these operations directly from C. Some compilers allow you to insert in-line assembly language statements into your C source code, which makes it quite easy to insert processor instructions to enable and disable interrupts. Other compilers contain language extensions to enable and disable interrupts directly from C.

To hide the implementation method chosen by the compiler manufacturer, µC/OS-II defines two macros to disable and enable interrupts: `OS_ENTER_CRITICAL()` and `OS_EXIT_CRITICAL()`, respectively. Because these macros are processor specific, they are found in a file called `OS_CPU.H`. Each processor port thus has its own `OS_CPU.H` file.

`OS_ENTER_CRITICAL()` and `OS_EXIT_CRITICAL()` are always used together to wrap critical sections of code as shown in the following segment:

```
{
    .
    .
    OS_ENTER_CRITICAL();
    /* µC/OS-II critical code section */
    OS_EXIT_CRITICAL();
    .
    .
}
```

3

Figure 3.1   *µC/OS-II file structure.*

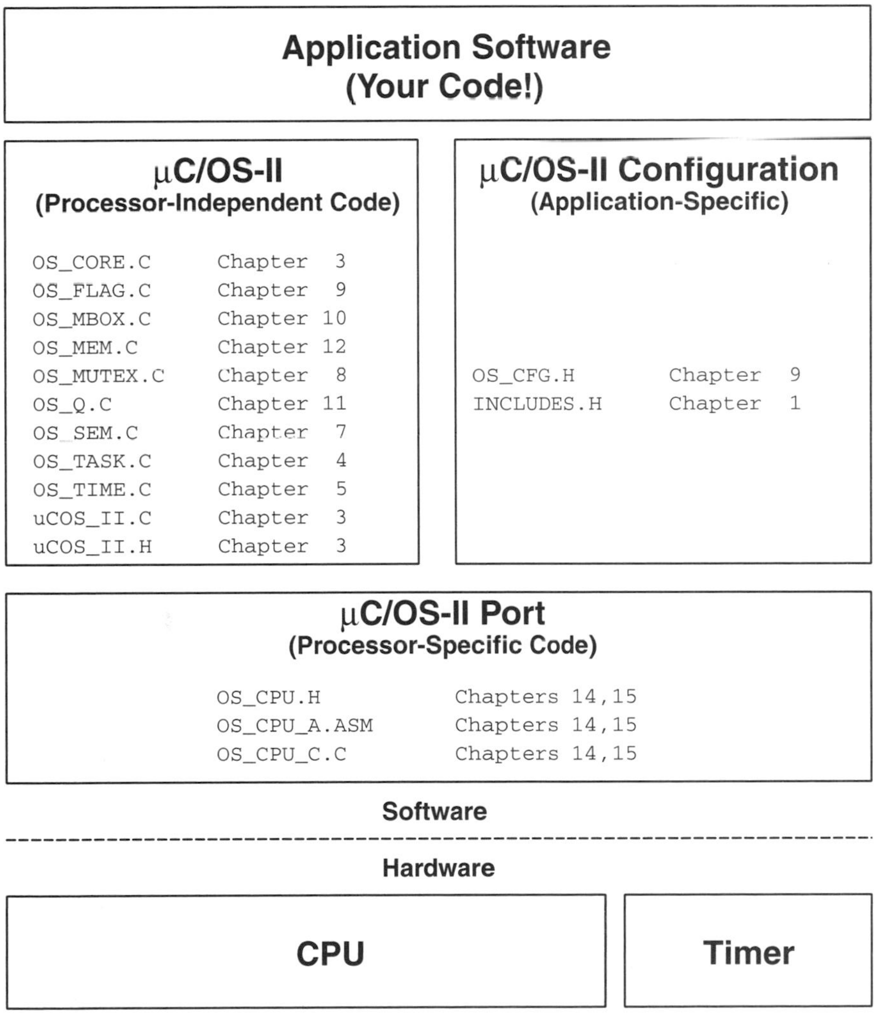

```
┌─────────────────────────────────────────────────────────────────┐
│                    Application Software                            │
│                       (Your Code!)                                │
└─────────────────────────────────────────────────────────────────┘

┌──────────────────────────────┐  ┌──────────────────────────────┐
│         µC/OS-II              │  │      µC/OS-II Configuration   │
│  (Processor-Independent Code) │  │      (Application-Specific)   │
│                               │  │                              │
│  OS_CORE.C     Chapter   3    │  │                              │
│  OS_FLAG.C     Chapter   9    │  │                              │
│  OS_MBOX.C     Chapter  10    │  │                              │
│  OS_MEM.C      Chapter  12    │  │                              │
│  OS_MUTEX.C    Chapter   8    │  │  OS_CFG.H     Chapter   9     │
│  OS_Q.C        Chapter  11    │  │  INCLUDES.H   Chapter   1     │
│  OS_SEM.C      Chapter   7    │  │                              │
│  OS_TASK.C     Chapter   4    │  │                              │
│  OS_TIME.C     Chapter   5    │  │                              │
│  uCOS_II.C     Chapter   3    │  │                              │
│  uCOS_II.H     Chapter   3    │  │                              │
└──────────────────────────────┘  └──────────────────────────────┘

┌─────────────────────────────────────────────────────────────────┐
│                       µC/OS-II Port                               │
│                  (Processor-Specific Code)                        │
│                                                                   │
│          OS_CPU.H          Chapters 14,15                         │
│          OS_CPU_A.ASM      Chapters 14,15                         │
│          OS_CPU_C.C        Chapters 14,15                         │
└─────────────────────────────────────────────────────────────────┘
                           Software
- - - - - - - - - - - - - - - - - - - - - - - - - - - - - - - - - - -
                           Hardware
┌──────────────────────────────────────┐  ┌───────────────────────┐
│                 CPU                   │  │        Timer          │
└──────────────────────────────────────┘  └───────────────────────┘
```

Your application can also use OS_ENTER_CRITICAL( ) and OS_EXIT_CRITICAL( ) to protect your own critical sections of code. Be careful, however, because your application will crash (i.e., hang) if you disable interrupts before calling a service such as OSTimeDly( ) (see Chapter 5). This problem happens because the task is suspended until time expires, but, because interrupts are disabled, you would never service the tick interrupt! Obviously, all the PEND calls are also subject to this problem, so be careful. As a general rule, you should always call μC/OS-II services with interrupts enabled!

OS_ENTER_CRITICAL() and OS_EXIT_CRITICAL() can be implemented using three different methods. The actual method used by your port depends on the capabilities of the processor, as well as the compiler used (see Chapter 13, Porting μC/OS-II). The method used is selected by the #define constant OS_CRITICAL_METHOD, which is defined in OS_CPU.H of the port you are using for your application (i.e., product).

OS_CRITICAL_METHOD == 1

The first and simplest way to implement these two macros is to invoke the processor instruction to disable interrupts for OS_ENTER_CRITICAL() and to enable interrupts instruction for OS_EXIT_CRITICAL(). However, there is a little problem with this scenario. If you call a μC/OS-II function with interrupts disabled, on return from a μC/OS-II service (i.e., function), interrupts are enabled! If you had disabled interrupts prior to calling μC/OS-II, you might want them to be disabled on return from the μC/OS-II function. In this case, this implementation is not adequate. However, with some processors/compilers, this method is the only one you can use.

OS_CRITICAL_METHOD == 2

The second way to implement OS_ENTER_CRITICAL() is to save the interrupt disable status onto the stack and then disable interrupts. OS_EXIT_CRITICAL() is simply implemented by restoring the interrupt status from the stack. Using this scheme, if you call a μC/OS-II service with interrupts either enabled or disabled, the status is preserved across the call. In other words, interrupts are enabled after the call if they were enabled before the call, and interrupts are disabled after the call if they were disabled before the call. Be careful when you call a μC/OS-II service with interrupts disabled because you are extending the interrupt latency of your application. The pseudocode for these macros is:

```
#define OS_ENTER_CRITICAL()    \
       asm(" PUSH    PSW")    \
       asm(" DI")


#define OS_EXIT_CRITICAL()    \
       asm(" POP     PSW")
```

Here, I'm assuming that your compiler allows you to execute in-line assembly language statements directly from your C code, as shown above. You need to consult your compiler documentation for this.

The PUSH PSW instruction pushes the processor status word (PSW) (also known as the condition code register or processor flags) onto the stack. The DI instruction stands for disable interrupts. Finally, the POP PSW instruction is assumed to restore the original state of the interrupt flag from the stack. The instructions I use are only for illustration purposes and might not be actual processor instructions.

Some compilers do not optimize in-line code very well, and thus this method might not work because the compiler might not be smart enough to know that the stack pointer was changed (by the PUSH instruction). Specifically, the processor you are using might provide a stack pointer relative addressing mode, which the compiler can use to access local variables or function arguments using an offset from the stack pointer. Of course, if the stack pointer is changed by the OS_ENTER_CRITICAL() macro, then all these stack offsets might be wrong and would most likely lead to incorrect behavior.

OS_CRITICAL_METHOD == 3

Some compilers provide you with extensions that allow you to obtain the current value of the processor status word (PSW) and save it into a local variable declared within a C function. The variable can then be used to restore the PSW, as shown in Listing 3.1.

Listing 3.1 Saving and restoring the PSW.

```
void Some_uCOS_II_Service (arguments)
{
    OS_CPU_SR  cpu_sr;                                    (1)



        .
    cpu_sr = get_processor_psw();                        (2)
    disable_interrupts();                                (3)
        .
    /* Critical section of code */                       (4)
        .
    set_processor_psw(cpu_sr);                            (5)
        .
}
```

L3.1(1)   OS_CPU_SR is a µC/OS-II data type that is declared in the processor-specific file OS_CPU.H. When you select this critical section method, OS_ENTER_CRITICAL() and OS_EXIT_CRITICAL(), always assume the presence of the cpu_sr variable. In other words, if you use this method to protect your own critical sections, you need to declare a cpu_sr variable in your function.

L3.1(2)   To enter a critical section, a function provided by the compiler vendor is called to obtain the current state of the PSW (condition code register, processor flags, or whatever else this register is called for your processor). I called this function get_processor_psw() for sake of discussion, but it likely has a different name for your compiler.

L3.1(3)   Another compiler-provided function (disable_interrupt()) is of course called to disable interrupts.

L3.1(4)   At this point, the critical code can execute.

L3.1(5)   After the critical section has completed, interrupts can be reenabled by calling another compiler-specific extension that, for sake of discussion, I call set_processor_psw(). The function receives as an argument the previous state of the PSW. It's assumed that this function restores the processor PSW to this value.

Because I don't know what the compiler functions are (there is no standard naming convention), the μC/OS-II macros are used to encapsulate the functionality as shown:

```
#define OS_ENTER_CRITICAL()              \
        cpu_sr = get_processor_psw(); \
        disable_interrupts();


#define OS_EXIT_CRITICAL()               \
        set_processor_psw(cpu_sr);
```

3.01   *Tasks*

A task is typically an infinite loop function, as shown in Listing 3.2.

Listing 3.2   *A task is an infinite loop.*

```
void YourTask (void *pdata)                                      (1)
{
    for (;;) {                                                   (2)
        /* USER CODE */
        Call one of uC/OS-II's services:
        OSFlagPend();
        OSMboxPend();
        OSMutexPend();
        OSQPend();
        OSSemPend();
        OSTaskDel(OS_PRIO_SELF);
        OSTaskSuspend(OS_PRIO_SELF);
        OSTimeDly();
        OSTimeDlyHMSM();
        /* USER CODE */
    }
}
```

L3.2(1)   The return type must always be declared `void`. An argument is passed to your task code when the task first starts executing. Notice that the argument is a pointer to a `void`, which allows your application to pass just about any kind of data to your task. The pointer is a universal vehicle used to pass your task the address of a variable, a structure, or even the address of a function if necessary! It is possible (see Example #1 in Chapter 1) to create many identical tasks, all using the same function (or task body). For example, you could have four asynchronous serial ports that each are managed by their own task. However, the task code is actually identical. Instead of copying the code four times, you can create a task that receives a pointer to a data structure that defines the serial port's parameters (for example, baud rate, I/O port addresses, and interrupt vector number.) as an argument.

L3.2(2) You could also use a `while (1)` statement, if you prefer. A task looks just like any other C function that containes a return type and an argument, but it never returns.

Alternatively, the task can delete itself upon completion, as shown in Listing 3.3. Note that the task code is not actually deleted; µC/OS-II simply doesn't know about the task anymore, so the task code does not run. Also, if the task calls `OSTaskDel()`, the task never returns.

Listing 3.3   *A task that deletes itself when done.*

```
void YourTask (void *pdata)
{
    /* USER CODE */
    OSTaskDel(OS_PRIO_SELF);
}
```

µC/OS-II can manage up to 64 tasks; however, the current version of µC/OS-II uses two tasks for system use. I recommend that you don't use priorities 0, 1, 2, 3, `OS_LOWEST_PRIO-3`, `OS_LOWEST_PRIO-2`, `OS_LOWEST_PRIO-1`, and `OS_LOWEST_PRIO` because I might use them in future versions of µC/OS-II. However, if you need to keep your application as tight as possible, then go ahead and use whatever priorities you need, as long as you don't use `OS_LOWEST_PRIO`. `OS_LOWEST_PRIO` is a `#define` constant, defined in the file `OS_CFG.H`. Therefore, you can have up to 63 of your own application tasks unless you decide to not use the top and bottom four priorities as I recommend. In this case, you "can" have up to 56 of your own tasks.

Each task must be assigned a unique priority level from 0 to `OS_LOWEST_PRIO-2`, inclusively. The lower the priority number, the higher the priority of the task. µC/OS-II always executes the highest priority task ready to run. In the current version of µC/OS-II, the task priority number also serves as the task identifier. The priority number (i.e., task identifier) is used by some kernel services, such as `OSTaskChangePrio()` and `OSTaskDel()`.

In order for µC/OS-II to manage your task, you must create a task by passing its address along with other arguments to one of two functions: `OSTaskCreate()` or `OSTaskCreateExt()`. `OSTaskCreateExt()` is an extended version of `OSTaskCreate()` and provides additional features. These two functions are explained in Chapter 4, "Task Management."

3.02 Task States

Figure 3.2 shows the state transition diagram for tasks under µC/OS-II. At any given time, a task can be in any one of five states.

The `TASK DORMANT` state corresponds to a task that resides in program space (ROM or RAM) but has not been made available to µC/OS-II. A task is made available to µC/OS-II by calling either `OSTaskCreate()` or `OSTaskCreateExt()`. These calls are simply used to tell µC/OS-II the starting address of your task, what priority you want to give to the task being created, how much stack space your task uses, and so on. When a task is created, it is made ready to run and placed in the `TASK READY` state. Tasks can be created before multitasking starts or dynamically by a running task. If multitasking has started and a task created by another task has a higher priority than its creator, the created task is given control of the CPU immediately. A task can return itself or another task to the dormant state by calling `OSTaskDel()`.

Multitasking is started by calling `OSStart()`. `OSStart()` **must** only be called once during startup and starts the highest priority task that has been created during your initialization code. The highest priority task is thus placed in the TASK RUNNING state. Only one task can be running at any given time. A ready task does not run until all higher priority tasks are either placed in the TASK WAITING state or are deleted.

Figure 3.2   Task states.

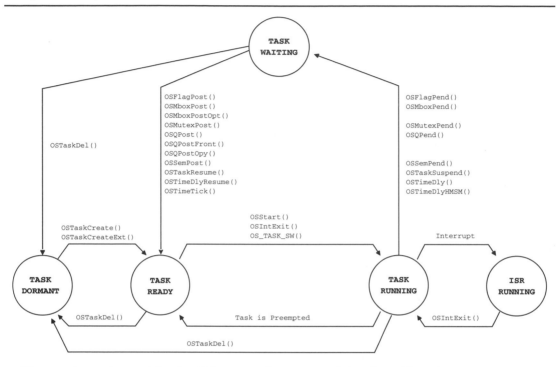

The running task can delay itself for a certain amount of time by calling either OSTimeDly() or OSTimeDlyHMSM(). This task would be placed in the TASK WAITING state until the time specified in the call expires. Both of these functions force an immediate context switch to the next highest priority task that is ready to run. The delayed task is made ready to run by OSTimeTick() when the desired time delay expires (see Section 3.11 "Clock Tick" on page 108). OSTimeTick() is an internal function to µC/OS-II and thus, you don't have to actually call this function from your code.

The running task may also need to wait until an event occurs by calling either OSFlagPend(), OSSemPend(), OSMutexPend(), OSMboxPend(), or OSQPend(). If the event did not already occur, the task that calls one of these functions is placed in the TASK WAITING state until the occurrence of the event. When a task pends on an event, the next highest priority task is immediately given control of the CPU. The task is made ready when the event occurs or when a timeout expires. The occurrence of an event can be signaled by either another task or an ISR.

A running task can always be interrupted, unless the task or µC/OS-II disables interrupts as we have seen. The task thus enters the ISR RUNNING state. When an interrupt occurs, execution of the task is suspended, and the ISR takes control of the CPU. The ISR can make one or more tasks ready to run by signaling one or more events. In this case, before returning from the ISR, µC/OS-II determines if the interrupted task is still the highest priority task ready to run. If the ISR makes a higher priority task ready to run, the new highest priority task is resumed; otherwise, the interrupted task is resumed.

When all tasks are waiting either for events or for time to expire, µC/OS-II executes an internal task called the idle task, OS_TaskIdle().

3.03 Task Control Blocks (*OS_TCB*)

When a task is created, it is assigned a *task control block*, OS_TCB (Listing 3.4). A task control block is a data structure that is used by μC/OS-II to maintain the state of a task when it is preempted. When the task regains control of the CPU, the task control block allows the task to resume execution exactly where it left off. All OS_TCBs reside in RAM. You should notice that I organized its fields to allow for data structure packing, while maintaining a logical grouping of members.

3

Listing 3.4   The μC/OS-II task control block.

```
typedef struct os_tcb {
    OS_STK          *OSTCBStkPtr;

#if OS_TASK_CREATE_EXT_EN > 0
    void            *OSTCBExtPtr;
    OS_STK          *OSTCBStkBottom;
    INT32U           OSTCBStkSize;
    INT16U           OSTCBOpt;
    INT16U           OSTCBId;
#endif

    struct os_tcb *OSTCBNext;
    struct os_tcb *OSTCBPrev;

#if ((OS_Q_EN > 0) && (OS_MAX_QS > 0)) || (OS_MBOX_EN > 0) || (OS_SEM_EN > 0) || (OS_MUTEX_EN > 0)
    OS_EVENT        *OSTCBEventPtr;
#endif

#if ((OS_Q_EN > 0) && (OS_MAX_QS > 0)) || (OS_MBOX_EN > 0)
    void            *OSTCBMsg;
#endif

#if (OS_VERSION >= 251) && (OS_FLAG_EN > 0) && (OS_MAX_FLAGS > 0)
#if OS_TASK_DEL_EN > 0
    OS_FLAG_NODE    *OSTCBFlagNode;
#endif
    OS_FLAGS         OSTCBFlagsRdy;
#endif

    INT16U           OSTCBDly;
    INT8U            OSTCBStat;
    INT8U            OSTCBPrio;

    INT8U            OSTCBX;
    INT8U            OSTCBY;
    INT8U            OSTCBBitX;
```

Listing 3.4   *The µC/OS-II task control block. (Continued)*

```
    INT8U           OSTCBBitY;


#if OS_TASK_DEL_EN > 0
    BOOLEAN         OSTCBDelReq;
#endif
} OS_TCB;
```

.OSTCBStkPtr

contains a pointer to the current top-of-stack for the task. µC/OS-II allows each task to have its own stack, but, just as importantly, each stack can be any size. Some commercial kernels assume that all stacks are the same size unless you write complex hooks. This limitation wastes RAM when all tasks have different stack requirements because the largest anticipated stack size has to be allocated for all tasks. .OSTCBStkPtr should be the only field in the OS_TCB data structure that is accessed from assembly language code (from the context-switching code). I decided to place .OSTCBStkPtr as the first entry in the structure to make accessing this field easier from assembly language code (it ought to be at offset zero).

.OSTCBExtPtr

is a pointer to a user-definable task control block extension, which allows you or the user of µC/OS-II to extend the task control block without having to change the source code for µC/OS-II. .OSTCBExtPtr is only used by OSTaskCreateExt(), so you need to set OS_TASK_CREATE_EXT_EN in OS_CFG.H to 1 to enable this field. After it is enabled, you can use .OSTCBExtPtr to point to a data structure that contains the name of the task, to keep track of the execution time of the task, or to track the number of times a task has been switched-in (see Example #3 in Chapter 1). Notice that I decided to place this pointer immediately after the stack pointer, in case you need to access this field from assembly language. This position makes calculating the offset from the beginning of the data structure easier.

.OSTCBStkBottom

is a pointer to the bottom of the task's stack. If the processor's stack grows from high to low memory locations, then .OSTCBStkBottom points at the lowest valid memory location for the stack. Similarly, if the processor's stack grows from low to high memory locations, then .OSTCBStkBottom points at the highest valid stack address. .OSTCBStkBottom is used by OSTaskStkChk() to check the size of a task's stack at run time, which allows you to determine the amount of free stack space available for each stack. Stack checking can only occur if you create a task with OSTaskCreateExt(), so you need to set OS_TASK_CREATE_EXT_EN in OS_CFG.H to 1 to enable this field.

.OSTCBStkSize

holds the size of the stack in number of elements instead of bytes (OS_STK is declared in OS_CPU.H), which means that if a stack contains 1,000 entries and each entry is 32-bits wide, then the actual size of the stack is 4,000 bytes. Similarly, a stack where entries are 16-bits wide contains 2,000 bytes for the same 1,000 entries. .OSTCBStkSize is used by OSTaskStkChk(). Again, this field is valid only if you set OS_TASK_CREATE_EXT_EN in OS_CFG.H to 1.

.OSTCBOpt

holds options that can be passed to OSTaskCreateExt(), so this field is valid only if you set OS_TASK_CREATE_EXT_EN in OS_CFG.H to 1. µC/OS-II currently defines only three options (see uCOS_II.H): OS_TASK_OPT_STK_CHK, OS_TASK_OPT_STK_CLR, and OS_TASK_OPT_SAVE_FP.

OS_TASK_OPT_STK_CHK is used to specify to OSTaskCreateExt() that stack checking is enabled for the task being created. µC/OS-II does not automatically perform stack checking because I didn't want to use valuable CPU time unless you actually want to do stack checking. Stack checking is performed by your application code by calling OSTaskStkChk() (see Chapter 4, "Task Management").

OS_TASK_OPT_STK_CLR indicates that the stack needs to be cleared (i.e., µC/OS-II writes zeros in every location of the stack) when the task is created. The stack only needs to be cleared if you intend to do stack checking. If you do not specify OS_TASK_OPT_STK_CLR and you then create and delete tasks, stack checking reports incorrect stack usage. If you never delete a task after it's created and your startup code clears all RAM, you can save valuable execution time by **not** specifying this option. Passing OS_TASK_OPT_STK_CLR increases the execution time of OSTaskCreateExt() because it clears the contents of the stack. The larger your stack, the longer it takes. Again, stack checking is invoked by your application code and not automatically by µC/OS-II.

OS_TASK_OPT_SAVE_FP tells OSTaskCreateExt() that the task will be doing floating-point computations. If the processor provides hardware-assisted floating-point capability, the floating-point registers need to be saved for the task being created and during a context switch.

.OSTCBId
> is used to hold an identifier for the task. This field is currently not used and has only been included for future expansion.

.OSTCBNext and .OSTCBPrev
> are used to doubly link OS_TCBs. OSTimeTick() uses the forward link (pointed to by .OSTCBNext) chain of OS_TCBs to update the .OSTCBDly field for each task. The OS_TCB for each task is linked (using both pointers) when the task is created, and the OS_TCB is removed from the list when the task is deleted. A doubly-linked list permits an element in the chain to be quickly inserted or removed.

.OSTCBEventPtr
> is a pointer to an event control block and is described later (see Chapter 6, "Kernel Structure").

.OSTCBMsg
> is a pointer to a message that is sent to a task. The use of this field is described later (see Chapters 10 and 11).

.OSTCBFlagNode
> is a pointer to an event flag node (see Chapter 9, "Event Flag Management"). This field is only used by OSTaskDel() when we delete a task that waits on an event flag group. This field is present in the OS_TCB only when OS_FLAG_EN in OS_CFG.H is set to 1.

.OSTCBFlagsRdy
> contains the event flags that made the task ready to run when the task was waiting on an event flag group (see Chapter 9, "Event Flag Management"). This field is present in the OS_TCB only when OS_FLAG_EN in OS_CFG.H is set to 1.

.OSTCBDly
> is used when a task needs to be delayed for a certain number of clock ticks or a task needs to pend for an event to occur with a timeout. In this case, this field contains the number of clock ticks the task is allowed to wait for the event to occur. When this variable is 0, the task is not delayed or has no timeout when waiting for an event.

.OSTCBStat

contains the state of the task. When .OSTCBStat is OS_STAT_READY, the task is ready to run. Other values can be assigned by µC/OS-II to .OSTCBStat, and these values are described in uCOS_II.H (see OS_STAT_???).

.OSTCBPrio

contains the task priority. A high-priority task has a low .OSTCBPrio value (i.e., the lower the number, the higher the actual priority).

.OSTCBX, .OSTCBY, .OSTCBBitX, and .OSTCBBitY

are used to accelerate the process of making a task ready to run or to make a task wait for an event (to avoid computing these values at run time). The values for these fields are computed when the task is created or when the task's priority is changed. The values are obtained as shown in Listing 3.5.

Listing 3.5   *Calculating* OS_TCB *members.*

```
.OSTCBY          = priority >> 3;
.OSTCBBitY       = OSMapTbl[priority >> 3];
.OSTCBX          = priority & 0x07;
.OSTCBBitX       = OSMapTbl[priority & 0x07];
```

.OSTCBDelReq

is a boolean used to indicate whether or not a task has requested that the current task be deleted. The use of this field is described later (see Chapter 4, "Task Management"). This field is present in the OS_TCB only when OS_TASK_DEL_EN in OS_CFG.H is set to 1.

You probably noticed that some of the fields in the OS_TCB structure are wrapped with conditional compilation statements. This wrapping is done to allow you to reduce the amount of RAM needed by µC/OS-II if you don't need all the features that µC/OS-II provides.

The maximum number of tasks (OS_MAX_TASKS) that an application can have is specified in OS_CFG.H and determines the number of OS_TCBs allocated for your application. You can reduce the amount of RAM needed by setting OS_MAX_TASKS to the actual number of tasks needed in your application. All OS_TCBs are placed in OSTCBTbl[]. Note that µC/OS-II allocates OS_N_SYS_TASKS (see uCOS_II.H) extra OS_TCBs for internal use. Currently, an OS_TCB is used for the idle task, and another is used for the statistic task (if OS_TASK_STAT_EN in OS_CFG.H is set to 1). When µC/OS-II is initialized, all OS_TCBs in the table are linked in a singly linked list of free OS_TCBs, as shown in Figure 3.3. When a task is created, the OS_TCB to which OSTCBFreeList points is assigned to the task, and OSTCBFreeList is adjusted to point to the next OS_TCB in the chain. When a task is deleted, its OS_TCB is returned to the list of free OS_TCBs.

Figure 3.3   *List of free* OS_TCBs.

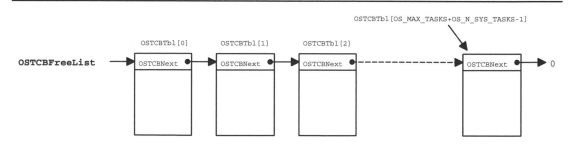

An OS_TCB is initialized by the function OS_TCBInit() (see Listing 3.6) when a task is created. OS_TCBInit() is called by either OSTaskCreate() or OSTaskCreateExt() (see Chapter 4,"Task Management"). OS_TCBInit() receives seven arguments:

prio	is the task priority.
ptos	is a pointer to the top of stack after the stack frame has been built by OSTaskStkInit() (described in Chapter 13, "Porting μC/OS-II") and is stored in the .OSTCBStkPtr field of the OS_TCB.
pbos	is a pointer to the stack bottom and is stored in the .OSTCBStkBottom field of the OS_TCB.
id	is the task identifier and is saved in the .OSTCBId field.
stk_size	is the total size of the stack and is saved in the .OSTCBStkSize field of the OS_TCB.
pext	is the value to place in the .OSTCBExtPtr field of the OS_TCB.
opt	are the OS_TCB options and are saved in the .OSTCBOpt field.

Listing 3.6   OS_TCBInit().

```
INT8U OS_TCBInit (INT8U  prio,      OS_STK *ptos,    OS_STK *pbos, INT16U id,
                  INT32U stk_size, void     *pext,    INT16U  opt)
{
#if OS_CRITICAL_METHOD == 3
    OS_CPU_SR   cpu_sr;
#endif
    OS_TCB      *ptcb;


    OS_ENTER_CRITICAL();
    ptcb = OSTCBFreeList;                                               (1)
    if (ptcb != (OS_TCB *)0) {                                         (2)
        OSTCBFreeList       = ptcb->OSTCBNext;
        OS_EXIT_CRITICAL();
        ptcb->OSTCBStkPtr    = ptos;                                   (3)
        ptcb->OSTCBPrio      = (INT8U)prio;
        ptcb->OSTCBStat      = OS_STAT_RDY;
        ptcb->OSTCBDly       = 0;
#if OS_TASK_CREATE_EXT_EN > 0
        ptcb->OSTCBExtPtr    = pext;                                   (4)
        ptcb->OSTCBStkSize   = stk_size;
        ptcb->OSTCBStkBottom = pbos;
        ptcb->OSTCBOpt       = opt;
        ptcb->OSTCBId        = id;
#else
        pext                = pext;
        stk_size            = stk_size;
        pbos                = pbos;
        opt                 = opt;
        id                  = id;
#endif
```

3

Listing 3.6   *OS_TCBInit(). (Continued)*

```
#if OS_TASK_DEL_EN > 0
    ptcb->OSTCBDelReq      = OS_NO_ERR;                                           (5)
#endif


    ptcb->OSTCBY           = prio >> 3;                                          (6)
    ptcb->OSTCBBitY        = OSMapTbl[ptcb->OSTCBY];
    ptcb->OSTCBX           = prio & 0x07;
    ptcb->OSTCBBitX        = OSMapTbl[ptcb->OSTCBX];

#if    OS_EVENT_EN > 0
    ptcb->OSTCBEventPtr  = (OS_EVENT *)0;                                        (7)
#endif


#if (OS_VERSION >= 251) && (OS_FLAG_EN > 0) && (OS_MAX_FLAGS > 0) && (OS_TASK_DEL_EN > 0)
    ptcb->OSTCBFlagNode  = (OS_FLAG_NODE *)0;                                    (8)
#endif

#if    OS_MBOX_EN || (OS_Q_EN && (OS_MAX_QS >= 2))
    ptcb->OSTCBMsg       = (void *)0;
#endif


#if OS_VERSION >= 204
    OSTCBInitHook(ptcb);                                                        (9)
#endif

    OSTaskCreateHook(ptcb);                                                    (10)

    OS_ENTER_CRITICAL();                                                       (11)
    OSTCBPrioTbl[prio]    = ptcb;                                              (12)
    ptcb->OSTCBNext       = OSTCBList;
    ptcb->OSTCBPrev       = (OS_TCB *)0;
    if (OSTCBList != (OS_TCB *)0) {
        OSTCBList->OSTCBPrev = ptcb;
    }
    OSTCBList             = ptcb;
    OSRdyGrp             |= ptcb->OSTCBBitY;                                    (13)
    OSRdyTbl[ptcb->OSTCBY] |= ptcb->OSTCBBitX;
    OS_EXIT_CRITICAL();
    return (OS_NO_ERR);                                                        (14)
    }
    OS_EXIT_CRITICAL();
    return (OS_NO_MORE_TCB);
}
```

L3.6(1)   OS_TCBInit() first tries to obtain an OS_TCB from the OS_TCB pool.

L3.6(2)

L3.6(3)   If the pool contains a free OS_TCB, it is initialized. Note that after an OS_TCB is allocated, OS_TCBInit() can re-enable interrupts because at this point the creator of the task owns the OS_TCB and it cannot be corrupted by another concurrent task creation. OS_TCBInit() can thus proceed to initialize some of the OS_TCB fields with interrupts enabled.

L3.6(4)   If you enabled code generation for OSTaskCreateExt()(OS_TASK_CREATE_EXT_EN is set to 1 in OS_CFG.H) then additional fields in OS_TCB are filled in.

L3.6(5)   The presence of the flag .OSTCBDelReq in OS_TCB depends on whether OS_TASK_DEL_EN has been enabled (see OS_CFG.H). In other words, if you never intend to delete tasks, you can save yourself the storage area of a BOOLEAN in every single OS_TCB.

L3.6(6)   In order to save a bit of processing time during scheduling, OS_TCBInit() precalculates some fields. I decided to exchange execution time in favor of data space storage.

L3.6(7)   If you don't intend to use any semaphores, mutexes, message mailboxes, and message queues in your application, then the field .OSTCBEventPtr in the OS_TCB is not be present.

L3.6(8)   If you enabled event flags (i.e., you set OS_FLAGS_EN to 1 in OS_CFG.H), then the pointer to an event flag node is intitialized to point to nothing because the task is not waiting for an event flag, it's only being created.

L3.6(9)   In μC/OS-II V2.04, I added a call to a function that can be defined in the processor's port file — OSTCBInitHook(). This function allows you to add extensions to the OS_TCB. For example, you could initialize and store the contents of floating-point registers, MMU registers, or anything else that can be associated with a task. However, you typically store this additional information in memory that is allocated by your application. Note that interrupts are enabled when OS_TCBInit() calls OSTCBInitHook().

L3.6(10) OS_TCBInit() then calls OSTaskCreateHook(), which is a user-specified function that allows you to extend the functionality of OSTaskCreate() or OSTaskCreateExt(). OSTaskCreateHook() can be declared either in OS_CPU_C.C (if OS_CPU_HOOKS_EN is set to 1) or elsewhere (if OS_CPU_HOOKS_EN is set to 0). Note that interrupts are enabled when OS_TCBInit() calls OSTaskCreateHook().

You should note that I could have called only one of the two hook functions: OSTCBInitHook() or OSTaskCreateHook(). The reason there are two functions is to allow you to group (i.e., encapsulate) items that are tied with the OS_TCB in OSTCBInitHook() and other task-related initialization in OSTaskCreateHook().

L3.6(11)

L3.6(12) OS_TCBInit() disables interrupts when it needs to insert the OS_TCB into the doubly linked list of tasks that have been created. The list starts at OSTCBList, and the OS_TCB of a new task is always inserted at the beginning of the list.

L3.6(13)

L3.6(14) Finally, the task is made ready to run, and OS_TCBInit() returns to its caller [OSTaskCreate() or OSTaskCreateExt()] with a code indicating that an OS_TCB has been allocated and initialized.

3.04   Ready List

Each task is assigned a unique priority level between 0 and OS_LOWEST_PRIO, inclusive (see OS_CFG.H). Task priority OS_LOWEST_PRIO is always assigned to the idle task when μC/OS-II is initialized. Note that OS_MAX_TASKS and OS_LOWEST_PRIO are unrelated. You can have only 10 tasks in an application while still having 32 priority levels (if you set OS_LOWEST_PRIO to 31).

Each task that is ready to run is placed in a ready list consisting of two variables, OSRdyGrp and OSRdyTbl[]. Task priorities are grouped (eight tasks per group) in OSRdyGrp. Each bit in OSRdyGrp indicates when a task in a group is ready to run. When a task is ready to run, it also sets its corresponding bit in the ready table, OSRdyTbl[]. The relationship between OSRdyGrp and OSRdyTbl[] is shown in Figure 3.4 and is given by the following rules:

> Bit 0 in OSRdyGrp is 1 when any bit in OSRdyTbl[0] is 1.
> Bit 1 in OSRdyGrp is 1 when any bit in OSRdyTbl[1] is 1.
> Bit 2 in OSRdyGrp is 1 when any bit in OSRdyTbl[2] is 1.
> Bit 3 in OSRdyGrp is 1 when any bit in OSRdyTbl[3] is 1.
> Bit 4 in OSRdyGrp is 1 when any bit in OSRdyTbl[4] is 1.
> Bit 5 in OSRdyGrp is 1 when any bit in OSRdyTbl[5] is 1.
> Bit 6 in OSRdyGrp is 1 when any bit in OSRdyTbl[6] is 1.
> Bit 7 in OSRdyGrp is 1 when any bit in OSRdyTbl[7] is 1.

The size of OSRdyTbl[] depends on OS_LOWEST_PRIO (see uCOS_II.H). This feature allows you to reduce the amount of RAM (data space) needed by μC/OS-II when your application requires few task priorities.

To determine which priority (and thus which task) will run next, the scheduler in μC/OS-II determines the lowest priority number that has its bit set in OSRdyTbl[].

The code in Listing 3.7 is used to place a task in the ready list. prio is the task's priority.

Listing 3.7   *Making a task ready to run.*

```
OSRdyGrp            |= OSMapTbl[prio >> 3];
OSRdyTbl[prio >> 3] |= OSMapTbl[prio & 0x07];
```

As you can see from Figure 3.4, the lower three bits of the task's priority are used to determine the bit position in OSRdyTbl[], and the next three most significant bits are used to determine the index into OSRdyTbl[]. Note that OSMapTbl[] (see OS_CORE.C) is in ROM and is used to equate an index from 0 to 7 to a bit mask, as shown in Table 3.2.

Figure 3.4   The µC/OS-II ready list.

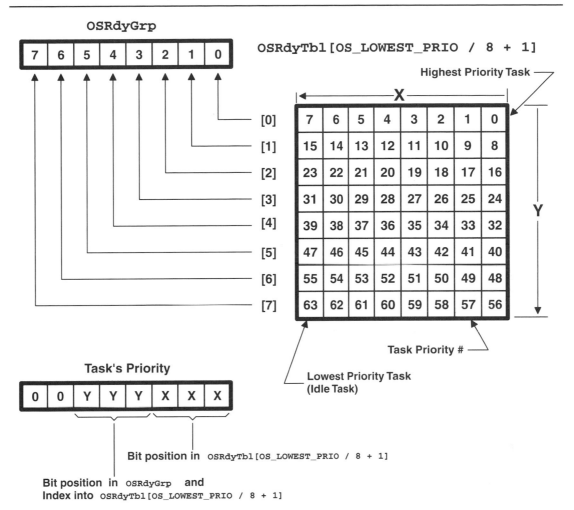

3

Table 3.2   Contents of `OSMapTbl[]`.

Index	Bit Mask (Binary)
0	00000001
1	00000010
2	00000100
3	00001000
4	00010000
5	00100000
6	01000000
7	10000000

A task is removed from the ready list by reversing the process using the code in Listing 3.8.

Listing 3.8   *Removing a task from the ready list.*

```
if ((OSRdyTbl[prio >> 3] &= ~OSMapTbl[prio & 0x07]) == 0)
    OSRdyGrp &= ~OSMapTbl[prio >> 3];
```

This code clears the ready bit of the task in OSRdyTbl[] and clears the bit in OSRdyGrp only if all tasks in a group are not ready to run; that is, all bits in OSRdyTbl[prio >> 3] are 0. Another table lookup is performed, rather than scanning through the table starting with OSRdyTbl[0], to find the highest priority task ready to run. OSUnMapTbl[256] is a priority resolution table (see OS_CORE.C). Eight bits represent when tasks are ready in a group. The least significant bit has the highest priority. Using this byte to index OSUnMapTbl[] returns the bit position of the highest priority bit set — a number between 0 and 7. Determining the priority of the highest priority task ready to run is accomplished with the code in Listing 3.9.

Listing 3.9   *Finding the highest priority task ready to run.*

```
y    = OSUnMapTbl[OSRdyGrp];    /* Determine Y position in OSRdyTbl[]  */
x    = OSUnMapTbl[OSRdyTbl[y]]; /* Determine X position in OSRdyTbl[Y] */
prio = (y << 3) + x;
```

For example, as shown in Figure 3.5, if OSRdyGrp contains 01101000 (binary) or 0x68, then the table lookup OSUnMapTbl[OSRdyGrp] yields a value of 3, which corresponds to bit 3 in OSRdyGrp. Note that bit positions are assumed to start on the right with bit 0 being the rightmost bit. Similarly, if OSRdyTbl[3] contains 11100100 (binary) or 0xE4, then OSUnMapTbl[OSRdyTbl[3]] results in a value of 2 (bit 2). The task priority (prio) is then 26 (i.e., $3 \times 8 + 2$). Getting a pointer to the OS_TCB for the corresponding task is done by indexing into OSTCBPrioTbl[] using the task's priority.

3.05   Task Scheduling

μC/OS-II always executes the highest priority task ready to run. The determination of which task has the highest priority, thus which task will be next to run, is determined by the scheduler. Task-level scheduling is performed by OS_Sched(). ISR-level scheduling is handled by another function [OSIntExit()] described later. The code for OS_Sched() is shown in Listing 3.10. μC/OS-II task-scheduling time is constant irrespective of the number of tasks created in an application.

Figure 3.5   *Finding the highest priority task ready to run.*

```
                                            ─── OSRdyGrp contains 0x68
INT8U  const  OSUnMapTbl[] = {
     0, 0, 1, 0, 2, 0, 1, 0, 3, 0, 1, 0, 2, 0, 1, 0,     /* 0x00 to 0x0F    */
     4, 0, 1, 0, 2, 0, 1, 0, 3, 0, 1, 0, 2, 0, 1, 0,     /* 0x10 to 0x1F    */
     5, 0, 1, 0, 2, 0, 1, 0, 3, 0, 1, 0, 2, 0, 1, 0,     /* 0x20 to 0x2F    */
     4, 0, 1, 0, 2, 0, 1, 0, 3, 0, 1, 0, 2, 0, 1, 0,     /* 0x30 to 0x3F    */
     6, 0, 1, 0, 2, 0, 1, 0, 3, 0, 1, 0, 2, 0, 1, 0,     /* 0x40 to 0x4F    */
     4, 0, 1, 0, 2, 0, 1, 0, 3, 0, 1, 0, 2, 0, 1, 0,     /* 0x50 to 0x5F    */
     5, 0, 1, 0, 2, 0, 1, 0, 3, 0, 1, 0, 2, 0, 1, 0,     /* 0x60 to 0x6F    */
     4, 0, 1, 0, 2, 0, 1, 0, 3, 0, 1, 0, 2, 0, 1, 0,     /* 0x70 to 0x7F    */
     7, 0, 1, 0, 2, 0, 1, 0, 3, 0, 1, 0, 2, 0, 1, 0,     /* 0x80 to 0x8F    */
     4, 0, 1, 0, 2, 0, 1, 0, 3, 0, 1, 0, 2, 0, 1, 0,     /* 0x90 to 0x9F    */
     5, 0, 1, 0, 2, 0, 1, 0, 3, 0, 1, 0, 2, 0, 1, 0,     /* 0xA0 to 0xAF    */
     4, 0, 1, 0, 2, 0, 1, 0, 3, 0, 1, 0, 2, 0, 1, 0,     /* 0xB0 to 0xBF    */
     6, 0, 1, 0, 2, 0, 1, 0, 3, 0, 1, 0, 2, 0, 1, 0,     /* 0xC0 to 0xCF    */
     4, 0, 1, 0, 2, 0, 1, 0, 3, 0, 1, 0, 2, 0, 1, 0,     /* 0xD0 to 0xDF    */
     5, 0, 1, 0, 2, 0, 1, 0, 3, 0, 1, 0, 2, 0, 1, 0,     /* 0xE0 to 0xEF    */
     4, 0, 1, 0, 2, 0, 1, 0, 3, 0, 1, 0, 2, 0, 1, 0      /* 0xF0 to 0xFF    */
};
                   ─── OSRdyTbl[3] contains 0xE4
```

```
 3  = OSUnMapTbl[  0x68 ];
 2  = OSUnMapTbl[  0xE4 ];
26  = ( 3 << 3) +  2;
```

Listing 3.10   *Task scheduler.*

```
void  OS_Sched (void)
{
#if OS_CRITICAL_METHOD == 3
    OS_CPU_SR  cpu_sr;
#endif
    INT8U      y;


    OS_ENTER_CRITICAL();
    if ((OSIntNesting == 0) && (OSLockNesting == 0)) {                          (1)
        y           = OSUnMapTbl[OSRdyGrp];                                     (2)
        OSPrioHighRdy = (INT8U)((y << 3) + OSUnMapTbl[OSRdyTbl[y]]);
        if (OSPrioHighRdy != OSPrioCur) {                                       (3)
            OSTCBHighRdy = OSTCBPrioTbl[OSPrioHighRdy];                         (4)
            OSCtxSwCtr++;                                                       (5)
            OS_TASK_SW();                                                       (6)
        }
    }
    OS_EXIT_CRITICAL();
}
```

L3.10(1)   OS_Sched() exits if called from an ISR (i.e., OSIntNesting > 0) or if scheduling has been disabled because your application called OSSchedLock() at least once (i.e., OSLockNesting > 0).

L3.10(2)   If OS_Sched() is not called from an ISR and the scheduler is enabled, then OS_Sched() determines the priority of the highest priority task that is ready to run. A task that is ready to run has its corresponding bit set in OSRdyTbl[].

L3.10(3)   After the highest priority task has been found, OS_Sched() verifies that the highest priority task is not the current task. Verification is done to avoid an unnecessary context switch, which would be time consuming. Note that µC/OS (V1.xx) obtained OSTCBHighRdy (a pointer) and compared it with OSTCBCur (another pointer). On 8- and some 16-bit processors, this operation was relatively slow because a comparison was made of pointers instead of 8-bit integers as it is now done in µC/OS-II. Also, there is no point in looking up OSTCBHighRdy in OSTCBPrioTbl[] (see L3.10(4)) unless you actually need to do a context switch. The combination of comparing 8-bit values instead of pointers and looking up OSTCBHighRdy only when needed should make µC/OS-II faster than µC/OS on 8- and some 16-bit processors.

L3.10(4)   To perform a context switch, OSTCBHighRdy must point to the OS_TCB of the highest priority task, which is done by indexing into OSTCBPrioTbl[], using OSPrioHighRdy.

L3.10(5)   Next, the statistic counter OSCtxSwCtr (a 32-bit variable) is incremented to keep track of the number of context switches. This counter serves no other purpose except that it allows you to determine the number of context switches in one second. Of course, do to this, you'd have to save OSCtxSwCtr in another variable (for example, OSCtxSwCtrPerSec) every second and then clear OSCtxSwCtr.

L3.10(6)   Finally, the macro OS_TASK_SW() is invoked to do the actual context switch.

A context switch consists of saving the processor registers on the stack of the task being suspended and restoring the registers of the higher priority task from its stack. In µC/OS-II, the stack frame for a ready task always looks as if an interrupt has just occurred and all processor registers were saved onto it. In other words, all that µC/OS-II has to do to run a ready task is restore all processor registers from the task's stack and execute a return from interrupt. To switch context, you implement OS_TASK_SW() so that you simulate an interrupt. Most processors provide either a software interrupt or TRAP instructions to accomplish this switch. The interrupt service routine (ISR) or trap handler (also called the exception handler) must vector to the assembly language function OSCtxSw(). OSCtxSw() expects to have OSTCBHighRdy point to the OS_TCB of the task to be switched in and to have OSTCBCur point to the OS_TCB of the task being suspended. Refer to Chapter 13, "Porting µC/OS-II," for additional details on OSCtxSw(). For now, you only need to know that OS_TASK_SW() suspends execution of the current task and allows the CPU to resume execution of the more important task.

All of the code in OS_Sched() is considered a critical section. Interrupts are disabled to prevent ISRs from setting the ready bit of one or more tasks during the process of finding the highest priority task ready to run. Note that OS_Sched() could be written entirely in assembly language to reduce scheduling time. OS_Sched() was written in C for readability and portability and to minimize use of assembly language.

3.06 *Task Level Context Switch, OS_TASK_SW()*

As we discussed in the previous section, after the scheduler has determined that a more important task needs to run, OS_TASK_SW() is called to perform a context switch. The context of a task is generally the contents of all of the CPU registers. The context-switch code simply needs to save the register values of the task being preempted and load into the CPU the values of the registers for the task to resume.

`OS_TASK_SW()` is a macro that normally invokes a microprocessor software interrupt because µC/OS-II assumes that context switching will be done by interrupt-level code. What µC/OS-II thus needs is a processor instruction that behaves just like a hardware interrupt (thus the name software interrupt). A macro is used to make µC/OS-II portable across multiple platforms by encapsulating the actual processor-specific software interrupt mechanism. Chapter 13, "Porting µC/OS-II" discusses how to implement `OS_TASK_SW()`.

Figure 3.6 shows the state of some µC/OS-II variables and data structures just prior to calling `OS_TASK_SW()`. For sake of discussion, I created a fictitious CPU containing seven registers:

A stack pointer (`SP`)
A program counter (`PC`)
A processor status word (`PSW`)
Four general purpose registers (`R1`, `R2`, `R3`, and `R4`)

Figure 3.6   *µC/OS-II structures when* `OS_TASK_SW()` *is called.*

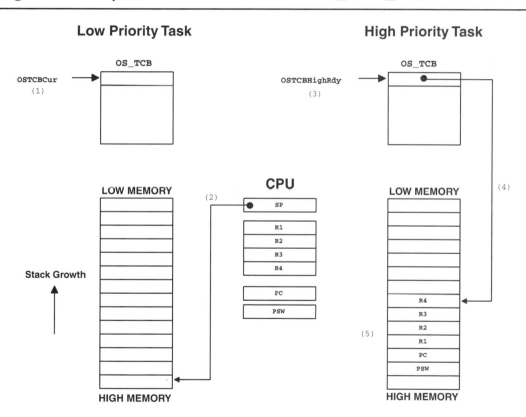

F3.6(1)   `OSTCBCur` points to the `OS_TCB` of the task being suspended (the low priority task).

F3.6(2)   The CPU's stack pointer (`SP` register) points to the current top-of-stack of the task being preempted.

F3.6(3)   `OSTCBHighRdy` points to the `OS_TCB` of the task that will execute after completing the context switch.

F3.6(4)   The .OSTCBStkPtr field in the OS_TCB points to the top-of-stack of the task to resume.

F3.6(5)   The stack of the task to resume contains the desired register values to load into the CPU. These values could have been saved by a previous context switch, as we will see shortly. For the time being, let's simply assume that they have the desired values.

Figure 3.7 shows the state of the variables and data structures after calling OS_TASK_SW() and after saving the context of the task to suspend.

Figure 3.7   *Saving the current task's context.*

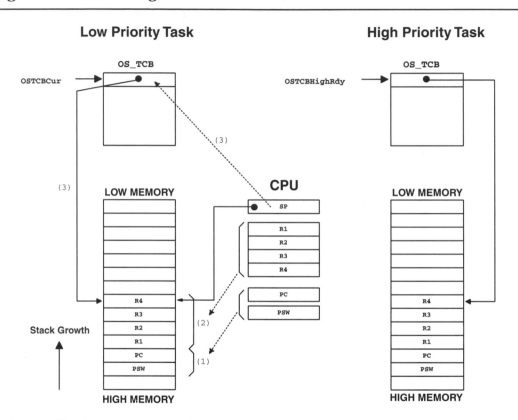

F3.7(1)   Calling OS_TASK_SW() invokes the software interrupt instruction, which forces the processor to save the current value of the PSW and the PC onto the current task's stack. The processor then vectors to the software interrupt handler, which is responsible for completing the remaining steps of the context switch.

F3.7(2)   The software interrupt handler starts by saving the general purpose registers, R1, R2, R3, and R4, in this order.

F3.7(3)   The stack pointer register is then saved into the current task's OS_TCB. At this point, both the CPU's SP register and OSTCBCur->OSTCBStkPtr are pointing to the same location into the current task's stack.

Figure 3.8 shows the state of the variables and data structures after executing the last part of the context-switch code.

Figure 3.8   *Resuming the current task.*

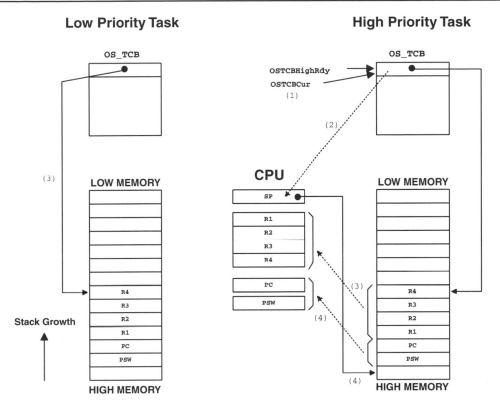

F3.8(1)   Because the new current task is now the task being resumed, the context-switch code copies OSTCBHighRdy to OSTCBCur.

F3.8(2)   The stack pointer of the task to resume is extracted from the OS_TCB (from OSTCBHighRdy->OSTCBStkPtr) and loaded into the CPU's SP register. At this point, the SP register points to the stack location containing the value of register R4.

F3.7(3)   The general purpose registers are popped from the stack in the reverse order (R4, R3, R2, and R1).

F3.8(4)   The PC and PSW registers are loaded back into the CPU by executing a return from interrupt instruction. Because the PC is changed, code execution resumes at the point to which the PC is pointing, which happens to be in the new task's code.

The pseudocode for the context switch is shown in Listing 3.11. OSCtxSw() is generally written in assembly language because most C compilers cannot manipulate CPU registers directly from C. Chapter 14, "80x86 Port; Real Mode, Large Model with Emulated Floating-Point Support" discusses how OSCtxSw(), as well as other μC/OS-II functions, look on a real processor, the Intel 80x86.

Listing 3.11   Context-switch pseudocode.

```
void  OSCtxSw (void)
{
   PUSH R1, R2, R3 and R4 onto the current stack;        See F3.6(2)
   OSTCBCur->OSTCBStkPtr = SP;                           See F3.6(3)
   OSTCBCur              = OSTCBHighRdy;                 See F3.7(1)
   SP                    = OSTCBHighRdy->OSTCBStkPtr;    See F3.7(2)
   POP R4, R3, R2 and R1 from the new stack;             See F3.7(3)
   Execute a return from interrupt instruction;          See F3.7(4)
}
```

3.07   Locking and Unlocking the Scheduler

The OSSchedLock() function (Listing 3.12) is used to prevent task rescheduling until its counterpart, OSSchedUnlock() (Listing 3.13), is called. The task that calls OSSchedLock() keeps control of the CPU even though other higher priority tasks are ready to run. Interrupts, however, are still recognized and serviced (assuming interrupts are enabled). OSSchedLock() and OSSchedUnlock() must be used in pairs. The variable OSLockNesting keeps track of the number of times OSSchedLock() has been called. Nested functions can thus contain critical code that other tasks cannot access. µC/OS-II allows nesting up to 255 levels deep. Scheduling is re-enabled when OSLockNesting is 0. OSSchedLock() and OSSchedUnlock() must be used with caution because they affect the normal management of tasks by µC/OS-II.

Listing 3.12   Locking the scheduler.

```
void  OSSchedLock (void)
{
#if OS_CRITICAL_METHOD == 3
    OS_CPU_SR  cpu_sr;
#endif

    if (OSRunning == TRUE) {                                    (1)
        OS_ENTER_CRITICAL();
        if (OSLockNesting < 255) {                              (2)
            OSLockNesting++;
        }
        OS_EXIT_CRITICAL();
    }
}
```

L3.12(1)   It only makes sense to lock the scheduler if multitasking has started (i.e., OSStart() was called).

L3.12(2)   Before incrementing OSLockNesting, we need to make sure that we have not exceeded the allowable number of nesting levels.

After calling OSSchedLock(), your application must not make any system calls that suspend execution of the current task; that is, your application cannot call OSFlagPend(), OSMboxPend(), OSMutexPend(), OSQPend(), OSSemPend(), OSTaskSuspend(OS_PRIO_SELF), OSTimeDly(), or OSTimeDlyHMSM() until OSLockNesting returns to 0 because OSSchedLock() prevents other tasks from running and thus your system will lock up.

You might want to disable the scheduler when a low-priority task needs to post messages to multiple mailboxes, queues, or semaphores (see Chapter 6, "Event Control Blocks") and you don't want a higher priority task to take control until all mailboxes, queues, and semaphores have been posted to.

Listing 3.13   *Unlocking the scheduler.*

```
void  OSSchedUnlock (void)
{
#if OS_CRITICAL_METHOD == 3
    OS_CPU_SR  cpu_sr;
#endif


    if (OSRunning == TRUE) {                                    (1)
        OS_ENTER_CRITICAL();
        if (OSLockNesting > 0) {                                (2)
            OSLockNesting--;                                    (3)
            if ((OSLockNesting == 0) && (OSIntNesting == 0)) {  (4)
                OS_EXIT_CRITICAL();
                OS_Sched();                                     (5)
            } else {
                OS_EXIT_CRITICAL();
            }
        } else {
            OS_EXIT_CRITICAL();
        }
    }
}
```

L3.13(1)   It only makes sense to unlock the scheduler if multitasking has started (i.e., OSStart() was called).

L3.13(2)   We make sure OSLockNesting is not already 0. If it were, it would be an indication that you called OSSchedUnlock() too many times. In other words, you would not have the same number of OSSchedLock() as OSSchedUnlock().

L3.13(3)   OSLockNesting is decremented.

L3.13(4)

L3.13(5)   We only want to allow the scheduler to execute when all nesting fuctions are complete. OSSchedUnlock() is called from a task because events could have made higher priority tasks ready to run while scheduling was locked.

3.08   Idle Task

µC/OS-II always creates a task (also called the *idle task*) that is executed when none of the other tasks are ready to run. The idle task, OS_TaskIdle(), is always set to the lowest priority, OS_LOWEST_PRIO. The code for the idle task is shown in Listing 3.14. The idle task can never be deleted by application software.

Listing 3.14   *The µC/OS-II idle task.*

```
void  OS_TaskIdle (void *pdata)
{
#if OS_CRITICAL_METHOD == 3
    OS_CPU_SR  cpu_sr;
#endif


    pdata = pdata;
    for (;;) {
        OS_ENTER_CRITICAL();
        OSIdleCtr++;                                           (1)
        OS_EXIT_CRITICAL();
        OSTaskIdleHook();                                      (2)
    }
}
```

L3.14(1)   OS_TaskIdle() increments a 32-bit counter called OSIdleCtr, which is used by the statistics task (see Section 3.09, "Statistics Task") to determine the percentage of CPU time actually being consumed by the application software. Interrupts are disabled and then enabled around the increment because on 8- and most 16-bit processors, a 32-bit increment requires multiple instructions that must be protected from being accessed by higher priority tasks or ISRs.

L3.14(2)   OS_TaskIdle() calls OSTaskIdleHook(), which is a function that you can write to do just about anything you want. You can use OSTaskIdleHook() to STOP the CPU so that it can enter low-power mode. This feature is useful when your application is battery powered. OS_TaskIdle() **must always** be ready to run, so don't call one of the PEND functions, OSTimeDly???() functions, or OSTaskSuspend() from OSTaskIdleHook().

3.09 *Statistics Task*

μC/OS-II contains a task that provides run-time statistics. This task is called OS_TaskStat() and is created by μC/OS-II if you set the configuration constant OS_TASK_STAT_EN (see OS_CFG.H) to 1. When enabled, OS_TaskStat() (see OS_CORE.C) executes every second and computes the percentage of CPU usage. In other words, OS_TaskStat() tells you how much of the CPU time is used by your application, as a percentage. This value is placed in the signed 8-bit integer variable, OSCPUUsage. The resolution of OSCPUUsage is 1 percent.

3

   If your application uses the statistic task, you must call OSStatInit() (see OS_CORE.C) from the first and only task created in your application during initialization. In other words, your startup code must create only one task before calling OSStart(). From this one task, you must call OSStatInit() before you create your other application tasks. The single task that you create is, of course, allowed to create other tasks, but only after calling OSStatInit(). The pseudocode in Listing 3.15 shows what needs to be done.

Listing 3.15   *Initializing the statistic task.*

```
void main (void)
{
    OSInit();                   /* Initialize uC/OS-II              (1)*/
    /* Install uC/OS-II's context switch vector */
    /* Create your startup task (for sake of discussion, TaskStart())  (2)*/
    OSStart();                  /* Start multitasking               (3)*/
}



void TaskStart (void *pdata)
{
    /* Install and initialize μC/OS-II's ticker                     (4)*/
    OSStatInit();               /* Initialize statistics task       (5)*/
    /* Create your application task(s) */
    for (;;) {
        /* Code for TaskStart() goes here! */
    }
}
```

   Because your application must create only one task, TaskStart(), μC/OS-II has only three tasks to manage when main() calls OSStart(): TaskStart(), OS_TaskIdle(), and OS_TaskStat(). Please note that you don't have to call the startup task: TaskStart() — you can call it anything you like. Your startup task has the highest priority because μC/OS-II sets the priority of the idle task to OS_LOWEST_PRIO and the priority of the statistic task to OS_LOWEST_PRIO − 1 internally.

   Figure 3.9 illustrates the flow of execution when initializing the statistic task.

Figure 3.9   *Statistic task initialization.*

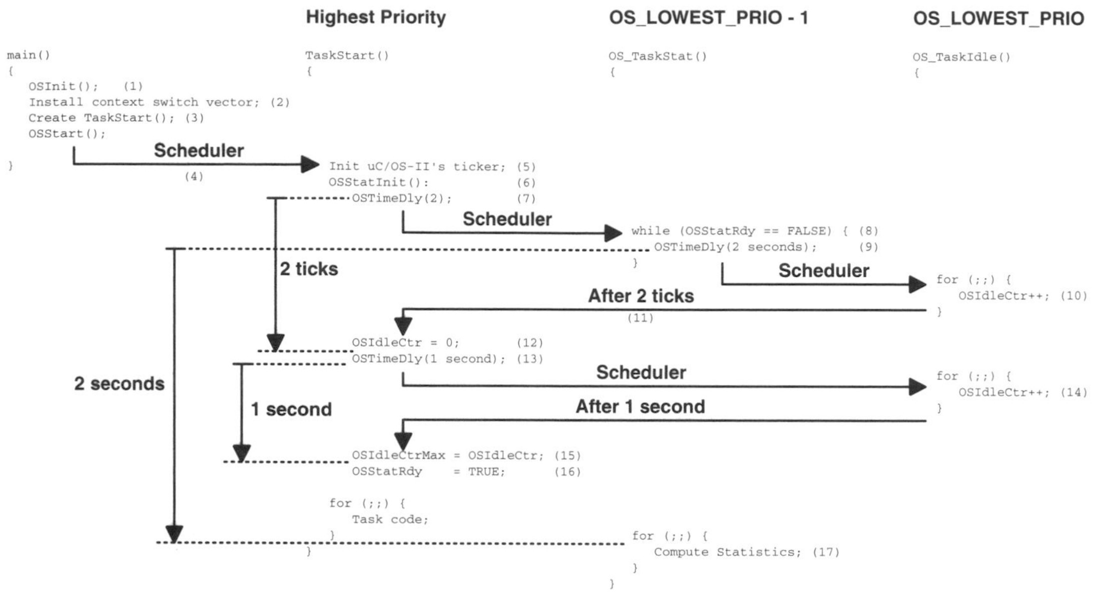

```
                         Highest Priority          OS_LOWEST_PRIO - 1          OS_LOWEST_PRIO

main()                   TaskStart()               OS_TaskStat()               OS_TaskIdle()
{                        {                         {                           {
   OSInit();   (1)
   Install context switch vector; (2)
   Create TaskStart(); (3)
   OSStart();
}                Scheduler
                                    Init uC/OS-II's ticker; (5)
                  (4)               OSStatInit():           (6)
                                    OSTimeDly(2);           (7)
                                          Scheduler
                                                    while (OSStatRdy == FALSE) { (8)
                                                      OSTimeDly(2 seconds);      (9)
                                                    }
                  2 ticks                               Scheduler
                                                                            for (;;) {
                                   After 2 ticks                              OSIdleCtr++; (10)
                                        (11)                                 }
                                   OSIdleCtr = 0;          (12)
                                   OSTimeDly(1 second); (13)
   2 seconds                                           Scheduler             for (;;) {
                                                                              OSIdleCtr++; (14)
                 1 second               After 1 second                      }

                                   OSIdleCtrMax = OSIdleCtr; (15)
                                   OSStatRdy    = TRUE;      (16)

                                   for (;;) {
                                       Task code;
                                   }                    for (;;) {
                                 }                          Compute Statistics; (17)
                                                        }
                                                      }
```

F3.9(1)   The first function that you must call in µC/OS-II is `OSInit()`, which initializes µC/OS-II.

F3.9(2)   Next, you need to install the interrupt vector that performs context switches. Note that on some processors (specifically the Motorola 68HC11), you do not need to install a vector because the vector is already resident in ROM.

F3.9(3)   You must create `TaskStart()` by calling either `OSTaskCreate()` or `OSTaskCreateExt()`.

F3.9(4)   After you are ready to multitask, call `OSStart()`, which schedules `TaskStart()` for execution because it has the highest priority.

F3.9(5)   `TaskStart()` is responsible for initializing and starting the ticker. You want to initialize the ticker in the first task to execute because you don't want to receive a tick interrupt until you are actually multitasking.

F3.9(6)   Next, `TaskStart()` calls `OSStatInit()`. `OSStatInit()` determines how high the idle counter (`OSIdleCtr`) can count if no other task in the application is executing. A Pentium II running at 333MHz increments this counter to a value of about 15,000,000. `OSIdleCtr` is still far from wrapping around the 4,294,967,296 limit of a 32-bit value. At the rate processor speeds are getting, it will not be too long before `OSIdleCtr` overflows. If overflow becomes a problem, you can always introduce some software delays in `OSTaskIdleHook()`. Because `OS_TaskIdle()` really doesn't execute any useful code, it's OK to throw away CPU cycles.

F3.9(7)   `OSStatInit()` starts off by calling `OSTimeDly()`, which puts `TaskStart()` to sleep for two ticks. This action is done to synchronize `OSStatInit()` with the ticker. µC/OS-II then picks the next highest priority task that is ready to run, which happens to be `OS_TaskStat()`.

F3.9(8)   The code for `OS_TaskStat()` is discussed later, but as a preview, the very first thing `OS_TaskStat()` does is check to see if the flag `OSStatRdy` is set to `FALSE` and then delays for two seconds if it is.

F3.9(9)   It so happens that OSStatRdy is initialized to FALSE by OSInit(), so OS_TaskStat() in fact puts itself to sleep for two seconds. This action causes a context switch to the only task that is ready to run, OS_TaskIdle().

F3.9(10)   The CPU stays in OS_TaskIdle() until the two ticks of TaskStart() expire.

F3.9(11)

F3.9(12)   After two ticks, TaskStart() resumes execution in OSStatInit(), and OSIdleCtr is cleared.

F3.9(13)   Then, OSStatInit() delays itself for one full second. Because no other task is ready to run, OS_TaskIdle() again gets control of the CPU.

F3.9(14)   During that time, OSIdleCtr is continuously incremented.

F3.9(15)   After one second, TaskStart() is resumed, still in OSStatInit(), and the value that OSIdleCtr reached during that one second is saved in OSIdleCtrMax.

F3.9(16)

F3.9(17)   OSStatInit() sets OSStatRdy to TRUE, which allows OS_TaskStat() to perform a CPU usage computation after its delay of two seconds expires.

The code for OSStatInit() is shown in Listing 3.16.

Listing 3.16   *Initializing the statistic task.*

```
void  OSStatInit (void)
{
#if OS_CRITICAL_METHOD == 3
    OS_CPU_SR  cpu_sr;
#endif


    OSTimeDly(2);
    OS_ENTER_CRITICAL();
    OSIdleCtr    = 0L;
    OS_EXIT_CRITICAL();
    OSTimeDly(OS_TICKS_PER_SEC);
    OS_ENTER_CRITICAL();
    OSIdleCtrMax = OSIdleCtr;
    OSStatRdy    = TRUE;
    OS_EXIT_CRITICAL();
}
```

The code for OS_TaskStat() is shown in Listing 3.17.

Listing 3.17   Statistics task.

```
void  OS_TaskStat (void *pdata)
{
#if OS_CRITICAL_METHOD == 3
    OS_CPU_SR   cpu_sr;
#endif
    INT32U      run;
    INT32U      max;
    INT8S       usage;


    pdata = pdata;
    while (OSStatRdy == FALSE) {                         (1)
        OSTimeDly(2 * OS_TICKS_PER_SEC);
    }
    max = OSIdleCtrMax / 100L;                           (2)
    for (;;) {
        OS_ENTER_CRITICAL();
        OSIdleCtrRun = OSIdleCtr;                        (3)
        run          = OSIdleCtr;
        OSIdleCtr    = 0L;
        OS_EXIT_CRITICAL();
        if (max > 0L) {
            usage = (INT8S)(100L - run / max);          (4)
            if (usage >= 0) {
                OSCPUUsage = usage;
            } else {
                OSCPUUsage = 0;
            }
        } else {
            OSCPUUsage = 0;
            max         = OSIdleCtrMax / 100L;
        }
        OSTaskStatHook();                               (5)
        OSTimeDly(OS_TICKS_PER_SEC);
    }
}
```

L3.17(1) I've already discussed why `OS_TaskStat()` has to wait for the flag `OSStatRdy` to be set to `TRUE` in the previous paragraphs. The task code executes every second and basically determines how much CPU time is actually consumed by all the application tasks. When you start adding application code, the idle task gets less of the processor's time, and `OSIdleCtr` is not allowed to count as high as it did when nothing else was running. Remember that `OSStatInit()` saved this maximum value in `OSIdleCtrMax`.

L3.17(3) Every second, the value of the idle counter is copied into the global variable `OSIdleCtrRun`. This variable thus holds the maximum value of the idle counter for the second that just passed. This value is not used anywhere else by µC/OS-II but can be monitored (and possibly displayed) by your application. The idle counter is then reset to 0 for the next measurement.

L3.17(4) CPU use (Equation [3.1]) is stored in the variable `OSCPUUsage`

[3.1]
$$OSCPUUsage_{(\%)} = 100 \times \left(1 - \frac{OSIdleCtr}{OSIdleCtrMax}\right)$$

L3.17(2) Equation 3.1 needs to be re-written because `OSIdleCtr` / `OSIdleCtrMax` will always yield 0 because of the integer operation. The new equation is

[3.2]
$$OSCPUUsage_{(\%)} = \left(100 - \frac{100 \times OSIdleCtr}{OSIdleCtrMax}\right)$$

Multiplying `OSIdleCtr` by 100 limits the maximum value that `OSIdleCtr` can take, especially on fast processors. In other words, in order for the multiplication of `OSIdleCtr` to not overflow, `OSIdleCtr` must never be higher than 42,949,672! With fast processors, it's quite likely that `OSIdleCtr` can reach this value. To correct this potential problem, all we need to do is divide `OSIdleCtrMax` by 100 instead as shown in Equation 3.3.

[3.3]
$$OSCPUUsage_{(\%)} = \left(100 - \frac{OSIdleCtr}{\left(\frac{OSIdleCtrMax}{100}\right)}\right)$$

The local variable `max` is thus precomputed to hold `OSIdleCtrMax`, divided by 100.

L3.17(5) After the computation is performed, `OS_TaskStat()` calls `OSTaskStatHook()`, a user-definable function that allows the statistic task to be expanded. Indeed, your application can compute and display the total execution time of all tasks, the percentage of time actually consumed by each task, and more (see Chapter 1, Example #3).

3.10   Interrupts Under µC/OS-II

µC/OS-II requires that an interrupt service routine (ISR) be written in assembly language. However, if your C compiler supports in-line assembly language, you can put the ISR code directly in a C source file.

The pseudocode for an ISR is shown in Listing 3.18.

Listing 3.18   ISRs under µC/OS-II.

```
YourISR:
    Save all CPU registers;                                          (1)
    Call OSIntEnter() or, increment OSIntNesting directly;           (2)
    if (OSIntNesting == 1) {                                         (3)
        OSTCBCur->OSTCBStkPtr = SP;                                  (4)
    }
    Clear interrupting device;                                       (5)
    Re-enable interrupts (optional)                                  (6)
    Execute user code to service ISR;                                (7)
    Call OSIntExit();                                                (8)
    Restore all CPU registers;                                       (9)
    Execute a return from interrupt instruction;                    (10)
```

L3.18(1)   Your code should save all CPU registers onto the current task stack. Note that on some processors, like the Motorola 68020 (and higher), a different stack is used when servicing an interrupt. µC/OS-II can work with such processors as long as the registers are saved on the interrupted task's stack when a context switch occurs.

L3.18(2)   µC/OS-II needs to know that you are servicing an ISR, so you need to either call OSIntEnter() or increment the global variable OSIntNesting. OSIntNesting can be incremented directly. Incrementing OSIntNesting directly is much faster than calling OSIntEnter() and is thus the preferred way.

Certain processors, such as the Motorola 68020, allow interrupts to be nested even though you are just starting to service an interrupt. The beginning of the ISR needs to be different for these processors. I do not discuss this issue here but, it might be worthwhile for you to download the CPU32 port from www.uCOS-II.com to see how to handle this situation.

L3.18(3)

L3.18(4)   We check to see if this level is the first interrupt level, and, if it is, we immediately save the stack pointer into the current task's OS_TCB. You should note that I added these two lines of code since µC/OS-II V2.04. If you have a port that assumes µC/OS-II V2.04 or earlier, you should simply add these two lines in **all** your ISRs.

L3.18(5)   You must clear the interrupt source because you stand the chance of re-entering the ISR if you decide to re-enable interrupts.

L3.18(6)   You can re-enable interrupts if you want to allow interrupt nesting. µC/OS-II allows you to nest interrupts because it keeps track of ISR nesting in OSIntNesting.

L3.18(7)   After you have done the previous steps, you can start servicing the interrupting device. This section is obviously application specific.

L3.18(8)   The conclusion of the ISR is marked by calling OSIntExit(), which decrements the interrupt nesting counter. When the nesting counter reaches 0, all nested interrupts are complete, and µC/OS-II needs to determine whether a higher priority task has been awakened by the ISR (or any other nested ISR). If a higher priority task is ready to run, µC/OS-II returns to the higher priority task rather than to the interrupted task.

L3.18(9)   If the interrupted task is still the most important task to run, `OSIntExit()` returns to the ISR.

L3.18(10) At that point, the saved registers are restored, and a return from interrupt instruction is executed. Note that µC/OS-II returns to the interrupted task if scheduling has been disabled (`OSLockNesting > 0`).

The previous description is further illustrated in Figure 3.10.

Figure 3.10   *Servicing an interrupt.*

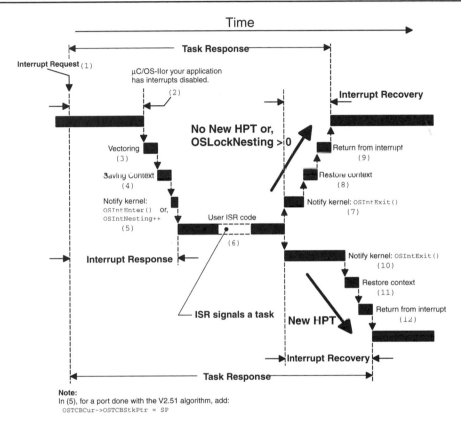

Note:
In (5), for a port done with the V2.51 algorithm, add:
`OSTCBCur->OSTCBStkPtr = SP`

F3.10(1)   The interrupt is received but is not recognized by the CPU, either because interrupts have been disabled by µC/OS-II or your application or, because the CPU has not completed executing the current instruction.

F3.10(2)

F3.10(3)   After the CPU recognizes the interrupt, the CPU vectors (at least on most microprocessors) to the ISR.

F3.10(4)   As described in Figure 3.10, the ISR saves the CPU registers (i.e., the CPU's context).

F3.10(5)   After the CPU registers are saved, your ISR notifies µC/OS-II by calling `OSIntEnter()` or by incrementing `OSIntNesting`. You also need to save the stack pointer into the current task's `OS_TCB`.

F3.10(6)   Your ISR code then executes. Your ISR should do as little work as possible and defer most of the work at the task level. A task is notified of the ISR by calling `OSFlagPost()`, `OSMboxPost()`,

OSQPost(), OSQPostFront(), or OSSemPost(). The receiving task might or might not be pending at the event flag, mailbox, queue, or semaphore when the ISR occurs and the post is made.

F3.10(7)   After the user ISR code has completed, you need to call OSIntExit(). As can be seen from the timing diagram, OSIntExit() takes less time to return to the interrupted task when there is no higher priority task (HPT) readied by the ISR.

F3.10(8)

F3.10(9)   In this case, the CPU registers are then simply restored and a return from interrupt instruction is executed.

F3.10(10) If the ISR makes a higher priority task ready to run, then OSIntExit() takes longer to execute because a context switch is now needed.

F3.10(11)

F3.10(12) The registers of the new task are restored, and a return from interrupt instruction is executed.

The code for OSIntEnter() is shown in Listing 3.19, and the code for OSIntExit() is shown in Listing 3.20. Very little needs to be said about OSIntEnter().

Listing 3.19   Notify µC/OS-II about beginning an ISR.

```
void  OSIntEnter (void)
{
    if (OSRunning == TRUE) {
        if (OSIntNesting < 255) {
            OSIntNesting++;
        }
    }
}
```

Listing 3.20   Notify µC/OS-II about leaving an ISR.

```
void  OSIntExit (void)
{
#if OS_CRITICAL_METHOD == 3
    OS_CPU_SR  cpu_sr;
#endif
```

3

Listing 3.20   *Notify µC/OS-II about leaving an ISR. (Continued)*

```
   OS_ENTER_CRITICAL();
   if (OSRunning == TRUE) {
      if (OSIntNesting > 0) {                                            (1)
         OSIntNesting--;
      }
      if ((OSIntNesting == 0) && (OSLockNesting == 0)) {
         OSIntExitY    = OSUnMapTbl[OSRdyGrp];                           (2)
         OSPrioHighRdy = (INT8U)((OSIntExitY << 3)
                         + OSUnMapTbl[OSRdyTbl[OSIntExitY]]);
         if (OSPrioHighRdy != OSPrioCur) {
            OSTCBHighRdy  = OSTCBPrioTbl[OSPrioHighRdy];
            OSCtxSwCtr++;
            OSIntCtxSw();                                                (3)
         }
      }
   }
   OS_EXIT_CRITICAL();
}
```

OSIntExit() looks strangely like OS_Sched() except for three differences:

L3.20(1)   The interrupt-nesting counter is decremented in OSIntExit(), and rescheduling occurs when both the interrupt-nesting counter and the lock-nesting counter (OSLockNesting) are 0.

L3.20(2)   The *Y* index needed for OSRdyTbl[] is stored in the global variable OSIntExitY because prior to µC/OS-II V2.51, OSIntCtxSw() needed to account for local variables and return addresses. As of µC/OS-II V2.51, OSIntCtxSw() doesn't need to account for these. However, I decided to leave OSIntExitY as a global for backwards compatibility with previous ports.

L3.20(3)   If a context switch is needed, OSIntExit() calls OSIntCtxSw() instead of OS_TASK_SW(), as it did in OS_Sched().

You need to call OSIntCtxSw(), instead of OS_TASK_SW(), because the ISR has already saved the CPU registers onto the interrupted task and thus shouldn't be saved again. Implementation details about OSIntCtxSw() are provided in Chapter 13, Porting µC/OS-II.

Some processors, such as the Motorola 68HC11, require that you implicitly re-enable interrupts in order to allow nesting. This process can be used to your advantage. Indeed, if your ISR needs to be serviced quickly and it doesn't need to notify a task about itself, you don't need to call OSIntEnter() (or increment OSIntNesting) or OSIntExit(), as long as you don't enable interrupts within the ISR. The pseudocode in Listing 3.21 shows this situation. In this case, the only way a task and this ISR can communicate is through global variables.

Listing 3.21   ISRs on a Motorola 68HC11.

```
M68HC11_ISR:                    /* Fast ISR, MUST NOT enable interrupts */
    All register saved automatically by the CPU;
    Execute user code to service the interrupt;
    Execute a return from interrupt instruction;
```

3.11   Clock Tick

µC/OS-II requires that you provide a periodic time source to keep track of time delays and timeouts. A tick should occur between 10 and 100 times per second, or Hertz. The faster the tick rate, the more overhead µC/OS-II imposes on the system. The actual frequency of the clock tick depends on the desired tick resolution of your application. You can obtain a tick source either by dedicating a hardware timer or by generating an interrupt from an AC power line (50/60Hz) signal.

You **must** enable ticker interrupts **after** multitasking has started, that is, after calling OSStart(). In other words, you should initialize ticker interrupts in the first task that executes following a call to OSStart(). A common mistake is to enable ticker interrupts after OSInit() and before OSStart(), as shown in Listing 3.22. Potentially, the tick interrupt could be serviced before µC/OS-II starts the first task. At this point, µC/OS-II is in an unknown state, so your application crashes.

Listing 3.22   Incorrect way to start the ticker.

```
void main(void)
{
    .
    .
    OSInit();                   /* Initialize _C/OS-II                      */
    .
    .

    /* Application initialization code ...                                  */
    /* ... Create at least one task by calling OSTaskCreate()              */
    .
    .

    Enable TICKER interrupts;   /* DO NOT DO THIS HERE!!!                   */
    .
    .

    OSStart();                  /* Start multitasking                       */
}
```

The µC/OS-II clock tick is serviced by calling OSTimeTick() from a *tick ISR*. OSTimeTick() keeps track of all of the task timers and timeouts. The tick ISR follows all the rules described in Section 3.10, "Interrupts Under µC/OS-II". The pseudocode for the tick ISR is shown in Listing 3.23. This code must be written in assembly language because you cannot access CPU registers directly from C. Because the tick ISR is always needed, it is generally provided with a port.

Listing 3.23   *Pseudocode for tick ISR.*

```
void OSTickISR(void)
{
    Save processor registers;
    Call OSIntEnter() or increment OSIntNesting;
    if (OSIntNesting == 1) {
        OSTCBCur->OSTCBStkPtr = SP;
    }
    Call OSTimeTick();
    Clear interrupting device;
    Re-enable interrupts (optional);
    Call OSIntExit();
    Restore processor registers;
    Execute a return from interrupt instruction;
}
```

The code for OSTimeTick() is shown in Listing 3.24.

Listing 3.24   *Service a tick,* `OSTimeTick()`.

```
void  OSTimeTick (void)
{
#if OS_CRITICAL_METHOD == 3
    OS_CPU_SR  cpu_sr;
#endif
    OS_TCB     *ptcb;


    OSTimeTickHook();                                                       (1)
#if OS_TIME_GET_SET_EN > 0
    OS_ENTER_CRITICAL();
    OSTime++;                                                               (2)
    OS_EXIT_CRITICAL();
#endif
    if (OSRunning == TRUE) {
        ptcb = OSTCBList;                                                   (3)
        while (ptcb->OSTCBPrio != OS_IDLE_PRIO) {                           (4)
            OS_ENTER_CRITICAL();
            if (ptcb->OSTCBDly != 0) {
                if (--ptcb->OSTCBDly == 0) {
                    if ((ptcb->OSTCBStat & OS_STAT_SUSPEND) == 0x00) {      (5)
                        OSRdyGrp                 |= ptcb->OSTCBBitY;        (6)
                        OSRdyTbl[ptcb->OSTCBY] |= ptcb->OSTCBBitX;
                    } else {
                        ptcb->OSTCBDly = 1;
```

Listing 3.24   Service a tick, OSTimeTick(). (Continued)

```
                }
            }
        }
        ptcb = ptcb->OSTCBNext;
        OS_EXIT_CRITICAL();
    }
  }
}
```

L3.24(1)   OSTimeTick() starts by calling the user-definable function OSTimeTickHook(), which can be used to extend the functionality of OSTimeTick(). I decided to call OSTimeTickHook() first to give your application a chance to do something as soon as the tick is serviced because you may have some time-critical work to do. Most of the work done by OSTimeTick() basically consists of decrementing the .OSTCBDly field for each OS_TCB (if it's nonzero).

L3.24(2)   OSTimeTick() also accumulates the number of clock ticks since power-up in an unsigned 32-bit variable called OSTime. Note that I disable interrupts before incrementing OSTime because on some processors, a 32-bit increment is likely to be done using multiple CPU instructions.

L3.24(3)

L3.24(4)   OSTimeTick() follows the chain of OS_TCB, starting at OSTCBList, until it reaches the idle task.

L3.24(6)   When the .OSTCBDly field of a task's OS_TCB is decremented to 0, the task is made ready to run.

L3.24(5)   The task is not readied, however, if it has been explicitly suspended by OSTaskSuspend().

The execution time of OSTimeTick() is directly proportional to the number of tasks created in an application; however, execution time is still very deterministic.

If you don't like to make ISRs any longer than they must be, OSTimeTick() can be called at the task level, as shown in Listing 3.25. To do this, create a task that has a higher priority than all your other application tasks. The tick ISR needs to signal this high-priority task by using either a semaphore or a message mailbox.

Listing 3.25   Service a tick, TickTask().

```
void TickTask (void *pdata)
{
    pdata = pdata;
    for (;;) {
        OSMboxPend(...);        /* Wait for signal from Tick ISR */
        OSTimeTick();
        OS_Sched();
    }
}
```

You obviously need to create a mailbox (with contents initialized to NULL) that will be used to signal the task that a tick interrupt has occurred (Listing 3.26).

Listing 3.26   *Service a tick,* `OSTickISR( )`.

```
void OSTickISR(void)
{
    Save processor registers;
    Call OSIntEnter() or increment OSIntNesting;
    if (OSIntNesting == 1) {
        OSTCBCur->OSTCBStkPtr = SP;
    }

    Post a 'dummy' message (e.g. (void *)1) to the tick mailbox;

    Call OSIntExit();
    Restore processor registers;
    Execute a return from interrupt instruction;
}
```

3.12   *μC/OS-II Initialization*

A requirement of μC/OS-II is that you call OSInit() before you call any of μC/OS-II's other services. OSInit() initializes all μC/OS-II variables and data structures (see OS_CORE.C). OSInit() creates the idle task OS_TaskIdle(), which is always ready to run. The priority of OS_TaskIdle() is always set to OS_LOWEST_PRIO. If OS_TASK_STAT_EN and OS_TASK_CREATE_EXT_EN (see OS_CFG.H) are both set to 1, OSInit() also creates the statistic task OS_TaskStat() and makes it ready to run. The priority of OS_TaskStat() is always set to OS_LOWEST_PRIO-1.

Figure 3.11 shows the relationship between some μC/OS-II variables and data structures after calling OSInit(). The illustration assumes that the following #define constants are set as follows in OS_CFG.H:

- OS_TASK_STAT_EN is set to 1,
- OS_FLAG_EN is set to 1,
- OS_LOWEST_PRIO is set to 63, and
- OS_MAX_TASKS is set to 62.

Figure 3.11   Variables and data structures after calling `OSInit()`.

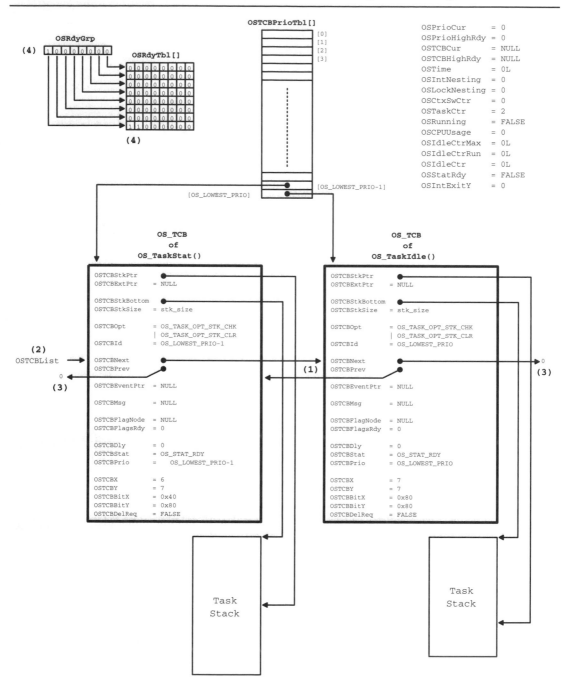

F3.11(1) Notice that the task control blocks (OS_TCBs) of OS_TaskIdle() and OS_TaskStat() are chained together in a doubly linked list.

F3.11(2) OSTCBList points to the beginning of this chain. When a task is created, it is always placed at the beginning of the list. In other words, OSTCBList always points to the OS_TCB of the last task created.

F3.11(3) Both ends of the doubly linked list point to NULL (i.e., 0).

F3.11(4) Because both tasks are ready to run, their corresponding bits in OSRdyTbl[] are set to 1. Also, because the bits of both tasks are on the same row in OSRdyTbl[], only one bit in OSRdyGrp is set to 1.

µC/OS-II also initializes five pools of free data structures, as shown in Figure 3.12. Each of these pools is a singly linked list and allows µC/OS-II to obtain and return an element from and to a pool quickly.

Figure 3.12   Free pools.

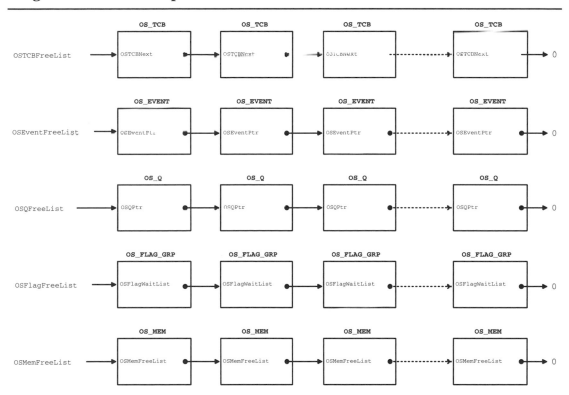

After OSInit() has been called, the OS_TCB pool contains OS_MAX_TASKS entries. The OS_EVENT pool contains OS_MAX_EVENTS entries, the OS_Q pool contains OS_MAX_QS entries, the OS_FLAG_GRP pool contains OS_MAX_FLAGS entries, and, finally, the OS_MEM pool contains OS_MAX_MEM_PART entries. Each of the free pools are NULL-pointer terminated to indicate the end. The pool is, of course, empty if any of the list pointers point to NULL. You define the size of these pools in OS_CFG.H.

3.13   Starting µC/OS-II

You start multitasking by calling OSStart(). However, before you start µC/OS-II, you must create at least one of your application tasks, as shown in Listing 3.27.

Listing 3.27   Initializing and starting µC/OS-II.

```
void main (void)
{
    OSInit();            /* Initialize uC/OS-II                        */
    .

    .
    Create at least 1 task using either OSTaskCreate() or OSTaskCreateExt();
    .

    .
    OSStart();           /* Start multitasking!  OSStart() will not return */
}
```

The code for OSStart() is shown in Listing 3.28.

Listing 3.28   Starting multitasking.

```
void OSStart (void)
{
    INT8U y;
    INT8U x;

    if (OSRunning == FALSE) {
        y             = OSUnMapTbl[OSRdyGrp];
        x             = OSUnMapTbl[OSRdyTbl[y]];
        OSPrioHighRdy = (INT8U)((y << 3) + x);
        OSPrioCur     = OSPrioHighRdy;
        OSTCBHighRdy  = OSTCBPrioTbl[OSPrioHighRdy];                    (1)
        OSTCBCur      = OSTCBHighRdy;
        OSStartHighRdy();                                              (2)
    }
}
```

L3.28(1) When called, OSStart() finds the OS_TCB (from the ready list) of the highest priority task that you have created.

L3.28(2) Then, OSStart() calls OSStartHighRdy(), which is found in OS_CPU_A.ASM for the processor being used (see Chapter 13, "Porting µC/OS-II"). Basically, OSStartHighRdy() restores the CPU registers by popping them off the task's stack and then executing a return from interrupt instruction, which forces the CPU to execute your task's code. Note that OSStartHighRdy() never returns to OSStart().

Figure 3.13 shows the contents of the variables and data structures after multitasking has started. Here, I assume that the task you created has a priority of 6. Notice that OSTaskCtr indicates that three tasks have been created: OSRunning is set to TRUE, indicating that multitasking has started; OSPrioCur and OSPrioHighRdy contain the priority of your application task; and OSTCBCur and OSTCBHighRdy both point to the OS_TCB of your task.

3

Figure 3.13   Variables and data structures after calling OSStart().

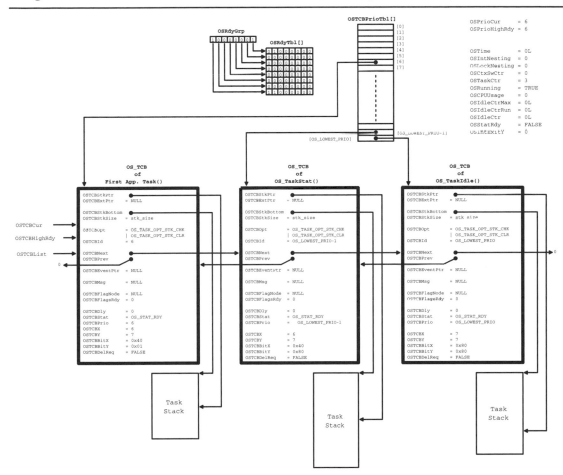

3.14   Obtaining the Current µC/OS-II Version

You can obtain the current version of µC/OS-II from your application by calling OSVersion() (Listing 3.29). OSVersion() returns the version number, multiplied by 100. In other words, µC/OS-II version 2.52 is returned as 252.

Listing 3.29   Getting the current µC/OS-II version.

```
INT16U OSVersion (void)
{
    return (OS_VERSION);
}
```

To find out about the latest version of µC/OS-II and how to obtain an upgrade, you should check the official µC/OS-II Web site at http://www.uCOS-II.com.

Chapter 4

Task Management

In the previous chapter, I specified that a task is either an infinite loop function or a function that deletes itself when it is done executing. Note that the task code is not actually deleted — μC/OS-II simply doesn't know about the task anymore, so that code will not run. A task looks just like any other C function, containing a return type and an argument, but the task must never return. The return type of a task must always be declared void. The functions described in this chapter are found in the file OS_TASK.C. A task must have one of the two structures:

```
void YourTask (void *pdata)
{
    for (;;) {
        /* USER CODE */
        Call one of uC/OS-II's services:
            OSFlagPend();
            OSMboxPend();
            OSMutexPend();
            OSQPend();
            OSSemPend();
            OSTaskSuspend(OS_PRIO_SELF);
            OSTimeDly();
            OSTimeDlyHMSM();
        /* USER CODE */
    }
}
```

or

```
void YourTask (void *pdata)
{
    /* USER CODE */
    OSTaskDel(OS_PRIO_SELF);
}
```

This chapter describes the services that allow your application to create a task, delete a task, change a task's priority, suspend and resume a task, and obtain information about a task.

μC/OS-II can manage up to 64 tasks, although I recommend reserving the four highest priority tasks and the four lowest priority tasks for future use by μC/OS-II. However, at this time, only two priority levels are actually used by μC/OS-II, OS_LOWEST_PRIO and OS_LOWEST_PRIO-1 (see OS_CFG.H). This leaves you with up to 56 application tasks. The lower the value of the priority, the higher the priority of the task. In the current version of μC/OS-II, the task priority number also serves as the task identifier.

4.00   *Creating a Task,* OSTaskCreate()

In order for μC/OS-II to manage your task, you must create it. You create a task by passing its address and other arguments to one of two functions: OSTaskCreate() or OSTaskCreateExt(). OSTaskCreate() is backward compatible with μC/OS, and OSTaskCreateExt() is an extended version of OSTaskCreate(), providing additional features. A task can be created using either function. A task can be created prior to the start of multitasking or by another task. You must create at least one task before you start multitasking [i.e., before you call OSStart()]. An ISR cannot create a task.

The code for OSTaskCreate() is shown in Listing 4.1. As can be seen, OSTaskCreate() requires four arguments: task is a pointer to the task code, pdata is a pointer to an argument that is passed to your task when it starts executing, ptos is a pointer to the top of the stack that is assigned to the task (see Section 4.02, "Task Stacks"), and prio is the desired task priority.

Listing 4.1   OSTaskCreate().

```
INT8U OSTaskCreate (void (*task)(void *pd), void *pdata, OS_STK *ptos, INT8U prio)
{
#if OS_CRITICAL_METHOD == 3
    OS_CPU_SR  cpu_sr;
#endif
    void    *psp;
    INT8U    err;

#if OS_ARG_CHK_EN > 0
    if (prio > OS_LOWEST_PRIO) {                                              (1)
        return (OS_PRIO_INVALID);
    }
#endif
    OS_ENTER_CRITICAL();
    if (OSTCBPrioTbl[prio] == (OS_TCB *)0) {                                  (2)
```

Listing 4.1   `OSTaskCreate()`. *(Continued)*

```
        OSTCBPrioTbl[prio] = (OS_TCB *)1;                                    (3)
        OS_EXIT_CRITICAL();                                                  (4)
        psp = (void *)OSTaskStkInit(task, pdata, ptos, 0);                   (5)
        err = OS_TCBInit(prio, psp, (void *)0, 0, 0, (void *)0, 0);          (6)
        if (err == OS_NO_ERR) {                                              (7)
            OS_ENTER_CRITICAL();
            OSTaskCtr++;                                                     (8)
            OS_EXIT_CRITICAL();
            if (OSRunning == TRUE) {                                         (9)
                OS_Sched();                                                  (10)
            }
        } else {
            OS_ENTER_CRITICAL();
            OSTCBPrioTbl[prio] = (OS_TCB *)0;                                (11)
            OS_EXIT_CRITICAL();
        }
        return (err);
    OS_EXIT_CRITICAL();
    return (OS_PRIO_EXIST);
}
```

L4.1(1)   If the configuration constant `OS_ARG_CHK_EN` (see file `OS_CFG.H`) is set to 1, `OSTaskCreate()` checks that the task priority is valid. The priority of a task must be a number between 0 and `OS_LOWEST_PRIO`, inclusive. Please note that `OS_LOWEST_PRIO` is reserved by μC/OS-II's idle task. Don't worry, your application can not call `OSTaskCreate()` and create a task at priority `OS_LOWEST_PRIO` because the priority will have already been 'reserved' for the idle task by `OSInit()`. If you try to, `OSTaskCreate()` returns `OS_PRIO_EXIST`.

L4.1(2)   Next, `OSTaskCreate()` makes sure that a task has not already been created at the desired priority. With μC/OS-II, all tasks must have a unique priority.

L4.1(3)   If the desired priority is free, μC/OS-II reserves the priority by placing a non-`NULL` pointer in `OSTCBPrioTbl[]`.

L4.1(4)   This allows `OSTaskCreate()` to re-enable interrupts while the function sets up the rest of the data structures for the task because no other concurrent calls to `OSTaskCreate()` can now use this priority.

L4.1(5)   `OSTaskCreate()` then calls `OSTaskStkInit()`, which is responsible for setting up the task stack. This function is processor specific and is found in `OS_CPU_C.C`. Refer to Chapter 13, "Porting μC/OS-II" for details on implementing `OSTaskStkInit()`. If you already have a port of μC/OS-II for the processor you are intending to use, you don't need to be concerned about implementation details. `OSTaskStkInit()` returns the new top-of-stack (`psp`), which will be saved in the task's `OS_TCB`. You should note that the fourth argument (`opt`) to `OSTaskStkInit()` is set to 0. Unlike `OSTaskCreateExt()`, however, `OSTaskCreate()` does not support options, so no options are available to pass to `OSTaskStkInit()`. μC/OS-II supports processors that have stacks that grow either from high to low memory or from low to high memory. When you call `OSTaskCreate()`, you must know how the stack grows (see

OS_STACK_GROWTH in OS_CPU.H of the processor you are using) because you must pass the task's top-of-stack to OSTaskCreate(), which can be either the lowest or the highest memory location of the stack.

L4.1(6)   After OSTaskStkInit() has completed setting up the stack, OSTaskCreate() calls OS_TCBInit() to obtain and initialize an OS_TCB from the pool of free OS_TCBs. The code for OS_TCBInit() was described in Section 3.03, "Task Control Blocks (OS_TCB)" and is found in OS_CORE.C instead of OS_TASK.C.

L4.1(7)

L4.1(8)   Upon return from OS_TCBInit(), OSTaskCreate() checks the return code and, upon success, increments OSTaskCtr, which keeps track of the number of tasks created.

L4.1(11)   If OS_TCBInit() failed, the priority level is relinquished by setting the entry in OSTCBPrioTbl[prio] to 0.

L4.1(9)

L4.1(10)   Finally, if OSTaskCreate() is called from a task (i.e., OSRunning is set to TRUE), the scheduler is called to determine whether the created task has a higher priority than its creator. Creating a higher priority task results in a context switch to the new task. If the task was created before multitasking has started [i.e., you did not call OSStart() yet], the scheduler is not called.

4.01 Creating a Task, OSTaskCreateExt()

Creating a task using OSTaskCreateExt() offers more flexibility but at the expense of additional overhead. The code for OSTaskCreateExt() is shown in Listing 4.2.

As can be seen, OSTaskCreateExt() requires nine arguments! The first four arguments (task, pdata, ptos, and prio) are exactly the same as in OSTaskCreate(), and they are located in the same order. I created the function this way to make it easier to migrate your code to use OSTaskCreateExt().

id   Establishes a unique identifier for the task being created. This argument has been added for future expansion and is otherwise unused by µC/OS-II. This identifier allows me to extend µC/OS-II beyond its limit of 64 tasks. For now, simply set the task's ID to the same value as the task's priority.

pbos   Is a pointer to the task's bottom-of-stack. This argument is used to perform stack checking.

stk_size   Specifies the size of the stack in number of elements. For example, if a stack entry is four bytes wide, then a stk_size of 1000 means that the stack has 4,000 bytes. Again, this argument is used for stack checking.

pext   Is a pointer to a user-supplied data area that can be used to extend the OS_TCB of the task. For example, you can add a name to a task (see Example #3 in Chapter 1), storage for the contents of floating-point registers (see Example #4 in Chapter 1) during a context switch, a port address to trigger an oscilloscope during a context switch, and more.

opt   Specifies options to OSTaskCreateExt(). This argument specifies whether stack checking is allowed, whether the stack will be cleared, and whether floating-point operations are performed by the task, among others. uCOS_II.H contains a list of available options (OS_TASK_OPT_STK_CHK, OS_TASK_OPT_STK_CLR, and `OS_TASK_OPT_SAVE_FP`). Each option consists of a bit. The option is selected when the bit is set (simply `OR` the above `OS_TASK_OPT_???` constants).

Listing 4.2   `OSTaskCreateExt()`.

```
INT8U  OSTaskCreateExt (void   (*task)(void *pd),
                        void   *pdata,
                        OS_STK *ptos,
                        INT8U  prio,
                        INT16U id,
                        OS_STK *pbos,
                        INT32U stk_size,
                        void   *pext,
                        INT16U opt)
{
#if OS_CRITICAL_METHOD == 3
    OS_CPU_SR  cpu_sr;
#endif
    OS_STK     *psp;
    INT8U      err;


#if OS_ARG_CHK_EN > 0
    if (prio > OS_LOWEST_PRIO) {                                    (1)
        return (OS_PRIO_INVALID);
    }
#endif
    OS_ENTER_CRITICAL();
    if (OSTCBPrioTbl[prio] == (OS_TCB *)0) {                        (2)
        OSTCBPrioTbl[prio] = (OS_TCB *)1;                          (3)

        OS_EXIT_CRITICAL();                                        (4)

        if (((opt & OS_TASK_OPT_STK_CHK) != 0x0000) ||             (5)
            ((opt & OS_TASK_OPT_STK_CLR) != 0x0000)) {
            #if OS_STK_GROWTH == 1
            (void)memset(pbos, 0, stk_size * sizeof(OS_STK));
            #else
            (void)memset(ptos, 0, stk_size * sizeof(OS_STK));
            #endif
        }
```

Listing 4.2   *OSTaskCreateExt(). (Continued)*

```
    psp = (OS_STK *)OSTaskStkInit(task, pdata, ptos, opt);          (6)
    err = OS_TCBInit(prio, psp, pbos, id, stk_size, pext, opt);     (7)
    if (err == OS_NO_ERR) {                                         (8)
        OS_ENTER_CRITICAL();                                        (9)
        OSTaskCtr++;
        OS_EXIT_CRITICAL();
        if (OSRunning == TRUE) {                                    (10)
            OS_Sched();                                             (11)
        }
    } else {
        OS_ENTER_CRITICAL();
        OSTCBPrioTbl[prio] = (OS_TCB *)0;
        OS_EXIT_CRITICAL();
    }
    return (err);
}
OS_EXIT_CRITICAL();
return (OS_PRIO_EXIST);
}
```

L4.2(1)   `OSTaskCreateExt()` starts by checking that the task priority is valid. The priority of a task must be a number between `0` and `OS_LOWEST_PRIO`, inclusive. Please note again that `OS_LOWEST_PRIO` is reserved by μC/OS-II's idle task. Your application can not call `OSTaskCreateExt()` and create a task at priority `OS_LOWEST_PRIO` because the priority will have already been 'reserved' for the idle task by `OSInit()`. If you try, `OSTaskCreateExt()` returns `OS_PRIO_EXIST`.

L4.2(2)   Next, `OSTaskCreateExt()` makes sure that a task has not already been created at the desired priority. With μC/OS-II, all tasks must have a unique priority.

L4.2(3)   If the desired priority is free, then μC/OS-II reserves the priority by placing a non-`NULL` pointer in `OSTCBPrioTbl[]`.

L4.2(4)   This allows `OSTaskCreateExt()` to re-enable interrupts while it sets up the rest of the data structures for the task.

L4.2(5)   In order to perform stack checking on a task (see Section 4.03 "Stack Checking, `OSTaskStkChk()`" on page 125), you must set the `OS_TASK_OPT_STK_CHK` flag in the `opt` argument. Also, stack checking requires that the stack contain zeros (i.e., it is cleared) when the task is created. To specify that a task gets cleared when it is created, set `OS_TASK_OPT_STK_CLR` in the `opt` argument. When both of these flags are set, `OSTaskCreateExt()` clears the stack. Note that I used `memset()` because it's an ANSI standard function and should be optimized by the compiler vendor.

L4.2(6)   `OSTaskCreateExt()` then calls `OSTaskStkInit()`, which is responsible for setting up the task stack. This function is processor specific and is found in `OS_CPU_C.C`. Refer to Chapter 13, "Porting μC/OS-II", for details on implementing `OSTaskStkInit()`. If you already have a port of μC/OS-II for the processor you are intending to use, then you don't need to be concerned about implementation details. OSTaskStkInit() returns the new top-of-stack (psp) which will be saved in the task's OS_TCB. µC/OS-II supports processors that have stacks that grow either from high to low memory or from low to high memory (see Section 4.02). When you call OSTaskCreateExt(), you must know how the stack grows (see OS_CPU.H of the processor you are using) because you must pass the task's top-of-stack, which can either be the lowest memory location of the stack (when OS_STK_GROWTH is 0) or the highest memory location of the stack (when OS_STK_GROWTH is 1), to OSTaskCreateExt().

L4.2(7)   After OSTaskStkInit() has completed setting up the stack, OSTaskCreateExt() calls OS_TCBInit() to obtain and initialize an OS_TCB from the pool of free OS_TCBs. The code for OS_TCBInit() is described in Section 3.03, "Task Control Blocks (OS_TCB)".

L4.2(8)

L4.2(9)   Upon return from OS_TCBInit(), OSTaskCreateExt() checks the return code and, upon success, increments OSTaskCtr, which keeps track of the number of tasks created.

L4.2(12) If OS_TCBInit() failed, the priority level is relinquished by setting the entry in OSTCBPrioTbl[prio] to 0.

L4.2(10)

L4.2(11) Finally, if OSTaskCreateExt() is called after multitasking has started (i.e., OSRunning is set to TRUE), the scheduler is called to determine whether the created task has a higher priority than its creator. Creating a higher priority task results in a context switch to the new task. If the task was created before multitasking started [i.e., you did not call OSStart() yet], the scheduler is not called.

4.02   Task Stacks

Each task must have its own stack space. A stack must be declared as being of type OS_STK and must consist of contiguous memory locations. You can allocate stack space either statically (at compile-time) or dynamically (at run-time). A static stack declaration is shown in Listings 4.3 and 4.4. Either declaration is made outside a function.

Listing 4.3   Static stack.

```
static OS_STK  MyTaskStack[stack_size];
```

or

Listing 4.4   Static stack.

```
OS_STK  MyTaskStack[stack_size];
```

You can allocate stack space dynamically by using the C compiler's malloc() function, as shown in Listing 4.5. However, you must be careful with fragmentation. Specifically, if you create and delete tasks, your memory allocator might not be able to return a stack for your task(s) because the heap eventually becomes fragmented.

Listing 4.5   Using `malloc()` to allocate stack space for a task.

```
OS_STK *pstk;


pstk = (OS_STK *)malloc(stack_size);
if (pstk != (OS_STK *)0) {        /* Make sure malloc() has enough space */
    Create the task;
}
```

Figure 4.1   Fragmentation.

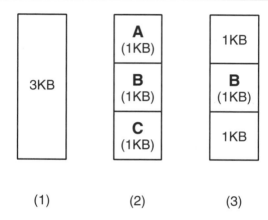

(1)   (2)   (3)

F4.1(1)   Figure 4.1 illustrates a heap containing 3KB of available memory that can be allocated with `malloc()`. For the sake of discussion, you create three tasks (tasks A, B, and C), each requiring 1KB.

F4.1(2)   Assume that the first 1KB is given to task A, the second to task B, and the third to task C.

F4.1(3)   Your application then deletes task A and task C and relinquishes the memory to the heap using `free()`. Your heap now has 2KB of memory free, but the memoy's not contiguous, which means that you cannot create another task (i.e., task D) that requires 2 KB because your heap is fragmented. If, however, you never delete a task, the use of `malloc()` is perfectly acceptable.

Because μC/OS-II supports processors with stacks that grow either from high to low memory or from low to high memory, you must know how the stack grows when you call either `OSTaskCreate()` or `OSTaskCreateExt()` because you need to pass the task's top-of-stack to these functions. When `OS_STK_GROWTH` is set to 0 in `OS_CPU.H`, you need to pass the lowest memory location of the stack to the task create function, as shown in Listing 4.6.

Listing 4.6   Stack grows from low to high memory.

```
OS_STK TaskStk[TASK_STK_SIZE];


OSTaskCreate(task, pdata, &TaskStk[0], prio);
```

When `OS_STK_GROWTH` is set to `1` in `OS_CPU.H`, you need to pass the highest memory location of the stack to the task create function, as shown in Listing 4.7.

Listing 4.7   Stack grows from high to low memory.

```
OS_STK  TaskStk[TASK_STK_SIZE];


OSTaskCreate(task, pdata, &TaskStk[TASK_STK_SIZE-1], prio);
```

This requirement affects code portability. If you need to port your code from a processor architecture that supports a downward-growing stack to one that supports an upward-growing stack, you might need to make your code handle both cases. Specifically, Listings 4.6 and 4.7 are rewritten, as shown in Listing 4.8.

Listing 4.8   Supporting stacks that grow in either direction.

```
OS_STK  TaskStk[TASK_STK_SIZE];



#if OS_STK_GROWTH == 0
    OSTaskCreate(task, pdata, &TaskStk[0], prio);
#else
    OSTaskCreate(task, pdata, &TaskStk[TASK_STK_SIZE-1], prio);
#endif
```

The size of the stack needed by your task is application specific. When sizing the stack, however, you must account for nesting of all the functions called by your task, the number of local variables that will be allocated by all functions called by your task, and the stack requirements for all nested interrupt service routines. In addition, your stack must be able to store all CPU registers.

4.03   Stack Checking, `OSTaskStkChk()`

Sometimes it is necessary to determine how much stack space a task actually uses. Stack checking allows you to reduce the amount of RAM needed by your application code by not overallocating stack space. µC/OS-II provides `OSTaskStkChk()`, which provides you with this valuable information.

In order to use the µC/OS-II stack-checking facilities, you must do the following:

- Set `OS_TASK_CREATE_EXT` to 1 in `OS_CFG.H`.
- Create a task using `OSTaskCreateExt()` and give the task much more space than you think it really needs. You can call `OSTaskStkChk()` for any task, from any task.
- Set the `opt` argument in `OSTaskCreateExt()` to `OS_TASK_OPT_STK_CHK` + `OS_TASK_OPT_STK_CLR`. Note that if your startup code clears all RAM and you never delete tasks after they are created, you don't need to set the `OS_TASK_OPT_STK_CLR` option. Not setting the option reduces the execution time of `OSTaskCreateExt()`.

- Call `OSTaskStkChk()` from a task by specifying the priority of the task you want to check. You can inquire about any task stack, not just the running task.

Figure 4.2   Stack checking.

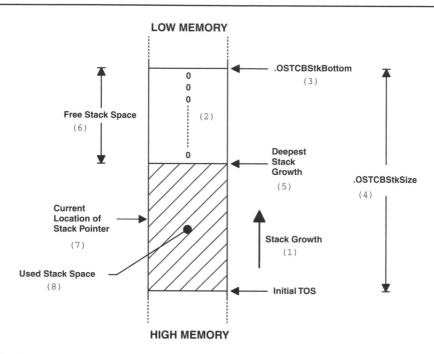

F4.2(1)   In Figure 4.2, I assume that the stack grows from high memory to low memory (i.e., `OS_STK_GROWTH` is set to 1), but the following discussion applies equally well to a stack growing in the opposite direction. μC/OS-II determines stack growth by looking at the contents of the stack itself. Stack checking is performed on demand, as opposed to continuously.

F4.2(2)   To perform stack checking, μC/OS-II requires that the stack be filled with zeros when the task is created.

F4.2(3)

F4.2(4)   Also, μC/OS-II needs to know the location of the bottom-of-stack (BOS) and the size of the stack you assigned to the task. These two values are stored in the task's `OS_TCB` when the task is created but only if the task was created with `OSTaskCreateExt()`.

F4.2(5)   `OSTaskStkChk()` computes the amount of free stack space by walking from the bottom of the stack and counting the number of zero-value entries on the stack until a nonzero value is found. Note that stack entries are checked using the data type of the stack (see `OS_STK` in `OS_CPU.H`). In other words, if a stack entry is 32-bits wide, the comparison for a zero value is done using 32 bits.

F4.2(6)

F4.2(8)   The amount of stack space used is obtained by subtracting the number of zero-value entries from the stack size you specified in `OSTaskCreateExt()`. `OSTaskStkChk()` actually places the number of bytes free and the number of bytes used in a data structure of type `OS_STK_DATA` (see `uCOS_II.H`).

F4.2(7)   Note that at any given time, the stack pointer for the task being checked might be pointing somewhere between the initial top-of-stack (TOS) and the deepest stack growth.

F4.2(5)   Also, every time you call `OSTaskStkChk()`, you may get a different value for the amount of free space on the stack until your task has reached its deepest growth.

You need to run the application long enough and under your worst-case conditions to get proper numbers. After `OSTaskStkChk()` provides you with the worst-case stack requirement, you can go back and set the final size of your stack. You should accommodate system expansion, so make sure you allocate between 10 and 100 percent more stack than what `OSTaskStkChk()` reports. What you should get from stack checking is a ballpark figure; you are not looking for an exact stack usage.

The code for `OSTaskStkChk()` is shown in Listing 4.9. The data structure `OS_STK_DATA` (see `uCOS_II.H`) is used to hold information about the task stack. I decided to use a data structure for two reasons. First, I consider `OSTaskStkChk()` to be a query-type function, and I wanted to have all query functions work the same way — return data about the query in a data structure. Second, passing data in a data structure is efficient and allows me to add additional fields in the future without changing the application programming interface (API) of `OSTaskStkChk()`. For now, `OS_STK_DATA` only contains two fields: `OSFree` and `OSUsed`. As you can see, you invoke `OSTaskStkChk()` by specifying the priority of the task on which you want to perform stack checking.

Listing 4.9   *Stack-checking function.*

```
INT8U  OSTaskStkChk (INT8U prio, OS_STK_DATA *pdata)
{
#if OS_CRITICAL_METHOD == 3
    OS_CPU_SR  cpu_sr;
#endif
    OS_TCB    *ptcb;
    OS_STK    *pchk;
    INT32U     free;
    INT32U     size;


#if OS_ARG_CHK_EN > 0
    if (prio > OS_LOWEST_PRIO && prio != OS_PRIO_SELF) {           (1)
        return (OS_PRIO_INVALID);
    }
#endif
    pdata->OSFree = 0;
    pdata->OSUsed = 0;
    OS_ENTER_CRITICAL();
    if (prio == OS_PRIO_SELF) {                                    (2)
        prio = OSTCBCur->OSTCBPrio;
    }
    ptcb = OSTCBPrioTbl[prio];
    if (ptcb == (OS_TCB *)0) {                                     (3)
```

Listing 4.9   *Stack-checking function. (Continued)*

```
        OS_EXIT_CRITICAL();
        return (OS_TASK_NOT_EXIST);
    }
    if ((ptcb->OSTCBOpt & OS_TASK_OPT_STK_CHK) == 0) {                    (4)
        OS_EXIT_CRITICAL();
        return (OS_TASK_OPT_ERR);
    }
    free = 0;                                                            (5)
    size = ptcb->OSTCBStkSize;
    pchk = ptcb->OSTCBStkBottom;
    OS_EXIT_CRITICAL();
#if OS_STK_GROWTH == 1
    while (*pchk++ == (OS_STK)0) {
        free++;
    }
#else
    while (*pchk-- == (OS_STK)0) {
        free++;
    }
#endif
    pdata->OSFree = free * sizeof(OS_STK);                               (6)
    pdata->OSUsed = (size - free) * sizeof(OS_STK);
    return (OS_NO_ERR);
}
```

L4.9(1)   If `OS_ARG_CHK_EN` is set to `1` in `OS_CFG.H`, `OSTaskStkChk()` verifies that the priority is within a valid range.

L4.9(2)   If you specify `OS_PRIO_SELF`, the function assumes that you want to know the stack information about the current task.

L4.9(3)   Obviously, the task must exist. Simply checking for the presence of a non-`NULL` pointer in `OSTCBPrioTbl[]` ensures that the task exists.

L4.9(4)   To perform stack checking, you must have created the task using `OSTaskCreateExt()`, and you must have passed the option `OS_TASK_OPT_STK_CHK`. If you called `OSTaskStkChk()` from a task that was created by `OSTaskCreate()` [instead of `OSTaskCreateExt()`], then the `opt` argument [passed to `OS_TCBInit()`] would have been `0`, and the test would fail.

L4.9(5)   If all of the proper conditions are met, `OSTaskStkChk()` computes the free stack space as described above by walking from the bottom of stack until a nonzero stack entry is encountered.

L4.9(6)   Finally, the information that is stored in `OS_STK_DATA` is computed. Note that the function computes the actual number of bytes free and the number of bytes used on the stack as opposed to the number of elements. Obviously, the actual stack size (in bytes) can be obtained by adding these two values.

4.04 Deleting a Task, `OSTaskDel()`

Sometimes it is necessary to delete a task. Deleting a task means that the task is returned to the dormant state (see Section 3.02, "Task States") and does not mean that the code for the task is actually "deleted." The task code is simply no longer scheduled by µC/OS-II. You delete a task by calling `OSTaskDel()` (Listing 4.10).

Listing 4.10   Task delete.

```
INT8U  OSTaskDel (INT8U prio)
{
#if OS_CRITICAL_METHOD == 3
    OS_CPU_SR    cpu_sr;
#endif

#if OS_EVENT_EN > 0
    OS_EVENT     *pevent;
#endif
#if (OS_VERSION >= 251) && (OS_FLAG_EN > 0) && (OS_MAX_FLAGS > 0)
    OS_FLAG_NODE *pnode;
#endif
    OS_TCB       *ptcb;
    BOOLEAN      self;


    if (OSIntNesting > 0) {                                            (1)
        return (OS_TASK_DEL_ISR);
    }
#if OS_ARG_CHK_EN > 0
    if (prio == OS_IDLE_PRIO) {                                        (2)
        return (OS_TASK_DEL_IDLE);
    }
    if (prio >= OS_LOWEST_PRIO && prio != OS_PRIO_SELF) {              (3)
        return (OS_PRIO_INVALID);
    }
#endif
    OS_ENTER_CRITICAL();
    if (prio == OS_PRIO_SELF) {                                       (4)
```

Listing 4.10   Task delete. (Continued)

```
           prio = OSTCBCur->OSTCBPrio;
       }
   ptcb = OSTCBPrioTbl[prio];
   if (ptcb != (OS_TCB *)0) {                                           (5)
       if ((OSRdyTbl[ptcb->OSTCBY] &= ~ptcb->OSTCBBitX) == 0x00) {      (6)
           OSRdyGrp &= ~ptcb->OSTCBBitY;
       }
#if OS_EVENT_EN > 0
       pevent = ptcb->OSTCBEventPtr;                                    (7)
       if (pevent != (OS_EVENT *)0) {
           if ((pevent->OSEventTbl[ptcb->OSTCBY] &= ~ptcb->OSTCBBitX) == 0) {
               pevent->OSEventGrp &= ~ptcb->OSTCBBitY;
           }
       }
#endif
#if (OS_VERSION >= 251) && (OS_FLAG_EN > 0) && (OS_MAX_FLAGS > 0)
       pnode = ptcb->OSTCBFlagNode;                                     (8)
       if (pnode != (OS_FLAG_NODE *)0) {
           OS_FlagUnlink(pnode);
       }
#endif
       ptcb->OSTCBDly  = 0;                                             (9)
       ptcb->OSTCBStat = OS_STAT_RDY;                                   (10)
       if (OSLockNesting < 255) {                                      (11)
           OSLockNesting++;
       }
       OS_EXIT_CRITICAL();                                             (12)
       OS_Dummy();                                                     (13)
       OS_ENTER_CRITICAL();
       if (OSLockNesting > 0) {                                        (14)
           OSLockNesting--;
       }
       OSTaskDelHook(ptcb);                                            (15)
       OSTaskCtr--;                                                    (16)
       OSTCBPrioTbl[prio] = (OS_TCB *)0;                               (17)
       if (ptcb->OSTCBPrev == (OS_TCB *)0) {                           (18)
           ptcb->OSTCBNext->OSTCBPrev = (OS_TCB *)0;
           OSTCBList                  = ptcb->OSTCBNext;
       } else {
```

Listing 4.10 *Task delete. (Continued)*

```
            ptcb->OSTCBPrev->OSTCBNext = ptcb->OSTCBNext;
            ptcb->OSTCBNext->OSTCBPrev = ptcb->OSTCBPrev;
        }
        ptcb->OSTCBNext = OSTCBFreeList;                                        (19)
        OSTCBFreeList   = ptcb;
        OS_EXIT_CRITICAL();
        OS_Sched();                                                            (20)
        return (OS_NO_ERR);
    }
    OS_EXIT_CRITICAL();
    return (OS_TASK_DEL_ERR);
}
```

L4.10(1) `OSTaskDel()` starts off by making sure you are not attempting to delete a task from within an ISR, because that's not allowed.

L4.10(2) `OSTaskDel()` checks that you are not attempting to delete the idle task because this is also not allowed.

L4.10(3) You are allowed to delete the statistic task (`OS_LOWEST_PRIO-1`) and all higher priority tasks (i.e., the task priority has a lower number).

L4.10(4) The caller can delete itself by specifying `OS_PRIO_SELF` as the argument.

L4.10(5) `OSTaskDel()` verifies that the task to delete does in fact exist. This test obviously passes if you specified `OS_PRIO_SELF`. I didn't want to create a separate case for this situation because it would have increased code size and thus execution time. If `OS_PRIO_SFI F` is specified, we simply obtain the priority of the current task, which is stored in its `OS_TCB`.

After all conditions are satisfied, the `OS_TCB` is removed from all possible µC/OS-II data structures. `OSTaskDel()` does this action in two parts to reduce interrupt latency.

L4.10(6) First, if the task is in the ready list, it is removed.

L4.10(7) If the task is in a list waiting for a mutex, mailbox, queue, or semaphore, it is removed from that list.

L4.10(8) If the task is in a list waiting for an event flag, it is removed from that list.

L4.10(9) Next, `OSTaskDel()` forces the delay count to zero to make sure that the tick ISR does not ready this task after I re-enable interrupts (see L4.10(12)).

L4.10(10) `OSTaskDel()` sets the task's `.OSTCBStat` flag to `OS_STAT_RDY`. Note that `OSTaskDel()` is not trying to make the task ready; it is simply preventing another task or an ISR from resuming this task [i.e., in case the other task or ISR calls `OSTaskResume()`]. This situation could occur because `OSTaskDel()` will be re-enabling interrupts (see L4.10(12)), so an ISR can make a higher priority task ready, which could resume the task you are trying to delete. Instead of setting the task's `.OSTCBStat` flag to `OS_STAT_RDY`, I simply could have cleared the `OS_STAT_SUSPEND` bit (which would have been clearer), but this action takes slightly more processing time.

L4.10(11) At this point, the task to delete cannot be made ready to run by another task or an ISR because it's been removed from the ready list, it's not waiting for an event to occur, it's not waiting for time to expire, and it cannot be resumed. For all intents and purposes, the task is dormant. Because the task is dormant, `OSTaskDel()` must prevent the scheduler from switching to another task because if the current task is almost deleted, it could not be rescheduled!

L4.10(12) At this point, `OSTaskDel()` re-enables interrupts in order to reduce interrupt latency. `OSTaskDel()` could thus service an interrupt, but, because it incremented `OSLockNesting`, the ISR would return to the interrupted task. Note that `OSTaskDel()` is still not done with the deletion process because it needs to unlink the `OS_TCB` from the TCB chain and return the `OS_TCB` to the free `OS_TCB` list.

L4.10(13) Note that I call the dummy function `OS_Dummy()` immediately after calling `OS_EXIT_CRITICAL()`. I want to make sure that the processor executes at least one instruction with interrupts enabled. On many processors, executing an interrupt-enable instruction forces the CPU to have interrupts disabled until the end of the next instruction! The Intel 80x86 and Zilog Z-80 processors actually work this way. Enabling and immediately disabling interrupts would behave just as if I didn't enable interrupts, which would, of course, increase interrupt latency. Calling `OS_Dummy()` thus ensures that I execute a call and a return instruction before re-disabling interrupts. You could certainly replace `OS_Dummy()` with a macro that executes a no-operation instruction and thus slightly reduce the execution time of `OSTaskDel()`. I didn't think it was worth the effort of creating yet another macro that would require porting.

L4.10(14) `OSTaskDel()` can now continue with the deletion process of the task. After `OSTaskDel()` re-disables interrupts, `OSTaskDel()` re-enables scheduling by decrementing the lock nesting counter.

L4.10(15) `OSTaskDel()` then calls the user-definable task delete hook `OSTaskDelHook()`, which allows user-defined `OS_TCB` extensions to be relinquished.

L4.10(16) Next, `OSTaskDel()` decrements the task counter to indicate that µC/OS-II is managing one less task.

L4.10(17) `OSTaskDel()` removes the `OS_TCB` from the priority table by simply replacing the link to the `OS_TCB` of the task being deleted with a `NULL` pointer.

L4.10(18) `OSTaskDel()` then removes the `OS_TCB` of the task being deleted from the doubly linked list of `OS_TCB`s that starts at `OSTCBList`. Note you do not need to check for the case where `ptcb->OSTCBNext == NULL` because `OSTaskDel()` cannot delete the idle task, which always happens to be at the end of the chain.

L4.10(19) The `OS_TCB` is returned to the free list of `OS_TCB`s to allow another task to be created.

L4.10(20) Finally, the scheduler is called to see if a higher priority task has been made ready to run by an ISR that would have occurred when `OSTaskDel()` re-enabled interrupts at step [L4.11(12)].

4.05 *Requesting to Delete a Task,* `OSTaskDelReq()`

Sometimes, a task owns resources such as memory buffers or a semaphore. If another task attempts to delete this task, the resources are not freed and thus are lost. This would lead to memory leaks which is not acceptable for just about any embedded system. In this type of situation, you somehow need to tell the task that owns these resources to delete itself when it's done with the resources. You can accomplish this with the `OSTaskDelReq()` function. Both the requester and the task to be deleted need to call `OSTaskDelReq()`. The requester code is shown in Listing 4.11.

Listing 4.11   *Requester code requesting a task to delete itself.*

```
void RequestorTask (void *pdata)
{
    INT8U err;


    pdata = pdata;
    for (;;) {
        /* Application code */
        if ('TaskToBeDeleted()' needs to be deleted) {                  (1)
            while (OSTaskDelReq(TASK_TO_DEL_PRIO) != OS_TASK_NOT_EXIST) {    (2)
                OSTimeDly(1);                                           (3)
            }
        }
        /* Application code */                                         (4)
    }
}
```

L4.11(1) The task that makes the request needs to determine what conditions can cause a request for the task to be deleted. In other words, your application determines what conditions lead to this decision.

L4.11(2) If the task needs to be deleted, call `OSTaskDelReq()` by passing the priority of the task to be deleted. If the task to delete does not exist, `OSTaskDelReq()` returns `OS_TASK_NOT_EXIST`. You get this response if the task to delete has already been deleted or has not been created yet. If the return value is `OS_NO_ERR`, the request has been accepted, but the task has not been deleted yet. You might want to wait until the task to be deleted does in fact delete itself.

L4.11(3) You can do this by delaying the requester for a certain amount of time. I decided to delay for one tick, but you can certainly wait longer if needed.

L4.11(4) When the requested task eventually deletes itself, the return value in L4.11(2) is `OS_TASK_NOT_EXIST`, and the loop exits.

The pseudocode for the task that needs to delete itself is shown in Listing 4.12. This task polls a flag that resides inside the task's `OS_TCB`. The value of this flag is obtained by calling `OSTaskDelReq(OS_PRIO_SELF)`.

Listing 4.12   *Task requesting to delete itself.*

```
void TaskToBeDeleted (void *pdata)
{
    INT8U err;
```

Listing 4.12   *Task requesting to delete itself. (Continued)*

```
    pdata = pdata;
    for (;;) {
        /* Application code */
        if (OSTaskDelReq(OS_PRIO_SELF) == OS_TASK_DEL_REQ) {           (1)
            Release any owned resources;                              (2)
            De-allocate any dynamic memory;
            OSTaskDel(OS_PRIO_SELF);                                  (3)
        } else {
            /* Application code */
        }
    }
}
```

L4.12(1) When OSTaskDelReq() returns OS_TASK_DEL_REQ to its caller, it indicates that another task has requested that this task needs to be deleted.

L4.12(2)

L4.12(3) In this case, the task to be deleted releases any resources owned and calls OSTaskDel(OS_PRIO_SELF) to delete itself. As previously mentioned, the code for the task is not actually deleted. Instead, µC/OS-II simply does not schedule the task for execution. In other words, the task code no longer runs. You can, however, recreate the task by calling either OSTaskCreate() or OSTaskCreateExt().

The code for OSTaskDelReq() is shown in Listing 4.13. As usual, OSTaskDelReq() needs to check for boundary conditions.

Listing 4.13   OSTaskDelReq().

```
INT8U  OSTaskDelReq (INT8U prio)
{
#if OS_CRITICAL_METHOD == 3
    OS_CPU_SR  cpu_sr;
#endif
    BOOLEAN    stat;
    INT8U      err;
    OS_TCB     *ptcb;


#if OS_ARG_CHK_EN > 0
    if (prio == OS_IDLE_PRIO) {                                       (1)
        return (OS_TASK_DEL_IDLE);
    }
```

Listing 4.13 *OSTaskDelReq().* *(Continued)*

```
    if (prio >= OS_LOWEST_PRIO && prio != OS_PRIO_SELF) {            (2)
        return (OS_PRIO_INVALID);
    }
#endif
    if (prio == OS_PRIO_SELF) {                                      (3)
        OS_ENTER_CRITICAL();
        stat = OSTCBCur->OSTCBDelReq;
        OS_EXIT_CRITICAL();
        return (stat);
    }
    OS_ENTER_CRITICAL();
    ptcb = OSTCBPrioTbl[prio];
    if (ptcb != (OS_TCB *)0) {                                       (4)
        ptcb->OSTCBDelReq = OS_TASK_DEL_REQ;                         (5)
        err               = OS_NO_ERR;
    } else {
        err               = OS_TASK_NOT_EXIST;                       (6)
    }
    OS_EXIT_CRITICAL();
    return (err);
}
```

L4.13(1)   First, `OSTaskDelReq()` notifies the caller in case the caller requests to delete the idle task.

L4.13(2)   Next, it must ensure that the caller is not trying to request to delete an invalid priority.

L4.13(3)   If the caller is the task to be deleted, the flag stored in the `OS_TCB` is returned.

L4.13(4)

L4.13(5)   If you specified a task with a priority other than `OS_PRIO_SELF` and the task exists, `OSTaskDelReq()` sets the internal flag for that task.

L4.13(6)   If the task does not exist, `OSTaskDelReq()` returns `OS_TASK_NOT_EXIST` to indicate that the task must have deleted itself.

4.06   Changing a Task's Priority, *OSTaskChangePrio( )*

When you create a task, you assign the task a priority. At runtime, you can change the priority of any task by calling OSTaskChangePrio( ). In other words, μC/OS-II allows you to change priorities dynamically. The code for OSTaskChangePrio( ) is shown in Listing 4.14.

Listing 4.14   *OSTaskChangePrio( ).*

```
INT8U  OSTaskChangePrio (INT8U oldprio, INT8U newprio)
{
#if OS_CRITICAL_METHOD == 3
    OS_CPU_SR    cpu_sr;
#endif

#if OS_EVENT_EN > 0
    OS_EVENT    *pevent;
#endif

    OS_TCB      *ptcb;
    INT8U       x;
    INT8U       y;
    INT8U       bitx;
    INT8U       bity;


#if OS_ARG_CHK_EN > 0
    if ((oldprio >= OS_LOWEST_PRIO && oldprio != OS_PRIO_SELF) ||          (1)
        newprio >= OS_LOWEST_PRIO) {
        return (OS_PRIO_INVALID);
    }
#endif
    OS_ENTER_CRITICAL();
    if (OSTCBPrioTbl[newprio] != (OS_TCB *)0) {                            (2)
        OS_EXIT_CRITICAL();
        return (OS_PRIO_EXIST);
    } else {
        OSTCBPrioTbl[newprio] = (OS_TCB *)1;                              (3)
        OS_EXIT_CRITICAL();
        y    = newprio >> 3;                                              (4)
        bity = OSMapTbl[y];
        x    = newprio & 0x07;
        bitx = OSMapTbl[x];
        OS_ENTER_CRITICAL();
        if (oldprio == OS_PRIO_SELF) {                                    (5)
            oldprio = OSTCBCur->OSTCBPrio;
```

Listing 4.14 *OSTaskChangePrio().* *(Continued)*

```
        }
        ptcb = OSTCBPrioTbl[oldprio];
        if (ptcb != (OS_TCB *)0) {                                          (6)
            OSTCBPrioTbl[oldprio] = (OS_TCB *)0;                            (7)
            if ((OSRdyTbl[ptcb->OSTCBY] & ptcb->OSTCBBitX) != 0x00) {      (8)
                if ((OSRdyTbl[ptcb->OSTCBY] &= ~ptcb->OSTCBBitX) == 0x00) {  (9)
                    OSRdyGrp &= ~ptcb->OSTCBBitY;
                }
                OSRdyGrp     |= bity;                                       (10)
                OSRdyTbl[y]  |= bitx;
#if OS_EVENT_EN > 0
            } else {
                pevent = ptcb->OSTCBEventPtr;
                if (pevent != (OS_EVENT *)0) {                              (11)
                    if ((pevent->OSEventTbl[ptcb->OSTCBY] &= ~ptcb->OSTCBBitX) == 0) {
                        pevent->OSEventGrp &= ~ptcb->OSTCBBitY;
                    }
                    pevent->OSEventGrp    |= bity;                          (12)
                    pevent->OSEventTbl[y] |= bitx;
                }
#endif
            }
            OSTCBPrioTbl[newprio] = ptcb;                                   (13)
            ptcb->OSTCBPrio     = newprio;                                  (14)
            ptcb->OSTCBY        = y;                                        (15)
            ptcb->OSTCBX        = x;
            ptcb->OSTCBBitY     = bity;
            ptcb->OSTCBBitX     = bitx;
            OS_EXIT_CRITICAL();
            OS_Sched();                                                     (16)
            return (OS_NO_ERR);
        } else {
            OSTCBPrioTbl[newprio] = (OS_TCB *)0;                            (17)
            OS_EXIT_CRITICAL();
            return (OS_PRIO_ERR);
        }
    }
}
```

L4.14(1) You cannot change the priority of the idle task. You can change either the priority of the calling task or another task. To change the priority of the calling task, specify either the old priority of that task or OS_PRIO_SELF, and OSTaskChangePrio() determines what the priority of the calling task is for you. You must also specify the new (i.e., desired) priority.

L4.14(2) Because µC/OS-II cannot have multiple tasks running at the same priority, OSTaskChangePrio() needs to check that the new desired priority is available.

L4.14(3) If the desired priority is available, µC/OS-II reserves the priority by loading something into OSTCBPrioTbl[newprio], thus reserving that entry, which allows OSTaskChangePrio() to re-enable interrupts and know that no other task can either create a task at the desired priority or have another task call OSTaskChangePrio() by specifying the same new priority.

L4.14(4) OSTaskChangePrio() precomputes some values that are stored in the task's OS_TCB. These values are used to put in or remove the task from the ready list (see Section 3.04, "Ready List").

L4.14(5) OSTaskChangePrio() then checks to see if the current task is attempting to change its own priority.

L4.14(6) Next, we see if the task for which OSTaskChangePrio() is trying to change the priority exists. Obviously, if it's the current task, this test succeeds.

L4.14(17) However, if OSTaskChangePrio() is trying to change the priority of a task that doesn't exist, it must relinquish the "reserved" priority back to the priority table, OSTCBPrioTbl[], and return an error code to the caller.

L4.14(7) OSTaskChangePrio() now removes the pointer to the OS_TCB of the task from the priority table by inserting a NULL pointer, which makes the old priority available for reuse.

L4.14(8) Then, we check to see if the task for which OSTaskChangePrio() is changing the priority is ready to run.

L4.14(9)

L4.14(10) If the task is ready to run, the task must be removed from the ready list at the current priority and inserted back into the ready list at the new priority. Note here that OSTaskChangePrio() uses the precomputed values [L4.14(4)] to insert the task in the ready list.

L4.14(11) If the task is not ready, it could be waiting on a semaphore, mutex, mailbox, or queue. OSTaskChangePrio() knows that the task is waiting for one of these events if the OSTCBEventPtr is non-NULL.

L4.14(12) If the task is waiting for an event, OSTaskChangePrio() must remove the task from the wait list (at the old priority) of the event control block (see Chapter 6, "Event Control Blocks") and insert the task back into the wait list, but this time at the new priority. The task could be waiting for time to expire (see Chapter 5, "Time Management") or the task could be suspended [see section 4.07, Suspending a Task, OSTaskSuspend()]. In these cases, items L4.14(8) through L4.14(12) are skipped.

L4.14(13) Next, OSTaskChangePrio() stores a pointer to the task's OS_TCB in OSTCBPrioTbl[].

L4.14(14)

L4.14(15) The new priority is saved in the OS_TCB, and the precomputed values are also saved in the OS_TCB.

L4.14(16) After OSTaskChangePrio() exits the critical section, the scheduler is called in case the new priority is higher than the old priority or the priority of the calling task.

4.07   *Suspending a Task,* `OSTaskSuspend()`

Sometimes it is useful to suspend the execution of a task explicitly. Suspension is accomplished with the `OSTaskSuspend()` function call. A suspended task can only be resumed by calling the `OSTaskResume()` function call. Task suspension is additive, which means that if the task being suspended is also waiting for time to expire, the suspension needs to be removed and the time needs to expire in order for the task to be ready to run. A task can suspend either itself or another task.

The code for `OSTaskSuspend()` is shown in Listing 4.15.

Listing 4.15   `OSTaskSuspend()`.

```
INT8U  OSTaskSuspend (INT8U prio)
{
#if OS_CRITICAL_METHOD == 3
    OS_CPU_SR  cpu_sr;
#endif
    BOOLEAN    self;
    OS_TCB     *ptcb;


#if OS_ARG_CHK_EN > 0
    if (prio == OS_IDLE_PRIO) {                                      (1)
        return (OS_TASK_SUSPEND_IDLE);
    }
    if (prio >= OS_LOWEST_PRIO && prio != OS_PRIO_SELF) {            (2)
        return (OS_PRIO_INVALID);
    }
#endif
    OS_ENTER_CRITICAL();
    if (prio == OS_PRIO_SELF) {                                      (3)
        prio = OSTCBCur->OSTCBPrio;
        self = TRUE;
    } else if (prio == OSTCBCur->OSTCBPrio) {                        (4)
        self = TRUE;
    } else {
        self = FALSE;
    }
    ptcb = OSTCBPrioTbl[prio];                                       (5)
    if (ptcb == (OS_TCB *)0) {
        OS_EXIT_CRITICAL();
        return (OS_TASK_SUSPEND_PRIO);
    }
```

4

Listing 4.15 *OSTaskSuspend( ). (Continued)*

```
if ((OSRdyTbl[ptcb->OSTCBY] &= ~ptcb->OSTCBBitX) == 0x00) {        (6)
    OSRdyGrp &= ~ptcb->OSTCBBitY;
}
ptcb->OSTCBStat |= OS_STAT_SUSPEND;                                 (7)
OS_EXIT_CRITICAL();
if (self == TRUE) {
    OS_Sched();                                                    (8)
}
return (OS_NO_ERR);
}
```

L4.15(1) OSTaskSuspend() ensures that your application is not attempting to suspend the idle task.

L4.15(2) Next, you must specify a valid priority. Remember that the highest valid priority number (i.e., lowest priority) is OS_LOWEST_PRIO-1. Note that you can suspend the statistic task. You might have noticed that the first test [L4.15(1)] is replicated in [L4.15(2)]. I replicated these tests to be backward compatible with µC/OS. The first test could be removed to save a little bit of processing time, but the amount is really insignificant so I decided to leave it.

L4.15(3) Next, OSTaskSuspend() checks to see if you specified to suspend the calling task by specifying OS_PRIO_SELF. In this case, the current task's priority is retrieved from its OS_TCB.

L4.15(4) You could also decided to suspend the calling task by specifying its priority. In both of these cases, the scheduler needs to be called, which is why I created the local variable self, which will be examined at the appropriate time. If you are not suspending the calling task, then OSTaskSuspend() does not need to run the scheduler because the calling task is suspending a lower priority task.

L4.15(5) OSTaskSuspend() then checks to see that the task to suspend exists.

L4.15(6) If so, the task is removed from the ready list. Note that the task to suspend might not be in the ready list because it could be waiting for an event or for time to expire. In this case, the corresponding bit for the task to suspend in OSRdyTbl[] would already be cleared (i.e., 0). Clearing it again is faster than checking to see if it's clear and then clearing it if it's not.

L4.15(7) Now OSTaskSuspend() sets the OS_STAT_SUSPEND flag in the task's OS_TCB to indicate that the task is now suspended.

L4.15(8) Finally, OSTaskSuspend() calls the scheduler only if the task being suspended is the calling task.

4.08 Resuming a Task, OSTaskResume( )

As mentioned in the previous section, a suspended task can only be resumed by calling OSTaskResume( ). The code for OSTaskResume( ) is shown in Listing 4.16.

Listing 4.16 OSTaskResume( ).

```
INT8U  OSTaskResume (INT8U prio)
{
#if OS_CRITICAL_METHOD == 3
    OS_CPU_SR  cpu_sr;
#endif
    OS_TCB    *ptcb;


#if OS_ARG_CHK_EN > 0
    if (prio >= OS_LOWEST_PRIO) {                               (1)
        return (OS_PRIO_INVALID);
    }
#endif
    OS_ENTER_CRITICAL();
    ptcb = OSTCBPrioTbl[prio];
    if (ptcb == (OS_TCB *)0) {                                  (2)
        OS_EXIT_CRITICAL();
        return (OS_TASK_RESUME_PRIO);
    }
    if ((ptcb->OSTCBStat & OS_STAT_SUSPEND) != 0x00) {          (3)
        if ((((ptcb->OSTCBStat &= ~OS_STAT_SUSPEND) == OS_STAT_RDY) &&    (4)
            (ptcb->OSTCBDly == 0)) {                            (5)
            OSRdyGrp                |= ptcb->OSTCBBitY;         (6)
            OSRdyTbl[ptcb->OSTCBY] |= ptcb->OSTCBBitX;
            OS_EXIT_CRITICAL();
            OS_Sched();                                         (7)
        } else {
            OS_EXIT_CRITICAL();
        }
        return (OS_NO_ERR);
    }
    OS_EXIT_CRITICAL();
    return (OS_TASK_NOT_SUSPENDED);
}
```

L4.16(1)   Because OSTaskSuspend() cannot suspend the idle task, it must verify that your application is not attempting to resume this task.   Note that this test also ensures that you are not trying to resume OS_PRIO_SELF (OS_PRIO_SELF is #defined to 0xFF, which is always greater than OS_LOWEST_PRIO), which wouldn't make sense — you can't resume *self* because *self* cannot possibly be suspended.

L4.16(2)

L4.16(3)   The task to resume must exist because you will be manipulating its OS_TCB and must also have been suspended.

L4.16(4)   OSTaskResume() removes the suspension by clearing the OS_STAT_SUSPEND bit in the .OSTCBStat field.

L4.16(5)   For the task to be ready to run, the .OSTCBDly field must be 0 because no flags exist in OSTCBStat to indicate that a task is waiting for time to expire.

L4.16(6)   The task is made ready to run only when both conditions are satisfied.

L4.16(7)   Finally, the scheduler is called to see if the resumed task has a higher priority than the calling task.

4.09   *Getting Information about a Task,* OSTaskQuery()

Your application can obtain information about itself or other application tasks by calling OSTaskQuery(). In fact, OSTaskQuery() obtains a copy of the contents of the desired task's OS_TCB. The fields available to you in the OS_TCB depend on the configuration of your application (see OS_CFG.H). Indeed, because µC/OS-II is scalable, it only includes the features that your application requires.

To call OSTaskQuery(), your application must allocate storage for an OS_TCB, as shown in Listing 4.17. This OS_TCB is in a totally different data space from the OS_TCBs allocated by µC/OS-II. After calling OSTaskQuery(), this OS_TCB contains a snapshot of the OS_TCB for the desired task. You need to be careful with the links to other OS_TCBs (i.e., .OSTCBNext and .OSTCBPrev); you don't want to change what these links are pointing to! In general, only use this function to see what a task is doing — a great tool for debugging.

Listing 4.17   *Obtaining information about a task.*

```
void MyTask (void *pdata)
{
    OS_TCB  MyTaskData;


    pdata = pdata;
    for (;;) {
        /* User code                      */
        err = OSTaskQuery(10, &MyTaskData);
        /* Examine error code ..          */
        /* User code                      */
    }
}
```

The code for `OSTaskQuery()` is shown in Listing 4.18.

Listing 4.18 *OSTaskQuery( ).*

```
INT8U  OSTaskQuery (INT8U prio, OS_TCB *pdata)
{
#if OS_CRITICAL_METHOD == 3
    OS_CPU_SR   cpu_sr;
#endif
    OS_TCB      *ptcb;


#if OS_ARG_CHK_EN > 0
    if (prio > OS_LOWEST_PRIO && prio != OS_PRIO_SELF) {          (1)
        return (OS_PRIO_INVALID);
    }
#endif
    OS_ENTER_CRITICAL();
    if (prio == OS_PRIO_SELF) {                                  (2)
        prio = OSTCBCur->OSTCBPrio;
    }
    ptcb = OSTCBPrioTbl[prio];
    if (ptcb == (OS_TCB *)0) {                                   (3)
        OS_EXIT_CRITICAL();
        return (OS_PRIO_ERR);
    }
    memcpy(pdata, ptcb, sizeof(OS_TCB));                         (4)
    OS_EXIT_CRITICAL();
    return (OS_NO_ERR);
}
```

L4.18(1) Note that I allow you to examine all the tasks, including the idle task. You need to be especially careful not to change what `.OSTCBNext` and `.OSTCBPrev` points to.

L4.18(2)

L4.18(3) As usual, `OSTaskQuery()` checks to see if you want information about the current task and that the task has been created.

L4.18(4) All fields are copied using the assignment shown instead of field by field. Using `memcpy()` is much faster than field-by-field copy or even-structure copies because the compiler will most likely generate memory-copy instructions.

5

Time Management

Section 3.11, "Clock Tick," established that μC/OS-II requires (as do most kernels) that you provide a periodic interrupt to keep track of time delays and timeouts. This periodic time source is called a *clock tick* and should occur between 10 and 100 times per second, or Hertz. The actual frequency of the clock tick depends on the desired tick resolution of your application. However, the higher the frequency of the ticker, the higher the overhead.

Section 3.10, "Interrupts Under μC/OS-II", discussed the tick ISR, as well as the function to call to notify μC/OS-II about the tick interrupt — OSTimeTick(). This chapter describes five services that deal with time issues:

- OSTimeDly(),
- OSTimeDlyHMSM(),
- OSTimeDlyResume(),
- OSTimeGet(), and
- OSTimeSet().

The functions described in this chapter are found in the file OS_TIME.C.

Some of the time management services must be enabled by setting configuration constants in OS_CFG.H. Specifically, Table 5.1 shows which services are compiled, based on the value of configuration constants found in OS_CFG.H.

Table 5.1   *Time management configuration constants in* OS_CFG.H.

μC/OS-II Time Management Service	*Enabled when set to 1 in* OS_CFG.H
OSTimeDly()	
OSTimeDlyHMSM()	OS_TIME_DLY_HMSM_EN
OSTimeDlyResume()	OS_TIME_DLY_RESUME_EN
OSTimeGet()	OS_TIME_GET_SET_EN
OSTimeSet()	OS_TIME_GET_SET_EN

145

5.00   *Delaying a Task,* `OSTimeDly()`

μC/OS-II provides a service that allows the calling task to delay itself for a user-specified number of clock ticks. This function is called `OSTimeDly()`. Calling this function causes a context switch and forces μC/OS-II to execute the next highest priority task that is ready to run. The task calling `OSTimeDly()` is made ready to run as soon as the time specified expires or if another task cancels the delay by calling `OSTimeDlyResume()`. Note that this task runs only when it's the highest priority task.

Listing 5.1 shows the code for `OSTimeDly()`. Your application calls this function by supplying the number of ticks to delay — a value between 1 and 65,535. A value of 0 specifies no delay.

Listing 5.1   `OSTimeDly()`.

```
void OSTimeDly (INT16U ticks)
{
    if (ticks > 0) {                                                  (1)
        OS_ENTER_CRITICAL();
        if ((OSRdyTbl[OSTCBCur->OSTCBY] &= ~OSTCBCur->OSTCBBitX) == 0) {   (2)
            OSRdyGrp &= ~OSTCBCur->OSTCBBitY;
        }
        OSTCBCur->OSTCBDly = ticks;                                    (3)
        OS_EXIT_CRITICAL();
        OSSched();                                                    (4)
    }
}
```

L5.1(1)   If you specify a value of 0, you are indicating that you don't want to delay the task, so the function returns immediately to the caller.

L5.1(2)   A nonzero value causes `OSTimeDly()` to remove the current task from the ready list.

L5.1(3)   Next, the number of ticks are stored in the `OS_TCB` of the current task, where `OSTimeTick()` decrements it on every clock tick. You should note that the calling task is not placed in any wait list. Simply having a non zero value in `.OSTCBDly` is sufficient for `OSTimeTick()` to know that the task is delayed.

L5.1(4)   Finally, because the task is no longer ready, the scheduler is called so that the next highest priority task that is ready to run is executed.

It is important to realize that the resolution of a delay is between zero and one tick. In other words, if you try to delay for only one tick, you could end up with an intermediate delay between zero and one tick. This is assuming, however, that your processor is not heavily loaded. Figure 5.1 illustrates what happens.

Figure 5.1   Delay resolution.

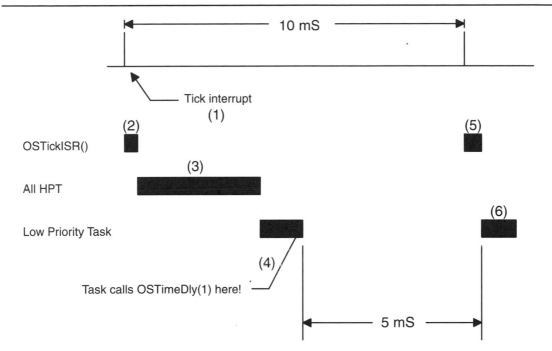

F5.1(1) A tick interrupt occurs every 10ms.

F5.1(2) Assuming that you are not servicing any other interrupts and that you have interrupts enabled, the tick ISR is invoked.

F5.1(3) You might have a few high priority tasks (HPT) waiting for time to expire, so they execute next.

F5.1(4) The low priority task (LPT) shown in Figure 5.1 then executes and, upon completion, calls `OSTimeDly(1)` at the moment shown. µC/OS-II puts the task to sleep until the next tick.

F5.1(5)

F5.1(6) When the next tick arrives, the tick ISR executes, but this time no HPTs exist to execute, and µC/OS-II executes the task that delayed itself for one tick. As you can see, the task actually delayed for less than one tick! On heavily loaded systems, the task can call `OSTimeDly(1)` a few tens of microseconds before the tick occurs, and thus the delay results in almost no delay because the task is immediately rescheduled. If your application must delay for at least one tick, you must call `OSTimeDly(2)` and thus specify a delay of two ticks.

5.01   *Delaying a Task,* `OSTimeDlyHMSM()`

`OSTimeDly()` is a very useful function, but your application needs to know time in terms of ticks. You can use the global #define constant `OS_TICKS_PER_SEC` (see `OS_CFG.H`) to convert time to ticks by declaring some #defines as follows:

```
#define  OS_TIME_100mS  (INT16U)((INT32U)OS_TICKS_PER_SEC * 100L / 1000L)
#define  OS_TIME_500mS  (INT16U)((INT32U)OS_TICKS_PER_SEC * 500L / 1000L)
#define  OS_TIME_2S     (INT16U)(OS_TICKS_PER_SEC * 2)
```

However, this process is somewhat awkward. I added the function `OSTimeDlyHMSM()` so that you can specify time in hours (H), minutes (M), seconds (S), and milliseconds (ms), which is more natural. Like calling `OSTimeDly()`, calling this function causes a context switch and forces µC/OS-II to execute the next highest priority task that is ready to run. The task calling `OSTimeDlyHMSM()` is made ready to run as soon as the time specified expires or if another task cancels the delay by calling `OSTimeDlyResume()` [see Section 5.02, "Resuming a Delayed Task,`OSTimeDlyResume()`"]. Again, this task runs only when it again becomes the highest priority task. Listing 5.2 shows the code for `OSTimeDlyHMSM()`. As you can see, your application calls this function by supplying the delay in hours, minutes, seconds, and milliseconds. In practice, you should avoid delaying a task for long periods of time because it's always a good idea to get some feedback activity from a task (for example increment a counter or blink an LED,). However, if you do need long delays, µC/OS-II can delay a task for 256 hours (close to 11 days).

Listing 5.2   `OSTimeDlyHMSM()`.

```
INT8U OSTimeDlyHMSM (INT8U hours, INT8U minutes, INT8U seconds, INT16U milli)
{
    INT32U ticks;
    INT16U loops;


    if (hours > 0 || minutes > 0 || seconds > 0 || milli > 0) {              (1)
        if (minutes > 59) {
            return (OS_TIME_INVALID_MINUTES);
        }
        if (seconds > 59) {
            return (OS_TIME_INVALID_SECONDS);
        }
        if (milli > 999) {
            return (OS_TIME_INVALID_MILLI);
        }
```

Listing 5.2 `OSTimeDlyHMSM()`. *(Continued)*

```
        ticks = (INT32U)hours    * 3600L * OS_TICKS_PER_SEC          (2)
              + (INT32U)minutes  *   60L * OS_TICKS_PER_SEC
              + (INT32U)seconds  *         OS_TICKS_PER_SEC
              + OS_TICKS_PER_SEC * ((INT32U)milli
              + 500L / OS_TICKS_PER_SEC) / 1000L;                    (3)
        loops = ticks / 65536L;                                     (4)
        ticks = ticks % 65536L;                                     (5)
        OSTimeDly(ticks);                                           (6)
        while (loops > 0) {                                         (7)
            OSTimeDly(32768);                                       (8)
            OSTimeDly(32768);
            loops--;
        }
        return (OS_NO_ERR);
    }
    return (OS_TIME_ZERO_DLY);                                      (9)
}
```

L5.2(1)   `OSTimeDlyHMSM()` starts by checking that you have specified valid values for its arguments.

L5.2(9)   As with `OSTimeDly()`, `OSTimeDlyHMSM()` exits if you specify no delay.

Because µC/OS-II only knows about ticks, the total number of ticks is computed from the specified time. The code shown in Listing 5.2 is obviously not very efficient. I just showed the equation this way so you can see how the total ticks are computed. The actual code efficiently factors in `OS_TICKS_PER_SEC`.

L5.2(3)   This portion of the equation determines the number of ticks given the specified milliseconds with rounding to the nearest tick. The value `500/OS_TICKS_PER_SECOND` basically corresponds to 0.5 ticks converted to milliseconds. For example, if the tick rate (`OS_TICKS_PER_SEC`) is set to 100Hz (10ms), a delay of 4ms results in no delay! A delay of 5ms results in a delay of 10ms, and so on.

L5.2(4)

L5.2(5)   µC/OS-II only supports delays of up to 65,535 ticks. To support longer delays, obtained by L5.2(2), `OSTimeDlyHMSM()` determines how many times you need to delay for more than 65,535 ticks, as well as the remaining number of ticks. For example, if `OS_TICKS_PER_SEC` is 100 and you want a delay of 15 minutes, then `OSTimeDlyHMSM()` has to delay for $15 \times 60 \times 100 = 90,000$ ticks. This delay is broken down into two delays of 32,768 ticks and one delay of 24,464 ticks (because you can't delay 65,536 ticks, only 65,535).

L5.2(6)

L5.2(7)

L5.2(8)   In this case, `OSTimeDlyHMSM()` takes care of the remainder first, then the number of times 65,535 is exceeded (i.e., two 32,768-tick delays).

Because of the way OSTimeDlyHMSM() is implemented, you cannot resume (see Section 5.02, "Resuming a Delayed Task, OSTimeDlyResume()") a task that calls OSTimeDlyHMSM() with a combined time that exceeds 65,535 clock ticks. In other words, if the clock tick runs at 100Hz, you cannot resume a delayed task that calls OSTimeDlyHMSM(0, 10, 55, 350) or higher.

5.02   *Resuming a Delayed Task,* OSTimeDlyResume()

Instead of waiting for time to expire, a delayed task can be made ready to run by another task that cancels the delay. This action is done by calling OSTimeDlyResume() and specifying the priority of the task to resume. In fact, OSTimeDlyResume() also can resume a task that is waiting for an event (see Chapters 7 through 11), although this action is not recommended. In this case, the task pending on the event thinks it timed out waiting for the event. The code for OSTimeDlyResume() is shown in Listing 5.3.

Listing 5.3   *Resuming a delayed task.*

```
INT8U  OSTimeDlyResume (INT8U prio)
{
#if OS_CRITICAL_METHOD == 3
    OS_CPU_SR  cpu_sr;
#endif
    OS_TCB    *ptcb;

    if (prio >= OS_LOWEST_PRIO) {                                            (1)
        return (OS_PRIO_INVALID);
    }
    OS_ENTER_CRITICAL();
    ptcb = (OS_TCB *)OSTCBPrioTbl[prio];
    if (ptcb != (OS_TCB *)0) {                                              (2)
        if (ptcb->OSTCBDly != 0) {                                         (3)
            ptcb->OSTCBDly  = 0;                                           (4)
            if ((ptcb->OSTCBStat & OS_STAT_SUSPEND) == OS_STAT_RDY) {      (5)
                OSRdyGrp                |= ptcb->OSTCBBitY;                 (6)
                OSRdyTbl[ptcb->OSTCBY] |= ptcb->OSTCBBitX;
                OS_EXIT_CRITICAL();
                OS_Sched();                                                (7)
            } else {
                OS_EXIT_CRITICAL();
            }
            return (OS_NO_ERR);
        } else {
            OS_EXIT_CRITICAL();
            return (OS_TIME_NOT_DLY);
        }
    }
    OS_EXIT_CRITICAL();
    return (OS_TASK_NOT_EXIST);
}
```

L5.3(1) `OSTimeDlyResume()` begins by making sure the task has a valid priority.

L5.3(2) Next, `OSTimeDlyResume()` verifies that the task to resume does in fact exist.

L5.3(3) If the task exists, `OSTimeDlyResume()` checks to see if the task is waiting for time to expire. Whenever the `OS_TCB` field `.OSTCBDly` contains a nonzero value, the task is waiting for time to expire because the task called either `OSTimeDly()`, `OSTimeDlyHMSM()`, or any of the `PEND` functions described in subsequent chapters.

L5.3(4) The delay is then canceled by forcing `.OSTCBDly` to 0.

L5.3(5) A delayed task might also have been suspended; thus, the task is only made ready to run if the task was not suspended.

L5.3(6) The task is placed in the ready list when the above conditions are satisfied.

L5.3(7) At this point, `OSTimeDlyResume()` calls the scheduler to see if the resumed task has a higher priority than the current task, which results in a context switch.

Note that you could also have a task delay itself by waiting on a semaphore, mutex, event flag, mailbox, or queue with a timeout (see Chapters 7 through 11). You resume such a task by simply posting to the semaphore, mutex, event flag, mailbox, or queue, respectively. The only problem with this scenario is that it requires you to allocate an event control block (see Section 6.00, "Placing a Task in the ECB Wait List"), so your application would consume a little bit more RAM.

5.03   System Time, `OSTimeGet()` and `OSTimeSet()`

Whenever a clock tick occurs, µC/OS-II increments a 32-bit counter. This counter starts at zero when you initiate multitasking by calling `OSStart()` and rolls over after 4,294,967,295 ticks. At a tick rate of 100Hz, this 32-bit counter rolls over every 497 days. You can obtain the current value of this counter by calling `OSTimeGet()`. You can also change the value of the counter by calling `OSTimeSet()`. The code for both functions is shown in Listing 5.4. Note that interrupts are disabled when accessing `OSTime` because incrementing and copying a 32-bit value on most 8-bit processors requires multiple instructions that must be treated indivisibly.

Listing 5.4   Obtaining and setting the system time.

```
INT32U  OSTimeGet (void)
{
#if OS_CRITICAL_METHOD == 3
    OS_CPU_SR  cpu_sr;
#endif
    INT32U     ticks;

    OS_ENTER_CRITICAL();
    ticks = OSTime;
    OS_EXIT_CRITICAL();
    return (ticks);
}
```

Listing 5.4   Obtaining and setting the system time. (Continued)

```c
void  OSTimeSet (INT32U ticks)
{
#if OS_CRITICAL_METHOD == 3
    OS_CPU_SR  cpu_sr;
#endif


    OS_ENTER_CRITICAL();
    OSTime = ticks;
    OS_EXIT_CRITICAL();
}
```

Chapter 6

Event Control Blocks

Figure 6.1 (page 153) shows how tasks and ISRs can interact with each other. A task or an ISR signals a task through a kernel object called an *event control block* (ECB). The signal is considered to be an event, which explains my choice of this name.

Figure 6.1   *Use of event control blocks.*

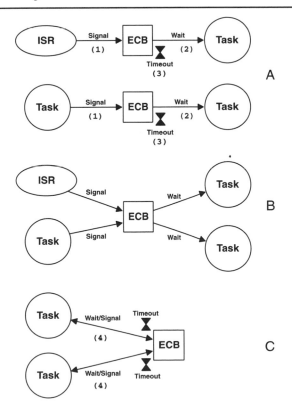

F6.1A(1) An ISR or a task can signal an ECB.

F6.1A(2) Only a task can wait for another task or an ISR to signal the ECB. An ISR is not allowed to wait on an ECB.

F6.1A(3) An optional timeout can be specified by the waiting task in case the object is not signaled within a specified time period.

F6.1B Multiple tasks can wait for a task or an ISR to signal an ECB. When the ECB is signaled, only the highest priority task waiting on the ECB is signaled and made ready to run. An ECB can be a semaphore, a message mailbox, or a message queue, as discussed later.

F6.1C(4) When an ECB is used as a semaphore, tasks can both wait on and signal the ECB.

An ECB is used as a building block to implement services, such as "Semaphore Management" (Chapter 7), "Mutual Exclusion Semaphores" (Chapter 8), "Message Mailbox Management" (Chapter 10), and "Message Queue Management" (Chapter 11).

μC/OS-II maintains the state of an ECB in a data structure called OS_EVENT (see uCOS_II.H). The state of an event consists of the event itself (a counter for a semaphore, a bit for a mutex, a pointer for a message mailbox, or an array of pointers for a queue) and a list of tasks waiting for the event to occur. Each semaphore, mutual exclusion semaphore, message mailbox, and message queue is assigned an ECB. The data structure for an ECB is shown in Listing 6.1 and also graphically in Figure 6.2 (page 155).

Listing 6.1   Event control block data structure.

```
typedef struct {
    INT8U   OSEventType;                  /* Event type                        */
    INT8U   OSEventGrp;                   /* Group for wait list               */
    INT16U  OSEventCnt;                   /* Count (when event is a semaphore) */
    void   *OSEventPtr;                   /* Ptr to message or queue structure */
    INT8U   OSEventTbl[OS_EVENT_TBL_SIZE]; /* Wait list for event to occur     */
} OS_EVENT;
```

.OSEventType

contains the type associated with the ECB and can have the following values: OS_EVENT_TYPE_SEM, OS_EVENT_TYPE_MUTEX, OS_EVENT_TYPE_MBOX, or OS_EVENT_TYPE_Q. This field is used to make sure you are accessing the proper object when you perform operations on these objects through μC/OS-II's service calls. .OSEventType is the first field (and first byte) of the data structure. This allows run-time checking to determine whether the pointer points to an ECB or an event flag (see Chapter 9).

.OSEventPtr

is only used when the ECB is assigned to a message mailbox or a message queue. It points to the message when used for a mailbox or to a data structure when used for a queue (see Chapter 10, "Message Mailbox Management" and Chapter 11, "Message Queue Management").

.OSEventTbl[] and .OSEventGrp

are similar to OSRdyTbl[] and OSRdyGrp, respectively, except that they contain a list of tasks waiting on the event instead of a list of tasks ready to run (see Section 3.04, "Ready List").

`.OSEventCnt`
> is used to hold the semaphore count when the ECB is used for a semaphore (see Chapter 7, "Semaphore Management") or the mutex and PIP when the ECB is used for a mutex (see Chapter 8, "Mutual Exclusion Semaphores").

Figure 6.2   Event Control Block (ECB).

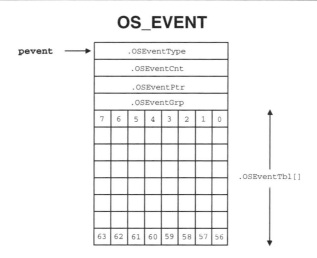

Each task that needs to wait for the event to occur is placed in the wait list, which consists of the two variables, `.OSEventGrp` and `.OSEventTbl[]`. Note that I used a dot (`.`) in front of the variable name to indicate that the variable is part of a data structure. Task priorities are grouped (eight tasks per group) in `.OSEventGrp`. Each bit in `.OSEventGrp` is used to indicate when any task in a group is waiting for the event to occur. When a task is waiting, its corresponding bit is set in the wait table, `.OSEventTbl[]`. The size (in bytes) of `.OSEventTbl[]` depends on `OS_LOWEST_PRIO` (see `uCOS_II.H`). This allows µC/OS-II to reduce the amount of RAM (i.e., data space) when the application requires just a few task priorities.

The task that is resumed when the event occurs is the highest priority task waiting for the event and corresponds to the lowest priority number that has a bit set in `.OSEventTbl[]`. The relationship between `.OSEventGrp` and `.OSEventTbl[]` is shown in Figure 6.3 and is given by the following rules.

> Bit 0 in `.OSEventGrp` is 1 when any bit in `.OSEventTbl[0]` is 1.
> Bit 1 in `.OSEventGrp` is 1 when any bit in `.OSEventTbl[1]` is 1.
> Bit 2 in `.OSEventGrp` is 1 when any bit in `.OSEventTbl[2]` is 1.
> Bit 3 in `.OSEventGrp` is 1 when any bit in `.OSEventTbl[3]` is 1.
> Bit 4 in `.OSEventGrp` is 1 when any bit in `.OSEventTbl[4]` is 1.
> Bit 5 in `.OSEventGrp` is 1 when any bit in `.OSEventTbl[5]` is 1.
> Bit 6 in `.OSEventGrp` is 1 when any bit in `.OSEventTbl[6]` is 1.
> Bit 7 in `.OSEventGrp` is 1 when any bit in `.OSEventTbl[7]` is 1.

Figure 6.3   Wait list for task waiting for an event to occur.

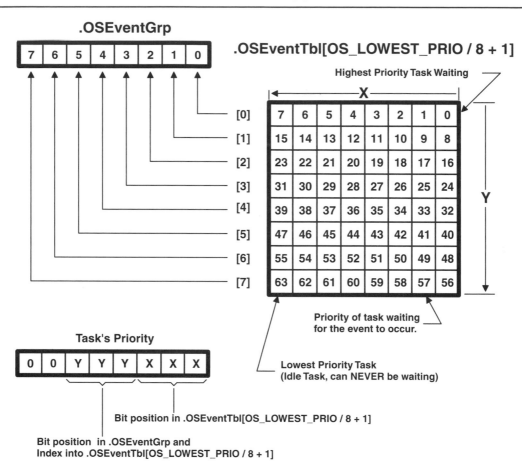

6.00   Placing a Task in the ECB Wait List

The code in Listing 6.2 places a task in the wait list:

Listing 6.2   Making a task wait for an event.

```
pevent->OSEventGrp            |= OSMapTbl[prio >> 3];
pevent->OSEventTbl[prio >> 3] |= OSMapTbl[prio & 0x07];
```

prio is the task's priority, and pevent is a pointer to the event control block.

You should realize from Listing 6.2 that the time required to insert a task in the wait list is constant and does not depend on how many tasks are in the system. Also, from Figure 6.3, the lower 3 bits of the task's priority are used to determine the bit position in .OSEventTbl[], and the next three most significant bits are used to determine the index into .OSEventTbl[]. Note that OSMapTbl[] (see OS_CORE.C) is a table in ROM, used to equate an index from 0 to 7 to a bit mask, as shown in the Table 6.1.

Table 6.1   Content of `OSMapTbl[]`.

Index	Bit Mask (Binary)
0	00000001
1	00000010
2	00000100
3	00001000
4	00010000
5	00100000
6	01000000
7	10000000

6

6.01   Removing a Task from an ECB Wait List

A task is removed from the wait list by reversing the process as in Listing 6.3.

Listing 6.3   Removing a task from a wait list.

```
if ((pevent->OSEventTbl[prio >> 3] &= ~OSMapTbl[prio & 0x07]) == 0) {
    pevent->OSEventGrp &= ~OSMapTbl[prio >> 3];
}
```

This code clears the bit corresponding to the task in `.OSEventTbl[]` and clears the bit in `.OSEventGrp`, only if all tasks in a group are not waiting; that is, all bits in `.OSEventTbl[prio >> 3]` are 0.

6.02   Finding the Highest Priority Task Waiting on an ECB

The code to find the highest priority task waiting for an event to occur is shown in Listing 6.4. Table lookups are again used for performance reasons because we don't want to scan the `.OSEventTbl[]` one bit at a time to locate the highest priority task waiting on the event.

Listing 6.4   Finding the highest priority task waiting for the event.

```
y    = OSUnMapTbl[pevent->OSEventGrp];                              (1)
x    = OSUnMapTbl[pevent->OSEventTbl[y]];                           (2)
prio = (y << 3) + x;                                                (3)
```

L6.4(1)   Using `.OSEventGrp` as an index into `OSUnMapTbl[]` (see Listing 6.5) you can quickly locate which entry in `.OSEventTbl[]` holds the highest priority task waiting for the ECB.

OSUnMapTbl[] returns the bit position of the highest priority bit set — a number between 0 and 7. This number corresponds to the *Y* position in .OSEventTbl[] (see Figure 6.3).

L6.4(2)   After we know which row (see Figure 6.3) contains the highest priority task waiting for the ECB, we can zoom in on the actual bit by performing another lookup in OSUnMapTbl[] but this time, with the entry in .OSEventTbl[] just found. Again, we get a number between 0 and 7. This number corresponds to the *X* position in .OSEventTbl[] (see Figure 6.3).

L6.4(3)   By combining the two previous operations, we can determine the priority number of the highest priority task waiting on the ECB. This number is between 0 and 63.

Listing 6.5   *OSUnMapTbl[].*

```
INT8U const OSUnMapTbl[] = {
    0, 0, 1, 0, 2, 0, 1, 0, 3, 0, 1, 0, 2, 0, 1, 0,     /* 0x00 to 0x0F */
    4, 0, 1, 0, 2, 0, 1, 0, 3, 0, 1, 0, 2, 0, 1, 0,     /* 0x10 to 0x1F */
    5, 0, 1, 0, 2, 0, 1, 0, 3, 0, 1, 0, 2, 0, 1, 0,     /* 0x20 to 0x2F */
    4, 0, 1, 0, 2, 0, 1, 0, 3, 0, 1, 0, 2, 0, 1, 0,     /* 0x30 to 0x3F */
    6, 0, 1, 0, 2, 0, 1, 0, 3, 0, 1, 0, 2, 0, 1, 0,     /* 0x40 to 0x4F */
    4, 0, 1, 0, 2, 0, 1, 0, 3, 0, 1, 0, 2, 0, 1, 0,     /* 0x50 to 0x5F */
    5, 0, 1, 0, 2, 0, 1, 0, 3, 0, 1, 0, 2, 0, 1, 0,     /* 0x60 to 0x6F */
    4, 0, 1, 0, 2, 0, 1, 0, 3, 0, 1, 0, 2, 0, 1, 0,     /* 0x70 to 0x7F */
    7, 0, 1, 0, 2, 0, 1, 0, 3, 0, 1, 0, 2, 0, 1, 0,     /* 0x80 to 0x8F */
    4, 0, 1, 0, 2, 0, 1, 0, 3, 0, 1, 0, 2, 0, 1, 0,     /* 0x90 to 0x9F */
    5, 0, 1, 0, 2, 0, 1, 0, 3, 0, 1, 0, 2, 0, 1, 0,     /* 0xA0 to 0xAF */
    4, 0, 1, 0, 2, 0, 1, 0, 3, 0, 1, 0, 2, 0, 1, 0,     /* 0xB0 to 0xBF */
    6, 0, 1, 0, 2, 0, 1, 0, 3, 0, 1, 0, 2, 0, 1, 0,     /* 0xC0 to 0xCF */
    4, 0, 1, 0, 2, 0, 1, 0, 3, 0, 1, 0, 2, 0, 1, 0,     /* 0xD0 to 0xDF */
    5, 0, 1, 0, 2, 0, 1, 0, 3, 0, 1, 0, 2, 0, 1, 0,     /* 0xE0 to 0xEF */
    4, 0, 1, 0, 2, 0, 1, 0, 3, 0, 1, 0, 2, 0, 1, 0      /* 0xF0 to 0xFF */
};
```

Let's look at an example, as shown in Figure 6.4, if .OSEventGrp contains 11001000 (binary) or 0xC8, OSUnMapTbl[.OSEventGrp] yields a value of 3, which corresponds to bit 3 in .OSEventGrp and also happens to be the index in .OSEventTbl[], which contains the first non-zero entry. Note that bit positions are assumed to start on the right with bit 0 being the rightmost bit. Similarly, if .OSEventTbl[3] contains 00010000 (binary) or 0x10, OSUnMapTbl[.OSEventTbl[3]] results in a value of 4 (bit 4). The priority of the task waiting (prio) is thus 28 (3 x 8 + 4), which corresponds to the number in .OSEventTbl[] of Figure 6.3.

Figure 6.4   Example of ECB wait list.

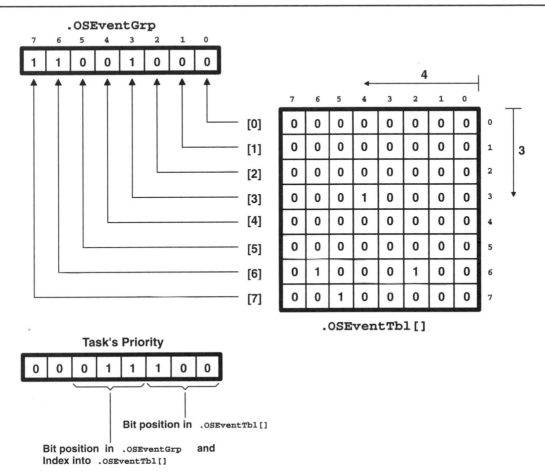

.OSEventTbl[]

Task's Priority

Bit position in .OSEventTbl[]

Bit position in .OSEventGrp and
Index into .OSEventTbl[]

6.03   List of Free ECBs

The number of ECBs to allocate depends on the number of semaphores, mutual exclusion semaphores, mailboxes, and queues needed for the application. The number of ECBs is established by the #define OS_MAX_EVENTS, which is found in OS_CFG.H. When OSInit() is called (see Section 3.12, "µC/OS-II Initialization"), all ECBs are linked in a singly linked list — the list of free ECBs (Figure 6.5). When a semaphore, mutex, mailbox, or queue is created, an ECB is removed from this list and initialized. ECBs can be returned to the list of free ECBs by invoking the OS???Del() functions for semaphore, mutex, mailbox, or queue services.

Figure 6.5   List of free ECBs.

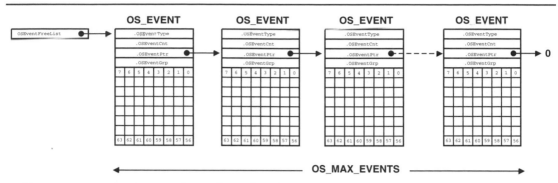

Four common operations can be performed on ECBs:

- initialize an ECB,
- make a task ready,
- make a task wait for an event, and
- make a task ready because a timeout occurred while waiting for an event.

To avoid duplicating code and thus to reduce code size, four functions have been created to perform these operations: OS_EventWaitListInit(), OS_EventTaskRdy(), OS_EventWait(), and OS_EventTO(), respectively.

6.04   Initializing an ECB, OS_EventWaitListInit()

Listing 6.6 shows the code for OS_EventWaitListInit(), which is a function called when a semaphore, mutex, message mailbox, or message queue is created [see OSSemCreate(), OSMutexCreate(), OSMboxCreate(), or OSQCreate()]. All that is accomplished by OS_EventWaitListInit() is to indicate that no task is waiting on the ECB. OS_EventWaitListInit() is passed a pointer to an event control block, which is assigned when the semaphore, mutex, message mailbox, or message queue is created. The code is implemented inline to avoid the overhead of a for loop.

Listing 6.6   Initializing the wait list.

```
void  OS_EventWaitListInit (OS_EVENT *pevent)
{
    INT8U  *ptbl;


    pevent->OSEventGrp = 0x00;
    ptbl               = &pevent->OSEventTbl[0];
```

Listing 6.6   *Initializing the wait list. (Continued)*

```
#if OS_EVENT_TBL_SIZE > 0
    *ptbl++            = 0x00;
#endif

#if OS_EVENT_TBL_SIZE > 1
    *ptbl++            = 0x00;
#endif

#if OS_EVENT_TBL_SIZE > 2
    *ptbl++            = 0x00;
#endif

#if OS_EVENT_TBL_SIZE > 3
    *ptbl++            = 0x00;
#endif

#if OS_EVENT_TBL_SIZE > 4
    *ptbl++            = 0x00;
#endif

#if OS_EVENT_TBL_SIZE > 5
    *ptbl++            = 0x00;
#endif

#if OS_EVENT_TBL_SIZE > 6
    *ptbl++            = 0x00;
#endif

#if OS_EVENT_TBL_SIZE > 7
    *ptbl             = 0x00;
#endif
}
```

6.05   *Making a Task Ready,* `OS_EventTaskRdy()`

Listing 6.7 shows the code for `OS_EventTaskRdy()`. This function is called by the POST functions for a semaphore, a mutex, a message mailbox, or a message queue when an ECB is signaled and the highest priority task waiting on the ECB needs to be made ready to run. In other words, `OS_EventTaskRdy()` removes the highest priority task (HPT) from the wait list of the ECB and makes this task ready to run.

Listing 6.7   Making a task ready to run.

```
INT8U  OS_EventTaskRdy (OS_EVENT *pevent, void *msg, INT8U msk)
{
    OS_TCB ^ptcb;
    INT8U  x;
    INT8U  y;
    INT8U  bitx;
    INT8U  bity;
    INT8U  prio;


    y    = OSUnMapTbl[pevent->OSEventGrp];                        (1)
    bity = OSMapTbl[y];                                           (2)
    x    = OSUnMapTbl[pevent->OSEventTbl[y]];                     (3)
    bitx = OSMapTbl[x];                                           (4)
    prio = (INT8U)((y << 3) + x);                                 (5)
    if ((pevent->OSEventTbl[y] &= ~bitx) == 0x00) {              (6)
        pevent->OSEventGrp &= ~bity;
    }
    ptcb               = OSTCBPrioTbl[prio];                      (7)
    ptcb->OSTCBDly     = 0;                                       (8)
    ptcb->OSTCBEventPtr = (OS_EVENT *)0;                          (9)
#if ((OS_Q_EN > 0) && (OS_MAX_QS > 0)) || (OS_MBOX_EN > 0)
    ptcb->OSTCBMsg     = msg;                                     (10)
#else
    msg                = msg;
#endif
    ptcb->OSTCBStat    &= ~msk;                                   (11)
    if (ptcb->OSTCBStat == OS_STAT_RDY) {                         (12)
        OSRdyGrp       |= bity;                                   (13)
        OSRdyTbl[y]    |= bitx;
    }
    return (prio);                                                (14)
}
```

L6.7(1)   OS_EventTaskRdy() starts by determining the index into .OSEventTbl[] of the HPT, a number between 0 and OS_LOWEST_PRIO/8 + 1.

L6.7(2)   Then the bit mask of the HPT in .OSEventGrp is obtained (see Table 6.1 for possible values).

L6.7(3)

L6.7(4) `OS_EventTaskRdy()` then determines the bit position of the task in `.OSEventTbl[]`, a value between 0 and `OS_LOWEST_PRIO/8 + 1`, and the bit mask of the HPT in `.OSEventTbl[]` (see Table 6.1 for possible values).

L6.7(5) The priority of the task being made ready to run is determined by combining the x and y indices.

L6.7(6) At this point, you can extract the task from the wait list. The code looks a little bit different than what was presented in Listing 6.3, but otherwise, it works just the same.

L6.7(7) The task control block (TCB) of the task being readied contains information that needs to be changed. Knowing the task's priority, you can obtain a pointer to that TCB.

L6.7(8) Because the HPT is not waiting anymore, you need to make sure that `OSTimeTick()` does not attempt to decrement the `.OSTCBDly` value of that task, which is done by forcing `.OSTCBDly` to 0.

L6.7(9) The pointer to the ECB is forced to `NULL` because the HPT is no longer waiting on this ECB.

L6.7(10) A message is sent to the HPT if `OS_EventTaskRdy()` is called by the `POST` functions for message mailboxes and message queues. This message is passed as an argument and needs to be placed in the task's TCB.

L6.7(11) When `OS_EventTaskRdy()` is called, the `msk` argument contains the appropriate bit mask to clear the bit in `.OSTCBStat`, which corresponds to the type of event signaled (`OS_STAT_SEM`, `OS_STAT_MUTEX`, `OS_STAT_MBOX`, or `OS_STAT_Q`).

L6.7(12)

L6.7(13) If `.OSTCBStat` indicates that the task is now ready to run, `OS_EventTaskRdy()` inserts this task in µC/OS-II's ready list. Note that the task might not be ready to run because it could have been explicitly suspended [see Section 4.07, "Suspending a Task, `OSTaskSuspend()`", and Section 4.08, "Resuming a Task, `OSTaskResume()`"].

L6.7(14) `OS_EventTaskRdy()` returns the priority of the task readied.

Note that `OS_EventTaskRdy()` is called with interrupts disabled.

6.06 *Making a Task Wait for an Event,* `OS_EventTaskWait()`

Listing 6.8 shows the code for `OS_EventTaskWait()`. This function is called by the `PEND` functions of a semaphore, mutex, message mailbox, and message queue when a task must wait on an ECB. In other words, `OS_EventTaskWait()` removes the current task from the ready list and places it in the wait list of the ECB.

Listing 6.8   *Making a task wait on an ECB.*

```
void  OS_EventTaskWait (OS_EVENT *pevent)
{
    OSTCBCur->OSTCBEventPtr = pevent;                                        (1)
    if ((OSRdyTbl[OSTCBCur->OSTCBY] &= ~OSTCBCur->OSTCBBitX) == 0x00) {      (2)
        OSRdyGrp &= ~OSTCBCur->OSTCBBitY;
    }
    pevent->OSEventTbl[OSTCBCur->OSTCBY] |= OSTCBCur->OSTCBBitX;             (3)
    pevent->OSEventGrp                   |= OSTCBCur->OSTCBBitY;
}
```

L6.8(1)   The pointer to the ECB is placed in the task's TCB, linking the task to the event control block.

L6.8(2)   The task is removed from the ready list.

L6.8(3)   The task is placed in the wait list for the ECB.

6.07   *Making a Task Ready Because of a Timeout,* OS_EventTO()

Listing 6.9 shows the code for OS_EventTO(). This function is called by PEND functions for a semaphore, mutex, message mailbox, and message queue when OSTimeTick() has readied a task to run, which means that the ECB was not signaled within the specified timeout period.

Listing 6.9   *Making a task ready because of a timeout.*

```
void  OS_EventTO (OS_EVENT *pevent)
{
    if ((pevent->OSEventTbl[OSTCBCur->OSTCBY] &= ~OSTCBCur->OSTCBBitX) == 0x00) {   (1)
        pevent->OSEventGrp &= ~OSTCBCur->OSTCBBitY;
    }
    OSTCBCur->OSTCBStat    = OS_STAT_RDY;                                           (2)
    OSTCBCur->OSTCBEventPtr = (OS_EVENT *)0;                                        (3)
}
```

L6.9(1)   OS_EventTO() must remove the task from the wait list of the ECB. The code look a little bit different than the code shown in Listing 6.3. However, it does the same thing.

L6.9(2)   The task is then marked as being ready.

L6.9(3)   The link to the ECB is finally removed from the task's TCB.

You should note that OS_EventTO() is also called with interrupts disabled.

Chapter 7

Semaphore Management

μC/OS-II semaphores consist of two elements: a 16-bit unsigned integer used to hold the semaphore count (0 to 65,535) and a list of tasks waiting for the semaphore count to be greater than 0. μC/OS-II provides six services to access semaphores: OSSemAccept(), OSSemCreate(), OSSemDel(), OSSemPend(), OSSemPost() and OSSemQuery().

To enable μC/OS-II semaphore services, you must set the configuration constants in OS_CFG.H. Specifically, Table 7.1 shows which services are compiled, based on the value of configuration constants found in OS_CFG.H. You should note that **none** of the semaphore services are enabled when OS_SEM_EN is set to 0. To enable the feature (i.e., service), simply set the configuration constant to 1. You should notice that OSSemCreate(), OSSemPend(), and OSSemPost() cannot be individually disabled as can the other services. That's because they are always needed when you enable μC/OS-II semaphore management.

Table 7.1   Semaphore configuration constants in OS_CFG.H.

μC/OS-II Semaphore Service	Enabled when set to 1 in OS_CFG.H
OSSemAccept()	OS_SEM_ACCEPT_EN
OSSemCreate()	
OSSemDel()	OS_SEM_DEL_EN
OSSemPend()	
OSSemPost()	
OSSemQuery()	OS_SEM_QUERY_EN

Figure 7.1 shows a flow diagram to illustrate the relationship between tasks, ISRs, and a semaphore. Note that the symbology used to represent a semaphore is either a key or a flag. You use a key symbol in such flow diagrams if the semaphore is used to access shared resources. The *N* next to the key represents how many resources are available. N is 1 for a binary semaphore. Use a flag symbol when a semaphore is used to signal the occurrence of an event. N in this case represents the number of times the event can be signaled. The hourglass represents a timeout that can be specified with the OSSemPend() call.

As you can see from Figure 7.1, a task or an ISR can call OSSemAccept(), OSSemPost(), or OSSemQuery(). However, only tasks are allowed to call OSSemDel() or OSSemPend().

Figure 7.1   *Relationships between tasks, ISRs, and a semaphore.*

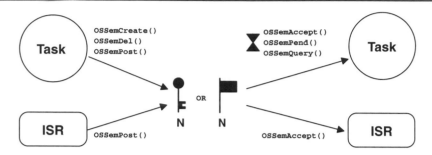

7.00   *Creating a Semaphore,* OSSemCreate()

A semaphore needs to be created before it can be used. You create a semaphore by calling OSSemCreate() and specifying the initial count of the semaphore. The initial value of a semaphore can be between 0 and 65,535. If you use the semaphore to signal the occurrence of one or more events, you typically initialize the semaphore to 0. If you use the semaphore to access a single shared resource, you need to initialize the semaphore to 1 (i.e., use it as a binary semaphore). Finally, if the semaphore allows your application to obtain any one of *n* identical resources, initialize the semaphore to *n* and use it as a counting semaphore.

The code to create a semaphore is shown in Listing 7.1.

Listing 7.1   *Creating a semaphore.*

```
OS_EVENT  *OSSemCreate (INT16U cnt)
{
#if OS_CRITICAL_METHOD == 3
    OS_CPU_SR  cpu_sr;                                              (1)
#endif
    OS_EVENT  *pevent;


    if (OSIntNesting > 0) {                                         (2)
        return ((OS_EVENT *)0);
    }
    OS_ENTER_CRITICAL();
    pevent = OSEventFreeList;                                       (3)
    if (OSEventFreeList != (OS_EVENT *)0) {                         (4)
        OSEventFreeList = (OS_EVENT *)OSEventFreeList->OSEventPtr;  (5)
    }
```

Listing 7.1   *Creating a semaphore. (Continued)*

```
    OS_EXIT_CRITICAL();
    if (pevent != (OS_EVENT *)0) {                          (6)
        pevent->OSEventType = OS_EVENT_TYPE_SEM;            (7)
        pevent->OSEventCnt  = cnt;                          (8)
        pevent->OSEventPtr  = (void *)0;                    (9)
        OS_EventWaitListInit(pevent);                      (10)
    }
    return (pevent);                                       (11)
}
```

L7.1(1)   A local variable called `cpu_sr` to support `OS_CRITICAL_METHOD #3` is allocated.

L7.1(2)   `OSSemCreate()` starts by making sure you are not calling this function from an ISR because this is not allowed. All kernel objects need to be created from task-level code or before multitasking starts.

L7.1(3)   `OSSemCreate()` then attempts to obtain an ECB from the free list of ECBs (see Figure 6.5, page 160).

L7.1(4)

L7.1(5)   The linked list of free ECBs is adjusted to point to the next free ECB.

L7.1(6)

L7.1(7)   If an ECB is available, the ECB type is set to `OS_EVENT_TYPE_SEM`. Other `OSSem???()` function calls check this structure member to make sure that the ECB is of the proper type (i.e., a semaphore). This prevents you from calling `OSSemPost()` on an ECB that was created for use as a message mailbox (see Chapter 10, "Message Mailbox Management").

L7.1(8)   Next, the desired initial count for the semaphore is stored in the ECB.

L7.1(9)   The `.OSEventPtr` field is then initialized to point to `NULL` because it doesn't belong to the free ECB linked list anymore.

L7.1(10) The wait list is then initialized by calling `OS_EventWaitListInit()` [see Section 6.04, "Initializing an ECB, `OS_EventWaitListInit()`"]. Because the semaphore is being initialized, there are no tasks waiting for it and thus, `OS_EventWaitListInit()` clears `.OSEventGrp` and `.OSEventTbl[]`.

L7.1(11) Finally, `OSSemCreate()` returns a pointer to the ECB. This pointer must be used in subsequent calls to manipulate semaphores `OSSemAccept()`, `OSSemDel()`, `OSSemPend()`, `OSSemPost()` and `OSSemQuery()`. The pointer is basically used as the semaphore's handle. If no more ECBs exist, `OSSemCreate()` returns a `NULL` pointer. You should make it a habit to check the return values to ensure that you are getting the desired results. Passing `NULL` pointers to μC/OS-II does not make it fail because μC/OS-II validates arguments (only if `OS_ARG_CHK_EN` is set to 1, though).

Figure 7.2 shows the content of the ECB just before `OSSemCreate()` returns.

Figure 7.2   *ECB just before* OSSemCreate() *returns.*

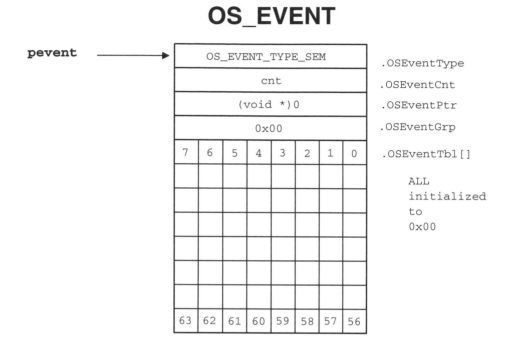

7.01   *Deleting a Semaphore,* OSSemDel()

The code to delete a semaphore is shown in Listing 7.2, and code is only generated by the compiler if OS_SEM_DEL_EN is set to 1 in OS_CFG.H. You must use this function with caution because multiple tasks could attempt to access a deleted semaphore. You should always use this function with great care. Generally speaking, before you delete a semaphore, you should first delete all the tasks that access the semaphore.

Listing 7.2   *Deleting a semaphore.*

```
OS_EVENT  *OSSemDel (OS_EVENT *pevent, INT8U opt, INT8U *err)
{
#if OS_CRITICAL_METHOD == 3
    OS_CPU_SR  cpu_sr;
#endif
    BOOLEAN    tasks_waiting;
```

Listing 7.2 *Deleting a semaphore. (Continued)*

```
    if (OSIntNesting > 0) {                                        (1)
        *err = OS_ERR_DEL_ISR;
        return (pevent);
    }
#if OS_ARG_CHK_EN > 0
    if (pevent == (OS_EVENT *)0) {                                 (2)
        *err = OS_ERR_PEVENT_NULL;
        return (pevent);
    }
    if (pevent->OSEventType != OS_EVENT_TYPE_SEM) {                (3)
        *err = OS_ERR_EVENT_TYPE;
        return (pevent);
    }
#endif
    OS_ENTER_CRITICAL();
    if (pevent->OSEventGrp != 0x00) {                              (4)
        tasks_waiting = TRUE;
    } else {
        tasks_waiting = FALSE;
    }
    switch (opt) {
        case OS_DEL_NO_PEND:
            if (tasks_waiting == FALSE) {                          (5)
                pevent->OSEventType = OS_EVENT_TYPE_UNUSED;        (6)
                pevent->OSEventPtr  = OSEventFreeList;             (7)
                OSEventFreeList     = pevent;
                OS_EXIT_CRITICAL();
                *err = OS_NO_ERR;
                return ((OS_EVENT *)0);                            (8)
            } else {
                OS_EXIT_CRITICAL();
                *err = OS_ERR_TASK_WAITING;
                return (pevent);
            }
```

7

Listing 7.2   *Deleting a semaphore. (Continued)*

```
      case OS_DEL_ALWAYS:                                         (9)
          while (pevent->OSEventGrp != 0x00) {                    (10)
              OS_EventTaskRdy(pevent, (void *)0, OS_STAT_SEM);
          }
          pevent->OSEventType = OS_EVENT_TYPE_UNUSED;             (11)
          pevent->OSEventPtr  = OSEventFreeList;                  (12)
          OSEventFreeList     = pevent;
          OS_EXIT_CRITICAL();
          if (tasks_waiting == TRUE) {
              OS_Sched();                                         (13)
          }
          *err = OS_NO_ERR;
          return ((OS_EVENT *)0);                                (14)

      default:
          OS_EXIT_CRITICAL();
          *err = OS_ERR_INVALID_OPT;
          return (pevent);
   }
}
```

L7.2(1)   `OSSemDel()` starts by making sure that this function is not called from an ISR because that's not allowed.

L7.2(2)

L7.2(3)   `OSSemDel()` validates `pevent` to ensure that it's not a `NULL` pointer and that it points to an ECB that was created as a semaphore.

L7.2(4)   `OSSemDel()` then determines whether there are any tasks waiting on the semaphore. The flag `tasks_waiting` is set accordingly.

Based on the option (i.e., `opt`) specified in the call, `OSSemDel()` either deletes the semaphore only if no tasks are pending on the semaphore (`opt == OS_DEL_NO_PEND`) or deletes the semaphore even if tasks are waiting (`opt == OS_DEL_ALWAYS`).

L7.2(5)

L7.2(6)

L7.2(7)   When `opt` is set to `OS_DEL_NO_PEND` and no task is waiting on the semaphore, `OSSemDel()` marks the ECB as unused, and the ECB is returned to the free list of ECBs. This action allows another semaphore (or any other ECB-based object) to be created.

L7.2(8)   You should note that `OSSemDel()` returns a `NULL` pointer because, at this point, the semaphore should no longer be accessed through the original pointer. `OSSemDel()` returns an error code if tasks are waiting on the semaphore (i.e., `OS_ERR_TASK_WAITING`) because, by specifying `OS_DEL_NO_PEND`, you indicated that you didn't want to delete the semaphore if tasks are waiting on the semaphore.

L7.2(9)

L7.2(10)   When `opt` is set to `OS_DEL_ALWAYS`, then all tasks waiting on the semaphore are readied. Each task thinks it has access to the semaphore. Of course, that's a dangerous outcome because the whole point of having a semaphore could be to protect against multiple accesses to a resource.

L7.2(11)

L7.2(12)   After all pending tasks are readied, `OSSemDel()` marks the ECB as unused, and the ECB is returned to the free list of ECBs.

L7.2(13)   The scheduler is called only if tasks were waiting on the semaphore.

L7.2(14)   Again, you should note that `OSSemDel()` returns a `NULL` pointer because, at this point, the semaphore should no longer be accessed through the original pointer.

7.02   *Waiting on a Semaphore (Blocking),* `OSSemPend()`

The code to wait on a semaphore is shown in Listing 7.3.

Listing 7.3   Waiting on a semaphore.

```
void  OSSemPend (OS_EVENT *pevent, INT16U timeout, INT8U *err)
{
#if OS_CRITICAL_METHOD == 3
    OS_CPU_SR  cpu_sr;
#endif

    if (OSIntNesting > 0) {                                            (1)
        *err = OS_ERR_PEND_ISR;
        return;
    }
#if OS_ARG_CHK_EN > 0
    if (pevent == (OS_EVENT *)0) {                                     (2)
        *err = OS_ERR_PEVENT_NULL;
        return;
    }
    if (pevent->OSEventType != OS_EVENT_TYPE_SEM) {                    (3)
        *err = OS_ERR_EVENT_TYPE;
        return;
    }
#endif
    OS_ENTER_CRITICAL();
```

Listing 7.3   *Waiting on a semaphore. (Continued)*

```
    if (pevent->OSEventCnt > 0) {                           (4)
        pevent->OSEventCnt--;                               (5)
        OS_EXIT_CRITICAL();
        *err = OS_NO_ERR;                                   (6)
        return;
    }
    OSTCBCur->OSTCBStat |= OS_STAT_SEM;                     (7)
    OSTCBCur->OSTCBDly   = timeout;                         (8)
    OS_EventTaskWait(pevent);                               (9)
    OS_EXIT_CRITICAL();
    OS_Sched();                                             (10)
    OS_ENTER_CRITICAL();
    if (OSTCBCur->OSTCBStat & OS_STAT_SEM) {                (11)
        OS_EventTO(pevent);                                 (12)
        OS_EXIT_CRITICAL();
        *err = OS_TIMEOUT;                                  (13)
        return;
    }
    OSTCBCur->OSTCBEventPtr = (OS_EVENT *)0;                (14)
    OS_EXIT_CRITICAL();
    *err = OS_NO_ERR;
}
```

L7.3(1)   OSSemPend() checks to see if an ISR called the function. It doesn't make sense to call OSSemPend() from an ISR because an ISR cannot be made to wait. Instead, you should call OSSemAccept() (see Section 7.04, "Getting a Semaphore Without Waiting (Non-blocking), OSSemAccept()").

L7.3(2)

L7.3(3)   If OS_ARG_CHK_EN is set to 1, OSSemPend() checks that pevent is not a NULL pointer and that OSSemCreate() has created the ECB.

L7.3(4)

L7.3(5)

L7.3(6)   If the semaphore is available (its count is nonzero), the count is decremented, and the function returns to its caller with an error code indicating success. If your code calls OSSemPend(), you want this outcome because it indicates that your code can proceed and access the resource (if OSSemPend() is used to guard a shared resource). This also happens to be the fastest path through OSSemPend().

L7.3(6)   If the semaphore is not available (the count was zero), OSSemPend() checks to see if an ISR called the function. It doesn't make sense to call OSSemPend() from an ISR because an ISR cannot be made to wait. Instead, you should call OSSemAccept() [see Section 7.04, "Getting a Semaphore Without Waiting (Non-blocking), OSSemAccept()"]. I decided to add this check just in case.

If the semaphore count is zero, the calling task needs to be put to sleep until another task (or an ISR) signals the semaphore [see Section 7.03, "Signaling a Semaphore, OSSemPost()"]. OSSemPend() allows you to specify a timeout value (in integral number of ticks) as one of its arguments (i.e., timeout). This feature is useful to avoid waiting indefinitely for the semaphore. If the value passed is nonzero, OSSemPend() suspends the task until the semaphore is signaled or the specified timeout period expires. Note that a timeout value of 0 indicates that the task is willing to wait forever for the semaphore to be signaled.

L7.3(7)   To put the calling task to sleep, OSSemPend() sets the status flag in the task's TCB to indicate that the task is suspended while waiting for a semaphore.

L7.3(8)   The timeout is also stored in the TCB so that it can be decremented by OSTimeTick(). You should recall (see Section 3.11, "Clock Tick") that OSTimeTick() decrements each of the created task's .OSTCBDly field if the count is nonzero.

L7.3(9)   The actual work of putting the task to sleep is done by OS_EventTaskWait() [see Section 6.06, "Making a Task Wait for an Event, OS_EventTaskWait()"].

L7.3(10)   Because the calling task is no longer ready to run, the scheduler is called to run the next highest priority task that is ready to run. As far as your task is concerned, it made a call to OSSemPend(), and it doesn't know that it is suspended until the semaphore is signaled.

L7.3(11)   When the semaphore is signaled (or the timeout period expires) OSSemPend() resumes execution immediately after the call to OS_Sched(). OSSemPend() then checks to see if the TCB status flag is still set to indicate that the task is waiting for the semaphore. If the task is still waiting for the semaphore, it must not have been signaled by an OSSemPost() call. Indeed, the task must have been readied by OSTimeTick(), indicating that the timeout period has expired.

L7.3(12)

L7.3(13)   In this case, the task is removed from the wait list for the semaphore by calling OS_EventTO(), and an error code is returned to the task that called OSSemPend() to indicate that a timeout occurred. If the status flag in the task's TCB doesn't have the OS_STAT_SEM bit set, the semaphore must have been signaled by OSSemPost() [see Section 7.03, "Signaling a Semaphore, OSSemPost()"] and the task that called OSSemPend() can now conclude that it has the semaphore.

L7.3(14)   Finally, the link to the ECB is removed.

7.03 *Signaling a Semaphore,* OSSemPost()

The code to signal a semaphore is shown in Listing 7.4.

Listing 7.4   *Signaling a semaphore.*

```
INT8U  OSSemPost (OS_EVENT *pevent)
{
#if OS_CRITICAL_METHOD == 3
    OS_CPU_SR  cpu_sr;
#endif
```

Listing 7.4   *Signaling a semaphore. (Continued)*

```
#if OS_ARG_CHK_EN > 0
    if (pevent == (OS_EVENT *)0) {                              (1)
        return (OS_ERR_PEVENT_NULL);
    }
    if (pevent->OSEventType != OS_EVENT_TYPE_SEM) {             (2)
        return (OS_ERR_EVENT_TYPE);
    }
#endif
    OS_ENTER_CRITICAL();
    if (pevent->OSEventGrp != 0x00) {                           (3)
        OS_EventTaskRdy(pevent, (void *)0, OS_STAT_SEM);        (4)
        OS_EXIT_CRITICAL();
        OS_Sched();                                             (5)
        return (OS_NO_ERR);
    }
    if (pevent->OSEventCnt < 65535) {
        pevent->OSEventCnt++;                                   (6)
        OS_EXIT_CRITICAL();
        return (OS_NO_ERR);
    }
    OS_EXIT_CRITICAL();
    return (OS_SEM_OVF);                                        (7)
}
```

L7.4(1)

L7.4(2)   If OS_ARG_CHK_EN is set to 1,   OSSemPost() checks that pevent is not a NULL pointer and that the ECB being pointed to by pevent has been created by OSSemCreate().

L7.4(3)   OSSemPost() then checks to see if any tasks are waiting on the semaphore. Tasks waiting are when the .OSEventGrp field in the ECB contains a nonzero value.

L7.4(4)

L7.4(5)   OS_EventTaskRdy() removes the highest priority task waiting for the semaphore from the wait list [see Section 6.05, "Making a Task Ready, OS_EventTaskRdy()"]. The task is ready-to-run. OS_Sched() is then called to see if the task made ready is now the highest priority task ready-to-run. If it is, a context switch results [only if OSSemPost() is called from a task] and the readied task is executed. In other words, the task that called OSSemPost() does **not** continue execution because OSSemPost() made a more important task ready to run and µC/OS-II does thus resume execution of that task. If the readied task is not the highest priority task, OS_Sched() returns, and the task that called OSSemPost()continues execution.

L7.4(6)

L7.4(7)   If no tasks are waiting on the semaphore, the semaphore count simply gets incremented. Note that a counting semaphore is implemented in μC/OS-II using a 16-bit variable, and `OSSemPost()` ensures that the semaphore does not overflow.

It's important to note that a context switch does **not** occur if an ISR calls `OSSemPost()` because context switching from an ISR can only occur when `OSIntExit()` is called at the completion of the ISR from the last nested ISR (see Section 3.10, "Interrupts Under μC/OS-II").

7.04   Getting a Semaphore Without Waiting (Non-blocking), `OSSemAccept()`

It is possible to obtain a semaphore without putting a task to sleep if the semaphore is not available. This action is accomplished by calling `OSSemAccept()`, as shown in Listing 7.5.

Listing 7.5   Getting a semaphore without waiting.

```
INT16U  OSSemAccept (OS_EVENT *pevent)
{
#if OS_CRITICAL_METHOD == 3
    OS_CPU_SR  cpu_sr;
#endif
    INT16U     cnt;


#if OS_ARG_CHK_EN > 0
    if (pevent == (OS_EVENT *)0) {                                    (1)
        return (0);
    }
    if (pevent->OSEventType != OS_EVENT_TYPE_SEM) {                   (2)
        return (0);
    }
#endif
    OS_ENTER_CRITICAL();
    cnt = pevent->OSEventCnt;                                         (3)
    if (cnt > 0) {                                                    (4)
        pevent->OSEventCnt--;                                         (5)
    }
    OS_EXIT_CRITICAL();
    return (cnt);                                                     (6)
}
```

7

L7.5(1)

L7.5(2)   If `OS_ARG_CHK_EN` is set to 1 in `OS_CFG.H`, `OSSemAccept()` starts by checking that `pevent` is not a `NULL` pointer and that the ECB being pointed to by `pevent` has been created by `OSSemCreate()`.

L7.5(3)

L7.5(4)   `OSSemAccept()` then gets the current semaphore count to determine whether the semaphore is available (i.e., a nonzero value).

L7.5(5)   The count is decremented only if the semaphore is available.

L7.5(6)   Finally, the original count of the semaphore is returned to the caller.

The code that calls `OSSemAccept()` needs to examine the returned value. A returned value of zero indicates that the semaphore is not available; a nonzero value indicates that the semaphore is available. Furthermore, a nonzero value indicates to the caller the number of resources that are available. Keep in mind that, in this case, one of the resources has been allocated to the calling task because the count has been decremented.

An ISR could use `OSSemAccept()`. However, it's not recommended to have a semaphore shared between a task and an ISR. Semaphores are supposed to be task-level objects. If a semaphore is used as a signalling object between an ISR and a task, the ISR should only `POST` to the semaphore.

7.05 *Obtaining the Status of a Semaphore,* `OSSemQuery()`

`OSSemQuery()` allows your application to take a snapshot of an ECB that is used as a semaphore (Listing 7.6). `OSSemQuery()` receives two arguments: `pevent` contains a pointer to the semaphore, which `OSSemCreate()` returns when the semaphore is created, and `pdata` is a pointer to a data structure (`OS_SEM_DATA`, see `uCOS_II.H`) that holds information about the semaphore. Your application thus needs to allocate a variable of type `OS_SEM_DATA` that is used to receive the information about the desired semaphore. I decided to use a new data structure because the caller should only be concerned with semaphore-specific data, as opposed to the more generic `OS_EVENT` data structure, which contains two additional fields (`.OSEventType` and `.OSEventPtr`). `OS_SEM_DATA` contains the current semaphore count (`.OSCnt`) and the list of tasks waiting on the semaphore (`.OSEventTbl[]` and `.OSEventGrp`).

Listing 7.6   *Obtaining the status of a semaphore.*

```
INT8U  OSSemQuery (OS_EVENT *pevent, OS_SEM_DATA *pdata)
{
#if OS_CRITICAL_METHOD == 3
    OS_CPU_SR  cpu_sr;
#endif
    INT8U      *psrc;
    INT8U      *pdest;
```

Listing 7.6   *Obtaining the status of a semaphore. (Continued)*

```c
#if OS_ARG_CHK_EN > 0
    if (pevent == (OS_EVENT *)0) {                                  (1)
        return (OS_ERR_PEVENT_NULL);
    }
    if (pevent->OSEventType != OS_EVENT_TYPE_SEM) {                 (2)
        return (OS_ERR_EVENT_TYPE);
    }
#endif
    OS_ENTER_CRITICAL();
    pdata->OSEventGrp = pevent->OSEventGrp;                         (3)
    psrc              = &pevent->OSEventTbl[0];
    pdest             = &pdata->OSEventTbl[0];
#if OS_EVENT_TBL_SIZE > 0
    *pdest++          = *psrc++;
#endif

#if OS_EVENT_TBL_SIZE > 1
    *pdest++          = *psrc++;
#endif

#if OS_EVENT_TBL_SIZE > 2
    *pdest++          = *psrc++;
#endif

#if OS_EVENT_TBL_SIZE > 3
    *pdest++          = *psrc++;
#endif

#if OS_EVENT_TBL_SIZE > 4
    *pdest++          = *psrc++;
#endif

#if OS_EVENT_TBL_SIZE > 5
    *pdest++          = *psrc++;
#endif

#if OS_EVENT_TBL_SIZE > 6
    *pdest++          = *psrc++;
#endif
```

7

Listing 7.6   *Obtaining the status of a semaphore. (Continued)*

```
#if OS_EVENT_TBL_SIZE > 7
    *pdest             = *psrc;
#endif
    pdata->OSCnt       = pevent->OSEventCnt;                           (4)
    OS_EXIT_CRITICAL();
    return (OS_NO_ERR);
}
```

L7.6(1)

L7.6(2)   As always, if OS_ARG_CHK_EN is set to 1, OSSemQuery() checks that pevent is not a NULL pointer and that it points to an ECB containing a semaphore.

L7.6(3)   OSSemQuery() then copies the wait list from the OS_EVENT structure to the OS_SEM_DATA structure. You should note that I decided to do the copy as inline code instead of using a loop for performance reasons.

L7.6(4)   Finally, OSSemQuery() copies the current semaphore count from the OS_EVENT structure to the OS_SEM_DATA structure.

Chapter 8

Mutual Exclusion Semaphores

Mutual exclusion semaphores (*mutexes*) are used by tasks to gain exclusive access to resources. Mutexes are binary semaphores that have additional features beyond the normal semaphores mechanism provided by µC/OS-II.

A mutex is used by your application code to reduce the priority inversion problem as described in Section 2.16. A priority inversion occurs when a low priority task owns a resource needed by a high priority task. In order to reduce priority inversion, the kernel can increase the priority of the lower priority task to the priority of the higher priority task until the lower priority task is done with the resource.

In order to implement mutexes, a real-time kernel needs to provide the ability to support multiple tasks at the same priority. Unfortunately, µC/OS-II doesn't allow multiple tasks at the same priority. However, there is a way around this problem. What if a priority just above the highest priority task that needs to access the mutex was reserved by the mutex to allow a lower priority task to be raised in priority?

Let's use an example to illustrate how µC/OS-II mutexes work. Listing 8.1 shows three tasks that might need to access a common resource. To access the resource, each task must pend on the mutex ResourceMutex. Task #1 has the highest priority (10), task #2 has a medium priority (15), and task #3, the lowest (20). An unused priority just above the highest task priority (i.e., priority 9) is reserved as the priority inheritance priority (PIP).

Listing 8.1   *Mutex use example.*

```
OS_EVENT *ResourceMutex;
OS_STK    TaskPrio10Stk[1000];
OS_STK    TaskPrio15Stk[1000];
OS_STK    TaskPrio20Stk[1000];
```

Listing 8.1   *Mutex use example. (Continued)*

```
void main (void)
{
    INT8U err;


    OSInit();                                                           (1)
    ---------- Application Initialization ----------
    OSMutexCreate(9, &err);                                             (2)
    OSTaskCreate(TaskPrio10, (void *)0, &TaskPrio10Stk[999], 10);       (3)
    OSTaskCreate(TaskPrio15, (void *)0, &TaskPrio15Stk[999], 15);
    OSTaskCreate(TaskPrio20, (void *)0, &TaskPrio20Stk[999], 20);
    ---------- Application Initialization ----------
    OSStart();                                                          (4)
}



void TaskPrio10 (void *pdata)                                   /* Task #1 */
{
    INT8U err;


    pdata = pdata;
    while (1) {
        --------- Application Code ----------
        OSMutexPend(ResourceMutex, 0, &err);
        ------- Access common resource ------
        OSMutexPost(ResourceMutex);
        --------- Application Code ----------
    }
}
```

Listing 8.1   Mutex use example. (Continued)

```
void TaskPrio15 (void *pdata)                                    /* Task #2 */
{
    INT8U err;


    pdata = pdata;
    while (1) {
        --------- Application Code ----------
        OSMutexPend(ResourceMutex, 0, &err);
        ------- Access common resource ------
        OSMutexPost(ResourceMutex);
        --------- Application Code ----------
    }
}


void TaskPrio20 (void *pdata)                                    /* Task #3 */
{
    INT8U err;


    pdata = pdata;
    while (1) {
        --------- Application Code ----------
        OSMutexPend(ResourceMutex, 0, &err);
        ------- Access common resource ------
        OSMutexPost(ResourceMutex);
        --------- Application Code ----------
    }
}
```

8

L8.1(1)

L8.1(2)   As shown in main(), μC/OS-II is initialized and a mutex is created by calling OSMutexCreate().
You should note that OSMutexCreate() is passed the PIP (i.e., 9).

L8.1(3)

L8.1(4)   The three tasks are then created, and μC/OS-II is started.

Suppose that this application has been running for a while and that, at some point, task #3 accesses
the common resource first and thus acquires the mutex. Task #3 runs for a while and then gets preempted by task #1. Task #1 needs the resource and thus attempts to acquire the mutex (by calling
OSMutexPend()). In this case, OSMutexPend() notices that a higher priority task needs the resource

and thus raises the priority of task #3 to 9, which forces a context switch back to task #3. Task #3 proceeds and hopefully releases the resource quickly. When done with the resource, task #3 calls `OSMutexPost()` to release the mutex. `OSMutexPost()` notices that the mutex was owned by a lower priority task that got its priority raised and thus, returns task #3 to its original priority. `OSMutexPost()` notices that a higher priority task (i.e., task #1) needs access to the resource, gives the resource to task #1, and perform a context switch to task #1.

µC/OS-II's mutexes consist of three elements: a flag indicating whether the mutex is available (0 or 1), a priority to assign the task that owns the mutex in case a higher priority task attempts to gain access to the mutex, and a list of tasks waiting for the mutex.

µC/OS-II provides six services to access mutexes: `OSMutexCreate()`, `OSMutexDel()`, `OSMutexPend()`, `OSMutexPost()`, `OSMutexAccept()`, and `OSMutexQuery()`.

To enable µC/OS-II mutex services, you must set the configuration constants in `OS_CFG.H`. Specifically, Table 8.1 shows which services are compiled, based on the value of configuration constants found in `OS_CFG.H`. You should note that **none** of the mutex services are enabled when `OS_MUTEX_EN` is set to 0. To enable specific features (i.e., services) listed in Table 8.1, set the configuration constant to 1. You should notice that `OSMutexCreate()`, `OSMutexPend()`, and `OSMutexPost()` cannot be individually disabled as can the other services. That's because they are always needed when you enable µC/OS-II's mutual exclusion semaphore management.

Table 8.1   *Mutex configuration constants in* `OS_CFG.H`.

µC/OS-II mutex service	*Enabled when set to* 1 *in* `OS_CFG.H`
`OSMutexAccept()`	`OS_MUTEX_ACCEPT_EN`
`OSMutexCreate()`	
`OSMutexDel()`	`OS_MUTEX_DEL_EN`
`OSMutexPend()`	
`OSMutexPost()`	
`OSMutexQuery()`	`OS_MUTEX_QUERY_EN`

Figure 8.1 shows a flow diagram to illustrate the relationship between tasks and a mutex. A mutex can only be accessed by tasks. Note that the symbology used to represent a mutex is a *key*. The key symbology shows that the mutex is used to access shared resources.

Figure 8.1   *Relationship between tasks and a mutex.*

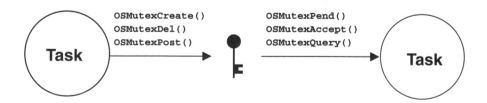

8.00 Creating a Mutex, OSMutexCreate()

A mutex needs to be created before it can be used. Creating a mutex is accomplished by calling OSMutexCreate(). The initial value of a mutex is always set to 1, which indicates that the resource is available. The code to create a mutex is shown in Listing 8.2.

Listing 8.2   Creating a mutex.

```
OS_EVENT *OSMutexCreate (INT8U prio, INT8U *err)
{
#if OS_CRITICAL_METHOD == 3
    OS_CPU_SR  cpu_sr;
#endif
    OS_EVENT *pevent;


    if (OSIntNesting > 0) {                                          (1)
        *err = OS_ERR_CREATE_ISR;
        return ((OS_EVENT *)0);
    }
#if OS_ARG_CHK_EN
    if (prio >= OS_LOWEST_PRIO) {                                    (2)
        *err = OS_PRIO_INVALID;
        return ((OS_EVENT *)0);
    }
#endif
    OS_ENTER_CRITICAL();
    if (OSTCBPrioTbl[prio] != (OS_TCB *)0) {                         (3)
        *err = OS_PRIO_EXIST;
        OS_EXIT_CRITICAL();
        return ((OS_EVENT *)0);
    }
    OSTCBPrioTbl[prio] = (OS_TCB *)1;                                (4)
    pevent             = OSEventFreeList;                            (5)
    if (pevent == (OS_EVENT *)0) {
        OSTCBPrioTbl[prio] = (OS_TCB *)0;
        OS_EXIT_CRITICAL();
        *err               = OS_ERR_PEVENT_NULL;
        return (pevent);
    }
    OSEventFreeList    = (OS_EVENT *)OSEventFreeList->OSEventPtr;     (6)
    OS_EXIT_CRITICAL();
```

8

Listing 8.2   Creating a mutex. (Continued)

```
pevent->OSEventType = OS_EVENT_TYPE_MUTEX;                              (7)
pevent->OSEventCnt  = (prio << 8) | OS_MUTEX_AVAILABLE;                 (8)
pevent->OSEventPtr  = (void *)0;                                       (9)
OSEventWaitListInit(pevent);                                          (10)
*err                = OS_NO_ERR;
return (pevent);                                                      (11)


    }
}
```

L8.2(1)   OSMutexCreate() starts by making sure it's not called from an ISR because that's not allowed.

L8.2(2)   OSMutexCreate() then verifies that the PIP is within a valid range, based on what you determined the lowest priority is for your application, as specified in OS_CFG.H.

L8.2(3)   OSMutexCreate() then checks to see that there isn't already a task assigned to the PIP. A NULL pointer in OSTCBPrioTbl[] indicates that the PIP is available.

L8.2(4)   If an entry is available, OSMutexCreate() reserves the priority by placing a non-NULL pointer in OSTCBPrioTbl[prio]. This action prevents you from using this priority to create other tasks or other mutexes using this priority.

L8.2(5)   OSMutexCreate() then attempts to obtain an event control block (ECB) from the free list of ECBs.

L8.2(6)   The linked list of free ECBs is adjusted to point to the next free ECB.

L8.2(7)   If an ECB is available, the ECB type is set to OS_EVENT_TYPE_MUTEX. Other µC/OS-II services check this field to make sure that the ECB is of the proper type. This check prevents you from calling OSMutexPost() on an ECB created for use as a message mailbox, for example.

L8.2(8)   OSMutexCreate() then sets the mutex value to available, and the PIP is stored.

It is worth noting that the .OSEventCnt field is used differently. Specifically, the upper 8 bits of .OSEventCnt are used to hold the PIP, and the lower 8 bits are used to hold either the value of the mutex when the resource is available (0xFF) or the priority of the task that owns the mutex (a value between 0 and 62). This configuration prevents having to add extra fields in an OS_EVENT structure and thus reduces the amount of RAM needed by µC/OS-II.

L8.2(9)   Because the mutex is being initialized, no tasks are waiting for it.

L8.2(10)   The wait list is then initialized by calling OSEventWaitListInit().

L8.2(11)   Finally, OSMutexCreate() returns a pointer to the ECB. This pointer **must** be used in subsequent calls to manipulate mutexes (OSMutexPend(), OSMutexPost(), OSMutexAccept(), OSMutexDel(), and OSMutexQuery()). The pointer is used as the mutex's handle. If there were no more ECBs, OSMutexCreate() would have returned a NULL pointer.

Figure 8.2 shows the ECB just before returning from OSMutexCreate().

Figure 8.2   *ECB just before* OSMutexCreate() *returns.*

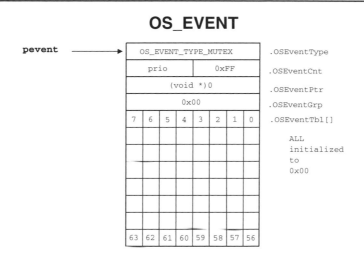

8.01   *Deleting a Mutex,* OSMutexDel()

The code to delete a mutex is shown in Listing 8.3, this service is available only if OS_MUTEX_DEL_EN is set to 1 in OS_CFG.H. This function is dangerous to use because multiple tasks could attempt to access a deleted mutex. You should always use this function with great care. Generally speaking, before you delete a mutex, you should first delete all the tasks that can access the mutex.

Listing 8.3   *Deleting a mutex.*

```
OS_EVENT  *OSMutexDel (OS_EVENT *pevent, INT8U opt, INT8U *err)
{
#if OS_CRITICAL_METHOD == 3
    OS_CPU_SR  cpu_sr;
#endif
    BOOLEAN    tasks_waiting;


    if (OSIntNesting > 0) {                                              (1)
        *err = OS_ERR_DEL_ISR;
        return (pevent);
    }
#if OS_ARG_CHK_EN
    if (pevent == (OS_EVENT *)0) {                                      (2)
        *err = OS_ERR_PEVENT_NULL;
        return (pevent);
    }
```

Listing 8.3   Deleting a mutex. (Continued)

```
    if (pevent->OSEventType != OS_EVENT_TYPE_MUTEX) {            (3)
        OS_EXIT_CRITICAL();
        *err = OS_ERR_EVENT_TYPE;
        return (pevent);
    }
#endif
    OS_ENTER_CRITICAL();
    if (pevent->OSEventGrp != 0x00) {                            (4)
        tasks_waiting = TRUE;
    } else {
        tasks_waiting = FALSE;
    }
    switch (opt) {
        case OS_DEL_NO_PEND:
            if (tasks_waiting == FALSE) {                        (5)
                pevent->OSEventType = OS_EVENT_TYPE_UNUSED;      (6)
                pevent->OSEventPtr  = OSEventFreeList;           (7)
                OSEventFreeList     = pevent;
                OS_EXIT_CRITICAL();
                *err = OS_NO_ERR;
                return ((OS_EVENT *)0);                          (8)
            } else {
                OS_EXIT_CRITICAL();
                *err = OS_ERR_TASK_WAITING;
                return (pevent);
            }

        case OS_DEL_ALWAYS:                                      (9)
            while (pevent->OSEventGrp != 0x00) {                 (10)
                OS_EventTaskRdy(pevent, (void *)0, OS_STAT_MUTEX);
            }
            pevent->OSEventType = OS_EVENT_TYPE_UNUSED;          (11)
            pevent->OSEventPtr  = OSEventFreeList;               (12)
            OSEventFreeList     = pevent;
            OS_EXIT_CRITICAL();
            if (tasks_waiting == TRUE) {                         (13)
                OS_Sched();
            }
            *err = OS_NO_ERR;
            return ((OS_EVENT *)0);                              (14)
```

Listing 8.3 *Deleting a mutex. (Continued)*

```
        default:
            OS_EXIT_CRITICAL();
            *err = OS_ERR_INVALID_OPT;
            return (pevent);
    }
}
```

L8.3(1)   OSMutexDel() makes sure that this function is not called from an ISR because that's not allowed.

L8.3(2)

L8.3(3)   We then check the arguments passed to it — pevent cannot be a NULL pointer, and pevent needs to point to a mutex.

L8.3(4)   OSMutexDel() then determines whether any tasks are waiting on the mutex. The flag tasks_waiting is set accordingly

Based on the option (i.e., opt) specified in the call, OSMutexDel() either deletes the mutex only if no tasks are pending on the mutex (opt == OS_DEL_NO_PEND) or deletes the mutex even if tasks are waiting (opt == OS_DEL_ALWAYS).

L8.3(5)

L8.3(6)

L8.3(7)   When opt is set to OS_DEL_NO_PEND and no task is waiting on the mutex, OSMutexDel() marks the ECB as unused, and the ECB is returned to the free list of ECBs. This process allows another mutex (or any other ECB-based object) to be created. You should note that OSMutexDel() returns a NULL pointer [L8.3(8)] because, at this point, the mutex should no longer be accessed through the original pointer.

L8.3(9)

L8.3(10)   When opt is set to OS_DEL_ALWAYS, all tasks waiting on the mutex are readied. Each task thinks it has access to the mutex. Of course, that's a dangerous outcome because the whole point of having a mutex is to protect against multiple accesses of a resource. Again, you should delete all the tasks that can access the mutex before you delete the mutex.

L8.3(11)

L8.3(12)   After all pending tasks are readied, OSMutexDel() marks the ECB as unused, and the ECB is returned to the free list of ECBs.

L8.3(13)   The scheduler is called only if tasks were waiting on the mutex.

L8.3(14)   You should note that OSMutexDel() returns a NULL pointer because, at this point, the mutex should no longer be accessed through the original pointer.

8

8.02   *Waiting on a Mutex (Blocking),* `OSMutexPend( )`

The code to wait on a mutex is shown in Listing 8.4.

Listing 8.4   *Waiting for a mutex.*

```
void OSMutexPend (OS_EVENT *pevent, INT16U timeout, INT8U *err)
{
#if OS_CRITICAL_METHOD == 3
    OS_CPU_SR  cpu_sr;
#endif
    INT8U      pip;
    INT8U      mprio;
    BOOLEAN    rdy;
    OS_TCB     *ptcb;


    if (OSIntNesting > 0) {                                              (1)
        *err = OS_ERR_PEND_ISR;
        return;
    }
#if OS_ARG_CHK_EN
    if (pevent == (OS_EVENT *)0) {                                       (2)
        *err = OS_ERR_PEVENT_NULL;
        return;
    }
#endif
    OS_ENTER_CRITICAL();
#if OS_ARG_CHK_EN
    if (pevent->OSEventType != OS_EVENT_TYPE_MUTEX) {                    (3)
        OS_EXIT_CRITICAL();
        *err = OS_ERR_EVENT_TYPE;
        return;
    }
#endif
                                                                        (4)
    if ((INT8U)(pevent->OSEventCnt & OS_MUTEX_KEEP_LOWER_8) == OS_MUTEX_AVAILABLE) {
        pevent->OSEventCnt &= OS_MUTEX_KEEP_UPPER_8;                     (5)
        pevent->OSEventCnt |= OSTCBCur->OSTCBPrio;                       (6)
        pevent->OSEventPtr  = (void *)OSTCBCur;                          (7)
        OS_EXIT_CRITICAL();
        *err  = OS_NO_ERR;
        return;
    }
```

Listing 8.4   *Waiting for a mutex. (Continued)*

```
    pip    = (INT8U)(pevent->OSEventCnt >> 8);                              (8)
    mprio  = (INT8U)(pevent->OSEventCnt & OS_MUTEX_KEEP_LOWER_8);           (9)
    ptcb   = (OS_TCB *)(pevent->OSEventPtr);                                (10)

    if (ptcb->OSTCBPrio != pip && mprio > OSTCBCur->OSTCBPrio) {            (11)
        if ((OSRdyTbl[ptcb->OSTCBY] & ptcb->OSTCBBitX) != 0x00) {          (12)
                                                                           (13)


            if ((OSRdyTbl[ptcb->OSTCBY] &= ~ptcb->OSTCBBitX) == 0x00) {
                OSRdyGrp &= ~ptcb->OSTCBBitY;
            }
            rdy = TRUE;                                                     (14)
        } else {
            rdy = FALSE;                                                    (15)
        }
        ptcb->OSTCBPrio      = pip;                                         (16)
        ptcb->OSTCBY         = ptcb->OSTCBPrio >> 3;
        ptcb->OSTCBBitY      = OSMapTbl[ptcb->OSTCBY];
        ptcb->OSTCBX         = ptcb->OSTCBPrio & 0x07;
        ptcb->OSTCBBitX      = OSMapTbl[ptcb->OSTCBX];
        if (rdy == TRUE) {                                                 (17)
            OSRdyGrp              |= ptcb->OSTCBBitY;
            OSRdyTbl[ptcb->OSTCBY] |= ptcb->OSTCBBitX;
        }
        OSTCBPrioTbl[pip]    = (OS_TCB *)ptcb;
    }
    OSTCBCur->OSTCBStat |= OS_STAT_MUTEX;                                   (18)
    OSTCBCur->OSTCBDly   = timeout;                                         (19)
    OS_EventTaskWait(pevent);                                              (20)
    OS_EXIT_CRITICAL();
    OS_Sched();                                                            (21)
    OS_ENTER_CRITICAL();
    if (OSTCBCur->OSTCBStat & OS_STAT_MUTEX) {                              (22)
        OS_EventTO(pevent);                                                (23)
        OS_EXIT_CRITICAL();
        *err = OS_TIMEOUT;                                                 (24)
        return;
    }
    OSTCBCur->OSTCBEventPtr = (OS_EVENT *)0;                                (25)
    OS_EXIT_CRITICAL();
    *err = OS_NO_ERR;
}
```

L8.4(1)   Like all µC/OS-II `pend` calls, `OSMutexPend()` cannot be called from an ISR, and thus `OSMutexPend()` checks for this condition first.

L8.4(2)

L8.4(3)   Assuming that the configuration constant `OS_ARG_CHK_EN` is set to 1, `OSMutexPend()` makes sure that the handle `pevent` is not a `NULL` pointer and that `OSMutexCreate()` has created the ECB being pointed to.

L8.4(4)

L8.4(5)

L8.4(6)   The mutex is available if the lower 8 bits of `.OSEventCnt` are set to `0xFF` (i.e., `OS_MUTEX_AVAILABLE`). If this is the case, `OSMutexPend()` grants the mutex to the calling task, and `OSMutexPend()` sets the lower 8 bits of `.OSEventCnt` to the calling task's priority.

L8.4(7)   `OSMutexPend()` then sets `.OSEventPtr` to point to the TCB of the calling task and returns. At this point, the caller can proceed with accessing the resource because the return error code is set to `OS_NO_ERR`. Obviously, if you want the mutex, this is the outcome you want. This also happens to be the fastest (normal) path through `OSMutexPend()`.

   If the mutex is owned by another task, the calling task needs to be put to sleep until the other task relinquishes the mutex [see `OSMutexPost()`]. `OSMutexPend()` allows you to specify a timeout value as one of its arguments (i.e., `timeout`). This feature is useful to avoid waiting indefinitely for the mutex. If the value passed is nonzero, then `OSMutexPend()` suspends the task until the mutex is signaled or the specified timeout period expires. Note that a timeout value of 0 indicates that the task is willing to wait forever for the mutex to be signaled.

L8.4(8)

L8.4(9)

L8.4(10)   Before the calling task is put to sleep, `OSMutexPend()` extracts the PIP of the mutex, the priority of the task that owns the mutex, and a pointer to the TCB of the task that owns the mutex.

L8.4(11)   If the owner's priority is lower (a higher number) than the task that calls `OSMutexPend()` then the priority of the task that owns the mutex is raised to the mutex's PIP. This action allows the owner of the mutex to relinquish the mutex sooner.

L8.4(12)   `OSMutexPend()` then determines if the task that owns the mutex is ready to run.

L8.4(13)

L8.4(14)   If the task is ready to run, that task is made no longer ready to run at the owner's priority, and the flag `rdy` is set indicating that the mutex owner was ready to run.

L8.4(15)   If the task was not ready to run, `rdy` is set accordingly. The reason the flag is set is to determine whether we need to make the task ready to run at the new, higher priority (i.e., at the PIP).

L8.4(16)   `OSMutexPend()` then computes task control block (TCB) elements at the PIP. You should note that I could have saved this information in the `OS_EVENT` data structure when the mutex was created in order to save processing time. However, saving this would have meant additional RAM for each `OS_EVENT` instantiation.

L8.4(17)   From this information and the state of the `rdy` flag, we determine whether the mutex owner needs to be made ready to run at the PIP.

L8.4(18) To put the calling task to sleep, `OSMutexPend()` sets the status flag in the task's TCB to indicate that the task is suspended while waiting for a mutex.

L8.4(19) The timeout is also stored in the TCB so that it can be decremented by `OSTimeTick()`. You should recall that `OSTimeTick()` decrements each of the created tasks `.OSTCBDly` fields if they are nonzero.

L8.4(20) The actual work of putting the task to sleep is done by `OS_EventTaskWait()`.

L8.4(21) Because the calling task is no longer ready to run, the scheduler is called to run the next highest priority task that is ready to run.

When the mutex is signaled (or the timeout period expires) and the task that called `OSMutexPend()` is again the highest priority task, `OS_Sched()` returns.

L8.4(22) `OSMutexPend()` then checks to see if the TCB's status flag is still set to indicate that the task is waiting for the mutex. If the task is still waiting for the mutex, then it must not have been signaled by an `OSMutexPost()` call. Indeed, the task must have be readied by `OSTimeTick()`, which indicates that the timeout period has expired.

L8.4(23)

L8.4(24) In this case, the task is removed from the wait list for the mutex by calling `OS_EventTO()`, and an error code is returned to the task that called `OSMutexPend()` to indicate that a timeout occurred.

If the status flag in the task's TCB doesn't have the `OS_STAT_MUTEX` bit set, then the mutex must have been signaled, and the task that called `OSMutexPend()` can now conclude that it has the mutex.

L8.4(25) Finally, the link to the ECB is removed.

8.03   *Signaling a Mutex,* `OSMutexPost()`

The code to signal a mutex is shown in Listing 8.5.

Listing 8.5   Signaling a mutex.

```
INT8U OSMutexPost (OS_EVENT *pevent)
{
#if OS_CRITICAL_METHOD == 3
    OS_CPU_SR  cpu_sr;
#endif
    INT8U      pip;
    INT8U      prio;


    if (OSIntNesting > 0) {                                                  (1)
        return (OS_ERR_POST_ISR);
    }
```

Listing 8.5   Signaling a mutex. (Continued)

```
#if OS_ARG_CHK_EN
    if (pevent == (OS_EVENT *)0) {                                              (2)
        return (OS_ERR_PEVENT_NULL);
    }
#endif
    OS_ENTER_CRITICAL();
    pip  = (INT8U)(pevent->OSEventCnt >> 8);
    prio = (INT8U)(pevent->OSEventCnt & OS_MUTEX_KEEP_LOWER_8);
#if OS_ARG_CHK_EN
    if (pevent->OSEventType != OS_EVENT_TYPE_MUTEX) {                           (3)
        OS_EXIT_CRITICAL();
        return (OS_ERR_EVENT_TYPE);
    }
    if (OSTCBCur->OSTCBPrio != pip ||
        OSTCBCur->OSTCBPrio != prio) {                                         (4)
        OS_EXIT_CRITICAL();
        return (OS_ERR_NOT_MUTEX_OWNER);
    }
#endif
    if (OSTCBCur->OSTCBPrio == pip) {                                          (5)

                                                                              (6)

        if ((OSRdyTbl[OSTCBCur->OSTCBY] &= ~OSTCBCur->OSTCBBitX) == 0) {
            OSRdyGrp &= ~OSTCBCur->OSTCBBitY;
        }
        OSTCBCur->OSTCBPrio        = prio;
        OSTCBCur->OSTCBY           = prio >> 3;
        OSTCBCur->OSTCBBitY        = OSMapTbl[OSTCBCur->OSTCBY];
        OSTCBCur->OSTCBX           = prio & 0x07;
        OSTCBCur->OSTCBBitX        = OSMapTbl[OSTCBCur->OSTCBX];
        OSRdyGrp                   |= OSTCBCur->OSTCBBitY;
        OSRdyTbl[OSTCBCur->OSTCBY] |= OSTCBCur->OSTCBBitX;
        OSTCBPrioTbl[prio]         = (OS_TCB *)OSTCBCur;
    }
    OSTCBPrioTbl[pip] = (OS_TCB *)1;
    if (pevent->OSEventGrp != 0x00) {                                          (7)
                                                                              (8)
        prio               = OS_EventTaskRdy(pevent, (void *)0, OS_STAT_MUTEX);
        pevent->OSEventCnt &= 0xFF00;                                          (9)
        pevent->OSEventCnt |= prio;
```

Listing 8.5   Signaling a mutex. (Continued)

```
       pevent->OSEventPtr  = OSTCBPrioTbl[prio];
       OS_EXIT_CRITICAL();
       OS_Sched();                                                      (10)
       return (OS_NO_ERR);
   }
   pevent->OSEventCnt |= 0x00FF;                                        (11)
   pevent->OSEventPtr  = (void *)0;
   OS_EXIT_CRITICAL();
   return (OS_NO_ERR);
}
```

L8.5(1)   Mutual exclusion semaphores must only be used by tasks, and thus a check is performed to make sure that `OSMutexPost()` is not called from an ISR.

L8.5(2)

L8.5(3)   Assuming that the configuration constant `OS_ARG_CHK_EN` is set to 1, `OSMutexPost()` checks that the handle `pevent` is not a `NULL` pointer and that `OSMutexCreate()` created the ECB being pointed to.

L8.5(4)   `OSMutexPost()` makes sure that the task that is signaling the mutex actually owns the mutex. The owner's priority must either be set to the PIP (`OSMutexPend()` could have raised the owner's priority) or the priority stored in the mutex itself.

L8.5(5)   `OSMutexPost()` then checks to see if the priority of the mutex owner had to be raised to the PIP because a higher priority task attempted to access the mutex. In this case, the priority of the owner is reduced to its original value. The original task priority is extracted from the lower 8 bits of `.OSEventCnt`.

L8.5(6)   The calling task is removed from the ready list at the PIP and placed in the ready list at the task's original priority. Note that the TCB fields are recomputed for the original task priority.

L8.5(7)   Next, we check to see if any tasks are waiting on the mutex. Tasks are waiting when the `.OSEventGrp` field in the ECB contains a nonzero value.

L8.5(8)   The highest priority task waiting for the mutex is removed from the wait list by `OS_EventTaskRdy()` [see Section 6.05, "Making a Task Ready, `OS_EventTaskRdy()`"], and this task is ready to run.

L8.5(9)   The priority of the new owner is saved in the mutex's ECB.

L8.5(10)   `OS_Sched()` is then called to see if the task made ready is now the highest priority task ready to run. If it is, a context switch results, and the readied task is resumed. If the readied task is not the highest priority task, then `OS_Sched()` returns, and the task that called `OSMutexPost()` will continue execution.

L8.5(11)   If no tasks are waiting on the mutex, the lower 8 bits of `.OSEventCnt` are set to `0xFF`, which indicates that the mutex is immediately available.

8

8.04   Getting a Mutex without Waiting (Non-blocking), *OSMutexAccept()*

It is possible to obtain a mutex without putting a task to sleep if the mutex is not available. This action is accomplished by calling OSMutexAccept(), and the code for this function is shown in Listing 8.6.

Listing 8.6   Getting a mutex without waiting.

```
INT8U OSMutexAccept (OS_EVENT *pevent, INT8U *err)
{
#if OS_CRITICAL_METHOD == 3
    OS_CPU_SR  cpu_sr;
#endif


    if (OSIntNesting > 0) {                                              (1)
        *err = OS_ERR_PEND_ISR;
        return (0);
    }
#if OS_ARG_CHK_EN
    if (pevent == (OS_EVENT *)0) {
        *err = OS_ERR_PEVENT_NULL;
        return (0);
    }
#endif
    OS_ENTER_CRITICAL();
#if OS_ARG_CHK_EN
    if (pevent->OSEventType != OS_EVENT_TYPE_MUTEX) {
        OS_EXIT_CRITICAL();
        *err = OS_ERR_EVENT_TYPE;
        return (0);
    }
#endif
    OS_ENTER_CRITICAL();
                                                                        (2)
```

Listing 8.6   *Getting a mutex without waiting. (Continued)*

```
    if ((pevent->OSEventCnt & OS_MUTEX_KEEP_LOWER_8) == OS_MUTEX_AVAILABLE) {
        pevent->OSEventCnt &= OS_MUTEX_KEEP_UPPER_8;                           (3)
        pevent->OSEventCnt |= OSTCBCur->OSTCBPrio;
        pevent->OSEventPtr  = (void *)OSTCBCur;                                (4)
        OS_EXIT_CRITICAL();
        *err = OS_NO_ERR;
        return (1);
    }
    OS_EXIT_CRITICAL();
    *err = OS_NO_ERR;
    return (0);
}
```

L8.6(1)   As with the other calls, if `OS_ARG_CHK_EN` is set to 1 in `OS_CFG.H`, `OSMutexAccept()` starts by ensuring that it's not called from an ISR and performs boundary checks.

L8.6(2)   `OSMutexAccept()` then checks to see if the mutex is available (the lower 8 bits of `.OSEventCnt` are set to `0xFF`).

L8.6(3)

L8.6(4)   If the mutex is available, `OSMutexAccept()` acquires the mutex by writing the priority of the mutex owner in the lower 8 bits of `.OSEventCnt` and by linking the owner's TCB.

The code that called `OSMutexAccept()` needs to examine the returned value. A returned value of 0 indicates that the mutex is not available. A return value of 1 indicates that the mutex is available, and the caller can access the resource.

8.05   *Obtaining the Status of a Mutex,* `OSMutexQuery()`

`OSMutexQuery()` allows your application to take a snapshot of an ECB that is used as a mutex. The code for this function is shown in Listing 8.7.

Listing 8.7   *Obtaining the status of a mutex.*

```
INT8U OSMutexQuery (OS_EVENT *pevent, OS_MUTEX_DATA *pdata)
{
#if OS_CRITICAL_METHOD == 3
    OS_CPU_SR  cpu_sr;
#endif
    INT8U     *psrc;
    INT8U     *pdest;
```

Listing 8.7   Obtaining the status of a mutex. (Continued)

```
    if (OSIntNesting > 0) {                                          (1)
        return (OS_ERR_QUERY_ISR);
    }
#if OS_ARG_CHK_EN
    if (pevent == (OS_EVENT *)0) {                                  (2)
        return (OS_ERR_PEVENT_NULL);
    }
#endif
    OS_ENTER_CRITICAL();
#if OS_ARG_CHK_EN
    if (pevent->OSEventType != OS_EVENT_TYPE_MUTEX) {               (3)
        OS_EXIT_CRITICAL();
        return (OS_ERR_EVENT_TYPE);
    }
#endif
    pdata->OSMutexPIP  = (INT8U)(pevent->OSEventCnt >> 8);          (4)
    pdata->OSOwnerPrio = (INT8U)(pevent->OSEventCnt & 0x00FF);
    if (pdata->OSOwnerPrio == 0xFF) {
        pdata->OSValue = 1;                                         (5)
    } else {
        pdata->OSValue = 0;                                         (6)
    }
    pdata->OSEventGrp  = pevent->OSEventGrp;                        (7)
    psrc               = &pevent->OSEventTbl[0];
    pdest              = &pdata->OSEventTbl[0];
#if OS_EVENT_TBL_SIZE > 0
    *pdest++           = *psrc++;
#endif

#if OS_EVENT_TBL_SIZE > 1
    *pdest++           = *psrc++;
#endif

#if OS_EVENT_TBL_SIZE > 2
    *pdest++           = *psrc++;
#endif

#if OS_EVENT_TBL_SIZE > 3
    *pdest++           = *psrc++;
#endif
```

Listing 8.7   Obtaining the status of a mutex. (Continued)

```
#if OS_EVENT_TBL_SIZE > 4
    *pdest++          = *psrc++;
#endif


#if OS_EVENT_TBL_SIZE > 5
    *pdest++          = *psrc++;
#endif


#if OS_EVENT_TBL_SIZE > 6
    *pdest++          = *psrc++;
#endif


#if OS_EVENT_TBL_SIZE > 7
    *pdest            = *psrc;
#endif
    OS_EXIT_CRITICAL();
    return (OS_NO_ERR);
}
```

8

OSMutexQuery() recieves two arguments: pevent contains a pointer to the mutex, which OSMutexCreate() returns when the mutex is created, and pdata, which is a pointer to a data structure (OS_MUTEX_DATA, see uCOS_II.H) that holds information about the mutex. Your application thus needs to allocate a variable of type OS_MUTEX_DATA that is used to receive the information about the desired mutex. I decided to use a new data structure because the caller should only be concerned with mutex-specific data, as opposed to the more generic OS_EVENT data structure. OS_MUTEX_DATA contains the mutex PIP (.OSMutexPIP), the priority of the task owning the mutex (.OSMutexPrio), and the value of the mutex (.OSMutexValue), which is set to 1 when the mutex is available and 0 if it's not. Note that .OSMutexPrio contains 0xFF if no task owns the mutex. Finally, OS_MUTEX_DATA contains the list of tasks waiting on the mutex (.OSEventTbl[] and .OSEventGrp).

L8.7(1)   As with all mutex calls, OSMutexQuery() determines whether the call is made from an ISR.

L8.7(2)

L8.7(3)   If the configuration constant OS_ARG_CHK_EN is set to 1, OSMutexQuery() checks that the handle pevent is not a NULL pointer and that OSMutexCreate() has created the ECB being pointed to.

L8.7(4)   OSMutexQuery() then loads the OS_MUTEX_DATA structure with the appropriate fields. We extract the PIP from the upper 8 bits of the .OSEventCnt field of the mutex.

L8.7(5)   Next, we obtain the mutex value from the lower 8 bits of the .OSEventCnt field of the mutex. If the mutex is available (i.e., lower 8 bits set to 0xFF), then the mutex value is assumed to be 1.

L8.7(6)   Otherwise, the mutex value is 0 (i.e., unavailable because it's owned by a task).

L8.7(7)   Finally, the mutex wait list is copied into the appropriate fields in OS_MUTEX_DATA. **For per**-formance reasons, I decided to use inline code instead of using a for loop.

Chapter 9

Event Flag Management

µC/OS-II event flags consist of two elements: a series of bits (either 8, 16, or 32) used to hold the current state of the events in the group and a list of tasks waiting for a combination of these bits to be either set (1) or cleared (0). µC/OS-II provides six services to access semaphores: `OSFlagAccept()`, `OSFlagCreate()`, `OSFlagDel()`, `OSFlagPend()`, `OSFlagPost()`, and `OSFlagQuery()`.

To enable µC/OS-II event-flag services, you must set the configuration constants in `OS_CFG.H`. Specifically, Table 9.1 shows which services are compiled, based on the value of configuration constants found in `OS_CFG.H`. You should note that **none** of the event flag services are enabled when `OS_FLAG_EN` is set to 0. To enable the feature (i.e., service), simply set the configuration constant to 1. You should notice that `OSFlagCreate()`, `OSFlagPend()`, and `OSFlagPost()` cannot be individually disabled like the other services because they are always needed when you enable µC/OS-II event flag management.

9

Table 9.1 **Event flag configuration constants in `OS_CFG.H`.**

µC/OS-II Event Flag Service	Enabled when set to 1 in `OS_CFG.H`
`OSFlagAccept()`	`OS_FLAG_ACCEPT_EN`
`OSFlagCreate()`	
`OSFlagDel()`	`OS_FLAG_DEL_EN`
`OSFlagPend()`	
`OSFlagPost()`	
`OSFlagQuery()`	`OS_FLAG_QUERY_EN`

Figure 9.1 shows a flow diagram to illustrate the relationship between tasks, ISRs, and event flags. Note that the symbology used to represent an event flag group is a series of 8 bits even though the event flag group can contain 8, 16, or 32 bits (see `OS_FLAGS` in `OS_CFG.H`). The hourglass represents a timeout that can be specified with the `OSFlagPend()` call.

As you can see from Figure 9.1, a task or an ISR can call `OSFlagAccept()`, `OSFlagPost()`, or `OSFlagQuery()`. However, only tasks are allowed to call `OSFlagCreate()`, `OSFlagDel()`, or `OSFlagPend()`.

199

Figure 9.1   µC/OS-II event flag services.

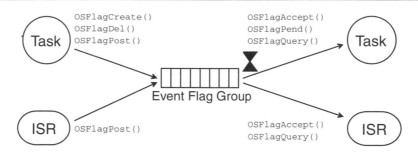

9.00   Event Flag Internals

A µC/OS-II's event flag group consist of three elements, as shown in the OS_FLAG_GRP structure (Listing 9.1).

Listing 9.1   Event flag group data structure.

```
typedef struct {
    INT8U    OSFlagType;                              (1)
    void    *OSFlagWaitList;                          (2)
    OS_FLAGS OSFlagFlags;                             (3)
} OS_FLAG_GRP;
```

L9.1(1)   .OSFlagType is a variable, which is used to make sure that you are pointing to an event flag group. This field is the first field of the structure because it allows µC/OS-II services to validate the type of structure to which you are pointing. For example, if you were to pass a pointer to an event flag group to OSSemPend(), µC/OS-II would return an error code indicating that you are not passing the proper object to the semaphore pend call. You should note that an event control block (ECB) also has its first byte containing the type of OS object (i.e., semaphore, mutex, message mailbox, or message queue).

L9.1(2)   .OSFlagWaitList contains a list of tasks waiting for events.

L9.1(3)   .OSFlagFlags is a series of flags (i.e., bits) that holds the current status of events. The number of bits used is decided at compile time and can either be 8, 16, or 32, depending on the data type you assign to OS_FLAGS in OS_CFG.H.

You should note that the wait list for event flags is different than the other wait lists in µC/OS-II. With event flags, the wait list is accomplished through a doubly linked list, as shown in Figure 9.2. Three data structures are involved. OS_FLAG_GRP (mentioned above), OS_TCB, which is the task control block, and OS_FLAG_NODE, which is used to keep track of the bits for which the task is waiting and the type of wait (AND or OR). As you can see, a lot of pointers are involved.

**Figure 9.2   *Relationship between event flag group, event flag nodes,
and TCBs.***

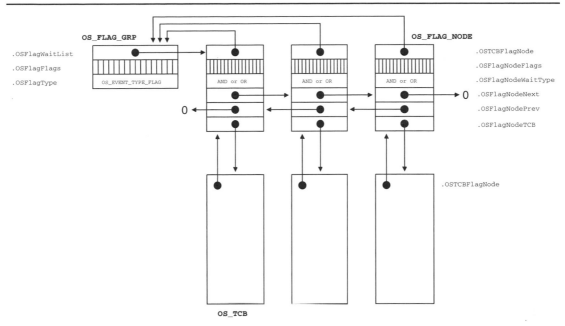

An OS_FLAG_NODE is created when a task desires to wait on bits of an event flag group, and the node is destroyed when the event(s) occur. In other words, a node is created by OSFlagPend() as we see shortly. Before we discuss this, let's look at the OS_FLAG_NODE data structure.

9

Listing 9.2   *Event flag group node data structure.*

```
typedef struct {
    void      *OSFlagNodeNext;                                        (1)
    void      *OSFlagNodePrev;
    void      *OSFlagNodeTCB;                                         (2)
    void      *OSFlagNodeFlagGrp;                                     (3)
    OS_FLAGS  OSFlagNodeFlags;                                        (4)
    INT8U     OSFlagNodeWaitType;                                     (5)
} OS_FLAG_NODE;
```

L9.2(1)   The .OSFlagNodeNext and .OSFlagNodePrev are used to maintain a doubly linked list of OS_FLAG_NODEs. The doubly linked list allows us to easily insert and especially remove nodes from the wait list.

L9.2(2)   .OSFlagNodeTCB is used to point to the TCB of the task waiting on flags belonging to the event flag group. In other words, this pointer allows us to know which task is waiting for the specified flags.

L9.2(3)   .OSFlagNodeFlagGrp allows a link back to the event flag group. This pointer is used when removing the node from the doubly linked list and is needed by OSTaskDel() when the pended task needs to be deleted.

L9.2(4)   The .OSFlagNodeFlags contains the bit-pattern of the flags for which the task is waiting. For example, your task might have performed an OSFlagPend() and specified that the task wants to wait for bits 0, 4, 6, and 7 (bit 0 is the rightmost bit). In this case, .OSFlagNodeFlags contains 0xD1. Depending on the size of the data type, OS_FLAGS, .OSFlagNodeFlags is either 8, 16, or 32 bits. OS_FLAGS is specified in your application configuration file, i.e., OS_CFG.H. Because µC/OS-II and the ports are provided in source form, you can easily change the number of bits in an event flag group to satisfy your requirements for a specific application or product. The reason you would limit the number of bits to 8 is to reduce both RAM and ROM for your application. However, for maximum portability of your applications, you should set OS_FLAGS to an INT32U data type.

L9.2(5)   The last member of the OS_FLAG_NODE data structure is OSFlagNodeWaitType, which determines whether the task is waiting for ALL (AND wait) the bits in the event flag group that match OSFlagNodeFlags or ANY (OR wait) of the bits in the event flag group that match OSFlagNodeFlags. OSFlagNodeWaitType can be set to

```
OS_FLAG_WAIT_CLR_ALL
OS_FLAG_WAIT_CLR_AND

OS_FLAG_WAIT_CLR_ANY
OS_FLAG_WAIT_CLR_OR

OS_FLAG_WAIT_SET_ALL
OS_FLAG_WAIT_SET_AND

OS_FLAG_WAIT_SET_ANY
OS_FLAG_WAIT_SET_OR
```

You should note that AND and ALL mean the same thing, and either one can be used. I prefer to use OS_FLAG_WAIT_???_ALL because it's more obvious, but you are certainly welcome to use OS_FLAG_WAIT_???_AND. Similarly, OR or ANY means the same thing, and either one can be used. Again, I prefer to use OS_FLAG_WAIT_???_ANY because it's more obvious, but, again, you can use OS_FLAG_WAIT_???_OR. The other thing to notice is that you can wait for either bits to be set or cleared.

9.01 Creating an Event Flag Group, `OSFlagCreate()`

The code to create an event flag group is shown in Listing 9.3.

Listing 9.3   *Creating an event flag group.*

```
OS_FLAG_GRP  *OSFlagCreate (OS_FLAGS flags, INT8U *err)
{
#if OS_CRITICAL_METHOD == 3
    OS_CPU_SR     cpu_sr;
#endif
    OS_FLAG_GRP *pgrp;


    If (OSIntNesting > 0) {                                              (1)
        *err = OS_ERR_CREATE_ISR;
        return ((OS_FLAG_GRP *)0);
    }
    OS_ENTER_CRITICAL();
    pgrp = OSFlagFreeList;                                              (2)
    if (pgrp != (OS_FLAG_GRP *)0) {                                     (3)
                                                                       (4)
        OSFlagFreeList        = (OS_FLAG_GRP *)OSFlagFreeList->OSFlagWaitList;
        pgrp->OSFlagType      = OS_EVENT_TYPE_FLAG;                     (5)
        pgrp->OSFlagFlags     = flags;                                  (6)
        pgrp->OSFlagWaitList = (void *)0;                              (7)
        OS_EXIT_CRITICAL();
        *err             = OS_NO_ERR;
    } else {
        OS_EXIT_CRITICAL();
        *err                 = OS_FLAG_GRP_DEPLETED;
    }
    return (pgrp);                                                      (8)
}
```

9

L9.3(1)   `OSFlagCreate()` starts by making sure it's not called from an ISR because that's not allowed.

L9.3(2)   `OSFlagCreate()` then attempts to get a free event flag group (i.e., an `OS_FLAG_GRP`) from the free list.

L9.3(3)   An non-`NULL` pointer indicates that an event flag group is available.

L9.3(4)   After a group is allocated, the free list pointer is adjusted. Note that the number of event flag groups that you can create is determined by the #define constant OS_MAX_FLAGS, which is defined in OS_CFG.H in your application.

L9.3(5)   OSFlagCreate() then fills in the fields in the event flag group. OS_EVENT_TYPE_FLAG indicates that this control block is an event flag group. Because this field is first in the data structure, it's at offset zero. In μC/OS-II, the first byte of an event flag group or an event control block used for semaphores, mailboxes, queues, and mutexes indicates the type of kernel object. This process allows us to check that we are pointing to the proper object.

L9.3(6)   OSFlagCreate() then stores the initial value of the event flags into the event flag group. Typically, you initialize the flags to all 0s, but, if you are checking for cleared bits then, you could initialize the flags to all 1s.

L9.3(7)   Because we are creating the group, no tasks are waiting on the group, and thus the wait list pointer is initialized to NULL.

L9.3(8)   The pointer to the created event flag group is returned. If no more groups are available, OSFlagCreate() returns a NULL pointer.

Figure 9.3   *Event flag group just before* OSFlagCreate() *returns.*

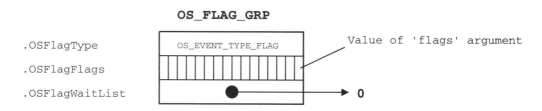

9.02   Deleting an Event Flag Group, OSFlagDel()

The code to delete an event flag group is shown in Listing 9.4.

Listing 9.4   Deleting an event flag group.

```
OS_FLAG_GRP  *OSFlagDel (OS_FLAG_GRP *pgrp, INT8U opt, INT8U *err)
{
#if OS_CRITICAL_METHOD == 3
    OS_CPU_SR      cpu_sr;
#endif
    BOOLEAN        tasks_waiting;
    OS_FLAG_NODE *pnode;
```

Listing 9.4   *Deleting an event flag group. (Continued)*

```
    if (OSIntNesting > 0) {                                          (1)
        *err = OS_ERR_DEL_ISR;
        return (pgrp);
    }
#if OS_ARG_CHK_EN > 0
    if (pgrp == (OS_FLAG_GRP *)0) {                                  (2)
        *err = OS_FLAG_INVALID_PGRP;
        return (pgrp);
    }
    if (pgrp->OSFlagType != OS_EVENT_TYPE_FLAG) {                    (3)
        *err = OS_ERR_EVENT_TYPE;
        return (pgrp);
    }
#endif
    OS_ENTER_CRITICAL();
    if (pgrp->OSFlagWaitList != (void *)0) {                         (4)
        tasks_waiting = TRUE;
    } else {
        tasks_waiting = FALSE;
    }
    switch (opt) {
        case OS_DEL_NO_PEND:                                         (5)
            if (tasks_waiting == FALSE) {
                pgrp->OSFlagType     = OS_EVENT_TYPE_UNUSED;
                pgrp->OSFlagWaitList = (void *)OSFlagFreeList;       (6)
                OSFlagFreeList       = pgrp;
                OS_EXIT_CRITICAL();
                *err                 = OS_NO_ERR;
                return ((OS_FLAG_GRP *)0);                           (7)
            } else {
                OS_EXIT_CRITICAL();
                *err                 = OS_ERR_TASK_WAITING;
                return (pgrp);
            }
```

9

Listing 9.4   Deleting an event flag group. (Continued)

```
          case OS_DEL_ALWAYS:                                              (8)
              pnode = pgrp->OSFlagWaitList;
              while (pnode != (OS_FLAG_NODE *)0) {                         (9)
                  OS_FlagTaskRdy(pnode, (OS_FLAGS)0);
                  pnode = pnode->OSFlagNodeNext;
              }
              pgrp->OSFlagType     = OS_EVENT_TYPE_UNUSED;
              pgrp->OSFlagWaitList = (void *)OSFlagFreeList;              (10)
              OSFlagFreeList       = pgrp;
              OS_EXIT_CRITICAL();
              if (tasks_waiting == TRUE) {                                (11)
                  OS_Sched();
              }
              *err = OS_NO_ERR;
              return ((OS_FLAG_GRP *)0);                                  (12)

          default:
              OS_EXIT_CRITICAL();
              *err = OS_ERR_INVALID_OPT;
              return (pgrp);
    }
}
```

You should use this function with caution because multiple tasks could attempt to access a deleted event flag group. Generally speaking, before you delete an event flag group, you first delete all the tasks that access the event flag group.

L9.4(1)   OSFlagDel() starts by making sure that this function is not called from an ISR because that's not allowed.

L9.4(2)

L9.4(3)   We then validate the arguments passed to OSFlagDel(). First, we make sure that pgrp is not a NULL pointer and that pgrp points to an event flag group. Note that this code is conditionally compiled, and thus, if OS_ARG_CHK_EN is set to 0, then this code is **not** compiled. This process is done to allow you to reduce the amount of code space needed by this module.

L9.4(4)   OSFlagDel() then determines whether any tasks are waiting on the event flag group and sets the local **boolean** variable tasks_waiting accordingly.

Based on the option (i.e., opt) passed in the call, OSFlagDel() either deletes the event flag group only if no tasks are pending on the event flag group (opt == OS_DEL_NO_PEND) or deletes the event flag group even if tasks are waiting (opt == OS_DEL_ALWAYS).

L9.4(5)

L9.4(6)   When `opt` is set to `OS_DEL_NO_PEND` and no task is waiting on the event flag group, `OSFlagDel()` marks the group as unused, and the event flag group is returned to the free list of groups. This process allows another event flag group to be created by reusing this event flag group.

L9.4(7)   You should note that `OSFlagDel()` returns a `NULL` pointer because, at this point, the event flag group should no longer be accessed through the original pointer.

L9.4(8)

L9.4(9)   When `opt` is set to `OS_DEL_ALWAYS`, all tasks waiting on the event flag group are readied. Each task thinks the event(s) that the task was waiting for occurred. We discuss `OS_FlagTaskRdy()` when we look at the code for `OSFlagPost()`.

L9.4(10)   After all pending tasks are readied, `OSFlagDel()` marks the event flag group as unused, and the group is returned to the free list of groups.

L9.4(11)   The scheduler is called only if tasks were waiting on the event flag group.

L9.4(12)   You should note that `OSFlagDel()` returns a `NULL` pointer because, at this point, the event flag group should no longer be accessed through the original pointer.

9.03   *Waiting for Event(s) of an Event Flag Group,* `OSFlagPend()`

The code to wait for event(s) of an event flag group is shown in Listing 9.5.

Listing 9.5   *Waiting for event(s) of an event flag group.*

```
OS_FLAGS  OSFlagPend (OS_FLAG_GRP *pgrp, OS_FLAGS flags, INT8U wait_type, INT16U timeout, INT8U *err)
{
#if OS_CRITICAL_METHOD == 3
    OS_CPU_SR       cpu_sr;
#endif
    OS_FLAG_NODE  node;
    OS_FLAGS      flags_cur;
    OS_FLAGS      flags_rdy;
    BOOLEAN       consume;


    if (OSIntNesting > 0) {                                 (1)
        *err = OS_ERR_PEND_ISR;
        return ((OS_FLAGS)0);
    }
#if OS_ARG_CHK_EN > 0
    if (pgrp == (OS_FLAG_GRP *)0) {                         (2)
        *err = OS_FLAG_INVALID_PGRP;
        return ((OS_FLAGS)0);
    }
```

9

Listing 9.5   Waiting for event(s) of an event flag group. (Continued)

```
        if (pgrp->OSFlagType != OS_EVENT_TYPE_FLAG) {                      (3)
            *err = OS_ERR_EVENT_TYPE;
            return ((OS_FLAGS)0);
        }
#endif
        if (wait_type & OS_FLAG_CONSUME) {                                 (4)
            wait_type &= ~OS_FLAG_CONSUME;
            consume    = TRUE;
        } else {
            consume    = FALSE;
        }
        OS_ENTER_CRITICAL();
        switch (wait_type) {                                              (5)
            case OS_FLAG_WAIT_SET_ALL:
                flags_rdy = pgrp->OSFlagFlags & flags;                    (6)
                if (flags_rdy == flags) {                                 (7)
                    if (consume == TRUE) {                                (8)
                        pgrp->OSFlagFlags &= ~flags_rdy;                  (9)
                    }
                    flags_cur = pgrp->OSFlagFlags;                        (10)
                    OS_EXIT_CRITICAL();
                    *err      = OS_NO_ERR;
                    return (flags_cur);                                   (11)
                } else {                                                  (12)
                    OS_FlagBlock(pgrp, &node, flags, wait_type, timeout);
                    OS_EXIT_CRITICAL();
                }
                break;

            case OS_FLAG_WAIT_SET_ANY:
                flags_rdy = pgrp->OSFlagFlags & flags;                    (13)
                if (flags_rdy != (OS_FLAGS)0) {                           (14)
                    if (consume == TRUE) {                                (15)
                        pgrp->OSFlagFlags &= ~flags_rdy;                  (16)
                    }
                    flags_cur = pgrp->OSFlagFlags;                        (17)
                    OS_EXIT_CRITICAL();
                    *err      = OS_NO_ERR;
                    return (flags_cur);                                   (18)
                } else {                                                  (19)
                    OS_FlagBlock(pgrp, &node, flags, wait_type, timeout);
                    OS_EXIT_CRITICAL();
                }
                break;
```

Listing 9.5   ***Waiting for event(s) of an event flag group. (Continued)***

```
#if OS_FLAG_WAIT_CLR_EN > 0
     case OS_FLAG_WAIT_CLR_ALL:
          flags_rdy = ~pgrp->OSFlagFlags & flags;
          if (flags_rdy == flags) {
              if (consume == TRUE) {
                  pgrp->OSFlagFlags |= flags_rdy;
              }
              flags_cur = pgrp->OSFlagFlags;
              OS_EXIT_CRITICAL();
              *err      = OS_NO_ERR;
              return (flags_cur);
          } else {
              OS_FlagBlock(pgrp, &node, flags, wait_type, timeout);
              OS_EXIT_CRITICAL();
          }
          break;

     case OS_FLAG_WAIT_CLR_ANY:
          flags_rdy = ~pgrp->OSFlagFlags & flags;
          if (flags_rdy != (OS_FLAGS)0) {
              if (consume == TRUE) {
                  pgrp->OSFlagFlags |= flags_rdy;
              }
              flags_cur = pgrp->OSFlagFlags;
              OS_EXIT_CRITICAL();
              *err      = OS_NO_ERR;
              return (flags_cur);
          } else {
              OS_FlagBlock(pgrp, &node, flags, wait_type, timeout);
              OS_EXIT_CRITICAL();
          }
          break;
#endif

     default:
          OS_EXIT_CRITICAL();
          flags_cur = (OS_FLAGS)0;
          *err      = OS_FLAG_ERR_WAIT_TYPE;
          return (flags_cur);
     }
     OS_Sched();                                                           (20)
     OS_ENTER_CRITICAL();
     if (OSTCBCur->OSTCBStat & OS_STAT_FLAG) {                             (21)
```

Listing 9.5   *Waiting for event(s) of an event flag group. (Continued)*

```
            OS_FlagUnlink(&node);                                                     (22)
            OSTCBCur->OSTCBStat = OS_STAT_RDY;
            OS_EXIT_CRITICAL();
            flags_cur          = (OS_FLAGS)0;
            *err               = OS_TIMEOUT;
        } else {
            if (consume == TRUE) {                                                    (23)
                switch (wait_type) {
                    case OS_FLAG_WAIT_SET_ALL:
                    case OS_FLAG_WAIT_SET_ANY:                                         (24)
                        pgrp->OSFlagFlags &= ~OSTCBCur->OSTCBFlagsRdy;
                        break;

                    case OS_FLAG_WAIT_CLR_ALL:
                    case OS_FLAG_WAIT_CLR_ANY:
                        pgrp->OSFlagFlags |= OSTCBCur->OSTCBFlagsRdy;
                        break;
                }
            }
            flags_cur = pgrp->OSFlagFlags;                                            (25)
            OS_EXIT_CRITICAL();
            *err      = OS_NO_ERR;
        }
    return (flags_cur);
}
```

L9.5(1)   As with all µC/OS-II `PEND` calls, `OSFlagPend()` cannot be called from an ISR, and thus `OSFlagPend()` checks for this condition first.

L9.5(2)

L9.5(3)   Assuming that the configuration constant `OS_ARG_CHK_EN` is set to 1, `OSFlagPend()` makes sure that the handle `pgrp` is not a `NULL` pointer and that `pgrp` points to an event flag group that should have been created by `OSFlagCreate()`.

OSFlagPend() allows you to specify whether you `SET` or `CLEAR` flags after they satisfy the condition for which you are waiting. This process is accomplished by ADDing (or ORing) `OS_FLAG_CONSUME` to the `wait_type` argument during the call to `OSFlagPend()`. For example, if you want to wait for `BIT0` to be `SET` in the event flag group and if `BIT0` is in fact `SET`, it is cleared by `OSFlagPend()` if you add `OS_FLAG_CONSUME` to the type of wait desired, as shown below

```
OSFlagPend(OSFlagMyGrp,
           (OS_FLAGS)0x01,
           FLAG_WAIT_SET_ANY + OS_FLAG_CONSUME,
           0,
           &err);
```

L9.5(4)   Because the consumption of the flag(s) is done later in the code, `OSFlagPend()` saves the consume option in the **boolean** variable called `consume`.

L9.5(5)   `OSFlagPend()` then executes code, based on the wait type specified in the function called. There are four choices:

> 1. wait for **all** bits specified to be **set** in the event flag group,
>
> 2. wait for **any** bit specified to be **set** in the event flag group,
>
> 3. wait for **all** bits specified to be **cleared** in the event flag group,
>
> 4. wait for **any** bit specified to be **cleared** in the event flag group.
>
> The last two choices are identical to the first two choices except that `OSFlagPend()` looks for the bits specified to be **cleared** (i.e., 0) instead of being **set** (i.e., 1). For this reason, I only discuss the first two choices. In fact, in order to conserve ROM, you might not need to look for bits to be cleared, and thus you can compile out all the corresponding code out by setting `OS_FLAG_WAIT_CLR_EN` to 0 in `OS_CFG.H`.

Wait for **all** of the specified bits to be **set**:

L9.5(6)   When `wait_type` is set to either `OS_FLAG_WAIT_SET_ALL` or `OS_FLAG_WAIT_SET_AND`, `OSFlagPend()` extracts the desired bits (which are specified in the flags argument) from the event flag group.

L9.5(7)   If all the bits extracted match the bits that you specified in the `flags` argument, then the event flags that the task wants are all set. Thus, the `PEND` call returns to the caller.

L9.5(8)

L9.5(9)   Before we return, we need to determine whether we need to consume the flags, and if so, we **clear** all the flags that satisfy the condition.

L9.5(10)

L9.5(11)   The new value of the event flag group is obtained and returned to the caller.

L9.5(12)   If **all** the desired bits in the event flag group were not **set**, then the calling task blocks (i.e., suspends) until **all** the bits are either **set** or a timeout occurs. Instead of repeating code for all four types of wait, I created a function [`OS_FlagBlock()`] to handle the details of blocking the calling task (described later).

Wait for **any** of the specified bits to be **set**:

L9.5(13)   When `wait_type` is set to either `OS_FLAG_WAIT_SET_ANY` or `OS_FLAG_WAIT_SET_OR`, `OSFlagPend()` extracts the desired bits (which are specified in the flags argument), from the event flag group.

L9.5(14)   If any of the bits extracted match the bits that you specified in the `flags` argument, then the `PEND` call returns to the caller.

L9.5(15)

L9.5(16)   Before we return, we need to determine whether we need to consume the flag(s), and if so, we need to **clear** all the flag(s) that satisfied the condition.

L9.5(17)

L9.5(18)   The new value of the event flag group is obtained and returned to the caller.

L9.5(19)   If **none** of the desired bits in the event flag group were not **set**, then the calling task will blocks (i.e., suspends) until **any** of the bits is either **set** or a timeout occurs.

9

As mentioned previously, if the desired bits and conditions of a PEND call are not satisfied the calling task is suspended until either the event or a timeout occurs. The task is suspended by OS_FlagBlock() (see Listing 9.6), which adds the calling task to the wait list of the event flag group. The process is shown in Figure 9.4.

Listing 9.6   Adding a task to the event flag group wait list.

```
static void OS_FlagBlock (OS_FLAG_GRP   *pgrp,
                          OS_FLAG_NODE  *pnode,
                          OS_FLAGS       flags,
                          INT8U          wait_type,
                          INT16U         timeout)
{
    OS_FLAG_NODE  *pnode_next;


    OSTCBCur->OSTCBStat      |= OS_STAT_FLAG;                               (1)
    OSTCBCur->OSTCBDly        = timeout;
#if OS_TASK_DEL_EN > 0
    OSTCBCur->OSTCBFlagNode   = pnode;                                      (2)
#endif
    pnode->OSFlagNodeFlags    = flags;                                     (3)
    pnode->OSFlagNodeWaitType = wait_type;
    pnode->OSFlagNodeTCB      = (void *)OSTCBCur;                          (4)
    pnode->OSFlagNodeNext     = pgrp->OSFlagWaitList;                      (5)
    pnode->OSFlagNodePrev     = (void *)0;                                 (6)
    pnode->OSFlagNodeFlagGrp  = (void *)pgrp;                              (7)
    pnode_next                = pgrp->OSFlagWaitList;
    if (pnode_next != (void *)0) {
        pnode_next->OSFlagNodePrev = pnode;                               (8)
    }
    pgrp->OSFlagWaitList = (void *)pnode;                                 (9)
                                                                         (10)

    if ((OSRdyTbl[OSTCBCur->OSTCBY] &= ~OSTCBCur->OSTCBBitX) == 0) {
        OSRdyGrp &= ~OSTCBCur->OSTCBBitY;
    }
}
```

L9.6(1)

F9.4(1)   OS_FlagBlock() starts by setting the appropriate fields in the task control block. You should note that an OS_FLAG_NODE is allocated on the stack of the calling task (see OSFlagPend(), Listing 9.5). This allocation means that we don't need to keep a separate free list of OS_FLAG_NODE because these data structures can simply be allocated on the stack of the calling task. That being said, the calling task must have sufficient stack space to allocate this structure on its stack.

L9.6(2)

F9.4(2)   We then link the `OS_FLAG_NODE` to the TCB but only if `OS_TASK_DEL_EN` is set to 1. This link allows `OSTaskDel()` to remove the task being suspended from the wait list, should another task decide to delete this task.

L9.6(3)

F9.4(3)   Next, `OS_FlagBlock()` saves the flags for which the task is waiting, as well as the wait type in the `OS_FLAG_NODE` structure.

Figure 9.4   *Adding the current task to the wait list of the event flag group.*

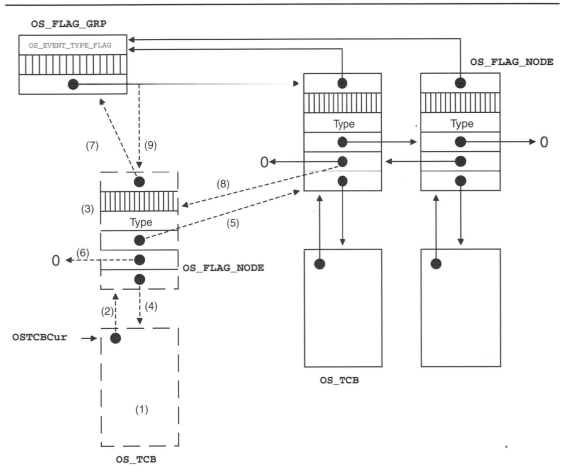

L9.6(4)

F9.4(4)   We then link the TCB to the `OS_FLAG_NODE`.

L9.6(5)

F9.4(5)   The `OS_FLAG_NODE` is then linked to the other `OS_FLAG_NODE`s in the wait list.

L9.6(6)

F9.4(6)   You should note that the `OS_FLAG_NODE` is simply inserted at the beginning of the doubly linked list for simplicity's sake.

L9.6(7)

F9.4(7)   We then link the event flag group to the `OS_FLAG_NODE`. This linkage is again done to allow us to delete the task that is being added to the wait list of the event flag group.

L9.6(8)

F9.4(8)   `OS_FlagBlock()` then links the previous first node in the wait list to the new `OS_FLAG_NODE`.

L9.6(9)

F9.4(9)

L9.6(10)   Finally, the pointer of the beginning of the wait list is updated to point to the new `OS_FLAG_NODE`, and the calling task is made **not** ready to run.

You should note that interrupts are disabled during the process of blocking the calling task.

L9.5(20)   When `OS_FlagBlock()` returns, the scheduler is called because, of course, the calling task is no longer able to run because the event(s) for which it was looking did not occur.

L9.5(21)   When μC/OS-II resumes the calling task, `OSFlagPend()` checks **how** the task was readied. If the status field in the TCB still indicates that the task is still waiting for event flags to be either set or cleared, then the task **must** have been readied because of a timeout.

L9.5(22)   In this case, the `OS_FLAG_NODE` is removed from the wait list by calling `OS_FlagUnlink()`, and an error code is returned to the caller indicating the outcome of the call. The code for `OS_FlagUnlink()` is not shown but should be quite obvious because we are simply removing a node from a doubly linked list. The code provided on the CD-ROM contains comments so you can easily follow what's going on.

L9.5(23)

L9.5(24)   If the calling task is **not** resumed because of a timeout, then it **must** have been resumed because the event flags for which it was waiting have been either set or cleared. In this case, we determine whether the calling task wanted to consume the event flags. If this is the case, the appropriate flags are either set or cleared based on the wait type.

L9.5(25)   Finally, `OSFlagPend()` obtains the current value of the event flags in the group in order to return this information to the caller.

9.04   Setting or Clearing Event(s) in an Event Flag Group, `OSFlagPost()`

The code for either setting or clearing bits in an event flag group is done by calling `OSFlagPost()`, and the code for this function is shown in Listing 9.7.

Listing 9.7   *Setting or clearing bits (i.e., events) in an event flag group.*

```
OS_FLAGS  OSFlagPost (OS_FLAG_GRP *pgrp, OS_FLAGS flags, INT8U opt, INT8U *err)
{
#if OS_CRITICAL_METHOD == 3
    OS_CPU_SR      cpu_sr;
#endif
    OS_FLAG_NODE *pnode;
    BOOLEAN       sched;
    OS_FLAGS      flags_cur;
    OS_FLAGS      flags_rdy;


#if OS_ARG_CHK_EN > 0
    if (pgrp == (OS_FLAG_GRP *)0) {                                      (1)
        *err = OS_FLAG_INVALID_PGRP;
        return ((OS_FLAGS)0);
    }
    if (pgrp->OSFlagType != OS_EVENT_TYPE_FLAG) {                        (2)
        *err = OS_ERR_EVENT_TYPE;
        return ((OS_FLAGS)0);
    }
#endif
    OS_ENTER_CRITICAL();
    switch (opt) {                                                      (3)
        case OS_FLAG_CLR:
             pgrp->OSFlagFlags &= ~flags;                               (4)
             break;

        case OS_FLAG_SET:
             pgrp->OSFlagFlags |= flags;                               (5)
             break;
```

Listing 9.7 ***Setting or clearing bits (i.e., events) in an event flag group. (Continued)***

```
        default:
             OS_EXIT_CRITICAL();
             *err = OS_FLAG_INVALID_OPT;
             return ((OS_FLAGS)0);
    }
    sched = FALSE;                                                   (6)
    pnode = pgrp->OSFlagWaitList;
    while (pnode != (OS_FLAG_NODE *)0) {                             (7)
        switch (pnode->OSFlagNodeWaitType) {
            case OS_FLAG_WAIT_SET_ALL:                               (8)
                flags_rdy = pgrp->OSFlagFlags & pnode->OSFlagNodeFlags;
                if (flags_rdy == pnode->OSFlagNodeFlags) {           (9)
                    if (OS_FlagTaskRdy(pnode, flags_rdy) == TRUE) {  (10)
                        sched = TRUE;                                (11)
                    }
                }
                break;


            case OS_FLAG_WAIT_SET_ANY:
                flags_rdy = pgrp->OSFlagFlags & pnode->OSFlagNodeFlags;
                if (flags_rdy != (OS_FLAGS)0) {
                    if (OS_FlagTaskRdy(pnode, flags_rdy) == TRUE) {
                        sched = TRUE;
                    }
                }
                break;

#if OS_FLAG_WAIT_CLR_EN > 0
            case OS_FLAG_WAIT_CLR_ALL:
                flags_rdy = ~pgrp->OSFlagFlags & pnode->OSFlagNodeFlags;
                if (flags_rdy == pnode->OSFlagNodeFlags) {
                    if (OS_FlagTaskRdy(pnode, flags_rdy) == TRUE) {
                        sched = TRUE;
                    }
                }
                break;
```

Listing 9.7   *Setting or clearing bits (i.e., events) in an event flag group. (Continued)*

```
                case OS_FLAG_WAIT_CLR_ANY:
                     flags_rdy = ~pgrp->OSFlagFlags & pnode->OSFlagNodeFlags;
                     if (flags_rdy != (OS_FLAGS)0) {
                         if (OS_FlagTaskRdy(pnode, flags_rdy) == TRUE) {
                             sched = TRUE;
                         }
                     }
                     break;
#endif
             }
             pnode = pnode->OSFlagNodeNext;                                    (12)
        }
    OS_EXIT_CRITICAL();
    if (sched == TRUE) {                                                       (13)
        OS_Sched();                                                           (14)
    }
    OS_ENTER_CRITICAL();
    flags_cur = pgrp->OSFlagFlags;                                           (15)
    OS_EXIT_CRITICAL();
    *err      = OS_NO_ERR;
    return (flags_cur);                                                       (16)
}
```

9

L9.7(1)

L9.7(2)   Assuming that the configuration constant `OS_ARG_CHK_EN` is set to 1, `OSFlagPost()` makes sure that the handle `pgrp` is not a `NULL` pointer and that `pgrp` points to an event flag group that should have been created by `OSFlagCreate()`.

L9.7(3)

L9.7(4)

L9.7(5)   Depending on the option you specified in the `opt` argument of `OSFlagPost()`, the flags specified in the flags argument are either **set** (when `opt == OS_FLAG_SET`) or **cleared** (when `opt == OS_FLAG_CLR`). If `opt` is not one of the two choices, the call is aborted, and an error code is returned to the caller.

L9.7(6)   We next start by assuming that **posting** doesn't make a higher priority task ready to run, and thus we set the **boolean** variable `sched` to `FALSE`. If this assumption is not verified because we make a higher priority task ready to run, then `sched` is simply be set to `TRUE`.

L9.7(7)   We then go through the wait list to see if any task is waiting on one or more events.

L9.7(15)

L9.7(16)   If the wait list is empty, we simply get the current state of the event flag bits and return this information to the caller.

L9.7(8)   If one or more tasks are waiting on the event flag group, we go through the list of OS_FLAG_NODEs to see if the new event flag bits now satisfy any of the waiting task conditions. Each one of the tasks can be waiting for one of four conditions:

1. **all** of the bits specified in the PEND call to be set.
2. **any** of the bits specified in the PEND call to be set.
3. **all** of the bits specified in the PEND call to be cleared.
4. **any** of the bits specified in the PEND call to be cleared.

L9.7(9)

L9.7(10)   Note that the last two conditions can be compiled out by setting OS_FLAG_WAIT_CLR_EN to 0 (see OS_CFG.H). You would do this if you didn't need the functionality of waiting for cleared bits and/or you need to reduce the amount of ROM in your product. When a waiting task's condition is satisfied, the waiting task is readied by calling OS_FlagTaskRdy() (see Listing 9.9). I only discuss the first wait condition because the other cases are similar enough.

L9.7(11)   Because a task is made ready to run, the scheduler has to be called. However, we only call the scheduler after going through all waiting tasks because there is no need to call the scheduler every time a task is made ready to run.

L9.7(12)   We proceed to the next node by following the linked list.

You should note that interrupts are disabled while we are going through the wait list. The implication is that OSFlagPost() can potentially disable interrupts for a long period of time, especially if multiple tasks are made ready to run. However, execution time is bounded and still deterministic.

L9.7(13)

L9.7(14)   When we have gone through the whole waiting list, we examine the sched flag to see if we need to run the scheduler and thus possibly perform a context switch to a higher priority task that just received the event flag(s) for which it was waiting.

L9.7(15)

L9.7(16)   OSFlagPost() returns the current state of the event flag group.

As previously mentioned, the code in Listing 9.8 is executed to make a task ready to run.

Listing 9.8   Make a waiting task ready to run.

```
static  BOOLEAN  OS_FlagTaskRdy (OS_FLAG_NODE *pnode, OS_FLAGS flags_rdy)
{
    OS_TCB    *ptcb;
    BOOLEAN    sched;


    ptcb                = (OS_TCB *)pnode->OSFlagNodeTCB;
    ptcb->OSTCBDly      = 0;
    ptcb->OSTCBFlagsRdy = flags_rdy;
```

Listing 9.8 *Make a waiting task ready to run. (Continued)*

```
    ptcb->OSTCBStat    &= ~OS_STAT_FLAG;
    if (ptcb->OSTCBStat == OS_STAT_RDY) {                    (1)
        OSRdyGrp                 |= ptcb->OSTCBBitY;
        OSRdyTbl[ptcb->OSTCBY] |= ptcb->OSTCBBitX;
        sched                    = TRUE;                     (2)
    } else {
        sched                    = FALSE;                    (3)
    }
    OS_FlagUnlink(pnode);                                    (4)
    return (sched);
}
```

L9.8(4)   This procedure is standard in µC/OS-II except for the fact that the OS_FLAG_NODE needs to be unlinked from the waiting list of the event flag group, as well as the task's OS_TCB (see Section 6.05, "Making a Task Ready, OS_EventTaskRdy()").

L9.8(1)

L9.8(2)

L9.8(3)   Note that even though this function removes the waiting task from the event flag group wait list, the task could still be suspended and might not be ready to run, which is why the **boolean** variable sched is used and returned to the caller.

The unlinking of the OS_FLAG_NODE is performed by the function OS_FlagUnlink(), as shown in Listing 9.9. Figure 9.5 shows the four possible locations of an OS_FLAG_NODE, which needs to be removed from the event flag wait list. The doubly linked list removal problem is classic except that other pointers must be adjusted.

9

Listing 9.9 *Unlinking an OS_FLAG_NODE.*

```
void  OS_FlagUnlink (OS_FLAG_NODE *pnode)
{
#if OS_TASK_DEL_EN > 0
    OS_TCB        *ptcb;
#endif
    OS_FLAG_GRP  *pgrp;
    OS_FLAG_NODE *pnode_prev;
    OS_FLAG_NODE *pnode_next;


    pnode_prev = pnode->OSFlagNodePrev;                      (1)
    pnode_next = pnode->OSFlagNodeNext;                      (2)
    if (pnode_prev == (OS_FLAG_NODE *)0) {                   (3)
        pgrp                 = pnode->OSFlagNodeFlagGrp;     (4)
        pgrp->OSFlagWaitList = (void *)pnode_next;           (5)
```

Listing 9.9   *Unlinking an* OS_FLAG_NODE. *(Continued)*

```
        if (pnode_next != (OS_FLAG_NODE *)0) {                          (6)
            pnode_next->OSFlagNodePrev = (OS_FLAG_NODE *)0;            (7)
        }
    } else {
        pnode_prev->OSFlagNodeNext = pnode_next;                       (8)
        if (pnode_next != (OS_FLAG_NODE *)0) {                         (9)
            pnode_next->OSFlagNodePrev = pnode_prev;                   (10)
        }
    }
#if OS_TASK_DEL_EN > 0
    ptcb                = (OS_TCB *)pnode->OSFlagNodeTCB;              (11)
    ptcb->OSTCBFlagNode = (void *)0;                                   (12)
#endif
}
```

Figure 9.5   *Removing an* OS_FLAG_NODE *from the wait list.*

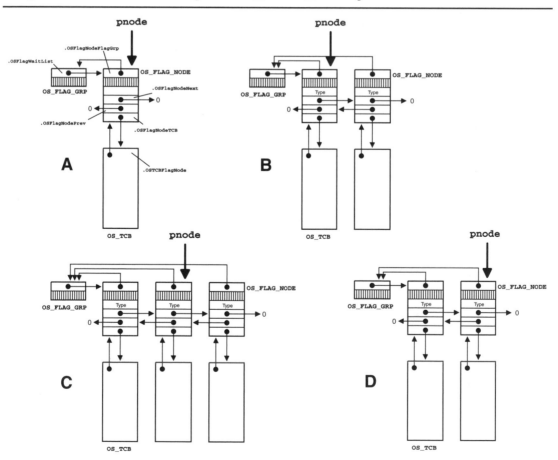

L9.9(1)

L9.9(2)   `OS_FlagUnlink()` starts off by setting up two local pointers: `pnode_next` and `pnode_prev`, which point to the next and previous `OS_FLAG_NODE` in the wait list, respectively.

L9.9(3)

F9.5(A,B)The previous pointer is examined to see if we have the first two cases of Figure 9.6 (an `OS_FLAG_NODE`, which is the first node in the wait list).

L9.9(4)

L9.9(5)   If the `OS_FLAG_NODE` is the first node, the wait-list pointer of the event flag group needs to point to the node immediately after the `OS_FLAG_NODE` to be removed.

L9.9(6)

L9.9(7)

F9.5(B)   If an `OS_FLAG_NODE` is to the right of the node to delete, then that node now points to where the previous pointer of the node to delete is pointing, which is, of course, a `NULL` pointer because the node to remove was the first one.

L9.9(8)

F9.5(C,D) Because the node to delete is not the first node in the wait list, the node to the left of the node to delete must now point to the node to the right of the node to delete.

L9.9(9)

L9.9(10)   If a node is to the right of the node to delete, the previous pointer of that node must now point to the previous node of the node to delete.

L9.9(11)

L9.9(12)   In all cases, the `.OSTCBFlagNode` field must now point to `NULL` because the node to be deleted will no longer exist after it's deallocated from the task that created the node in the first place.

9

Figures 9.6 through 9.9 show the before and after for each case mentioned. The number in parenthesis corresponds to the number in parenthesis of list Listing 9.9. You should notice that `OS_FlagUnlink()` updates three pointers at most. Because the node being removed exists on the stack of the task being readied (it was allocated by `OSFlagPend()`), that node automatically disappears! As far as the task that pended on the event flag is concerned, it doesn't even know about the `OS_FLAG_NODE`.

Figure 9.6 ***Removing an*** OS_FLAG_NODE ***from the wait list, Case A.***

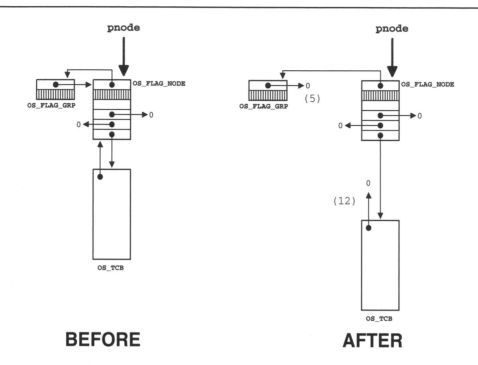

BEFORE   **AFTER**

Figure 9.7 ***Removing an*** OS_FLAG_NODE ***from the wait list, Case B.***

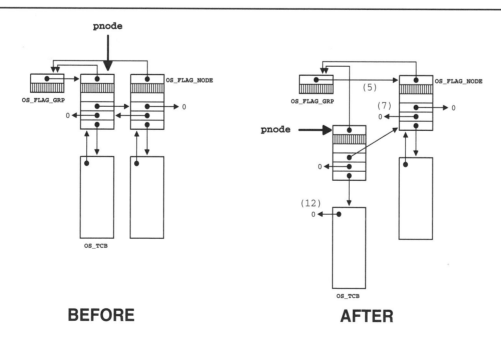

BEFORE   **AFTER**

Figure 9.8   *Removing an* `OS_FLAG_NODE` *from the wait list, Case C.*

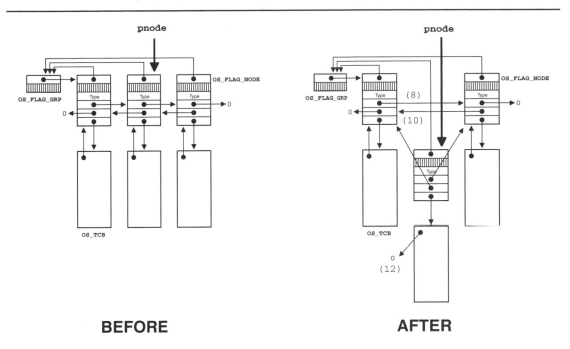

BEFORE   **AFTER**

Figure 9.9   *Removing an* `OS_FLAG_NODE` *from the wait list, Case D.*

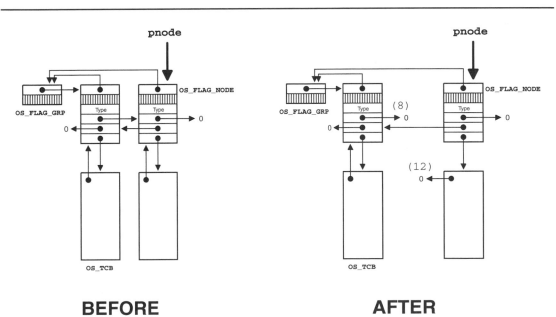

BEFORE   **AFTER**

9

9.05   *Looking for Event(s) of an Event Flag Group,* OSFlagAccept()

The code to look for desired event(s) from an event flag group without waiting is shown in Listing 9.10. This function is quite similar to OSFlagPend() except that the caller is not suspended (i.e., blocked) should the event(s) not be present. The only two different things are:

1. OSFlagAccept() can be called from an ISR, unlike some of the other calls.

2. If the conditions are **not** met, the call does not block and simply returns an error code that the caller should check.

Listing 9.10   *Looking for event flags without waiting.*

```
OS_FLAGS  OSFlagAccept (OS_FLAG_GRP *pgrp, OS_FLAGS flags, INT8U wait_type, INT8U *err)
{
#if OS_CRITICAL_METHOD == 3
    OS_CPU_SR      cpu_sr;
#endif
    OS_FLAGS       flags_cur;
    OS_FLAGS       flags_rdy;
    BOOLEAN        consume;


#if OS_ARG_CHK_EN > 0
    if (pgrp == (OS_FLAG_GRP *)0) {
        *err = OS_FLAG_INVALID_PGRP;
        return ((OS_FLAGS)0);
    }
    if (pgrp->OSFlagType != OS_EVENT_TYPE_FLAG) {
        *err = OS_ERR_EVENT_TYPE;
        return ((OS_FLAGS)0);
    }
#endif
    if (wait_type & OS_FLAG_CONSUME) {
        wait_type &= ~OS_FLAG_CONSUME;
        consume    = TRUE;
    } else {
        consume    = FALSE;
    }

    OS_ENTER_CRITICAL();
    switch (wait_type) {
```

Listing 9.10   *Looking for event flags without waiting. (Continued)*

```
    case OS_FLAG_WAIT_SET_ALL:
         flags_rdy = pgrp->OSFlagFlags & flags;
         if (flags_rdy == flags) {
             if (consume == TRUE) {
                 pgrp->OSFlagFlags &= ~flags_rdy;
             }
             flags_cur = pgrp->OSFlagFlags;
             OS_EXIT_CRITICAL();
             *err      = OS_NO_ERR;
         } else {
             flags_cur = pgrp->OSFlagFlags;
             OS_EXIT_CRITICAL();
             *err       = OS_FLAG_ERR_NOT_RDY;
         }
         break;


    case OS_FLAG_WAIT_SET_ANY:
         flags_rdy = pgrp->OSFlagFlags & flags;
         if (flags_rdy != (OS_FLAGS)0) {
             if (consume == TRUE) {
                 pgrp->OSFlagFlags &= ~flags_rdy;
             }
             flags_cur = pgrp->OSFlagFlags;
             OS_EXIT_CRITICAL();
             *err       = OS_NO_ERR;
         } else {
             flags_cur = pgrp->OSFlagFlags;
             OS_EXIT_CRITICAL();
             *err       = OS_FLAG_ERR_NOT_RDY;
         }
         break;

#if OS_FLAG_WAIT_CLR_EN > 0
    case OS_FLAG_WAIT_CLR_ALL:
         flags_rdy = ~pgrp->OSFlagFlags & flags;
         if (flags_rdy == flags) {
             if (consume == TRUE) {
                 pgrp->OSFlagFlags |= flags_rdy;
             }
```

Listing 9.10 *Looking for event flags without waiting. (Continued)*

```
            flags_cur = pgrp->OSFlagFlags;
            OS_EXIT_CRITICAL();
            *err      = OS_NO_ERR;
        } else {
            flags_cur = pgrp->OSFlagFlags;
            OS_EXIT_CRITICAL();
            *err      = OS_FLAG_ERR_NOT_RDY;
        }
        break;


    case OS_FLAG_WAIT_CLR_ANY:
        flags_rdy = ~pgrp->OSFlagFlags & flags;
        if (flags_rdy != (OS_FLAGS)0) {
            if (consume == TRUE) {
                pgrp->OSFlagFlags |= flags_rdy;
            }
            flags_cur = pgrp->OSFlagFlags;
            OS_EXIT_CRITICAL();
            *err      = OS_NO_ERR;
        } else {
            flags_cur = pgrp->OSFlagFlags;
            OS_EXIT_CRITICAL();
            *err      = OS_FLAG_ERR_NOT_RDY;
        }
        break;
#endif

    default:
        OS_EXIT_CRITICAL();
        flags_cur = (OS_FLAGS)0;
        *err      = OS_FLAG_ERR_WAIT_TYPE;
        break;
    }
    return (flags_cur);
}
```

9.06   *Querying an Event Flag Group,* `OSFlagQuery()`

`OSFlagQuery()` allows your code to get the current value of the event flag group. The code for this function is shown in Listing 9.11.

Listing 9.11   *Obtaining the current flags of an event flag group.*

```
OS_FLAGS  OSFlagQuery (OS_FLAG_GRP *pgrp, INT8U *err)
{
#if OS_CRITICAL_METHOD == 3
    OS_CPU_SR  cpu_sr;
#endif
    OS_FLAGS    flags;


#if OS_ARG_CHK_EN > 0
    if (pgrp == (OS_FLAG_GRP *)0) {                             (1)
        *err = OS_FLAG_INVALID_PGRP;
        return ((OS_FLAGS)0);
    }
    if (pgrp->OSFlagType != OS_EVENT_TYPE_FLAG) {               (2)
        *err = OS_ERR_EVENT_TYPE;
        return ((OS_FLAGS)0);
    }
#endif
    OS_ENTER_CRITICAL();
    flags = pgrp->OSFlagFlags;                                  (3)
    OS_EXIT_CRITICAL();
    *err = OS_NO_ERR;
    return (flags);                                            (4)
}
```

`OSFlagQuery()` is passed two arguments: `pgrp` contains a pointer to the event flag group, which was returned by `OSFlagCreate()` when the event flag group is created; and `err`, which is a pointer to an error code that lets the caller know whether the call was successful or not.

L9.11(1)

L9.11(2)   As with all μC/OS-II calls, `OSFlagQuery()` performs argument checking if this feature is enabled when `OS_ARG_CHK_EN` is set to 1 in `OS_CFG.H`.

L9.11(3)

L9.11(4)   If no errors exist, `OSFlagQuery()` obtains the current state of the event flags and returns this information to the caller.

Chapter 10

Message Mailbox Management

A *message mailbox* (or simply a mailbox) is a µC/OS-II object that allows a task or an ISR to send a pointer-sized variable to another task. The pointer is typically initialized to point to some applicationspecific data structure containing a message. µC/OS-II provides six services to access mailboxes: OSMboxCreate(), OSMboxPend(), OSMboxPost(), OSMboxPostOpt(), OSMboxAccept(), and OSMboxQuery().

To enable µC/OS-II message-mailbox services, you must set configuration constants in OS_CFG.H. Specifically, Table 10.1 shows which services are compiled, based on the value of configuration constants found in OS_CFG.H. You should note that **none** of the mailbox services are enabled when OS_MBOX_EN is set to 0. To enable specific features (i.e., services) listed in Table 10.1, simply set the configuration constant to 1. You should notice that OSMboxCreate() and OSMboxPend() cannot be individually disabled like the other services. That's because they are always needed when you enable µC/OS-II message mailbox management. You **must** enable at least one of the post services: OSMboxPost() and OSMboxPostOpt().

Table 10.1   *Mailbox configuration constants in* OS_CFG.H.

µC/OS-II Event Flag Service	*Enabled when set to 1 in* OS_CFG.H
OSMboxAccept()	OS_MBOX_ACCEPT_EN
OSMboxCreate()	
OSMboxDel()	OS_MBOX_DEL_EN
OSMboxPend()	
OSMboxPost()	OS_MBOX_POST_EN
OSMboxPostOpt()	OS_MBOX_POST_OPT_EN
OSMboxQuery()	OS_MBOX_QUERY_EN

Figure 10.1 shows a flow diagram to illustrate the relationship between tasks, ISRs, and a message mailbox. Note that the symbology used to represent a mailbox is an I-beam. The hourglass represents a timeout that can be specified with the OSMboxPend() call. The content of the mailbox is a pointer to a

message. What the pointer points to is application specific. A mailbox can only contain one pointer (mailbox is full) or a pointer to NULL (mailbox is empty).

As you can see from Figure 10.1, a task or an ISR can call OSMboxPost() or OSMboxPostOpt(). However, only tasks are allowed to call OSMboxDel(), OSMboxPend(), and OSMboxQuery(). Your application can have just about any number of mailboxes. The limit is set by OS_MAX_EVENTS in OS_CFG.H.

Figure 10.1   Relationships between tasks, ISRs, and a message mailbox.

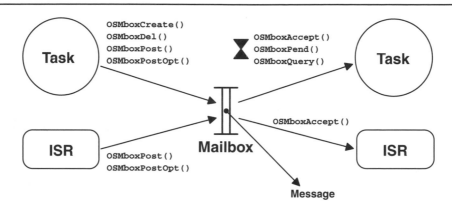

10.00 Creating a Mailbox, OSMboxCreate()

A mailbox needs to be created before it can be used. Creating a mailbox is accomplished by calling OSMboxCreate() and specifying the initial value of the pointer. Typically, the initial value is a NULL pointer, but a mailbox can initially contain a message. If you use the mailbox to signal the occurrence of an event (i.e., send a message), you typically initialize it to a NULL pointer because the event (most likely) has not occurred. If you use the mailbox to access a shared resource, you initialize the mailbox with a non-NULL pointer. In this case, you basically use the mailbox as a binary semaphore.

The code to create a mailbox is shown in Listing 10.1.

Listing 10.1   Creating a mailbox.

```
OS_EVENT  *OSMboxCreate (void *msg)
{
#if OS_CRITICAL_METHOD == 3
    OS_CPU_SR  cpu_sr;                                                          (1)
#endif
    OS_EVENT  *pevent;


    if (OSIntNesting > 0) {                                                     (2)
        return ((OS_EVENT *)0);
    }
```

Listing 10.1 *Creating a mailbox. (Continued)*

```
        OS_ENTER_CRITICAL();
        pevent = OSEventFreeList;                                    (3)
        if (OSEventFreeList != (OS_EVENT *)0) {                      (4)
            OSEventFreeList = (OS_EVENT *)OSEventFreeList->OSEventPtr; (5)
        }
        OS_EXIT_CRITICAL();
        if (pevent != (OS_EVENT *)0) {                              (6)
            pevent->OSEventType = OS_EVENT_TYPE_MBOX;               (7)
            pevent->OSEventCnt  = 0;                                (8)
            pevent->OSEventPtr  = msg;                              (9)
            OS_EventWaitListInit(pevent);                          (10)
        }
        return (pevent);                                           (11)
    }
```

L10.1(1) A local variable called `cpu_sr` to support `OS_CRITICAL_METHOD #3` is allocated.

L10.1(2) `OSMboxCreate()` starts by making sure you are not calling this function from an ISR because that's not allowed. All kernel objects need to be created from task-level code or before multitasking starts.

L10.1(3) `OSMboxCreate()` then attempts to obtain an event control block (ECB) from the free list of ECBs (see Figure 6.5).

L10.1(4)

L10.1(5) The linked list of free ECBs is adjusted to point to the next free ECB.

L10.1(6)

L10.1(7) If an ECB is available, the ECB type is set to `OS_EVENT_TYPE_MBOX`. Other `OSMbox???()` function calls checks this structure member to make sure that the ECB is of the proper type (i.e., a mailbox). This check prevents you from calling `OSMboxPost()` on an ECB that was created for use as a message queue.

L10.1(8) The `.OSEventCnt` field is then initialized to zero because this field is not used by message mailboxes.

L10.1(9) The initial value of the message is stored in the ECB.

L10.1(10) The wait list is then initialized by calling `OS_EventWaitListInit()` [see Section 6.04, "Initializing an ECB, `OS_EventWaitListInit()`"]. Because the mailbox is being initialized, no tasks are waiting for it, and thus `OS_EventWaitListInit()` clears the `.OSEventGrp` and `.OSEventTbl[]` fields of the ECB.

L10.1(11) Finally, `OSMboxCreate()` returns a pointer to the ECB. This pointer must be used in subsequent calls to manipulate mailboxes [`OSMboxAccept()`, `OSMboxDel()`, `OSMboxPend()`, `OSMboxPost()`, `OSMboxPostOpt()`, and `OSMboxQuery()`]. The pointer is basically used as the mailbox handle. If no more ECBs are present, `OSMboxCreate()` returns a `NULL` pointer. You should make it a habit to check return values to ensure that you are getting the desired results. Passing NULL pointers to µC/OS-II does not make it fail because µC/OS-II validates arguments (only if OS_ARG_CHK_EN is set to 1, though). Figure 10.2 shows the content of the ECB just before OSMboxCreate() returns.

Figure 10.2   *ECB just before* OSMboxCreate() *returns.*

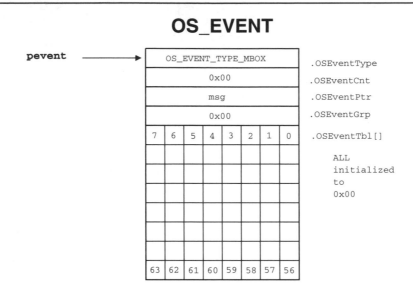

10.01 *Deleting a Mailbox,* OSMboxDel()

The code to delete a mailbox is shown in Listing 10.2, and this code is only generated by the compiler if OS_MBOX_DEL_EN is set to 1 in OS_CFG.H. You must use this function with caution because multiple tasks could attempt to access a deleted mailbox. Generally speaking, before you delete a mailbox, you first delete all the tasks that can access the mailbox.

Listing 10.2   *Deleting a mailbox.*

```
OS_EVENT  *OSMboxDel (OS_EVENT *pevent, INT8U opt, INT8U *err)
{
#if OS_CRITICAL_METHOD == 3
    OS_CPU_SR  cpu_sr;
#endif
    BOOLEAN    tasks_waiting;


    if (OSIntNesting > 0) {                                           (1)
        *err = OS_ERR_DEL_ISR;
        return (pevent);
    }
```

Listing 10.2   Deleting a mailbox. (Continued)

```
#if OS_ARG_CHK_EN > 0
    if (pevent == (OS_EVENT *)0) {                                  (2)
        *err = OS_ERR_PEVENT_NULL;
        return (pevent);
    }
    if (pevent->OSEventType != OS_EVENT_TYPE_MBOX) {                (3)
        *err = OS_ERR_EVENT_TYPE;
        return (pevent);
    }
#endif
    OS_ENTER_CRITICAL();
    if (pevent->OSEventGrp != 0x00) {                              (4)
        tasks_waiting = TRUE;
    } else {
        tasks_waiting = FALSE;
    }
    switch (opt) {
        case OS_DEL_NO_PEND:
            if (tasks_waiting == FALSE) {
                pevent->OSEventType = OS_EVENT_TYPE_UNUSED;        (5)
                pevent->OSEventPtr  = OSEventFreeList;             (6)
                OSEventFreeList     = pevent;                     (7)
                OS_EXIT_CRITICAL();
                *err = OS_NO_ERR;
                return ((OS_EVENT *)0);                           (8)
            } else {
                OS_EXIT_CRITICAL();
                *err = OS_ERR_TASK_WAITING;
                return (pevent);
            }

        case OS_DEL_ALWAYS:
            while (pevent->OSEventGrp != 0x00) {                  (9)
                OS_EventTaskRdy(pevent, (void *)0, OS_STAT_MBOX); (10)
            }
            pevent->OSEventType = OS_EVENT_TYPE_UNUSED;          (11)
            pevent->OSEventPtr  = OSEventFreeList;               (12)
            OSEventFreeList     = pevent;
            OS_EXIT_CRITICAL();
            if (tasks_waiting == TRUE) {
```

10

Listing 10.2   Deleting a mailbox. (Continued)

```
        OS_Sched();                                            (13)
    }
    *err = OS_NO_ERR;
    return ((OS_EVENT *)0);                                    (14)


 default:
    OS_EXIT_CRITICAL();
    *err = OS_ERR_INVALID_OPT;
    return (pevent);
    }
 }
```

L10.2(1)   OSMboxDel() starts by making sure that this function is not called from an ISR because that's not allowed.

L10.2(2)

L10.2(3)   We then validate pevent to ensure that it's not a NULL pointer and that it points to an ECB that was created as a mailbox.

L10.2(4)   OSMboxDel() then determines whether any tasks are waiting on the mailbox. The flag tasks_waiting is set accordingly.

   Based on the option (i.e., opt) specified in the call, OSMboxDel() either deletes the mailbox only if no tasks are pending on the mailbox (opt == OS_DEL_NO_PEND) or deletes the mailbox even if tasks are waiting (opt == OS_DEL_ALWAYS).

L10.2(5)

L10.2(6)

L10.2(7)   When opt is set to OS_DEL_NO_PEND and no task is waiting on the mailbox, OSMboxDel() marks the ECB as unused, and the ECB is returned to the free list of ECBs. This process allows another mailbox (or any other ECB-based object) to be created.

L10.2(8)   You should note that OSMboxDel() returns a NULL pointer because, at this point, the mailbox should no longer be accessed through the original pointer. You ought to call OSMboxDel() as follows

```
MbxPtr = OSMboxDel(MbxPtr, opt, &err);
```

   This feature allows the pointer to the mailbox to be altered by the call. OSMboxDel() returns an error code if any tasks are waiting on the mailbox (i.e., OS_ERR_TASK_WAITING) because by specifying OS_DEL_NO_PEND you indicated that you didn't want to delete the mailbox if tasks are waiting on the mailbox.

L10.2(9)

L10.2(10) When opt is set to OS_DEL_ALWAYS, then all tasks waiting on the mailbox are readied. Each task thinks it received a NULL message. Each task should examine the returned pointer to make sure it's non-NULL. Also, you should note that interrupts are disabled while each task is being readied. This feature, of course, increases the interrupt latency of your system.

L10.2(11)

L10.2(12) After all pending tasks are readied, `OSMboxDel()` marks the ECB as unused, and the ECB is returned to the free list of ECBs.

L10.2(13) The scheduler is called only if tasks are waiting on the mailbox.

L10.2(14) Again, you should note that `OSMboxDel()` returns a `NULL` pointer because, at this point, the mailbox should no longer be accessed through the original pointer.

10.02 Waiting for a Message at a Mailbox, `OSMboxPend()`

The code to wait for a message to arrive at a mailbox is shown in Listing 10.3.

Listing 10.3   Waiting for a message at a mailbox (blocking), `OSMboxPend()`.

```
void  *OSMboxPend (OS_EVENT *pevent, INT16U timeout, INT8U *err)
{
#if OS_CRITICAL_METHOD == 3
    OS_CPU_SR  cpu_sr;
#endif
    void       *msg;


    if (OSIntNesting > 0) {                                          (1)
        *err = OS_ERR_PEND_ISR;
        return ((void *)0);
    }
#if OS_ARG_CHK_EN > 0
    if (pevent == (OS_EVENT *)0) {                                   (2)
        *err = OS_ERR_PEVENT_NULL;
        return ((void *)0);
    }
    if (pevent->OSEventType != OS_EVENT_TYPE_MBOX) {                 (3)
        *err = OS_ERR_EVENT_TYPE;
        return ((void *)0);
    }
#endif
```

10

Listing 10.3   *Waiting for a message at a mailbox (blocking),*
OSMboxPend( ). (Continued)

```
    OS_ENTER_CRITICAL();
    msg = pevent->OSEventPtr;                               (4)
    if (msg != (void *)0) {
        pevent->OSEventPtr = (void *)0;                     (5)
        OS_EXIT_CRITICAL();
        *err = OS_NO_ERR;
        return (msg);                                       (6)
    }
    OSTCBCur->OSTCBStat  |= OS_STAT_MBOX;                    (7)
    OSTCBCur->OSTCBDly    = timeout;                         (8)
    OS_EventTaskWait(pevent);                               (9)
    OS_EXIT_CRITICAL();
    OS_Sched();                                            (10)
    OS_ENTER_CRITICAL();
    msg = OSTCBCur->OSTCBMsg;
    if (msg != (void *)0) {                                (11)
        OSTCBCur->OSTCBMsg      = (void *)0;
        OSTCBCur->OSTCBStat     = OS_STAT_RDY;
        OSTCBCur->OSTCBEventPtr = (OS_EVENT *)0;
        OS_EXIT_CRITICAL();
        *err              = OS_NO_ERR;
        return (msg);                                      (12)
    }
    OS_EventTO(pevent);                                    (13)
    OS_EXIT_CRITICAL();
    *err = OS_TIMEOUT;
    return ((void *)0);                                    (14)
}
```

L10.3(1) OSMboxPend( ) checks to see if the function was called by an ISR. It doesn't make sense to
call OSMboxPend( ) from an ISR because an ISR cannot be made to wait. Instead, you should
call OSMboxAccept( ) (see Section Section 10.05, "Getting a Message without Waiting
(Non-blocking), OSMboxAccept( )").

L10.3(2)

L10.3(3) If OS_ARG_CHK_EN (see OS_CFG.H) is set to 1, OSMboxPend( ) checks that pevent is not a NULL
pointer and that the ECB to which pevent is pointing has been created by OSMboxCreate( ).

L10.3(4)

L10.3(5)

L10.3(6) If a message has been deposited in the mailbox (non-`NULL` pointer), the message is extracted from the mailbox and replaced with a `NULL` pointer, and the function returns to its caller with the message that was in the mailbox. An error code is also set indicating success. If your code calls `OSMboxPend()`, this outcome is the one for which you are looking because it indicates that another task or an ISR already deposited a message. This path is the fastest through `OSMboxPend()`.

If the mailbox is empty, the calling task needs to be put to sleep until another task (or an ISR) sends a message through the mailbox [see Section 10.04, "Sending a Message to a Mailbox, `OSMboxPostOpt()`"]. `OSMboxPend()` allows you to specify a timeout value (in integral number of ticks) as one of its arguments (i.e., `timeout`). This feature is useful to avoid waiting indefinitely for a message to arrive at the mailbox. If the timeout value is non-zero, `OSMboxPend()` suspends the task until the mailbox receives a message or the specified timeout period expires. Note that a timeout value of 0 indicates that the task is willing to wait forever for a message to arrive.

L10.3(7) To put the calling task to sleep, `OSMboxPend()` sets the status flag in the task's task control block (TCB) to indicate that the task is suspended waiting at a mailbox.

L10.3(8) The timeout is also stored in the TCB so that it can be decremented by `OSTimeTick()`. You should recall (see Section 3.11, "Clock Tick") that `OSTimeTick()` decrements each of the created task's `.OSTCBDly` field if it's nonzero.

L10.3(9) The actual work of putting the task to sleep is done by `OS_EventTaskWait()` [see Section 6.06, "Making a Task Wait for an Event, `OS_EventTaskWait()`"].

L10.3(10) Because the calling task is no longer ready to run, the scheduler is called to run the next highest priority task that is ready to run. As far as your task is concerned, it made a call to `OSMboxPend()`, and it doesn't know that it is suspended until a message arrives. When the mailbox receives a message (or the timeout period expires), `OSMboxPend()` resumes execution immediately after the call to `OS_Sched()`.

L10.3(11) When `OS_Sched()` returns, `OSMboxPend()` checks to see if a message has been placed in the task's TCB by `OSMboxPost()`.

L10.3(12) If so, the call is successful, and the message is returned to the caller.

L10.3(13) If a message is not received, then `OS_Sched()` must have returned because of a timeout. The calling task is then removed from the mailbox wait list by calling `OS_EventTO()`.

L10.3(14) Note that the returned pointer is set to `NULL` because no message is available to return. The calling task should either examine the contents of the return pointer or the return code to determine whether a valid message has been received.

10

10.03 *Sending a Message to a Mailbox,* `OSMboxPost()`

The code to deposit a message in a mailbox is shown in Listing 10.4.

Listing 10.4   *Posting a message to a mailbox,* `OSMboxPost()`.

```
INT8U  OSMboxPost (OS_EVENT *pevent, void *msg)
{
#if OS_CRITICAL_METHOD == 3
    OS_CPU_SR  cpu_sr;
#endif


#if OS_ARG_CHK_EN > 0
    if (pevent == (OS_EVENT *)0) {                              (1)
        return (OS_ERR_PEVENT_NULL);
    }
    if (msg == (void *)0) {
        return (OS_ERR_POST_NULL_PTR);
    }
    if (pevent->OSEventType != OS_EVENT_TYPE_MBOX) {
        return (OS_ERR_EVENT_TYPE);
    }
#endif
    OS_ENTER_CRITICAL();
    if (pevent->OSEventGrp != 0x00) {                           (2)
        OS_EventTaskRdy(pevent, msg, OS_STAT_MBOX);             (3)
        OS_EXIT_CRITICAL();
        OS_Sched();                                             (4)
        return (OS_NO_ERR);
    }
    if (pevent->OSEventPtr != (void *)0) {                      (5)
        OS_EXIT_CRITICAL();
        return (OS_MBOX_FULL);
    }
    pevent->OSEventPtr = msg;                                   (6)
    OS_EXIT_CRITICAL();
    return (OS_NO_ERR);
}
```

L10.4(1)   If OS_ARG_CHK_EN is set to 1 in OS_CFG.H, OSMboxPost() checks to see that pevent is not a NULL pointer, that the message being posted is not a NULL pointer, and finally makes sure that the ECB is a mailbox.

L10.4(2)   OSMboxPost() then checks to see if any task is waiting for a message to arrive at the mailbox. Tasks are waiting when the .OSEventGrp field in the ECB contains a nonzero value.

L10.4(3)   The highest priority task waiting for the message is removed from the wait list by OS_EventTaskRdy() [see Section 6.05, "Making a Task Ready, OS_EventTaskRdy()"], and this task is made ready to run.

L10.4(4)   OS_Sched() is then called to see if the task made ready is now the highest priority task ready to run. If it is, a context switch results [only if OSMboxPost() is called from a task], and the readied task is executed. If the readied task is not the highest priority task, OS_Sched() returns, and the task that called OSMboxPost() continues execution.

L10.4(5)   At this point, no tasks are waiting for a message at the specified mailbox. OSMboxPost() then checks to see that a message isn't already in the mailbox. Because the mailbox can only hold one message, an error code is returned if we get this outcome.

L10.4(6)   If no tasks are waiting for a message to arrive at the mailbox, then the pointer to the message is saved in the mailbox. Storing the pointer in the mailbox allows the next task to call OSMboxPend() to get the message immediately.

Note that a context switch does not occur if OSMboxPost() is called by an ISR because context switching from an ISR only occurs when OSIntExit() is called at the completion of the ISR and from the last nested ISR (see Section 3.10, "Interrupts Under µC/OS-II").

10.04 Sending a Message to a Mailbox, OSMboxPostOpt()

You can also post a message to a mailbox using an alternate and more powerful function called OSMboxPostOpt(). There are two post calls for backwards compatibility with previous versions of µC/OS-II. OSMboxPostOpt() is the newer function and can replace OSMboxPost(). In addition, OSMboxPostOpt() allows posting a message to all tasks (i.e., broadcast) waiting on the mailbox. The code to deposit a message in a mailbox is shown in Listing 10.5.

Listing 10.5   Posting a message to a mailbox, OSMboxPostOpt().

```
INT8U  OSMboxPostOpt (OS_EVENT *pevent, void *msg, INT8U opt)
{
#if OS_CRITICAL_METHOD == 3
    OS_CPU_SR  cpu_sr;
#endif
```

Listing 10.5   *Posting a message to a mailbox,*
OSMboxPostOpt( ). (Continued)

```
#if OS_ARG_CHK_EN > 0
    if (pevent == (OS_EVENT *)0) {                              (1)
        return (OS_ERR_PEVENT_NULL);
    }
    if (msg == (void *)0) {
        return (OS_ERR_POST_NULL_PTR);
    }
    if (pevent->OSEventType != OS_EVENT_TYPE_MBOX) {
        return (OS_ERR_EVENT_TYPE);
    }
#endif
    OS_ENTER_CRITICAL();
    if (pevent->OSEventGrp != 0x00) {                           (2)
        if ((opt & OS_POST_OPT_BROADCAST) != 0x00) {           (3)
            while (pevent->OSEventGrp != 0x00) {               (4)
                OS_EventTaskRdy(pevent, msg, OS_STAT_MBOX);     (5)
            }
        } else {
            OS_EventTaskRdy(pevent, msg, OS_STAT_MBOX);         (6)
        }
        OS_EXIT_CRITICAL();
        OS_Sched();                                             (7)
        return (OS_NO_ERR);
    }
    if (pevent->OSEventPtr != (void *)0) {                      (8)
        OS_EXIT_CRITICAL();
        return (OS_MBOX_FULL);
    }
    pevent->OSEventPtr = msg;                                   (9)
    OS_EXIT_CRITICAL();
    return (OS_NO_ERR);
}
```

L10.5(1)   If `OS_ARG_CHK_EN` is set to 1 in `OS_CFG.H`, `OSMboxPostOpt()` checks to see that `pevent` is not a `NULL` pointer, that the message being posted is not a `NULL` pointer, and finally checks to make sure that the ECB is a mailbox.

L10.5(2)   `OSMboxPost()` then checks to see if any task is waiting for a message to arrive at the mailbox. Tasks are waiting when the `.OSEventGrp` field in the ECB contains a nonzero value.

L10.5(3)

L10.5(4)

L10.5(5)   If you set the `OS_POST_OPT_BROADCAST` bit in the `opt` argument, then all tasks waiting for a message receives the message. All tasks waiting for the message are removed from the wait list by `OS_EventTaskRdy()` [see Section 6.05, "Making a Task Ready, `OS_EventTaskRdy()`"]. You should notice that interrupt-disable time is proportional to the number of tasks waiting for a message from the mailbox.

L10.5(6)   If a broadcast was not requested, then only the highest priority task waiting for a message is made ready to run. The highest priority task waiting for the message is removed from the wait list by `OS_EventTaskRdy()`.

L10.5(7)   `OS_Sched()` is then called to see if the task made ready is now the highest priority task ready to run. If it is, a context switch results [only if `OSMboxPostOpt()` is called from a task], and the readied task is executed. If the readied task is not the highest priority task, `OS_Sched()` returns, and the task that called `OSMboxPostOpt()` continues execution.

L10.5(8)   If nothing is waiting for a message, the message to post needs to be placed in the mailbox. In this case, `OSMboxPostOpt()` makes sure that a message isn't already in the mailbox. Remember that a mailbox can only contain one message. An error code is returned if an attempt is made to add a message to an already full mailbox.

L10.5(9)   `OSMboxPostOpt()` then deposits the message in the mailbox.

Note that a context switch does not occur if `OSMboxPostOpt()` is called by an ISR because context switching from an ISR only occurs when `OSIntExit()` is called at the completion of the ISR and from the last nested ISR (see Section 3.10, "Interrupts Under µC/OS-II").

10.05 Getting a Message without Waiting (Non-blocking), *OSMboxAccept()*

You can obtain a message from a mailbox without putting a task to sleep if the mailbox is empty. This action is accomplished by calling `OSMboxAccept()`, shown in Listing 10.6.

Listing 10.6   Getting a message without waiting.

```
void  *OSMboxAccept (OS_EVENT *pevent)
{
#if OS_CRITICAL_METHOD == 3
    OS_CPU_SR  cpu_sr;
#endif
    void       *msg;


#if OS_ARG_CHK_EN > 0
    if (pevent == (OS_EVENT *)0) {                                    (1)
        return ((void *)0);
```

10

Listing 10.6   *Getting a message without waiting. (Continued)*

```
    }
    if (pevent->OSEventType != OS_EVENT_TYPE_MBOX) {                        (2)
        return ((void *)0);
    }
#endif
    OS_ENTER_CRITICAL();
    msg                 = pevent->OSEventPtr;                               (3)
    pevent->OSEventPtr = (void *)0;                                         (4)
    OS_EXIT_CRITICAL();
    return (msg);                                                           (5)
}
```

L10.6(1)

L10.6(2)   If OS_ARG_CHK_EN is set to 1 in OS_CFG.H, OSMboxAccept() starts by checking that pevent is not a NULL pointer and that the ECB to which pevent is pointing has been created by OSMboxCreate().

L10.6(3)   OSMboxAccept() then gets the current contents of the mailbox in order to determine whether a message is available (i.e., a non-NULL pointer).

L10.6(4)   If a message is available, the mailbox is emptied. You should note that this operation is done even if the message already contains a NULL pointer. This operation is done for performance considerations.

L10.6(5)   Finally, the original contents of the mailbox is returned to the caller.

The code that calls OSMboxAccept() must examine the returned value. If OSMboxAccept() returns a NULL pointer, then a message was not available. A non-NULL pointer indicates that a message has been deposited in the mailbox. An ISR should use OSMboxAccept() instead of OSMboxPend().

You can use OSMboxAccept() to flush (i.e., empty) the contents of a mailbox.

10.06 Obtaining the Status of a Mailbox, OSMboxQuery()

OSMboxQuery() allows your application to take a snapshot of an ECB used for a message mailbox. The code for this function is shown in Listing 10.7. OSMboxQuery() is passed two arguments: pevent contains a pointer to the message mailbox, which is returned by OSMboxCreate() when the mailbox is created; and pdata is a pointer to a data structure (OS_MBOX_DATA, see uCOS_II.H) that holds information about the message mailbox. Your application needs to allocate a variable of type OS_MBOX_DATA that can be used to receive the information about the desired mailbox. I decided to use a new data structure because the caller should only be concerned with mailbox-specific data, as opposed to the more generic OS_EVENT data structure, which contains two additional fields (.OSEventCnt and .OSEventType).

OS_MBOX_DATA contains the current contents of the message (.OSMsg) and the list of tasks waiting for a message to arrive (.OSEventTbl[] and .OSEventGrp).

Listing 10.7   Obtaining the status of a mailbox.

```
INT8U  OSMboxQuery (OS_EVENT *pevent, OS_MBOX_DATA *pdata)
{
#if OS_CRITICAL_METHOD == 3
    OS_CPU_SR  cpu_sr;
#endif
    INT8U      *psrc;
    INT8U      *pdest;


#if OS_ARG_CHK_EN > 0
    if (pevent == (OS_EVENT *)0) {                                      (1)
        return (OS_ERR_PEVENT_NULL);
    }
    if (pevent->OSEventType != OS_EVENT_TYPE_MBOX) {                    (2)
        return (OS_ERR_EVENT_TYPE);
    }
#endif
    OS_ENTER_CRITICAL();
    pdata->OSEventGrp = pevent->OSEventGrp;                             (3)
    psrc              = &pevent->OSEventTbl[0];
    pdest             = &pdata->OSEventTbl[0];

#if OS_EVENT_TBL_SIZE > 0
    *pdest++          = *psrc++;
#endif

#if OS_EVENT_TBL_SIZE > 1
    *pdest++          = *psrc++;
#endif

#if OS_EVENT_TBL_SIZE > 2
    *pdest++          = *psrc++;
#endif

#if OS_EVENT_TBL_SIZE > 3
    *pdest++          = *psrc++;
#endif
```

10

Listing 10.7   Obtaining the status of a mailbox. (Continued)

```
#if OS_EVENT_TBL_SIZE > 4
    *pdest++         = *psrc++;
#endif

#if OS_EVENT_TBL_SIZE > 5
    *pdest++         = *psrc++;
#endif

#if OS_EVENT_TBL_SIZE > 6
    *pdest++         = *psrc++;
#endif

#if OS_EVENT_TBL_SIZE > 7
    *pdest           = *psrc;
#endif
    pdata->OSMsg = pevent->OSEventPtr;                                    (4)
    OS_EXIT_CRITICAL();
    return (OS_NO_ERR);
}
```

L10.7(1)

L10.7(2)   As always, if OS_ARG_CHK_EN is set to 1, OSMboxQuery() checks that pevent is not a NULL pointer and that it points to an ECB containing a mailbox.

L10.7(3)   OSMboxQuery() then copies the wait list. You should note that I decided to do the copy as in-line code instead of using a loop for performance reasons.

L10.7(4)   Finally, the current message, from the OS_EVENT structure, is copied to the OS_MBOX_DATA structure.

10.07 Using a Mailbox as a Binary Semaphore

A message mailbox can be used as a binary semaphore by initializing the mailbox with a non-NULL pointer [(void *)1 works well]. A task requesting the semaphore calls OSMboxPend() and releases the semaphore by calling OSMboxPost(). Listing 10.8 shows how this process works. You can use this technique to conserve code space if your application only needs binary semaphores and mailboxes. In this case, set OS_MBOX_EN to 1 and OS_SEM_EN to 0 so that you use only mailboxes instead of both mailboxes and semaphores.

Listing 10.8   *Using a mailbox as a binary semaphore.*

```
OS_EVENT *MboxSem;


void Task1 (void *pdata)
{
    INT8U err;

    for (;;) {
        OSMboxPend(MboxSem, 0, &err);   /* Obtain access to resource(s)  */
        .
        .    /* Task has semaphore, access resource(s)                  */
        .
        OSMboxPost(MboxSem, (void *)1); /* Release access to resource(s) */
    }
}
```

10.08 *Using a Mailbox Instead of* OSTimeDly()

The timeout feature of a mailbox can be used to simulate a call to OSTimeDly(). As shown in Listing 10.9, Task1() resumes execution after the time period expires if no message is received within the specified timeout. This process is basically identical to OSTimeDly(TIMEOUT). However, the task can be resumed by Task2() when Task(2) posts a dummy message to the mailbox before the timeout expires. This operation is the same as calling OSTimeDlyResume() had Task1() called OSTimeDly(). Note that the returned message is ignored because you are not actually looking to get a message from another task or an ISR.

10

Listing 10.9   *Using a mailbox as a time delay.*

```
OS_EVENT *MboxTimeDly;


void Task1 (void *pdata)
{
    INT8U err;

    for (;;) {
        OSMboxPend(MboxTimeDly, TIMEOUT, &err);   /* Delay task                   */
        .
        .      /* Code executed after time delay or dummy message is received  */
        .
    }
}


void Task2 (void *pdata)
{
    INT8U err;


    for (;;) {
        OSMboxPost(MboxTimeDly, (void *)1);        /* Cancel delay for Task1  */
        .
        .
    }
}
```

Chapter 11

Message Queue Management

A *message queue* (or simply a queue) is a µC/OS-II object that allows a task or an ISR to send pointer-sized variables to another task. Each pointer typically is initialized to point to some application-specific data structure containing a message. µC/OS-II provides nine services to access message queues: OSQCreate(), OSQDel(), OSQPend(), OSQPost(), OSQPostFront(), OSQPostOpt(), OSQAccept(), OSQFlush(), and OSQQuery().

To enable µC/OS-II message-queue services, you must set configuration constants in OS_CFG.H. Specifically, Table 11.1 shows which services are compiled, based on the value of configuration constants found in OS_CFG.H. You should note that **none** of the queue services are enabled when OS_Q_EN is set to 0 or OS_MAX_QS is set to 0. To enable a specific feature (i.e., service), simply set the corresponding configuration constant to 1. You should notice that OSQCreate() and OSQPend() cannot be individually disabled like the other services. That's because they are always needed when you enable µC/OS-II message queue management. You must enable at least one of the post services: OSQPost(), OSQPostFront(), and OSQPostOpt().

11

Table 11.1   *Message queue configuration constants in* OS_CFG.H.

µC/OS-II Event Flag Service	Enabled when set to 1 in OS_CFG.H
OSQAccept()	OS_Q_ACCEPT_EN
OSQCreate()	
OSQDel()	OS_Q_DEL_EN
OSQFlush()	OS_Q_FLUSH_EN
OSQPend()	
OSQPost()	OS_Q_POST_EN
OSQPostFront()	OS_Q_POST_FRONT_EN
OSQPostOpt()	OS_Q_POST_OPT_EN
OSQQuery()	OS_Q_QUERY_EN

Figure 11.1 shows a flow diagram to illustrate the relationship between tasks, ISRs, and a message queue. Note that the symbology used to represent a queue looks like a mailbox with multiple entries. In fact, you can think of a queue as an array of mailboxes, except that only one wait list is associated with the queue. The hourglass represents a timeout that can be specified with the OSQPend() call. Again, what the pointers point to is application specific. *N* represents the number of entries the queue holds. The queue is full when your application calls OSQPost() [or OSQPostFront() or OSQPostOpt()] *N* times before your application has called OSQPend() or OSQAccept().

As you can see from Figure 11.1, a task or an ISR can call OSQPost(), OSQPostFront(), OSQPostOpt(), OSQFlush(), or OSQAccept(). However, only tasks are allowed to call OSQDel(), OSQPend(), and OSQQuery().

Figure 11.1   Relationships between tasks, ISRs, and a message queue.

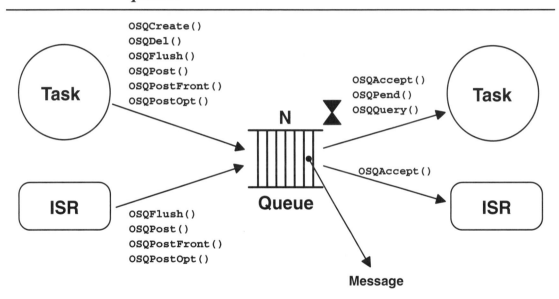

Figure 11.2 Data structures used in a message queue.

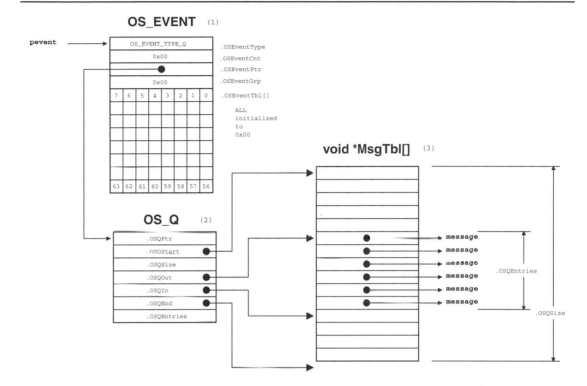

Figure 11.2 shows the different data structures needed to implement a message queue.

F11.2(1) An ECB is required because you need a wait list, and using an ECB allows queue services to use some of the same code used by semaphores, mutexes, and mailboxes.

F11.2(2) When a message queue is created, a queue control block (i.e., an OS_Q, see OS_Q.C) is allocated and linked to the ECB using the .OSEventPtr field in OS_EVENT.

F11.2(3) Before you create a queue, however, you need to allocate an array of pointers that contains the desired number of queue entries. In other words, the number of elements in the array corresponds to the number of entries in the queue. The starting address of the array is passed to OSQCreate() as an argument, as well as the size (in number of elements) of the array. In fact, you don't actually need to use an array as long as the memory occupies contiguous locations.

The configuration constant OS_MAX_QS in OS_CFG.H specifies how many queues you are allowed to have in your application and must be greater than 0. When µC/OS-II is initialized, a list of free queue control blocks is created, as shown in Figure 11.3.

11

Figure 11.3   List of free queue control blocks.

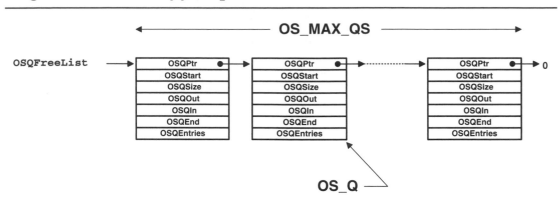

A *queue control block* is a data structure used to maintain information about the queue. It contains the fields described in the following list. Note that the fields are preceded with a dot to show that they are members of a structure, as opposed to simple variables.

.OSQPtr links queue control blocks in the list of free queue control blocks. After the queue is created, this field is not used.

.OSQStart contains a pointer to the start of the message queue storage area. Your application must declare this storage area before creating the queue.

.OSQEnd is a pointer to one location past the end of the queue. This pointer is used to make the queue a circular buffer.

.OSQIn is a pointer to the location in the queue where the next message will be inserted. .OSQIn is adjusted back to the beginning of the message storage area when .OSQIn equals .OSQEnd.

.OSQOut is a pointer to the next message to be extracted from the queue. .OSQOut is adjusted back to the beginning of the message storage area when .OSQOut equals .OSQEnd. .OSQOut is also used to insert a message [see OSQPostFront() and OSQPostOpt()].

.OSQSize contains the size of the message storage area. The size of the queue is determined by your application when the queue is created. Note that µC/OS-II allows the queue to contain up to 65,535 entries.

.OSQEntries contains the current number of entries in the message queue. The queue is empty when .OSQEntries is 0 and full when it equals .OSQSize. The message queue is empty when the queue is created.

A message queue is basically a circular buffer, as shown in Figure 11.4.

Figure 11.4   *A message queue as a circular buffer of pointers.*

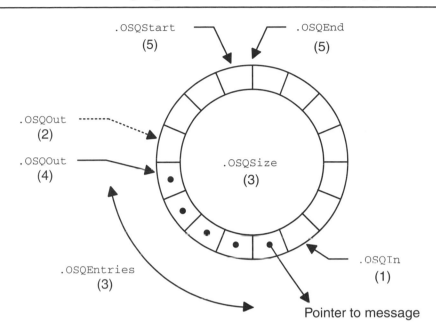

F11.4(1)

F11.4(3)   Each entry contains a pointer. The pointer to the next message is deposited at the entry to which `.OSQIn` points, unless the queue is full (i.e., `.OSQEntries == .OSQSize`). Depositing the pointer at `.OSQIn` implements a First-In-First-Out (FIFO) queue, which is what `OSQPost()` does.

F11.4(2)   μC/OS-II implements a Last-In-First-Out (LIFO) queue by pointing to the entry preceding `.OSQOut` and depositing the pointer at that location [see `OSQPostFront()` and `OSQPostOpt()`].

F11.4(4)   The pointer is also considered full when `.OSQEntries == .OSQSize`. Message pointers are always extracted from the entry to which `.OSQOut` points.

F11.4(5)   The pointers `.OSQStart` and `.OSQEnd` are simply markers used to establish the beginning and end of the array so that `.OSQIn` and `.OSQOut` can wrap around to implement this circular motion.

11.00 Creating a Message Queue, *OSQCreate()*

A message queue (or simply a queue) needs to be created before it can be used. Creating a queue is accomplished by calling `OSQCreate()` and passing it two arguments: a pointer to an array that holds the messages and the size of this array. The array must be declared as an array of pointers to `void`, as follows

```
void *MyArrayOfMsg[SIZE];
```

You would pass the address of `MyArrayOfMsg[]` to `OSQCreate()`, as well as the size of this array. The message queue is assumed to be initially empty — it doesn't contain any messages.

The code to create a queue is shown in Listing 11.1.

Listing 11.1   Creating a message queue.

```
OS_EVENT  *OSQCreate (void **start, INT16U size)
{
#if OS_CRITICAL_METHOD == 3
    OS_CPU_SR  cpu_sr;                                                (1)
#endif
    OS_EVENT  *pevent;
    OS_Q      *pq;


    if (OSIntNesting > 0) {                                           (2)
        return ((OS_EVENT *)0);
    }
    OS_ENTER_CRITICAL();
    pevent = OSEventFreeList;                                         (3)
    if (OSEventFreeList != (OS_EVENT *)0) {
        OSEventFreeList = (OS_EVENT *)OSEventFreeList->OSEventPtr;
    }
    OS_EXIT_CRITICAL();
    if (pevent != (OS_EVENT *)0) {                                    (4)
        OS_ENTER_CRITICAL();
        pq = OSQFreeList;
        if (pq != (OS_Q *)0) {
            OSQFreeList          = OSQFreeList->OSQPtr;
            OS_EXIT_CRITICAL();
            pq->OSQStart       = start;                               (5)
            pq->OSQEnd         = &start[size];
            pq->OSQIn          = start;
            pq->OSQOut         = start;
            pq->OSQSize        = size;
            pq->OSQEntries     = 0;
            pevent->OSEventType = OS_EVENT_TYPE_Q;                    (6)
            pevent->OSEventCnt  = 0;
            pevent->OSEventPtr  = pq;
            OS_EventWaitListInit(pevent);                            (7)
        } else {
            pevent->OSEventPtr = (void *)OSEventFreeList;            (8)
            OSEventFreeList    = pevent;
            OS_EXIT_CRITICAL();
```

Listing 11.1   Creating a message queue. (Continued)

```
        pevent = (OS_EVENT *)0;
     }
  }
  return (pevent);                                    (9)
}
```

L11.1(1)   A local variable called `cpu_sr` to support `OS_CRITICAL_METHOD` #3 is allocated.

L11.1(2)   `OSQCreate()` starts by making sure you are not calling this function from an ISR because that's not allowed. All kernel objects need to be created from task-level code or before multitasking starts.

L11.1(3)   `OSQCreate()` then attempts to obtain an ECB from the free list of ECBs (see Figure 6.5) and adjusts the linked list accordingly.

L11.1(4)   If an ECB is available, `OSQCreate()` attempts to allocate a queue control block (OS_Q) from the free list of queue control blocks (refer to Figure 11.3) and adjusts the linked list accordingly.

L11.1(5)

L11.1(6)   If a queue control block is available from the free list, the fields of the queue control block are initialized, followed by the ones of the ECB. You should note that the `.OSEventType` field is set to `OS_EVENT_TYPE_Q` so that subsequent message-queue services can check the validity of the ECB.

L11.1(7)   The wait list is cleared, indicating that no task is currently waiting on the message queue.

L11.1(8)   If an ECB is available but a queue control block is not, then the ECB is returned to the free list because we cannot satisfy the request to create a queue unless we also have a queue control block.

L11.1(9)   `OSQCreate()` returns either a pointer to the ECB upon successfully creating a message queue or a `NULL` pointer if not. This pointer must be used (if not `NULL`) in subsequent calls that operate on message queues. The pointer is used as the queue's handle.

11

11.01 Deleting a Message Queue, `OSQDel()`

The code to delete a message queue is shown in Listing 11.2, and this code is only generated by the compiler if `OS_Q_DEL_EN` is set to 1 in `OS_CFG.H`. You must use this function with caution because multiple tasks could attempt to access a deleted message queue. Generally speaking, before you delete a message queue, you first delete all the tasks that can access the message queue.

Listing 11.2   Deleting a message queue.

```
OS_EVENT  *OSQDel (OS_EVENT *pevent, INT8U opt, INT8U *err)
{
#if OS_CRITICAL_METHOD == 3
    OS_CPU_SR  cpu_sr;
```

Listing 11.2   *Deleting a message queue. (Continued)*

```
#endif
    BOOLEAN     tasks_waiting;
    OS_Q        *pq;


    if (OSIntNesting > 0) {                                              (1)
        *err = OS_ERR_DEL_ISR;
        return ((OS_EVENT *)0);
    }
#if OS_ARG_CHK_EN > 0
    if (pevent == (OS_EVENT *)0) {                                      (2)
        *err = OS_ERR_PEVENT_NULL;
        return (pevent);
    }
    if (pevent->OSEventType != OS_EVENT_TYPE_Q) {                       (3)
        *err = OS_ERR_EVENT_TYPE;
        return (pevent);
    }
#endif
    OS_ENTER_CRITICAL();
    if (pevent->OSEventGrp != 0x00) {                                   (4)
        tasks_waiting = TRUE;
    } else {
        tasks_waiting = FALSE;
    }
    switch (opt) {
        case OS_DEL_NO_PEND:
            if (tasks_waiting == FALSE) {
                pq                   = pevent->OSEventPtr;              (5)
                pq->OSQPtr           = OSQFreeList;
                OSQFreeList          = pq;
                pevent->OSEventType = OS_EVENT_TYPE_UNUSED;             (6)
                pevent->OSEventPtr  = OSEventFreeList;                  (7)
                OSEventFreeList      = pevent;
                OS_EXIT_CRITICAL();
                *err = OS_NO_ERR;
                return ((OS_EVENT *)0);                                 (8)
```

Listing 11.2   *Deleting a message queue. (Continued)*

```
        } else {
            OS_EXIT_CRITICAL();
            *err = OS_ERR_TASK_WAITING;
            return (pevent);
        }

    case OS_DEL_ALWAYS:
        while (pevent->OSEventGrp != 0x00) {                           (9)
            OS_EventTaskRdy(pevent, (void *)0, OS_STAT_Q);           (10)
        }
        pq                    = pevent->OSEventPtr;                   (11)
        pq->OSQPtr            = OSQFreeList;
        OSQFreeList          = pq;
        pevent->OSEventType = OS_EVENT_TYPE_UNUSED;                   (12)
        pevent->OSEventPtr  = OSEventFreeList;                        (13)
        OSEventFreeList      = pevent;
        OS_EXIT_CRITICAL();
        if (tasks_waiting == TRUE) {
            OS_Sched();                                               (14)
        }
        *err = OS_NO_ERR;
        return ((OS_EVENT *)0);                                       (15)

    default:
        OS_EXIT_CRITICAL();
        *err = OS_ERR_INVALID_OPT;
        return (pevent);
    }
}
```

L11.2(1)   OSQDel() starts by making sure that this function is not called from an ISR because that's not allowed.

L11.2(2)

L11.2(3)   If OS_ARG_CHK_EN (see OS_CFG.H) is set to 1, OSQDel() validates pevent to ensure that it's not a NULL pointer and that it points to an ECB that was created as a queue.

L11.2(4)   OSQDel() then determines whether any tasks are waiting on the queue. The flag tasks_waiting is set accordingly.

Based on the option (i.e., opt) specified in the call, OSQDel() either deletes the queue only if no tasks are pending on the queue (opt == OS_DEL_NO_PEND) or deletes the queue even if tasks are waiting (opt == OS_DEL_ALWAYS).

11

L11.2(5)   When `opt` is set to `OS_DEL_NO_PEND` and no task is waiting on the queue, `OSQDel()` starts by returning the queue control block to the free list.

L11.2(6)

L11.2(7)   `OSQDel()` then marks the ECB as unused, and the ECB is returned to the free list of ECBs. This process allows another message queue (or any other ECB-based object) to be created.

L11.2(8)   You should note that `OSQDel()` returns a `NULL` pointer because, at this point, the queue should no longer be accessed through the original pointer. You should call `OSQDel()` as follows

```
QPtr = OSQDel(QPtr, opt, &err);
```

`OSQDel()` returns an error code if any tasks are waiting on the queue (i.e., `OS_ERR_TASK_WAITING`) because by specifying `OS_DEL_NO_PEND` you indicated that you didn't want to delete the queue if tasks are waiting on the queue.

L11.2(9)

L11.2(10)   When `opt` is set to `OS_DEL_ALWAYS`, then all tasks waiting on the queue are readied. Each task thinks it received a message when in fact no message has been sent. The task should examine the pointer returned to it to make sure it's non-`NULL`. Also, you should note that interrupts are disabled while each task is being readied. This feature, of course, increases the interrupt latency of your system.

L11.2(11)   `OSQDel()` then returns the queue control block to the free list.

L11.2(12)

L11.2(13)   After all pending tasks are readied, `OSQDel()` marks the ECB as unused, and the ECB is returned to the free list of ECBs.

L11.2(14)   The scheduler is called only if tasks were waiting on the queue.

L11.2(15)   Again, you should note that `OSQDel()` returns a `NULL` pointer because, at this point, the queue should no longer be accessed through the original pointer.

11.02 *Waiting for a Message at a Queue (Blocking),* `OSQPend()`

The code to wait for a message to arrive at a queue is shown in Listing 11.3.

Listing 11.3   *Waiting for a message to arrive at a queue.*

```
void  *OSQPend (OS_EVENT *pevent, INT16U timeout, INT8U *err)
{
#if OS_CRITICAL_METHOD == 3
    OS_CPU_SR  cpu_sr;
#endif
    void      *msg;
    OS_Q      *pq;
```

Listing 11.3   Waiting for a message to arrive at a queue. (Continued)

```
    if (OSIntNesting > 0) {                                   (1)
        *err = OS_ERR_PEND_ISR;
        return ((void *)0);
    }
#if OS_ARG_CHK_EN > 0
    if (pevent == (OS_EVENT *)0) {                           (2)
        *err = OS_ERR_PEVENT_NULL;
        return ((void *)0);
    }
    if (pevent->OSEventType != OS_EVENT_TYPE_Q) {            (3)
        *err = OS_ERR_EVENT_TYPE;
        return ((void *)0);
    }
#endif
    OS_ENTER_CRITICAL();
    pq = (OS_Q *)pevent->OSEventPtr;
    if (pq->OSQEntries > 0) {                                (4)
        msg = *pq->OSQOut++;                                 (5)
        pq->OSQEntries--;                                    (6)
        if (pq->OSQOut == pq->OSQEnd) {                      (7)
            pq->OSQOut = pq->OSQStart;                       (8)
        }
        OS_EXIT_CRITICAL();
        *err = OS_NO_ERR;
        return (msg);                                        (9)
    }
    OSTCBCur->OSTCBStat |= OS_STAT_Q;                        (10)
    OSTCBCur->OSTCBDly    = timeout;                         (11)
    OS_EventTaskWait(pevent);                                (12)
    OS_EXIT_CRITICAL();
    OS_Sched();                                              (13)
    OS_ENTER_CRITICAL();
    msg = OSTCBCur->OSTCBMsg;                                (14)
```

11

Listing 11.3   Waiting for a message to arrive at a queue. (Continued)

```
    if (msg != (void *)0) {
        OSTCBCur->OSTCBMsg      = (void *)0;                    (15)
        OSTCBCur->OSTCBStat     = OS_STAT_RDY;
        OSTCBCur->OSTCBEventPtr = (OS_EVENT *)0;
        OS_EXIT_CRITICAL();
        *err                    = OS_NO_ERR;
        return (msg);
    }
    OS_EventTO(pevent);                                        (16)
    OS_EXIT_CRITICAL();
    *err = OS_TIMEOUT;
    return ((void *)0);                                       (17)
}
```

L11.3(1)   It doesn't make sense to call `OSQPend()` from an ISR because an ISR cannot be made to wait. Instead, you should call `OSQAccept()` (see Section 11.06, "Getting a Message Without Waiting, `OSQAccept()`").

L11.3(2)

L11.3(3)   If `OS_ARG_CHK_EN` (see `OS_CFG.H`) is set to 1, `OSQPend()` verifies that `pevent` is not a `NULL` pointer and that the ECB to which `pevent` is pointing has been created by `OSQCreate()`.

L11.3(4)

L11.3(5)   A message is available when `.OSQEntries` is greater than 0. In this case, `OSQPend()` gets the message to which the `.OSQOut` field of the queue control block is pointing, stores the pointer to the message in `msg`, and moves the `.OSQOut` pointer so that it points to the next entry in the queue.

L11.3(6)   `OSQPend()` then decrements the number of entries left in the queue because the previous operation consumed the entry (i.e., removed the oldest message).

L11.3(7)

L11.3(8)   Because a message queue is a circular buffer, `OSQPend()` needs to check that `.OSQOut` has not moved past the last valid entry in the array. When this event happens, however, `.OSQOut` is adjusted to point back to the beginning of the array.

L11.3(9)   The message extracted from the queue is then returned to the caller of `OSQPend()`. This path is what you are looking for when calling `OSQPend()`. It also happens to be the fastest path.

   If the message queue is empty, the calling task needs to be put to sleep until another task (or an ISR) sends a message through the queue (see Section 11.04, "Sending a Message to a Queue (LIFO), `OSQPostFront()`"). `OSQPend()` allows you to specify a timeout value (specified in integral number of ticks) as one of its arguments (i.e., timeout). This feature is useful to avoid waiting indefinitely for a message to arrive at the queue. If the timeout value is nonzero, `OSQPend()` suspends the task until the queue receives a message or the specified timeout period expires. Note that a timeout value of 0 indicates that the task is willing to wait forever for a message to arrive.

L11.3(10) To put the calling task to sleep, `OSQPend()` sets the status flag in the task's TCB to indicate that the task is suspended waiting for a queue.

L11.3(11) The timeout is also stored in the TCB so that it can be decremented by `OSTimeTick()`. You should recall (see Section 3.11, "Clock Tick") that `OSTimeTick()` decrements each of the created task's `.OSTCBDly` field if it's nonzero.

L11.3(12) The actual work of putting the task to sleep is done by `OS_EventTaskWait()` [see Section 6.06, "Making a Task Wait for an Event, `OS_EventTaskWait()`"].

L11.3(13) Because the calling task is no longer ready to run, the scheduler is called to run the next highest priority task that is ready to run. As far as your task is concerned, it made a call to `OSQPend()`, and it doesn't know that it is suspended until a message arrives. When the queue receives a message (or the timeout period expires), `OSQPend()` resumes execution immediately after the call to `OS_Sched()`.

L11.3(14) When `OS_Sched()` returns, `OSQPend()` checks to see if a message has been placed in the task's TCB by `OSQPost()`.

L11.3(15) If so, the call is successful, and the message is returned to the caller.

L11.3(16) If a message is not received, then `OS_Sched()` must have returned because of a timeout. The calling task is then removed from the queue wait list by calling `OS_EventTO()`.

L11.3(17) Note that the returned pointer is set to `NULL` because no message is available to return. The calling task should either examine the contents of the return pointer or the return code to determine whether a valid message has been received.

11.03 Sending a Message to a Queue (FIFO), `OSQPost()`

The code to deposit a message in a queue is shown in Listing 11.4.

Listing 11.4   Depositing a message in a queue (FIFO), `OSQPost()`.

11

```
INT8U  OSQPost (OS_EVENT *pevent, void *msg)
{
#if OS_CRITICAL_METHOD == 3
    OS_CPU_SR  cpu_sr;
#endif
    OS_Q      *pq;


#if OS_ARG_CHK_EN > 0
    if (pevent == (OS_EVENT *)0) {                              (1)
        return (OS_ERR_PEVENT_NULL);
    }
```

Listing 11.4   *Depositing a message in a queue (FIFO),*
   OSQPost( ). (Continued)

```
        if (msg == (void *)0) {                                        (2)
            return (OS_ERR_POST_NULL_PTR);
        }
        if (pevent->OSEventType != OS_EVENT_TYPE_Q) {                  (3)
            return (OS_ERR_EVENT_TYPE);
        }
#endif
    OS_ENTER_CRITICAL();
    if (pevent->OSEventGrp != 0x00) {                                  (4)
        OS_EventTaskRdy(pevent, msg, OS_STAT_Q);                       (5)
        OS_EXIT_CRITICAL();
        OS_Sched();                                                    (6)
        return (OS_NO_ERR);
    }
    pq = (OS_Q *)pevent->OSEventPtr;
    if (pq->OSQEntries >= pq->OSQSize) {                               (7)
        OS_EXIT_CRITICAL();
        return (OS_Q_FULL);
    }
    *pq->OSQIn++ = msg;                                                (8)
    pq->OSQEntries++;                                                  (9)
    if (pq->OSQIn == pq->OSQEnd) {                                     (10)
        pq->OSQIn = pq->OSQStart;
    }
    OS_EXIT_CRITICAL();
    return (OS_NO_ERR);
}
```

L11.4(1)

L11.4(2)

L11.4(3)   If OS_ARG_CHK_EN is set to 1 in OS_CFG.H, OSQPost( ) checks to see that pevent is not a NULL pointer, that the message being posted is also not a NULL pointer, and finally checks to make sure that the ECB is a queue.

L11.4(4)   OSQPost( ) then checks to see if any task is waiting for a message to arrive at the queue. Tasks are waiting when the .OSEventGrp field in the ECB contains a nonzero value.

L11.4(5)   The highest priority task waiting for the message is removed from the wait list by OS_EventTaskRdy( ) [see Section 6.05, "Making a Task Ready, OS_EventTaskRdy( )"], and this task is made ready to run.

L11.4(6)   `OS_Sched()` is then called to see if the task made ready is now the highest priority task ready to run. If it is, a context switch results [only if `OSQPost()` is called from a task], and the readied task is executed. If the readied task is not the highest priority task, `OS_Sched()` returns, and the task that called `OSQPost()` continues execution.

L11.4(7)   If no task is waiting for a message, the message to post needs to be placed in the queue. In this case, `OSQPost()` makes sure that there is still room in the queue. An error code is returned if an attempt is made to add a message to an already full queue.

L11.4(8)

L11.4(9)   If no tasks are waiting for a message to arrive at the queue and the queue is not already full, then the message to post is inserted in the next free location (FIFO), and the number of entries in the queue is incremented.

L11.4(10) Finally, `OSQPost()` adjusts the circular-buffer pointer to prepare for the next post.

Note that a context switch does not occur if `OSQPost()` is called by an ISR because context switching from an ISR only occurs when `OSIntExit()` is called at the completion of the ISR and from the last nested ISR (see Section 3.10, "Interrupts Under µC/OS-II").

11.04 Sending a Message to a Queue (LIFO), `OSQPostFront()`

`OSQPostFront()` is basically identical to `OSQPost()`, except that `OSQPostFront()` uses `.OSQOut` instead of `.OSQIn` as the pointer to the next entry to insert. The code is shown in Listing 11.5.

Listing 11.5   Depositing a message in a queue (LIFO), `OSQPostFront()`.

```
INT8U OSQPostFront (OS_EVENT *pevent, void *msg)
{
#if OS_CRITICAL_METHOD == 3
    OS_CPU_SR  cpu_sr;
#endif
    OS_Q       *pq;


#if OS_ARG_CHK_EN > 0
    if (pevent == (OS_EVENT *)0) {
        return (OS_ERR_PEVENT_NULL);
    }
    if (msg == (void *)0) {
        return (OS_ERR_POST_NULL_PTR);
    }
    if (pevent->OSEventType != OS_EVENT_TYPE_Q) {
        return (OS_ERR_EVENT_TYPE);
```

11

Listing 11.5   *Depositing a message in a queue (LIFO),*
`OSQPostFront( )`. *(Continued)*

```
    }
#endif
    OS_ENTER_CRITICAL();
    if (pevent->OSEventGrp != 0x00) {
        OS_EventTaskRdy(pevent, msg, OS_STAT_Q);
        OS_EXIT_CRITICAL();
        OS_Sched();
        return (OS_NO_ERR);
    }
    pq = (OS_Q *)pevent->OSEventPtr;
    if (pq->OSQEntries >= pq->OSQSize) {
        OS_EXIT_CRITICAL();
        return (OS_Q_FULL);
    }
    if (pq->OSQOut == pq->OSQStart) {                                    (1)
        pq->OSQOut = pq->OSQEnd;                                         (2)
    }
    pq->OSQOut--;                                                        (3)
    *pq->OSQOut = msg;
    pq->OSQEntries++;
    OS_EXIT_CRITICAL();
    return (OS_NO_ERR);
}
```

L11.5(1)

L11.5(2)   You should note that `.OSQOut` points to an already inserted entry, so `.OSQOut` must be made
            to point to the previous entry. If `.OSQOut` points at the beginning of the array, then a decre-
            ment really means positioning `.OSQOut` at the end of the array.

L11.5(3)   However, `.OSQEnd` points to one entry past the array, and thus `.OSQOut` needs to be adjusted
            to be within range. `OSQPostFront( )` implements a LIFO queue because the next message
            extracted by `OSQPend( )` is the last message inserted by `OSQPostFront( )`.

11.05 *Sending a Message to a Queue (FIFO or LIFO),*
`OSQPostOpt( )`

You can also post a message to a queue using an alternate and more flexible function called
`OSQPostOpt( )`. There are three post calls for backwards compatibility with previous versions of
µC/OS-II. `OSQPostOpt( )` is the newer function and can replace both `OSQPost( )` and `OSQPostFront( )`

with a single call. In addition, `OSQPostOpt()` allows posting a message to all tasks (i.e., broadcast) waiting on the queue. The code to deposit a message in a queue is shown in Listing 11.6.

Listing 11.6   *Depositing a message in a queue (Broadcast, FIFO, or LIFO),* `OSQPostOpt()`.

```
INT8U  OSQPostOpt (OS_EVENT *pevent, void *msg, INT8U opt)
{
#if OS_CRITICAL_METHOD == 3
    OS_CPU_SR  cpu_sr;
#endif
    OS_Q       *pq;



#if OS_ARG_CHK_EN > 0
    if (pevent == (OS_EVENT *)0) {                               (1)
        return (OS_ERR_PEVENT_NULL);
    }
    if (msg == (void *)0) {                                      (2)
        return (OS_ERR_POST_NULL_PTR);
    }
    if (pevent->OSEventType != OS_EVENT_TYPE_Q) {                (3)
        return (OS_ERR_EVENT_TYPE);
    }
#endif
    OS_ENTER_CRITICAL();
    if (pevent->OSEventGrp != 0x00) {                            (4)
        if ((opt & OS_POST_OPT_BROADCAST) != 0x00) {            (5)
            while (pevent->OSEventGrp != 0x00) {                (6)
                OS_EventTaskRdy(pevent, msg, OS_STAT_Q);
            }
        } else {
            OS_EventTaskRdy(pevent, msg, OS_STAT_Q);            (7)
        }
        OS_EXIT_CRITICAL();
        OS_Sched();                                             (8)
        return (OS_NO_ERR);
    }
```

11

Listing 11.6   *Depositing a message in a queue (Broadcast, FIFO, or LIFO),* `OSQPostOpt()`. *(Continued)*

```
    pq = (OS_Q *)pevent->OSEventPtr;
    if (pq->OSQEntries >= pq->OSQSize) {                          (9)
        OS_EXIT_CRITICAL();
        return (OS_Q_FULL);
    }
    if ((opt & OS_POST_OPT_FRONT) != 0x00) {                      (10)
        if (pq->OSQOut == pq->OSQStart) {                         (11)
            pq->OSQOut = pq->OSQEnd;
        }
        pq->OSQOut--;
        *pq->OSQOut = msg;
    } else {
        *pq->OSQIn++ = msg;                                       (12)
        if (pq->OSQIn == pq->OSQEnd) {
            pq->OSQIn = pq->OSQStart;
        }
    }
    pq->OSQEntries++;                                             (13)
    OS_EXIT_CRITICAL();
    return (OS_NO_ERR);
}
```

L11.6(1)

L11.6(2)

L11.6(3)   If `OS_ARG_CHK_EN` is set to 1 in `OS_CFG.H`, `OSQPostOpt()` checks to see that `pevent` is not a `NULL` pointer, checks that the message being posted is also not a `NULL` pointer, and finally checks to make sure that the ECB is a queue.

L11.6(4)   `OSQPost()` then checks to see if any task is waiting for a message to arrive at the queue. Tasks are waiting when the `.OSEventGrp` field in the ECB contains a nonzero value.

L11.6(5)

L11.6(6)   If you set the `OS_POST_OPT_BROADCAST` bit in the `opt` argument, then all tasks waiting for a message receive the message. All tasks waiting for the message are removed from the wait list by `OS_EventTaskRdy()` [see Section 6.05, "Making a Task Ready, `OS_EventTaskRdy()`"]. You should notice that interrupt-disable time is proportional to the number of tasks waiting for a message from the queue.

L11.6(7)   If a broadcast was not requested, then only the highest priority task waiting for a message is made ready to run. The highest priority task waiting for the message is removed from the wait list by `OS_EventTaskRdy()`.

L11.6(8)   `OS_Sched()` is then called to see if a task made ready is now the highest priority task ready to run. If it is, a context switch results [only if `OSQPostOpt()` is called from a task], and the readied task is executed. If the readied task is not the highest priority task, `OS_Sched()` returns, and the task that called `OSQPostOpt()` continues execution.

L11.6(9)   If no task is waiting for a message, the message to post needs to be placed in the queue. In this case, `OSQPostOpt()` makes sure that room is still available in the queue. An error code would be returned if an attempt is made to add a message to an already full queue.

L11.6(10) `OSQPostOpt()` then checks the `opt` argument to see if the calling task desires to post the message in FIFO or LIFO (setting `opt` to `OS_POST_OPT_FRONT`) order.

L11.6(11) If LIFO order is selected, `OSQPostOpt()` emulates `OSQPostFront()`.

L11.6(12) If FIFO order, `OSQPostOpt()` emulates `OSQPost()`.

L11.6(13) In either case, the number of entries in the queue is incremented.

Note that a context switch does not occur if `OSQPostOpt()` is called by an ISR because context switching from an ISR only occurs when `OSIntExit()` is called at the completion of the ISR and from the last nested ISR (see Section 3.10, "Interrupts Under µC/OS-II").

11.06 Getting a Message Without Waiting, `OSQAccept()`

You can obtain a message from a queue without putting a task to sleep by calling `OSQAccept()` if the queue is empty. The code for this function is shown in Listing 11.7.

Listing 11.7   Getting a message without waiting (non-blocking), `OSQAccept()`.

```
void  *OSQAccept (OS_EVENT *pevent)
{
#if OS_CRITICAL_METHOD == 3
    OS_CPU_SR  cpu_sr;
#endif
    void      *msg;
    OS_Q      *pq;


#if OS_ARG_CHK_EN > 0
    if (pevent == (OS_EVENT *)0) {                              (1)
        return ((void *)0);
    }
    if (pevent->OSEventType != OS_EVENT_TYPE_Q) {              (2)
        return ((void *)0);
    }
```

Listing 11.7   *Getting a message without waiting (non-blocking),* OSQAccept( ). *(Continued)*

```
#endif
    OS_ENTER_CRITICAL();
    pq = (OS_Q *)pevent->OSEventPtr;
    if (pq->OSQEntries > 0) {                                (3)
        msg = *pq->OSQOut++;                                 (4)
        pq->OSQEntries--;                                    (5)
        if (pq->OSQOut == pq->OSQEnd) {                      (6)
            pq->OSQOut = pq->OSQStart;
        }
    } else {
        msg = (void *)0;                                     (7)
    }
    OS_EXIT_CRITICAL();
    return (msg);
}
```

L11.7(1)

L11.7(2)   If OS_ARG_CHK_EN is set to 1 in OS_CFG.H, OSQAccept() starts by checking that pevent is not a NULL pointer and that the ECB to which pevent is pointing has been created by OSQCreate().

L11.7(3)   OSQAccept() then checks to see if any entries are in the queue by looking at the .OSQEntries queue control block field.

L11.7(4)

L11.7(5)   If a message is available, the oldest message (FIFO) is retrieved from the queue and copied to the local pointer msg, and the number of entries in the queue is decreased by one to reflect the extraction.

L11.7(6)   OSQAccept() then adjusts the circular queue pointer by moving the .OSQOut pointer to the next entry.

L11.7(7)   If no entries are in the queue, the local pointer is set to NULL.

The code that calls OSQAccept() needs to examine the returned value. If OSQAccept() returns a NULL pointer, then a message was not available. You don't want your application to dereference a NULL pointer because, by convention, a NULL pointer is invalid. A non-NULL pointer indicates that a message pointer is available. An ISR can use OSQAccept().

11.07 Flushing a Queue, OSQFlush()

OSQFlush() allows you to remove all the messages posted to a queue and basically start with a fresh queue. The code for this function is shown in Listing 11.8.

Listing 11.8 Flushing the contents of a queue.

```
INT8U  OSQFlush (OS_EVENT *pevent)
{
#if OS_CRITICAL_METHOD == 3
    OS_CPU_SR  cpu_sr;
#endif
    OS_Q       *pq;


#if OS_ARG_CHK_EN > 0
    if (pevent == (OS_EVENT *)0) {                              (1)
        return (OS_ERR_PEVENT_NULL);
    }
    if (pevent->OSEventType != OS_EVENT_TYPE_Q) {              (2)
        return (OS_ERR_EVENT_TYPE);
    }
#endif
    OS_ENTER_CRITICAL();
    pq              = (OS_Q *)pevent->OSEventPtr;              (3)
    pq->OSQIn       = pq->OSQStart;
    pq->OSQOut      = pq->OSQStart;
    pq->OSQEntries = 0;
    OS_EXIT_CRITICAL();
    return (OS_NO_ERR);
}
```

11

L11.8(1)

L11.8(2) If OS_ARG_CHK_EN is set to 1 in OS_CFG.H, OSQFlush() starts by checking that pevent is not a NULL pointer and that the ECB to which pevent is pointing has been created by OSQCreate().

L11.8(3) The IN and OUT pointers are reset to the beginning of the array, and the number of entries is cleared. I decided not to check to see if any tasks were pending on the queue because it is irrelevant anyway and takes more processing time. In other words, if tasks are waiting on the queue, then .OSQEntries is already set to 0. The only difference is that .OSQIn and .OSQOut might be pointing elsewhere in the array. There is also no need to fill the queue with NULL pointers.

11.08 Obtaining the Status of a Queue, `OSQQuery()`

`OSQQuery()` allows your application to take a snapshot of the contents of a message queue. The code for this function is shown in Listing 11.9. `OSQQuery()` is passed two arguments: `pevent` contains a pointer to the message queue, which is returned by `OSQCreate()` when the queue is created; and `pdata` is a pointer to a data structure (`OS_Q_DATA`, see `uCOS_II.H`) that holds information about the message queue. Your application thus needs to allocate a variable of type `OS_Q_DATA` that can receive the information about the desired queue. `OS_Q_DATA` contains the following fields:

`.OSMsg` contains the contents to which `.OSQOut` points if entries are in the queue. If the queue is empty, `.OSMsg` will contains a `NULL` pointer.

`.OSNMsgs` contains the number of messages in the queue (i.e., a copy of `.OSQEntries`).

`.OSQSize` contains the size of the queue (in number of entries).

`.OSEventTbl[]`

`.OSEventGrp` contains a snapshot of the message queue wait list. The caller to `OSQQuery()` can thus determine how many tasks are waiting for the queue.

Listing 11.9   Obtaining the status of a queue.

```
INT8U  OSQQuery (OS_EVENT *pevent, OS_Q_DATA *pdata)
{
#if OS_CRITICAL_METHOD == 3
    OS_CPU_SR  cpu_sr;
#endif
    OS_Q       *pq;
    INT8U      *psrc;
    INT8U      *pdest;


#if OS_ARG_CHK_EN > 0
    if (pevent == (OS_EVENT *)0) {                               (1)
        return (OS_ERR_PEVENT_NULL);
    }
    if (pevent->OSEventType != OS_EVENT_TYPE_Q) {                (2)
        return (OS_ERR_EVENT_TYPE);
    }
#endif
    OS_ENTER_CRITICAL();
    pdata->OSEventGrp = pevent->OSEventGrp;                      (3)
    psrc              = &pevent->OSEventTbl[0];
    pdest             = &pdata->OSEventTbl[0];
#if OS_EVENT_TBL_SIZE > 0
    *pdest++          = *psrc++;
#endif
```

Listing 11.9 *Obtaining the status of a queue. (Continued)*

```c
#if OS_EVENT_TBL_SIZE > 1
    *pdest++          = *psrc++;
#endif

#if OS_EVENT_TBL_SIZE > 2
    *pdest++          = *psrc++;
#endif

#if OS_EVENT_TBL_SIZE > 3
    *pdest++          = *psrc++;
#endif

#if OS_EVENT_TBL_SIZE > 4
    *pdest++          = *psrc++;
#endif

#if OS_EVENT_TBL_SIZE > 5
    *pdest++          = *psrc++;
#endif

#if OS_EVENT_TBL_SIZE > 6
    *pdest++          = *psrc++;
#endif

#if OS_EVENT_TBL_SIZE > 7
    *pdest            = *psrc;
#endif
    pq = (OS_Q *)pevent->OSEventPtr;
    if (pq->OSQEntries > 0) {                                           (4)
        pdata->OSMsg = *pq->OSQOut;
    } else {
        pdata->OSMsg = (void *)0;
    }
    pdata->OSNMsgs = pq->OSQEntries;                                    (5)
    pdata->OSQSize = pq->OSQSize;                                       (6)
    OS_EXIT_CRITICAL();
    return (OS_NO_ERR);
}
```

11

L11.9(1)

L11.9(2)   As always, if `OS_ARG_CHK_EN` is set to 1, `OSQQuery()` checks that `pevent` is not a `NULL` pointer and that it points to an ECB containing a queue.

L11.9(3)   `OSQQuery()` then copies the wait list. You should note that I decided to do the copy as in-line code instead of using a loop for performance reasons.

L11.9(4)   If the queue is not empty, the oldest message is extracted (but not removed) from the queue and copied to `.OSMsg`. In other words, `OSQQuery()` does not move the `.OSQOut` pointer. If no messages are in the queue, the `.OSMsg` contains a `NULL` pointer.

L11.9(5)

L11.9(6)   Finally, the current number of entries and the queue size are placed in the `.OSNMsgs` and `.OSQSize` fields of the `OS_Q_DATA` structure, respectively.

11.09 Using a Message Queue When Reading Analog Inputs

It is often useful in control applications to read analog inputs at regular intervals. To accomplish this task, create a task, called `OSTimeDly()` [see Section 5.00, "Delaying a Task, `OSTimeDly()`"] and specify the desired sampling period.

As shown in Listing 11.5, you could use a message queue instead and have your task pend on the queue with a timeout. The timeout corresponds to the desired sampling period. If no other task sends a message to the queue, the task is resumed after the specified timeout, which basically emulates the `OSTimeDly()` function.

You are probably wondering why I decided to use a queue when `OSTimeDly()` does the trick just fine. By adding a queue, you can have other tasks abort the wait by sending a message, thus forcing an immediate conversion. If you add some intelligence to your messages, you can tell the analog to digital converter (ADC) task to convert a specific channel, tell the task to increase the sampling rate, and more. In other words, you can say to the task: "Can you convert analog input 3 for me now?" After servicing the message, the task initiates the pend on the queue, which restarts the scanning process.

Figure 11.5   Reading analog inputs.

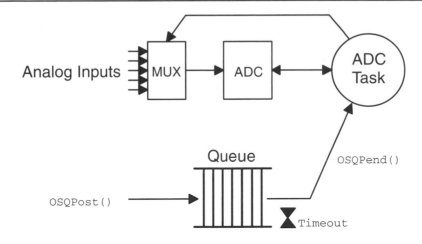

11.10 Using a Queue as a Counting Semaphore

A message queue can be used as a counting semaphore by initializing and loading a queue with as many non-NULL pointers [(void *)1 works well] as resources are available. A task requesting the semaphore calls OSQPend() and releases the semaphore by calling OSQPost(). Listing 11.10 shows how this process works. You can use this technique to conserve code space if your application only needs counting semaphores and message queues (you then have no need for the semaphore services). In this case, set OS_SEM_EN to 0 and only use queues instead of both queues and semaphores. Note that this technique consumes a pointer-sized variable for each resource that the semaphore is guarding and requires a queue control block. In other words, you are sacrificing data space (i.e. RAM) in order to save code space. Also, message queue services are slower than semaphore services. This technique is very inefficient if your counting semaphore (in this case, a queue) is guarding a large amount of resources (because you would need a large array of pointers).

11

Listing 11.10   *Using a queue as a counting semaphore.*

```
OS_EVENT *QSem;
void     *QMsgTbl[N_RESOURCES]


void main (void)
{
    OSInit();
    .
    .
    QSem = OSQCreate(&QMsgTbl[0], N_RESOURCES);
    for (i = 0; i < N_RESOURCES; i++) {
        OSQPost(QSem, (void *)1);
    }
    .
    .
    OSTaskCreate(Task1, .., .., ..);
    .
    .
    OSStart();
}


void Task1 (void *pdata)
{
    INT8U err;


    for (;;) {
        OSQPend(&QSem, 0, &err);      /* Obtain access to resource(s)   */
        .
        .    /* Task has semaphore, access resource(s)              */
        .
        OSMQPost(QSem, (void*)1);    /* Release access to resource(s)  */
    }
}
```

Chapter 12

Memory Management

Your application can allocate and free dynamic memory using any ANSI C compiler's `malloc()` and `free()` functions, respectively. However, using `malloc()` and `free()` in an embedded real-time system is dangerous because, eventually, you might not be able to obtain a single contiguous memory area due to *fragmentation*. Fragmentation is the development of a large number of separate free areas (i.e., the total free memory is fragmented into small, non-contiguous pieces). Execution time of `malloc()` and `free()` are also generally nondeterministic because of the algorithms used to locate a contiguous block of free memory.

μC/OS-II provides an alternative to `malloc()` and `free()` by allowing your application to obtain fixed-sized *memory blocks* from a *partition* made of a contiguous memory area, as illustrated in Figure 12.1. All memory blocks are the same size, and the partition contains an integral number of blocks. Allocation and deallocation of these memory blocks is done in constant time and is deterministic.

As shown in Figure 12.2, more than one memory partition can exist, so your application can obtain memory blocks of different sizes. However, a specific memory block must be returned to the partition from which it came. This type of memory management is not subject to fragmentation.

To enable μC/OS-II memory management services, you must set configuration constants in `OS_CFG.H`. Specifically, Table 12.1 shows which services are compiled based on the value of configuration constants found in `OS_CFG.H`. You should note that **none** of the memory management services are enabled when `OS_MEM_EN` is set to 0. To enable specific features (i.e. service) listed in Table 12.1, simply set the configuration constant to 1. You will notice that `OSMemCreate()`, `OSMemGet()` and `OSMemPut()` cannot be individually disabled like the other services. That's because they are always needed when you enable μC/OS-II memory management.

12

Table 12.1   *Memory management configuration constants in* OS_CFG.H.

µC/OS-II Memory Service	Enabled when set to 1 in OS_CFG.H
OSMemCreate()	
OSMemGet()	
OSMemPut()	
OSMemQuery()	OS_MEM_QUERY_EN

12.00 Memory Control Blocks

µC/OS-II keeps track of memory partitions through the use of a data structure called a *memory control block* (Listing 12.1). Each memory partition requires its own memory control block.

Listing 12.1   *Memory control block data structure.*

```
typedef struct {
    void    *OSMemAddr;
    void    *OSMemFreeList;
    INT32U  OSMemBlkSize;
    INT32U  OSMemNBlks;
    INT32U  OSMemNFree;
} OS_MEM;
```

.OSMemAddr is a pointer to the beginning (base) of the memory partition from which memory blocks are allocated. This field is initialized when you create a partition [see Section 12.01, "Creating a Partition, OSMemCreate()"] and is not used thereafter.

.OSMemFreeList is a pointer used by µC/OS-II to point either to the next free memory control block or to the next free memory block. The use depends on whether the memory partition has been created or not (see Section 12.01, "Creating a Partition, OSMemCreate()").

.OSMemBlkSize determines the size of each memory block in the partition and is a parameter you specify when the memory partition is created (see Section 12.01, "Creating a Partition, OSMemCreate()").

.OSMemNBlks establishes the total number of memory blocks available from the partition. This parameter is specified when the partition is created (see Section 12.01, "Creating a Partition, OSMemCreate()").

.OSMemNFree is used to determine how many memory blocks are available from the partition.

Figure 12.1   Memory partition.

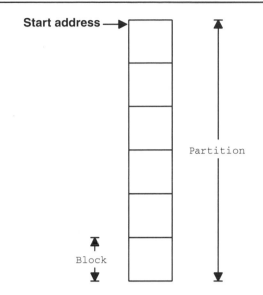

Figure 12.2   Multiple memory partitions.

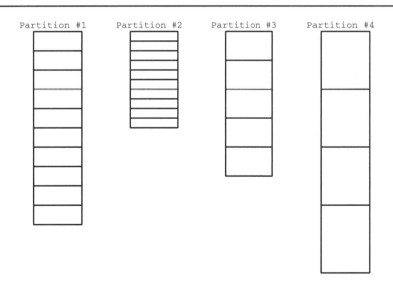

µC/OS-II initializes the memory manager if you configure OS_MEM_EN to 1 in OS_CFG.H. Initialization is done by OS_MemInit() [called by OSInit()] and consists of creating a linked list of memory control blocks, as shown in Figure 12.3. You specify the maximum number of memory partitions with the configuration constant OS_MAX_MEM_PART (see OS_CFG.H), which must be set at least to 2.

As you can see, the OSMemFreeList field of the control block is used to chain the free control blocks.

12

Figure 12.3   List of free memory control blocks.

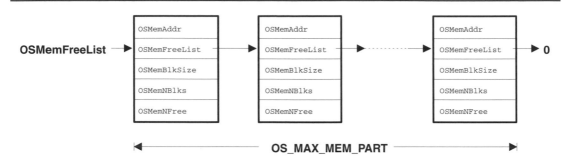

12.01 Creating a Partition, *OSMemCreate()*

Your application must create each partition before it can be used and is this done by calling OSMemCreate(). Listing 12.2 shows how you could create a memory partition containing 100 blocks of 32 bytes each.

Listing 12.2   Creating a memory partition.

```
OS_MEM *CommTxBuf;
INT8U   CommTxPart[100][32];


void main (void)
{
    INT8U err;


    OSInit();
    .

    .
    CommTxBuf = OSMemCreate(CommTxPart, 100, 32, &err);
    .

    .
    OSStart();
}
```

The code to create a memory partition is shown in Listing 12.3. OSMemCreate() requires four arguments: the beginning address of the memory partition, the number of blocks to be allocated from this partition, the size (in bytes) of each block, and a pointer to a variable that contains an error code. OSMemCreate() returns a NULL pointer if OSMemCreate() fails. On success, OSMemCreate() returns a pointer to the allocated memory control block. This pointer must be used in subsequent calls to memory management services [see `OSMemGet()`, `OSMemPut()`, and `OSMemQuery()` in Sections 12.02–12.04].

Listing 12.3 *OSMemCreate().*

```
OS_MEM  *OSMemCreate (void *addr, INT32U nblks, INT32U blksize, INT8U *err)
{
#if OS_CRITICAL_METHOD == 3
    OS_CPU_SR  cpu_sr;
#endif
    OS_MEM    *pmem;
    INT8U     *pblk;
    void      **plink;
    INT32U     i;


#if OS_ARG_CHK_EN > 0
    if (addr == (void *)0) {                                          (1)
        *err = OS_MEM_INVALID_ADDR;
        return ((OS_MEM *)0);
    }
    if (nblks < 2) {                                                  (2)
        *err = OS_MEM_INVALID_BLKS;
        return ((OS_MEM *)0);
    }
    if (blksize < sizeof(void *)) {                                   (3)
        *err = OS_MEM_INVALID_SIZE;
        return ((OS_MEM *)0);
    }
#endif
    OS_ENTER_CRITICAL();
    pmem = OSMemFreeList;                                             (4)
    if (OSMemFreeList != (OS_MEM *)0) {
        OSMemFreeList = (OS_MEM *)OSMemFreeList->OSMemFreeList;
    }
    OS_EXIT_CRITICAL();
    if (pmem == (OS_MEM *)0) {                                        (5)
        *err = OS_MEM_INVALID_PART;
        return ((OS_MEM *)0);
    }
    plink = (void **)addr;                                            (6)
    pblk  = (INT8U *)addr + blksize;
```

12

Listing 12.3   *OSMemCreate( ) (Continued).*

```
    for (i = 0; i < (nblks - 1); i++) {
        *plink = (void *)pblk;
        plink  = (void **)pblk;
        pblk   = pblk + blksize;
    }
    *plink               = (void *)0;
    pmem->OSMemAddr      = addr;                          (7)
    pmem->OSMemFreeList  = addr;
    pmem->OSMemNFree     = nblks;
    pmem->OSMemNBlks     = nblks;
    pmem->OSMemBlkSize   = blksize;
    *err                 = OS_NO_ERR;
    return (pmem);                                        (8)
}
```

L12.3(1)   You must pass a valid pointer to the memory allocated that will be used as a partition.

L12.3(2)   Each memory partition must contain at least two memory blocks.

L12.3(3)   Each memory block must be able to hold the size of a pointer because a pointer is used to chain all the memory blocks together.

L12.3(4)   Next, OSMemCreate( ) obtains a memory control block from the list of free memory control blocks. The memory control block contains run-time information about the memory partition.

L12.3(5)   OSMemCreate( ) cannot create a memory partition unless a memory control block is available.

L12.3(6)   If a memory control block is available and all the previous conditions are satisfied, the memory blocks within the partition are linked together in a singly linked list. A singly linked list is used because insertion and removal of elements in the list is always done from the top of the list.

L12.3(7)   When all the blocks are linked, the memory control block is filled with information about the partition.

L12.3(8)   OSMemCreate( ) returns the pointer to the memory control block, so it can be used in subsequent calls to access the memory blocks from this partition.

Figure 12.4 shows how the data structures look when OSMemCreate( ) completes successfully. Note that the memory blocks are shown linked one after the other. At run time, as you allocate and deallocate memory blocks, the blocks will most likely not be in the same order.

Figure 12.4   Memory partition created by `OSMemCreate()`.

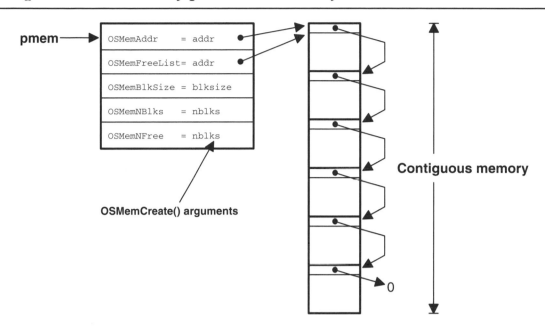

OSMemCreate() arguments

12.02 Obtaining a Memory Block, `OSMemGet()`

Your application can get a memory block from one of the created memory partitions by calling `OSMemGet()`. You must use the pointer returned by `OSMemCreate()` in the call to `OSMemGet()` to specify from which partition the memory block will come. Obviously, your application needs to know how big the memory block obtained is, so that it doesn't exceed its storage capacity. In other words, you must not use more memory than is available from the memory block. For example, if a partition contains 32-byte blocks, then your application can use up to 32 bytes. When you are done using the block, you must return it to the proper memory partition [see Section 12.03, "Returning a Memory Block, `OSMemPut()`"]. Listing 12.4 shows the code for `OSMemGet()`.

Listing 12.4   `OSMemGet()`.

```
void  *OSMemGet (OS_MEM *pmem, INT8U *err)                             (1)
{
#if OS_CRITICAL_METHOD == 3
    OS_CPU_SR  cpu_sr;
#endif
    void      *pblk;
```

12

Listing 12.4   *OSMemGet( ). (Continued)*

```
#if OS_ARG_CHK_EN > 0
    if (pmem == (OS_MEM *)0) {                                          (2)
        *err = OS_MEM_INVALID_PMEM;
        return ((OS_MEM *)0);
    }
#endif
    OS_ENTER_CRITICAL();
    if (pmem->OSMemNFree > 0) {                                         (3)
        pblk                = pmem->OSMemFreeList;                      (4)
        pmem->OSMemFreeList = *(void **)pblk;                           (5)
        pmem->OSMemNFree--;                                             (6)
        OS_EXIT_CRITICAL();
        *err = OS_NO_ERR;
        return (pblk);                                                  (7)
    }
    OS_EXIT_CRITICAL();
    *err = OS_MEM_NO_FREE_BLKS;
    return ((void *)0);
}
```

L12.4(1)   The pointer passed to OSMemGet( ) specifies the partition from which you want to get a memory block.

L12.4(2)   If you enabled argument checking (i.e., OS_ARG_CHK_EN is set to 1 in OS_CFG.H), then OSMemGet( ) makes sure that you didn't pass a NULL pointer instead of a pointer to a partition. Unfortunately, OSMemGet( ) doesn't know whether a non-NULL is actually pointing to a valid partition (pmem could point to anything).

L12.4(3)   OSMemGet( ) checks to see if free blocks are available.

L12.4(4)   If a block is available, it is removed from the free list.

L12.4(5)

L12.4(6)   The free list is then updated so that it points to the next free memory block, and the number of blocks is decremented, indicating that the block has been allocated.

L12.4(7)   The pointer to the allocated block is finally returned to your application.

Note that you can call this function from an ISR because, if a memory block is not available, there is no waiting and the ISR simply receives a NULL pointer.

12.03 *Returning a Memory Block,* OSMemPut( )

When your application is done with a memory block, it must be returned to the appropriate partition. This operation is accomplished by calling OSMemPut( ). You should note that OSMemPut( ) has no way of knowing whether the memory block returned to the partition belongs to that partition. In other words, if you allocate a memory block from a partition containing blocks of 32 bytes, then you should not return this block to a memory partition containing blocks of 120 bytes. The next time an application requests a block from the 120-byte partition, it will only get 32 valid bytes; the remaining 88 bytes might belong to some other task(s). This issue could certainly make your system crash.

Listing 12.5 shows the code for OSMemPut( ).

Listing 12.5   OSMemPut( ).

```
INT8U  OSMemPut (OS_MEM  *pmem, void *pblk)                           (1)
{
#if OS_CRITICAL_METHOD == 3
    OS_CPU_SR  cpu_sr;
#endif


#if OS_ARG_CHK_EN > 0
    if (pmem == (OS_MEM *)0) {                                        (2)
        return (OS_MEM_INVALID_PMEM);
    }
    if (pblk == (void *)0) {
        return (OS_MEM_INVALID_PBLK);
    }
#endif
    OS_ENTER_CRITICAL();
    if (pmem->OSMemNFree >= pmem->OSMemNBlks) {                       (3)
        OS_EXIT_CRITICAL();
        return (OS_MEM_FULL);
    }
    *(void **)pblk      = pmem->OSMemFreeList;                        (4)
    pmem->OSMemFreeList = pblk;
    pmem->OSMemNFree++;                                               (5)
    OS_EXIT_CRITICAL();
    return (OS_NO_ERR);
}
```

12

L12.5(1)   You pass to OSMemPut( ) the address of the memory control block (pmem) to which the memory block belongs (pblk).

L12.5(2)   OSMemPut( ) then checks that the pointers being passed to the function are non-NULL. Unfortunately, OSMemPut( ) doesn't know whether the block returned actually belongs to the partition. It is assumed that your application is returning the block to its proper place.

L12.5(3)   Next, we check to see that the memory partition is not already full. This situation would certainly indicate that something went wrong during the allocation/deallocation process. Indeed, you are returning a block to a partition that thinks it has all of its blocks already returned to it.

L12.5(4)   If the memory partition can accept another memory block, it is inserted into the linked list of free blocks.

L12.5(5)   Finally, the number of memory blocks in the memory partition is incremented.

12.04 Obtaining Status of a Memory Partition, *OSMemQuery()*

OSMemQuery() is used to obtain information about a memory partition. For example, your application can determine how many memory blocks are free, how many memory blocks have been used (i.e., allocated), and the size of each memory block (in bytes). This information is placed in a data structure called OS_MEM_DATA, as shown in Listing 12.6. The code for OSMemQuery() is shown in Listing 12.7.

Listing 12.6   *Data structure used to obtain status from a partition.*

```
typedef struct {
    void  *OSAddr;      /* Points to beginning address of memory partition    */
    void  *OSFreeList; /* Points to beginning of free list of memory blocks   */
    INT32U OSBlkSize;  /* Size (in bytes) of each memory block                */
    INT32U OSNBlks;    /* Total number of blocks in the partition             */
    INT32U OSNFree;    /* Number of memory blocks free                        */
    INT32U OSNUsed;    /* Number of memory blocks used                        */
} OS_MEM_DATA;
```

Listing 12.7   *OSMemQuery().*

```
INT8U  OSMemQuery (OS_MEM *pmem, OS_MEM_DATA *pdata)
{
#if OS_CRITICAL_METHOD == 3
    OS_CPU_SR  cpu_sr;
#endif



#if OS_ARG_CHK_EN > 0
    if (pmem == (OS_MEM *)0) {                                             (1)
        return (OS_MEM_INVALID_PMEM);
    }
    if (pdata == (OS_MEM_DATA *)0) {
        return (OS_MEM_INVALID_PDATA);
    }
#endif
    OS_ENTER_CRITICAL();
    pdata->OSAddr     = pmem->OSMemAddr;                                   (2)
    pdata->OSFreeList = pmem->OSMemFreeList;
```

Listing 12.7   `OSMemQuery()`.

```
    pdata->OSBlkSize  = pmem->OSMemBlkSize;
    pdata->OSNBlks    = pmem->OSMemNBlks;
    pdata->OSNFree    = pmem->OSMemNFree;
    OS_EXIT_CRITICAL();
    pdata->OSNUsed    = pdata->OSNBlks - pdata->OSNFree;                    (3)
    return (OS_NO_ERR);
}
```

L12.7(1)   As usual, we start off by checking the arguments passed to the function.

L12.7(2)   All the fields found in OS_MEM are copied to the OS_MEM_DATA data structure with interrupts disabled. This process ensures that the fields are not altered until they are all copied.

L12.7(3)   You should also notice that computation of the number of blocks used is performed outside of the critical section because it's done using the local copy of the data.

12.05 *Using Memory Partitions*

Figure 12.5 shows an example of how you can use the dynamic memory allocation feature of μC/OS-II, as well as its message-passing capability (see Chapter 11, "Message Queue Management"). Also, refer to Listing 12.9 for the pseudocode of the two tasks shown. The numbers in parentheses in Figure 12.5 correspond to the appropriate action in Listing 12.9.

Figure 12.5   *Using dynamic memory allocation.*

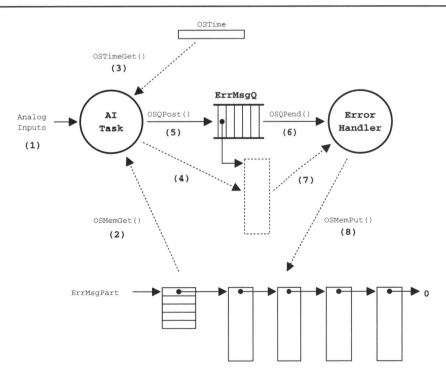

The first task reads and checks the value of analog inputs (pressures, temperatures, and voltages) and sends a message to the second task if any of the analog inputs exceed a threshold. The message sent contains a time stamp, information about which channel had the error, an error code, an indication of the severity of the error, and any other information you can think of.

Error handling in this example is centralized. This means that other tasks, or even ISRs, can post error messages to the error-handling task. The error-handling task can be responsible for displaying error messages on a monitor (a display), logging errors to a disk, or dispatching other tasks that could take corrective actions based on the error.

Listing 12.8   *Scanning analog inputs and reporting errors.*

```
AnalogInputTask()
{
    for (;;) {
        for (all analog inputs to read) {
            Read analog input;                                          (1)
            if (analog input exceeds threshold) {
                Get memory block;                                       (2)
                Get current system time (in clock ticks);               (3)
                Store the following items in the memory block.          (4)
                    System time (i.e. a time stamp);
                    The channel that exceeded the threshold;
                    An error code;
                    The severity of the error;
                    Etc.
                Post the error message to error queue;                  (5)
                    (A pointer to the memory block containing the data)
            }
        }
        Delay task until it's time to sample analog inputs again;
    }
}




ErrorHandlerTask()
{
    for (;;) {
        Wait for message from error queue;                             (6)
            (Gets a pointer to a memory block containing information
             about the error reported)
```

Listing 12.8   *Scanning analog inputs and reporting errors. (Continued)*

```
        Read the message and take action based on error reported;    (7)
        Return the memory block to the memory partition;             (8)
    }
}
```

12.06 *Waiting for Memory Blocks from a Partition*

Sometimes it's useful to have a task wait for a memory block in case a partition runs out of blocks. µC/OS-II doesn't support pending on partitions, but you can support this requirement by adding a counting semaphore (see Chapter 7, "Semaphore Management") to guard the memory partition. To obtain a memory block, simply obtain a semaphore and then call OSMemGet(). To release a block, simply return the block to its partition and post to the semaphore. The whole process is shown in Listing 12.9.

Listing 12.9   *Waiting for memory blocks from a partition.*

```
OS_EVENT   *SemaphorePtr;                                          (1)
OS_MEM     *PartitionPtr;
INT8U      Partition[100][32];
OS_STK     TaskStk[1000];


void main (void)
{
    INT8U err;

    OSInit();                                                     (2)
    .

    .
    SemaphorePtr = OSSemCreate(100);                              (3)
    PartitionPtr = OSMemCreate(Partition, 100, 32, &err);        (4)
    .
    OSTaskCreate(Task, (void *)0, &TaskStk[999], &err);          (5)
    .
    OSStart();                                                    (6)
}

void Task (void *pdata)
{
    INT8U  err;
```

12

Listing 12.9   Waiting for memory blocks from a partition. (Continued)

```
    INT8U *pblock;


    for (;;) {
        OSSemPend(SemaphorePtr, 0, &err);                        (7)
        pblock = OSMemGet(PartitionPtr, &err);                   (8)
        .

        .  /* Use the memory block */

        .
        OSMemPut(PartitionPtr, pblock);                          (9)
        OSSemPost(SemaphorePtr);                                 (10)
    }

}
```

L12.9(1)   First, declare your system objects. Note that I used hard-coded constants for clarity. You would certainly create `#define` constants in a real application.

L12.9(2)

L12.9(3)   Initialize μC/OS-II by calling `OSInit()` and then create a semaphore with an initial count corresponding to the number of blocks in the partition.

L12.9(4)   Next, create the partition and one of the tasks that will be accessing the partition.

L12.9(5)   By now, you should be able to figure out what you need to do to add the other tasks. It obviously does not make much sense to use a semaphore if only one task is using memory blocks — there is no need to ensure mutual exclusion! In fact, it doesn't even make sense to use partitions unless you intend to share memory blocks with other tasks.

L12.9(6)   Multitasking is then started by calling `OSStart()`.

L12.9(7)

L12.9(8)   When the task executes, it obtains a memory block only if a semaphore is available. After the semaphore is available, the memory block is obtained. There is no need to check for an error code from `OSSemPend()` because the only way μC/OS-II can return to this task is if a memory block is released because a timeout of 0 is specified. Also, you don't need the error code from `OSMemGet()` for the same reason — you must have at least one block in the partition in order for the task to resume.

L12.9(9)

L12.9(10) When the task is finished with a memory block, the task simply returns the memory block to the partition and signals the semaphore.

Chapter 13

Porting µC/OS-II

This chapter describes in general terms what needs to be done to adapt µC/OS-II to different processors. Adapting a real-time kernel to a microprocessor or a microcontroller is called a *port*. Most of µC/OS-II is written in C for portability; however, it is still necessary to write some processor-specific code in C and assembly language. Specifically, µC/OS-II manipulates processor registers, which can only be done through assembly language. Porting µC/OS-II to different processors is relatively easy because µC/OS-II was designed to be portable. If you already have a port for the processor you are intending to use, you don't need to read this chapter, unless of course you want to know how µC/OS-II processor-specific code works.

A processor can run µC/OS-II if the processor satisfies the following general requirements:

1. The processor has a C compiler that generates reentrant code.

2. The processor supports interrupts and can provide an interrupt that occurs at regular intervals (typically between 10 and 100Hz).

3. Interrupts can be disabled and enabled from C.

4. The processor supports a hardware stack that can accommodate a fair amount of data (possibly many kilobytes).

5. The processor has instructions to load and store the stack pointer and other CPU registers, either on the stack or in memory.

Processors, such as the Motorola 6805 series, do not satisfy requirements 4 and 5, so µC/OS-II cannot run on such processors.

Figure 13.1 shows the µC/OS-II architecture and its relationship with the hardware. When you use µC/OS-II in an application, you are responsible for providing the application software and the µC/OS-II configuration sections. This book and companion CD contains all the source code for the processor-independent code section, as well as the processor-specific code section for the Intel 80x86, real mode, large model. If you intend to use µC/OS-II on a different processor, you need either to obtain a copy of a port for the processor you intend to use or to write one yourself if the desired processor port has not already been ported. Check the official µC/OS-II Web site at `www.uCOS-II.com` for a list of available ports. In fact, you might want to look at other ports and learn from the experience of others.

13

Figure 13.1 μC/OS-II hardware/software architecture.

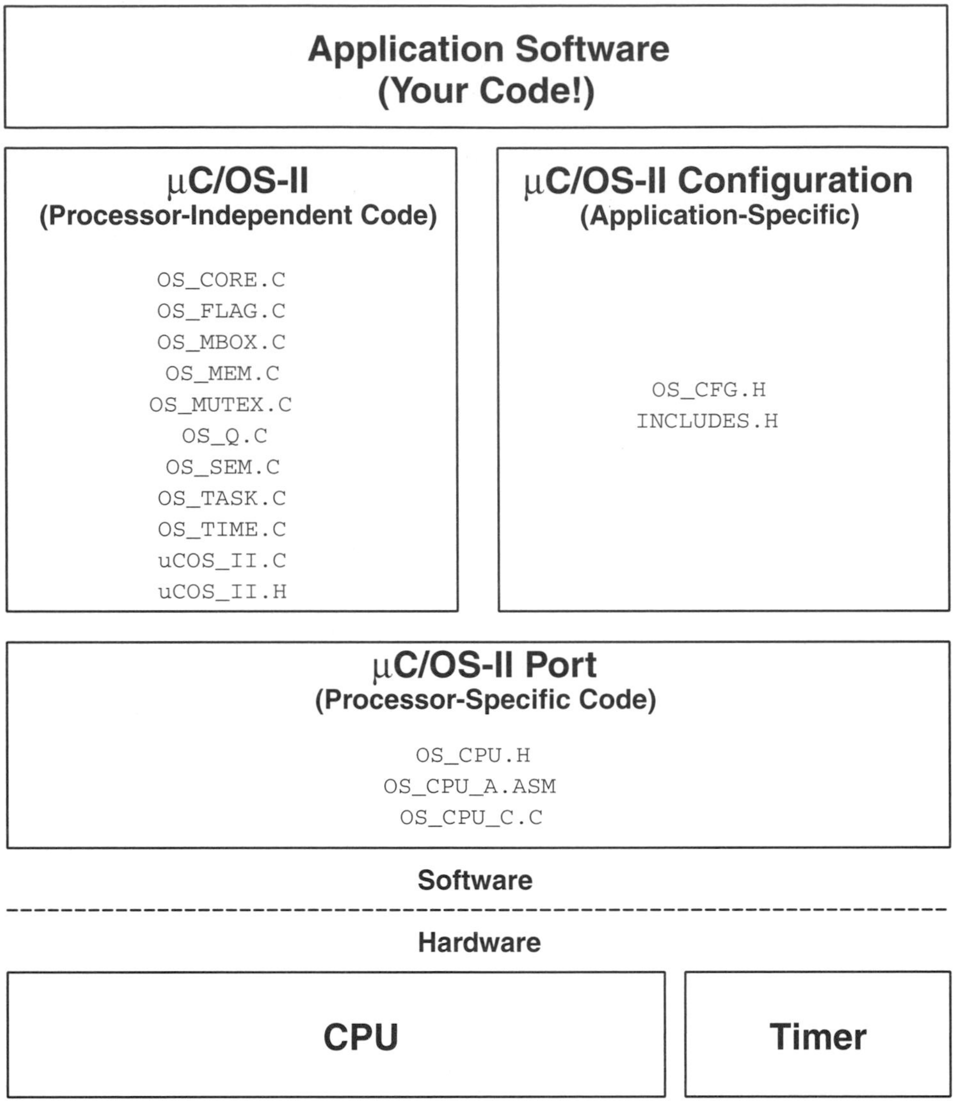

Porting μC/OS-II is actually quite straightforward after you understand the subtleties of the target processor and the C compiler you are using. Depending on the processor, a port can consist of writing or changing between 50 and 300 lines of code and could take anywhere from a few hours to about a week to accomplish. The easiest thing to do, however, is to modify an existing port from a processor that is similar to the one you intend to use. Table 13.1 summarizes the code you must write or modify. I decided to add a column that indicates the relative complexity involved: 1 means easy, 2 means average, and 3 means more complicated.

Table 13.1   Port summary.

Name	Type	File	C or Assembly?	Complexity
BOOLEAN	Data Type	OS_CPU.H	C	1
INT8U	Data Type	OS_CPU.H	C	1
INT8S	Data Type	OS_CPU.H	C	1
INT16U	Data Type	OS_CPU.H	C	1
INT16S	Data Type	OS_CPU.H	C	1
INT32U	Data Type	OS_CPU.H	C	1
INT32S	Data Type	OS_CPU.H	C	1
FP32	Data Type	OS_CPU.H	C	1
FP64	Data Type	OS_CPU.H	C	1
OS_STK	Data Type	OS_CPU.H	C	2
OS_CPU_SR	Data Type	OS_CPU.H	C	2
OS_CRITICAL_METHOD	#define	OS_CPU.H	C	3
OS_STK_GROWTH	#define	OS_CPU.H	C	1
OS_ENTER_CRITICAL()	Macro	OS_CPU.H	C	3
OS_EXIT_CRITICAL()	Macro	OS_CPU.H	C	3
OSStartHighRdy()	Function	OS_CPU_A.ASM	Assembly	2
OSCtxSw()	Function	OS_CPU_A.ASM	Assembly	3
OSIntCtxSw()	Function	OS_CPU_A.ASM	Assembly	3
OSTickISR()	Function	OS_CPU_A.ASM	Assembly	3
OSTaskStkInit()	Function	OS_CPU_C.C	C	3
OSInitHookBegin()	Function	OS_CPU_C.C	C	1
OSInitHookEnd()	Function	OS_CPU_C.C	C	1
OSTaskCreateHook()	Function	OS_CPU_C.C	C	1
OSTaskDelHook()	Function	OS_CPU_C.C	C	1
OSTaskSwHook()	Function	OS_CPU_C.C	C	1
OSTaskStatHook()	Function	OS_CPU_C.C	C	1
OSTCBInitHook()	Function	OS_CPU_C.C	C	1
OSTimeTickHook()	Function	OS_CPU_C.C	C	1
OSTaskIdleHook()	Function	OS_CPU_C.C	C	1

13

13.00 Development Tools

As previously stated, because µC/OS-II is written mostly in ANSI C, you need an ANSI C compiler for the processor you intend to use. Also, because µC/OS-II is a preemptive kernel, you should only use a C compiler that generates reentrant code.

Your tools should also include an assembler because some of the port requires saving and restoring CPU registers that are generally not accessible from C. However, some C compilers do have extensions that allow you to manipulate CPU registers directly from C or allow you to write in-line assembly language statements.

Most C compilers designed for embedded systems also include a linker and a locator. The linker is used to combine object files (compiled and assembled files) from different modules, while the locator allows you to place the code and data anywhere in the memory map of the target processor.

Your C compiler must also provide a mechanism to disable and enable interrupts from C. Some compilers allow you to insert in-line assembly language statements into your C source code, which makes it easy to insert the proper processor instructions to enable and disable interrupts. Other compilers actually contain language extensions to enable and disable interrupts directly from C.

13.01 Directories and Files

The installation program provided on the companion CD installs µC/OS-II and the port for the Intel 80x86 (real mode, large model) on your hard drive. I devised a consistent directory structure that allows you to find the files for the desired target processor easily. If you add a port for another processor, you should consider following the same conventions.

All ports should be placed under \SOFTWARE\uCOS-II on your hard drive. You should note that I don't specify on which disk drive these files should reside; I leave this decision up to you. The source code for each microprocessor or microcontroller port must be found in either two or three files: OS_CPU.H, OS_CPU_C.C, and, optionally, OS_CPU_A.ASM. The assembly language file is optional because some compilers allow you to have in-line assembly language, so you can place the needed assembly language code directly in OS_CPU_C.C. The directory in which the port is located determines which processor you are using. Examples of directories where different ports are stored are shown in the Table 13.2. Note that each directory contains the same filenames, even though they have totally different targets. Also, the directory structure accounts for different C compilers. For example, the µC/OS-II port files for the Paradigm C (see www.DevTools.com) compiler should be placed in a Paradigm sub-directory. Similarly, the port files for the Borland C (see www.Borland.com) compiler v4.5 should be placed in a BC45 sub-directory. The port files for other processors, such as the Motorola 68HC11 processor using a COSMIC compiler (see www.Cosmic-US.com), should be placed as shown in Table 13.2.

Table 13.2   *Examples of port directories.*

Intel/AMD 80186	\SOFTWARE\uCOS-II\Ix86L\PARADIGM
	\OS_CPU.H
	\OS_CPU_A.ASM
	\OS_CPU_C.C
	\SOFTWARE\uCOS-II\Ix86L\BC45
	\OS_CPU.H
	\OS_CPU_A.ASM
	\OS_CPU_C.C

Table 13.2   ***Examples of port directories. (Continued)***

Motorola 68HC11	\SOFTWARE\uCOS-II\68HC11\COSMIC
	\OS_CPU.H
	\OS_CPU_A.ASM
	\OS_CPU_C.C

13.02   INCLUDES.H

As mentioned in Chapter 1, INCLUDES.H is a *master* include file found at the top of all .C files

```
#include "includes.h"
```

INCLUDES.H allows every .C file in your project to be written without concern about which header file is actually needed. The only drawback to having a master include file is that INCLUDES.H can include header files that are not pertinent to the actual .C file being compiled. Each file therefore will require extra time to compile. This inconvenience is offset by code portability. I assume that you have an INCLUDES.H in each project that uses µC/OS-II. You can edit the INCLUDES.H file that I provide and add your own header files, but your header files should be added at the end of the list. INCLUDES.H is not actually considered part of a port, but I decided to mention it here because every µC/OS-II file assumes it.

13.03   OS_CPU.H

OS_CPU.H contains processor- and implementation-specific #define constants, macros, and typedefs. The general layout of OS_CPU.H is shown in Listing 13.1.

Listing 13.1   OS_CPU.H.

```
/*
*********************************************************************
*                         DATA TYPES
*                      (Compiler Specific)
*********************************************************************
*/

typedef unsigned char   BOOLEAN;                                          (1)
typedef unsigned char   INT8U;     /* Unsigned  8 bit quantity     */
typedef signed   char   INT8S;     /* Signed    8 bit quantity     */
typedef unsigned int    INT16U;    /* Unsigned 16 bit quantity     */
typedef signed   int    INT16S;    /* Signed   16 bit quantity     */
typedef unsigned long   INT32U;    /* Unsigned 32 bit quantity     */
typedef signed   long   INT32S;    /* Signed   32 bit quantity     */
```

13

Listing 13.1   *OS_CPU.H. (Continued)*

```
typedef float          FP32;      /* Single precision floating point    */        (2)
typedef double         FP64;      /* Double precision floating point    */

typedef unsigned int   OS_STK;    /* Each stack entry is 16-bit wide    */        (3)
typedef unsigned short OS_CPU_SR; /* Define size of CPU status register */        (4)


/*
*********************************************************************************
*                            Processor Specifics
*********************************************************************************
*/
#define  OS_CRITICAL_METHOD    ??                                                  (5)


#if      OS_CRITICAL_METHOD == 1
#define  OS_ENTER_CRITICAL()   ????                                               (6)
#define  OS_EXIT_CRITICAL()    ????
#endif


#if      OS_CRITICAL_METHOD == 2
#define  OS_ENTER_CRITICAL()   ????                                               (7)
#define  OS_EXIT_CRITICAL()    ????
#endif


#if      OS_CRITICAL_METHOD == 3
#define  OS_ENTER_CRITICAL()   ????                                               (8)
#define  OS_EXIT_CRITICAL()    ????
#endif



#define  OS_STK_GROWTH         1          /* Stack growth (0=Up, 1=Down) */       (9)


#define  OS_TASK_SW()          ????                                               (10)
```

13.03.01 Compiler-Specific Data Types

Because different microprocessors have different word lengths, the port of μC/OS-II includes a series of type definitions that ensures portability. Specifically, μC/OS-II code never makes use of C's short, int, and long data types because they are inherently nonportable.

To complete the data-type section, you need to consult your compiler documentation and find the standard C data types that correspond to the types expected by μC/OS-II.

L13.1(1) I defined integer data types that are both portable and intuitive. The INT16U data type, for example, always represents a 16-bit unsigned integer. μC/OS-II and your application code can now assume that the range of values for variables declared with this type is from 0 to

65,535. A µC/OS-II port to a 32-bit processor means that an INT16U is actually declared as an unsigned short instead of an unsigned int. Where µC/OS-II is concerned, however, it still deals with an INT16U. All you have to do is determine from your compiler documentation what combination of standard C data types map to the data types µC/OS-II expects.

L13.1(2)   Also, for convenience, I have included floating-point data types even though µC/OS-II doesn't make use of floating-point numbers.

L13.1(3)   You must tell µC/OS-II the data type of a task's stack, which is done by declaring the proper C data type for OS_STK. If stack elements on your processor are 32 bit, you can declare OS_STK as

```
typedef  INT32U  OS_STK;
```

This example assumes that the declaration of INT32U precedes that of OS_STK. When you create a task and you declare a stack for this task, then you **must** always use OS_STK as its data type.

L13.1(4)   If you use OS_CRITICAL_METHOD #3 (see next section), you need to declare the data type for the processor status word (PSW) . The PSW is also called the processor flag or status register. If the PSW of your processor is 16-bit wide, simply declare it as

```
typedef  INT16U  OS_CPU_SR;
```

13.03.02 *OS_ENTER_CRITICAL() and OS_EXIT_CRITICAL()*

This section is similiar to Section 3.00, "Critical Sections, OS_ENTER_CRITICAL() and OS_EXIT_CRITICAL()," with some items removed and others added. I decided to repeat this text here to avoid having you flip back and forth between sections. µC/OS-II, like all real-time kernels, needs to disable interrupts in order to access critical sections of code and to reenable interrupts when done. This ability allows µC/OS-II to protect critical code from being entered simultaneously from either multiple tasks or ISRs.

Processors generally provide instructions to disable/enable interrupts, and your C compiler must have a mechanism to perform these operations directly from C. Some compilers allow you to insert in-line assembly language statements into your C source code, which makes it quite easy to insert processor instructions to enable and disable interrupts. Other compilers contain language extensions to enable and disable interrupts directly from C.

To hide the implementation method chosen by the compiler manufacturer, µC/OS-II defines two macros to disable and enable interrupts: OS_ENTER_CRITICAL() and OS_EXIT_CRITICAL(), respectively [see L13.1(5) through L13.1(8)].

OS_ENTER_CRITICAL() and OS_EXIT_CRITICAL() are always together to wrap critical sections of code as shown in Listing 13.2.

13

Listing 13.2   Use of critical section.

```
{
     .

     .

    OS_ENTER_CRITICAL();
    /* µC/OS-II critical code section */
    OS_EXIT_CRITICAL();

     .

     .

}
```

Your application can also use OS_ENTER_CRITICAL() and OS_EXIT_CRITICAL() to protect your own critical sections of code. Be careful, however, because your application will crash (i.e., hang) if you disable interrupts before calling a service, such as OSTimeDly() (see Chapter 5). This problem happens because the task is suspended until time expires, but because interrupts are disabled, you would never service the tick interrupt! Obviously, all the PEND calls are also subject to this problem, so be careful. As a general rule, you should always call µC/OS-II services with interrupts enabled!

OS_ENTER_CRITICAL() and OS_EXIT_CRITICAL() can be implemented using three different methods. You only need one of the three methods, even though I show OS_CPU.H (Listing 13.1) containing three different methods. The actual method used by your application depends on the capabilities of the processor, as well as the compiler used. The method used is selected by the #define constant OS_CRITICAL_METHOD, which is defined in OS_CPU.H of the port you are using for your application (i.e., product). The #define constant OS_CRITICAL_METHOD is necessary in OS_CPU.H because µC/OS-II allocates a local variable called cpu_sr if OS_CRITICAL_METHOD is set to 3.

OS_CRITICAL_METHOD == 1

The first and simplest way to implement these two macros is to invoke the processor instruction to disable interrupts for OS_ENTER_CRITICAL() and the enable interrupts instruction for OS_EXIT_CRITICAL(). However, there is a little problem with this scenario. If you call a µC/OS-II function with interrupts disabled, on return from a µC/OS-II service (i.e., function), interrupts are enabled! If you had disabled interrupts prior to calling µC/OS-II, you might want them to be disabled on return from the µC/OS-II function. In this case, this implementation is not adequate. However, with some processors/compilers, this method is the only one you can use. An example declaration is shown in Listing 13.3. Here, I assume that the compiler you are using provides you with two functions to disable and enable interrupts, respectively. The names disable_int() and enable_int() are arbitrarily chosen for sake of illustration. You compiler can have different names for them.

Listing 13.3   Critical method #1.

```
#define  OS_ENTER_CRITICAL()  disable_int()    /* Disable interrupts        */
#define  OS_EXIT_CRITICAL()   enable_int()     /* Enable  interrupts        */
```

OS_CRITICAL_METHOD == 2

The second way to implement OS_ENTER_CRITICAL() is to save the interrupt disable status onto the stack and then disable interrupts. OS_EXIT_CRITICAL() is implemented by restoring the interrupt status from the stack. Using this scheme, if you call a μC/OS-II service with interrupts either enabled or disabled, the status is preserved across the call. In other words, interrupts are enabled after the call if they were enabled before the call, and interrupts are disabled after the call if they were disabled before the call. Be careful when you call a μC/OS-II service with interrupts disabled because you are extending the interrupt latency of your application. The pseudocode for these macros is shown in Listing 13.4.

Listing 13.4   Critical method #2.

```
#define OS_ENTER_CRITICAL()    \
      asm(" PUSH    PSW");   \
      asm(" DI");
#define OS_EXIT_CRITICAL()     \
      asm(" POP     PSW");
```

Here, I'm assuming that your compiler allows you to execute in-line assembly language statements directly from your C code, as shown in Listing 13.4 (thus the asm() pseudo-function). You need to consult your compiler documentation for this.

The PUSH PSW instruction pushes the 'Processor Startus Word', PSW (also known as the condition code register or, processor flags) onto the stack. The DI instruction stands for 'Disable Interrupts'. Finally, the POP PSW instruction is assumed to restore the original state of the interrupt flag from the stack. The instructions I used are only for illustration purposes and may not be actual processor instructions.

Some compilers do not optimize inline code real well and thus, this method may not work because the compiler may not be 'smart' enough to know that the stack pointer was changed (by the PUSH instruction). Specifically, the processor you are using may provide a 'stack pointer relative' addressing mode which the compiler can use to access local variables or function arguments using and offset from the stack pointer. Of course, if the stack pointer is changed by the OS_ENTER_CRITICAL() macro then all these stack offsets may be wrong and would most likely lead to incorrect behavior.

OS_CRITICAL_METHOD == 3

Some compilers provide you with extensions that allow you to obtain the current value of the PSW and save it into a local variable declared within a C function. The variable can then be used to restore the PSW, as shown in Listing 13.5.

Listing 13.5   Saving and restoring the PSW.

```
void Some_uCOS_II_Service (arguments)
{
  OS_CPU_SR  cpu_sr                                              (1)


    cpu_sr = get_processor_psw();                                (2)
    disable_interrupts();                                        (3)

    .
    /* Critical section of code */                               (4)
```

13

Listing 13.5   Saving and restoring the PSW. (Continued)

```
    .
    set_processor_psw(cpu_sr);                                           (5)
    .
}
```

L13.5(1)   OS_CPU_SR is a µC/OS-II data type that is declared in the processor-specific file OS_CPU.H. When you select this critical section method, OS_ENTER_CRITICAL() and OS_EXIT_CRITICAL() always assume the presence of the cpu_sr variable. In other words, if you use this method to protect your own critical sections, you need to declare a cpu_sr variable in your function. However, you do not need to declare this variable in any of the µC/OS-II functions because that's already done.

L13.5(2)   To enter a critical section, a function provided by the compiler vendor is called to obtain the current state of the PSW (condition code register, processor flags, or whatever else this register is called for your processor). I called this function get_processor_psw() for sake of discussion, but it likely has a different name.

L13.5(3)   Another compiler-provided function (disable_interrupt()) is called, of course, to disable interrupts.

L13.5(4)   At this point, the critical code can execute.

L13.5(5)   After the critical section has completed, interrupts can be reenabled by calling another compiler-specific extension that, for sake of discussion, I call set_processor_psw(). The function receives as an argument the previous state of the PSW. It's assumed that this function restores the processor PSW to this value.

Because I don't know what the compiler functions are (there is no standard naming convention), the µC/OS-II macros are used to encapsulate the functionality as shown

Listing 13.6   Critical method #3.

```
#define OS_ENTER_CRITICAL()          \
        cpu_sr = get_processor_psw(); \
        disable_interrupts();


#define OS_EXIT_CRITICAL()           \
        set_processor_psw(cpu_sr);
```

13.03.03   OS_STK_GROWTH

The stack on most microprocessors and microcontrollers grows from high to low memory. However, some processors work the other way around.

L13.1(9)   µC/OS-II has been designed to be able to handle either flavor by specifying which way the stack grows through the configuration constant OS_STK_GROWTH, as shown.

Set OS_STK_GROWTH to 0 for low-to-high memory stack growth.

Set OS_STK_GROWTH to 1 for high-to-low memory stack growth.

The reason this #define constant is provided is twofold. First, OSInit() needs to know where the top-of-stack is when it's creating OS_TaskIdle() and OS_TaskStat(). Second, if you call OSTaskStkChk(), μC/OS-II needs to know where the bottom-of-stack is (high-memory or low-memory) in order to determine stack usage.

13.03.04   *OS_TASK_SW( )*

L13.1(10) OS_TASK_SW() is a macro that is invoked when μC/OS-II switches from a low priority task to the highest priority task. OS_TASK_SW() is always called from task-level code. Another mechanism, OSIntExit(), is used to perform a context switch when an ISR makes a higher priority task ready for execution. A context switch simply consists of saving the processor registers on the stack of the task being suspended and restoring the registers of the higher priority task from its stack.

In μC/OS-II, the stack frame for a ready task always looks as if an interrupt has just occurred and all processor registers are saved onto it. In other words, all that μC/OS-II has to do to run a ready task is to restore all processor registers from the task's stack and execute a return from interrupt. You thus need to implement OS_TASK_SW() to simulate an interrupt. Most processors provide either software interrupt or **trap** instructions to accomplish this task. The ISR or trap handler (also called the exception handler) must vector to the assembly language function OSCtxSw() (see Section Section 13.04.02, "OSTaskCreateHook( ),").

For example, a port for an Intel or AMD 80x86 processor uses an INT instruction, as shown in Listing 13.7. The interrupt handler needs to vector to OSCtxSw(). You must determine how to do this with your compiler/processor.

Listing 13.7   *Critical method #3.*

```
#define  OS_TASK_SW()        asm  INT  080H
```

A port for the Motorola 68HC11 processor most likely uses the SWI instruction. Again, the SWI handler is OSCtxSw(). Finally, a port for a Motorola 680x0/CPU32 processor probably uses one of the 16 TRAP instructions. Of course, the selected **trap** handler is none other than OSCtxSw().

Some processors, such as the Zilog Z80, do not provide a software interrupt mechanism. In this case, you need to simulate the stack frame as closely to an interrupt stack frame as you can. OS_TASK_SW() calls OSCtxSw() instead of vectoring to it. The Z80 is a processor that has been ported to μC/OS and is thus portable to μC/OS-II.

13.04   *OS_CPU_C.C*

13

A μC/OS-II port requires that you write 10 fairly simple C functions:

```
OSTaskStkInit()
OSTaskCreateHook()
OSTaskDelHook()
OSTaskSwHook()
OSTaskIdleHook()
OSTaskStatHook()
OSTimeTickHook()
OSInitHookBegin()
```

```
OSInitHookEnd()
OSTCBInitHook()
```

The only required function is OSTaskStkInit(). The other nine functions must be declared but do not need to contain any code. Function prototypes, as well as a reference manual, is provided at the end of this chapter.

13.04.01   *OSTaskStkInit()*

This function is called by OSTaskCreate() and OSTaskCreateExt() to initialize the stack frame of a task so that the stack looks as if an interrupt has just occurred and all the processor registers have been pushed onto that stack. The pseudocode for OSTaskStkInit() is shown in Listing 13.8.

Listing 13.8   *Pseudocode for OSTaskStkInit().*

```
OS_STK *OSTaskStkInit (void  (*task)(void *pd),
                       void   *pdata,
                       OS_STK *ptos,
                       INT16U  opt);
{
    Simulate call to function with an argument (i.e. pdata);          (1)
    Simulate ISR vector;                                             (2)
    Setup stack frame to contain desired initial values of all registers;   (3)
    Return new top-of-stack pointer to caller;                       (4)
}
```

Figure 13.2 shows what OSTaskStkInit() needs to put on the stack of the task being created. Note that I assume a stack grows from high to low memory. The discussion that follows applies just as well for a stack growing in the opposite direction.

Listing 13.9 shows the function prototypes for OSTaskCreate(), OSTaskCreateExt(), and OSTaskStkInit(). The arguments in bold font are passed from the create calls to OSTaskStkInit(). When OSTaskCreate() calls OSTaskStkInit(), OSTaskCreate() sets the opt argument to 0x0000 because OSTaskCreate() doesn't support additional options.

Listing 13.9   *Function prototypes.*

```
INT8U  OSTaskCreate (void  (*task)(void *pd),
                     Void   *pdata,
                     OS_STK *ptos,
                     INT8U   prio)
INT8U  OSTaskCreateExt (void    (*task)(void *pd),
                        void     *pdata,
                        OS_STK   *ptos,
                        INT8U     prio,
                        INT16U    id,
                        OS_STK   *pbos,
                        INT32U    stk_size,
                        void     *pext,
                        INT16U    opt)
```

Listing 13.9   Function prototypes. (Continued)

```
OS_STK *OSTaskStkInit (void  (*task)(void *pd),
                       void   *pdata,
                       OS_STK *ptos,
                       INT16U  opt);
```

Figure 13.2   Stack-frame initialization with `pdata` passed to the stack.

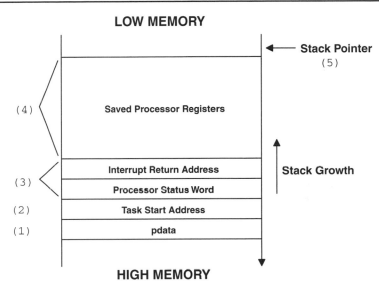

Listing 13.10   Task code.

```
void MyTask (void *pdata)
{
    /* Do something with argument 'pdata' */
    for (;;) {
        /* Task code                     */
    }
}
```

Recall that under μC/OS-II, a task is an infinite loop but otherwise looks just like any other C function. When the task is started by μC/OS-II, the task receives an argument just as if it were called by another function, as shown in Listing 13.10.

If I were to call `MyTask()` from another function, the C compiler might push the argument onto the stack followed by the return address of the function calling `MyTask()`. `OSTaskStkInit()` needs to simulate this behavior. Some compilers actually pass `pdata` in one or more registers. I'll discuss this situation later.

13

F13.2(1)

L13.8(1)   Assuming `pdata` is pushed onto the stack, `OSTaskStkInit()` simulates the scenario and loads the stack accordingly.

F13.2(2)

L13.8(1)   Unlike a C function call, the return address of the caller is unknown because the task was never really called (we are just trying to set up the stack frame of a task, as if the code were called). All `OSTaskStkInit()` knows about is the start address of the task (it's passed as an argument). It turns out that you really don't need the return address because the task is not supposed to return to another function anyway.

F13.2(3)

L13.8(2)   At this point, `OSTaskStkInit()` needs to put the registers on the stack. The registers are automatically pushed by the processor when the function recognizes and starts servicing an interrupt. Some processors stack all of the registers; others stack just a few. Generally speaking, a processor stacks at least the value of the program counter of the instruction to which to return upon returning from an interrupt and the processor status word. Obviously, you must match the order exactly.

F13.2(4)

L13.8(3)   Next, `OSTaskStkInit()` needs to put the rest of the processor registers on the stack. The stacking order depends on whether your processor gives you a choice or not. Some processors have one or more instructions that push many registers at once. You would have to emulate the stacking order of such instructions. For example, the Intel 80x86 has the `PUSHA` instruction, which pushes eight registers onto the stack. On the Motorola 68HC11 processor, all registers are automatically pushed onto the stack during an interrupt response, so you would also need to match the stacking order.

F13.2(5)

L13.8(4)   After you've initialized the stack, `OSTaskStkInit()` needs to return the address to where the stack pointer points after the stacking is complete. `OSTaskCreate()` or `OSTaskCreateExt()` takes this address and saves it in the task control block. The processor documentation tells you whether the stack pointer should point to the next free location on the stack or the location of the last stored value. For example, on an Intel 80x86 processor, the stack pointer points to the last stored data, whereas on a Motorola 68HC11 processor, the stack pointer points at the next free location.

Now it's time to returns to the issue of what to do if your C compiler passes the `pdata` argument in registers instead of on the stack.

F13.3(1)   Similarly to the previous case, `OSTaskStkInit()` saves the task address onto the stack in order to simulate a call to your task code.

F13.3(2)   Again, `OSTaskStkInit()` needs to put the registers on the stack. The registers are automatically pushed by the processor when the function recognizes and starts servicing an interrupt. Some processors stack all of registers; others stack just a few. Generally speaking, a processor stacks at least the value of the program counter for the instruction to which to return upon returning from an interrupt and the processor status word. Obviously, you must match the order exactly.

F13.3(3)   Next, `OSTaskStkInit()` needs to put the rest of the processor registers on the stack. The stacking order depends on whether your processor gives you a choice or not. Some processors have one or more instructions that push many registers at once. You would have to emulate the stacking order of such instructions. Because the compiler passed arguments to a function in registers (at least some of them), you need to find out from the compiler documentation the register in which pdata is stored. pdata is placed on the stack in the same area in which you save the corresponding register.

F13.3(4)   After you've initialized the stack, OSTaskStkInit() needs to return the address to which the stack pointer points after the stacking is complete. OSTaskCreate() or OSTaskCreateExt() takes this address and saves it in the task control block (OS_TCB). Again, the processor documentation tells you whether the stack pointer should point to the next free location on the stack or the location of the last stored value.

Figure 13.3   **Stack frame initialization with** pdata **passed in register.**

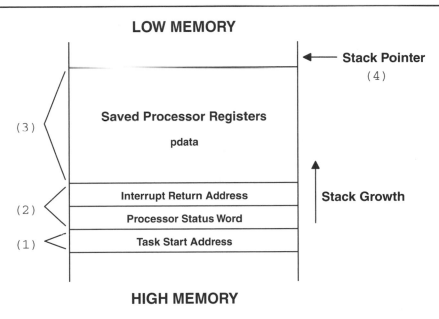

13.04.02 *OSTaskCreateHook()*

OSTaskCreateHook() is called by OS_TCBInit() whenever a task is created. This function allows you or the user of your port to extend the functionality of µC/OS-II. OSTaskCreateHook() is called when µC/OS-II is done setting up most of the OS_TCB but before the OS_TCB is linked to the active task chain and before the task is made ready to run. Interrupts are enabled when this function is called.

When called, OSTaskCreateHook() receives a pointer to the OS_TCB of the task created and can thus access all of the structure elements. OSTaskCreateHook() has limited capability when the task is created with OSTaskCreate(). However, with OSTaskCreateExt(), you get access to a TCB extension pointer (OSTCBExtPtr) in OS_TCB that can be used to access additional data about the task, such as the contents of floating-point registers, Memory Management Unit (MMU) registers, task counters, and debug information. You might want to examine OS_TCBInit() to see exactly what's being done. Chapter 15 shows how you can use this function.

13

Note about OS_CPU_HOOKS_EN

The code for the hook functions (OS???Hook()) that are described in this and the following sections is generated from the file OS_CPU_C.C only if OS_CPU_HOOKS_EN is set to 1 in OS_CFG.H. The OS???Hook() functions are always needed, and the #define constant OS_CPU_HOOKS_EN doesn't mean that the code will not be called. All OS_CPU_HOOKS_EN means is that the hook functions are in OS_CPU_C.C (when 1) or elsewhere, in another file (when 0). This feature allows the user of your port to redefine all the hook functions in a different file. Obviously, users of your port need access to the source to compile it with OS_CPU_HOOKS_EN set to 0 in order to prevent multiply defined symbols at link time. If you don't need to use hook functions because you don't intend to extend the functionality of µC/OS-II through this mechanism, then you can leave the function bodies empty. Again, µC/OS-II always expects that the hook functions exist (i.e., they must always be declared somewhere).

13.04.03   *OSTaskDelHook()*

OSTaskDelHook() is called by OSTaskDel() after removing the task from either the ready list or a wait list (if the task was waiting for an event to occur). It is called before unlinking the task from µC/OS-II's internal linked list of active tasks. When called, OSTaskDelHook() receives a pointer to the OS_TCB of the task being deleted and can access all structure members. OSTaskDelHook() can see if a TCB extension has been created (a non-NULL pointer) and is thus responsible for performing cleanup operations. OSTaskDelHook() is called with interrupts disabled, which means that your OSTaskDelHook() can affect interrupt latency if it's too long. You might want to study OSTaskDel() and see exactly what is accomplished before calling OSTaskDelHook(). Chapter 15 shows how you can use this function.

13.04.04   *OSTaskSwHook()*

OSTaskSwHook() is called whenever a task switch occurs. The call happens whether the task switch is performed by OSCtxSw() or OSIntCtxSw() (see Section 13.05, "OS_CPU_A.ASM,"). OSTaskSwHook() can access OSTCBCur and OSTCBHighRdy directly because they are global variables. OSTCBCur points to the OS_TCB of the task being switched out, and OSTCBHighRdy points to the OS_TCB of the new task. Note that interrupts are always disabled during the call to OSTaskSwHook(), so you should keep additional code to a minimum because additional code affects interrupt latency. OSTaskSwHook() has no arguments and is not expected to return anything. Chapter 15 shows how you can use this function.

13.04.05   *OSTaskStatHook()*

OSTaskStatHook() is called once every second by OSTaskStat(). You can extend the statistics capability with OSTaskStatHook(). For instance, you can keep track of and display the execution time of each task, the percentage of the CPU used by each task, how often each task executes, and more. OSTaskStatHook() has no arguments and is not expected to return anything. You might want to examine OS_TaskStat(). Example #3 in Chapter 1 shows how you can use this function.

13.04.06 *OSTimeTickHook( )*

OSTaskTimeHook( ) is called by OSTimeTick( ) at every system tick. In fact, OSTimeTickHook( ) is called before a tick is actually processed by μC/OS-II in order to give your port or application first claim to the tick. OSTimeTickHook( ) has no arguments and is not expected to return anything.

13.04.07 *OSTCBInitHook( )*

OSTCBInitHook( ) is called by OS_TCBInit( ) immediately before it calls OSTaskCreateHook( ), which is also called by OS_TCBInit( ). I did this so that you could initialize OS_TCB-related data with OSTCBInitHook( ) and task-related data with OSTaskCreateHook( ) (there can be a difference). It's up to you to decide whether you need to populate both of these functions. Like OSTaskCreateHook( ), OSTCBInitHook( ) receives a pointer to the newly created task's OS_TCB after initializing most of the field but before linking the OS_TCB to the chain of created tasks. You might want to examine OS_TCBInit( ).

13.04.08 *OSTaskIdleHook()*

Many microprocessors allow you to execute instructions that bring the CPU into a low-power mode. The CPU exits low power mode when it receives an interrupt. OSTaskIdleHook( ) is called by OS_TaskIdle( ) and, as shown in Listing 13.11, can be made to use this CPU feature.

Listing 13.11   Use of *OSTaskIdleHook( )*.

```
void  OS_TaskIdle (void *pdata)
{
#if OS_CRITICAL_METHOD == 3
    OS_CPU_SR  cpu_sr;
#endif


    pdata = pdata;
    for (;;) {
        OS_ENTER_CRITICAL();
        OSIdleCtr++;                                            (1)
        OS_EXIT_CRITICAL();
        OSTaskIdleHook();                                       (2)
    }
}


void  OSTaskIdleHook (void)
{
    asm(" STOP");                                               (3)
    /* Interrupt received and serviced */                      (4)
}
```

13

L13.11(1) As you know, OS_TaskIdle() is executed whenever no other task is ready to run. OS_TaskIdle() increments the idle counter, OSIdleCtr.

L13.11(2) Next, OS_TaskIdle() calls the hook function OSTaskIdleHook() that you declare in the port file OS_CPU_C.C.

L13.11(3) OSTaskIdleHook() immediately invokes the CPU instruction to bring the CPU into low-power mode. I assume, for sake of illustration, that your compiler supports in-line assembly language and that the instruction to execute is called STOP. Other compilers might not allow you to do in-line assembly language and, in those cases, you could declare OSTaskIdleHook() in the assembly language file OS_CPU_A.ASM but make sure you include a return from the call. Also, the instruction to bring the CPU into low-power mode can be called something else.

L13.11(4) When an interrupt occurs, the CPU exits low-power mode and processes the ISR. The ISR signals a higher priority task, which executes upon completion of the ISR because the ISR calls OSIntExit(). When all tasks are again waiting for events to occur, µC/OS-II switches back to the idle task immediately after item L13.9(4), OSTaskIdleHook() returns to OS_TaskIdle(), and the same process repeats.

You could also use OSTaskIdleHook() to blink an LED, which could be used as an indication of how busy the CPU is. A dim LED would indicate a very busy CPU, while a bright LED indicates a lightly loaded CPU.

13.04.09   *OSInitHookBegin()*

OSInitHookBegin() is called immediately upon entering OSInit(). The reason I added this function is to encapsulate OS-related initialization within OSInit(). This encapsulation allows you to extend OSInit() with your own port-specific code. The user of your port still only sees OSInit(), and the code is cleaner.

13.04.10 *OSInitHookEnd()*

OSInitHookEnd() is similar to OSInitHookBegin(), except that the hook is called at the end of OSInit() just before returning to OSInit()'s caller. The reason is the same as above and you can see an example of the use of OSInitHookEnd() in Chapter 15.

13.05 OS_CPU_A.ASM

A µC/OS-II port requires that you write four assembly language functions:

```
OSStartHighRdy()
OSCtxSw()
OSIntCtxSw()
OSTickISR()
```

If your compiler supports in-line assembly language, you could actually place these functions in OS_CPU_C.C, instead of having a separate assembly language file.

13.05.01 *OSStartHighRdy()*

OSStartHighRdy() is called by OSStart() to start the highest priority task ready to run. The pseudocode for this function is shown in Listing 13.12. You need to convert this pseudocode to assembly language.

Listing 13.12 *Pseudocode for OSStartHighRdy().*

```
void OSStartHighRdy (void)
{
    Call user definable OSTaskSwHook();                         (1)
    OSRunning = TRUE;                                           (2)
    Get the stack pointer of the task to resume:               (3)
        Stack pointer = OSTCBHighRdy->OSTCBStkPtr;


    Restore all processor registers from the new task's stack; (4)
    Execute a return from interrupt instruction:               (5)

}
```

L13.12(1) OSStartHighRdy() must call OSTaskSwHook(). However, OSStartHighRdy() only does half a context switch — you are only restoring the registers of the highest priority task and **not** saving the register of a task. OSTaskSwHook() needs to examine OSRunning to tell whether OSTaskSwHook() was called from OSStartHighRdy() (OSRunning is FALSE) or from a regular context switch (OSRunning is TRUE).

L13.12(2) OSStartHighRdy() sets OSRunning to TRUE before the highest priority task is restored but after calling OSTaskSwHook().

You should note that I should have placed the previous two statements in OSStart() instead of requiring that you place them in OSStartHighRdy() because they don't need to be done in assembly language. Unfortunately, I didn't notice this fact when I first wrote OSStart(). If I were to change OSStart() at this point, a large number of ports might not work properly. I have thus decided to leave these statements in OSStartHighRdy() in order to avoid a lot of e-mail messages!

L13.12(3) OSStartHighRdy() then needs to load the stack pointer of the CPU with the top-of-stack pointer of the highest priority task. OSStartHighRdy() assumes that OSTCBHighRdy points to the OS_TCB of the task with the highest priority. To simplify things, the stack pointer is always stored at the beginning of the OS_TCB. In other words, the stack pointer of the task to resume is always stored at offset 0 in the OS_TCB.

L13.12(4) In µC/OS-II, the stack frame for a ready task always looks as if an interrupt has just occurred and all processor registers have been saved onto it. To run the highest priority task, all you need to do is restore all processor registers from the task's stack in the proper order and execute a return from interrupt. In this step, OSStartHighRdy() retrieves the contents of all the CPU registers from the stack. It's important to pop the registers in the reverse order from the way they were placed onto the stack by OSTaskStkInit() (see Section 13.04.01, "OSTaskStkInit(),").

L13.12(5) The last step is to execute a return-from-interrupt instruction, which causes the CPU to retrieve the program counter and possibly the CPU flags register (also called the status register) from the stack. This action causes the CPU to resume execution at the first instruction of the highest priority task.

Remember that before you can call OSStart(), however, you must have created at least one of your tasks [see OSTaskCreate() and OSTaskCreateExt()].

13.05.02   *OSCtxSw()*

A task-level context switch is accomplished by issuing a software-interrupt instruction or, depending on the processor, executing a TRAP instruction. The interrupt service routine, trap, or exception handler must vector to OSCtxSw().

The sequence of events that leads µC/OS-II to vector to OSCtxSw() begins when the current task calls a service provided by µC/OS-II, which causes a higher priority task to be ready to run. At the end of the service call, µC/OS-II calls OS_Sched(), which concludes that the current task is no longer the most important task to run. OS_Sched() loads the address of the highest priority task into OSTCBHighRdy and then executes the software interrupt or TRAP instruction by invoking the macro OS_TASK_SW(). Note that the variable OSTCBCur already contains a pointer to the current task's, OS_TCB. The software interrupt instruction (or TRAP) forces some of the processor registers (most likely the return address and the processor's status word) onto the current task's stack and then the processor vectors to OSCtxSw().

The pseudocode for OSCtxSw() is shown in Listing 13.13. This code must be written in assembly language because you cannot access CPU registers directly from C. Note that interrupts are disabled during OSCtxSw() and also during execution of the user-definable function OSTaskSwHook(). When OSCtxSw() is invoked, it is assumed that the processor's program counter (PC) and possibly the flag register (or status register) are pushed onto the stack by the software-interrupt instruction, which is invoked by the OS_TASK_SW() macro.

Listing 13.13   *Pseudocode for OSCtxSw().*

```
void OSCtxSw(void)
{
    Save processor registers;                                        (1)
    Save the current task's stack pointer into the current task's OS_TCB:  (2)
        OSTCBCur->OSTCBStkPtr = Stack pointer;
    OSTaskSwHook();                                                  (3)
    OSTCBCur  = OSTCBHighRdy;                                        (4)
    OSPrioCur = OSPrioHighRdy;                                       (5)
    Get the stack pointer of the task to resume:                    (6)
        Stack pointer = OSTCBHighRdy->OSTCBStkPtr;
    Restore all processor registers from the new task's stack;      (7)
    Execute a return from interrupt instruction;                    (8)
}
```

L13.13(1) OSCtxSw() saves all the processor registers (except the ones already saved by the software interrupt) in the **same** order in which OSTaskStkInit() placed them on the stack by.

L13.13(2) After all CPU registers are on the stack of the task to suspend, OSCtxSw() saves the stack pointer into the task's OS_TCB.

L13.13(3) OSCtxSw() calls OSTaskSwHook() in case your port needs to extend the functionality of a context switch. Note that OSTaskSwHook() is **always** called whether this function is declared in OS_CPU_C.C or elsewhere.

L13.13(4) OSCtxSw() then needs to make the pointer to the current OS_TCB point to the OS_TCB of the task being resumed. In other words, the new task becomes the current task.

L13.13(5) OSCtxSw() needs to copy the new task's priority into the current task priority.

L13.13(6) The new task's stack pointer is then retrieved from the new task's OS_TCB.

L13.13(7) OSCtxSw() then needs to restore the value of the CPU registers for the task that is being resumed. You must restore the registers in exactly the reverse order as they were saved. For example, if your processor has four registers called R1, R2, R3, and R4 and you saved them in that order, then you must retrieve them starting from R4 and ending with R1.

L13.13(8) Because the value of the high priority task's program counter (and possibly the status register) are still on the stack, a return from interrupt causes the program counter and status register to be popped off the stack and loaded into the CPU. This action causes your task code to be resumed.

You can see an animation of a context switch for an Intel 80x86 CPU by visiting www.uCOS-II.com.

13.05.03 *OSTickISR()*

µC/OS-II requires you to provide a periodic time source to keep track of time delays and timeouts. A tick should occur between 10 and 100 times per second, or Hertz. To provide an appropriate time source, either dedicate a hardware timer or obtain 50/60Hz from an AC power line.

You must enable ticker interrupts after multitasking has started, that is, after calling OSStart(). Note that you really can't do this because OSStart() never returns. However, you can and should initialize and tick interrupts in the first task that executes following a call to OSStart(). This task is the highest priority that you create before calling OSStart(). A common mistake is to enable ticker interrupts between calling OSInit() and OSStart(), as shown in Listing 13.14. This issue is a problem because the tick interrupt could be serviced before µC/OS-II starts the first task and, at that point, µC/OS-II is in an unknown state and your application can crash.

Listing 13.14 *Incorrect place to start the tick interrupt.*

```
void main(void)
{
    .

    .

    OSInit();                      /* Initialize µC/OS-II           */
    .

    .

    /* Application initialization code ...                          */
    /* ... Create at least on task by calling OSTaskCreate()        */
    .
```

13

Listing 13.14   Incorrect place to start the tick interrupt.

```
    .
    Enable TICKER interrupts; /* DO NOT DO THIS HERE!!!          */
    .
    .
    OSStart();                   /* Start multitasking          */
}
```

The pseudocode for the tick ISR is shown in Listing 13.15. This code must be written in assembly language because you cannot access CPU registers directly from C.

Listing 13.15   Pseudocode for tick ISR.

```
void OSTickISR(void)
{
    Save processor registers;                                   (1)
    Call OSIntEnter() or increment OSIntNesting;                (2)
    if (OSIntNesting == 1) {                                     (3)
        OSTCBCur->OSTCBStkPtr = Stack Pointer;
    }
    Clear interrupting device;                                   (4)
    Re-enable interrupts (optional);                             (5)
    OSTimeTick();                                                (6)
    OSIntExit();                                                 (7)
    Restore processor registers;                                (8)
    Execute a return from interrupt instruction;                (9)
}
```

L13.15(1) The tick ISR (as with any ISR) needs to save all the CPU registers onto the current task's stack. Of course, they need to be saved in the same order as they are placed in OSTaskStkInit().

L13.15(2) It is assumed that interrupts are disabled at this point so you can directly increment OSIntNesting without fear of data corruption from another ISR. In the past, I recommended that you calle OSIntEnter(), which handles the increment. At the time, I wanted to encapsulate the increment in case I needed to do more processing at the beginning of the ISR. It turns out that I added a boundary check in OSIntEnter() to ensure that interrupt nesting never exceeds 255 levels. If don't expect to nest this deep, you can increment OSIntNesting without this boundary check. If you want to be safe, simply call OSIntEnter(). However, calling OSIntEnter() adds overhead to the ISR. It's up to you to decide which way you want to implement your port.

L13.15(3) The tick ISR then needs to check the value of OSIntNesting, and, if it's one, you need to save the contents of the stack pointer into the current task's OS_TCB. This step has been added in v2.51, and, although it complicates the ISR slightly, it does make a port more compiler-independent.

L13.15(4) Depending on the source of the interrupt, the interrupting device might need to be cleared to acknowledge the interrupt.

L13.15(5) You might want to re-enable interrupts at this point in order to allow higher priority interrupts to be recognized. This step is optional because you might not want to allow nested interrupts because they consume stack space.

L13.15(6) OSTickISR() must call OSTimeTick(), which is responsible for maintaining µC/OS-II's internal timers. The timers allow tasks to be suspended for a certain amount of time or allow timeouts on PEND-type calls.

L13.15(7) Because we are done servicing this ISR, we need to call OSIntExit(). As you probably remember, OSIntExit() determines whether a higher priority task has been made ready to run because of this ISR. If a higher priority task is ready to run, OSIntExit() does not return to the interrupted task but instead performs context switch to this higher priority task.

L13.15(8) If there is no higher priority task, then OSIntExit() returns, and we simply restore the CPU registers from the values stacked at the beginning of the ISR. Again, the registers must be restored in the reverse order.

L13.15(9) OSTickISR() needs to execute a return from interrupt in order to resume execution of the interrupted task.

13.05.04   *OSIntCtxSw()*

OSIntCtxSw() is called by OSIntExit() to perform a context switch from an ISR. Because OSIntCtxSw() is called from an ISR, we assume that all the processor registers are properly saved onto the interrupted task's stack (see Section 13.05.03, "OSTickISR(),").

The pseudocode for OSIntCtxSw() is shown in Listing 13.16. This code must be written in assembly language because you cannot access CPU registers directly from C. If your C compiler supports in-line assembly, put the code for OSIntCtxSw() in OS_CPU_C.C instead of OS_CPU_A.ASM. You should note that this pseudocode is for v2.51 (and higher) because prior to v2.51, OSIntCtxSw() required a few extra steps. If you have a port that was done for a version prior to v2.51, I highly recommend that you change it to match the algorithm shown in Listing 13.16.

A lot of the code is identical to OSCtxSw() except that we don't save the CPU registers onto the current task because that's already done by the ISR. In fact, you can reduce the amount of code in the port by jumping to the appropriate section of code in OSCtxSw() if you want. Because of the similarity between OSCtxSw() and OSIntCtxSw(), after you figure out how to do OSCtxSw(), you have automatically figured out how to do OSIntCtxSw()!

Listing 13.16   *Pseudocode for OSIntCtxSw() for v2.51 and higher.*

13

```
void OSIntCtxSw(void)
{
    Call user-definable OSTaskSwHook();
    OSTCBCur  = OSTCBHighRdy;
    OSPrioCur = OSPrioHighRdy;
    Get the stack pointer of the task to resume:
```

Listing 13.16   Pseudocode for *OSIntCtxSw( )* for v2.51 and higher. *(Continued)*

```
        Stack pointer = OSTCBHighRdy->OSTCBStkPtr;
    Restore all processor registers from the new task's stack;
    Execute a return from interrupt instruction;
}
```

Listing 13.17 shows the pseudocode for OSIntCtxSw( ) for a port made for a version of µC/OS-II prior to v2.51. You should recognize such a port because of the added two items before calling OSTaskSwHook( ): L13.17(1) and L13.17(2). ISRs for such a port also do not have the statements shown in L13.15(3) to save the stack pointer into the OS_TCB of the interrupted task. Therefore, OSIntCtxSw( ) had to do these operations [again, L13.17(1) and L13.17(2)]. However, because the stack pointer was not pointing to the proper stack-frame location (when OSIntCtxSw( ) starts executing, the return address of OSIntExit( ) and OSIntCtxSw( ) were placed on the stack by the calls), the stack pointer needed to be adjusted. The solution was to add an offset to the stack pointer. The value of this offset was dependent on the compiler options and generated more e-mail messages than I expected or cared for. One of these e-mail messages was from a clever individual named Nicolas Pinault who pointed out how this stack-adjustment business could all be avoided as previously described. Because of Nicolas, µC/OS-II is no longer dependent on compiler options. Thanks again Nicolas!

Listing 13.17   Pseudocode for *OSIntCtxSw( )* prior to v2.51.

```
void OSIntCtxSw(void)
{
    Adjust the stack pointer to remove calls to:                             (1)
        OSIntExit();
        OSIntCtxSw();
    Save the current task's stack pointer into the current task's OS_TCB:    (2)
        OSTCBCur->OSTCBStkPtr = Stack Pointer;
    Call user-definable OSTaskSwHook();
    OSTCBCur  = OSTCBHighRdy;
    OSPrioCur = OSPrioHighRdy;
    Get the stack pointer of the task to resume:
        Stack pointer = OSTCBHighRdy->OSTCBStkPtr;
    Restore all processor registers from the new task's stack;
    Execute a return from interrupt instruction;
}
```

13.06 Testing a Port

After you have a port of µC/OS-II for your processor, you need to verify its operation. This part is probably the most complicated part of writing a port. You should test your port without application code. In other words, test the operations of the kernel by itself. There are two reasons to do this. First, you don't want to complicate things anymore than they need to be. Second, if something doesn't work, you know that the problem lies in the port as opposed to your application. Start with a couple of simple tasks and the ticker interrupt service routine. After you get multitasking going, it's quite simple to add your application tasks.

You can use a number of techniques to test your port depending on your level of experience with embedded systems and processors in general. When I write a port, I generally follow the following four steps:

> Ensure that the code compiles, assembles, and links
> Verify `OSTaskStkInit()` and `OSStartHighRdy()`
> Verify `OSCtxSw()`
> Verify `OSIntCtxSw()` and `OSTickISR()`

13.06.01 *Ensure that the Code Compiles, Assembles, and Links*

After you complete the port, you need to compile, assemble, and link it along with the µC/OS-II processor-independent code. This step is obviously compiler specific, and you need to consult your compiler documentation to determine how to do this step.

I generally set up a simple test directory, as follows

> `\SOFTWARE\uCOS-II\processor\compiler\TEST`

where,

> `processor` is the name of the processor or microcontroller for which you have done the port.
> `compiler` is the name of the compiler you used.

Table 13.2 shows the directories you will need to work with, along with the files found in those directories. In the `TEST` directory, you should have at least three files: `TEST.C`, `INCLUDES.H`, and `OS_CFG.H`. Depending on the processor used, you might also need to have an interrupt-vector table, which I assumed is called `VECTORS.C`, but it could certainly be called something else.

The `TEST` directory could also contain a `MAKEFILE`, which specifies compiler, assembler, and linker directives to build your project. A `MAKEFILE` assumes, of course, that you use a make utility. If your compiler provides an integrated development environment (IDE), you might not have a `MAKEFILE`, but instead you could have project files specific to the IDE.

The port you did (refer to Section 13.01, "Directories and Files,") should be found in the following directory:

> `\SOFTWARE\uCOS-II\processor\compiler`

Table 13.3   *Files needed to test a port.*

Directory	File
`\SOFTWARE\uCOS-II\processor\compiler\TEST`	`TEST.C`
	`OS_CFG.H`
	`INCLUDES.H`
	`VECTORS.C`
	`MAKEFILE` or IDE project file(s)
`\SOFTWARE\uCOS-II\processor\compiler`	`OS_CPU_A.ASM`
	`OS_CPU_C.C`
	`OS_CPU.H`

13

Table 13.3   Files needed to test a port.

\SOFTWARE\uCOS-II\SOURCE	OS_CORE.C
	OS_FLAG.C
	OS_MBOX.C
	OS_MEM.C
	OS_MUTEX.C
	OS_Q.C
	OS_SEM.C
	OS_TASK.C
	OS_TIME.C
	uCOS_II.C
	uCOS_II.H

Listing 13.18 shows the contents of a typical INCLUDES.H. STRING.H is needed because OSTaskCreateExt() uses the ANSI C function memset() to initialize the stack of a task. The other standard C header files (STDIO.H, CTYPE.H, and STDLIB.H) are not actually used by μC/OS-II but are included in case your application needs them.

Listing 13.18   Typical INCLUDES.H.

```
#include    <stdio.h>
#include    <string.h>
#include    <ctype.h>
#include    <stdlib.h>

#include    "os_cpu.h"
#include    "os_cfg.h"
#include    "ucos_ii.h"
```

Listing 13.19 shows the contents of OS_CFG.H, which was set up to enable all the features of μC/OS-II. You can find a similar file in the \SOFTWARE\uCOS-II\EX1_x86L\BC45\SOURCE directory of the companion CD so that you can use it as a starting point, instead of typing an OS_CFG.H from scratch.

Listing 13.19   OS_CFG.H that enables all μC/OS-II features.

```
                                /* --------------------- MISCELLANEOUS ----------------- */
#define OS_ARG_CHK_EN        1  /* Enable (1) or Disable (0) argument checking            */

#define OS_CPU_HOOKS_EN      1  /* uC/OS-II hooks are found in the processor port files   */

#define OS_LOWEST_PRIO      63  /* Defines the lowest priority that can be assigned ...    */
                                /* ... MUST NEVER be higher than 63!                      */
```

Listing 13.19   OS_CFG.H *that enables all µC/OS-II*
**   *features. (Continued)***

```
#define OS_MAX_EVENTS           20    /* Max. number of event control blocks in your application ...   */
                                      /* ... MUST be > 0                                               */
#define OS_MAX_FLAGS            10    /* Max. number of Event Flag Groups     in your application ...  */
                                      /* ... MUST be > 0                                               */
#define OS_MAX_MEM_PART         10    /* Max. number of memory partitions ...                          */
                                      /* ... MUST be > 0                                               */
#define OS_MAX_QS               10    /* Max. number of queue control blocks in your application ...   */
                                      /* ... MUST be > 0                                               */
#define OS_MAX_TASKS            63    /* Max. number of tasks in your application ...                  */
                                      /* ... MUST be >= 2                                              */


#define OS_SCHED_LOCK_EN         1    /*     Include code for OSSchedLock() and OSSchedUnlock()        */


#define OS_TASK_IDLE_STK_SIZE   512   /* Idle task stack size (# of OS_STK wide entries)               */


#define OS_TASK_STAT_EN          1    /* Enable (1) or Disable(0) the statistics task                 */
#define OS_TASK_STAT_STK_SIZE   512   /* Statistics task stack size (# of OS_STK wide entries)         */


#define OS_TICKS_PER_SEC        200   /* Set the number of ticks in one second                        */



                                      /* -------------------- EVENT FLAGS -------------------- */
#define OS_FLAG_EN               1    /* Enable (1) or Disable (0) code generation for EVENT FLAGS     */
#define OS_FLAG_WAIT_CLR_EN      1    /* Include code for Wait on Clear EVENT FLAGS                    */
#define OS_FLAG_ACCEPT_EN        1    /*     Include code for OSFlagAccept()                           */
#define OS_FLAG_DEL_EN           1    /*     Include code for OSFlagDel()                              */
#define OS_FLAG_QUERY_EN         1    /*     Include code for OSFlagQuery()                            */



                                      /* ------------------- MESSAGE MAILBOXES ------------------- */
#define OS_MBOX_EN               1    /* Enable (1) or Disable (0) code generation for MAILBOXES       */
#define OS_MBOX_ACCEPT_EN        1    /*     Include code for OSMboxAccept()                           */
#define OS_MBOX_DEL_EN           1    /*     Include code for OSMboxDel()                              */
#define OS_MBOX_POST_EN          1    /*     Include code for OSMboxPost()                             */
#define OS_MBOX_POST_OPT_EN      1    /*     Include code for OSMboxPostOpt()                          */
#define OS_MBOX_QUERY_EN         1    /*     Include code for OSMboxQuery()                            */



                                      /* ------------------- MEMORY MANAGEMENT ------------------- */
#define OS_MEM_EN                1    /* Enable (1) or Disable (0) code generation for MEMORY MANAGER */
#define OS_MEM_QUERY_EN          1    /*     Include code for OSMemQuery()                             */



                                      /* ---------------- MUTUAL EXCLUSION SEMAPHORES ---------------- */
#define OS_MUTEX_EN              1    /* Enable (1) or Disable (0) code generation for MUTEX           */
```

13

Listing 13.19 OS_CFG.H *that enables all µC/OS-II features. (Continued)*

```
#define OS_MUTEX_ACCEPT_EN      1    /*      Include code for OSMutexAccept()                 */
#define OS_MUTEX_DEL_EN         1    /*      Include code for OSMutexDel()                    */
#define OS_MUTEX_QUERY_EN       1    /*      Include code for OSMutexQuery()                  */


                                     /* --------------------- MESSAGE QUEUES --------------------- */
#define OS_Q_EN                 1    /* Enable (1) or Disable (0) code generation for QUEUES  */
#define OS_Q_ACCEPT_EN          1    /*      Include code for OSQAccept()                     */
#define OS_Q_DEL_EN             1    /*      Include code for OSQDel()                        */
#define OS_Q_FLUSH_EN           1    /*      Include code for OSQFlush()                      */
#define OS_Q_POST_EN            1    /*      Include code for OSQPost()                       */
#define OS_Q_POST_FRONT_EN      1    /*      Include code for OSQPostFront()                  */
#define OS_Q_POST_OPT_EN        1    /*      Include code for OSQPostOpt()                    */
#define OS_Q_QUERY_EN           1    /*      Include code for OSQQuery()                      */


                                     /* --------------------- SEMAPHORES --------------------- */
#define OS_SEM_EN               1    /* Enable (1) or Disable (0) code generation for SEMAPHORES */
#define OS_SEM_ACCEPT_EN        1    /*      Include code for OSSemAccept()                   */
#define OS_SEM_DEL_EN           1    /*      Include code for OSSemDel()                      */
#define OS_SEM_QUERY_EN         1    /*      Include code for OSSemQuery()                    */


                                     /* --------------------- TASK MANAGEMENT --------------------- */
#define OS_TASK_CHANGE_PRIO_EN  1    /*      Include code for OSTaskChangePrio()              */
#define OS_TASK_CREATE_EN       1    /*      Include code for OSTaskCreate()                  */
#define OS_TASK_CREATE_EXT_EN   1    /*      Include code for OSTaskCreateExt()               */
#define OS_TASK_DEL_EN          1    /*      Include code for OSTaskDel()                     */
#define OS_TASK_SUSPEND_EN      1    /*      Include code for OSTaskSuspend() and OSTaskResume() */
#define OS_TASK_QUERY_EN        1    /*      Include code for OSTaskQuery()                   */


                                     /* --------------------- TIME MANAGEMENT --------------------- */
#define OS_TIME_DLY_HMSM_EN     1    /*      Include code for OSTimeDlyHMSM()                 */
#define OS_TIME_DLY_RESUME_EN   1    /*      Include code for OSTimeDlyResume()               */
#define OS_TIME_GET_SET_EN      1    /*      Include code for OSTimeGet() and OSTimeSet()     */


typedef INT16U          OS_FLAGS;    /* Date type for event flag bits (8, 16 or 32 bits)     */
```

Listing 13.20 shows the contents of a simple TEST.C file with which you can start to prove your compile process. For this first step, there is no need for any more code because all we are trying to accomplish is a build. At this point, it's up to you to resolve any compiler, assembler, and/or linker errors. You might also get some warnings, and you need to determine whether the warnings are severe enough to be a problem.

Listing 13.20   Minimal *TEST.C for step #1.*

```
#include    "includes.h"


void  main (void)
{
    OSInit();
    OSStart();
}
```

13.06.02 Verify *OSTaskStkInit()* and *OSStartHighRdy()*

After you achieve a successful build, you are actually ready to start testing your port. As the title of this section suggests, this step verifies the proper operation of OSTaskStkInit() and OSStartHighRdy().

Testing with a Source Level Debugger

If you have a source-level debugger, you should be able to verify this step fairly quickly. I assume you already know how to use your debugger.

Start by modifying OS_CFG.H to disable the statistic task by setting OS_TASK_STAT_EN to 0. Because your TEST.C file (see Listing 13.20) doesn't create any application task, the only task created is the μC/OS-II idle task: OS_TaskIdle(). You will step into the code until μC/OS-II switches to OS_TaskIdle().

You should load the code into the debugger and start single-stepping into main(). You should step **over** the function OSInit() and then step **into** the code for OSStart() (shown in Listing 13.21). Step through the code until you reach the call to OSStartHighRdy() [the last statement in OSStart()] and then step **into** the code for OSStartHighRdy(). At this point, your debugger should switch to assembly-language mode because OSStartHighRdy() is written in assembly language. This is the code you wrote to start the first task, and, because we didn't create any task other than OS_TaskIdle(), OSStartHighRdy() should start this task.

Listing 13.21 *OSStart()*.

```
void  OSStart (void)
{
    INT8U y;
    INT8U x;


    if (OSRunning == FALSE) {
        y             = OSUnMapTbl[OSRdyGrp];
        x             = OSUnMapTbl[OSRdyTbl[y]];
        OSPrioHighRdy = (INT8U)((y << 3) + x);
        OSPrioCur     = OSPrioHighRdy;
        OSTCBHighRdy  = OSTCBPrioTbl[OSPrioHighRdy];
```

13

Listing 13.21   *OSStart( ). (Continued)*

```
    OSTCBCur      = OSTCBHighRdy;
    OSStartHighRdy();
  }
}
```

Step through your code and verify that it does what you expect. Specifically, OSStartHighRdy() should start populating CPU registers in the reverse order that they were placed onto the task stack by OSTaskStkInit() (see OS_CPU_C.C). If the order isn't correct, you most likely misaligned the stack pointer. In this case, you must correct OSTaskStkInit() accordingly. The last instruction in OSStartHighRdy() should be a return from interrupt, and, as soon as you execute that code, your debugger should be positioned at the first instruction of OS_TaskIdle(). If this action doesn't happen, you might not have placed the proper start address of the task onto the task stack, and you will most likely have to correct this problem in OSTaskStkInit(). If your debugger ends up in OS_TaskIdle() and you can execute a few times through the infinite loop, you are done with this step and have successfully verified OSTaskStkInit() and OSStartHighRdy().

Go/No Go Testing

If you don't have access to a source-level debugger but have an LED on your target system, you can write a Go/No Go test. Start by turning **off** the LED. If OSTaskStkInit() and OSStartHighRdy() works, the LED is turned **on** by the idle task. In fact, the LED is turned **on** and **off** very quickly and appears to always be **on**. If you have an oscilloscope, you should be able to confirm that the LED is blinking at a roughly 50% duty cycle.

For this test, you need to *temporarily* modify three files: OS_CFG.H, OS_CPU_C.C, and TEST.C. In OS_CFG.H, you need to disable the statistic task by setting OS_TASK_STAT_EN to 0. In TEST.C, you need to add code to turn **off** the LED, as shown in Listing 13.22. In OS_CPU_C.C, you need to modify OSTaskIdleHook() to toggle the LED as shown in the pseudocode of Listing 13.23.

The next step is to load the code in your target system and run it. If the LED doesn't toggle, you need to find out what's wrong in either OSTaskStkInit() or OSStartHighRdy(). With such limited and primitive tools, the best you can do is carefully inspect your code until you find what you did wrong!

Listing 13.22   *Modifying* main( ) *in TEST.C.*

```
#include    "includes.h"


void  main (void)
{
    OSInit();
    Turn OFF LED;
    OSStart();
}
```

Listing 13.23   Modifying `OSTaskIdleHook()` in `OS_CPU_C.C.`

```
void  OSTaskIdleHook (void)
{
    if (LED is ON) {            /* Toggle LED              */
        Turn OFF LED;
    } else {
        Turn ON LED;
    }
}
```

13.06.03   Verify `OSCtxSw()`

This step should be easy because in the previous step, we verified that the stack frame of a task is correctly initialized by `OSTaskStkInit()`. For this test, we create an application task and force a context switch back to the idle task. For this test, you need to ensure that you have correctly set up the software interrupt or `TRAP` to vector to `OSCtxSw()`. You'll have to determine how to do this.

Testing with a Source-Level Debugger

Start by modifying `main()` in `TEST.C`, as shown in Listing 13.24. For sake of discussion, I decided to assume that the stack of your processor grows downwards from high to low memory and that 100 entries are sufficient stack space for the test task. Of course, you should modify this code according to your own processor requirements.

Listing 13.24   Testing `OSCtxSw()` using a debugger.

```
#include    "includes.h"
OS_STK  TestTaskStk[100];

void  main (void)
{
    OSInit();
    OSTaskCreate(TestTask, (void *)0, &TestTaskStk[99], 0);          (1)
    OSStart();
}



void  TestTask (void *pdata)                                        (2)
{
    pdata = pdata;
    while (1) {
        OSTimeDly(1);                                               (3)
    }
}
```

13

L13.24(1) We create a high priority task. I decided to use priority level 0, but you can use anything below OS_LOWEST_PRIO (see OS_CFG.H).

L13.24(2) Because we proved in Section 13.06.02, "Verify OSTaskStkInit() and OSStartHighRdy()," that OSStartHighRdy() works, μC/OS-II should start executing TestTask() as its first task instead of executing the idle task. You can step through the code until you get to the beginning of TestTask().

L13.24(3) TestTask() enters an infinite loop that continuously calls OSTimeDly(1). In other words, TestTask() doesn't really do anything except wait for time to expire. Because we didn't enable interrupts nor did we start the clock tick, OSTimeDly(1) never returns to TestTask()!

You can now step into OSTimeDly(). OSTimeDly() calls OS_Sched(), and OS_Sched() in turn calls the assembly-language function OSCtxSw(). In most cases, the call is accomplished through a TRAP or software-interrupt mechanism. In other words, if you set up the software interrupt or TRAP correctly, this instruction should cause the CPU to start executing OSCtxSw(). You can step through the code for OSCtxSw() and see the registers of TestTask() being saved onto its stack and the value of the registers for OS_TaskIdle() being loaded into the CPU. When the return from interrupt is executed (for the software interrupt or TRAP), you should be in OS_TaskIdle()!

If OSCtxSw() doesn't bring you into OS_TaskIdle() you need to find out why and make the necessary corrections to OSCtxSw().

Go/No Go Testing

Modify main() in TEST.C, as shown in Listing 13.25. I decided to assume that the stack of your processor grows downwards from high to low memory and that 100 entries are sufficient stack space for the test task.

Listing 13.25   Testing *OSCtxSw( )* using an LED.

```
#include    "includes.h"


OS_STK  TestTaskStk[100];


void  main (void)
{
    OSInit();
    Turn OFF LED;                                             (1)
    OSTaskCreate(TestTask, (void *)0, &TestTaskStk[99], 0);   (2)
    OSStart();
}
```

Listing 13.25 Testing OSCtxSw() using an LED. (Continued)

```
void  TestTask (void *pdata)                                                    (3)
{
    pdata = pdata;
    while (1) {
        OSTimeDly(1);                                                           (4)
    }
}
```

L13.25(1) You need to turn **off** the LED before you run the rest of the code so that if the test fails, hopefully the LED is turned **off**. I say hopefully because the processor could crash and still turn the LED **on**. However, if OSCtxSw() is written correctly, the LED should toggle very quickly, and you can thus verify this with an oscilloscope.

L13.25(2) We create a high priority task. I decided to use priority level 0, but you can use anything below OS_LOWEST_PRIO (see OS_CFG.H).

L13.25(3) Because we proved in "Verify OSTaskStkInit() and OSStartHighRdy()" (Section 13.06.02) that OSStartHighRdy() works, μC/OS-II should start executing TestTask() as its first task instead of executing the idle task.

L13.25(4) TestTask() enters an infinite loop that continuously calls OSTimeDly(1). In other words, TestTask() doesn't really do anything except wait for time to expire. Because we didn't enable interrupts nor did we start the clock tick, OSTimeDly(1) never returns to TestTask()! When OSTimeDly(1) is called, a context switch to the idle task should occur (if OSCtxSw() is properly written), and you should get the LED to blink very quickly. In fact, it blinks so fast that it appears to be always **on**. You should verify that it blinks using an oscilloscope (if one is available). If the LED is not blinking or is **off**, you need to find out why and make the necessary corrections to OSCtxSw().

13.06.04 Verify OSIntCtxSw() and OSTickISR()

This step should be easy because OSIntCtxSw() is similar to but simpler than OSCtxSw(). In fact, most of the code for OSIntCtxSw() can be borrowed from OSCtxSw(). For this test, you need to set up an interrupt vector for the clock tick ISR. We then initialize the clock tick and enable interrupts.

Start by modifying main() in TEST.C, as shown in Listing 13.26.

Listing 13.26 Testing OSIntCtxSw() and OSTickISR().

```
#include    "includes.h"

OS_STK   TestTaskStk[100];
```

13

Listing 13.26 Testing *OSIntCtxSw( ) and*
**   ** *OSTickISR( ). (Continued)*

```
void  main (void)
{
    OSInit();
    Turn LED OFF;                                                    (1)
    Install the clock tick interrupt vector;                        (2)
    OSTaskCreate(TestTask, (void *)0, &TestTaskStk[99], 0);         (3)
    OSStart();
}



void  TestTask (void *pdata)                                        (4)
{
    BOOLEAN  led_state;


    pdata = pdata;
    Initialize the clock tick interrupt (i.e. timer);              (5)
    Enable interrupts;                                             (6)
    led_state = FALSE;
    Turn ON LED;                                                   (7)
    while (1) {
        OSTimeDly(1);                                              (8)
        if (led_state == FALSE) {                                 (9)
            led_state = TRUE;
            Turn ON LED;
        } else {
            led_state = FALSE;
            Turn OFF LED;
        }
    }
}
```

L13.26(1) Regardless of whether you have a degugger or not, it's useful for this test to have access to an LED (or some display device). You need to turn **off** the LED before you run the rest of the code.

L13.26(2) You need to install the clock-tick-interrupt vector. You need to consult your compiler or processor documentation to determine how to perform the installation. Some processors do not allow you to install interrupt vectors at run time (e.g., the Motorola 68HC11 assumes that vectors reside in ROM). The tick interrupt needs to vector to your port's `OSTickISR()`.

L13.26(3) We create a high priority task. I decided to use priority level 0, but you can use anything below `OS_LOWEST_PRIO` (see `OS_CFG.H`).

L13.26(4) Again, because we proved in Section 13.06.02, "Verify `OSTaskStkInit()` and `OSStartHighRdy()`," that `OSStartHighRdy()` works, µC/OS-II should start executing `TestTask()` as its first task.

L13.26(5) Upon entry into `TestTask()`, you should intialize the device (typically a timer) to generate a clock-tick interrupt at the desired rate. I would recommend making the tick rate 10Hz or so, in order to be able to make the LED blink at 5Hz. This tick rate should match what you set `OS_TICKS_PER_SEC` to in `OS_CFG.H`.

L13.26(6) You can now enable interrupts to allow the tick interrupt to invoke `OSTickISR()`.

L13.26(7) Turn **on** the LED to show that you made it to `TestTask()`.

L13.26(8) The call to `OSTimeDly()` causes a context switch to the idle task using `OSCtxSw()`. The idle task spins until the tick interrupt is received. The tick interrupt should invoke `OSTickISR()`, which in turn calls `OSTimeTick()`. `OSTimeTick()` decrements the `.OSTCBDly` count of `TestTask()` to 0 and makes this task ready to run. When `OSTickISR()` completes and calls `OSIntExit()`, `OSIntExit()` should notice that the more important task, `TestTask()`, is ready to run. The ISR, therefore, does not return to the idle task, but instead performs a context switch back to `TestTask()`. Of course, all this assumes that `OSIntCtxSw()` and `OSTickISR()` are both working.

L13.26(9) If `OSIntCtxSw()` does work, you ought to see the LED blink at 5Hz if you set the tick rate at 10Hz.

If the LED is not blinking and you are using a debugger, you can set a breakpoint in `OSTickISR()` and follow what's going on. I would also suggest trying to run the ISR without having it call `OSIntExit()`. In this case, you could simply have the ISR blink the LED (or another LED). If the LED is blinking, then the problem is with `OSIntCtxSw()`. Again, because `OSIntCtxSw()` should have been derived from `OSCtxSw()`, I suspect that the problem is in the `OSTickISR()`.

At this point, your port should work, and you can now start adding application tasks. Have fun!

13

OSCtxSw()

`void OSCtxSw(void)`

File	Called from	
OS_CPU_A.ASM	OS_TASK_SW()	Always needed

This function is called to perform a task-level context switch. Generally, this function is invoked via a software-interrupt instruction (also called a TRAP instruction). The pseudocode for this function is

```
void  OSCtxSw (void)
{
    Save processor registers;
    Save the current task's stack pointer into the current task's OS_TCB:
        OSTCBCur->OSTCBStkPtr = Stack pointer;
    OSTaskSwHook();
    OSTCBCur  = OSTCBHighRdy;
    OSPrioCur = OSPrioHighRdy;
    Get the stack pointer of the task to resume:
        Stack pointer = OSTCBHighRdy->OSTCBStkPtr;
    Restore all processor registers from the new task's stack;
    Execute a return from interrupt instruction;
}
```

Arguments

Return Values

Notes/Warnings

1. Interrupts are disabled when this function is called.
2. Some compilers allow you to create software interrupts (or TRAPS) directly in C, and thus you could place this function in OS_CPU_C.C. In some cases, the compiler also requires that you declare the prototype for this function differently. In this case, you can define the #define constant OS_ISR_PROTO_EXT in your INCLUDES.H, which allows you to delare OSCtxSw() differently. In other words, you are not forced to use the void OSCtxSw(void) prototype.

Example

OSInitHookBegin()

`void OSInitHookBegin(void)`

File	Called from	Code enabled in OS_CPU_C.C if
OS_CPU_C.C	OSInit()	OS_CPU_HOOKS_EN == 1

This function is called by OSInit() at the very beginning of OSInit(). This function allows you to perform CPU (or other) initialization as part of OSInit(). For example, you can initialize I/O devices from OSInitHookBegin(). The function encapsulates the initialization as part of the port. In other words, it prevents requiring that the user of µC/OS-II know anything about such additional initialization.

Arguments

Return Values

Notes/Warnings

Example

13

OSInitHookEnd()

`void OSInitHookEnd(void)`

File	Called from	Code enabled in `OS_CPU_C.C` if
OS_CPU_C.C	OSInit()	OS_CPU_HOOKS_EN == 1

This function is called by `OSInit()` at the very end of `OSInit()`. This function allows you to perform CPU (or other) initialization as part of `OSInit()`. For example, you can initialize I/O devices from `OSInitHookEnd()`. The function encapsulates the initialization as part of the port. The users of µC/OS-II, therefore, do no need to know anything about such additional initialization.

Arguments

Return Values

Notes/Warnings

Example

OSIntCtxSw()

`void OSIntCtxSw(void)`

File	*Called from*	
OS_CPU_A.ASM	OSIntExit()	Always needed

This function is called from OSIntExit() when OSIntExit() determines that a higher priority task must be executed because of an ISR. The pseudocode for this function is

```
void  OSIntCtxSw (void)
{
    OSTaskSwHook();
    OSTCBCur  = OSTCBHighRdy;
    OSPrioCur = OSPrioHighRdy;
    Get the stack pointer of the task to resume:
        Stack pointer = OSTCBHighRdy->OSTCBStkPtr;
    Restore all processor registers from the new task's stack;
    Execute a return from interrupt instruction;
}
```

Arguments

Return Values

Notes/Warnings

1. Interrupts are disabled when this function is called.

Example

13

OSStartHighRdy()

`void OSStartHighRdy(void)`

File	Called from	
OS_CPU_A.ASM	OSStart()	Always needed

This function is called from OSStart() to start the highest priority task that you created before you called OSStart(). The pseudocode for this function is

```
void OSStartHighRdy (void)
{
    OSTaskSwHook();
    OSRunning = TRUE;
    Get the stack pointer of the task to resume:
        Stack pointer = OSTCBHighRdy->OSTCBStkPtr;

    Restore all processor registers from the new task's stack;
    Execute a return from interrupt instruction;
}
void OSStartHighRdy (void)
```

Arguments

Return Values

Notes/Warnings

1. Interrupts are disabled when this function is called.

Example

OSTaskCreateHook()

`void OSTaskCreateHook(OS_TCB *ptcb)`

File	*Called from*	*Code enabled in OS_CPU_C.C if*
OS_CPU_C.C	OSTaskCreate() and OSTaskCreateExt()	OS_CPU_HOOKS_EN == 1

This function is called whenever a task is created, after a TCB has been allocated and initialized and after the stack frame of the task is initialized. OSTaskCreateHook() allows you to extend the functionality of the task-creation function with your own features. For example, you can initialize and store the contents of floating-point registers, MMU registers, or anything else that can be associated with a task. Typically, you store this additional information in memory allocated by your application. You should note that OSTaskCreateHook() is called immediately after another hook function called OSTCBInitHook(). In other words, either of these functions can be used to initialize the TCB. However, you ought to use OSTCBInitHook() for TCB-related items and OSTaskCreateHook() for other task-related items. You could also use OSTaskCreateHook() to trigger an oscilloscope or a logic analyzer or to set a breakpoint.

Arguments

ptcb   is a pointer to the TCB of the task created.

Return Values

Notes/Warnings

1. Interrupts are enabled when this function is called. You, therefore, might need to call OS_ENTER_CRITICAL() and OS_EXIT_CRITICAL() to protect critical sections inside OSTaskCreateHook().

Example

This example assumes that you have created a task using OSTaskCreateExt() because the function expects to have the .OSTCBExtPtr field in the task's OS_TCB contain a pointer to storage for floating-point registers.

```
void OSTaskCreateHook (OS_TCB *ptcb)
{
    if (ptcb->OSTCBExtPtr != (void *)0) {
        /* Save contents of floating-point registers in .. */
        /* .. the TCB extension                            */
    }
}
```

13

OSTaskDelHook()

`void OSTaskDelHook(OS_TCB *ptcb)`

File	*Called from*	*Code enabled in* $OS\_CPU\_C.C$ *if*
OS_CPU_C.C	OSTaskDel()	OS_CPU_HOOKS_EN == 1

This function is called whenever you delete a task by calling OSTaskDel(). You can dispose of memory you have allocated through the task-create hook, OSTaskCreateHook(). OSTaskDelHook() is called just before the TCB is removed from the TCB chain. You can also use OSTaskCreateHook() to trigger an oscilloscope or a logic analyzer or to set a breakpoint.

Arguments

ptcb   is a pointer to the TCB of the task being deleted.

Return Values

Notes/Warnings

1. Interrupts are disabled when this function is called. You, therefore, should keep the code in this function to a minimum because it directly affects interrupt latency.

Example

```
void OSTaskDelHook (OS_TCB *ptcb)
{
    /* Output signal to trigger an oscilloscope          */
}
```

OSTaskIdleHook()

`void OSTaskIdleHook(void)`

File	*Called from*	*Code enabled in OS_CPU_C.C if*
OS_CPU_C.C	OS_TaskIdle()	OS_CPU_HOOKS_EN == 1

This function is called by the idle task [OS_TaskIdle()] when no other higher priority task is ready to run. OSTaskIdleHook() can be used to force the CPU in low-power mode for battery-operated products to conserve energy when none of your tasks need to be serviced.

Arguments

Return Values

Notes/Warnings

1. OSTaskIdleHook() is called with interrupts enabled.

Example

```
void OSTaskIdleHook (void)
{
    /* Put the CPU in low power mode.                    */
}
```

13

OSTaskStatHook()

void OSTaskStatHook(void)

File	Called from	Code enabled in OS_CPU_C.C if
OS_CPU_C.C	OS_TaskStat()	OS_CPU_HOOKS_EN == 1

This function is called every second by µC/OS-II's statistic task. OSTaskStatHook() allows you to add your own statistics.

Arguments

Return Values

Notes/Warnings

1. The statistic task starts executing about five seconds after calling OSStart(). Note that this function is not called if either OS_TASK_STAT_EN or OS_TASK_CREATE_EXT_EN is set to 0.

Example

```
void OSTaskStatHook (void)
{
    /* Compute the total execution time of all the tasks    */
    /* Compute the percentage of execution of each task     */
}
```

OSTaskStkInit()

```
OS_STK *OSTaskStkInit(void (*task)(void *pd),
                      void *pdata,
                      OS_STK *ptos,
                      INT16U opt);
```

File	Called from	
OS_CPU_C.C	OSTaskCreate() or OSTaskCreateExt()	Always needed

This function is called by either OSTaskCreate() or OSTaskCreateExt() to initialize the stack frame of a task. Generally speaking, the stack frame is made to look as if an interrupt has just occurred and all the CPU registers have been saved onto it. The pseudocode for this function is

```
OS_STK *OSTaskStkInit (void  (*task)(void *pd),
                       void  *pdata,
                       OS_STK *ptos,
                       INT16U opt);
{

    Simulate call to function with an argument (i.e. pdata);
    Simulate ISR vector;
    Setup stack frame to contain desired initial values of all registers;
    Return new top-of-stack pointer to caller;

}
```

Arguments

task   is a pointer to the task code (i.e., the address of the function that you want to declare as a task).

pdata   is a pointer to a user-supplied data area that is be passed to the task when the task first executes. Sometimes, the compiler will pass pdata into registers while other compilers will pass pdata on the stack. You will need to consult your compiler documentation for the actual method used.

ptos   is a pointer to the top of the stack. It is assumed that ptos points to a free entry on the task stack. If OS_STK_GROWTH is set to 1, then ptos contains the **highest** valid address of the stack. Similarly, if OS_STK_GROWTH is set to 0, ptos contains the **lowest** valid address of the stack.

opt   specifies options that can be used to alter the behavior of OSTaskStkInit(). See uCOS_II.H for OS_TASK_OPT_???.

Return Values

A pointer to the new top-of-stack.

13

Notes/Warnings

1. Interrupts are enabled when this function is called.

Example

OSTaskSwHook()

`void OSTaskSwHook(void)`

File	*Called from*	*Code enabled in OS_CPU_C.C if*
OS_CPU_C.C	OSCtxSw() and OSIntCtxSw()	OS_CPU_HOOKS_EN == 1

This function is called whenever a context switch is performed. The global variable OSTCBHighRdy points to the TCB of the task that gets the CPU, and OSTCBCur points to the TCB of the task being switched out. OSTaskSwHook() is called just after saving the task's registers and after saving the stack pointer into the current task's TCB. You can use this function to save/restore the contents of floating-point registers or MMU registers, to keep track of task-execution time and of how many times the task has been switched in, and more. OSTaskSwHook() is also called by OSStartHighRdy(). You, therefore, need to verify the flag OSRunning in OSTaskSwHook(), so you don't perform any action as you would when a task is switched out (see the example).

Arguments

Return Values

Notes/Warnings

1. Interrupts are disabled when this function is called. You, therefore, should keep the code in this function to a minimum because it directly affects interrupt latency.

Example

```
void OSTaskSwHook (void)
{
    if (OSRunning == TRUE) {
        /* Save floating-point registers in current task's TCB ext. */
    }
    /* Restore floating-point registers from new task's TCB ext.    */
}
```

13

OSTCBInitHook()

void OSTCBInitHook(OS_TCB *ptcb)

File	Called from	Code enabled in *OS_CPU_C.C* if
OS_CPU_C.C	OS_TCBInit()	OS_CPU_HOOKS_EN == 1

This function is called whenever a task is created, after a TCB has been allocated and initialized and when the stack frame of the task is initialized. OSTCBInitHook() allows you to extend the functionality of the TCB-creation function with your own features. For example, you can initialize and store the contents of floating-point registers, MMU registers, or anything else that can be associated with a task. Typically, you store this additional information in memory allocated by your application. You should note that OSTCBInitHook() is called immediately before OSTaskCreateHook(). In other words, either of these functions can be used to initialize the TCB. However, you ought to use OSTCBInitHook() for TCB-related items and OSTaskCreateHook() for other task-related items.

Arguments

ptcb   is a pointer to the TCB of the task created.

Return Values

Notes/Warnings

1. Interrupts are enabled when this function is called. You, therefore, might need to call OS_ENTER_CRITICAL() and OS_EXIT_CRITICAL() to protect critical sections inside OSTCBInitHook().

Example

This example assumes that you have created a task using OSTaskCreateExt() because the function expects to have the .OSTCBExtPtr field in the task's OS_TCB contain a pointer to storage for floating-point registers.

```
void OSTCBInitHook (OS_TCB *ptcb)
{
    if (ptcb->OSTCBExtPtr != (void *)0) {
        /* Save contents of floating-point registers in .. */
        /* .. the TCB extension                            */
    }
}
```

OSTickISR()

`void OSTickISR(void)`

File	Called from	
OS_CPU_A.ASM	Tick Interrupt	Always needed

When a tick interrupt occurs, the CPU needs to vector to this ISR. The pseudocode for the ISR is

```
Void  OSTickISR (void)
{
   Save processor registers;
   Call OSIntEnter() or increment OSIntNesting;
   if (OSIntNesting == 1) {
      OSTCBCur->OSTCBStkPtr = Stack Pointer;
   }
   Clear interrupting device;
   Re-enable interrupts (optional);
   OSTimeTick();
   OSIntExit();
   Restore processor registers;
   Execute a return from interrupt instruction;
}
```

Arguments

Return Values

Notes/Warnings

1. The interrupting device that causes the call to OSTickISR() should generally be set up to generate an interrupt every 10 to 100ms.

2. Some compilers allow you to create ISRs directly in C, and thus you could place this function in OS_CPU_C.C. In some cases, the compiler also requires that you declare the prototype for this function differently. In this case, you can define the #define constant OS_ISR_PROTO_EXT in your INCLUDES.H, which allows you to delare OSTickISR() differently. In other words, you are not forced to use the void OSTickISR(void) prototype.

Example

13

OSTimeTickHook()

`void OSTimeTickHook(void)`

File	*Called from*	*Code enabled in* `OS_CPU_C.C` *if*
OS_CPU_C.C	OSTimeTick()	OS_CPU_HOOKS_EN == 1

This function is called by `OSTimeTick()`, which in turn is called whenever a clock tick occurs. `OSTimeTickHook()` is called immediately upon entering `OSTimeTick()` and allows execution of time-critical code in your application. You can also use this function to trigger an oscilloscope for debugging, trigger a logic analyzer, or establish a breakpoint for an emulator.

Arguments

Return Values

Notes/Warnings

1. `OSTimeTick()` is generally called by an ISR, so the execution time of the tick ISR is increased by the code you provide in this function. Interrupts might or might not be enabled when `OSTimeTickHook()` is called, depending on how the processor port has been implemented. If interrupts are disabled, this function affects interrupt latency.

Example

```
void OSTimeTickHook (void)
{
    /* Trigger an oscilloscope                          */
}
```

Chapter 14

80x86 Port

Real Mode, Large Model
with Emulated Floating-Point Support

This chapter describes how μC/OS-II has been ported to the Intel 80x86 series of processors running in *real mode, large model* for the Borland C++ v4.51 tools. This port assumes that your application does not do any floating-point math, or, if it does, it uses the Borland Floating-Point Emulation library. In other words, I assume that you are using this port with embedded 80186, 80286, 80386, or even plain 8086 class processors that rely only on integer math. This port can also be adapted (i.e., changed) to run plain 8086 processors but requires that you replace the use of the PUSHA/POPA instructions with the proper number of PUSH/POP instructions.

The Intel 80x86 series includes the 80186, 80286, 80386, 80486, Pentiums™ (all models), and Celeron, as well most 80x86 processors from AMD, NEC (V-series), and others. Literally millions of 80x86 CPUs are sold each year. Most of these end up in desktop computers, but a growing number of processors are making their way into embedded systems. It's predicted that we will see 10GHz processors by 2005.

Most C compilers that support 80x86 processors running in real mode offer different memory models, each suited for a different program and data size. Each model uses memory differently. The *large model* allows your application (code and data) to reside in a 1MB memory space. Pointers in this model require 32 bits, although they only address up to 1MB. The next section shows why a 32-bit pointer in this model can only address 20 bits worth of memory.

Figure 14.1 shows the programming model of an 80x86 processor running in real mode. All registers are 16-bits wide, and they all need to be saved during a context switch. As can be seen, there are no floating-point registers because these are emulated by the Borland compiler library using the integer registers.

The 80x86 provides a clever mechanism to access up to 1MB of memory with its 16-bit registers. Memory addressing relies on using a *segment* and an *offset* register. Physical-address calculation is done by shifting a segment register by four (multiplying it by 16) and adding one of five other registers

14

(BP, SP, SI, DI, or IP). The result is a 20-bit address that can access up to 1MB Figure 14.2 shows how the registers are combined. Each segment points to a block of 16 memory locations called a *paragraph*. A 16-bit segment register can point to any of 65,536 different paragraphs of 16 bytes and thus can address 1,048,576 bytes. Because the offset is also 16 bits, a single segment of code cannot exceed 64KB. In practice, however, programs are made up of many smaller segments.

Figure 14.1   80x86 real-mode register model.

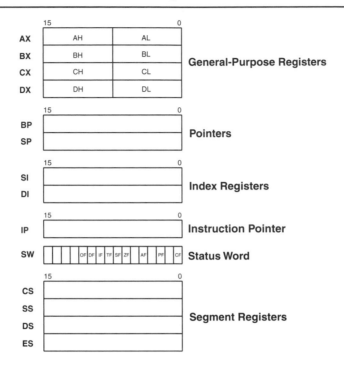

Figure 14.2   Addressing with a segment and an offset register.

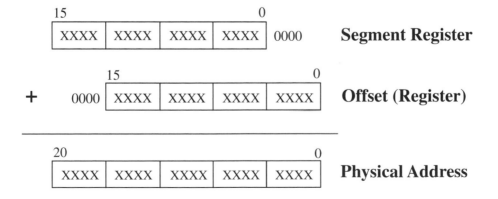

The *code segment* register (CS) points to the base of the program currently executing. The *stack segment* register (SS) points to the base of the stack. The *data segment* register (DS) points to the base of one data area. The *extra segment* register (ES) points to the base of another area where data can be stored. Each time the CPU needs to generate a memory address, one of the segment registers is automatically chosen, and its contents are added to an offset register. It is common to find the segment-colon-offset notation in literature in order to reference a memory location. For example, `1000:00FF` represents physical memory location `0x100FF`.

14.00 Development Tools

I used the Borland C/C++ v4.51 compiler, along with the Borland Turbo Assembler, to port and test the 80x86 port. This compiler generates reentrant code and provides in-line assembly language instructions that can be inserted in C code. The compiler comes with a floating-point emulation library that simulates the floating-point hardware found on 80x86 processors that are equipped with floating-point hardware. Once compiled, the code is executed on a PC. I tested the code on a 300MHz Pentium-II-based computer running the Microsoft Windows 2000 operating system. In fact, I configured the compiler to generate a DOS executable, which was run in a DOS window.

I thought of changing compilers because some readers have complained that they can't find the Borland tools anymore, which makes it harder to build the example code provided in this book. It turns out that a similar compiler and assembler that can compile the example code is available from Borland for only $70 USD (circa 2002). Borland calls it the *Turbo C++ Suite for DOS,* and you can order a copy by visiting the Borland Web site at `www.Borland.com` and following the links to this product.

You can also get professional 80x86-level tools from Paradigm (`www.DevTools.com`) that contain not only a Borland-compatible compiler and assembler but also an IDE, a utility that allows you to locate your code for deployment in embedded systems, a source-level debugger, and more. Paradigm calls their package, the *Paradigm C++ Professional Real.*

Finally, you can also adapt the port provided in this chapter to other 80x86 compilers as long as they generate real-mode code. You will most likely have to change some of the compiler options and assembler directives if you use a different development environment.

Table 14.1 shows the Borland C/C++ compiler v4.51 options (i.e., flags) supplied on the command line. These settings are used to compile the port, as well as the example code provided in Chapter 1.

Table 14.1   *Compiler options used to compile port and examples.*

Option (i.e., Setting)	Description
-1	Generate 80186 code
-B	Compile and call assembler
-c	Compiler to .OBJ
-G	Select code for speed
-I	Path to compiler include files is `C:\BC45\INCLUDE`
-k-	Standard stack frame
-L	Path to compiler libraries is `C:\BC45\LIB`

14

Table 14.1   ***Compiler options used to compile port and examples. (Continued)***

-ml	Large-memory model
-N-	Do not check for stack overflow
-n..\obj	Path where to place object files is ..\OBJ
-O	Optimize jumps
-Ob	Dead code elimination
-Oe	Global register allocation
-Og	Optimize globally
-Oi	Expand common intrinsic functions in-line
-Ol	Loop optimization
-Om	Invariant code motion
-Op	Copy propagation
-Ov	Induction variable
-v	Source debugging **on**
-vi	Turn in-line expansion **on**
-wpro	Error reporting: call to functions with no prototype
-Z	Suppress redundant loads

Table 14.2 shows the Borland Turbo Assembler v4.0 options (i.e., flags) supplied on the command line. These settings are used to assemble the port's OS_CPU_A.ASM.

Table 14.2   ***Assembler options used to assemble .ASM files.***

Option (i.e., Setting)	Description
/MX	Case sensitive on globals
/ZI	Full debugging info
/O	Generate overlay code

14.01 Directories and Files

The installation program provided on the companion CD installs the port for the Intel 80x86 (real mode, large model) on your hard disk. The port is found under the \SOFTWARE\uCOS II\Ix86L\BC45 directory. The directory name stands for **Intel 80x86** real mode, **Large** model and is placed in the **Bor**land **C++** v**4.5**x directory. The source code for the port is found in the following files: OS_CPU.H, OS_CPU_C.C, and OS_CPU_A.ASM.

14.02 INCLUDES.H

INCLUDES.H is a master include file and is found at the top of all .C files. INCLUDES.H allows every .C file in your project to be written without concern about which header file is actually needed. The only drawbacks to having a master include file are that INCLUDES.H might include header files that are not pertinent to the actual .C file being compiled and that the compilation process might take longer. These inconveniences are offset by code portability. You can edit INCLUDES.H to add your own header files, but your header files should be added at the end of the list. Listing 14.1 shows the contents of INCLUDES.H for the 80x86 port.

INCLUDES.H is not really part of the port but is described here because it is needed to compile the port files.

Listing 14.1   INCLUDES.H.

```
#include    <stdio.h>
#include    <string.h>
#include    <ctype.h>
#include    <stdlib.h>
#include    <conio.h>
#include    <dos.h>
#include    <math.h>
#include    <setjmp.h>

#include    "os_cpu.h"
#include    "os_cfg.h"
#include    "ucos_ll.h"
#include    "pc.h"
```

14.03 OS_CPU.H

OS_CPU.H contains processor- and implementation-specific #defines constants, macros, and typedefs. OS_CPU.H for the 80x86 port is shown in Listing 14.2.

OS_CPU_GLOBALS and OS_CPU_EXT allows you to declare global variables that are specific to this port (described later).

Listing 14.2   OS_CPU.H.

```
#ifdef  OS_CPU_GLOBALS
#define OS_CPU_EXT
#else
#define OS_CPU_EXT  extern
#endif
```

14

Listing 14.2   OS_CPU.H (Continued)

```
typedef unsigned char   BOOLEAN;                                    (1)
typedef unsigned char   INT8U;
typedef signed   char   INT8S;
typedef unsigned int    INT16U;
typedef signed   int    INT16S;
typedef unsigned long   INT32U;
typedef signed   long   INT32S;
typedef float           FP32;                                      (2)
typedef double          FP64;


typedef unsigned int    OS_STK;                                    (3)
typedef unsigned short  OS_CPU_SR;                                 (4)


#define BYTE            INT8S                                      (5)
#define UBYTE           INT8U
#define WORD            INT16S
#define UWORD           INT16U
#define LONG            INT32S
#define ULONG           INT32U
```

14.03.01 OS_CPU.H, Data Types

L14.2(1)   If you consult the Borland compiler documentation, you find that an int is 16 bits and a long is 32 bits.

L14.2(2)   Floating-point data types are included even though µC/OS-II doesn't make use of floating-point numbers.

L14.2(3)   A stack entry for the 80x86 processor running in real mode is 16-bits wide; thus, OS_STK is declared accordingly. All task stacks must be declared using OS_STK as the data type.

L14.2(4)   The status register (also called the processor flags) on the 80x86 processor running in real mode is 16-bits wide. The OS_CPU_SR data type is used only if OS_CRITICAL_METHOD is set to 3, which it isn't for this port. I included the OS_CPU_SR data type anyway, in case you use a different compiler and need to use OS_CRITICAL_METHOD #3.

L14.2(5)   I also included data types to allow for backward compatibility with older µC/OS v1.xx applications. These are not necessary if you don't have any applications written with µC/OS v1.xx (you can simply delete these lines).

14.03.02 *OS_CPU.H, OS_ENTER_CRITICAL( ), and OS_EXIT_CRITICAL( )*

Listing 14.2   *OS_CPU.H (Continued)*

```
#define  OS_CRITICAL_METHOD    2                                          (6)


#if      OS_CRITICAL_METHOD == 1
#define  OS_ENTER_CRITICAL()  asm  CLI                                    (7)
#define  OS_EXIT_CRITICAL()   asm  STI
#endif


#if      OS_CRITICAL_METHOD == 2
#define  OS_ENTER_CRITICAL()  asm  {PUSHF; CLI}                           (8)
#define  OS_EXIT_CRITICAL()   asm  POPF
#endif


#if      OS_CRITICAL_METHOD == 3
#define  OS_ENTER_CRITICAL()  (cpu_sr = OSCPUSaveSR())                    (9)
#define  OS_EXIT_CRITICAL()   (OSCPURestoreSR(cpu_sr))
#endif


#if OS_CRITICAL_METHOD == 3                                               (10)
OS_CPU_SR  OSCPUSaveSR(void);
void       OSCPURestoreSR(OS_CPU_SR cpu_sr);
#endif
```

L14.2(6)   µC/OS-II, as with all real-time kernels, needs to disable interrupts in order to access critical sections of code and re-enable interrupts when done. Because the Borland compiler supports in-line assembly language, it's quite easy to specify the instructions to disable and enable interrupts. µC/OS-II defines two macros to disable and enable interrupts: OS_ENTER_CRITICAL( ) and OS_EXIT_CRITICAL( ), respectively. I actually allow you to use one of three methods for disabling and enabling interrupts. For this port, the preferred one is the second method because it's directly supported by the compiler.

OS_CRITICAL_METHOD == 1

L14.2(7)   The first and simplest way to implement these two macros is to invoke the processor instruction to disable interrupts (CLI) for OS_ENTER_CRITICAL( ) and to enable interrupts (STI) for OS_EXIT_CRITICAL( ).

OS_CRITICAL_METHOD == 2

L14.2(8)   The second way to implement OS_ENTER_CRITICAL( ) is to save the interrupt-disable status onto the stack and then disable interrupts. This action is accomplished on the 80x86 by executing the PUSHF instruction, followed by the CLI instruction. OS_EXIT_CRITICAL( ) simply needs to execute a POPF instruction to restore the original contents of the processor's SW register.

OS_CRITICAL_METHOD == 3

14

L14.2(9)   The third way to implement OS_ENTER_CRITICAL() is to write a function that saves the status register of the CPU in a variable. OS_EXIT_CRITICAL() invokes another function to restore the status register from the variable. I didn't include this code in the port, but, if you are familiar with assembly language, you should be able to write this easily.

L14.2(10)   I recommend that you call the functions expected in OS_ENTER_CRITICAL() and OS_EXIT_CRITICAL(): OSCPUSaveSR() and OSCPURestoreSR(), respectively. You would declare the code for these two functions in OS_CPU_A.ASM.

14.03.03 *OS_CPU.H, Stack Growth*

L14.2(11)   The stack on an 80x86 processor grows from high to low memory, which means that OS_STK_GROWTH must be set to 1.

Listing 14.2   OS_CPU.H (Continued)

```
#define   OS_STK_GROWTH           1                                              (11)
```

14.03.04 *OS_CPU.H, OS_TASK_SW()*

Listing 14.2   OS_CPU.H (Continued)

```
#define   uCOS                    0x80                                           (12)


#define   OS_TASK_SW()            asm   INT   uCOS                               (13)
```

L14.2(13)   To switch context, OS_TASK_SW() needs to simulate an interrupt. The 80x86 provides 256 software interrupts to accomplish this. The interrupt service routine (ISR) (also called the exception handler) must vector to the assembly-language function OSCtxSw() (see OS_CPU_A.ASM). We thus need to ensure that the pointer at vector 0x80 points to OSCtxSw().

L14.2(12)   I tested the code on a PC, and I decided to use interrupt number 128 (0x80) because I found it to be available. Actually, the original PC used interrupts 0x80 through 0xF0 for the BASIC interpreter. Few, if any PCs, come with a BASIC interpreter built in anymore, so it should be safe to use these vectors. Optionally, you can also use vectors 0x4B to 0x5B, 0x5D to 0x66, or 0x68 to 0x6F. If you use this port on an embedded processor, such as the 80186, you are most likely not as restricted in your choice of vectors.

14.03.05 *OS_CPU.H, Tick Rate*

The tick rate for an RTOS should generally be set between 10 and 100Hz. It is always preferable (but not necessary) to set the tick rate to a round number. Unfortunately, on the PC, the default tick rate is 18.20648Hz, which is not what I would call a nice, round number. For this port, I decided to change the tick rate of the PC from the standard 18.20648Hz to 200Hz (i.e., 5ms between ticks). There are three reasons to do this:

1. 200Hz happens to be almost exactly 11 times faster than 18.20648Hz. The port needs to chain into DOS once every 11 ticks. In DOS, the tick handler is responsible for some system maintenance that is expected to happen every 54.93ms.

2. It's useful to have a 5.00ms-time resolution for time delays and timeouts. If you are running the example code on an 80386 PC, you might find the overhead of a 200Hz tick rate unacceptable. However, on today's fast Pentium-class processors, a 200Hz tick rate is not likely to be a problem.

3. Even if it's possible to change the tick rate on a PC to be exactly 20Hz or even 100Hz, it would be difficult to chain into the DOS-tick handler at exactly 18.20648Hz. That's why I chose an exact multiple and thus had to choose 200Hz. Of course, I could also have used 22 as a multiple and would have obtained 400Hz (2.5ms). On a fast PC, you should have no problems running at this tick rate or even faster.

Listing 14.2   OS_CPU.H (Continued)

```
OS_CPU_EXT  INT8U  OSTickDOSCtr;                                    (14)
```

L14.2(14)   This statement declares an 8-bit variable (OSTickDOSCtr) that keeps track of the number of times the ticker is called. Every 11th time, the DOS-tick handler is called. OSTickDOSCtr is used in OS_CPU_A.ASM and really only applies to a PC environment. You most likely would not use this scheme if you designed an embedded system around a non-PC architecture, because you would set the tick rate to the proper value in the first place.

14.03.06 OS_CPU.H, Floating-Point Emulation

As previously mentioned, the Borland compiler provides a floating-point emulation library. However, this library is non-reentrant.

Listing 14.2   OS_CPU.H (Continued)

```
void    OSTaskStkInit_FPE_x86(OS_STK **pptos, OS_STK **ppbos, INT32U *psize);    (15)
```

L14.2(15)   A function has been added to allow you to pre-condition the stack of a task in order to make the Borland library think it only has one task and thus make the library reentrant. This function will be discussed in Section 14.04.02, "OSTaskStkInit_FPE_x86()".

14.04 OS_CPU_C.C

A μC/OS-II port requires that you write ten fairly simple C functions:

OSTaskStkInit()	OSTaskStatHook()
OSTaskCreateHook()	OSTimeTickHook()
OSTaskDelHook()	OSInitHookBegin()
OSTaskSwHook()	OSInitHookEnd()
OSTaskIdleHook()	OSTCBInitHook()

μC/OS-II only requires OSTaskStkInit(). The other nine functions must be declared but don't need to contain any code. In the case of this port, I did just that. The #define constant OS_CPU_HOOKS_EN (see OS_CFG.H) should be set to 1.

14

14.04.01   `OSTaskStkInit()`

This function is called by `OSTaskCreate()` and `OSTaskCreateExt()` to initialize the stack frame of a task so that it looks as if an interrupt has just occurred and that all processor registers have been pushed onto it. Figure 14.3 shows what `OSTaskStkInit()` puts on the stack of the task being created. Note that the diagram doesn't show the stack frame of the code calling `OSTaskStkInit()` but rather the stack frame of the task being created.

Figure 14.3   Stack frame initialization with `pdata` *passed on the stack.*

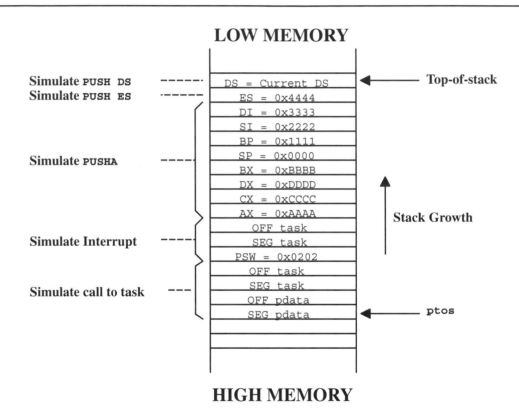

When you create a task, you pass the start address of the task (`task`), a pointer (`pdata`), the task's top-of-stack (`ptos`), and the task's priority (`prio`) to `OSTaskCreate()` or `OSTaskCreateExt()`. `OSTaskCreateExt()` requires additional arguments, but these are irrelevant in discussing

OSTaskStkInit(). To properly initialize the stack frame, OSTaskStkInit() (Listing 14.3) requires only the first three arguments just mentioned (i.e., task, pdata, and ptos).

Listing 14.3 *OS_CPU_C.C, OSTaskStkInit( ).*

```c
OS_STK  *OSTaskStkInit (void  (*task)(void *pd),
                        void   *pdata,
                        OS_STK *ptos,
                        INT16U  opt)
{
    INT16U *stk;


    opt     = opt;
    stk     = (INT16U *)ptos;                    (1)
    *stk-- = (INT16U)FP_SEG(pdata);              (2)
    *stk-- = (INT16U)FP_OFF(pdata);
    *stk-- = (INT16U)FP_SEG(task);               (3)
    *stk-- = (INT16U)FP_OFF(task);
    *stk-- = (INT16U)0x0202;                     (4)
    *stk-- = (INT16U)FP_SEG(task);
    *stk-- = (INT16U)FP_OFF(task);
    *stk-- = (INT16U)0xAAAA;                     (5)
    *stk-- = (INT16U)0xCCCC;
    *stk-- = (INT16U)0xDDDD;
    *stk-- = (INT16U)0xBBBB;
    *stk-- = (INT16U)0x0000;
    *stk-- = (INT16U)0x1111;
    *stk-- = (INT16U)0x2222;
    *stk-- = (INT16U)0x3333;
    *stk-- = (INT16U)0x4444;
    *stk    = _DS;                               (6)
    return ((OS_STK *)stk);                      (7)
}
```

L14.3(1)   OSTaskStkInit() creates and initializes a local pointer to 16-bit elements because stack entries are 16-bits wide on the 80x86. Note that μC/OS-II requires that the pointer ptos points to an empty stack entry.

L14.3(2)   The Borland C compiler passes the argument pdata on the stack instead of registers. Therefore, pdata is placed on the stack frame with the offset register and segment in the order shown.

14

L14.3(3)   The address of your task is placed on the stack next. In theory, this address should be the return address of your task. However, in μC/OS-II, a task must never return, so what is placed here is not really critical.

L14.3(4)   The status word (SW) and the task address are placed on the stack to simulate the behavior of the processor in response to an interrupt. The SW register is initialized to 0x0202, which allows the task to have interrupts enabled when it starts. You can in fact start all your tasks with interrupts disabled by forcing SW to 0x0002 instead. μC/OS-II contains no options to selectively enable interrupts upon startup for some tasks and disable interrupts upon task startup for others. In other words, either all tasks have interrupts disabled upon startup or all tasks have them disabled. You could, however, overcome this limitation by passing the desired interrupt-startup state of a task by using the pdata or the opt arguments for tasks created with OSTaskCreateExt(). However, the latter is not currently implemented. If you chose to have interrupts disabled, each task needs to enable them when they execute. In this case, you also have to modify the code for OS_TaskIdle() and OS_TaskStat() to enable interrupts in those functions. If you don't, your application crashes! I thus recommend that you leave SW initialized to 0x0202 and have interrupts enabled when the task starts.

L14.3(5)   The remaining registers are placed on the stack to simulate the PUSHA, PUSH ES, and PUSH DS instructions, which are assumed to be found at the beginning of every ISR. Note that the AX, BX, CX, DX, SP, BP, SI, and DI registers are placed to satisfy the order of the PUSHA instruction. If you port this code to a 'plain' 8086 processor, you may want to simulate the PUSHA instruction or place the registers in a neater order. You should also note that each register has a unique value instead of all zeros, which is useful for debugging.

L14.3(6)   Also, the Borland compiler supports pseudo-registers (i.e., the _DS keyword notifies the compiler to obtain the value of the DS register), which in this case is used to copy the current value of the DS register to the simulated stack frame.

L14.3(7)   After the task is completed, OSTaskStkInit() returns the address of the new top-of-stack. OSTaskCreate() or OSTaskCreateExt() takes this address and saves it in the task's OS_TCB.

14.04.02   *OSTaskStkInit_FPE_x86()*

When floating-point emulation is enabled (see the Borland documentation), the stack of the Borland-compiled program is organized as shown in Figure 14.3. The compiler assumes that the application runs in a single-threaded (i.e., tasking) environment.

Figure 14.4 Borland floating-point emulation stack.

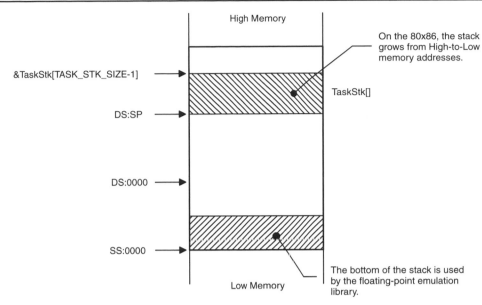

The Borland C Floating-Point Emulation (FPE) library assumes that about 300 bytes starting at SS:0x0000 are reserved to hold floating-point emulation variables. As far as I can tell, this information applies to the large-memory model only. To accommodate this feature, a special function [OSTaskStkInit_FPE_x86()] must be called prior to calling either OSTaskCreate() or OSTaskCreateExt() in order to properly initialize the stack frame of each task that needs to perform floating-point operations. This function applies to Borland v3.x and v4.5x compilers, and thus OSTaskStkInit_FPE_x86() is most likely not included in a port using a different compiler.

The floating-point emulation library stores its data within the reserved space in relation to the current SS register value, assuming that some space starting from SS up (from SS:0x0000 up) is reserved for floating-point operations.

μCOS-II's task stacks are generally allocated statically as shown

```
OS_STK Task1Stk[TASK_STK_SIZE]; /* stack table for task 1 */
OS_TSK Task2Stk[TASK_STK_SIZE]; /* stack table for task 2 */
```

When a task is created by μCOS-II, the highest-table address of the stack is passed to OSTaskCreate() (or OSTaskCreateExt()) as shown

```
OSTaskCreate(Task1, (void*)0, &Task1Stk[TASK_STK_SIZE-1], prio1);
OSTaskCreate(Task2, (void*)0, &Task2Stk[TASK_STK_SIZE-1], prio2);
```

The stack of Task1() starts at DS:&Task1Stk[TASK_STK_SIZE-1] while the stack of Task2() starts at DS:&Task2Stk[TASK_STK_SIZE-1]. After μC/OS-II performs the initialization, the task's top-of-stack (TOS) is saved in the task's OS_TCB.

The stack of the two tasks created from the previous code is shown in Figure 14.5. As can be seen, both tasks are part of the same segment, and, more importantly, they share the same segment base

14

because both stacks are allocated from the same data segment. When μC/OS-II loads a task during a context switch, it sets the SS register to the value of the DS register of the stack. This causes a problem because both tasks have to share the same floating-point emulation variables!

Figure 14.5   Borland floating-point emulation stack.

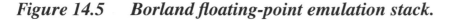

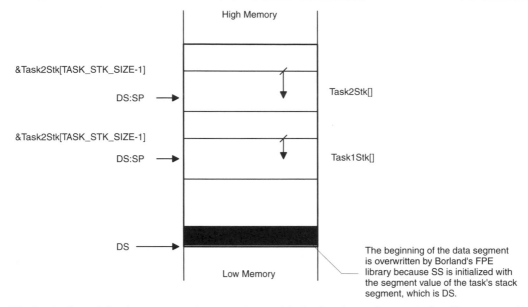

The beginning of the data segment is overwritten with the floating-point emulation library even if we were to use a semaphore to guard access to the region. Protecting this resource with a semaphore allows exclusive access to the floating-point variables, but it does not protect the data segment from being over-writen. Even a single μCOS-II task using floating-point variables overwrites the data segment! Further system behavior depends on what data is overwritten, and typically data-segment overwriting crashes the system.

A similar situation occurs when the stacks are allocated from the heap, because we don't know what part of memory is being overwritten. Typically, the heap is corrupted because the floating-point emulation library overwrites the header of the heap-allocated block.

To fix this problem, the function OSTaskStkInit_FPE_x86(), shown in Listing 14.4, needs to be called prior to creating a task. This function basically normalizes the stack so that every stack starts at SS:0x0000, and the function reserves and properly initializes the floating-point emulation variables for the task being created.

Listing 14.4   *OS_CPU_C.C,*
OSTaskStkInit_FPE_x86().

```
void  OSTaskStkInit_FPE_x86 (OS_STK **pptos,
                             OS_STK **ppbos,
                             INT32U  *psize)

{
    INT32U  lin_tos;
    INT32U  lin_bos;
```

Listing 14.4 *OS_CPU_C.C,*
OSTaskStkInit_FPE_x86( ). (Continued)

```
    INT16U   seg;
    INT16U   off;
    INT32U   bytes;


    seg       = FP_SEG(*pptos);                              (1)
    off       = FP_OFF(*pptos);
    lin_tos   = ((INT32U)seg << 4) + (INT32U)off;            (2)
    bytes     = *psize * sizeof(OS_STK);                     (3)
    lin_bos   = (lin_tos - bytes + 15) & 0xFFFFFFF0L;        (4)


    seg       = (INT16U)(lin_bos >> 4);                      (5)
    *ppbos    = (OS_STK *)MK_FP(seg, 0x0000);                (6)
    memcpy(*ppbos, MK_FP(_SS, 0), 384);                      (7)
    bytes     = bytes - 16;                                  (8)
    *pptos    = (OS_STK *)MK_FP(seg, (INT16U)bytes);         (9)
    *ppbos    = (OS_STK *)MK_FP(seg, 384);                   (10)
    bytes     = bytes - 384;                                 (11)
    *psize    = bytes / sizeof(OS_STK);                      (12)
}
```

As can be seen from the code, you need to pass three arguments to `OSTaskStkInit_FPE_x86()`:

pptos   is a pointer to the task's top-of-stack (TOS) pointer (a pointer to a pointer). The task's TOS is passed to `OSTaskCreate()` or `OSTaskCreateExt()` when you create a task. The stack is allocated from the data space and consists of a value for the DS register and an offset from this segment register. Because `OSTaskStkInit_FPE_x86()` normalizes the TOS, a pointer to the initial TOS is passed to this function so that it can be altered.

ppbos   is a pointer to the task's bottom-of-stack (BOS) pointer (a pointer to a pointer). The task's BOS is not passed to `OSTaskCreate()`; however, it is passed to `OSTaskCreateExt()`. In other words, `ppbos` is necessary for `OSTaskCreateExt()`. The bottom of this stack is generally not located at `DS:0000` but instead, at some offset from the DS register. Because `OSTaskStkInit_FPE_x86()` normalizes the BOS, a pointer to the initial BOS is passed to this function so that it can be altered.

psize   is a pointer to a variable that contains the size of the stack. The task's size is not needed by `OSTaskCreate()`, but the size is needed for `OSTaskCreateExt()`. Because `OSTaskStkInit_FPE_x86()` reserves storage for the floating-point emulation variables, the available stack size is actually altered by this function, which is why a pointer to the size is passed. You must ensure that you pass `OSTaskStkInit_FPE_x86()` a stack large enough to hold the floating-point emulation variables plus the anticipated stack space needed by your application task.

14

L14.4(1)   `OSTaskStkInit_FPE_x86()` starts by decomposing the TOS into its segment and offset components.

L14.4(2)   We then convert the address of the TOS into a linear address. Remember that on the 80x86 (real mode), the segment is multiplied by 16 and added to the offset to form the actual memory address.

L14.4(3)   We then determine the size of the stack (in number of bytes). Remember that with μC/OS-II, you must declare a stack using the `OS_STK` data type, which can represent an 8-bit wide stack, a 16-bit wide stack, or a 32-bit wide stack. For the Borland compiler, the stack width is 16 bits, but it's always better to use the C operator `sizeof()`.

L14.4(4)   The linear address for the BOS is then determined by subtracting the number of bytes allocated to the stack from the TOS address. You should note that I added 15 bytes to the bottom of the stack and ANDed it with `0xFFFFFFF0L` so that I align the BOS on a paragraph boundary (i.e., a 16-byte boundary).

L14.4(5)   From the BOS's linear address, we determine the new segment of the BOS.

L14.4(6)   A far pointer with an offset of `0x0000` is then created and assigned to the new BOS pointer.

L14.4(7)   To initialize the floating-point emulation variables of the task's stack, we can simply copy the bottom of the calling task's stack into the new stack. You should note that the calling task **must** have also been created from a task that has it stack initialized with the floating-point emulation variables. Failure to do this can cause unpredictable results. The Borland Floating-Point Emulation (FPE) library assumes that about 300 bytes, starting at `SS:0x0000`, are reserved to hold floating-point emulation variables. This information applies to the 'large-memory model' only. Note that I decided to copy 384 bytes (`0x0180`). It turns out that you don't need to copy this many bytes, but I find it safe to add a little extra in case of expansion. Your task stack, therefore, **must** have at least 384 bytes **plus** the anticipated stack requirements of your task (including ISR nesting, of course). Note that _SS is a Borland pseudo-register that allows the code to obtain the current value of the CPU's stack segment register. Also, I decided to use the ANSI function `memcpy()` because Borland most likely optimized this function.

L14.4(8)   The next step to to determine the normalized address of the TOS. We first need to subtract 16 bytes because we aligned the stack on a page boundary. If I could guarantee that you would always align your stacks to a paragraph boundary, I would not have to do this.

L14.4(9)   The new TOS is determined by making a far pointer using the new segment [found in L14.4(6)] and the new size of the stack (aligned to a paragraph).

L14.4(10)   The final step is to move the BOS up by 384 bytes in case the BOS is used to perform stack checking [i.e., if your application calls `OSTaskStkChk()`].

L14.4(11)

L14.4(12)   If you use stack checking, μC/OS-II needs to know the size of the new stack. Of course, we don't want to start the stack check from the bottom of the original stack but in fact the new stack.

Figure 14.6 shows what `OSTaskStkInit_FPE_x86()` does. Note that paragraph alignment is not shown.

Figure 14.6 **Stack normalization by** `OSTaskStkInit_FPE_x86()`.

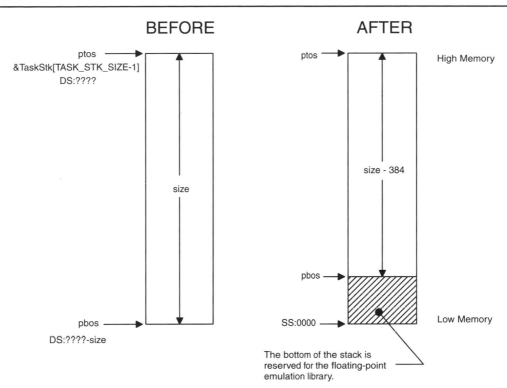

You use `OSTaskStkInit_FPE_x86()`, as shown in Listing 14.5, which contains an example with both `OSTaskCreate()` and `OSTaskCreateExt()`. The code shows that if your task is to do floating-point math, `OSTaskStkInit_FPE_x86()` **must** be called **before** calling either `OSTaskCreate()` or `OSTaskCreateExt()` in order to initialize the task's stack as just described. The returned pointers (`ptos` and `pbos`) **must** be used in the task-creation call. Note that `pbos` is passed to `OSTaskCreateExt()` as the new bottom of stack. You should note that if you were to call `OSTaskStkChk()` [only if the task is created with `OSTaskCreateExt()`] to determine the size of the task's stack at run time, then `OSTaskStkChk()` would report that the stack contains 384 bytes less than it's original size (see the **after** case of Figure 14.6)!

Listing 14.5 **OS_CPU_C.C, using** `OSTaskStkInit_FPE_x86()`.

```
OS_STK Task1Stk[1000];
OS_STK Task2Stk[1000];
```

14

Listing 14.5   *OS_CPU_C.C, using*
                    OSTaskStkInit_FPE_x86(). (Continued)

```
void main (void)
{
    OS_STK *ptos;
    OS_STK *pbos;
    INT32U  size;


    OSInit();
        .
        .
    ptos = &Task1Stk[999];
    pbos = &Task1Stk[0];
    size = 1000;
    OSTaskStkInit_FPE_x86(&ptos, &pbos, &size);
    OSTaskCreate(Task1,
                 (void *)0,
                 ptos,
                 10);
        .
        .
    ptos = &Task2Stk[999];
    pbos = &Task2Stk[0];
    size = 1000;
    OSTaskStkInit_FPE_x86(&ptos, &pbos, &size);
    OSTaskCreateExt(Task2,
                    (void *)0,
                    ptos,
                    11,
                    11,
                    pbos,
                    size,
                    (void *)0,
                    OS_TASK_OPT_SAVE_FP);
        .
        .
    OSStart();
}
```

You should be careful that your code doesn't generate any floating-point exceptions (e.g., divide by zero) because the floating-point library does not work properly under these circumstances. Run-time exceptions can, however, be avoided by adding range-testing code.

14.04.03 *OSTaskCreateHook( )*

As previously mentioned, OS_CPU_C.C does not define code for this function. In other words, no additional work is done by the port when a task is created. The assignment of ptcb to ptcb is done so that the compiler doesn't complain about OSTaskCreateHook( ) not doing anything with the argument.

Listing 14.6 *OS_CPU_C.C, OSTaskCreateHook( ).*

```
void  OSTaskCreateHook (OS_TCB *ptcb)
{
    ptcb = ptcb;
}
```

14.04.04 *OSTaskDelHook( )*

As previously mentioned, OS_CPU_C.C does not define code for this function. In other words, no additional work is done by the port when a task is deleted. The assignment of ptcb to ptcb is again done so that the compiler doesn't complain about OSTaskDelHook( ) not doing anything with the argument.

Listing 14.7 *OS_CPU_C.C, OSTaskDelHook( ).*

```
void  OSTaskDelHook (OS_TCB *ptcb)
{
    ptcb = ptcb;
}
```

14.04.05 *OSTaskSwHook( )*

OS_CPU_C.C doesn't do anything in this function. You should note that I added the skeleton of the code you need if you were to actually do something in OSTaskSwHook( ).

Listing 14.8 *OS_CPU_C.C, OSTaskSwHook( ).*

```
void  OSTaskSwHook (void)
{
#if 0
    if (OSRunning == TRUE) {
        /* Save for task being 'switched-out' */
    }
    /* Code for task being 'switched-in'      */
#endif
}
```

14

14.04.06 `OSTaskIdleHook()`

`OS_CPU_C.C` doesn't do anything in this function.

Listing 14.9   `OS_CPU_C.C, OSTaskIdleHook().`

```
void   OSTaskIdleHook (void)
{
}
```

14.04.07 `OSTaskStatHook()`

`OS_CPU_C.C` doesn't do anything in this function. See Example 3 in Chapter 1 for an example on what you can do with this function.

Listing 14.10   `OS_CPU_C.C, OSTaskStatHook().`

```
void   OSTaskStatHook (void)
{
}
```

14.04.08 `OSTimeTickHook()`

`OS_CPU_C.C` doesn't do anything in this function.

Listing 14.11   `OS_CPU_C.C, OSTimeTickHook().`

```
void   OSTimeTickHook (void)
{
}
```

14.04.09 `OSInitHookBegin()`

`OS_CPU_C.C` doesn't do anything in this function.

Listing 14.12   `OS_CPU_C.C, OSInitHookBegin().`

```
void   OSInitHookBegin (void)
{
}
```

14.04.10 *OSInitHookEnd()*

OS_CPU_C.C doesn't do anything in this function.

Listing 14.13 *OS_CPU_C.C, OSInitHookEnd().*

```
void  OSInitHookEnd (void)
{
}
```

14.04.11 *OSTCBInitHook()*

OS_CPU_C.C doesn't do anything in this function.

Listing 14.14 *OS_CPU_C.C, OSTCBInitHook().*

```
void  OSTCBInitHook (void)
{
}
```

14.05 *OS_CPU_A.ASM*

A µC/OS-II port requires that you write four assembly-language functions:
```
OSStartHighRdy()
OSCtxSw()
OSIntCtxSw()
OSTickISR()
```

14.05.01 *OSStartHighRdy()*

This function is called by OSStart() to start the highest priority task ready to run. However, before you can call OSStart(), you must call OSInit() and create at least one task [see OSTaskCreate() and OSTaskCreateExt()]. OSStart() sets up OSTCBHighRdy so that it points to the TCB of the task with the highest priority. Figure 14.7 shows the stack frame for an 80x86 real-mode task created by either OSTaskCreate() or OSTaskCreateExt() just before OSStart() calls OSStartHighRdy(). The code for OSStartHighRdy() is shown in Listing 14.5.

Listing 14.15 *OSStartHighRdy().*

```
_OSStartHighRdy  PROC FAR

          MOV     AX, SEG _OSTCBHighRdy
          MOV     DS, AX
;
          CALL    FAR PTR _OSTaskSwHook                          (1)
;
          MOV     AL, 1                                          (2)
```

14

Listing 14.15   OSStartHighRdy(). (Continued)

```
        MOV     BYTE PTR DS:_OSRunning, AL
;
        LES     BX, DWORD PTR DS:_OSTCBHighRdy              (3)
        MOV     SS, ES:[BX+2]
        MOV     SP, ES:[BX+0]
;
        POP     DS                                         (4)
        POP     ES
        POPA
;
        IRET                                               (5)


_OSStartHighRdy  ENDP
```

Figure 14.7   80x86 stack frame when task is created.

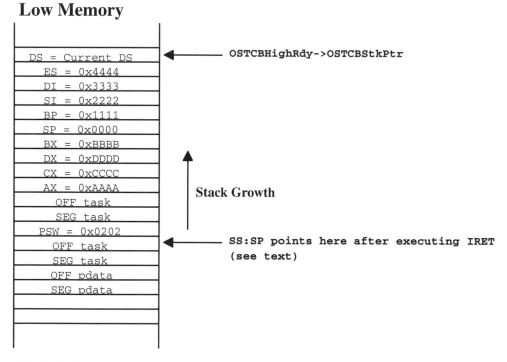

Low Memory

DS = Current DS	◄─── **OSTCBHighRdy->OSTCBStkPtr**
ES = 0x4444
DI = 0x3333
SI = 0x2222
BP = 0x1111
SP = 0x0000
BX = 0xBBBB
DX = 0xDDDD
CX = 0xCCCC
AX = 0xAAAA	**Stack Growth**
OFF task
SEG task
PSW = 0x0202
OFF task	◄─── **SS:SP points here after executing IRET**
SEG task	**(see text)**
OFF pdata
SEG pdata

High Memory

L14.15(1)   As mentioned in Chapter 13, OSStartHighRdy() must call OSTaskSwHook() when it starts.
            Remember that your OSTaskSwHook() function must check the state of OSRunning (which

should be `FALSE` at this point) so that the function only performs a restore-context operation instead of a save-and-restore-context operation.

L14.15(2) `OSStartHighRdy()` then sets `OSRunning` to `TRUE` so that subsequent calls to `OSTaskSwHook()` are able to perform both save and restore operations. Because the code is done in assembly language, there is no way to get the exact value of `TRUE` from the C compiler. I'm thus assuming that `TRUE` is 1.

L14.15(3) `OSStartHighRdy()` then retrieves and loads the stack pointer from the task's `OS_TCB`. As mentioned before, I decided to store the stack pointer at the beginning of the TCB (i.e., its `OS_TCB`) to make it easier to access the pointer from assembly language.

L14.15(4) `OSStartHighRdy()` then restores the contents of all the CPU-integer registers from the task's stack.

L14.15(5) The `IRET` instruction is executed in order to perform a return from interrupt. Remember that the stack frame of the task was created so that it looks as if an interrupt has occurred and all the CPU registers has been pushed onto the task's stack. The `IRET` instruction pulls the task address and places it into the CS:IP registers, followed by the value (called status word or flags) to load into the SW register.

As seen in Figure 14.7, upon executing the `IRET` instruction, the stack pointer (`SS:SP`) points to the return address of the task and looks as if the task were called by a normal function. `SS:SP+4` points to the argument `pdata`, which is passed to the task. In other words, your task does not know whether it was called by `OSStartHighRdy()` or by any other function!

14.05.02 *OSCtxSw()*

A task-level context switch is accomplished on the 80x86 processor by executing a software-interrupt instruction. The ISR must vector to `OSCtxSw()`. The sequence of events that leads μC/OS-II to vector to `OSCtxSw()` begins when the current task calls a service provided by μC/OS-II, which causes a higher priority task to be ready to run. At the end of the service call, μC/OS-II calls the function `OS_Sched()`, which concludes that the current task is no longer the most important task to run. `OS_Sched()` loads the address of the `OS_TCB` of the highest priority task into `OSTCBHighRdy` and then executes the software-interrupt instruction by invoking the macro `OS_TASK_SW()`. Note that the variable `OSTCBCur` already contains a pointer to the current task's `OS_TCB`. The code for `OSCtxSw()` is shown in Listing 14.16. Figure 14.8 shows the stack frames of the task being suspended and the task being resumed.

Listing 14.16 *OSCtxSw()*.

```
_OSCtxSw      PROC    FAR                                          (1)
;
              PUSHA                                                (2)
              PUSH    ES
              PUSH    DS
;
              MOV     AX, SEG _OSTCBCur
              MOV     DS, AX
;
```

Listing 14.16   OSCtxSw( ). *(Continued)*

```
        LES     BX, DWORD PTR DS:_OSTCBCur                    (3)
        MOV     ES:[BX+2], SS
        MOV     ES:[BX+0], SP
;

        CALL    FAR PTR _OSTaskSwHook                         (4)
;

        MOV     AX, WORD PTR DS:_OSTCBHighRdy+2               (5)
        MOV     DX, WORD PTR DS:_OSTCBHighRdy
        MOV     WORD PTR DS:_OSTCBCur+2, AX
        MOV     WORD PTR DS:_OSTCBCur, DX
;

        MOV     AL, BYTE PTR DS:_OSPrioHighRdy                (6)
        MOV     BYTE PTR DS:_OSPrioCur, AL
;

        LES     BX, DWORD PTR DS:_OSTCBHighRdy               (7)
        MOV     SS, ES:[BX+2]
        MOV     SP, ES:[BX]
;

        POP     DS                                           (8)
        POP     ES
        POPA
;

        IRET                                                 (9)
;
_OSCtxSw    ENDP
```

F14.8(1)

L14.16(1)   On the 80x86 processor, the software-interrupt instruction forces the SW register to be pushed onto the current task's stack, followed by the return address (segment and then offset) of the task that executed the INT instruction [i.e., the task that invoked OS_TASK_SW( )].

F14.8(2)

L14.16(2)   The remaining CPU registers of the task to suspend are saved onto the current task's stack.

F14.8(3)

L14.16(3)   The pointer to the new stack frame is saved into the task's OS_TCB. This pointer is composed of the stack segment (SS register) and the stack pointer (SP register). The OS_TCB in μC/OS-II is organized such that the stack pointer is placed at the beginning of the OS_TCB structure to make it easier to save and restore the stack pointer using assembly language.

L14.16(4)   The user-definable task-switch hook OSTaskSwHook( ) is then called. Note that when OSTaskSwHook( ) is called, OSTCBCur points to the current task's OS_TCB, while OSTCBHighRdy points to the new task's OS_TCB. You can thus access each task's OS_TCB from `OSTaskSwHook()`. If you never intend to use the context-switch hook, you can comment out the call and save yourself a few clock cycles during the context switch. In other words, there is no point in going through the overhead of calling and returning from a funtion if your port doesn't use `OSTaskSwHook()`. As a general rule, however, I like to make the call to be consistent between ports.

L14.16(5) Upon returning from `OSTaskSwHook()`, `OSTCBHighRdy` is copied to `OSTCBCur` because the new task is now also the current task.

L14.16(6) Also, `OSPrioHighRdy` is copied to `OSPrioCur` for the same reason.

F14.8(4)

L14.16(7) At this point, `OSCtxSw()` loads the processor's registers with the new task's context. This action is done by retrieving the SS and SP registers from the new task's `OS_TCB`.

F14.8(5)

L14.16(8) The remaining CPU registers are pulled from the new task's stack.

F14.8(6)

L14.16(9) An `IRET` instruction is executed in order to load the new task's program counter and status word. After this instruction, the processor resumes execution of the new task.

Figure 14.8   80x86 stack frames during a task-level context switch.

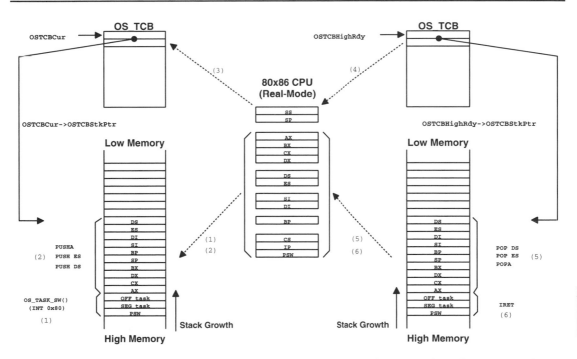

Note that interrupts are disabled during `OSCtxSw()` and also during execution of the user-definable function `OSTaskSwHook()`.

Note: You can see an animation of a context switch for the Intel 80x86 processor by visiting www.uCOS-II.com.

14.05.03 *OSIntCtxSw( )*

OSIntCtxSw( ) is called by OSIntExit( ) to perform a context switch from an ISR. Because OSIntCtxSw( ) is called from an ISR, it is assumed that all the processor registers are already properly saved onto the interrupted task's stack.

The code shown in Listing 14.17 is identical to OSCtxSw( ), except for the fact that there is no need to save the registers (i.e., no PUSHA, PUSH ES, or PUSH DS) onto the stack because it is assumed that the beginning of the ISR has already done that. Also, it is assumed that the stack pointer is saved into the task's OS_TCB by the ISR. Figure 14.9 shows the context-switch process, from OSIntCtxSw( )'s point of view.

To understand the difference, let's assume that the processor receives an interrupt. Let's also suppose that interrupts are enabled. The processor completes the current instruction and initiates an interrupt-handling procedure.

F14.9(1)   The 80x86 automatically pushes the processor's SW register, followed by the return address of the interrupted task, onto the stack. The CPU then vectors to the proper ISR. µC/OS-II requires that your ISR begin by saving the rest of the processor registers. After the registers are saved, µC/OS-II requires that you also save the contents of the stack pointer in the task's OS_TCB.

Your ISR then needs either to call OSIntEnter( ) or to increment the global variable OSIntNesting by one. At this point, we can assume that the task is suspended and that we could, if needed, switch to a different task.

The ISR can now start servicing the interrupting device and possibly make a higher priority task ready. This action occurs if the ISR sends a message to a task by calling OSFlagPost( ), OSMboxPost( ), OSMboxPostOpt( ), OSQPostFront( ), OSQPost( ), or OSQPostOpt( ). A higher priority task can also be resumed if the ISR calls OSTaskResume( ), OSTimeTick( ), or OSTimeDlyResume( ).

Assume that a higher priority task is made ready to run by the ISR. µC/OS-II requires that an ISR calls OSIntExit( ) when it has finished servicing the interrupting device. OSIntExit( ) basically tells µC/OS-II that it's time to return to task-level code if all nested interrupts have completed. In other words, when OSIntNesting is decremented to 0 by OSIntExit( ), OSIntExit( ) returns to task-level code.

When OSIntExit( ) executes, it notices that the interrupted task is no longer the task that needs to run because a higher priority task is now ready. In this case, the pointer OSTCBHighRdy is made to point to the new task's OS_TCB, and OSIntExit( ) calls OSIntCtxSw( ) to perform the context switch.

Listing 14.17 *OSIntCtxSw( ).*

```
_OSIntCtxSw PROC    FAR
;
            CALL    FAR PTR _OSTaskSwHook                    (1)
;
            MOV     AX, SEG _OSTCBCur
            MOV     DS, AX
```

Listing 14.17 *OSIntCtxSw( ). (Continued)*

```
;
            MOV     AX, WORD PTR DS:_OSTCBHighRdy+2                    (2)
            MOV     DX, WORD PTR DS:_OSTCBHighRdy
            MOV     WORD PTR DS:_OSTCBCur+2, AX
            MOV     WORD PTR DS:_OSTCBCur, DX
;
            MOV     AL, BYTE PTR DS:_OSPrioHighRdy                     (3)
            MOV     BYTE PTR DS:_OSPrioCur, AL
;
            LES     BX, DWORD PTR DS:_OSTCBHighRdy                     (4)
            MOV     SS, ES:[BX+2]
            MOV     SP, ES:[BX]
;
            POP     DS                                                (5)
            POP     ES
            POPA
;
            IRET                                                      (6)
;
_OSIntCtxSw ENDP
```

L14.17(1) The first thing OSIntCtxSw( ) does is call the user-definable task-switch hook OSTaskSwHook( ). Note that when OSTaskSwHook( ) is called, OSTCBCur points to the current task's OS_TCB, while OSTCBHighRdy points to the new task's OS_TCB. You can thus access each task's OS_TCB from OSTaskSwHook( ). Again, if you never intend to use the context-switch hook, you can comment out the call and save yourself a few clock cycles during the context switch.

L14.17(2) Upon returning from OSTaskSwHook( ), OSTCBHighRdy is copied to OSTCBCur because the new task is now also the current task.

L14.17(3) OSPrioHighRdy is also copied to OSPrioCur for the same reason.

F14.9(2)

L14.17(4) At this point, OSCtxSw( ) loads the processor's registers with the new task's context. This action is done by retrieving the SS and SP registers from the new task's OS_TCB.

F14.9(3)

L14.17(5) The remaining CPU registers are pulled from the stack.

F14.9(4)

L14.17(6) An IRET instruction is executed in order to load the new task's program counter and status word. After this instruction, the processor resumes execution of the new task.

Note that interrupts are disabled during OSIntCtxSw( ) and also during execution of the user-definable function OSTaskSwHook( ).

14

Figure 14.9 *80x86 stack frames during an interrupt-level context switch.*

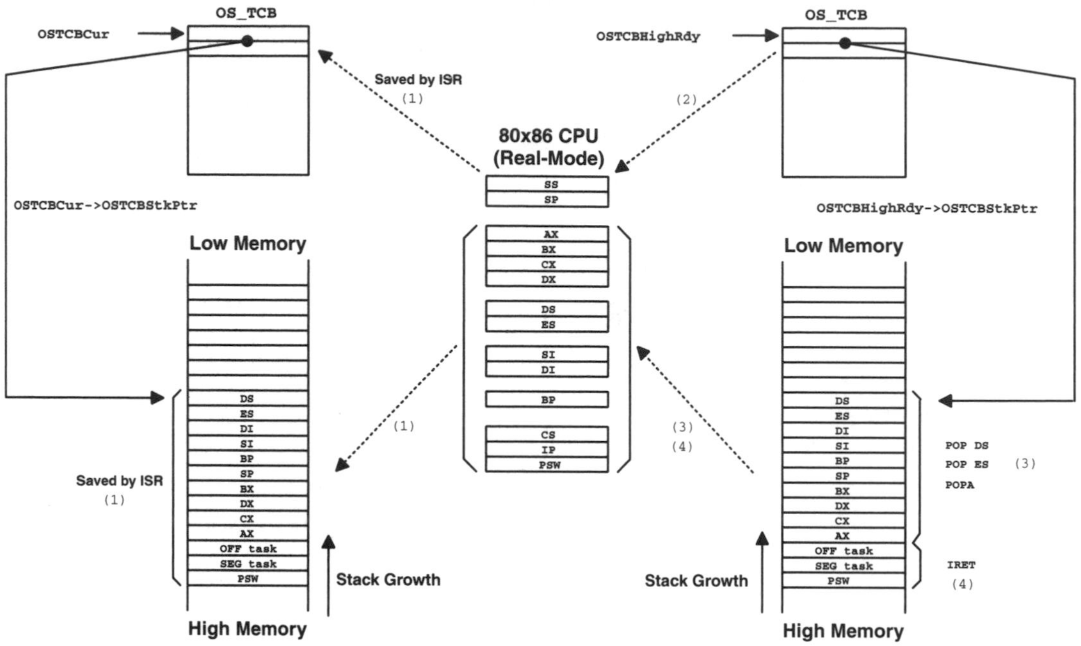

14.05.04 OSTickISR()

As mentioned in Section 14.03.05, "OS_CPU.H, Tick Rate", the tick rate of an RTOS should be set between 10 and 100Hz. On the PC, the ticker occurs every 54.93ms (18.20648Hz) and is obtained by a hardware timer that interrupts the CPU. Recall that I reprogrammed the tick rate to 200Hz. The ticker on the PC is assigned to vector 0x08, but µC/OS-II redefined it so that it vectors to OSTickISR() instead. Because of this change, the PC's tick handler is saved [see PC.C, PC_DOSSaveReturn()] in vector 129 (0x81). To satisfy DOS, however, the PC's handler is called every 54.93ms (described shortly). Figure 14.10 shows the contents of the interrupt-vector table (IVT) before and after installing µC/OS-II.

With µC/OS-II, it is very important that you enable ticker interrupts after multitasking has started, that is, after calling OSStart(). In the case of the PC, however, ticker interrupts are already occurring before you actually execute your µC/OS-II application.

To prevent the ISR from invoking OSTickISR() until µC/OS-II is ready, do the following:
main()

    Call OSInit() to initialize µC/OS-II.

    Call PC_DOSSaveReturn() (see PC.C)

    Call PC_VectSet() to install context switch-vector OSCtxSw() at vector 0x80

    Create at least one application task

    Call OSStart() when you are ready to multitask

The first task to execute needs to

    Install OSTickISR() at vector 0x08

Change the tick rate from 18.20648 to 200Hz

The tick handler on the PC is somewhat tricky, so I explain it using the pseudocode shown in Listing 14.18. This code would normally be written in assembly language.

Listing 14.18 *Pseudocode for* `OSTickISR()`.

```
void  OSTickISR (void)
{
    Save all registers on the current task's stack;            (1)
    OSIntNesting++;                                            (2)
    if (OSIntNesting == 1) {                                   (3)
        OSTCBCur->OSTCBStkPtr = SS:SP                          (4)
    }
    OSTickDOSCtr--;                                            (5)
    if (OSTickDOSCtr == 0) {                                   (6)
        OSTickDOSCtr = 11;                                     (7)
        INT 81H;        /* Interrupt will be cleared by DOS */
    } else {
        Send EOI to PIC;                                      (8)
    }
    OSTimeTick();                                              (9)
    OSIntExit();                                              (10)
    Restore all registers that were save on the current task's stack;  (11)
    Return from Interrupt;                                    (12)
}
```

L14.18(1)   Like all µC/OS-II ISRs, all registers need to be saved onto the current task's stack.

L14.18(2)   Upon entering an ISR, you need to tell µC/OS-II that you are starting an ISR by either calling `OSIntEnter()` or directly incrementing `OSIntNesting`. I like to increment `OSIntNesting` directly because it's faster. However, `OSIntEnter()` checks that you don't increment `OSIntNesting` beyond 255 and thus is safer if you nest your ISRs.

L14.18(3)

L14.18(4)   If this ISR is the first nested ISR, you need to save the stack pointer into the current task's `OS_TCB`.

L14.18(5)

L14.18(6)

L14.18(7)   Next, the counter `OSTickDOSCtr` is decremented, and, when it reaches 0, the DOS-ticker handler is called, which happens every 54.93ms.

L14.18(8)   Ten times out of 11, however, a command is sent to the priority interrupt controller (PIC) to clear the interrupt. Note that this action is unnecesary when the DOS ticker is called because the DOS-tick handler directly clears the interrupt source.

14

L14.18(9)   OSTickISR() then calls OSTimeTick() so that µC/OS-II can update all tasks waiting for time to expire or pending for some event to occur, with a timeout.

L14.18(10)   At the completion of all ISRs, OSIntExit() is called. If a higher priority task has been made ready by this ISR (or any other nested ISRs) and this is the last nested ISR, then OSIntExit() does not return to OSTickISR()! Instead, OSIntCtxSw() restores the processor's context of the new task and issues an IRET instruction. If the ISR is not the last nested ISR or the ISR did not cause a higher priority task to be ready, then OSIntExit() returns to OSTickISR().

L14.18(11)

L14.18(12)   If OSIntExit() returns, it's because OSIntExit() didn't find any higher priority task to run, and thus the contents of the interrupt task's processor registers are restored. When the IRET instruction is executed, the ISR returns to the interrupted task.

Figure 14.10   The PC interrupt-vector table (IVT).

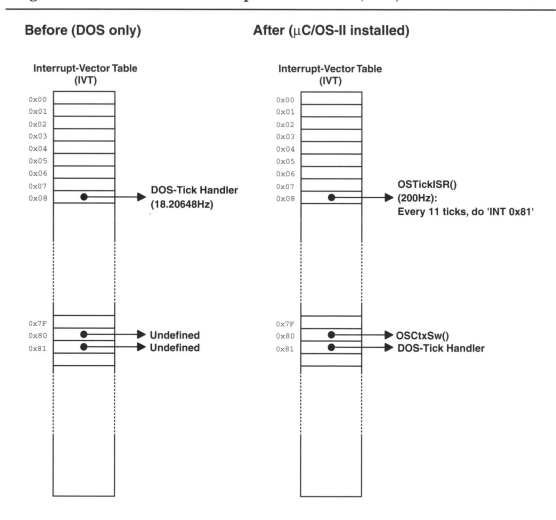

The actual code for OSTickISR() is shown in Listing 14.19. The number in Listing 14.19 corresponds to the same item in Listing 14.18. You should note that the actual code in the file contains comments.

Listing 14.19 *OSTickISR().*

```
_OSTickISR   PROC    FAR
;
             PUSHA                                                (1)
             PUSH    ES
             PUSH    DS
;
             MOV     AX, SEG(_OSIntNesting)                       (2)
             MOV     DS, AX
             INC     BYTE PTR DS:_OSIntNesting
;
             CMP     BYTE PTR DS:_OSIntNesting, 1                 (3)
             JNE     SHORT _OSTickISR1
             MOV     AX, SEG(_OSTCBCur)
             MOV     DS, AX
             LES     BX, DWORD PTR DS:_OSTCBCur                   (4)
             MOV     ES:[BX+2], SS
             MOV     ES:[BX+0], SP
;
_OSTickISR1:
             MOV     AX, SEG(_OSTickDOSCtr)                       (5)
             MOV     DS, AX
             DEC     BYTE PTR DS:_OSTickDOSCtr
             CMP     BYTE PTR DS:_OSTickDOSCtr, 0                 (6)
             JNE     SHORT _OSTickISR2
;
             MOV     BYTE PTR DS:_OSTickDOSCtr, 11                (7)
             INT     081H
             JMP     SHORT _OSTickISR3

_OSTickISR2:
             MOV     AL, 20H                                      (8)
             MOV     DX, 20H
             OUT     DX, AL
;
_OSTickISR3:
             CALL    FAR PTR _OSTimeTick                         (9)
```

14

Listing 14.19   OSTickISR( ). *(Continued)*

```
;
           CALL    FAR PTR _OSIntExit                                  (10)
;
           POP     DS                                                  (11)
           POP     ES
           POPA
;
           IRET                                                        (12)
;
_OSTickISR  ENDP
```

You can simplify OSTickISR( ) by not increasing the tick rate from 18.20648 to 200Hz, as shown in the pseudocode in Listing 14.20. The actual code is shown in Listing 14.21 and matches the same item from Listing 14.20. This code is included so that you can model your ISRs after it.

Listing 14.20   Pseudocode for 18.2Hz OSTickISR( ).

```
void OSTickISR (void)
{
    Save all registers on the current task's stack;                   (1)
    OSIntNesting++;                                                    (2)
    if (OSIntNesting == 1) {                                           (3)
        OSTCBCur->OSTCBStkPtr = SS:SP                                  (4)
    }
    INT 81H;                                                           (5)
    OSTimeTick();                                                      (6)
    OSIntExit();                                                       (7)
    Restore all registers that were save on the current task's stack; (8)
    Return from Interrupt;                                             (9)
}
```

L14.20(1)   As with all µC/OS-II ISRs, all registers need to be saved onto the current task's stack.

L14.20(2)   Upon entering an ISR, you need to tell µC/OS-II that you are starting an ISR by either calling OSIntEnter( ) or directly incrementing OSIntNesting. I like to increment OSIntNesting directly because it's faster.

L14.20(3)

L14.20(4)   If this ISR is the first nested ISR, you need to save the stack pointer into the current task's OS_TCB.

L14.20(5)   Next, the DOS-tick handler is called by issuing an INT 81H instruction (see the remapping of the IVT, Figure 14.10). Note that you do not need to clear the interrupt because the DOS ticker performs this action.

L14.20(6)   Call OSTimeTick() so that µC/OS-II can update all tasks waiting for time to expire or pending some event to occur with a timeout. If your ISR is not for the DOS tick, this place is where you put the code to service your own interrupt.

L14.20(7)   When you are done servicing the ISR, call OSIntExit(). If the ISR makes a higher priority task ready to run, OSIntExit() does not return to this ISR but instead performs context switch to the new, higher priority task.

L14.20(8)   The processor registers are restored.

L14.20(9)   The ISR returns to the interrupted source by executing an IRET instruction.

Note that you must not change the tick rate by calling PC_SetTickRate() if you are using this version of the code. In other words, you must leave the tick rate alone. You also have to change the configuration constant OS_TICKS_PER_SEC (see OS_CFG.H) from 200 to 18. You should note that the tick rate is not actually 18 but 18.20648. You need to be aware of this information, especially if you want to delay a task for 10 seconds. You would specify 10 * OS_TICKS_PER_SEC ticks, actually ends up being only 9.8866 seconds!

Listing 14.21   *18.2Hz version of* OSTickISR( ).

```
_OSTickISR   PROC    FAR
;
             PUSHA                                              (1)
             PUSH    ES
             PUSH    DS
;
             MOV     AX, SEG(_OSIntNesting)                     (2)
             MOV     DS, AX
             INC     BYTE PTR DS:_OSIntNesting
;
             CMP     BYTE PTR DS:_OSIntNesting, 1               (3)
             JNE     SHORT _OSTickISR1
             MOV     AX, SEG(_OSTCBCur)
             MOV     DS, AX
             LES     BX, DWORD PTR DS:_OSTCBCur                 (4)
             MOV     ES:[BX+2], SS
             MOV     ES:[BX+0], SP
;
_OSTickISR1:
             INT     081H                                       (5)
;
             CALL    FAR PTR _OSTimeTick                        (6)
;
             CALL    FAR PTR _OSIntExit                         (7)
;
```

14

Listing 14.21   *18.2Hz version of* `OSTickISR( ). (Continued)`

```
            POP     DS                                          (8)
            POP     ES
            POPA
;
            IRET                                                (9)
;
_OSTickISR  ENDP
```

14.06 Memory Usage

Table 14.3 shows the amount of memory (both code and data space) used by µC/OS-II, based on the value of configuration constants. *Data* in this case means RAM, and *code* means ROM if µC/OS-II is used in an embedded system.

The spreadsheet is actually provided on the companion CD:

`\SOFTWARE\uCOS-II\Ix86L\BC45\DOC\80x86L-ROM-RAM.XLS`

You need Microsoft Excel for Office 2000 (or higher) to use this file. The spreadsheet allows you to do what-if scenarios based on the options you select. You can change the configuration values (in **red**) and see how they affect µC/OS-II's ROM and RAM usage on the 80x86. For the ???_EN values, you **must** use either 0 or 1.

I set up the Borland compiler to generate the fastest code. The number of bytes shown are not meant to be accurate but are simply provided to give you a relative idea of how much code space each of the µC/OS-II group of services requires. For example, if you don't need message-queue services (`OS_Q_EN` is set to 0), then you save between 1,900 and 2,200 bytes of code space.

The spreadsheet also shows you the difference in code size based on the value of `OS_ARG_CHK_EN` in your `OS_CFG.H`. You don't need to change the value of `OS_ARG_CHK_EN` to see the difference.

The Data column is not as straightforward. Notice that the stacks for both the idle task and the statistics task have been set to 1,024 bytes (1KB) each. Based on your own requirements, these numbers might be higher or lower. As a minimum, µC/OS-II requires about 3,500 bytes of RAM for µC/OS-II internal data structures if you configure the maximum number of tasks (62 application tasks).

Table 14.4 shows how µC/OS-II can scale down the amount of memory required with most of the services disabled. In this case, I allowed only 16 tasks with 20 priority levels (0 to 19). Notice that the code space is now between 2,400 and 2,700 bytes and that data space for µC/OS-II internals is only about 500 bytes. However, just about the only service you can use in your tasks is `OSTimeDly( )`! Of course you will still be able to do multitasking.

If you use an 80x86 processor, you will most likely not be too restricted with memory, and thus µC/OS-II will most likely not be the largest user of memory.

Table 14.3   *Maximum µC/OS-II configuration.*

Configuration Parameters	Value in OS_CFG.H	DATA (bytes)	CODE (bytes) OS_ARG_CHK_EN == 0	CODE (bytes) OS_ARG_CHK_EN == 1	Delta CODE (bytes)	Delta CODE (%)
TOTAL:		**5523**	**13048**	**14919**	**1871**	**14%**
OS_MAX_EVENTS	10	164				
OS_MAX_FLAGS	2	14				
OS_MAX_MEM_PART	2	44				
OS_MAX_QS	2	52				
OS_MAX_TASKS	62	2,880				
OS_LOWEST_PRIO	63	264				
OS_TASK_IDLE_STK_SIZE	512	1,024				
OS_TASK_STAT_EN	1	10	351	351		
OS_TASK_STAT_STK_SIZE	512	1,024				
OS_ARG_CHK_EN	1					
OS_CPU_HOOKS_EN	1					
MINIMUM			2,177	2,493	316	
OS_FLAG_EN	1		2,174	2,539	82	
OS_FLAG_WAIT_CLR_EN	1				108	
OS_FLAG_ACCEPT_EN	1				41	
OS_FLAG_DEL_EN	1				95	
OS_FLAG_QUERY_EN	1				39	
OS_MBOX_EN	1		958	1,185	55	
OS_MBOX_ACCEPT_EN	1				23	
OS_MBOX_DEL_EN	1				49	
OS_MBOX_POST_EN	1				36	
OS_MBOX_POST_OPT_EN	1				39	
OS_MBOX_QUERY_EN	1				25	

14

Table 14.3   Maximum µC/OS-II configuration. (Continued)

Configuration Parameters	Value in OS_CFG.H	DATA (bytes)	CODE (bytes) OS_ARG_CHK_EN == 0	CODE (bytes) OS_ARG_CHK_EN == 1	Delta CODE (bytes)	Delta CODE (%)
OS_MEM_EN	1		689	838	123	
OS_MEM_QUERY_EN	1				26	
OS_MUTEX_EN	1		1,596	1,792	83	
OS_MUTEX_ACCEPT_EN	1				39	
OS_MUTEX_DEL_EN	1				47	
OS_MUTEX_QUERY_EN	1				27	
OS_Q_EN	1		1,917	2,206	45	
OS_Q_ACCEPT_EN	1				23	
OS_Q_DEL_EN	1				49	
OS_Q_FLUSH_EN	1				25	
OS_Q_POST_EN	1				40	
OS_Q_POST_FRONT_EN	1				40	
OS_Q_POST_OPT_EN	1				40	
OS_Q_QUERY_EN	1				27	
OS_SEM_EN	1		707	864	62	
OS_SEM_ACCEPT_EN	1				21	
OS_SEM_DEL_EN	1				49	
OS_SEM_QUERY_EN	1				25	
OS_TASK_CHANGE_PRIO_EN	1		444	466	22	
OS_TASK_CREATE_EN	1		185	196	11	
OS_TASK_CREATE_EXT_EN	1		441	467	26	
OS_TASK_DEL_EN	1		527	578	51	
OS_TASK_SUSPEND_EN	1		264	300	36	
OS_TASK_QUERY_EN	1		87	103	16	
OS_TIME_DLY_HMSM_EN	1		248	248		
OS_TIME_DLY_RESUME_EN	1		122	132	10	
OS_TIME_GET_SET_EN	1		59	59		

Table 14.3 Maximum µC/OS-II configuration. (Continued)

Configuration Parameters	Value in OS_CFG.H	DATA (bytes)	CODE (bytes) OS_ARG_CHK_EN = 0	CODE (bytes) OS_ARG_CHK_EN = 1	Delta CODE (bytes)	Delta CODE (%)
OS_SCHED_LOCK_EN	1		102	102		
µC/OS-II Internals		47				
Total Application Stacks		0				
Total Application RAM		0				

Table 14.4 Minimum µC/OS-II configuration.

Configuration Parameters	Value in OS_CFG.H	DATA (bytes)	CODE (bytes) OS_ARG_CHK_EN = 0	CODE (bytes) OS_ARG_CHK_EN = 1	Delta CODE (bytes)	Delta CODE (%)
TOTAL:		**1508**	**2362**	**2689**	**327**	**14%**
OS_MAX_EVENTS	10					
OS_MAX_FLAGS	2					
OS_MAX_MEM_PART	2					
OS_MAX_QS	2					
OS_MAX_TASKS	16	360				
OS_LOWEST_PRIO	20	87				
OS_TASK_IDLE_STK_SIZE	512	1,024				
OS_TASK_STAT_EN	0					
OS_TASK_STAT_STK_SIZE	512					
OS_ARG_CHK_EN	1					
OS_CPU_HOOKS_EN	1					
MINIMUM			2,177	2,493	316	
OS_FLAG_EN	0					
OS_FLAG_WAIT_CLR_EN	1					
OS_FLAG_ACCEPT_EN	1					

14

Table 14.4   Minimum µC/OS-II configuration. (Continued)

Configuration Parameters	Value in OS_CFG.H	DATA (bytes)	CODE (bytes) OS_ARG_CHK_EN = 0	CODE (bytes) OS_ARG_CHK_EN = 1	Delta CODE (bytes)	Delta CODE (%)
OS_FLAG_DEL_EN	1					
OS_FLAG_QUERY_EN	1					
OS_MBOX_EN	0					
OS_MBOX_ACCEPT_EN	1					
OS_MBOX_DEL_EN	1					
OS_MBOX_POST_EN	1					
OS_MBOX_POST_OPT_EN	1					
OS_MBOX_QUERY_EN	1					
OS_MEM_EN	0					
OS_MEM_QUERY_EN	1					
OS_MUTEX_EN	0					
OS_MUTEX_ACCEPT_EN	1					
OS_MUTEX_DEL_EN	1					
OS_MUTEX_QUERY_EN	1					
OS_Q_EN	0					
OS_Q_ACCEPT_EN	1					
OS_Q_DEL_EN	1					
OS_Q_FLUSH_EN	1					
OS_Q_POST_EN	1					
OS_Q_POST_FRONT_EN	1					
OS_Q_POST_OPT_EN	1					
OS_Q_QUERY_EN	1					
OS_SEM_EN	0					
OS_SEM_ACCEPT_EN	1					
OS_SEM_DEL_EN	1					
OS_SEM_QUERY_EN	1					
OS_TASK_CHANGE_PRIO_EN	0					

Table 14.4   Minimum µC/OS-II configuration. (Continued)

Configuration Parameters	Value in OS_ CFG.H	DATA (bytes)	CODE (bytes) OS_ARG_CHK_EN == 0	CODE (bytes) OS_ARG_CHK_EN == 1	Delta CODE (bytes)	Delta CODE (%)
OS_TASK_CREATE_EN	1		185	196	11	
OS_TASK_CREATE_EXT_EN	0					
OS_TASK_DEL_EN	0					
OS_TASK_SUSPEND_EN	0					
OS_TASK_QUERY_EN	0					
OS_TIME_DLY_HMSM_EN	0					
OS_TIME_DLY_RESUME_EN	0					
OS_TIME_GET_SET_EN	0					
OS_SCHED_LOCK_EN	0					
µC/OS-II Internals		37				
Total Application Stacks	0					
Total Application RAM	0					

Table 14.5   80x86 data sizes.

Data Structures	#Bytes
Compiler Alignment	2
BOOLEAN	1
INT8S	1
INT8U	1
INT16U	2
INT32U	4
OS_FLAGS	2
OS_STK	2
POINTER	4

14

Chapter 15

80x86 Port

Real Mode, Large Model with Hardware Floating-Point Support

This chapter describes how µC/OS-II has been ported to the Intel 80x86 series of processors that provides a floating-point unit (FPU). Some of the processors that can make use of this port are the Intel 80486™, Pentiums™ (all models), Xeon™, AMD Athlon™, K6™-series, ElanSC520™, and more. The port assumes that you are using the Borland C/C++ compiler v4.51, which was set up to generate code for the *large-memory model*. The processor is assumed to be running in *real mode*. The code for this port is very similar to the one presented in Chapter 14, and, in some cases, I am only presenting the differences.

This port assumes that you have enabled code generation for OSTaskCreateExt() (by setting OS_TASK_CREATE_EXT_EN to 1 in OS_CFG.H) and that you have enabled µC/OS-II's memory-management services (by setting OS_MEM_EN to 1 in OS_CFG.H). Of course, you must set OS_MAX_MEM_PART to at least 1. Finally, tasks that perform floating-point operations **must** be created by using OSTaskCreateExt() and setting the OS_TASK_OPT_SAVE_FP option.

Figure 15.1 shows the programming model of an 80x86 processor running in real mode. The integer registers are identical to those presented in Chapter 14. In fact, they are saved and restored using the same technique. The only difference between this port and the one presented in Chapter 14 is that we also need to save and restore the FPU registers, which is done by using the context-switch-hook functions.

15.00 Development Tools

As with Chapter 14, I used the Borland C/C++ v4.51 compiler, along with the Borland Turbo Assembler for porting and testing. This compiler generates reentrant code and provides in-line assembly language instructions that can be inserted into C code. The compiler can be directed to generate code specifically

15

to make use of the FPU. I tested the code on a 300MHz Pentium-II-based computer running the Microsoft Windows 2000 operating system. In fact, I configured the compiler to generate a DOS executable, which was run in a DOS window.

Finally, you can also adapt the port provided in this chapter to other 80x86 compilers as long as they generate real-mode code. You will most likely have to change some of the compiler options and assembler directives if you use a different development environment.

Table 15.1 shows the Borland C/C++ compiler v4.51 options (i.e., flags) supplied on the command line. These settings are used to compile the port, as well as example code provided in Chapter 1.

Figure 15.1   80x86 real-mode register model.

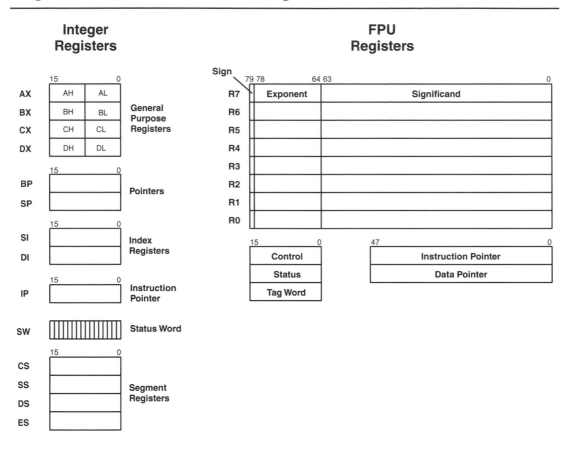

Table 15.1   *Compiler options used to compile port and examples.*

Option (i.e., setting)	Description
-1	Generate 80186 code
-B	Compile and call assembler
-c	Compiler to .OBJ
-d	Merge duplicate strings
-f287	Use FPU hardware instructions
-G	Select code for speed
-I	Path to compiler include files is C:\BC45\INCLUDE
-k-	Standard stack frame
-L	Path to compiler libraries is C:\BC45\LIB
-ml	Large-memory model
-N-	Do not check for stack overflow
-n..\obj	Path where to place object files is ..\OBJ
-O	Optimize jumps
-Ob	Dead code elimination
-Oe	Global register allocation
-Og	Optimize globally
-Oi	Expand common intrinsic functions in-line
-Ol	Loop optimization
-Om	Invariant code motion
-Op	Copy propagation
-Ov	Induction variable
-v	Source debugging **on**
-vi	Turn in-line expansion **on**
-wpro	Error reporting: call to functions with no prototype
-Z	Suppress redundant loads

15

Table 15.2 shows the Borland Turbo Assembler v4.0 options (i.e., flags) supplied on the command line. These settings are used to assemble OS_CPU_A.ASM.

Table 15.2   *Assembler options used to assemble .ASM files.*

Option (i.e., setting)	Description
/MX	Case sensitive on globals
/ZI	Full debugging info
/O	Generate overlay code

15.01 Directories and Files

The installation program provided on the companion CD installs the port for the Intel 80x86 (real mode, large model with FPU support) on your hard disk. The port is found under the
    \SOFTWARE\uCOS-II\Ix86L-FP\BC45
directory. The directory name stands for **I**ntel 80**x86** real mode, **L**arge model with hardware **F**loating-**P**oint instructions and is placed in the **B**orland **C**++ v**4.5**x directory. The source code for the port is found in the following files: OS_CPU.H, OS_CPU_C.C, and OS_CPU_A.ASM.

15.02 INCLUDES.H

Listing 15.1 shows the contents of INCLUDES.H for this 80x86 port. It is identical to the one used in Chapter 14. INCLUDES.H is not really part of the port but is described here because it is needed to compile the port files.

Listing 15.1   INCLUDES.H.

```
#include    <stdio.h>
#include    <string.h>
#include    <ctype.h>
#include    <stdlib.h>
#include    <conio.h>
#include    <dos.h>
#include    <math.h>
#include    <setjmp.h>

#include    "os_cpu.h"
#include    "os_cfg.h"
#include    "ucos_ii.h"
#include    "pc.h"
```

15.03 *OS_CPU.H*

OS_CPU.H contains processor- and implementation-specific #defines constants, macros, and typedefs. OS_CPU.H for the 80x86 port are shown in Listing 15.2. Most of OS_CPU.H is identical to the OS_CPU.H of Chapter 14.

Listing 15.2 *OS_CPU.H.*

```
#ifdef  OS_CPU_GLOBALS
#define OS_CPU_EXT
#else
#define OS_CPU_EXT  extern
#endif


typedef unsigned char   BOOLEAN;                                    (1)
typedef unsigned char   INT8U;
typedef signed   char   INT8S;
typedef unsigned int    INT16U;
typedef signed   int    INT16S;
typedef unsigned long   INT32U;
typedef signed   long   INT32S;
typedef float           FP32;                                      (2)
typedef double          FP64;


typedef unsigned int    OS_STK;                                    (3)
typedef unsigned short  OS_CPU_SR;                                 (4)
```

15.03.01 *OS_CPU.H, Data Types*

L15.2(1) If you consult the Borland compiler documentation, you find that an int and a short are 16 bits and a long is 32 bits.

L15.2(2) Floating-point data types are included because it's assumed that you are performing floating-point operations in your tasks. However, μC/OS-II itself doesn't make use of floating-point numbers.

L15.2(3) A stack entry for the 80x86 processor running in real mode is 16-bits wide; thus, OS_STK is declared accordingly. The stack width doesn't change because of this port. All task stacks must be declared using OS_STK as the data type.

L15.2(4) The status register (also called the processor flags) on the 80x86 processor running in real mode is 16-bits wide. The OS_CPU_SR data type is used only if OS_CRITICAL_METHOD is set to 3, which it isn't for this port. I included the OS_CPU_SR data type anyway, in case you use a different compiler and need to use OS_CRITICAL_METHOD #3.

15

15.03.02 *OS_CPU.H, OS_ENTER_CRITICAL( ), and OS_EXIT_CRITICAL( )*

Listing 15.2 *OS_CPU.H. (Continued)*

```
#define   OS_CRITICAL_METHOD   2                                            (5)

#define   OS_ENTER_CRITICAL()   asm {PUSHF; CLI}                            (6)
#define   OS_EXIT_CRITICAL()    asm  POPF
```

L15.2(5)   For this port, the preferred critical method is the second one because it's directly supported by the compiler.

L15.2(6)   OS_ENTER_CRITICAL( ) is implemented by saving the interrupt-disable status onto the stack and then disabling interrupts. This action is accomplished on the 80x86 by executing the PUSHF instruction, followed by the CLI instruction. OS_EXIT_CRITICAL( ) simply needs to execute a POPF instruction to restore the original contents of the processor's SW register.

15.03.03 *OS_CPU.H, Stack Growth*

Listing 15.2 *OS_CPU.H. (Continued)*

```
#define   OS_STK_GROWTH   1                                                 (7)
```

L15.2(7)   The stack on an 80x86 processor grows from high to low memory, which means that OS_STK_GROWTH must be set to 1.

15.03.04 *OS_CPU.H, OS_TASK_SW( )*

Listing 15.2 *OS_CPU.H. (Continued)*

```
#define  uCOS              0x80                                             (8)

#define  OS_TASK_SW()      asm  INT  uCOS                                   (9)
```

L15.2(9)   To switch context, OS_TASK_SW( ) needs to simulate an interrupt. The 80x86 provides 256 software interrupts to accomplish the simulation. The ISR (also called the exception handler) must vector to the assembly-language function OSCtxSw( ) (see OS_CPU_A.ASM). We thus need to ensure that the pointer at vector 0x80 points to OSCtxSw( ).

L15.2(8)   I tested the code on a PC, and I decided to use interrupt number 128 (0x80).

15.03.05 *OS_CPU.H, Tick Rate*

I also decided (see Chapter 14 for additional details) to change the tick rate of the PC from the standard 18.20648Hz to 200Hz (i.e., 5ms between ticks).

Listing 15.2 *OS_CPU.H. (Continued)*

```
OS_CPU_EXT  INT8U  OSTickDOSCtr;                                    (10)
```

L15.2(10) This statement declares an 8-bit variable (OSTickDOSCtr) that keeps track of the number of times the ticker is called. Every 11th time, the DOS-tick handler is called. OSTickDOSCtr is used in OS_CPU_A.ASM and really only applies to a PC environment.

15.03.06 *OS_CPU.H, Floating-Point Functions*

This port defines three special functions that are specific to the floating-point capabilities of the 80x86. In other words, I had to add three new functions to the port to handle the floating-point hardware.

Listing 15.2 *OS_CPU.H. (Continued)*

```
void      OSFPInit(void);                                          (11)
void      OSFPRestore(void *pblk);                                 (12)
void      OSFPSave(void *pblk);                                    (13)
```

L15.2(11) A function has been added to initialize the floating-point handling mechanism described in this port.

L15.2(12) OSFPRestore() is called to retrieve the value of the floating-point registers when a task is being switched in. OSFPRestore() is actually written in assembly language and is thus found in OS_CPU_A.ASM.

L15.2(13) OSFPSave() is called to save the current value of the floating-point registers when a task is being suspended. OSFPSave() is also written in assembly language and found in OS_CPU_A.ASM.

15.04 *OS_CPU_C.C*

As mentioned in Chapters 13 and 14, the µC/OS-II port requires that you write ten fairly simple C functions:

```
OSTaskStkInit()          OSTaskStatHook()
OSTaskCreateHook()       OSTimeTickHook()
OSTaskDelHook()          OSInitHookBegin()
OSTaskSwHook()           OSInitHookEnd()
OSTaskIdleHook()         OSTCBInitHook()
```

15

µC/OS-II itself only requires OSTaskStkInit(). The other nine functions must be declared but don't need to contain any code. However, this port uses OSTaskCreateHook(), OSTaskDelHook(), OSTaskSwHook(), and OSInitHookEnd().

The #define constant OS_CPU_HOOKS_EN (see OS_CFG.H) should be set to 1.

15.04.01 OSTaskStkInit()

This function is called by OSTaskCreate() and OSTaskCreateExt() and is identical to the OSTaskStkInit() presented in Section 14.04.01. You might recall that OSTaskStkInit() is called to initialize the stack frame of a task so that it looks as if an interrupt has just occurred and that all of the processor-integer registers have been pushed onto it. Figure 15.2 (identical to Figure 14.3) shows what OSTaskStkInit() puts on the stack of the task being created. Note that the diagram doesn't show the stack frame of the code calling OSTaskStkInit() but rather the stack frame of the task being created. Also, the stack frame only contains the contents of the integer registers and nothing about the floating point registers. I discuss how we handle the FPU registers shortly.

Figure 15.2   Stack frame initialization with pdata passed on the stack.

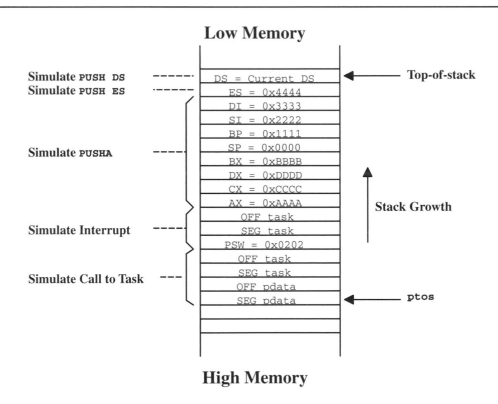

For reference, Listing 15.3 shows the code for OSTaskStkInit(), which is identical to the one shown in Chapter 14 (Listing 14.3).

Listing 15.3   *OS_CPU_C.C, OSTaskStkInit().*

```
OS_STK  *OSTaskStkInit (void  (*task)(void *pd),
                        void   *pdata,
                        OS_STK *ptos,
                        INT16U  opt)
{
    INT16U *stk;


    opt     = opt;
    stk     = (INT16U *)ptos;
    *stk-- = (INT16U)FP_SEG(pdata);
    *stk-- = (INT16U)FP_OFF(pdata);
    *stk-- = (INT16U)FP_SEG(task);
    *stk-- = (INT16U)FP_OFF(task);
    *stk-- = (INT16U)0x0202;
    *stk-- = (INT16U)FP_SEG(task);
    *stk-- = (INT16U)FP_OFF(task);
    *stk-- = (INT16U)0xAAAA;
    *stk-- = (INT16U)0xCCCC;
    *stk-- = (INT16U)0xDDDD;
    *stk-- = (INT16U)0xBBBB;
    *stk-- = (INT16U)0x0000;
    *stk-- = (INT16U)0x1111;
    *stk-- = (INT16U)0x2222;
    *stk-- = (INT16U)0x3333;
    *stk-- = (INT16U)0x4444;
    *stk    = _DS;
    return ((OS_STK *)stk);
}
```

15.04.02 OSFPInit()

OSFPInit() is called by OSInitHookEnd() when OSInit() is done initializing µC/OS-II's internal structures. OSFPInit() is basically used to initialize the floating-point context-switching mechanism presented in this chapter. OSFPInit() assumes that you enabled µC/OS-II's memory-management

15

functions (i.e., you must set OS_MEM_EN to 1 in OS_CFG.H). The code for OSFPInit() is shown in Listing 15.4.

Listing 15.4   OS_CPU_C.C, OSFPInit().

```
#define OS_NTASKS_FP          (OS_MAX_TASKS + OS_N_SYS_TASKS - 1)           (1)
#define OS_FP_STORAGE_SIZE 128                                             (2)


static  OS_MEM *OSFPPartPtr;                                              (3)
static  INT32U  OSFPPart[OS_NTASKS_FP][OS_FP_STORAGE_SIZE / sizeof(INT32U)]; (4)



void  OSFPInit (void)
{
    INT8U   err;
#if OS_TASK_STAT_EN
    OS_TCB  *ptcb;
    void    *pblk;
#endif

    OSFPPartPtr = OSMemCreate(&OSFPPart[0][0],                            (5)
                   OS_NTASKS_FP,
                   OS_FP_STORAGE_SIZE,
                   &err);

#if OS_TASK_STAT_EN && OS_TASK_CREATE_EXT_EN
    ptcb            = OSTCBPrioTbl[OS_STAT_PRIO];                         (6)
    ptcb->OSTCBOpt |= OS_TASK_OPT_SAVE_FP;                               (7)
    pblk            = OSMemGet(OSFPPartPtr, &err);                        (8)
    if (pblk != (void *)0) {                                             (9)
       ptcb->OSTCBExtPtr = pblk;                                         (10)
       OSFPSave(pblk);                                                   (11)
    }
#endif
}
```

L15.4(1)   Although not actually part of OSFPInit(), I defined this constant that is used to determine how many storage buffers are needed to save FPU register values. In this case, I decided to have as many buffers as I have tasks plus one for the statistic task as described below.

L15.4(2)   The 80x86 FPU requires 108 bytes of storage. I decided to allocate 128 bytes for future expansion. If you are tight on memory, you could save 20 bytes per task by setting this value to 108.

L15.4(3)   We are using a µC/OS-II memory partition for the storage of all the FPU contexts. OSFPPartPtr is a pointer to the partition created for this purpose. Because OSFPPartPtr is declared static, your application does not know it exists.

L15.4(4)   OSFPPart[][] is the actual partition that holds the storage for all of the FPU registers of all the tasks. As you can probably tell, you need to have at least

(OS_MAX_TASKS + 1) * 128

bytes of RAM (i.e., data space) for this partition. Because OSFPPart[][] is declared static, your application does not know it exists.

L15.4(5)   OSFPInit() tells µC/OS-II about this partition. You might recall that OSMemCreate() breaks the partition into memory blocks (each of 128 bytes) and links these blocks in a singly linked list. If an FPU storage block is needed, we simply need to call OSMemGet() (discussed in OSTaskCreateHook()).

L15.4(6)   I decided to change the attributes of OS_TaskStat() to allow it to perform floating-point math. You might wonder why I do this because OS_TaskStat() does not perform any floating-point operations. I did this because you might decide to extend the functionality of OS_TaskStat() through OSTaskStatHook() and possibly perform floating-point calculations. OSFPInit() finds the pointer to the statistic task's OS_TCB.

L15.4(7)   The .OSTCBOpt flag is set indicating that OS_TaskStat() is a task that needs to save and restore floating-point registers because µC/OS-II doesn't set this option by default.

L15.4(8)   I get a storage buffer that holds the contents of the floating-point registers for OS_TaskStat() when OS_TaskStat() is switched out.

L15.4(9)   It is always prudent to check for an invalid pointer.

L15.4(10) The pointer to the FPU storage area is saved in the OS_TCB extension pointer, .OSTCBExtPtr. This process allows the context-switch code to know where floating-point registers are saved.

L15.4(11) The function OSFPSave() (see OS_CPU_A.ASM) is called to store the current contents of the FPU registers at the location to which pblk points. It doesn't really matter what the FPU registers contain when we do this. The important thing to realize is that the FPU registers contain valid values, whatever they are. OSFPSave() is discussed in Section 15.05.05, "OSFPSave()."

You should be careful that your code doesn't generate any floating-point exceptions (e.g., divide by zero) because µC/OS-II will not do anything about them. Run-time exceptions can, however, be avoided by adding range-testing code to your application. In fact, you should make it a practice to check for possible divide by zero and the like.

15

15.04.03 *OSTaskCreateHook( )*

Listing 15.5 shows the code for OSTaskCreateHook( ). Recall that OSTaskCreateHook( ) is called by OS_TCBInit( ) [which in turn is called by OSTaskCreate( ) or OSTaskCreateExt( )].

Listing 15.5   OS_CPU_C.C, OSTaskCreateHook( ).

```
void  OSTaskCreateHook (OS_TCB *ptcb)
{
    INT8U  err;
    void  *pblk;


    if (ptcb->OSTCBOpt & OS_TASK_OPT_SAVE_FP) {                          (1)
        pblk = OSMemGet(OSFPPartPtr, &err);                             (2)
        if (pblk != (void *)0) {                                       (3)
            ptcb->OSTCBExtPtr = pblk;                                  (4)
            OSFPSave(pblk);                                            (5)
        }
    }
}
```

L15.5(1)   If you create a task that performs floating-point calculations, you must set the OS_TASK_OPT_ SAVE_FP bit in opt argument of OSTaskCreateExt( ). This option tells OSTaskCreateHook( ) that the task uses the FPU, and thus we need to save and restore the values of these registers during a context switch into or out of this task.

L15.5(2)   Because we are creating a task that uses the FPU, we need to allocate storage for the FPU registers.

L15.5(3)   Again, it's a good idea to validate the pointer.

L15.5(4)   The pointer to the storage area is saved in the OS_TCB of the task being created.

L15.5(5)   Again, the function OSFPSave( ) (see OS_CPU_A.ASM) is called to store the current contents of the FPU registers at the location to which pblk points. It doesn't really matter what the FPU registers contain when we do this. The important thing to realize is that the FPU registers contain valid values, whatever they are. OSFPSave( ) is discussed in Section 15.05.05, "OSFPSave( )".

   Figure 15.3 shows the relationship between some of the data structures after OSTaskCreateHook( ) has executed.

Figure 15.3   Initialized stack and FPU register storage.

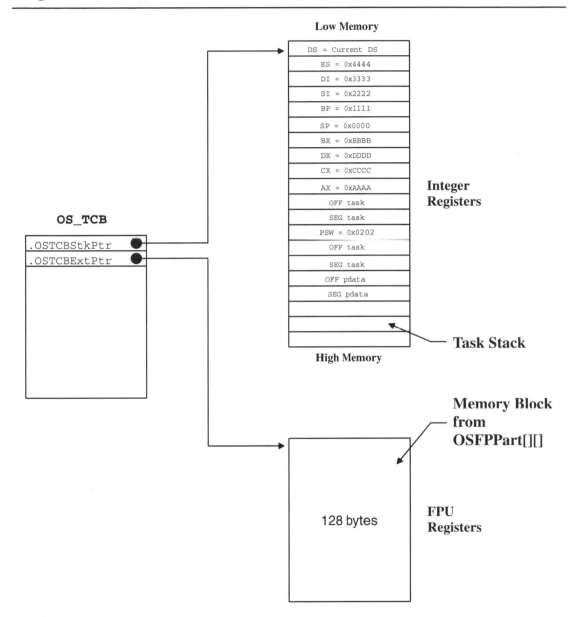

15.04.04 *OSTaskDelHook()*

You might recall that OSTaskDelHook() is called by OSTaskDel() to extend the functionality of OSTaskDel(). Because we allocated a memory block to hold the contents of the floating-point registers when the task was created, we need to deallocate the block when the task is deleted. Listing 15.6 shows how OSTaskDelHook() accomplishes this action.

Listing 15.6　*OS_CPU_C.C, OSTaskDelHook().*

```
void OSTaskDelHook (OS_TCB *ptcb)
{
    if (ptcb->OSTCBOpt & OS_TASK_OPT_SAVE_FP) {            (1)
        if (ptcb->OSTCBExtPtr != (void *)0) {             (2)
            OSMemPut(OSFPPartPtr, ptcb->OSTCBExtPtr);      (3)
        }
    }
}
```

L15.6(1)

L15.6(2)　We first need to confirm that we allocated a memory block that was used for floating-point context storage.

L15.6(3)　The memory block is returned to its proper memory partition.

15.04.05 *OSTaskSwHook()*

OSTaskSwHook() is used to extend the functionality of the context-switch code. You might recall that OSTaskSwHook() is called by OSStartHighRdy(), the task-level context-switch function OSCtxSw(), and the ISR context-switch function OSIntCtxSw(). Listing 15.7 shows how OSTaskSwHook() is implemented.

Listing 15.7　*OS_CPU_C.C, OSTaskSwHook().*

```
void  OSTaskSwHook (void)
{
    INT8U  err;
    void  *pblk;

    if (OSRunning == TRUE) {                              (1)
        if (OSTCBCur->OSTCBOpt & OS_TASK_OPT_SAVE_FP) {   (2)
            pblk = OSTCBCur->OSTCBExtPtr;
            if (pblk != (void *)0) {                      (3)
                OSFPSave(pblk);                           (4)
            }
        }
    }
}
```

Listing 15.7   OS_CPU_C.C, OSTaskSwHook(). (Continued)

```
    if (OSTCBHighRdy->OSTCBOpt & OS_TASK_OPT_SAVE_FP) {          (5)
        pblk = OSTCBHighRdy->OSTCBExtPtr;
        if (pblk != (void *)0) {                                (6)
            OSFPRestore(pblk);                                  (7)
        }
    }
}
```

L15.7(1)   When OSStartHighRdy() calls OSTaskSwHook(), it is trying to restore the contents of the floating-point registers of the highest priority task. When OSStartHighRdy() is called, OSRunning is FALSE indicating that we haven't started multitasking yet, and thus OSTaskSwHook() must not save the floating-point registers.

L15.7(2)   If OSTaskSwHook() is called by either OSCtxSw() or OSIntCtxSw(), then we are switching out a task (i.e., suspending a lower priority task), and thus we check to see if this task was created with the floating-point option.

L15.7(3)   Just to be sure, we also check the contents of the .OSTCBExtPtr to ensure that the contents do not contain a NULL pointer; it shouldn't.

L15.7(4)   As usual, we call OSFPSave() to save the current contents of the floating-point registers to the memory block allocated for that purpose.

L15.7(5)   We then check to see if the task to be switched in (i.e., the higher priority task) was created with the floating-point option. In other words, the function checks whether you told OSTaskCreateExt() that this task will be doing floating-point operations.

L15.7(6)   Just to be sure, we also check the contents of the .OSTCBExtPtr to ensure that the contents do not contain a NULL pointer.

L15.7(7)   The function OSFPRestore() (see OS_CPU_A.ASM) is called to restore the current contents of the FPU registers from the location to which pblk points. OSFPRe<Code>store() is discussed in Section 15.05.06, "OSFPRestore(),".

15.04.06 OSTaskIdleHook()

OS_CPU_C.C doesn't do anything in this function.

Listing 15.8   OS_CPU_C.C, OSTaskIdleHook().

```
void  OSTaskIdleHook (void)
{
}
```

15

15.04.07 *OSTaskStatHook()*

OS_CPU_C.C doesn't do anything in this function. See Example 3 in Chapter 1 for an example on what you can do with OSTaskStatHook().

Listing 15.9   *OS_CPU_C.C, OSTaskStatHook().*

```
void  OSTaskStatHook (void)
{
}
```

15.04.08 *OSTimeTickHook()*

OS_CPU_C.C doesn't do anything in this function.

Listing 15.10   *OS_CPU_C.C, OSTimeTickHook().*

```
void  OSTimeTickHook (void)
{
}
```

15.04.09 *OSInitHookBegin()*

OS_CPU_C.C doesn't do anything in this function.

Listing 15.11   *OS_CPU_C.C, OSInitHookBegin().*

```
void  OSInitHookBegin (void)
{
}
```

15.04.10 *OSInitHookEnd()*

OSInitHookEnd() is called just before OSInit() returns, which means that OSInit() initialized µC/OS-II's memory-partition services (which to use this port you should have set OS_MEM_EN to 1 in OS_CFG.H). OSInitHook() simply calls OSFPInit() (see Section 15.04.02, "OSFPInit()") which is responsible for setting up the memory partition reserved to hold the contents of floating-point registers for each task. The code for OSInitHookEnd() is shown in Listing 15.12.

Listing 15.12 *OS_CPU_C.C, OSInitHookEnd().*

```
void  OSInitHookEnd (void)
{
    OSFPInit();
}
```

15.04.11 *OSTCBInitHook()*

OS_CPU_C.C doesn't do anything in this function.

Listing 15.13 *OS_CPU_C.C, OSTCBInitHook().*

```
void  OSTCBInitHook (void)
{
}
```

15.05 *OS_CPU_A.ASM*

A µC/OS-II port requires that you write four assembly-language functions:

```
OSStartHighRdy()
OSCtxSw()
OSIntCtxSw()
OSTickISR()
```

This port adds two functions called OSFPSave() and OSFPRestore(), which are found in OS_CPU_A.ASM. These functions are responsible for saving and restoring the contents of floating-point registers during a context switch, respectively.

15.05.01 *OSStartHighRdy()*

This function is called by OSStart() to start the highest priority task ready to run. It is identical to the OSStartHighRdy() presented in Chapter 14 (see Section 14.05.01, "OSStartHighRdy()"). The code is shown again in Listing 15.14 for your convenience.

Listing 15.14 *OSStartHighRdy().*

```
_OSStartHighRdy  PROC FAR

         MOV     AX, SEG _OSTCBHighRdy
         MOV     DS, AX
;
         CALL    FAR PTR _OSTaskSwHook
;
         MOV     AL, 1
         MOV     BYTE PTR DS:_OSRunning, AL
;
         LES     BX, DWORD PTR DS:_OSTCBHighRdy
         MOV     SS, ES:[BX+2]
         MOV     SP, ES:[BX+0]
;
```

15

Listing 15.14   *OSStartHighRdy( ). (Continued)*

```
                POP     DS
                POP     ES
                POPA
;

                IRET


_OSStartHighRdy ENDP
```

15.05.02 *OSCtxSw( )*

A task-level context switch is accomplished on the 80x86 processor by executing a software-interrupt instruction. The ISR must vector to OSCtxSw( ). The sequence of events that leads µC/OS-II to vector to OSCtxSw( ) begins when the current task calls a service provided by µC/OS-II, which causes a higher priority task to be ready to run. At the end of the service call, µC/OS-II calls the function OS_Sched( ), which concludes that the current task is no longer the most important task to run. OS_Sched( ) loads the address of the OS_TCB of the highest priority task into OSTCBHighRdy and then executes the software-interrupt instruction by invoking the macro OS_TASK_SW( ). Note that the variable OSTCBCur already contains a pointer to the current task's OS_TCB. The code for OSCtxSw( ), which is identical to the one presented in Chapter 14, is shown in Listing 15.15. OSCtxSw( ) is discussed again because of the added complexity of the floating-point context switch.

Listing 15.15   *OSCtxSw( ).*

```
_OSCtxSw    PROC    FAR                                         (1)
;

            PUSHA                                               (2)
            PUSH    ES
            PUSH    DS
;

            MOV     AX, SEG _OSTCBCur
            MOV     DS, AX
;

            LES     BX, DWORD PTR DS:_OSTCBCur                   (3)
            MOV     ES:[BX+2], SS
            MOV     ES:[BX+0], SP
;

            CALL    FAR PTR _OSTaskSwHook                        (4)
;

            MOV     AX, WORD PTR DS:_OSTCBHighRdy+2              (5)
            MOV     DX, WORD PTR DS:_OSTCBHighRdy
            MOV     WORD PTR DS:_OSTCBCur+2, AX
            MOV     WORD PTR DS:_OSTCBCur, DX
```

Listing 15.15   *OSCtxSw( ). (Continued)*

```
;
        MOV     AL, BYTE PTR DS:_OSPrioHighRdy                    (6)
        MOV     BYTE PTR DS:_OSPrioCur, AL
;
        LES     BX, DWORD PTR DS:_OSTCBHighRdy                    (7)
        MOV     SS, ES:[BX+2]
        MOV     SP, ES:[BX]
;
        POP     DS                                               (8)
        POP     ES
        POPA
;
        IRET                                                     (9)
;
_OSCtxSw    ENDP
```

Figure 15.4 shows the stack frames, as well as the FPU storage areas of the task being suspended and the task being resumed.

Figure 15.4   *80x86 stack frames and FPU storage during a task-level context switch.*

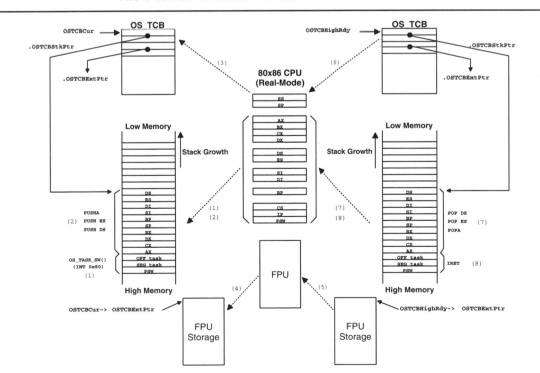

15

F15.4(1)

L15.15(1) On the 80x86 processor, the software-interrupt instruction forces the SW register to be pushed onto the current task's stack, followed by the return address (segment and then offset) of the task that executed the INT instruction [i.e., the task that invoked OS_TASK_SW()].

F15.4(2)

L15.15(2) The remaining CPU registers of the task to suspend are saved onto the current task's stack.

F15.4(3)

L15.15(3) The pointer to the new stack frame is saved into the task's OS_TCB. This pointer is composed of the stack segment (SS register) and the stack pointer (SP register). The OS_TCB in µC/OS-II is organized such that the stack pointer is placed at the beginning of the OS_TCB structure to make it easier to save and restore the stack pointer using assembly language.

F15.4(4)

F15.4(5)

L15.15(4) The task-switch hook OSTaskSwHook() is then called. Note that when OSTaskSwHook() is called, OSTCBCur points to the current task's OS_TCB, while OSTCBHighRdy points to the new task's OS_TCB. You can thus access each task's OS_TCB from OSTaskSwHook(). OSTaskSwHook() first saves the current contents of the FPU registers into the storage area allocated to the current task. This storage is pointed to by the .OSTCBExtPtr field of the current task's OS_TCB. The FPU registers are then loaded with the values stored in the new task's storage area. Again, the .OSTCBExtPtr field of the new task points to the storage area of the floating-point registers. Of course, storage and retrieval is contingent on the .OSTCBExtPtr of each task being non-NULL. However, it is quite possible for the new task to not require floating-point and thus not have any storage area for it. In this case, OSTaskSwHook() does not change the contents of the FPU.

L15.15(5) Upon returning from OSTaskSwHook(), OSTCBHighRdy is copied to OSTCBCur because the new task is now also the current task.

L15.15(6) Also, OSPrioHighRdy is copied to OSPrioCur for the same reason.

F15.4(6)

L15.15(7) At this point, OSCtxSw() loads the processor's registers with the new task's context. This action is done by retrieving the SS and SP registers from the new task's OS_TCB.

F15.4(7)

L15.15(8) The remaining CPU registers are pulled from the new task's stack.

F15.4(8)

L15.15(9) An IRET instruction is executed in order to load the new task's program counter and status word. After this instruction, the processor resumes execution of the new task.

Note that interrupts are disabled during OSCtxSw() and also during execution of OSTaskSwHook().

15.05.03 OSIntCtxSw()

OSIntCtxSw() is called by OSIntExit() to perform a context switch from an ISR. Because OSIntCtxSw() is called from an ISR, it is assumed that all the processor's integer registers are already properly saved onto the interrupted task's stack.

The code is shown in Listing 15.16 and is identical to the `OSIntCtxSw()` presented in Chapter 14. The floating-point registers are handled by `OSTaskSwHook()`. Figure 15.5 shows the context-switch process from `OSIntCtxSw()`'s point of view.

Figure 15.5   *80x86 stack frames and FPU storage during an interrupt-level context switch.*

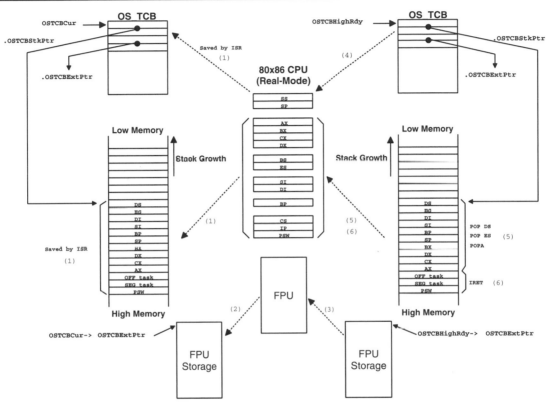

As in Chapter 14, let's assume that the processor receives an interrupt. Let's also suppose that interrupts are enabled. The processor completes the current instruction and initiates an interrupt-handling procedure.

F15.5(1)   The 80x86 automatically pushes the processor's SW register, followed by the return address of the interrupted task, onto the stack. The CPU then vectors to the proper ISR. μC/OS-II requires that your ISR begin by saving the rest of the processor's integer registers. After the registers are saved, μC/OS-II requires that you also save the contents of the stack pointer in the task's `OS_TCB`.

Your ISR then needs either to call `OSIntEnter()` or to increment the global variable `OSIntNesting` by one. At this point, we can assume that the task is suspended and that we could, if needed, switch to a different task.

The ISR can now start servicing the interrupting device and possibly make a higher priority task ready. This action occurs if the ISR sends a message to a task by calling `OSFlagPost()`, `OSMboxPost()`, `OSMboxPostOpt()`, `OSQPostFront()`, `OSQPost()`, or `OSQPostOpt()`. A higher priority task can also be resumed if the ISR calls `OSTaskResume()`, `OSTimeTick()`, or `OSTimeDlyResume()`.

15

Assume that a higher priority task is made ready to run by the ISR. µC/OS-II requires that an ISR calls OSIntExit() when it has finished servicing the interrupting device. OSIntExit() basically tells µC/OS-II that it's time to return to task-level code if all nested interrupts have completed. In other words, when OSIntNesting is decremented to 0 by OSIntExit(), OSIntExit() returns to task-level code.

When OSIntExit() executes, it notices that the interrupted task is no longer the task that needs to run because a higher priority task is now ready. In this case, the pointer OSTCBHighRdy is made to point to the new task's OS_TCB, and OSIntExit() calls OSIntCtxSw() to perform the context switch.

Listing 15.16 OSIntCtxSw().

```
_OSIntCtxSw PROC    FAR
;
            CALL    FAR PTR _OSTaskSwHook                        (1)
;
            MOV     AX, SEG _OSTCBCur
            MOV     DS, AX
;
            MOV     AX, WORD PTR DS:_OSTCBHighRdy+2              (2)
            MOV     DX, WORD PTR DS:_OSTCBHighRdy
            MOV     WORD PTR DS:_OSTCBCur+2, AX
            MOV     WORD PTR DS:_OSTCBCur, DX
;
            MOV     AL, BYTE PTR DS:_OSPrioHighRdy              (3)
            MOV     BYTE PTR DS:_OSPrioCur, AL
;
            LES     BX, DWORD PTR DS:_OSTCBHighRdy              (4)
            MOV     SS, ES:[BX+2]
            MOV     SP, ES:[BX]
;
            POP     DS                                          (5)
            POP     ES
            POPA
;
            IRET                                                (6)
;
_OSIntCtxSw ENDP
```

F15.5(2)

F15.5(3)

L15.16(1) The first thing OSIntCtxSw() does is call OSTaskSwHook(). Note that when OSTaskSwHook() is called, OSTCBCur points to the current task's OS_TCB, while OSTCBHighRdy points to the new task's OS_TCB. You can thus access each task's OS_TCB from

OSTaskSwHook(). As previously discussed, OSTaskSwHook() first saves the current contents of the FPU registers into the storage area allocated to the current task. This storage is pointed to by the .OSTCBExtPtr field of the current task's OS_TCB. The FPU registers are then loaded with the values stored in the new task's storage area. Again, the .OSTCBExtPtr field of the new task points to the storage area of the floating-point registers.

L15.16(2) Upon returning from OSTaskSwHook(), OSTCBHighRdy is copied to OSTCBCur because the new task is now also the current task.

L15.16(3) OSPrioHighRdy is also copied to OSPrioCur for the same reason.

F15.5(4)

L15.16(4) At this point, OSCtxSw() loads the processor's registers with the new task's context. This action is done by retrieving the SS and SP registers from the new task's OS_TCB.

F15.5(5)

L15.16(5) The remaining CPU registers are pulled from the stack.

F15.5(6)

L15.16(6) An IRET instruction is executed in order to load the new task's program counter and status word. After this instruction, the processor resumes execution of the new task.

Note that interrupts are disabled during OSIntCtxSw() and also during execution of OSTaskSwHook().

15.05.04 *OSTickISR()*

As mentioned in Section 15.03.05, "OS_CPU.H, Tick Rate", the tick rate of an RTOS should be set between 10 and 100Hz. On the PC, however, the ticker occurs every 54.93ms (18.20648Hz) and is obtained by a hardware timer that interrupts the CPU. Recall that I reprogrammed the tick rate to 200Hz because it was a multiple of 18.20648Hz. The ticker on the PC is assigned to vector 0x08, but µC/OS-II redefined it so that it vectors to OSTickISR() instead. Because of this change, the PC's tick handler is saved [see PC.C, PC_DOSSaveReturn()] in vector 129 (0x81). To satisfy DOS, however, the PC's handler is called every 54.93ms. OSTickISR() for this port is identical to the OSTickISR() presented in Section 14.05.04, "OSTickISR()", and thus there is no need to repeat the description here. I did, however, include the code in Listing 15.17 for your convenience.

Listing 15.17 OSTickISR().

```
_OSTickISR    PROC     FAR
;
              PUSHA
              PUSH     ES
              PUSH     DS
;
              MOV      AX, SEG(_OSIntNesting)
              MOV      DS, AX
              INC      BYTE PTR DS:_OSIntNesting
;
              CMP      BYTE PTR DS:_OSIntNesting, 1
```

15

Listing 15.17   *OSTickISR( ). (Continued)*

```
            JNE     SHORT _OSTickISR1
            MOV     AX, SEG(_OSTCBCur)
            MOV     DS, AX
            LES     BX, DWORD PTR DS:_OSTCBCur
            MOV     ES:[BX+2], SS
            MOV     ES:[BX+0], SP
;
_OSTickISR1:
            MOV     AX, SEG(_OSTickDOSCtr)
            MOV     DS, AX
            DEC     BYTE PTR DS:_OSTickDOSCtr
            CMP     BYTE PTR DS:_OSTickDOSCtr, 0
            JNE     SHORT _OSTickISR2
;
            MOV     BYTE PTR DS:_OSTickDOSCtr, 11
            INT     081H
            JMP     SHORT _OSTickISR3

_OSTickISR2:
            MOV     AL, 20H
            MOV     DX, 20H
            OUT     DX, AL
;
_OSTickISR3:
            CALL    FAR PTR _OSTimeTick
;
            CALL    FAR PTR _OSIntExit
;
            POP     DS
            POP     ES
            POPA
;
            IRET
;
_OSTickISR  ENDP
```

15.05.05 *OSFPSave( )*

OSFPSave( ) is not normally part of a µC/OS-II port. OSFPSave( ) basically takes the contents of the floating-point registers and saves them at the address passed to OSFPSave( ). OSFPSave( ) is called from C but is written in assembly language because the function must execute an FPU instruction that is not available from C. OSFPSave() is called by the C functions OSFPInit(), OSTaskCreateHook(), and OSTaskSwHook() as follows

```
OSFPSave((void *pblk);
```

where pblk is the address of a storage area large enough to hold the FPU context and must be at least 108 bytes. Listing 15.18 shows the code for OSFPSave().

Listing 15.18 *OSFPSave().*

```
_OSFPSave       PROC    FAR
;
                PUSH    BP                              (1)
                MOV     BP,SP
                PUSH    ES
                PUSH    BX
;
                LES     BX, DWORD PTR [BP+6]            (2)
;
                FSAVE   ES:[BX]                         (3)
;
                POP     BX                              (4)
                POP     ES
                POP     BP
;
                RET                                     (5)
;
_OSFPSave       ENDP
```

L15.18(1) OSFPSave() saves integer registers onto the current task's stack because they are needed by this function.

L15.18(2) The pointer passed to OSFPSave() as an argument is loaded into ES:BX.

L15.18(3) The FPU instruction FSAVE is executed. This instruction saves the whole context of the FPU (108 bytes worth) at the address found in ES:BX.

L15.18(4) The temporary registers are retrieved from the stack.

L15.18(5) OSFPSave() returns to its caller.

15.05.06 *OSFPRestore()*

OSFPRestore() is also not normally part of a μC/OS-II port. OSFPRestore() basically loads the FPU registers with the contents of a memory buffer pointed to by the address passed to OSFPRestore(). OSFPRestore() is called from C but is written in assembly language because the function must execute

15

an FPU instruction that is not available from C. OSFPRestore() is only called by OSTaskSwHook() as follows

```
OSFPRestore(void *pblk);
```

where pblk is the address of a storage area large enough to hold the FPU context and must be at least 108 bytes. Listing 15.19 shows the code for OSFPRestore().

Listing 15.19   OSFPRestore().

```
_OSFPRestore PROC    FAR
;
             PUSH    BP                                              (1)
             MOV     BP,SP
             PUSH    ES
             PUSH    BX
;
             LES     BX, DWORD PTR [BP+6]                            (2)
;
             FRSTOR ES:[BX]                                          (3)
;
             POP     BX                                              (4)
             POP     ES
             POP     BP
;
             RET                                                     (5)
;
_OSFPRestore ENDP
```

L15.19(1) OSFPRestore() saves integer registers onto the current task's stack because they are needed by this function.

L15.19(2) The pointer passed to OSFPRestore() as an argument is loaded into ES:BX.

L15.19(3) The FPU instruction FRSTOR is executed. This instruction loads the FPU with the contents of the memory location pointed to by ES:BX.

L15.19(4) The temporary registers are retrieved from the stack.

L15.19(5) OSFPRestore() returns to its caller.

15.06 Memory Usage

The only code that has changed in this chapter from the code provided in Chapter 14 is OS_CPU_A.ASM, OS_CPU_C.C, and OS_CPU.H. These files add only an additional 164bytes of code space (ROM).

You **must** include the code for `OSTaskCreateExt()` (set `OS_TASK_CREATE_EXT` to 1 in `OS_CFG.H`) and the memory-management services (set `OS_MEM_EN` to 1 in `OS_CFG.H`) because this port does not work without them.

With respect to data space, this port requires a memory buffer of 128 bytes (although we only need 108 bytes) for each task that performs floating-point operations.

Note: The spreadsheet for this port is found on the companion CD; see:
`\SOFTWARE\uCOS-II\Ix86L-FP\BC45\DOC\80x86L-FP-ROM-RAM.XLS`
You need Microsoft Excel for Office 2000 (or higher) to use this file. The spreadsheet allows you to do what-if scenarios based on the options you select. You can change the configuration values (in **red**) and see how they affect µC/OS-II's ROM and RAM usage on the 80x86. For the `???_EN` values, you **must** use either 0 or 1.

As with Chapter 14, I set up the Borland compiler to generate the fastest code. The number of bytes shown are not meant to be accurate but are simply provided to give you a relative idea of how much code space each of the µC/OS-II group of services requires.

The spreadsheet also shows you the difference in code size based on the value of `OS_ARG_CHK_EN` in your `OS_CFG.H`. You don't need to change the value of `OS_ARG_CHK_EN` to see the difference.

The Data column is not as straightforward. Notice that the stacks for both the idle task and the statistics task have been set to 1,024 bytes (1KB) each. Based on your own requirements, these numbers might be higher or lower. As a minimum, µC/OS-II requires about 3,500 bytes of RAM for µC/OS-II internal data structures if you configure the maximum number of tasks (62 application tasks). I added an entry that specifies the number of tasks that can do floating-point operations. Remember that each such task requires a buffer of 128 bytes. One buffer is always allocated because I changed the statistic task to allow floating-point operations.

If you use an 80x86 processor, you will most likely not be too restricted with memory, and thus µC/OS-II will most likely not be the largest user of memory.

15

μC/OS-II Reference Manual

This chapter provides a reference to μC/OS-II services. Each of the user-accessible kernel services is presented in alphabetical order. The following information is provided for each of the services:

- A brief description
- The function prototype
- The filename of the source code
- The #define constant needed to enable the code for the service
- A description of the arguments passed to the function
- A description of the returned value(s)
- Specific notes and warnings on using the service
- One or two examples of how to use the function

OS_ENTER_CRITICAL()
OS_EXIT_CRITICAL()

Chapter	File	Called from	Code enabled by
3	OS_CPU.H	Task or ISR	N/A

OS_ENTER_CRITICAL() and OS_EXIT_CRITICAL() are macros used to disable and enable, respectively, the processor's interrupts.

Arguments

Returned Values

Notes/Warnings

1. These macros must be used in pairs.

2. If OS_CRITICAL_METHOD is set to 3, your code is assumed to have allocated local storage for a variable of type OS_CPU_SR, which is called cpu_sr, as follows

```
#if OS_CRITICAL_METHOD == 3      /* Allocate storage for CPU status register */
    OS_CPU_SR  cpu_sr;
#endif
```

Example

```
void TaskX(void *pdata)
{
#if OS_CRITICAL_METHOD == 3
     OS_CPU_SR    cpu_sr;
#endif

    for (;;) {
       .

       .
       OS_ENTER_CRITICAL();   /* Disable interrupts    */
       .                      /* Access critical code  */
       OS_EXIT_CRITICAL();    /* Enable  interrupts    */
       .

       .
    }
}
```

OSFlagAccept()

```
OS_FLAGS OSFlagAccept(OS_FLAG_GRP *pgrp,
                      OS_FLAGS flags,
                      INT8U wait_type,
                      INT8U *err);
```

Chapter	File	Called from	Code enabled by
9	OS_FLAG.C	Task	OS_FLAG_EN && OS_FLAG_ACCEPT_EN

OSFlagAccept() allows you to check the status of a combination of bits to be either set or cleared in an event flag group. Your application can check for **any** bit to be set/cleared or **all** bits to be set/cleared. This function behaves exactly as OSFlagPend() does, except that the caller does NOT block if the desired event flags are not present.

Arguments

pgrp   is a pointer to the event flag group. This pointer is returned to your application when the event flag group is created [see OSFlagCreate()].

flags   is a bit pattern indicating which bit(s) (i.e., flags) you wish to check. The bits you want are specified by setting the corresponding bits in flags.

wait_type   specifies whether you want **all** bits to be set/cleared or **any** of the bits to be set/cleared. You can specify the following arguments:

OS_FLAG_WAIT_CLR_ALL   You check **all** bits in flags to be clear (0)

OS_FLAG_WAIT_CLR_ANY   You check **any** bit in flags to be clear (0)

OS_FLAG_WAIT_SET_ALL   You check **all** bits in flags to be set (1)

OS_FLAG_WAIT_SET_ANY   You check **any** bit in flags to be set (1)

You can add OS_FLAG_CONSUME if you want the event flag(s) to be consumed by the call. For example, to wait for **any** flag in a group and then clear the flags that are present, set wait_type to

OS_FLAG_WAIT_SET_ANY + OS_FLAG_CONSUME

err   a pointer to an error code and can be any of the following:

OS_NO_ERR   No error

OS_ERR_EVENT_TYPE   You are not pointing to an event flag group

OS_FLAG_ERR_WAIT_TYPE   You didn't specify a proper wait_type argument.

OS_FLAG_INVALID_PGRP   You passed a NULL pointer instead of the event flag handle.

OS_FLAG_ERR_NOT_RDY   The desired flags for which you are waiting are not available.

Returned Values

The state of the flags in the event flag group.

16

Notes/Warnings

1. The event flag group must be created before it is used.
2. This function does **not** block if the desired flags are not present.

Example

```c
#define  ENGINE_OIL_PRES_OK    0x01
#define  ENGINE_OIL_TEMP_OK    0x02
#define  ENGINE_START          0x04


OS_FLAG_GRP *EngineStatus;


void Task (void *pdata)
{
    INT8U    err;
    OS_FLAGS  value;


    pdata = pdata;
    for (;;) {
        value = OSFlagAccept(EngineStatus,
                        ENGINE_OIL_PRES_OK + ENGINE_OIL_TEMP_OK,
                        OS_FLAG_WAIT_SET_ALL,
                        &err);
        switch (err) {
            case OS_NO_ERR:
                /* Desired flags are available */
                break;

            case OS_FLAG_ERR_NOT_RDY:
                /* The desired flags are NOT available */
                break;
        }
        .
        .
    }
}
```

OSFlagCreate()

`OS_FLAG_GRP *OSFlagCreate(OS_FLAGS flags, INT8U *err);`

Chapter	File	Called from	Code enabled by
9	OS_FLAG.C	Task or startup code	OS_FLAG_EN

OSFlagCreate() is used to create and initialize an event flag group.

Arguments

flags   contains the initial value to store in the event flag group.

err   is a pointer to a variable that is used to hold an error code. The error code can be one of the following:

OS_NO_ERR   if the call is successful and the event flag group has been created.

OS_ERR_CREATE_ISR   if you attempt to create an event flag group from an ISR.

OS_FLAG_GRP_DEPLETED   if no more event flag groups are available. You need to increase the value of OS_MAX_FLAGS in OS_CFG.H.

Returned Values

A pointer to the event flag group if a free event flag group is available. If no event flag group is available, OSFlagCreate() returns a NULL pointer.

Notes/Warnings

1.   Event flag groups must be created by this function before they can be used by the other services.

Example

```
OS_FLAG_GRP *EngineStatus;

void main (void)
{
    INT8U  err;


    .
    OSInit();         /* Initialize µC/OS-II */
    .

    .
                      /* Create a flag group containing the engine's status */
    EngineStatus = OSFlagCreate(0x00, &err);
    .

    .
    OSStart();        /* Start Multitasking  */
}
```

16

OSFlagDel()

`OS_FLAG_GRP *OSFlagDel(OS_FLAG_GRP *pgrp, INT8U opt, INT8U *err);`

Chapter	File	Called from	Code enabled by
9	OS_FLAG.C	Task	OS_FLAG_EN and OS_FLAG_DEL_EN

`OSFlagDel()` is used to delete an event flag group. This function is dangerous to use because multiple tasks could be relying on the presence of the event flag group. You should always use this function with great care. Generally speaking, before you delete an event flag group, you must first delete all the tasks that access the event flag group.

Arguments

pgrp   is a pointer to the event flag group. This pointer is returned to your application when the event flag group is created [see `OSFlagCreate()`].

opt   specifies whether you want to delete the event flag group only if there are no pending tasks (`OS_DEL_NO_PEND`) or whether you always want to delete the event flag group regardless of whether tasks are pending or not (`OS_DEL_ALWAYS`). In this case, all pending task are readied.

err   is a pointer to a variable that is used to hold an error code. The error code can be one of the following:

OS_NO_ERR	if the call is successful and the event flag group has been deleted.
OS_ERR_DEL_ISR	if you attempt to delete an event flag group from an ISR.
OS_FLAG_INVALID_PGRP	if you pass a NULL pointer in pgrp.
OS_ERR_EVENT_TYPE	if pgrp is not pointing to an event flag group.
OS_ERR_INVALID_OPT	if you do not specify one of the two options mentioned in the opt argument.
OS_ERR_TASK_WAITING	if one or more task are waiting on the event flag group and you specify OS_DEL_NO_PEND.

Returned Values

A NULL pointer if the event flag group is deleted or pgrp if the event flag group is not deleted. In the latter case, you need to examine the error code to determine the reason for the error.

Notes/Warnings

1. You should use this call with care because other tasks might expect the presence of the event flag group.

2. This call can potentially disable interrupts for a long time. The interrupt-disable time is directly proportional to the number of tasks waiting on the event flag group.

Example

```c
OS_FLAG_GRP *EngineStatusFlags;


void Task (void *pdata)
{
    INT8U        err;
    OS_FLAG_GRP *pgrp;


    pdata = pdata;
    while (1) {
        .
        .
        pgrp = OSFlagDel(EngineStatusFlags, OS_DEL_ALWAYS, &err);
        if (pgrp == (OS_FLAG_GRP *)0) {
            /* The event flag group was deleted */
        }
        .
        .
    }
}
```

16

OSFlagPend()

```
OS_FLAGS OSFlagPend(OS_FLAG_GRP *pgrp,
                    OS_FLAGS flags,
                    INT8U wait_type,
                    INT16U timeout,
                    INT8U *err);
```

Chapter	*File*	*Called from*	*Code enabled by*
9	OS_FLAG.C	Task only	OS_FLAG_EN

OSFlagPend() is used to have a task wait for a combination of conditions (i.e., events or bits) to be set (or cleared) in an event flag group. You application can wait for **any** condition to be set or cleared or for **all** conditions to be set or cleared. If the events that the calling task desires are not available, then the calling task is blocked until the desired conditions are satisfied or the specified timeout expires.

Arguments

pgrp   is a pointer to the event flag group. This pointer is returned to your application when the event flag group is created [see OSFlagCreate()].

flags   is a bit pattern indicating which bit(s) (i.e., flags) you wish to check. The bits you want are specified by setting the corresponding bits in flags.

wait_type   specifies whether you want **all** bits to be set/cleared or **any** of the bits to be set/cleared. You can specify the following arguments:

OS_FLAG_WAIT_CLR_ALL	You check **all** bits in flags to be clear (0)
OS_FLAG_WAIT_CLR_ANY	You check **any** bit in flags to be clear (0)
OS_FLAG_WAIT_SET_ALL	You check **all** bits in flags to be set (1)
OS_FLAG_WAIT_SET_ANY	You check **any** bit in flags to be set (1)

You can also specify whether the flags are consumed by adding OS_FLAG_CONSUME to the wait_type. For example, to wait for **any** flag in a group and then **clear** the flags that satisfy the condition, set wait_type to

OS_FLAG_WAIT_SET_ANY + OS_FLAG_CONSUME

err   is a pointer to an error code and can be:

OS_NO_ERR	No error.
OS_ERR_PEND_ISR	You try to call OSFlagPend from an ISR, which is not allowed.
OS_FLAG_INVALID_PGRP	You pass a NULL pointer instead of the event flag handle.
OS_ERR_EVENT_TYPE	You are not pointing to an event flag group.
OS_TIMEOUT	The flags are not available within the specified amount of time.
OS_FLAG_ERR_WAIT_TYPE	You don't specify a proper wait_type argument.

Returned Value

The value of the flags in the event flag group after they are consumed (if OS_FLAG_CONSUME is specified) or the state of the flags just before OSFlagPend() returns. OSFlagPend() returns 0 if a timeout occurs.

Notes/Warnings

1. The event flag group must be created before it's used.

Example

```
#define  ENGINE_OIL_PRES_OK    0x01
#define  ENGINE_OIL_TEMP_OK    0x02
#define  ENGINE_START          0x04


OS_FLAG_GRP *EngineStatus;


void Task (void *pdata)
{
    INT8U     err;
    OS_FLAGS  value;


    pdata = pdata;
    for (;;) {
        value = OSFlagPend(EngineStatus,
                           ENGINE_OIL_PRES_OK  + ENGINE_OIL_TEMP_OK,
                           OS_FLAG_WAIT_SET_ALL + OS_FLAG_CONSUME,
                           10,
                           &err);
        switch (err) {
            case OS_NO_ERR:
                /* Desired flags are available */
                break;

            case OS_TIMEOUT:
                /* The desired flags were NOT available before 10 ticks occurred */
                break;
        }
        .
        .
    }
}
```

16

OSFlagPost()

```
OS_FLAGS OSFlagPost(OS_FLAG_GRP *pgrp,
                    OS_FLAGS flags,
                    INT8U opt,
                    INT8U *err);
```

Chapter	File	Called from	Code enabled by
9	OS_FLAG.C	Task or ISR	OS_FLAG_EN

You set or clear event flag bits by calling OSFlagPost(). The bits set or cleared are specified in a *bit mask*. OSFlagPost() readies each task that has its desired bits satisfied by this call. You can set or clear bits that are already set or cleared.

Arguments

pgrp   is a pointer to the event flag group. This pointer is returned to your application when the event flag group is created [see OSFlagCreate()].

flags   specifies which bits you want set or cleared. If opt is OS_FLAG_SET, each bit that is set in flags sets the corresponding bit in the event flag group. For example to set bits 0, 4, and 5, you set flags to 0x31 (note, bit 0 is the least significant bit). If opt is OS_FLAG_CLR, each bit that is set in flags will **clears** the corresponding bit in the event flag group. For example to clear bits 0, 4, and 5, you specify flags as 0x31 (note, bit 0 is the least significant bit).

opt   indicates whether the flags are set (OS_FLAG_SET) or cleared (OS_FLAG_CLR).

err   is a pointer to an error code and can be:

OS_NO_ERR   The call is successful.

OS_FLAG_INVALID_PGRP   You pass a NULL pointer.

OS_ERR_EVENT_TYPE   You are not pointing to an event flag group.

OS_FLAG_INVALID_OPT   You specify an invalid option.

Returned Value

The new value of the event flags.

Notes/Warnings

1. Event flag groups must be created before they are used.

2. The execution time of this function depends on the number of tasks waiting on the event flag group. However, the execution time is deterministic.

3. The amount of time interrupts are **disabled** also depends on the number of tasks waiting on the event flag group.

Example

```
#define   ENGINE_OIL_PRES_OK    0x01
#define   ENGINE_OIL_TEMP_OK    0x02
#define   ENGINE_START          0x04


OS_FLAG_GRP  *EngineStatusFlags;


void  TaskX (void *pdata)
{
    INT8U  err;


    pdata = pdata;
    for (;;) {
        .
        .
        err = OSFlagPost(EngineStatusFlags, ENGINE_START, OS_FLAG_SET, &err);
        .
        .
    }
}
```

16

OSFlagQuery()

`OS_FLAGS OSFlagQuery(OS_FLAG_GRP *pgrp, INT8U *err);`

Chapter	File	Called from	Code enabled by
9	OS_FLAG.C	Task or ISR	OS_FLAG_EN && OS_FLAG_QUERY_EN

`OSFlagQuery()` is used to obtain the current value of the event flags in a group. At this time, this function does **not** return the list of tasks waiting for the event flag group.

Arguments

pgrp   is a pointer to the event flag group. This pointer is returned to your application when the event flag group is created [see `OSFlagCreate()`].

err   is a pointer to an error code and can be:

OS_NO_ERR   The call is successful.

OS_FLAG_INVALID_PGRP   You pass a NULL pointer.

OS_ERR_EVENT_TYPE   You are not pointing to an event flag groups.

Returned Value

The state of the flags in the event flag group.

Notes/Warnings

1. The event flag group to query must be created.

2. You can call this function from an ISR.

Example

```
OS_FLAG_GRP *EngineStatusFlags;

void Task (void *pdata)
{
    OS_FLAGS flags;
    INT8U    err;

    pdata = pdata;
    for (;;) {
        .
        .
        flags = OSFlagQuery(EngineStatusFlags, &err);
        .
        .
    }
}
```

OSInit()

void OSInit(void);

Chapter	File	Called from	Code enabled by
3	OS_CORE.C	Startup code only	N/A

OSInit() initializes µC/OS-II and must be called prior to calling OSStart(), which actually starts multitasking.

Arguments

Returned Values

Notes/Warnings

1.   OSInit() must be called before OSStart().

Example

```
void main (void)
{
    .

    .

    OSInit();      /* Initialize uC/OS-II */
    .

    .

    OSStart();      /* Start Multitasking  */
}
```

16

OSIntEnter()

`void OSIntEnter(void);`

Chapter	File	Called from	Code enabled by
3	OS_CORE.C	ISR only	N/A

`OSIntEnter()` notifies μC/OS-II that an ISR is being processed, which allows μC/OS-II to keep track of interrupt nesting. `OSIntEnter()` is used in conjunction with `OSIntExit()`.

Arguments

Returned Values

Notes/Warnings

1. This function must not be called by task-level code.

2. You can increment the interrupt-nesting counter (`OSIntNesting`) directly in your ISR to avoid the overhead of the function call/return. It's safe to increment `OSIntNesting` in your ISR because interrupts are assumed to be disabled when `OSIntNesting` needs to be incremented.

3. You are allowed to nest interrupts up to 255 levels deep.

Example 1

(Intel 80x86, real mode, large model)

Use `OSIntEnter()` for backward compatibility with μC/OS.

```
    ISRx PROC    FAR
         PUSHA                           ; Save interrupted task's context
         PUSH    ES
         PUSH    DS
;
         CALL    FAR PTR _OSIntEnter      ; Notify μC/OS-II of start of ISR
         .
         .
         POP     DS                       ; Restore processor registers
         POP     ES
         POPA
         IRET                            ; Return from interrupt
    ISRx ENDP
```

Example 2

(Intel 80x86, real mode, large model)

```
     ISRx    PROC    FAR
             PUSHA                                  ; Save interrupted task's context
             PUSH    ES
             PUSH    DS
     ;
             MOV     AX, SEG(_OSIntNesting)  ; Reload DS
             MOV     DS, AX
     ;
             INC     BYTE PTR _OSIntNesting  ; Notify uC/OS-II of start of ISR
               .
               .
               .
             POP     DS                             ; Restore processor registers
             POP     ES
             POPA
             IRET                                   ; Return from interrupt
     ISRx    ENDP
```

16

OSIntExit()

void OSIntExit(void);

Chapter	File	Called from	Code enabled by
3	OS_CORE.C	ISR only	N/A

OSIntExit() notifies µC/OS-II that an ISR is complete, which allows µC/OS-II to keep track of interrupt nesting. OSIntExit() is used in conjunction with OSIntEnter(). When the last nested interrupt completes, OSIntExit() determines if a higher priority task is ready to run, in which case, the interrupt returns to the higher priority task instead of the interrupted task.

Arguments

Returned Value

Notes/Warnings

1. This function must not be called by task-level code. Also, if you decided to increment OSIntNesting, you still need to call OSIntExit().

Example

(Intel 80x86, real mode, large model)

```
    ISRx    PROC    FAR
            PUSHA                       ; Save processor registers
            PUSH    ES
            PUSH    DS
             .
             .
            CALL    FAR PTR _OSIntExit ; Notify µC/OS-II of end of ISR
            POP     DS                  ; Restore processor registers
            POP     ES
            POPA
            IRET                        ; Return to interrupted task
    ISRx    ENDP
```

OSMboxAccept()

```
void *OSMboxAccept(OS_EVENT *pevent);
```

Chapter	File	Called from	Code enabled by
10	OS_MBOX.C	Task or ISR	OS_MBOX_EN && OS_MBOX_ACCEPT_EN

OSMboxAccept() allows you to see if a message is available from the desired mailbox. Unlike OSMboxPend(), OSMboxAccept() does not suspend the calling task if a message is not available. In other words, OSMboxAccept() is non-blocking. If a message is available, the message is returned to your application, and the content of the mailbox is cleared. This call is typically used by ISRs because an ISR is not allowed to wait for a message at a mailbox.

Arguments

pevent   is a pointer to the mailbox from which the message is received. This pointer is returned to your application when the mailbox is created [see OSMboxCreate()].

Returned Value

A pointer to the message if one is available; NULL if the mailbox does not contain a message.

Notes/Warnings

1.   Mailboxes must be created before they are used.

Example

```
OS_EVENT *CommMbox;


void Task (void *pdata)
{
    void *msg;

    pdata = pdata;
    for (;;) {
        msg = OSMboxAccept(CommMbox); /* Check mailbox for a message */
        if (msg != (void *)0) {
                                      /* Message received, process   */
            .

            .
        } else {
                                      /* Message not received, do .. */
            .
                                      /* .. something else */
            .
        }
        .

        .
    }
}
```

16

OSMboxCreate()

`OS_EVENT *OSMboxCreate(void *msg);`

Chapter	*File*	*Called from*	*Code enabled by*
10	OS_MBOX.C	Task or startup code	OS_MBOX_EN

OSMboxCreate() creates and initializes a mailbox. A mailbox allows tasks or ISRs to send a pointer-sized variable (message) to one or more tasks.

Arguments

msg   is used to initialize the contents of the mailbox. The mailbox is empty when msg is a NULL pointer. The mailbox initially contains a message when msg is non-NULL.

Returned Value

A pointer to the event control block allocated to the mailbox. If no event control block is available, OSMboxCreate() returns a NULL pointer.

Notes/Warnings

1. Mailboxes must be created before they are used.

Example

```
OS_EVENT *CommMbox;


void main (void)
{
    .
    .
    OSInit();                              /* Initialize uC/OS-II  */
    .
    .
    CommMbox = OSMboxCreate((void *)0);   /* Create COMM mailbox  */
    OSStart();                             /* Start Multitasking   */
}
```

OSMboxDel()

```
OS_EVENT *OSMboxDel(OS_EVENT *pevent, INT8U opt, INT8U *err);
```

Chapter	File	Called from	Code enabled by
10	OS_MBOX.C	Task	OS_MBOX_EN and OS_MBOX_DEL_EN

OSMboxDel() is used to delete a message mailbox. This function is dangerous to use because multiple tasks could attempt to access a deleted mailbox. You should always use this function with great care. Generally speaking, before you delete a mailbox, you must first delete all the tasks that can access the mailbox.

Arguments

pevent   is a pointer to the mailbox. This pointer is returned to your application when the mailbox is created [see OSMboxCreate()].

opt   specifies whether you want to delete the mailbox only if there are no pending tasks (OS_DEL_NO_PEND) or whether you always want to delete the mailbox regardless of whether tasks are pending or not (OS_DEL_ALWAYS). In this case, all pending task are readied.

err   is a pointer to a variable that is used to hold an error code. The error code can be one of the following:

OS_NO_ERR	if the call is successful and the mailbox has been deleted.
OS_ERR_DEL_ISR	if you attempt to delete the mailbox from an ISR.
OS_ERR_INVALID_OPT	if you don't specify one of the two options mentioned in the opt argument.
OS_ERR_TASK_WAITING	One or more tasks is waiting on the mailbox.
OS_ERR_EVENT_TYPE	if pevent is not pointing to a mailbox.
OS_ERR_PEVENT_NULL	if no more OS_EVENT structures are available.

Returned Value

A NULL pointer if the mailbox is deleted or pevent if the mailbox is not deleted. In the latter case, you need to examine the error code to determine the reason.

Notes/Warnings

1. You should use this call with care because other tasks might expect the presence of the mailbox.
2. Interrupts are disabled when pended tasks are readied, which means that interrupt latency depends on the number of tasks that are waiting on the mailbox.
3. OSMboxAccept() callers do not know that the mailbox has been deleted.

16

Example

```
OS_EVENT *DispMbox;

void Task (void *pdata)
{
    INT8U  err;

    pdata = pdata;
    while (1) {
        .
        .
        DispMbox = OSMboxDel(DispMbox, OS_DEL_ALWAYS, &err);
        if (DispMbox == (OS_EVENT *)0) {
            /* Mailbox has been deleted */
        }
        .
        .
    }
}
```

OSMboxPend()

```
void *OSMboxPend(OS_EVENT *pevent, INT16U timeout, INT8U *err);
```

Chapter	File	Called from	Code enabled by
10	OS_MBOX.C	Task only	OS_MBOX_EN

OSMboxPend() is used when a task expects to receive a message. The message is sent to the task either by an ISR or by another task. The message received is a pointer-sized variable, and its use is application specific. If a message is present in the mailbox when OSMboxPend() is called, the message is retrieved, the mailbox is emptied, and the retrieved message is returned to the caller. If no message is present in the mailbox, OSMboxPend() suspends the current task until either a message is received or a user-specified timeout expires. If a message is sent to the mailbox and multiple tasks are waiting for the message, µC/OS-II resumes the highest priority task waiting to run. A pended task that has been suspended with OSTaskSuspend() can receive a message. However, the task remains suspended until it is resumed by calling OSTaskResume().

Arguments

pevent   is a pointer to the mailbox from which the message is received. This pointer is returned to your application when the mailbox is created [see OSMboxCreate()].

timeout   allows the task to resume execution if a message is not received from the mailbox within the specified number of clock ticks. A timeout value of 0 indicates that the task wants to wait forever for the message. The maximum timeout is 65,535 clock ticks. The timeout value is not synchronized with the clock tick. The timeout count begins decrementing on the next clock tick, which could potentially occur immediately.

err   is a pointer to a variable that holds an error code. OSMboxPend() sets *err to one of the following:

OS_NO_ERR	if a message is received.
OS_TIMEOUT	if a message is not received within the specified timeout period.
OS_ERR_EVENT_TYPE	if pevent is not pointing to a mailbox.
OS_ERR_PEND_ISR	if you call this function from an ISR and µC/OS-II suspends it. In general, you should not call OSMboxPend() from an ISR, but µC/OS-II checks for this situation anyway.
OS_ERR_PEVENT_NULL	if pevent is a NULL pointer.

Returned Value

OSMboxPend() returns the message sent by either a task or an ISR, and *err is set to OS_NO_ERR. If a message is not received within the specified timeout period, the returned message is a NULL pointer, and *err is set to OS_TIMEOUT.

16

Notes/Warnings

1. Mailboxes must be created before they are used.
2. You should not call OSMboxPend() from an ISR.

Example

```
OS_EVENT *CommMbox;


void CommTask(void *pdata)
{
    INT8U  err;
    void   *msg;


    pdata = pdata;
    for (;;) {
        .

        .
        msg = OSMboxPend(CommMbox, 10, &err);
        if (err == OS_NO_ERR) {
            .
            .  /* Code for received message                 */
            .
        } else {
            .
            .  /* Code for message not received within timeout */
            .
        }
        .

        .
    }
}
```

OSMboxPost()

`INT8U OSMboxPost(OS_EVENT *pevent, void *msg);`

Chapter	File	Called from	Code enabled by
10	OS_MBOX.C	Task or ISR	OS_MBOX_EN && OS_MBOX_POST_EN

OSMboxPost() sends a message to a task through a mailbox. A message is a pointer-sized variable and, its use is application specific. If a message is already in the mailbox, an error code is returned indicating that the mailbox is full. OSMboxPost() then immediately returns to its caller, and the message is not placed in the mailbox. If any task is waiting for a message at the mailbox, the highest priority task waiting receives the message. If the task waiting for the message has a higher priority than the task sending the message, the higher priority task is resumed, and the task sending the message is suspended. In other words, a context switch occurs.

Arguments

pevent   is a pointer to the mailbox into which the message is deposited. This pointer is returned to your application when the mailbox is created [see OSMboxCreate()].

msg   is the actual message sent to the task. msg is a pointer-sized variable and is application specific. You must never post a NULL pointer because this pointer indicates that the mailbox is empty.

Returned Value

OSMboxPost() returns one of these error codes:

OS_NO_ERR	if the message is deposited in the mailbox.
OS_MBOX_FULL	if the mailbox already contains a message.
OS_ERR_EVENT_TYPE	if pevent is not pointing to a mailbox.
OS_ERR_PEVENT_NULL	if pevent is a pointer to NULL.
OS_ERR_POST_NULL_PTR	if you are attempting to post a NULL pointer. By convention a NULL pointer is not supposed to point to anything.

Notes/Warnings

1. Mailboxes must be created before they are used.
2. You must never post a NULL pointer because this pointer indicates that the mailbox is empty.

16

Example

```
OS_EVENT *CommMbox;
INT8U    CommRxBuf[100];


void CommTaskRx (void *pdata)
{
    INT8U  err;

    pdata = pdata;
    for (;;) {
        .
        .
        err = OSMboxPost(CommMbox, (void *)&CommRxBuf[0]);
        .
        .
    }
}
```

OSMboxPostOpt()

```
INT8U OSMboxPostOpt(OS_EVENT *pevent, void *msg, INT8U opt);
```

Chapter	File	Called from	Code enabled by
10	OS_MBOX.C	Task or ISR	OS_MBOX_EN and OS_MBOX_POST_OPT_EN

OSMboxPostOpt() works just like OSMboxPost() except that it allows you to post a message to **multiple** tasks. In other words, OSMboxPostOpt() allows the message posted to be broadcast to **all** tasks waiting on the mailbox. OSMboxPostOpt() can actually replace OSMboxPost() because it can emulate OSMboxPost().

OSMboxPostOpt() is used to send a message to a task through a mailbox. A message is a pointer-sized variable, and its use is application specific. If a message is already in the mailbox, an error code is returned indicating that the mailbox is full. OSMboxPostOpt() then immediately returns to its caller, and the message is not placed in the mailbox. If any task is waiting for a message at the mailbox, OSMboxPostOpt() allows you either to post the message to the highest priority task waiting at the mailbox (opt set to OS_POST_OPT_NONE) or to all tasks waiting at the mailbox (opt is set to OS_POST_OPT_BROADCAST). In either case, scheduling occurs and, if any of the tasks that receives the message have a higher priority than the task that is posting the message, then the higher priority task is resumed, and the sending task is suspended. In other words, a context switch occurs.

Arguments

pevent   is a pointer to the mailbox. This pointer is returned to your application when the mailbox is created [see OSMboxCreate()].

msg   is the actual message sent to the task(s). msg is a pointer-sized variable and is application specific. You must never post a NULL pointer because this pointer indicates that the mailbox is empty.

opt   specifies whether you want to send the message to the highest priority task waiting at the mailbox (when opt is set to OS_POST_OPT_NONE) or to **all** tasks waiting at the mailbox (when opt is set to OS_POST_OPT_BROADCAST).

Returned Value

err   is a pointer to a variable that is used to hold an error code. The error code can be one of the following:

OS_NO_ERR	if the call is successful and the message has been sent.
OS_MBOX_FULL	if the mailbox already contains a message. You can only send **one** message at a time to a mailbox, and thus the message **must** be consumed before you are allowed to send another one.
OS_ERR_EVENT_TYPE	if pevent is not pointing to a mailbox.
OS_ERR_PEVENT_NULL	if pevent is a NULL pointer.
OS_ERR_POST_NULL_PTR	if you are attempting to post a NULL pointer. By convention, a NULL pointer is not supposed to point to anything.

16

Notes/Warnings

1. Mailboxes must be created before they are used.

2. You must **never** post a NULL pointer to a mailbox because this pointer indicates that the mailbox is empty.

3. If you need to use this function and want to reduce code space, you can disable code generation of OSMboxPost() because OSMboxPostOpt() can emulate OSMboxPost().

4. The execution time of OSMboxPostOpt() depends on the number of tasks waiting on the mailbox if you set opt to OS_POST_OPT_BROADCAST.

Example

```c
OS_EVENT *CommMbox;
INT8U    CommRxBuf[100];


void CommRxTask (void *pdata)
{
    INT8U   err;


    pdata = pdata;
    for (;;) {

        .
        .
        err = OSMboxPostOpt(CommMbox, (void *)&CommRxBuf[0], OS_POST_OPT_BROADCAST);
        .
        .

    }
}
```

OSMboxQuery()

INT8U OSMboxQuery(OS_EVENT *pevent, OS_MBOX_DATA *pdata);

Chapter	File	Called from	Code enabled by
10	OS_MBOX.C	Task or ISR	OS_MBOX_EN && OS_MBOX_QUERY_EN

OSMboxQuery() obtains information about a message mailbox. Your application must allocate an OS_MBOX_DATA data structure, which is used to receive data from the event control block of the message mailbox. OSMboxQuery() allows you to determine whether any tasks are waiting for a message at the mailbox and how many tasks are waiting (by counting the number of 1s in the .OSEventTbl[] field). You can also examine the current contents of the mailbox. Note that the size of .OSEventTbl[] is established by the #define constant OS_EVENT_TBL_SIZE (see uCOS_II.H).

Arguments

pevent   is a pointer to the mailbox. This pointer is returned to your application when the mailbox is created [see OSMboxCreate()].

pdata   is a pointer to a data structure of type OS_MBOX_DATA, which contains the following fields:

```
void  *OSMsg;                    /* Copy of the message stored in the mailbox */
INT8U  OSEventTbl[OS_EVENT_TBL_SIZE];    /* Copy of the mailbox wait list  */
INT8U  OSEventGrp;
```

Returned Value

OSMboxQuery() returns one of these error codes:

        OS_NO_ERR   if the call is successful.

        OS_ERR_PEVENT_NULL   if pevent is a NULL pointer.

        OS_ERR_EVENT_TYPE   if you don't pass a pointer to a message mailbox.

Notes/Warnings

1.   Message mailboxes must be created before they are used.

16

Example

```
OS_EVENT *CommMbox;


void Task (void *pdata)
{
     OS_MBOXDATA mbox_data;
     INT8U       err;


     pdata = pdata;
     for (;;) {
        .

        .
        err = OSMboxQuery(CommMbox, &mbox_data);
        if (err == OS_NO_ERR) {
           .   /* Mailbox contains a message if mbox_data.OSMsg is not NULL*/
        }
        .

        .
     }
}
```

OSMemCreate()

`OS_MEM *OSMemCreate(void *addr, INT32U nblks, INT32U blksize, INT8U *err);`

Chapter	File	Called from	Code enabled by
12	OS_MEM.C	Task or startup code	OS_MEM_EN

`OSMemCreate()` creates and initializes a memory partition. A memory partition contains a user-specified number of fixed-size memory blocks. Your application can obtain one of these memory blocks and, when done, release the block back to the partition.

Arguments

addr
: is the address of the start of a memory area that is used to create fixed-size memory blocks. Memory partitions can be created either using static arrays or `malloc()` during startup.

nblks
: contains the number of memory blocks available from the specified partition. You must specify at least two memory blocks per partition.

blksize
: specifies the size (in bytes) of each memory block within a partition. A memory block must be large enough to hold at least a pointer.

err
: is a pointer to a variable that holds an error code. `OSMemCreate()` sets *err to:

OS_NO_ERR	if the memory partition is created successfully
OS_MEM_INVALID_ADDR	if you are specifying an invalid address (i.e., addr is a NULL pointer)
OS_MEM_INVALID_PART	if a free memory partition is not available
OS_MEM_INVALID_BLKS	if you don't specify at least two memory blocks per partition
OS_MEM_INVALID_SIZE	if you don't specify a block size that can contain at least a pointer variable

Returned Value

`OSMemCreate()` returns a pointer to the created memory-partition control block if one is available. If no memory-partition control block is available, `OSMemCreate()` returns a NULL pointer.

Notes/Warnings

1. Memory partitions must be created before they are used.

16

Example

```
OS_MEM *CommMem;
INT8U   CommBuf[16][128];



void main (void)
{
    INT8U err;


    OSInit();                           /* Initialize µC/OS-II      */
    .
    .
    CommMem = OSMemCreate(&CommBuf[0][0], 16, 128, &err);
    .
    .
    OSStart();                          /* Start Multitasking       */
}
```

OSMemGet()

```
void *OSMemGet(OS_MEM *pmem, INT8U *err);
```

Chapter	File	Called from	Code enabled by
12	OS_MEM.C	Task or ISR	OS_MEM_EN

OSMemGet obtains a memory block from a memory partition. It is assumed that your application knows the size of each memory block obtained. Also, your application must return the memory block [using OSMemPut()] when it no longer needs it. You can call OSMemGet() more than once until all memory blocks are allocated.

Arguments

pmem   is a pointer to the memory-partition control block that is returned to your application from the OSMemCreate() call.

err   is a pointer to a variable that holds an error code. OSMemGet() sets *err to one of the following:

     OS_NO_ERR   if a memory block is available and returned to your application.

     OS_MEM_NO_FREE_BLKS   if the memory partition doesn't contain any more memory blocks to allocate.

     OS_MEM_INVALID_PMEM   if pmem is a NULL pointer.

Returned Value

OSMemGet() returns a pointer to the allocated memory block if one is available. If no memory block is available from the memory partition, OSMemGet() returns a NULL pointer.

Notes/Warnings

1. Memory partitions must be created before they are used.

16

Example

```
OS_MEM *CommMem;

void Task (void *pdata)
{
    INT8U *msg;

    pdata = pdata;
    for (;;) {
      msg = OSMemGet(CommMem, &err);
      if (msg != (INT8U *)0) {
        .                            /* Memory block allocated, use it. */
        .
      }
      .
      .
    }
}
```

OSMemPut()

`INT8U OSMemPut(OS_MEM *pmem, void *pblk);`

Chapter	File	Called from	Code enabled by
12	OS_MEM.C	Task or ISR	OS_MEM_EN

OSMemPut() returns a memory block to a memory partition. It is assumed that you return the memory block to the appropriate memory partition.

Arguments

pmem   is a pointer to the memory-partition control block that is returned to your application from the OSMemCreate() call.

pblk   is a pointer to the memory block to be returned to the memory partition.

Returned Value

OSMemPut()   returns one of the following error codes:

OS_NO_ERR   if a memory block is available and returned to your application.

OS_MEM_FULL   if the memory partition can not accept more memory blocks. This code is surely an indication that something is wrong because you are returning more memory blocks than you obtained using OSMemGet().

OS_MEM_INVALID_PMEM   if pmem is a NULL pointer.

OS_MEM_INVALID_PBLK   if pblk is a NULL pointer.

Notes/Warnings

1. Memory partitions must be created before they are used.

2. You must return a memory block to the proper memory partition.

16

Example

```
OS_MEM *CommMem;
INT8U  *CommMsg;



void Task (void *pdata)
{
    INT8U err;


    pdata = pdata;
    for (;;) {
        err = OSMemPut(CommMem, (void *)CommMsg);
        if (err == OS_NO_ERR) {
            .                          /* Memory block released        */
            .
        }
        .
        .
    }
}
```

OSMemQuery()

`INT8U OSMemQuery(OS_MEM *pmem, OS_MEM_DATA *pdata);`

Chapter	File	Called from	Code enabled by
12	OS_MEM.C	Task or ISR	OS_MEM_EN && OS_MEM_QUERY_EN

OSMemQuery() obtains information about a memory partition. Basically, this function returns the same information found in the OS_MEM data structure but in a new data structure called OS_MEM_DATA. OS_MEM_DATA also contains an additional field that indicates the number of memory blocks in use.

Arguments

pmem   is a pointer to the memory-partition control block that is returned to your application from the OSMemCreate() call.

pdata   is a pointer to a data structure of type OS_MEM_DATA, which contains the following fields

```
void   *OSAddr;     /* Points to beginning address of the memory partition  */
void   *OSFreeList; /* Points to beginning of the free list of memory blocks */
INT32U OSBlkSize;   /* Size (in bytes) of each memory block                  */
INT32U OSNBlks;     /* Total number of blocks in the partition               */
INT32U OSNFree;     /* Number of memory blocks free                          */
INT32U OSNUsed;     /* Number of memory blocks used                          */
```

Returned Value

OSMemQuery() returns one of the following error codes:

OS_NO_ERR   if a memory block is available and returned to your application.

OS_MEM_INVALID_PMEM   if pmem is a NULL pointer.

OS_MEM_INVALID_PDATA   if pdata is a NULL pointer.

Notes/Warnings

1. Memory partitions must be created before they are used.

16

Example

```
OS_MEM       *CommMem;


void Task (void *pdata)
{
    INT8U        err;
    OS_MEM_DATA  mem_data;


    pdata = pdata;
    for (;;) {
        .
        .
        err = OSMemQuery(CommMem, &mem_data);
        .
        .
    }
}
```

OSMutexAccept()

`INT8U OSMutexAccept(OS_EVENT *pevent, INT8U *err);`

Chapter	File	Called from	Code enabled by
8	OS_MUTEX.C	Task	OS_MUTEX_EN

OSMutexAccept() allows you to check to see if a resource is available. Unlike OSMutexPend(), OSMutexAccept() does not suspend the calling task if the resource is not available. In other words, OSMutexAccept() is non-blocking.

Arguments

pevent   is a pointer to the mutex that guards the resource. This pointer is returned to your application when the mutex is created [see OSMutexCreate()].

err   is a pointer to a variable used to hold an error code. OSMutexAccept() sets *err to one of the following:

OS_NO_ERR   if the call is successful.

OS_ERR_EVENT_TYPE   if pevent is not pointing to a mutex.

OS_ERR_PEVENT_NULL   if pevent is a NULL pointer.

OS_ERR_PEND_ISR   if you call OSMutexAccept() from an ISR.

Returned Value

If the mutex is available, OSMutexAccept() returns 1. If the mutex is owned by another task, OSMutexAccept() returns 0.

Notes/Warnings

1. Mutexes must be created before they are used.
2. This function **must not** be called by an ISR.
3. If you acquire the mutex through OSMutexAccept(), you **must** call OSMutexPost() to release the mutex when you are done with the resource.

16

Example

```
OS_EVENT *DispMutex;


void Task (void *pdata)
{
    INT8U  err;
    INT8U  value;


    pdata = pdata;
    for (;;) {
        value = OSMutexAccept(DispMutex, &err);
        if (value == 1) {
            .                            /* Resource available, process */
            .
        } else {
            .                            /* Resource NOT available      */
            .
        }
        .
        .
    }
}
```

OSMutexCreate()

`OS_EVENT *OSMutexCreate(INT8U prio, INT8U *err);`

Chapter	File	Called from	Code enabled by
8	OS_MUTEX.C	Task or startup code	OS_MUTEX_EN

OSMutexCreate() is used to create and initialize a mutex. A mutex is used to gain exclusive access to a resource.

Arguments

prio   is the priority inheritance priority (PIP) that is used when a high priority task attempts to acquire the mutex that is owned by a low priority task. In this case, the priority of the low priority task is *raised* to the PIP until the resource is released.

err   is a pointer to a variable that is used to hold an error code. The error code can be one of the following:

OS_NO_ERR	if the call is successful and the mutex has been created.
OS_ERR_CREATE_ISR	if you attempt to create a mutex from an ISR.
OS_PRIO_EXIST	if a task at the specified priority inheritance priority already exists.
OS_ERR_PEVENT_NULL	if no more OS_EVENT structures are available.
OS_PRIO_INVALID	if you specify a priority with a higher number than OS_LOWEST_PRIO.

Returned Value

A pointer to the event control block allocated to the mutex. If no event control block is available, OSMutexCreate() returns a NULL pointer.

Notes/Warnings

1. Mutexes must be created before they are used.

2. You **must** make sure that prio has a higher priority than **any** of the tasks that use the mutex to access the resource. For example, if three tasks of priority 20, 25, and 30 are going to use the mutex, then prio must be a number **lower** than 20. In addition, there **must not** already be a task created at the specified priority.

16

Example

```
OS_EVENT *DispMutex;

void main (void)
{
    INT8U  err;


    .

    .
    OSInit();                              /* Initialize μC/OS-II         */
    .

    .
    DispMutex = OSMutexCreate(20, &err);  /* Create Display Mutex        */
    .

    .
    OSStart();                             /* Start Multitasking          */
}
```

OSMutexDel()

OS_EVENT *OSMutexDel(OS_EVENT *pevent, INT8U opt, INT8U *err);

Chapter	File	Called from	Code enabled by
8	OS_MUTEX.C	Task	OS_MUTEX_EN and OS_MUTEX_DEL_EN

OSMutexDel() is used to delete a mutex. This function is dangerous to use because multiple tasks could attempt to access a deleted mutex. You should always use this function with great care. Generally speaking, before you delete a mutex, you must first delete all the tasks that can access the mutex.

Arguments

pevent   is a pointer to the mutex. This pointer is returned to your application when the mutex is created [see OSMutexCreate()].

opt   specifies whether you want to delete the mutex only if there are no pending tasks (OS_DEL_NO_PEND) or whether you always want to delete the mutex regardless of whether tasks are pending or not (OS_DEL_ALWAYS). In this case, all pending task are readied.

err   is a pointer to a variable that is used to hold an error code. The error code can be one of the following:

OS_NO_ERR	if the call is successful and the mutex has been deleted.
OS_ERR_DEL_ISR	if you attempt to delete a mutex from an ISR.
OS_ERR_INVALID_OPT	if you don't specify one of the two options mentioned in the opt argument.
OS_ERR_TASK_WAITING	if one or more task are waiting on the mutex and you specify OS_DEL_NO_PEND.
OS_ERR_EVENT_TYPE	if pevent is not pointing to a mutex.
OS_ERR_PEVENT_NULL	if no more OS_EVENT structures are available.

Returned Value

A NULL pointer if the mutex is deleted or pevent if the mutex is not deleted. In the latter case, you need to examine the error code to determine the reason.

Notes/Warnings

1. You should use this call with care because other tasks might expect the presence of the mutex.

16

Example

```
OS_EVENT *DispMutex;


void Task (void *pdata)
{
    INT8U  err;


    pdata = pdata;
    while (1) {
        .
        .
        DispMutex = OSMutexDel(DispMutex, OS_DEL_ALWAYS, &err);
        if (DispMutex == (OS_EVENT *)0) {
            /* Mutex has been deleted */
        }
        .
        .
    }
}
```

OSMutexPend( )

```
void OSMutexPend(OS_EVENT *pevent, INT16U timeout, INT8U *err);
```

Chapter	File	Called from	Code enabled by
8	OS_MUTEX.C	Task only	OS_MUTEX_EN

OSMutexPend( ) is used when a task desires to get exclusive access to a resource. If a task calls OSMutexPend( ) and the mutex is available, then OSMutexPend( ) gives the mutex to the caller and returns to its caller. Note that nothing is actually given to the caller except for the fact that if err is set to OS_NO_ERR, the caller can assume that it owns the mutex. However, if the mutex is already owned by another task, OSMutexPend( ) places the calling task in the wait list for the mutex. The task thus waits until the task that owns the mutex releases the mutex and thus the resource or until the specified timeout expires. If the mutex is signaled before the timeout expires, µC/OS-II resumes the highest priority task that is waiting for the mutex. Note that if the mutex is owned by a lower priority task, then OSMutexPend( ) raises the priority of the task that owns the mutex to the PIP, as specified when you created the mutex [see OSMutexCreate( )].

Arguments

pevent   is a pointer to the mutex. This pointer is returned to your application when the mutex is created [see OSMutexCreate( )].

timeout   is used to allow the task to resume execution if the mutex is not signaled (i.e., posted to) within the specified number of clock ticks. A timeout value of 0 indicates that the task desires to wait forever for the mutex. The maximum timeout is 65,535 clock ticks. The timeout value is not synchronized with the clock tick. The timeout count starts being decremented on the next clock tick, which could potentially occur immediately.

err   is a pointer to a variable that is used to hold an error code. OSMutexPend( ) sets *err to one of the following:

OS_NO_ERR   if the call is successful and the mutex is available.

OS_TIMEOUT   if the mutex is not available within the specified timeout.

OS_ERR_EVENT_TYPE   if you don't pass a pointer to a mutex to OSMutexPend( ).

OS_ERR_PEVENT_NULL   if pevent is a NULL pointer.

OS_ERR_PEND_ISR   if you attempt to acquire the mutex from an ISR.

Returned Value

16

Notes/Warnings

1. Mutexes must be created before they are used.

2. You should **not** suspend the task that owns the mutex, have the mutex owner wait on any other µC/OS-II objects (i.e., semaphore, mailbox, or queue), and delay the task that owns the mutex. In other words, your code should hurry up and release the resource as quickly as possible.

Example

```
OS_EVENT *DispMutex;


void  DispTask (void *pdata)
{
    INT8U  err;


    pdata = pdata;
    for (;;) {
        .

        .

        OSMutexPend(DispMutex, 0, &err);
        .                         /* The only way this task continues is if … */
        .                         /* … the mutex is available or signaled!    */
    }
}
```

OSMutexPost()

`INT8U OSMutexPost(OS_EVENT *pevent);`

Chapter	File	Called from	Code enabled by
8	OS_MUTEX.C	Task	OS_MUTEX_EN

A mutex is signaled (i.e., released) by calling `OSMutexPost()`. You call this function only if you acquire the mutex by first calling either `OSMutexAccept()` or `OSMutexPend()`. If the priority of the task that owns the mutex has been raised when a higher priority task attempts to acquire the mutex, the original task priority of the task is restored. If one or more tasks are waiting for the mutex, the mutex is given to the highest priority task waiting on the mutex. The scheduler is then called to determine if the awakened task is now the highest priority task ready to run, and if so, a context switch is done to run the readied task. If no task is waiting for the mutex, the mutex value is simply set to available (`0xFF`).

Arguments

pevent   is a pointer to the mutex. This pointer is returned to your application when the mutex is created [see `OSMutexCreate()`].

Returned Value

`OSMutexPost()` returns one of these error codes:

OS_NO_ERR	if the call is successful and the mutex is released.
OS_ERR_EVENT_TYPE	if you don't pass a pointer to a mutex to `OSMutexPost()`.
OS_ERR_PEVENT_NULL	if pevent is a NULL pointer.
OS_ERR_POST_ISR	if you attempt to call `OSMutexPost()` from an ISR.
OS_ERR_NOT_MUTEX_OWNER	if the task posting (i.e., signaling the mutex) doesn't actually own the mutex.

Notes/Warnings

1. Mutexes must be created before they are used.
2. You cannot call this function from an ISR.

16

Example

```c
OS_EVENT  *DispMutex;


void  TaskX (void *pdata)
{
    INT8U  err;


    pdata = pdata;
    for (;;) {
        .
        .
        err = OSMutexPost(DispMutex);
        switch (err) {
          case OS_NO_ERR: /* Mutex signaled        */
               .
               .
               break;

          case OS_ERR_EVENT_TYPE:
               .
               .
               break;

          case OS_ERR_PEVENT_NULL:
               .
               .
               break;

          case OS_ERR_POST_ISR:
               .
               .
               break;

        }
        .
        .
    }
}
```

OSMutexQuery()

INT8U OSMutexQuery(OS_EVENT *pevent, OS_MUTEX_DATA *pdata);

Chapter	File	Called from	Code enabled by
8	OS_MUTEX.C	Task	OS_MUTEX_EN && OS_MUTEX_QUERY_EN

OSMutexQuery() is used to obtain run-time information about a mutex. Your application must allocate an OS_MUTEX_DATA data structure that is used to receive data from the event control block of the mutex. OSMutexQuery() allows you to determine whether any task is waiting on the mutex, how many tasks are waiting (by counting the number of 1s) in the .OSEventTbl[] field, obtain the PIP, and determine whether the mutex is available (1) or not (0). Note that the size of .OSEventTbl[] is established by the #define constant OS_EVENT_TBL_SIZE (see uCOS_II.H).

Arguments

pevent   is a pointer to the mutex. This pointer is returned to your application when the mutex is created [see OSMutexCreate()].

pdata   is a pointer to a data structure of type OS_MUTEX_DATA, which contains the following fields

```
INT8U   OSMutexPIP;     /* The PIP of the mutex                       */
INT8U   OSOwnerPrio;    /* The priority of the mutex owner            */
INT8U   OSValue;        /* The current mutex value, 1 means available, */
                        /* 0 means unavailable                        */
INT8U   OSEventGrp;     /* Copy of the mutex wait list                */
INT8U   OSEventTbl[OS_EVENT_TBL_SIZE];
```

Returned Value

OSMutexQuery() returns one of these error codes:

OS_NO_ERR	if the call is successful.
OS_ERR_EVENT_TYPE	if you don't pass a pointer to a mutex to OSMutexQuery().
OS_ERR_PEVENT_NULL	if pevent is a NULL pointer.
OS_ERR_QUERY_ISR	if you attempt to call OSMutexQuery() from an ISR.

Notes/Warnings

1. Mutexes must be created before they are used.
2. You cannot call this function from an ISR.

16

Example

In this example, we check the contents of the mutex to determine the highest priority task that is waiting for it.

```
OS_EVENT *DispMutex;


void Task (void *pdata)
{
    OS_MUTEX_DATA mutex_data;
    INT8U         err;
    INT8U         highest;        /* Highest priority task waiting on mutex */
    INT8U         x;
    INT8U         y;


    pdata = pdata;
    for (;;) {
        .

        .
        err = OSMutexQuery(DispMutex, &mutex_data);
        if (err == OS_NO_ERR) {
            if (mutex_data.OSEventGrp != 0x00) {
                y       = OSUnMapTbl[mutex_data.OSEventGrp];
                x       = OSUnMapTbl[mutex_data.OSEventTbl[y]];
                highest = (y << 3) + x;
                .
                .
            }
        }
        .

        .
    }
}
```

OSQAccept()

`void *OSQAccept(OS_EVENT *pevent);`

Chapter	File	Called from	Code enabled by
11	OS_Q.C	Task or ISR	OS_Q_EN

OSQAccept() checks to see if a message is available in the desired message queue. Unlike OSQPend(), OSQAccept() does not suspend the calling task if a message is not available. In other words, OSQAccept() is non-blocking. If a message is available, it is extracted from the queue and returned to your application. This call is typically used by ISRs because an ISR is not allowed to wait for messages at a queue.

Arguments

pevent   is a pointer to the message queue from which the message is received. This pointer is returned to your application when the message queue is created [see OSQCreate()].

Returned Value

A pointer to the message if one is available; NULL if the message queue does not contain a message.

Notes/Warnings

1.   Message queues must be created before they are used.

Example

```
OS_EVENT *CommQ;

void Task (void *pdata)
{
     void *msg;

     pdata = pdata;
     for (;;) {
         msg = OSQAccept(CommQ);        /* Check queue for a message   */
         if (msg != (void *)0) {
             .                          /* Message received, process   */
             .
             .
         } else {
             .                          /* Message not received, do .. */
             .                          /* .. something else           */
         }
         .
         .
     }
}
```

16

OSQCreate()

`OS_EVENT *OSQCreate(void **start, INT8U size);`

Chapter	File	Called from	Code enabled by
11	OS_Q.C	Task or startup code	OS_Q_EN

`OSQCreate()` creates a message queue. A message queue allows tasks or ISRs to send pointer-sized variables (messages) to one or more tasks. The meaning of the messages sent are application specific.

Arguments

start   is the base address of the message storage area. A message storage area is declared as an array of pointers to voids.

size   is the size (in number of entries) of the message storage area.

Returned Value

`OSQCreate()` returns a pointer to the event control block allocated to the queue. If no event control block is available, `OSQCreate()` returns a NULL pointer.

Notes/Warnings

1. Queues must be created before they are used.

Example

```
OS_EVENT *CommQ;
void     *CommMsg[10];


void main (void)
{
     OSInit();                                  /* Initialize _C/OS-II    */
     .
     .
     CommQ = OSQCreate(&CommMsg[0], 10);        /* Create COMM Q          */
     .
     .
     OSStart();                                 /* Start Multitasking     */
}
```

OSQDel()

```
OS_EVENT *OSQDel(OS_EVENT *pevent, INT8U opt, INT8U *err);
```

Chapter	File	Called from	Code enabled by
11	OS_Q.C	Task	OS_Q_EN and OS_Q_DEL_EN

OSQDel() is used to delete a message queue. This function is dangerous to use because multiple tasks could attempt to access a deleted queue. You should always use this function with great care. Generally speaking, before you delete a queue, you must first delete all the tasks that can access the queue.

Arguments

pevent   is a pointer to the queue. This pointer is returned to your application when the queue is created [see OSQCreate()].

opt   specifies whether you want to delete the queue only if there are no pending tasks (OS_DEL_NO_PEND) or whether you always want to delete the queue regardless of whether tasks are pending or not (OS_DEL_ALWAYS). In this case, all pending task are readied.

err   is a pointer to a variable that is used to hold an error code. The error code can be one of the following:

OS_NO_ERR	if the call is successful and the queue has been deleted.
OS_ERR_DEL_ISR	if you attempt to delete the queue from an ISR.
OS_ERR_INVALID_OPT	if you don't specify one of the two options mentioned in the opt argument.
OS_ERR_TASK_WAITING	if one or more tasks are waiting for messages at the message queue.
OS_ERR_EVENT_TYPE	if pevent is not pointing to a queue.
OS_ERR_PEVENT_NULL	if no more OS_EVENT structures are available.

Returned Value

A NULL pointer if the queue is deleted or pevent if the queue is not deleted. In the latter case, you need to examine the error code to determine the reason.

Notes/Warnings

1. You should use this call with care because other tasks might expect the presence of the queue.

2. Interrupts are disabled when pended tasks are readied, which means that interrupt latency depends on the number of tasks that are waiting on the queue.

16

Example

```
OS_EVENT *DispQ;



void Task (void *pdata)
{
    INT8U  err;



    pdata = pdata;
    while (1) {
        .

        .
        DispQ = OSQDel(DispQ, OS_DEL_ALWAYS, &err);
        if (DispQ == (OS_EVENT *)0) {
            /* Queue has been deleted */
        }
        .

        .
    }
}
```

OSQFlush()

`INT8U *OSQFlush(OS_EVENT *pevent);`

Chapter	File	Called from	Code enabled by
11	OS_Q.C	Task or ISR	OS_Q_EN && OS_Q_FLUSH_EN

OSQFlush() empties the contents of the message queue and eliminates all the messages sent to the queue. This function takes the same amount of time to execute regardless of whether tasks are waiting on the queue (and thus no messages are present) or the queue contains one or more messages.

Arguments

pevent   is a pointer to the message queue. This pointer is returned to your application when the message queue is created [see OSQCreate()].

Returned Value

OSQFlush() returns one of the following codes:

OS_NO_ERR   if the message queue is flushed.

OS_ERR_EVENT_TYPE   if you attempt to flush an object other than a message queue.

OS_ERR_PEVENT_NULL   if pevent is a NULL pointer.

Notes/Warnings

1. Queues must be created before they are used.

Example

```
OS_EVENT *CommQ;


void main (void)
{
      INT8U err;

      OSInit();                             /* Initialize µC/OS-II    */
      .
      .
      err = OSQFlush(CommQ);
      .
      .
      OSStart();                            /* Start Multitasking     */
}
```

16

OSQPend()

`void *OSQPend(OS_EVENT *pevent, INT16U timeout, INT8U *err);`

Chapter	File	Called from	Code enabled by
11	OS_Q.C	Task only	OS_Q_EN

OSQPend() is used when a task wants to receive messages from a queue. The messages are sent to the task either by an ISR or by another task. The messages received are pointer-sized variables, and their use is application specific. If at least one message is present at the queue when OSQPend() is called, the message is retrieved and returned to the caller. If no message is present at the queue, OSQPend() suspends the current task until either a message is received or a user-specified timeout expires. If a message is sent to the queue and multiple tasks are waiting for such a message, then µC/OS-II resumes the highest priority task that is waiting. A pended task that has been suspended with OSTaskSuspend() can receive a message. However, the task remains suspended until it is resumed by calling OSTaskResume().

Arguments

pevent   is a pointer to the queue from which the messages are received. This pointer is returned to your application when the queue is created [see OSQCreate()].

timeout   allows the task to resume execution if a message is not received from the mailbox within the specified number of clock ticks. A timeout value of 0 indicates that the task wants to wait forever for the message. The maximum timeout is 65,535 clock ticks. The timeout value is not synchronized with the clock tick. The timeout count starts decrementing on the next clock tick, which could potentially occur immediately.

err   is a pointer to a variable used to hold an error code. OSQPend() sets *err to one of the following:

OS_NO_ERR	if a message is received.
OS_TIMEOUT	if a message is not received within the specified timeout.
OS_ERR_EVENT_TYPE	if pevent is not pointing to a message queue.
OS_ERR_PEVENT_NULL	if pevent is a NULL pointer.
OS_ERR_PEND_ISR	if you call this function from an ISR and µC/OS-II has to suspend it. In general, you should not call OSQPend() from an ISR. µC/OS-II checks for this situation anyway.

Returned Value

OSQPend() returns a message sent by either a task or an ISR, and *err is set to OS_NO_ERR. If a timeout occurs, OSQPend() returns a NULL pointer and sets *err to OS_TIMEOUT.

Notes/Warnings

1. Queues must be created before they are used.
2. You should not call OSQPend() from an ISR.

Example

```c
OS_EVENT *CommQ;



void CommTask(void *data)
{
    INT8U  err;
    void   *msg;



    pdata = pdata;
    for (;;) {
        .
        .
        msg = OSQPend(CommQ, 100, &err);
        if (err == OS_NO_ERR) {
            .
            .              /* Message received within 100 ticks!       */
            .
        } else {
            .
            .              /* Message not received, must have timed out  */
            .
        }
        .
        .
    }
}
```

16

OSQPost()

`INT8U OSQPost(OS_EVENT *pevent, void *msg);`

Chapter	*File*	*Called from*	*Code enabled by*
11	OS_Q.C	Task or ISR	OS_Q_EN && OS_Q_POST_EN

`OSQPost()` sends a message to a task through a queue. A message is a pointer-sized variable, and its use is application specific. If the message queue is full, an error code is returned to the caller. In this case, `OSQPost()` immediately returns to its caller, and the message is not placed in the queue. If any task is waiting for a message at the queue, the highest priority task receives the message. If the task waiting for the message has a higher priority than the task sending the message, the higher priority task resumes, and the task sending the message is suspended; that is, a context switch occurs. Message queues are first-in first-out (FIFO), which means that the first message sent is the first message received.

Arguments

pevent   is a pointer to the queue into which the message is deposited. This pointer is returned to your application when the queue is created [see `OSQCreate()`].

msg   is the actual message sent to the task. `msg` is a pointer-sized variable and is application specific. You must never post a `NULL` pointer.

Returned Value

`OSQPost()` returns one of these error codes:

OS_NO_ERR	if the message is deposited in the queue.
OS_Q_FULL	if the queue is already full.
OS_ERR_EVENT_TYPE	if `pevent` is not pointing to a message queue.
OS_ERR_PEVENT_NULL	if `pevent` is a `NULL` pointer.
OS_ERR_POST_NULL_PTR	if you are posting a `NULL` pointer. By convention, a `NULL` pointer is not supposed to point to anything valid.

Notes/Warnings

1. Queues must be created before they are used.
2. You must never post a `NULL` pointer.

Example

```
OS_EVENT *CommQ;
INT8U    CommRxBuf[100];



void CommTaskRx (void *pdata)
{
     INT8U  err;



     pdata = pdata;
     for (;;) {

       .

       .

       err = OSQPost(CommQ, (void *)&CommRxBuf[0]);
       switch (err) {
          case OS_NO_ERR:
               /* Message was deposited into queue    */
               break;

          case OS_Q_FULL:
               /* Queue is full                       */
               Break;

          .

       }

       .

       .

     }
}
```

16

OSQPostFront()

`INT8U OSQPostFront(OS_EVENT *pevent, void *msg);`

Chapter	*File*	*Called from*	*Code enabled by*
11	OS_Q.C	Task or ISR	OS_Q_EN && OS_Q_POST_FRONT_EN

OSQPostFront() sends a message to a task through a queue. OSQPostFront() behaves very much like OSQPost(), except that the message is inserted at the front of the queue. This means that OSQPostFront() makes the message queue behave like a last-in first-out (LIFO) queue instead of a first-in first-out (FIFO) queue. The message is a pointer-sized variable, and its use is application specific. If the message queue is full, an error code is returned to the caller. OSQPostFront() immediately returns to its caller, and the message is not placed in the queue. If any tasks are waiting for a message at the queue, the highest priority task receives the message. If the task waiting for the message has a higher priority than the task sending the message, the higher priority task is resumed, and the task sending the message is suspended; that is, a context switch occurs.

Arguments

pevent   is a pointer to the queue into which the message is deposited. This pointer is returned to your application when the queue is created [see OSQCreate()].

msg   is the actual message sent to the task. msg is a pointer-sized variable and is application specific. You must never post a NULL pointer.

Returned Value

OSQPostFront() returns one of these error codes:

OS_NO_ERR	if the message is deposited in the queue.
OS_Q_FULL	if the queue is already full.
OS_ERR_EVENT_TYPE	if pevent is not pointing to a message queue.
OS_ERR_PEVENT_NULL	if pevent is a NULL pointer.
OS_ERR_POST_NULL_PTR	if you are posting a NULL pointer. By convention, a NULL pointer is not supposed to point to anything valid.

Notes/Warnings

1. Queues must be created before they are used.
2. You must never post a NULL pointer.

Example

```
OS_EVENT *CommQ;
INT8U     CommRxBuf[100];



void CommTaskRx (void *pdata)
{
    INT8U  err;



    pdata = pdata;
    for (;;) {
        .

        .
        err = OSQPostFront(CommQ, (void *)&CommRxBuf[0]);
        switch (err) {
            case OS_NO_ERR:
                /* Message was deposited into queue    */
                break;

            case OS_Q_FULL:
                /* Queue is full                       */
                break;
            .
        }
        .

        .
    }
}
```

16

OSQPostOpt()

`INT8U OSQPostOpt(OS_EVENT *pevent, void *msg, INT8U opt);`

Chapter	File	Called from	Code enabled by
11	OS_Q.C	Task or ISR	OS_Q_EN && OS_Q_POST_OPT_EN

OSQPostOpt() is used to send a message to a task through a queue. A message is a pointer-sized variable, and its use is application specific. If the message queue is full, an error code is returned indicating that the queue is full. OSQPostOpt() then immediately returns to its caller, and the message is not placed in the queue. If any task is waiting for a message at the queue, OSQPostOpt() allows you to either post the message to the highest priority task waiting at the queue (opt set to OS_POST_OPT_NONE) or to all tasks waiting at the queue (opt is set to OS_POST_OPT_BROADCAST). In either case, scheduling occurs, and, if any of the tasks that receive the message have a higher priority than the task that is posting the message, then the higher priority task is resumed, and the sending task is suspended. In other words, a context switch occurs.

OSQPostOpt() emulates both OSQPost() and OSQPostFront() and also allows you to post a message to **multiple** tasks. In other words, it allows the message posted to be broadcast to **all** tasks waiting on the queue. OSQPostOpt() can actually replace OSQPost() and OSQPostFront() because you specify the mode of operation via an option argument, opt. Doing this allows you to reduce the amount of code space needed by µC/OS-II.

Arguments

pevent   is a pointer to the queue. This pointer is returned to your application when the queue is created [see OSQCreate()].

msg   is the actual message sent to the task(s). msg is a pointer-sized variable, and what msg points to is application specific. You must never post a NULL pointer.

opt   determines the type of POST performed:

OS_POST_OPT_NONE	POST to a single waiting task [identical to OSQPost()].
OS_POST_OPT_BROADCAST	POST to **all** tasks waiting on the queue.
OS_POST_OPT_FRONT	POST as LIFO [simulates OSQPostFront()].

Below is a list of **all** the possible combination of these flags:

OS_POST_OPT_NONE	is identical to OSQPost()
OS_POST_OPT_FRONT	is identical to OSQPostFront()
OS_POST_OPT_BROADCAST	is identical to OSQPost() but broadcasts msg to **all** waiting tasks
OS_POST_OPT_FRONT + OS_POST_OPT_BROADCAST	is identical to OSQPostFront() except that broadcasts msg to **all** waiting tasks.

Returned Value

err   is a pointer to a variable that is used to hold an error code. The error code can be one of
                   the following:

OS_NO_ERR	if the call is successful and the message has been sent.
OS_Q_FULL	if the queue can no longer accept messages because it is full.
OS_ERR_EVENT_TYPE	if pevent is not pointing to a mailbox.
OS_ERR_PEVENT_NULL	if pevent is a NULL pointer.
OS_ERR_POST_NULL_PTR	if you are attempting to post a NULL pointer.

Notes/Warnings

1. Queues must be created before they are used.

2. You must **never** post a NULL pointer to a queue.

3. If you need to use this function and want to reduce code space, you can disable code generation of OSQPost() (set OS_Q_POST_EN to 0 in OS_CFG.H) and OSQPostFront() (set OS_Q_POST_FRONT_EN to 0 in OS_CFG.H) because OSQPostOpt() can emulate these two functions.

4. The execution time of OSQPostOpt() depends on the number of tasks waiting on the queue if you set opt to OS_POST_OPT_BROADCAST.

Example

```
OS_EVENT *CommQ;
INT8U    CommRxBuf[100];



void CommRxTask (void *pdata)
{
    INT8U  err;


    pdata = pdata;
    for (;;) {
        .

        .
        err = OSQPostOpt(CommQ, (void *)&CommRxBuf[0], OS_POST_OPT_BROADCAST);
        .

        .

    }
}
```

16

OSQQuery()

`INT8U OSQQuery(OS_EVENT *pevent, OS_Q_DATA *pdata);`

Chapter	File	Called from	Code enabled by
11	OS_Q.C	Task or ISR	OS_Q_EN && OS_QUERY_EN

`OSQQuery()` obtains information about a message queue. Your application must allocate an `OS_Q_DATA` data structure used to receive data from the event control block of the message queue. `OSQQuery()` allows you to determine whether any tasks are waiting for messages at the queue, how many tasks are waiting (by counting the number of 1s in the `.OSEventTbl[]` field), how many messages are in the queue, and what the message queue size is. `OSQQuery()` also obtains the next message that is returned if the queue is not empty. Note that the size of `.OSEventTbl[]` is established by the #define constant `OS_EVENT_TBL_SIZE` (see uCOS_II.H).

Arguments

pevent   is a pointer to the message queue. This pointer is returned to your application when the queue is created [see `OSQCreate()`].

pdata   is a pointer to a data structure of type `OS_Q_DATA`, which contains the following fields

```
void  *OSMsg;                    /* Next message if one available      */
INT16U OSNMsgs;                  /* Number of messages in the queue    */
INT16U OSQSize;                  /* Size of the message queue          */
INT8U  OSEventTbl[OS_EVENT_TBL_SIZE];    /* Message queue wait list    */
INT8U  OSEventGrp;
```

Returned Value

`OSQQuery()` returns one of these error codes:

OS_NO_ERR	if the call is successful.
OS_ERR_EVENT_TYPE	if you don't pass a pointer to a message queue.
OS_ERR_PEVENT_NULL	if pevent is a NULL pointer.

Notes/Warnings

1. Message queues must be created before they are used.

Example

```
OS_EVENT *CommQ;


void Task (void *pdata)
{
    OS_Q_DATA qdata;
    INT8U     err;


    pdata = pdata;
    for (;;) {
        .

        .
        err = OSQQuery(CommQ, &qdata);
        if (err == OS_NO_ERR) {
            .   /* 'qdata' can be examined! */
        }
        .

        .
    }
}
```

16

OSSchedLock()

void OSSchedLock(void);

Chapter	File	Called from	Code enabled by
3	OS_CORE.C	Task or ISR	OS_SCHED_LOCK_EN

OSSchedLock() prevents task rescheduling until its counterpart, OSSchedUnlock(), is called. The task that calls OSSchedLock() keeps control of the CPU even though other higher priority tasks are ready to run. However, interrupts are still recognized and serviced (assuming interrupts are enabled). OSSchedLock() and OSSchedUnlock() must be used in pairs. µC/OS-II allows OSSchedLock() to be nested up to 255 levels deep. Scheduling is enabled when an equal number of OSSchedUnlock() calls have been made.

Arguments

Returned Value

Notes/Warnings

1. After calling OSSchedLock(), your application must not make system calls that suspend execution of the current task; that is, your application cannot call OSTimeDly(), OSTimeDlyHMSM(), OSFlagPend(), OSSemPend(), OSMutexPend(), OSMboxPend(), or OSQPend(). Because the scheduler is locked out, no other task is allowed to run, and your system will lock up.

Example

```
void TaskX (void *pdata)
{
    pdata = pdata;
    for (;;) {
        .
        OSSchedLock();          /* Prevent other tasks to run          */
        .
        .                       /* Code protected from context switch */
        .
        OSSchedUnlock();        /* Enable other tasks to run           */
        .
    }
}
```

OSSchedUnlock()

```
void OSSchedUnlock(void);
```

Chapter	File	Called from	Code enabled by
3	OS_CORE.C	Task or ISR	OS_SCHED_LOCK_EN

OSSchedUnlock() re-enables task scheduling whenever it is paired with OSSchedLock().

Arguments

Returned Value

Notes/Warnings

1. After calling OSSchedLock(), your application must not make system calls that suspend execution of the current task; that is, your application cannot call OSTimeDly(), OSTimeDlyHMSM(), OSFlagPend(), OSSemPend(), OSMutexPend(), OSMboxPend(), or OSQPend(). Because the scheduler is locked out, no other task is allowed to run, and your system will lock up.

Example

```
void TaskX (void *pdata)
{
    pdata = pdata;
    for (;;) {
        .
        OSSchedLock();     /* Prevent other tasks to run         */
        .
                           /* Code protected from context switch */
        .
        OSSchedUnlock();   /* Enable other tasks to run          */
        .
    }
}
```

16

OSSemAccept()

```
INT16U OSSemAccept(OS_EVENT *pevent);
```

Chapter	*File*	*Called from*	*Code enabled by*
7	OS_SEM.C	Task or ISR	OS_SEM_EN && OS_SEM_ACCEPT_EN

OSSemAccept() checks to see if a resource is available or an event has occurred. Unlike OSSemPend(), OSSemAccept() does not suspend the calling task if the resource is not available. In other words, OSSemAccept() is non-blocking. Use OSSemAccept() from an ISR to obtain the semaphore.

Arguments

pevent   is a pointer to the semaphore that guards the resource. This pointer is returned to your application when the semaphore is created [see OSSemCreate()].

Returned Value

When OSSemAccept() is called and the semaphore value is greater than 0, the semaphore value is decremented, and the value of the semaphore before the decrement is returned to your application. If the semaphore value is 0 when OSSemAccept() is called, the resource is not available, and 0 is returned to your application.

Notes/Warnings

1.   Semaphores must be created before they are used.

Example

```
OS_EVENT *DispSem;

void Task (void *pdata)
{
    INT16U value;


    pdata = pdata;
    for (;;) {
        value = OSSemAccept(DispSem);          /* Check resource availability */
        if (value > 0) {

                                               /* Resource available, process */
            .

            .
        }
        .

        .
    }
}
```

OSSemCreate()

`OS_EVENT *OSSemCreate(INT16U value);`

Chapter	File	Called from	Code enabled by
7	OS_SEM.C	Task or startup code	OS_SEM_EN

OSSemCreate() creates and initializes a semaphore. A semaphore

- allows a task to synchronize with either an ISR or a task (you initialize the semaphore to 0),
- gains exclusive access to a resource (you initialize the semaphore to a value greater than 0), and
- signals the occurrence of an event (you initialize the semaphore to 0).

Arguments

value   is the initial value of the semaphore and can be between 0 and 65,535. A value of 0 indicates that a resource is not available or an event has not occurred.

Returned Value

OSSemCreate() returns a pointer to the event control block allocated to the semaphore. If no event control block is available, OSSemCreate() returns a NULL pointer.

Notes/Warnings

1. Semaphores must be created before they are used.

Example

```
OS_EVFNT *DispSem;



void main (void)
{
    .

    .
    OSInit();                   /* Initialize µC/OS-II          */
    .

    .
    DispSem = OSSemCreate(1);   /* Create Display Semaphore     */
    .

    .
    OSStart();                  /* Start Multitasking           */
}
```

16

OSSemDel()

`OS_EVENT *OSSemDel(OS_EVENT *pevent, INT8U opt, INT8U *err);`

Chapter	File	Called from	Code enabled by
7	OS_SEM.C	Task	OS_SEM_EN and OS_SEM_DEL_EN

OSSemDel() is used to delete a semaphore. This function is dangerous to use because multiple tasks could attempt to access a deleted semaphore. You should always use this function with great care. Generally speaking, before you delete a semaphore, you must first delete all the tasks that can access the semaphore.

Arguments

pevent   is a pointer to the semaphore. This pointer is returned to your application when the semaphore is created [see OSSemCreate()].

opt   specifies whether you want to delete the semaphore only if there are no pending tasks (OS_DEL_NO_PEND) or whether you always want to delete the semaphore regardless of whether tasks are pending or not (OS_DEL_ALWAYS). In this case, all pending task are readied.

err   is a pointer to a variable that is used to hold an error code. The error code can be one of the following:

OS_NO_ERR	if the call is successful and the semaphore has been deleted.
OS_ERR_DEL_ISR	if you attempt to delete the semaphore from an ISR.
OS_ERR_INVALID_OPT	if you don't specify one of the two options mentioned in the opt argument.
OS_ERR_TASK_WAITING	if one or more tasks are waiting on the semaphore.
OS_ERR_EVENT_TYPE	if pevent is not pointing to a semaphore.
OS_ERR_PEVENT_NULL	if no more OS_EVENT structures are available.

Returned Value

A NULL pointer if the semaphore is deleted or pevent if the semaphore is not deleted. In the latter case, you need to examine the error code to determine the reason.

Notes/Warnings

1. You should use this call with care because other tasks might expect the presence of the semaphore.

2. Interrupts are disabled when pended tasks are readied, which means that interrupt latency depends on the number of tasks that are waiting on the semaphore.

Example

```c
OS_EVENT *DispSem;


void Task (void *pdata)
{
    INT8U  err;


    pdata = pdata;
    while (1) {
        .

        .
        DispSem = OSSemDel(DispSem, OS_DEL_ALWAYS, &err);
        if (DispSem == (OS_EVENT *)0) {
            /* Semaphore has been deleted */
        }
        .

        .

    }
}
```

16

OSSemPend()

```
void OSSemPend(OS_EVENT *pevent, INT16U timeout, INT8U *err);
```

Chapter	File	Called from	Code enabled by
7	OS_SEM.C	Task only	OS_SEM_EN

OSSemPend() is used when a task wants exclusive access to a resource, needs to synchronize its activities with an ISR or a task, or is waiting until an event occurs. If a task calls OSSemPend() and the value of the semaphore is greater than 0, OSSemPend() decrements the semaphore and returns to its caller. However, if the value of the semaphore is 0, OSSemPend() places the calling task in the waiting list for the semaphore. The task waits until a task or an ISR signals the semaphore or the specified timeout expires. If the semaphore is signaled before the timeout expires, μC/OS-II resumes the highest priority task waiting for the semaphore. A pended task that has been suspended with OSTaskSuspend() can obtain the semaphore. However, the task remains suspended until it is resumed by calling OSTaskResume().

Arguments

pevent   is a pointer to the semaphore. This pointer is returned to your application when the semaphore is created [see OSSemCreate()].

timeout   allows the task to resume execution if a message is not received from the mailbox within the specified number of clock ticks. A timeout value of 0 indicates that the task waits forever for the message. The maximum timeout is 65,535 clock ticks. The timeout value is not synchronized with the clock tick. The timeout count begins decrementing on the next clock tick, which could potentially occur immediately.

err   is a pointer to a variable used to hold an error code. OSSemPend() sets *err to one of the following:

OS_NO_ERR	if the semaphore is available.
OS_TIMEOUT	if the semaphore is not signaled within the specified timeout.
OS_ERR_EVENT_TYPE	if pevent is not pointing to a semaphore.
OS_ERR_PEND_ISR	if you called this function from an ISR and μC/OS-II has to suspend it. You should not call OSSemPend() from an ISR. μC/OS-II checks for this situation.
OS_ERR_PEVENT_NULL	if pevent is a NULL pointer.

Returned Value

Notes/Warnings

1.   Semaphores must be created before they are used.

Example

```
OS_EVENT *DispSem;


void DispTask (void *pdata)
{
    INT8U  err;


    pdata = pdata;
    for (;;) {
        .

        .

        OSSemPend(DispSem, 0, &err);
        .                   /* The only way this task continues is if … */
        .                   /* … the semaphore is signaled!             */
    }
}
```

16

OSSemPost()

`INT8U OSSemPost(OS_EVENT *pevent);`

Chapter	File	Called from	Code enabled by
7	OS_SEM.C	Task or ISR	OS_SEM_EN

A semaphore is signaled by calling `OSSemPost()`. If the semaphore value is 0 or more, it is incremented, and `OSSemPost()` returns to its caller. If tasks are waiting for the semaphore to be signaled, `OSSemPost()` removes the highest priority task pending for the semaphore from the waiting list and makes this task ready to run. The scheduler is then called to determine if the awakened task is now the highest priority task ready to run.

Arguments

pevent   is a pointer to the semaphore. This pointer is returned to your application when the semaphore is created [see `OSSemCreate()`].

Returned Value

`OSSemPost()` returns one of these error codes:

OS_NO_ERR	if the semaphore is signaled successfully.
OS_SEM_OVF	if the semaphore count overflows.
OS_ERR_EVENT_TYPE	if pevent is not pointing to a semaphore.
OS_ERR_PEVENT_NULL	if pevent is a NULL pointer.

Notes/Warnings

1.   Semaphores must be created before they are used.

Example

```
OS_EVENT *DispSem;


void TaskX (void *pdata)
{
    INT8U  err;


    pdata = pdata;
    for (;;) {
        .

        .
        err = OSSemPost(DispSem);
        switch (err) {
            case OS_NO_ERR:
                /* Semaphore signaled       */
                break;

            case OS_SEM_OVF:
                /* Semaphore has overflowed */
                break;
            .

            .
        }
        .

        .
    }
}
```

16

OSSemQuery()

`INT8U OSSemQuery(OS_EVENT *pevent, OS_SEM_DATA *pdata);`

Chapter	*File*	*Called from*	*Code enabled by*
7	OS_SEM.C	Task or ISR	OS_SEM_EN && OS_SEM_QUERY_EN

`OSSemQuery()` obtains information about a semaphore. Your application must allocate an `OS_SEM_DATA` data structure used to receive data from the event control block of the semaphore. `OSSemQuery()` allows you to determine whether any tasks are waiting on the semaphore and how many tasks are waiting (by counting the number of 1s in the `.OSEventTbl[]` field) and obtains the semaphore count. Note that the size of `.OSEventTbl[]` is established by the `#define` constant `OS_EVENT_TBL_SIZE` (see `uCOS_II.H`).

Arguments

pevent   is a pointer to the semaphore. This pointer is returned to your application when the semaphore is created [see `OSSemCreate()`].

pdata   is a pointer to a data structure of type `OS_SEM_DATA`, which contains the following fields

```
INT16U OSCnt;                           /* Current semaphore count    */
INT8U  OSEventTbl[OS_EVENT_TBL_SIZE];   /* Semaphore wait list        */
INT8U  OSEventGrp;
```

Returned Value

`OSSemQuery()` returns one of these error codes:

         OS_NO_ERR   if the call is successful.

         OS_ERR_EVENT_TYPE   if you don't pass a pointer to a semaphore.

         OS_ERR_PEVENT_NULL   if `pevent` is is a `NULL` pointer.

Notes/Warnings

1. Semaphores must be created before they are used.

Example

In this example, the contents of the semaphore is checked to determine the highest priority task waiting at the time the function call was made.

```
OS_EVENT *DispSem;


void Task (void *pdata)
{
    OS_SEM_DATA sem_data;
    INT8U       err;
    INT8U       highest; /* Highest priority task waiting on sem. */
    INT8U       x;
    INT8U       y;



    pdata = pdata;
    for (;;) {
        .
        .
        err = OSSemQuery(DispSem, &sem_data);
        if (err == OS_NO_ERR) {
            if (sem_data.OSEventGrp != 0x00) {
                y       = OSUnMapTbl[sem_data.OSEventGrp];
                x       = OSUnMapTbl[sem_data.OSEventTbl[y]];
                highest = (y << 3) + x;
                .
                .
            }
        }
        .
        .
    }
}
```

OSStart()

```
void OSStart(void);
```

Chapter	File	Called from	Code enabled by
3	OS_CORE.C	Startup code only	N/A

OSStart() starts multitasking under µC/OS-II. This function is typically called from your startup code but after you call OSInit().

Arguments

Returned Value

Notes/Warnings

1. OSInit() must be called prior to calling OSStart(). OSStart() should only be called once by your application code. If you do call OSStart() more than once, it does not do anything on the second and subsequent calls.

Example

```
void main (void)
{
       .                          /* User Code          */
       .
       .
    OSInit();                      /* Initialize uC/OS-II */
       .                          /* User Code          */
       .
       .
    OSStart();                     /* Start Multitasking  */
    /* Any code here should NEVER be executed! */
}
```

OSStatInit()

`void OSStatInit(void);`

Chapter	File	Called from	Code enabled by
3	OS_CORE.C	Startup code only	OS_TASK_STAT_EN && OS_TASK_CREATE_EXT_EN

OSStatInit() determines the maximum value that a 32-bit counter can reach when no other task is executing. This function must be called when only one task is created in your application and when multitasking has started; that is, this function must be called from the first and, only, task created.

Arguments

Returned Value

Notes/Warnings

Example

```
void FirstAndOnlyTask (void *pdata)
{
    .
    .
    OSStatInit();              /* Compute CPU capacity with no task running */
    .
    OSTaskCreate(…);           /* Create the other tasks                    */
    OSTaskCreate(…);
    .
    for (;;) {
        .
        .
    }
}
```

16

OSTaskChangePrio()

`INT8U OSTaskChangePrio(INT8U oldprio, INT8U newprio);`

Chapter	File	Called from	Code enabled by
4	OS_TASK.C	Task only	OS_TASK_CHANGE_PRIO_EN

OSTaskChangePrio() changes the priority of a task.

Arguments

oldprio   is the priority number of the task to change.

newprio   is the new task's priority.

Returned Value

OSTaskChangePrio() returns one of the following error codes:

OS_NO_ERR	if the task's priority is changed.
OS_PRIO_INVALID	if either the old priority or the new priority is equal to or exceeds OS_LOWEST_PRIO.
OS_PRIO_EXIST	if newprio already exists.
OS_PRIO_ERR	if no task with the specified old priority exists (i.e., the task specified by oldprio does not exist).

Notes/Warnings

1. The desired priority must not already have been assigned; otherwise, an error code is returned. Also, OSTaskChangePrio() verifies that the task to change exists.

Example

```
void TaskX (void *data)
{
    INT8U  err;


    for (;;) {
        .
        .
        err = OSTaskChangePrio(10, 15);
        .
        .
    }
}
```

OSTaskCreate()

```
INT8U OSTaskCreate(void (*task)(void *pd),
                   void *pdata,
                   OS_STK *ptos,
                   INT8U prio);
```

Chapter	File	Called from	Code enabled by
4	OS_TASK.C	Task or startup code	OS_TASK_CREATE_EN

OSTaskCreate() creates a task so it can be managed by µC/OS-II. Tasks can be created either prior to the start of multitasking or by a running task. A task cannot be created by an ISR. A task must be written as an infinite loop, as shown below, and must not return.

OSTaskCreate() is used for backward compatibility with µC/OS and when the added features of OSTaskCreateExt() are not needed.

Depending on how the stack frame is built, your task has interrupts either enabled or disabled. You need to check with the processor-specific code for details.

```
void Task (void *pdata)
{
    .                       /* Do something with 'pdata'         */
    for (;;) {              /* Task body, always an infinite loop. */
        .

        .

        /* Must call one of the following services:        */
        /*      OSMboxPend()                               */
        /*      OSFlagPend()                               */
        /*      OSMutexPend()                              */
        /*      OSQPend()                                  */
        /*      OSSemPend()                                */
        /*      OSTimeDly()                                */
        /*      OSTimeDlyHMSM()                            */
        /*      OSTaskSuspend()    (Suspend self)          */
        /*      OSTaskDel()        (Delete  self)          */

        .

        .

    }
}
```

16

Arguments

task   is a pointer to the task's code.

pdata   is a pointer to an optional data area used to pass parameters to the task when it is cre-
                ated. Where the task is concerned, it thinks it is invoked and passes the argument pdata.
                pdata can be used to pass arguments to the task created. For example, you can create a
                generic task that handles an asynchronous serial port. pdata can be used to pass this
                task information about the serial port it has to manage: the port address, the baud rate,
                the number of bits, the parity, and more.

ptos   is a pointer to the task's top-of-stack. The stack is used to store local variables, func-
                tion parameters, return addresses, and CPU registers during an interrupt. The size of
                the stack is determined by the task's requirements and the anticipated interrupt nest-
                ing. Determining the size of the stack involves knowing how many bytes are required
                for storage of local variables for the task itself and all nested functions, as well as
                requirements for interrupts (accounting for nesting). If the configuration constant
                OS_STK_GROWTH is set to 1, the stack is assumed to grow downward (i.e., from high to
                low memory). ptos thus needs to point to the highest *valid* memory location on the
                stack. If OS_STK_GROWTH is set to 0, the stack is assumed to grow in the opposite direc-
                tion (i.e., from low to high memory).

prio   is the task priority. A unique priority number must be assigned to each task, and the
                lower the number, the higher the priority (i.e., the task importance).

Returned Value

OSTaskCreate() returns one of the following error codes:

OS_NO_ERR	if the function is successful.
OS_PRIO_EXIST	if the requested priority already exists.
OS_PRIO_INVALID	if prio is higher than OS_LOWEST_PRIO.
OS_NO_MORE_TCB	if µC/OS-II doesn't have any more OS_TCBs to assign.

Notes/Warnings

1. The stack for the task must be declared with the OS_STK type.

2. A task must always invoke one of the services provided by µC/OS-II to wait for time to expire, sus-
    pend the task, or wait for an event to occur (wait on a mailbox, queue, or semaphore). This allows
    other tasks to gain control of the CPU.

3. You should not use task priorities 0, 1, 2, 3, OS_LOWEST_PRIO-3, OS_LOWEST_PRIO-2,
    OS_LOWEST_PRIO-1, and OS_LOWEST_PRIO because they are reserved for use by µC/OS-II. This
    leaves you with up to 56 application tasks.

Example 1

This example shows that the argument that Task1() receives is not used, so the pointer pdata is set to NULL. Note that I assume the stack grows from high to low memory because I pass the address of the highest valid memory location of the stack Task1Stk[]. If the stack grows in the opposite direction for the processor you are using, pass &Task1Stk[0] as the task's top-of-stack.

Assigning pdata to itself is used to prevent compilers from issuing a warning about the fact that pdata is not being used. In other words, if I had not added this line, some compilers would have complained about 'WARNING - variable pdata not used.'

```c
OS_STK  Task1Stk[1024];


void main (void)
{
    INT8U err;


    .
    OSInit();                       /* Initialize µC/OS-II        */
    .
    OSTaskCreate(Task1,
                 (void *)0,
                 &Task1Stk[1023],
                 25);
    .
    OSStart();                      /* Start Multitasking         */
}


void Task1 (void *pdata)
{
    pdata = pdata;                  /* Prevent compiler warning   */
    for (;;) {
                                    /* Task code                  */
        .
        .
    }
}
```

Example 2

You can create a generic task that can be instantiated more than once. For example, a task that handles a serial port could be passed the address of a data structure that characterizes the specific port (i.e., port address and baud rate). Note that each task has its own stack space and its own (different) priority. In this example, I arbitrarily decided that COM1 is the most important port of the two.

16

```
OS_STK    *Comm1Stk[1024];
COMM_DATA  Comm1Data;              /* Data structure containing COMM port   */
                                   /* Specific data for channel 1           */


OS_STK    *Comm2Stk[1024];
COMM_DATA  Comm2Data;              /* Data structure containing COMM port   */
                                   /* Specific data for channel 2           */



void main (void)
{
    INT8U err;


    .
    OSInit();                      /* Initialize µC/OS-II                   */
    .
                                   /* Create task to manage COM1            */
    OSTaskCreate(CommTask,
                 (void *)&Comm1Data,
                 &Comm1Stk[1023],
                 25);
                                   /* Create task to manage COM2            */
    OSTaskCreate(CommTask,
                 (void *)&Comm2Data,
                 &Comm2Stk[1023],
                 26);

    .
    OSStart();                     /* Start Multitasking                    */
}



void CommTask (void *pdata)        /* Generic communication task            */
{
    for (;;) {
        .                          /* Task code                             */
        .
    }
}
```

OSTaskCreateExt()

```
INT8U OSTaskCreateExt(void (*task)(void *pd),
                      void    *pdata,
                      OS_STK  *ptos,
                      INT8U   prio,
                      INT16U  id,
                      OS_STK  *pbos,
                      INT32U  stk_size,
                      void    *pext,
                      INT16U  opt);
```

Chapter	File	Called from	Code enabled by
4	OS_TASK.C	Task or startup code	N/A

OSTaskCreateExt() creates a task to be managed by μC/OS-II. This function serves the same purpose as OSTaskCreate(), except that it allows you to specify additional information about your task to μC/OS-II. Tasks can be created either prior to the start of multitasking or by a running task. A task cannot be created by an ISR. A task must be written as an infinite loop, as shown below, and must not return. Depending on how the stack frame is built, your task has interrupts either enabled or disabled. You need to check with the processor-specific code for details. Note that the first four arguments are exactly the same as the ones for OSTaskCreate(). This was done to simplify the migration to this new and more powerful function. It is highly recommended that you use OSTaskCreateExt() instead of the older OSTaskCreate() function because it's much more flexible.

```
void Task (void *pdata)
{
    .                       /* Do something with 'pdata'           */
    for (;;) {              /* Task body, always an infinite loop. */
        .
        .

        /* Must call one of the following services:                */
        /*     OSMboxPend()                                         */
        /*     OSFlagPend()                                         */
        /*     OSMutexPend()                                        */
        /*     OSQPend()                                            */
        /*     OSSemPend()                                          */
        /*     OSTimeDly()                                          */
        /*     OSTimeDlyHMSM()                                      */
        /*     OSTaskSuspend()    (Suspend self)                    */
        /*     OSTaskDel()        (Delete  self)                    */
        .
        .

    }
}
```

16

Arguments

task   is a pointer to the task's code.

pdata   is a pointer to an optional data area, which is used to pass parameters to the task when it is created. Where the task is concerned, it thinks it is invoked and passes the argument pdata. pdata can be used to pass arguments to the task created. For example, you can create a generic task that handles an asynchronous serial port. pdata can be used to pass this task information about the serial port it has to manage: the port address, the baud rate, the number of bits, the parity, and more.

ptos   is a pointer to the task's top-of-stack. The stack is used to store local variables, function parameters, return addresses, and CPU registers during an interrupt.

The size of this stack is determined by the task's requirements and the anticipated interrupt nesting. Determining the size of the stack involves knowing how many bytes are required for storage of local variables for the task itself and all nested functions, as well as requirements for interrupts (accounting for nesting).

If the configuration constant OS_STK_GROWTH is set to 1, the stack is assumed to grow downward (i.e., from high to low memory). ptos thus needs to point to the highest *valid* memory location on the stack. If OS_STK_GROWTH is set to 0, the stack is assumed to grow in the opposite direction (i.e., from low to high memory).

prio   is the task priority. A unique priority number must be assigned to each task: the lower the number, the higher the priority (i.e., the importance) of the task.

id   is the task's ID number. At this time, the ID is not currently used in any other function and has simply been added in OSTaskCreateExt() for future expansion. You should set id to the same value as the task's priority.

pbos   is a pointer to the task's bottom-of-stack. If the configuration constant OS_STK_GROWTH is set to 1, the stack is assumed to grow downward (i.e., from high to low memory); thus, pbos must point to the lowest valid stack location. If OS_STK_GROWTH is set to 0, the stack is assumed to grow in the opposite direction (i.e., from low to high memory); thus, pbos must point to the highest valid stack location. pbos is used by the stack-checking function OSTaskStkChk().

stk_size   specifies the size of the task's stack in number of elements. If OS_STK is set to INT8U, then stk_size corresponds to the number of bytes available on the stack. If OS_STK is set to INT16U, then stk_size contains the number of 16-bit entries available on the stack. Finally, if OS_STK is set to INT32U, then stk_size contains the number of 32-bit entries available on the stack.

pext   is a pointer to a user-supplied memory location (typically a data structure) used as a TCB extension. For example, this user memory can hold the contents of floating-point registers during a context switch, the time each task takes to execute, the number of times the task is switched in, and so on.

opt   contains task-specific options. The lower 8 bits are reserved by μC/OS-II, but you can use the upper 8 bits for application-specific options. Each option consists of one or more bits. The option is selected when the bit(s) is set. The current version of μC/OS-II supports the following options:

OS_TASK_OPT_STK_CHK	specifies whether stack checking is allowed for the task.
OS_TASK_OPT_STK_CLR	specifies whether the stack needs to be cleared.
OS_TASK_OPT_SAVE_FP	specifies whether floating-point registers are saved. This option is only valid if your processor has floating-point hardware and the processor-specific code saves the floating-point registers.

Refer to uCOS_II.H for other options.

Returned Value

OSTaskCreateExt() returns one of the following error codes:

OS_NO_ERR	if the function is successful.
OS_PRIO_EXIST	if the requested priority already exists.
OS_PRIO_INVALID	if prio is higher than OS_LOWEST_PRIO.
OS_NO_MORE_TCB	if μC/OS-II doesn't have any more OS_TCBs to assign.

Notes/Warnings

1. The stack must be declared with the OS_STK type.
2. A task must always invoke one of the services provided by μC/OS-II to wait for time to expire, suspend the task, or wait an event to occur (wait on a mailbox, queue, or semaphore). This allows other tasks to gain control of the CPU.
3. You should not use task priorities 0, 1, 2, 3, OS_LOWEST_PRIO-3, OS_LOWEST_PRIO-2, OS_LOWEST_PRIO-1, and OS_LOWEST_PRIO because they are reserved for use by μC/OS-II. This leaves you with up to 56 application tasks.

16

Example 1

E1(1)   The task control block is extended using a user-defined data structure called OS_TASK_USER_DATA, which in this case contains the name of the task as well as other fields.

E1(2)   The task name is initialized with the standard library function strcpy().

E1(4)   Note that stack checking has been enabled for this task, so you are allowed to call OSTaskStkChk().

E1(3)   Also, assume here that the stack grows downward on the processor used (i.e., OS_STK_GROWTH is set to 1; TOS stands for top-of-stack and BOS stands for bottom-of-stack).

```
typedef struct {                        /*  User defined data structure */    (1)
    char    OSTaskName[20];
    INT16U  OSTaskCtr;
    INT16U  OSTaskExecTime;
    INT32U  OSTaskTotExecTime;
} OS_TASK_USER_DATA;



OS_STK              TaskStk[1024];
TASK_USER_DATA      TaskUserData;



void main (void)
{
    INT8U err;


    .
    OSInit();                              /* Initialize µC/OS-II*/
    .
    strcpy(TaskUserData.TaskName, "MyTaskName");  /* Name of task */        (2)
    err = OSTaskCreateExt(Task,
            (void *)0,
            &TaskStk[1023],                /*  Stack grows down (TOS) */    (3)


            10,
            &TaskStk[0],                   /*  Stack grows down (BOS) */    (3)
            1024,
            (void *)&TaskUserData,         /*  TCB Extension*/
            OS_TASK_OPT_STK_CHK);          /*  Stack checking enabled */    (4)

    .
    OSStart();                             /* Start Multitasking*/
}
```

```
void Task(void *pdata)
{
     pdata = pdata;                              /* Avoid compiler warning*/
     for (;;) {

          .                                      /* Task code*/

          .

     }
}
```

16

Example 2

E2(1)   Now create a task, but this time on a processor for which the stack grows upward. The Intel MCS-51 is an example of such a processor. In this case, OS_STK_GROWTH is set to 0.

E2(2)   Note that stack checking has been enabled for this task so you are allowed to call OSTaskStkChk() (TOS stands for top-of-stack and BOS stands for bottom-of-stack).

```
OS_STK *TaskStk[1024];


void main (void)
{
    INT8U err;


    .
    OSInit();                              /* Initialize µC/OS-II    */
    .
    err = OSTaskCreateExt(Task,
            (void *)0,
            &TaskStk[0],                   /*  Stack grows up (TOS)  */   (1)
            10,
            10,
            &TaskStk[1023],                /*  Stack grows up (BOS)  */   (1)
            1024,
            (void *)0,
            OS_TASK_OPT_STK_CHK);          /*  Stack checking enabled */  (2)
    .
    OSStart();                             /* Start Multitasking     */
}


void Task (void *pdata)
{
    pdata = pdata;                         /* Avoid compiler warning */
    for (;;) {
                                           /* Task code              */
        .
        .
    }
}
```

OSTaskDel()

```
INT8U OSTaskDel(INT8U prio);
```

Chapter	File	Called from	Code enabled by
4	OS_TASK.C	Task only	OS_TASK_DEL_EN

OSTaskDel() deletes a task by specifying the priority number of the task to delete. The calling task can be deleted by specifying its own priority number or OS_PRIO_SELF (if the task doesn't know its own priority number). The deleted task is returned to the dormant state. The deleted task can be re-created by calling either OSTaskCreate() or OSTaskCreateExt() to make the task active again.

Arguments

prio   is the priority number of the task to delete. You can delete the calling task by passing OS_PRIO_SELF, in which case the next highest priority task is executed.

Returned Value

OSTaskDel() returns one of the following error codes:

OS_NO_ERR	if the task doesn't delete itself.
OS_TASK_DEL_IDLE	if you try to delete the idle task, which is of course is not allowed.
OS_TASK_DEL_ERR	if the task to delete does not exist.
OS_PRIO_INVALID	if you specify a task priority higher than OS_LOWEST_PRIO.
OS_TASK_DEL_ISR	if you try to delete a task from an ISR.

Notes/Warnings

1. OSTaskDel() verifies that you are not attempting to delete the µC/OS-II idle task.

2. You must be careful when you delete a task that owns resources. Instead, consider using OSTaskDelReq() as a safer approach.

16

Example

```
void TaskX (void *pdata)
{
    INT8U err;

    for (;;) {
        .
        .
        err = OSTaskDel(10);        /* Delete task with priority 10  */
        if (err == OS_NO_ERR) {
            .                       /* Task was deleted              */
            .
        }
        .
        .
    }
}
```

OSTaskDelReq()

INT8U OSTaskDelReq(INT8U prio);

Chapter	File	Called from	Code enabled by
4	OS_TASK.C	Task only	OS_TASK_DEL_EN

OSTaskDelReq() requests that a task delete itself. Basically, use OSTaskDelReq() when you need to delete a task that can potentially own resources (e.g., the task might own a semaphore). In this case, you don't want to delete the task until the resource is released. The requesting task calls OSTaskDelReq() to indicate that the task needs to be deleted. Deletion of the task is, however, deferred to the task being deleted. In other words, the task is actually deleted when it regains control of the CPU. For example, suppose Task 10 needs to be deleted. The task wanting to delete this task (example Task 5) calls OSTaskDelReq(10). When Task 10 executes, it calls OSTaskDelReq(OS_PRIO_SELF) and monitors the return value. If the return value is OS_TASK_DEL_REQ, then Task 10 is asked to delete itself. At this point, Task 10 calls OSTaskDel(OS_PRIO_SELF). Task 5 knows whether Task 10 has been deleted by calling OSTaskDelReq(10) and checking the return code. If the return code is OS_TASK_NOT_EXIST, then Task 5 knows that Task 10 has been deleted. Task 5 might have to check periodically until OS_TASK_NOT_EXIST is returned.

Arguments

prio   is the task's priority number of the task to delete. If you specify OS_PRIO_SELF, you are asking whether another task wants the current task to be deleted.

Returned Value

OSTaskDelReq() returns one of the following error codes:

OS_NO_ERR	if the task deletion has been registered.
OS_TASK_NOT_EXIST	if the task does not exist. The requesting task can monitor this return code to see if the task is actually deleted.
OS_TASK_DEL_IDLE	if you ask to delete the idle task (which is obviously not allowed).
OS_PRIO_INVALID	if you specify a task priority higher than OS_LOWEST_PRIO or do not specify OS_PRIO_SELF.
OS_TASK_DEL_REQ	if a task (possibly another task) requests that the running task be deleted.

Notes/Warnings

1. OSTaskDelReq() verifies that you are not attempting to delete the µC/OS-II idle task.

16

Example

```
void TaskThatDeletes (void *pdata)    /* My priority is 5                    */
{
    INT8U err;


    for (;;) {
      .
      .
      err = OSTaskDelReq(10);      /* Request task #10 to delete itself */
      if (err == OS_NO_ERR) {
        while (err != OS_TASK_NOT_EXIST) {
          err = OSTaskDelReq(10);
          OSTimeDly(1);            /* Wait for task to be deleted       */
        }
        .                         /* Task #10 has been deleted          */
      }
      .
      .
    }
}


void TaskToBeDeleted (void *pdata)    /* My priority is 10                   */
{
  .
  .
  pdata = pdata;
  for (;;) {
    OSTimeDly(1);
    if (OSTaskDelReq(OS_PRIO_SELF) == OS_TASK_DEL_REQ) {
      /* Release any owned resources;                                    */
      /* De-allocate any dynamic memory;                                 */
      OSTaskDel(OS_PRIO_SELF);
    }
  }
}
```

OSTaskQuery()

```
INT8U OSTaskQuery(INT8U prio, OS_TCB *pdata);
```

Chapter	*File*	*Called from*	*Code enabled by*
4	OS_TASK.C	Task or ISR	N/A

OSTaskQuery() obtains information about a task. Your application must allocate an OS_TCB data structure to receive a snapshot of the desired task's control block. Your copy contains *every* field in the OS_TCB structure. You should be careful when accessing the contents of the OS_TCB structure, especially OSTCBNext and OSTCBPrev, because they point to the next and previous OS_TCBs in the chain of created tasks, respectively. You could use this function to provide a debugger kernel awareness.

Arguments

prio is the priority of the task from which you wish to obtain data. You can obtain information about the calling task by specifying OS_PRIO_SELF.

pdata is a pointer to a structure of type OS_TCB, which contains a copy of the task's control block.

Returned Value

OSTaskQuery() returns one of these error codes:

OS_NO_ERR if the call is successful.

OS_PRIO_ERR if you try to obtain information from an invalid task.

OS_PRIO_INVALID if you specify a priority higher than OS_LOWEST_PRIO.

Notes/Warnings

1. The fields in the task control block depend on the following configuration options (see OS_CFG.H):

    *   OS_TASK_CREATE_EN
    *   OS_Q_EN
    *   OS_FLAG_EN
    *   OS_MBOX_EN
    *   OS_SEM_EN
    *   OS_TASK_DEL_EN

16

Example

```
void Task (void *pdata)
{
    OS_TCB  task_data;
    INT8U   err;
    void    *pext;
    INT8U   status;


    pdata = pdata;
    for (;;) {
      .
      .
      err = OSTaskQuery(OS_PRIO_SELF, &task_data);
      if (err == OS_NO_ERR) {
         pext   = task_data.OSTCBExtPtr; /* Get TCB extension pointer  */
         status = task_data.OSTCBStat;   /* Get task status            */
         .
         .
      }
      .
      .
    }
}
```

OSTaskResume()

INT8U OSTaskResume(INT8U prio);

Chapter	File	Called from	Code enabled by
4	OS_TASK.C	Task only	OS_TASK_SUSPEND_EN

OSTaskResume() resumes a task suspended through the OSTaskSuspend() function. In fact, OSTaskResume() is the only function that can unsuspend a suspended task.

Arguments

prio   specifies the priority of the task to resume.

Returned Value

OSTaskResume() returns one of the these error codes:

OS_NO_ERR	if the call is successful.
OS_TASK_RESUME_PRIO	if the task you are attempting to resume does not exist.
OS_TASK_NOT_SUSPENDED	if the task to resume has not been suspended.
OS_PRIO_INVALID	if prio is higher or equal to OS_LOWEST_PRIO.

Notes/Warnings

Example

```
void TaskX (void *pdata)
{
    INT8U err;


    for (;;) {
        .

        .
        err = OSTaskResume(10);          /* Resume task with priority 10    */
        if (err == OS_NO_ERR) {
                                         /* Task was resumed                */
            .

            .
        }
        .

        .
    }
}
```

16

OSTaskStkChk()

INT8U OSTaskStkChk(INT8U prio, OS_STK_DATA *pdata);

Chapter	File	Called from	Code enabled by
4	OS_TASK.C	Task code	OS_TASK_CREATE_EXT

OSTaskStkChk() determines a task's stack statistics. Specifically, it computes the amount of free stack space, as well as the amount of stack space used by the specified task. This function requires that the task be created with OSTaskCreateExt() and that you specify OS_TASK_OPT_STK_CHK in the opt argument.

Stack sizing is done by walking from the bottom of the stack and counting the number of 0 entries on the stack until a nonzero value is found. Of course, this assumes that the stack is cleared when the task is created. For that purpose, you need to set OS_TASK_OPT_STK_CLR to 1 as an option when you create the task. You could set OS_TASK_OPT_STK_CLR to 0 if your startup code clears all RAM and you never delete your tasks. This reduces the execution time of OSTaskCreateExt().

Arguments

prio   is the priority of the task about which you want to obtain stack information. You can check the stack of the calling task by passing OS_PRIO_SELF.

pdata   is a pointer to a variable of type OS_STK_DATA, which contains the following fields:

```
    INT32U OSFree;      /* Number of bytes free on the stack      */
    INT32U OSUsed;      /* Number of bytes used on the stack      */
```

Returned Value

OSTaskStkChk() returns one of the these error codes:

OS_NO_ERR   if you specify valid arguments and the call is successful.

OS_PRIO_INVALID   if you specify a task priority higher than OS_LOWEST_PRIO or you don't specify OS_PRIO_SELF.

OS_TASK_NOT_EXIST   if the specified task does not exist.

OS_TASK_OPT_ERR   if you do not specify OS_TASK_OPT_STK_CHK when the task was created by OSTaskCreateExt() or if you create the task by using OSTaskCreate().

Notes/Warnings

1. Execution time of this task depends on the size of the task's stack and is thus nondeterministic.

2. Your application can determine the total task stack space (in number of bytes) by adding the two fields .OSFree and .OSUsed of the OS_STK_DATA data structure.

3. Technically, this function can be called by an ISR, but because of the possibly long execution time, it is not advisable.

Example

```
void Task (void *pdata)
{
    OS_STK_DATA stk_data;
    INT32U      stk_size;


    for (;;) {
        .
        .
        err = OSTaskStkChk(10, &stk_data);
        if (err == OS_NO_ERR) {
            stk_size = stk_data.OSFree + stk_data.OSUsed;
        }
        .
        .
    }
}
```

16

OSTaskSuspend()

`INT8U OSTaskSuspend(INT8U prio);`

Chapter	File	Called from	Code enabled by
4	OS_TASK.C	Task only	OS_TASK_SUSPEND_EN

OSTaskSuspend() suspends (or blocks) execution of a task unconditionally. The calling task can be suspended by specifying its own priority number or OS_PRIO_SELF if the task doesn't know its own priority number. In this case, another task needs to resume the suspended task. If the current task is suspended, rescheduling occurs, and µC/OS-II runs the next highest priority task ready to run. The only way to resume a suspended task is to call OSTaskResume().

Task suspension is additive, which means that if the task being suspended is delayed until *n* ticks expire, the task is resumed only when both the time expires and the suspension is removed. Also, if the suspended task is waiting for a semaphore and the semaphore is signaled, the task is removed from the semaphore-wait list (if it is the highest priority task waiting for the semaphore), but execution is not resumed until the suspension is removed.

Arguments

prio   specifies the priority of the task to suspend. You can suspend the calling task by passing OS_PRIO_SELF, in which case, the next highest priority task is executed.

Returned Value

OSTaskSuspend() returns one of the these error codes:

OS_NO_ERR	if the call is successful.
OS_TASK_SUSPEND_IDLE	if you attempt to suspend the µC/OS-II idle task, which is not allowed.
OS_PRIO_INVALID	if you specify a priority higher than the maximum allowed (i.e., you specify a priority of OS_LOWEST_PRIO or more) or you don't specify OS_PRIO_SELF.
OS_TASK_SUSPEND_PRIO	if the task you are attempting to suspend does not exist.

Notes/Warnings

1.   OSTaskSuspend() and OSTaskResume() must be used in pairs.

2.   A suspended task can only be resumed by OSTaskResume().

Example

```
void TaskX (void *pdata)
{
    INT8U err;


    for (;;) {
       .
       .
       err = OSTaskSuspend(OS_PRIO_SELF);      /* Suspend current task      */
       .                       /* Execution continues when ANOTHER task ..  */
       .                       /* .. explicitly resumes this task.          */
       .

    }
}
```

16

OSTimeDly()

```
void OSTimeDly(INT16U ticks);
```

Chapter	File	Called from	Code enabled by
5	OS_TIME.C	Task only	N/A

OSTimeDly() allows a task to delay itself for an integral number of clock ticks. Rescheduling always occurs when the number of clock ticks is greater than zero. Valid delays range from one to 65,535 ticks. A delay of 0 means that the task is not delayed, and OSTimeDly() returns immediately to the caller. The actual delay time depends on the tick rate (see OS_TICKS_PER_SEC in the configuration file OS_CFG.H).

Arguments

ticks   is the number of clock ticks to delay the current task.

Returned Value

Notes/Warnings

1. Note that calling this function with a value of 0 results in no delay, and the function returns immediately to the caller.

2. To ensure that a task delays for the specified number of ticks, you should consider using a delay value that is one tick higher. For example, to delay a task for at least 10 ticks, you should specify a value of 11.

Example

```
void TaskX (void *pdata)
{
    for (;;) {
        .
        .
        OSTimeDly(10);                 /* Delay task for 10 clock ticks */
        .
        .
    }
}
```

OSTimeDlyHMSM()

`void OSTimeDlyHMSM (INT8U hours, INT8U minutes, INT8U seconds, INT8U milli);`

Chapter	File	Called from	Code enabled by
5	OS_TIME.C	Task only	N/A

OSTimeDlyHMSM() allows a task to delay itself for a user-specified amount of time specified in hours, minutes, seconds, and milliseconds. This format is more convenient and natural than ticks. Rescheduling always occurs when at least one of the parameters is nonzero.

Arguments

hours   is the number of hours the task is delayed. The valid range of values is 0 to 255.

minutes   is the number of minutes the task is delayed. The valid range of values is 0 to 59.

seconds   is the number of seconds the task is delayed. The valid range of values is 0 to 59.

milli   is the number of milliseconds the task is delayed. The valid range of values is 0 to 999. Note that the resolution of this argument is in multiples of the tick rate. For instance, if the tick rate is set to 100Hz, a delay of 4ms results in no delay. The delay is rounded to the nearest tick. Thus, a delay of 15ms actually results in a delay of 20ms.

Returned Value

OSTimeDlyHMSM() returns one of the these error codes:

OS_NO_ERR   if you specify valid arguments and the call is successful.

OS_TIME_INVALID_MINUTES   if the minutes argument is greater than 59.

OS_TIME_INVALID_SECONDS   if the seconds argument is greater than 59.

OS_TIME_INVALID_MILLI   if the milliseconds argument is greater than 999.

OS_TIME_ZERO_DLY   if all four arguments are 0.

Notes/Warnings

1. Note that OSTimeDlyHMSM(0,0,0,0) (i.e., hours, minutes, seconds, milliseconds) results in no delay, and the function returns to the caller. Also, if the total delay time is longer than 65,535 clock ticks, you cannot abort the delay and resume the task by calling OSTimeDlyResume().

16

Example

```
void TaskX (void *pdata)
{
    for (;;) {
        .
        .
        OSTimeDlyHMSM(0, 0, 1, 0);  /* Delay task for 1 second */
        .
        .
    }
}
```

OSTimeDlyResume()

`INT8U OSTimeDlyResume(INT8U prio);`

Chapter	File	Called from	Code enabled by
5	OS_TIME.C	Task only	N/A

OSTimeDlyResume() resumes a task that has been delayed through a call to either OSTimeDly() or OSTimeDlyHMSM().

Arguments

prio   specifies the priority of the task to resume.

Returned Value

OSTimeDlyResume() returns one of the these error codes:

OS_NO_ERR	if the call is successful.
OS_PRIO_INVALID	if you specify a task priority greater than OS_LOWEST_PRIO.
OS_TIME_NOT_DLY	if the task is not waiting for time to expire.
OS_TASK_NOT_EXIST	if the task has not been created.

Notes/Warnings

1. Note that you must not call this function to resume a task that is waiting for an event with timeout. This situation makes the task look like a timeout occurred (unless you desire this effect).

2. You cannot resume a task that has called OSTimeDlyHMSM() with a combined time that exceeds 65,535 clock ticks. In other words, if the clock tick runs at 100Hz, you cannot resume a delayed task that called OSTimeDlyHMSM(0, 10, 55, 350) or higher.

   `(10 minutes * 60 + (55 + 0.35) seconds) * 100 ticks/second`

Example

```
void TaskX (void *pdata)
{
   INT8U err;

   pdata = pdata;
   for (;;) {
      .
      err = OSTimeDlyResume(10);        /* Resume task with priority 10    */
      if (err == OS_NO_ERR) {
                                        /* Task was resumed                */
         .
         .
      }
      .
   }
}
```

16

OSTimeGet()

```
INT32U OSTimeGet(void);
```

Chapter	File	Called from	Code enabled by
5	OS_TIME.C	Task or ISR	N/A

OSTimeGet() obtains the current value of the system clock. The system clock is a 32-bit counter that counts the number of clock ticks since power was applied or since the system clock was last set.

Arguments

Returned Value

The current system clock value (in number of ticks).

Notes/Warnings

Example

```
void TaskX (void *pdata)
{
    INT32U clk;


    for (;;) {
        .
        .
        clk = OSTimeGet();  /* Get current value of system clock */
        .
        .
    }
}
```

OSTimeSet()

```
void OSTimeSet(INT32U ticks);
```

Chapter	File	Called from	Code enabled by
5	OS_TIME.C	Task or ISR	N/A

OSTimeSet() sets the system clock. The system clock is a 32-bit counter that counts the number of clock ticks since power was applied or since the system clock was last set.

Arguments

ticks is the desired value for the system clock, in ticks.

Returned Value

Notes/Warnings

Example

```c
void TaskX (void *pdata)
{
    for (;;) {
        .
        .
        OSTimeSet(0L);      /* Reset the system clock  */
        .
        .
    }
}
```

16

OSTimeTick()

void OSTimeTick(void);

Chapter	File	Called from	Code enabled by
5	OS_TIME.C	Task or ISR	N/A

OSTimeTick() processes a clock tick. µC/OS-II checks all tasks to see if they are either waiting for time to expire [because they called OSTimeDly() or OSTimeDlyHMSM()] or waiting for events to occur until they timeout.

Arguments

Returned Value

Notes/Warnings

1. The execution time of OSTimeTick() is directly proportional to the number of tasks created in an application. OSTimeTick() can be called by either an ISR or a task. If called by a task, the task priority should be very high (i.e., have a low priority number) because this function is responsible for updating delays and timeouts.

Example

(Intel 80x86, real mode, large model)

```
_OSTickISR PROC FAR
           PUSHA                                 ; Save processor context
           PUSH ES
           PUSH DS
;
           MOV     AX, SEG(_OSIntNesting)        ; Reload DS
           MOV     DS, AX
           INC     BYTE PTR DS:_OSIntNesting     ; Notify uC/OS-II of ISR
;
           CMP     BYTE PTR DS:_OSIntNesting, 1  ; if (OSIntNesting == 1)
           JNE     SHORT _OSTickISR1
           MOV     AX, SEG(_OSTCBCur)            ;     Reload DS
           MOV     DS, AX
           LES     BX, DWORD PTR DS:_OSTCBCur    ;     OSTCBCur->OSTCBStkPtr = SS:SP
           MOV     ES:[BX+2], SS                 ;
           MOV     ES:[BX+0], SP                 ;
           CALL  FAR  PTR  _OSTimeTick           ; Process clock tick
           .                                     ; User Code to clear interrupt
           .
           CALL FAR PTR _OSIntExit               ; Notify _C/OS-II of end of ISR
           POP   DS                              ; Restore processor registers
           POP   ES
           POPA
;
           IRET                                  ; Return to interrupted task
_OSTickISR ENDP
```

16

OSVersion()

```
INT16U OSVersion(void);
```

Chapter	File	Called from	Code enabled by
3	OS_CORE.C	Task or ISR	N/A

OSVersion() obtains the current version of µC/OS-II.

Arguments

Returned Value

The version is returned as *x.yy* multiplied by 100. For example, v2.52 is returned as 252.

Notes/Warnings

Example

```c
void TaskX (void *pdata)
{
    INT16U os_version;


    for (;;) {
        .
        .
        os_version = OSVersion();  /* Obtain µC/OS-II's version   */
        .
        .
    }
}
```

μC/OS-II Configuration Manual

This chapter provides a description of the configurable elements of μC/OS-II. Because μC/OS-II is provided in source form, configuration is done through a number of #define constants, which are found in OS_CFG.H and should exist for each project/product that you develop. In other words, configuration is done via conditional compilation.

This section describes each of the #define constants in OS_CFG.H.

17.00 Miscellaneous

OS_ARG_CHK_EN

OS_ARG_CHK_EN indicates whether you want most of μC/OS-II functions to perform argument checking. When set to 1, μC/OS-II will ensure that pointers passed to functions are non-NULL, that arguments passed are within allowable range and more. OS_ARG_CHK_EN was added to reduce the amount of code space and processing time required by μC/OS-II. Set OS_ARG_CHK_EN to 0 if you must reduce code space to a minimum. In general, you should always enable argument checking and thus set OS_ARG_CHK_EN to 1.

OS_CPU_HOOKS_EN

OS_CPU_HOOKS_EN indicates whether OS_CPU_C.C declares the hook function (when set to 1) or not (when set to 0). Recall that μC/OS-II expects the presence of nine functions that can be defined either in the port (i.e., in OS_CPU_C.C) or by the application code. These functions are

OSInitHookBegin()	OSTaskStatHook()
OSInitHookEnd()	OSTaskSwHook()
OSTaskCreateHook()	OSTCBInitHook()
OSTaskDelHook()	OSTimeTickHook()
OSTaskIdleHook()	

513

OS_LOWEST_PRIO

OS_LOWEST_PRIO specifies the lowest task priority (i.e., highest number) that you intend to use in your application and is provided to reduce the amount of RAM needed by µC/OS-II. Remember that µC/OS-II priorities can go from 0 (highest priority) to a maximum of 63 (lowest possible priority). Setting OS_LOWEST_PRIO to a value less than 63 means that your application cannot create tasks with a priority number higher than OS_LOWEST_PRIO. In fact, µC/OS-II reserves priorities OS_LOWEST_PRIO and OS_LOWEST_PRIO-1 for itself; OS_LOWEST_PRIO is reserved for the idle task, OS_TaskIdle(), and OS_LOWEST_PRIO-1 is reserved for the statistic task, OS_TaskStat(). The priorities of your application tasks can thus take a value between 0 and OS_LOWEST_PRIO-2 (inclusive). The lowest task priority specified by OS_LOWEST_PRIO is independent of OS_MAX_TASKS. For example, you can set OS_MAX_TASKS to 10 and OS_LOWEST_PRIO to 32 and have up to 10 application tasks, each of which can have a task priority value between 0 and 30 (inclusive). Note that each task must still have a different priority value. You must always set OS_LOWEST_PRIO to a value greater than the number of application tasks in your system. For example, if you set OS_MAX_TASKS to 20 and OS_LOWEST_PRIO to 10, you can not create more than eight application tasks (0, ... , 7). You are simply wasting RAM.

OS_MAX_EVENTS

OS_MAX_EVENTS specifies the maximum number of event control blocks that can be allocated. An event control block is needed for every message mailbox, message queue, mutual exclusion semaphore, or semaphore object. For example, if you have 10 mailboxes, five queues, four mutexes, and three semaphores, you must set OS_MAX_EVENTS to at least 22. OS_MAX_EVENTS must be greater than 0. See also OS_MBOX_EN, OS_Q_EN, OS_MUTEX_EN, and OS_SEM_EN.

OS_MAX_FLAGS

OS_MAX_FLAGS specifies the maximum number of event flags that you need in your application. OS_MAX_FLAGS must be greater than 0. To use event-flag services, you also need to set OS_FLAG_EN to 1.

OS_MAX_MEM_PART

OS_MAX_MEM_PART specifies the maximum number of memory partitions that can be managed by the memory-partition manager found in OS_MEM.C. To use a memory partition, however, you also need to set OS_MEM_EN to 1. If you intend to use memory partitions, OS_MAX_MEM_PART must be greater than 0. In other words, you are allowed to only have one memory partition.

OS_MAX_QS

OS_MAX_QS specifies the maximum number of message queues that your application can create. To use message-queue services, you also need to set OS_Q_EN to 1. OS_MAX_QS must be greater than 0. In other words, you are allowed to only have one message queue.

OS_MAX_TASKS

OS_MAX_TASKS specifies the maximum number of *application* tasks that can exist in your application. Note that OS_MAX_TASKS cannot be greater than 62 because µC/OS-II currently reserves two tasks for itself (see OS_N_SYS_TASKS in uCOS_II.H). If you set OS_MAX_TASKS to the exact number of tasks in your system, you need to make sure that you revise this value when you add additional tasks. Conversely, if you make OS_MAX_TASKS much higher than your current task requirements (for future expansion), you are wasting valuable RAM. If RAM is not a problem for your product, you should set OS_MAX_TASKS to 62.

OS_TASK_IDLE_STK_SIZE

OS_TASK_IDLE_STK_SIZE specifies the size of the µC/OS-II idle-task stack. The size is specified not in bytes but in number of elements. This is because a stack is declared to be of type OS_STK. The size of the idle-task stack depends on the processor you are using and the deepest anticipated interrupt-nesting level. Very little is being done in the idle task, but you should allow at least enough space to store all processor registers on the stack and enough storage to handle all nested interrupts.

OS_TASK_STAT_EN

OS_TASK_STAT_EN specifies whether or not you can enable the µC/OS-II statistic task, as well as its initialization function. When set to 1, the statistic task OS_TaskStat() and the statistic-task-initialization function are enabled. OS_TaskStat() computes the CPU usage of your application. When enabled, it executes every second and computes the 8-bit variable OSCPUUsage, which provides the percentage of CPU use of your application. OS_TaskStat() calls OSTaskStatHook() every time it executes so that you can add your own statistics as needed. See OS_CORE.C for details on the statistic task. The priority of OS_TaskStat() is always set to OS_LOWEST_PRIO-1.

    The global variables OSCPUUsage, OSIdleCtrMax, OSIdleCtrRun, OSTaskStatStk[], and OSStatRdy are not declared when OS_TASK_STAT_EN is set to 0, which reduces the amount of RAM needed by µC/OS-II if you don't intend to use the statistic task. OSIdleCtrRun contains a snapshot of OSIdleCtr just before OSIdleCtr is cleared to zero every second. OSIdleCtrRun is not used by µC/OS-II for any other purpose. However, you can read and display OSIdleCtrRun if needed.

OS_TASK_STAT_STK_SIZE

OS_TASK_STAT_STK_SIZE specifies the size of the µC/OS-II statistic-task stack. The size is specified not in bytes but in number of elements. This is because a stack is declared as being of type OS_STK. The size of the statistic-task stack depends on the processor you are using and the maximum of the following actions:

- The stack growth associated with performing 32-bit arithmetic (subtraction and division)
- The stack growth associated with calling OSTimeDly()
- The stack growth associated with calling OSTaskStatHook()
- The deepest anticipated interrupt-nesting level

    If you want to run stack checking on this task and determine its actual stack requirements, you must enable code generation for OSTaskCreateExt() by setting OS_TASK_CREATE_EXT_EN to 1. Again, the priority of OS_TaskStat() is always set to OS_LOWEST_PRIO-1.

OS_SHED_LOCK_EN

This constant enables (when set to 1) or disables (when set to 0) code generation for the two functions OSShedLock() and OSShedUnlock().

OS_TICKS_PER_SEC

OS_TICKS_PER_SEC specifies the rate at which you call OSTimeTick(). It is up to your initialization code to ensure that OSTimeTick() is invoked at this rate. This constant is used by OSStatInit(), OS_TaskStat(), and OSTimeDlyHMSM().

17.01 Event Flags

OS_FLAG_EN

OS_FLAG_EN enables (when set to 1) or disables (when set to 0) code generation of **all** the event-flag services and data structures, which reduces the amount of code and data space needed when your application does not require the use of event flags. When OS_FLAG_EN is set to 0, you do not need to enable or disable any of the other #define constants in this section.

OS_FLAG_WAIT_CLR_EN

OS_FLAG_WAIT_CLR_EN enables (when set to 1) or disables (when set to 0) the code generation used to wait for event flags to be 0 instead of 1. Generally, you want to wait for event flags to be set. However, you might also want to wait for event flags to be clear, and thus you need to enable this option.

OS_FLAG_ACCEPT_EN

OS_FLAG_ACCEPT_EN enables (when set to 1) or disables (when set to 0) the code generation of the function OSFlagAccept().

OS_FLAG_DEL_EN

OS_FLAG_DEL_EN enables (when set to 1) or disables (when set to 0) the code generation of the function OSFlagDel().

OS_FLAG_QUERY_EN

OS_FLAG_QUERY_EN enables (when set to 1) or disables (when set to 0) the code generation of the function OSFlagQuery().

17.02 Message Mailboxes

OS_MBOX_EN

This constant enables (when set to 1) or disables (when set to 0) the code generation of **all** message-mailbox services and data structures, which reduces the amount of code space needed when your application does not require the use of message mailboxes. When OS_MBOX_EN is set to 0, you do not need to enable or disable any of the other #define constants in this section.

OS_MBOX_ACCEPT_EN

This constant enables (when set to 1) or disables (when set to 0) the code generation of the function OSMboxAccept().

OS_MBOX_DEL_EN

This constant enables (when set to 1) or disables (when set to 0) the code generation of the function `OSMboxDel()`.

OS_MBOX_POST_EN

`OS_MBOX_POST_EN` enables (when set to 1) or disables (when set to 0) the code generation of the function `OSMboxPost()`. You can disable code generation for this function if you decide to use the more powerful function `OSMboxPostOpt()` instead.

OS_MBOX_POST_OPT_EN

`OS_MBOX_POST_OPT_EN` enables (when set to 1) or disables (when set to 0) the code generation of the function `OSMboxPostOpt()`. You can disable code generation for this function if you do not need the additional functionality provided by `OSMboxPostOpt()`. `OSMboxPost()` generates less code.

OS_MBOX_QUERY_EN

`OS_MBOX_QUERY_EN` enables (when set to 1) or disables (when set to 0) the code generation of the function `OSMboxQuery()`.

17.03 Memory Management

OS_MEM_EN

`OS_MEM_EN` enables (when set to 1) or disables (when set to 0) **all** code generation of the µC/OS-II partition-memory manager and its associated data structures. This feature reduces the amount of code and data space needed when your application does not require the use of memory partitions.

OS_MEM_QUERY_EN

`OS_MEM_QUERY_EN` enables (when set to 1) or disables (when set to 0) the code generation of the function `OSMemQuery()`.

17.04 Mutual Exclusion Semaphores

OS_MUTEX_EN

`OS_MUTEX_EN` enables (when set to 1) or disables (when set to 0) the code generation of **all** mutual-exclusion-semaphore services and data structures, which reduces the amount of code and data space needed when your application does not require the use of mutexes. When `OS_MUTEX_EN` is set to 0, you do not need to enable or disable any of the other #define constants in this section.

OS_MUTEX_ACCEPT_EN

`OS_MUTEX_ACCEPT_EN` enables (when set to 1) or disables (when set to 0) the code generation of the function `OSMutexAccept()`.

OS_MUTEX_DEL_EN

OS_MUTEX_DEL_EN enables (when set to 1) or disables (when set to 0) the code generation of the function OSMutexDel().

OS_MUTEX_QUERY_EN

OS_MUTEX_QUERY_EN enables (when set to 1) or disables (when set to 0) the code generation of the function OSMutexQuery().

17.05 Message Queues

OS_Q_EN

OS_Q_EN enables (when set to 1) or disables (when set to 0) the code generation of **all** message-queue services and data structures, which reduces the amount of code space needed when your application does not require the use of message queues. When OS_Q_EN is set to 0, you do not need to enable or disable any of the other #define constants in this section. Note that if OS_Q_EN is set to 0, the #define constant OS_MAX_QS is irrelevant.

OS_Q_ACCEPT_EN

OS_Q_ACCEPT_EN enables (when set to 1) or disables (when set to 0) the code generation of the function OSQAccept().

OS_Q_DEL_EN

OS_Q_DEL_EN enables (when set to 1) or disables (when set to 0) the code generation of the function OSQDel().

OS_Q_FLUSH_EN

OS_Q_FLUSH_EN enables (when set to 1) or disables (when set to 0) the code generation of the function OSQFlush().

OS_Q_POST_EN

OS_Q_POST_EN enables (when set to 1) or disables (when set to 0) the code generation of the function OSQPost(). You can disable code generation for this function if you decide to use the more powerful function OSQPostOpt() instead.

OS_Q_POST_FRONT_EN

OS_Q_POST_FRONT_EN enables (when set to 1) or disables (when set to 0) the code generation of the function OSQPostFront(). You can disable code generation for this function if you decide to use the more powerful function OSQPostOpt() instead.

OS_Q_POST_OPT_EN

OS_Q_POST_OPT_EN enables (when set to 1) or disables (when set to 0) the code generation of the function OSQPostOpt(). You can disable code generation for this function if you do not need the additional functionality provided by OSQPostOpt(). OSQPost() generates less code.

OS_Q_QUERY_EN

OS_Q_QUERY_EN enables (when set to 1) or disables (when set to 0) the code generation of the function OSQQuery().

17.06 Semaphores

OS_SEM_EN

OS_SEM_EN enables (when set to 1) or disables (when set to 0) **all** code generation of the µC/OS-II semaphore manager and its associated data structures, which reduces the amount of code and data space needed when your application does not require the use of semaphores. When OS_SEM_EN is set to 0, you do not need to enable or disable any of the other #define constants in this section.

OS_SEM_ACCEPT_EN

OS_SEM ACCEPT_EN enables (when set to 1) or disables (when set to 0) the code generation of the function OSSemAccept().

OS_SEM_DEL_EN

OS_SEM_DEL_EN enables (when set to 1) or disables (when set to 0) the code generation of the function OSSemDel().

OS_SEM_QUERY_EN

OS_SEM_QUERY_EN enables (when set to 1) or disables (when set to 0) the code generation of the function OSSemQuery().

17.07 Task Management

OS_TASK_CHANGE_PRIO_EN

OS_TASK_CHANGE_PRIO_EN enables (when set to 1) or disables (when set to 0) the code generation of the function OSTaskChangePrio(). If your application never changes task priorities after they are assigned, you can reduce the amount of code space used by µC/OS-II by setting OS_TASK_CHANGE_PRIO_EN to 0.

OS_TASK_CREATE_EN

OS_TASK_CREATE_EN enables (when set to 1) or disables (when set to 0) the code generation of the OSTaskCreate() function. Enabling this function makes µC/OS-II backward compatible with the µC/OS task-creation function. If your application always uses OSTaskCreateExt() (recommended), you can reduce the amount of code space used by µC/OS-II by setting OS_TASK_CREATE_EN to 0. Note that you must set at least OS_TASK_CREATE_EN or OS_TASK_CREATE_EXT_EN to 1. If you wish, you can use both.

OS_TASK_CREATE_EXT_EN

OS_TASK_CREATE_EN enables (when set to 1) or disables (when set to 0) the code generation of the function OSTaskCreateExt(), which is the extended, more powerful version of the two task-creation functions. If your application never uses OSTaskCreateExt(), you can reduce the amount of code space used by μC/OS-II by setting OS_TASK_CREATE_EXT_EN to 0. Note that you need the extended task-create function to use the stack-checking function OSTaskStkChk().

OS_TASK_DEL_EN

OS_TASK_DEL_EN enables (when set to 1) or disables (when set to 0) code generation of the function OSTaskDel(), which deletes tasks. If your application never uses this function, you can reduce the amount of code space used by μC/OS-II by setting OS_TASK_DEL_EN to 0.

OS_TASK_SUSPEND_EN

OS_TASK_SUSPEND_EN enables (when set to 1) or disables (when set to 0) code generation of the functions OSTaskSuspend() and OSTaskResume(), which allows you to explicitly suspend and resume tasks, respectively. If your application never uses these functions, you can reduce the amount of code space used by μC/OS-II by setting OS_TASK_SUSPEND_EN to 0.

OS_TASK_QUERY_EN

OS_TASK_QUERY_EN enables (when set to 1) or disables (when set to 0) code generation of the function OSTaskQuery(). If your application never uses this function, you can reduce the amount of code space used by μC/OS-II by setting OS_TASK_QUERY_EN to 0.

17.08 Time Management

OS_TIME_DLY_HMSM_EN

OS_TIME_DLY_HMSM_EN enables (when set to 1) or disables (when set to 0) the code generation of the function OSTimeDlyHMSM(), which is used to delay a task for a specified number of hours, minutes, seconds, and milliseconds.

OS_TIME_DLY_RESUME_EN

OS_TIME_DLY_RESUME_EN enables (when set to 1) or disables (when set to 0) the code generation of the function OSTimeDlyResume().

OS_TIME_GET_SET_EN

OS_TIME_GET_SET_EN enables (when set to 1) or disables (when set to 0) the code and data generation of the functions OSTimeGet() and OSTimeSet(). If you don't need to use the 32-bit tick counter OSTime, then you can save yourself 4 bytes of data space and code space by not having the code for these functions generated by the compiler.

17.09 Function Summary

Table 17.1 lists each μC/OS-II function by type (**Service**), indicates which variables enable the code (**Set to** 1), and lists other configuration constants that affect the function (**Other Constants**).

Of course, OS_CFG.H must be included when μC/OS-II is built, in order for the desired configuration to take effect.

Table 17.1 *µC/OS-II functions and* #define *configuration constants.*

17

Service	Set to 1	Other Constants
Miscellaneous		
OSInit()	N/A	OS_MAX_EVENTS OS_Q_EN and OS_MAX_QS OS_MEM_EN OS_TASK_IDLE_STK_SIZE OS_TASK_STAT_EN OS_TASK_STAT_STK_SIZE
OSSchedLock()	OS_SCHED_LOCK_EN	N/A
OSSchedUnlock()	OS_SCHED_LOCK_EN	N/A
OSStart()	N/A	N/A
OSStatInit()	OS_TASK_STAT_EN && OS_TASK_CREATE_EXT_EN	OS_TICKS_PER_SEC
OSVersion()	N/A	N/A
Interrupt Management		
OSIntEnter()	N/A	N/A
OSIntExit()	N/A	N/A
Event Flags		
OSFlagAccept()	OS_FLAG_EN	OS_FLAG_ACCEPT_EN
OSFlagCreate()	OS_FLAG_EN	OS_MAX_FLAGS
OSFlagDel()	OS_FLAG_EN	OS_FLAG_DEL_EN
OSFlagPend()	OS_FLAG_EN	OS_FLAG_WAIT_CLR_EN
OSFlagPost()	OS_FLAG_EN	N/A
OSFlagQuery()	OS_FLAG_EN	OS_FLAG_QUERY_EN
Message Mailboxes		
OSMboxAccept()	OS_MBOX_EN	OS_MBOX_ACCEPT_EN
OSMboxCreate()	OS_MBOX_EN	OS_MAX_EVENTS
OSMboxDel()	OS_MBOX_EN	OS_MBOX_DEL_EN
OSMboxPend()	OS_MBOX_EN	N/A
OSMboxPost()	OS_MBOX_EN	OS_MBOX_POST_EN
OSMboxPostOpt()	OS_MBOX_EN	OS_MBOX_POST_OPT_EN
OSMboxQuery()	OS_MBOX_EN	OS_MBOX_QUERY_EN
Memory Partition Management		
OSMemCreate()	OS_MEM_EN	OS_MAX_MEM_PART
OSMemGet()	OS_MEM_EN	N/A
OSMemPut()	OS_MEM_EN	N/A
OSMemQuery()	OS_MEM_EN	OS_MEM_QUERY_EN

Table 17.1   *µC/OS-II functions and* #define *configuration constants. (Continued)*

Service	Set to 1	Other Constants
Mutex Management		
OSMutexAccept()	OS_MUTEX_EN	OS_MUTEX_ACCEPT_EN
OSMutexCreate()	OS_MUTEX_EN	OS_MAX_EVENTS
OSMutexDel()	OS_MUTEX_EN	OS_MUTEX_DEL_EN
OSMutexPend()	OS_MUTEX_EN	N/A
OSMutexPost()	OS_MUTEX_EN	N/A
OSMutexQuery()	OS_MUTEX_EN	OS_MUTEX_QUERY_EN
Message Queues		
OSQAccept()	OS_Q_EN	OS_Q_ACCEPT_EN
OSQCreate()	OS_Q_EN	OS_MAX_EVENTS OS_MAX_QS
OSQDel()	OS_Q_EN	OS_Q_DEL_EN
OSQFlush()	OS_Q_EN	OS_Q_FLUSH_EN
OSQPend()	OS_Q_EN	N/A
OSQPost()	OS_Q_EN	OS_Q_POST_EN
OSQPostFront()	OS_Q_EN	OS_Q_POST_FRONT_EN
OSQPostOpt()	OS_Q_EN	OS_Q_POST_OPT_EN
OSQQuery()	OS_Q_EN	OS_Q_QUERY_EN
Semaphore Management		
OSSemAccept()	OS_SEM_EN	OS_SEM_ACCEPT_EN
OSSemCreate()	OS_SEM_EN	OS_MAX_EVENTS
OSSemDel()	OS_SEM_EN	OS_SEM_DEL_EN
OSSemPend()	OS_SEM_EN	N/A
OSSemPost()	OS_SEM_EN	N/A
OSSemQuery()	OS_SEM_EN	OS_SEM_QUERY_EN
Task Management		
OSTaskChangePrio()	OS_TASK_CHANGE_PRIO_EN	OS_LOWEST_PRIO
OSTaskCreate()	OS_TASK_CREATE_EN	OS_MAX_TASKS
OSTaskCreateExt()	OS_TASK_CREATE_EXT_EN	OS_MAX_TASKS OS_TASK_STK_CLR
OSTaskDel()	OS_TASK_DEL_EN	OS_MAX_TASKS
OSTaskDelReq()	OS_TASK_DEL_EN	OS_MAX_TASKS
OSTaskResume()	OS_TASK_SUSPEND_EN	OS_MAX_TASKS
OSTaskStkChk()	OS_TASK_CREATE_EXT_EN	OS_MAX_TASKS
OSTaskSuspend()	OS_TASK_SUSPEND_EN	OS_MAX_TASKS
OSTaskQuery()	OS_TASK_QUERY_EN	OS_MAX_TASKS

Table 17.1   *µC/OS-II functions and #define configuration constants. (Continued)*

Service	Set to 1	Other Constants
Time Management		
OSTimeDly()	N/A	N/A
OSTimeDlyHMSM()	OS_TIME_DLY_HMSM_EN	OS_TICKS_PER_SEC
OSTimeDlyResume()	OS_TIME_DLY_RESUME_EN	OS_MAX_TASKS
OSTimeGet()	OS_TIME_GET_SET_EN	N/A
OSTimeSet()	OS_TIME_GET_SET_EN	N/A
OSTimeTick()	N/A	N/A
User-Defined Functions		
OSTaskCreateHook()	OS_CPU_HOOKS_EN	N/A
OSTaskDelHook()	OS_CPU_HOOKS_EN	N/A
OSTaskStatHook()	OS_CPU_HOOKS_EN	N/A
OSTaskSwHook()	OS_CPU_HOOKS_EN	N/A
OSTimeTickHook()	OS_CPU_HOOKS_EN	N/A

17

PC Services

The code in this book was tested on a PC. It was convenient to create a number of services (i.e., functions) to access some of the capabilities of a PC. These services are invoked from the test code and are encapsulated in a file called PC.C. The functions provided in this chapter could be of some use to you, because industrial PCs are so popular as embedded systems platforms. These services assume that you are running under DOS or a DOS box under Microsoft Windows 95, 98, NT, or 2000. You should note that under these environments, you have an emulated DOS (i.e., a virtual x86 session) and not an actual one. The behavior of some functions might be altered because of this.

The files PC.C and PC.H are found in the \SOFTWARE\BLOCKS\PC\BC45 directory. These functions encapsulate services that are available on a PC. Encapsulation allows you to easily adapt the code to a different compiler. PC.C basically contains three types of services: character-based display, elapsed-time measurement, and miscellaneous. All functions start with the prefix PC_.

18.00 Character-Based Display

PC.C provides services to display ASCII (and special) characters on a PC's VGA display. In normal mode (i.e., character mode), a PC's display can hold up to 2,000 characters organized as 25 rows (i.e., Y) by 80 columns (i.e., X), as shown in Figure 18.1. Please disregard the aspect ratio of the figure. The actual aspect ratio of a monitor is generally 4×3. Video memory on a PC is *memory mapped* and, on a VGA monitor, video memory starts at absolute memory location 0x000B8000 (or using segment:offset notation, B800:0000).

Figure 18.1   80 x 25 characters on a VGA monitor.

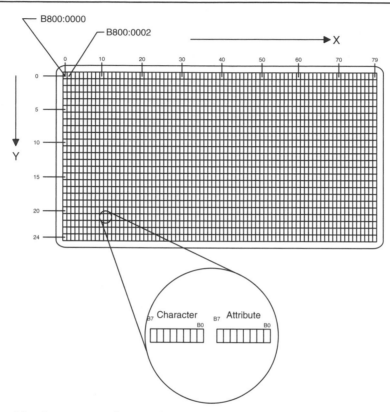

Each displayable *character* requires two bytes to display. The first byte (lowest memory location) is the character that you want to display, while the second byte (next memory location) is an attribute that determines the foreground/background-color combination of the character. The foreground color is specified in the lower four bits of the attribute, while the background color appears in bits four to six. Finally, the most significant bit determines whether the character blinks (when 1) or not (when 0). The character and attribute bytes are shown in Figure 18.2.

Figure 18.2   Character and attribute bytes on a VGA monitor.

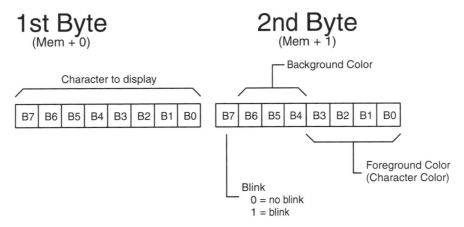

Table 18.1 shows the possible colors that can be obtained from the PC's VGA character mode.

Table 18.1   Attribute byte values.

Blink (B7)

Blink?	#define	Hex
No		0x00
Yes	DISP_BLINK	0x80

Background Color (B6 B5 B4)

Color	#define	Hex
Black	DISP_BGND_BLACK	0x00
Blue	DISP_BGND_BLUE	0x10
Green	DISP_BGND_GREEN	0x20
Cyan	DISP_BGND_CYAN	0x30
Red	DISP_BGND_RED	0x40
Purple	DISP_BGND_PURPLE	0x50
Brown	DISP_BGND_BROWN	0x60
Light Gray	DISP_BGND_LIGHT_GRAY	0x70

Table 18.1   Attribute byte values. (Continued)

Blink (B7)

Foreground Color (B3 B2 B1 B0)

Color	#define	Hex
Black	DISP_FGND_BLACK	0x00
Blue	DISP_FGND_BLUE	0x01
Green	DISP_FGND_GREEN	0x02
Cyan	DISP_FGND_CYAN	0x03
Red	DISP_FGND_RED	0x04
Purple	DISP_FGND_PURPLE	0x05
Brown	DISP_FGND_BROWN	0x06
Light Gray	DISP_FGND_LIGHT_GRAY	0x07
Dark Gray	DISP_FGND_DARK_GRAY	0x08
Light Blue	DISP_FGND_LIGHT_BLUE	0x09
Light Green	DISP_FGND_LIGHT_GREEN	0x0A
Light Cyna	DISP_FGND_LIGHT_CYAN	0x0B
Light Red	DISP_FGND_LIGHT_RED	0x0C
Light Purple	DISP_FGND_LIGHT_PURPLE	0x0D
Yellow	DISP_FGND_YELLOW	0x0E
White	DISP_FGND_WHITE	0x0F

You should note that you can only have eight possible background colors but a choice of 16 foreground colors. PC.H contains #defines that allow you to select the proper combination of foreground and background colors. These #defines are shown in Table 18.1. For example, to obtain a non-blinking **white** character on a **black** background, you simply add DISP_FGND_WHITE and DISP_BGND_BLACK (FGND means foreground, and BGND is background). This value corresponds to a hexadecimal value of 0x07, which happens to be the default video attribute of a displayable character on a PC. You should note that because DISP_BGND_BLACK has a value of 0x00, you don't actually need to specify it, and thus the attribute for the same **white** character could just as well have been specified as DISP_FGND_WHITE. You should use the #define constants instead of the hexadecimal values to make your code more readable.

The display functions in PC.C are used to write ASCII (and special) characters anywhere on the screen using X and Y coordinates. The coordinate system of the display is shown in Figure 18.1. You should note that position 0,0 is located at the upper-left corner — as opposed to the bottom left-corner as you might expect, which makes the computation of the location of each character to display easier to determine. The address in video memory for any character on the screen is given by

```
Address of Character = 0x000B8000 + Y * 160 + X * 2
```

The address of the attribute byte is at the next memory location or

```
Address of Attribute = 0x000B8000 + Y * 160 + X * 2 + 1
```

The display functions provided in PC.C perform direct writes to video RAM even though BIOS services in most PCs can do the same thing but in a portable fashion. I chose to write directly to video memory for performance reasons.

PC.C contains the following five functions, which are further described in the interface section of this chapter.

PC_DispChar()	To display a single ASCII character anywhere on the screen
PC_DispClrCol()	To clear a single column
PC_DispClrRow()	To clear a single row (or line)
PC_DispClrScr()	To clear the screen
PC_DispStr()	To display an ASCII string anywhere on the screen

18.01 *Saving and Restoring DOS's Context*

The current DOS environment is saved by calling PC_DOSSaveReturn() (see Listing 18.1) and is called by main() to:

1. Set up µC/OS-II's context switch vector,

2. Set up the tick ISR vector,

3. Save DOS's context so that we can return to DOS when we need to terminate execution of a µC/OS-II based application.

A lot happens in PC_DOSSaveReturn() so you might need to look at the code in Listing 18.1 to follow along.

Listing 18.1   *Saving the DOS environment.*

```
void PC_DOSSaveReturn (void)
{
    PC_ExitFlag  = FALSE;                               (1)
    OSTickDOSCtr =    1;                                (2)
    PC_TickISR   = PC_VectGet(VECT_TICK);               (3)


    OS_ENTER_CRITICAL();
    PC_VectSet(VECT_DOS_CHAIN, PC_TickISR);             (4)
    OS_EXIT_CRITICAL();


    setjmp(PC_JumpBuf);                                 (5)
```

Listing 18.1   Saving the DOS environment. (Continued)

```
    if (PC_ExitFlag == TRUE) {
        OS_ENTER_CRITICAL();
        PC_SetTickRate(18);                                      (6)
        PC_VectSet(VECT_TICK, PC_TickISR);                       (7)
        OS_EXIT_CRITICAL();
        PC_DispClrScr(DISP_FGND_WHITE + DISP_BGND_BLACK);        (8)
        exit(0);                                                 (9)
    }
}
```

L18.1(1)   PC_DOSSaveReturn() starts by setting the flag PC_ExitFlag to FALSE, indicating that we are not returning to DOS.

L18.1(2)   Then, PC_DOSSaveReturn() initializes OSTickDOSCtr to 1 because this variable is decremented in OSTickISR(). A value of 0 causes this value to wrap around to 255 when decremented by OSTickISR().

L18.1(3)

L18.1(4)   PC_DOSSaveReturn() then saves DOS's tick handler in a free vector-table entry so it can be called by μC/OS-II's tick handler (this is called chaining the vectors).

L18.1(5)   Next, PC_DOSSaveReturn() calls setjmp(), which captures the state of the processor (i.e., the contents of all important registers) in a structure called PC_JumpBuf. Capturing the processor's context allows us to return to PC_DOSSaveReturn() (from anywhere) and execute the code immediately following the call to setjmp(). Because PC_ExitFlag was initialized to FALSE [see L18.1(1)], PC_DOSSaveReturn() skips the code in the if statement and returns to the caller [i.e., main()].

L18.2(1)

L18.2(2)   When you want to return to DOS, all you have to do is call PC_DOSReturn() (see Listing 18.2), which sets PC_ExitFlag to TRUE and executes a longjmp().

L18.1(5)   This action brings the processor back in PC_DOSSaveReturn() [just after the call to setjmp()].

L18.1(6)   This time, however, PC_ExitFlag is TRUE, and the code following the if statement is executed.

L18.1(7)

L18.1(8)

L18.1(9)   PC_DOSSaveReturn() changes the tick rate back to 18.2Hz, restores the PC's tick-ISR handler, clears the screen, and returns to the DOS prompt through the exit(0) function.

Listing 18.2   Setting up to return to DOS.

```
void PC_DOSReturn (void)
{
    PC_ExitFlag = TRUE;                                          (1)
    longjmp(PC_JumpBuf, 1);                                      (2)
}
```

18.02 Elapsed-Time Measurement

The elapsed-time-measurement functions are used to determine how much time a function takes to execute. Time measurement is performed by using the PC's 82C54 timer #2. You make time measurement by wrapping the code to measure by the two functions PC_ElapsedStart() and PC_ElapsedStop(). However, before you can use these two functions, you need to call the function PC_ElapsedInit(). PC_ElapsedInit() basically computes the overhead associated with the other two functions. This way, the execution time (in microseconds) returned by PC_ElapsedStop() consists exclusively of the code you are measuring. Note that none of these functions are reentrant, and thus you must be careful that you do not invoke them from multiple tasks at the same time.

18.03 Miscellaneous

PC_GetDateTime() is a function that obtains the PC's current date and time and formats this information into an ASCII string. The format is

      "YYYY-MM-DD HH:MM:SS"

and you need at least 21 characters (including the NULL character) to hold this string. You should note that there are two spaces between the date and the time, which explains why you need 21 characters instead of 20. PC_GetDateTime() uses the Borland C/C++ library functions gettime() and getdate(), which should have their equivalents on other DOS compilers.

PC_GetKey() is a function that checks to see if a key has been pressed and, if so, obtains that key, and returns it to the caller. PC_GetKey() uses the Borland C/C++ library functions kbhit() and getch(), which again have their equivalents on other DOS compilers.

PC_SetTickRate() allows you to change the tick rate for μC/OS-II by specifying the desired frequency. Under DOS, a tick occurs 18.20648 times per second, or every 54.925 ms. This is because the 82C54 chip used didn't get its counter initialized and the default value of 65,535 takes effect. Had the chip been initialized with a divide by 59,659, the tick rate would have been a very nice 20.000Hz! I decided to change the tick rate to something more exciting and thus decided to use about 200Hz (actually 199.9966). The code found in OS_CPU_A.ASM calls the DOS-tick handler one time out of 11. This action is done to ensure that some of the housekeeping needed in DOS is maintained. You would not need to do this if you were to set the tick rate to 20Hz. Before returning to DOS, PC_SetTickRate() is called by specifying 18 as the desired frequency. PC_SetTickRate() knows that you actually mean 18.2Hz and correctly sets the 82C54.

The last two functions in PC.C are used to get and set an interrupt vector. PC_VectGet() and PC_VectSet() should be compiler-independent as long as the compiler support the macros MK_FP() (make far pointer), FP_OFF() (get the offset portion of a far pointer), and FP_SEG() (get the segment of a far pointer).

18.04 Interface Functions

The following section provides a reference section for the PC services.

PC_DispChar()

```
void PC_DispChar(INT8U x, INT8U y, INT8U c, INT8U color)
```

PC_DispChar() allows you to display a single ASCII (or special) character anywhere on the display.

Arguments

x and y   specifies the coordinates (col, row) where the character will appear. Rows (i.e., lines) are numbered from 0 to DISP_MAX_Y - 1, and columns are numbered from 0 to DISP_MAX_X - 1 (see PC.C).

c   is the character to display. You can specify any ASCII or special characters if *c* has a value higher than 128.

color   specifies the contents of the attribute byte and thus the color combination of the character to be displayed. You can add one DISP_FGND_??? (see PC.H) and one DISP_BGND_??? (see PC.H) to obtain the desired color combination.

Returned Values

Notes/Warnings

Example

```
void Task (void *pdata)
  {
       .
       .
       .
      for (;;) {
           .
          PC_DispChar(0, 0, '$', DISP_FGND_WHITE);
           .
           .
      }
  }
```

PC_DispClrCol()

```
void PC_DispClrCol(INT8U x, INT8U color)
```

PC_DispClrCol() allows you to clear the contents of a column (all 25 characters).

Arguments

x   specifies which column cleared. Columns are numbered from 0 to DISP_MAX_X − 1
                 (see PC.C).

color   specifies the contents of the attribute byte. Because the character used to clear a column
                 is the space character (i.e., ' '), only the background color appears. You can thus specify
                 any of the DISP_BGND_??? colors.

Returned Values

Notes/Warnings

Example

```
void Task (void *pdata)
{
    .
    .
    for (;;) {
        .
        PC_DispClrCol(0, DISP_BGND_BLACK);
        .
        .
    }
}
```

PC_DispClrRow()

```
void PC_DispClrRow(INT8U y, INT8U color)
```

PC_DispClrRow() allows you to clear the contents of a row (all 80 characters).

Arguments

y   specifies which row (i.e., line) is cleared. Rows are numbered from 0 to DISP_MAX_Y − 1 (see PC.C).

color   specifies the contents of the attribute byte. Because the character used to clear a row is the space character (i.e., ' '), only the background color appears. You can thus specify any of the DISP_BGND_??? colors.

Returned Values

Notes/Warnings

Example

```c
void Task (void *pdata)
{
    .
    .
    for (;;) {
        .
        PC_DispClrRow(10, DISP_BGND_BLACK);
        .
        .
    }
}
```

PC_DispClrScr()

`void PC_DispClrScr(INT8U color)`

`PC_DispClrScr()` allows you to clear the entire display.

Arguments

`color`   specifies the contents of the attribute byte. Because the character used to clear the
screen is the space character (i.e., ' '), only the background color appears. You can thus
specify any of the `DISP_BGND_???` colors.

Returned Values

Notes/Warnings

1. You should use `DISP_FGND_WHITE` instead of `DISP_BGND_BLACK` because you don't want to leave the
   attribute field with black on black.

Example

```
void Task (void *pdata)
{
    .
    .
    PC_DispClrScr(DISP_FGND_WHITE);
    for (;;) {
        .
        .
        .
    }
}
```

PC_DispStr()

```
void PC_DispStr(INT8U x, INT8U y, INT8U *s, INT8U color)
```

PC_DispStr() allows you to display an ASCII string. In fact, you could display an array containing any of 255 characters, as long as the array itself is NULL terminated.

Arguments

x and y   specifies the coordinates (col, row) where the first character will appear. Rows (i.e., lines) are numbered from 0 to DISP_MAX_Y - 1, and columns are numbered from 0 to DISP_MAX_X - 1 (see PC.C).

s   is a pointer to the array of characters to display. The array **must** be NULL terminated. Note that you can display any characters from 0x01 to 0xFF.

color   specifies the contents of the attribute byte and thus the color combination of the characters to be displayed. You can add one DISP_FGND_??? (see PC.H) and one DISP_BGND_??? (see PC.H) to obtain the desired color combination.

Returned Values

Notes/Warnings

1. All the characters of the string or array are displayed with the same color attributes.

Example #1

The code below displays the current value of a global variable called Temperature. The color used depends on whether the temperature is below 100 (white), below 200 (yellow), or exceeds 200 (blinking white on a red background).

```
FP32 Temperature;


void Task (void *pdata)
{
    char s[20];


    .

    .

    PC_DispStr(0, 0, "Temperature:", DISP_FGND_YELLOW + DISP_BGND_BLUE);
    for (;;) {
        sprintf(s, "%6.1f", Temperature);
        if (Temperature < 100.0) {
            color = DISP_FGND_WHITE;
        } else if (Temperature < 200.0) {
            color = DISP_FGND_YELLOW;
        } else {
```

```
            color = DISP_FGND_WHITE + DISP_BGND_RED + DISP_BLINK;
    }
    PC_DispStr(13, 0, s, color);
    .
    .
    .
    }
}
```

Example #2

The code below displays a square box 10 characters wide by seven characters high in the center of the screen.

```
INT8U  Box[7][11] = {
    {0xDA, 0xC4, 0xC4, 0xC4, 0xC4, 0xC4, 0xC4, 0xC4, 0xC4, 0xBF, 0x00},
    {0xB3, 0x20, 0x20, 0x20, 0x20, 0x20, 0x20, 0x20, 0x20, 0xB3, 0x00},
    {0xB3, 0x20, 0x20, 0x20, 0x20, 0x20, 0x20, 0x20, 0x20, 0xB3, 0x00},
    {0xB3, 0x20, 0x20, 0x20, 0x20, 0x20, 0x20, 0x20, 0x20, 0xB3, 0x00},
    {0xB3, 0x20, 0x20, 0x20, 0x20, 0x20, 0x20, 0x20, 0x20, 0xB3, 0x00},
    {0xB3, 0x20, 0x20, 0x20, 0x20, 0x20, 0x20, 0x20, 0x20, 0xB3, 0x00},
    {0xC0, 0xC4, 0xC4, 0xC4, 0xC4, 0xC4, 0xC4, 0xC4, 0xC4, 0xD9, 0x00}
};


void Task (void *pdata)
{
    INT8U i;


    .

    .

    for (i = 0; i < 7; i++) {
        PC_DispStr(35, i + 9, Box[i], DISP_FGND_WHITE);
    }
    for (;;) {
        .

        .

    }
}
```

PC_DOSReturn()

`void PC_DOSReturn(void)`

`PC_DOSReturn()` allows your application to return to DOS. It is assumed that you have previously called `PC_DOSSaveReturn()` to save the processor's important registers in order to properly return to DOS. See Chapter 1 for a description of how to use this function.

Arguments

Returned Values

Notes/Warnings

1. You **must** have called `PC_DOSSaveReturn()` prior to calling `PC_DOSReturn()`.

Example

```
void Task (void *pdata)
{
    INT16U key;

    .
    .

    for (;;) {

        .
        .

        if (PC_GetKey(&key) == TRUE) {
            if (key == 0x1B) {
                PC_DOSReturn();                    /* Return to DOS */
            }
        }

        .
        .

    }
}
```

PC_DOSSaveReturn()

```
void PC_DOSSaveReturn(void)
```

PC_DOSSaveReturn() allows your application to save the processor's important registers in order to properly return to DOS before you actually start multitasking with μC/OS-II. You normally call this function from main(), as shown in the example code.

Arguments

Returned Values

Notes/Warnings

1. You **must** call this function prior to setting μC/OS-II's context-switch vector as shown with example.

Example

```
void  main (void)
{
    OSInit();                    /* Initialize uC/OS-II            */
    .
    PC_DOSSaveReturn();          /* Save DOS's environment         */
    .
    PC_VectSet(uCOS, OSCtxSw); /* uC/OS-II's context switch vector */
    OSTaskCreate(…);
    .

    .
    OSStart();                   /* Start multitasking             */
}
```

PC_ElapsedInit()

`void PC_ElapsedInit(void)`

`PC_ElapsedInit()` is invoked to compute the overhead associated with the `PC_ElapsedStart()` and `PC_ElapsedStop()` calls. This allows `PC_ElapsedStop()` to return the execution time (in microseconds) of the code you are trying to measure.

18

Arguments

Returned Values

Notes/Warnings

1. You **must** call this function prior to calling either `PC_ElapsedStart()` or `PC_ElapsedStop()`.

Example

```
void  main (void)
{
    OSInit();                   /* Initialize uC/OS-II          */
    .
    .
    PC_ElapsedInit();           /* Compute overhead of elapse meas. */
    .
    .
    OSStart();                  /* Start multitasking           */
}
```

PC_ElapsedStart()

`void PC_ElapsedStart(void)`

`PC_ElapsedStart()` is used in conjunction with `PC_ElapsedStop()` to measure the execution time of some of your application code.

Arguments

Returned Values

Notes/Warnings

1. You **must** call `PC_ElapsedInit()` before you use either `PC_ElapsedStart()` or `PC_ElapsedStop()`.

2. This function is non-reentrant and cannot be called by multiple tasks without proper protection mechanisms (i.e., semaphores, locking the scheduler, etc.).

3. The execution time of your code must be less than 54.93ms in order for the elapsed-time-measurement functions to work properly.

Example

```
void  main (void)
{
    OSInit();                    /* Initialize uC/OS-II            */
    .
    .
    PC_ElapsedStart();            /* Compute overhead of elapse meas. */
    .
    .
    OSStart();                   /* Start multitasking             */
}
```

Example

```
void Task (void *pdata)
{
    INT16U time_us;

    .
    .

    for (;;) {

        .
        .
        PC_ElapsedStart();
        /* Code you want to measure the execution time */
        time_us = PC_ElaspedStop();
        .
        .

    }
}
```

PC_ElapsedStop()

`INT16U PC_ElapsedStop(void)`

`PC_ElapsedStop()` is used in conjunction with `PC_ElapsedStart()` to measure the execution time of some of your application code.

Arguments

Returned Values

The execution time of your code that was wrapped between `PC_ElapsedStart()` and `PC_ElapsedStop()` is returned in microseconds.

Notes/Warnings

1. You **must** call `PC_ElapsedInit()` before you use either `PC_ElapsedStart()` or `PC_ElapsedStop()`.

2. This function is non-reentrant and cannot be called by multiple tasks without proper protection mechanisms (i.e., semaphores, locking the scheduler, etc.).

3. The execution time of your code must be less than 54.93ms in order for the elapsed-time-measurement functions to work properly.

Example

See `PC_ElapsedStart()`, page 542.

PC_GetDateTime()

`void PC_GetDateTime(char *s)`

`PC_GetDateTime()` is used to obtain the current date and time from the PC's real-time clock chip and return this information in an ASCII string that can hold at least 21 characters.

18

Arguments

s
is a pointer to the storage area where the ASCII string will be deposited. The format of the ASCII string is

`"YYYY-MM-DD  HH:MM:SS"`

and requires 21 bytes of storage (note that there are two spaces between the date and the time).

Returned Values

Notes/Warnings

Example

```
void Task (void *pdata)
{
    char s[80];
    .
    .
    for (;;) {
        .
        .
        PC_GetDateTime(&s[0]);
        PC_DispStr(0, 24, s, DISP_FGND_WHITE);
        .
        .
    }
}
```

PC_GetKey()

```
BOOLEAN PC_GetDateTime(INT16S *key)
```

PC_GetKey() is used to see if a key has been pressed on the PC's keyboard, and if so, obtain the value of the key pressed. You normally invoke this function every so often (i.e., poll the keyboard) to see if a key has been pressed. Note that the PC actually obtains key presses through an ISR and buffers key presses. Up to 10 keys are buffered by the PC.

Arguments

key   is a pointer to where the key value will be stored. If no key has been pressed, the value contains 0x0000.

Returned Values

TRUE is a key has been pressed, and FALSE otherwise.

Notes/Warnings

Example

```
void Task (void *pdata)
{
   INT16S    key;
   BOOLEAN   avail;


   .

   .

   for (;;) {

      .

      .

      avail = PC_GetKey(&key);
      if (avail == TRUE) {
         /* Process key pressed */
      }

      .

      .

   }
}
```

PC_SetTickRate()

```
void PC_SetTickRate(INT16U freq)
```

18

`PC_SetTickRate()` is used to change the PC's tick rate from the standard 18.20648Hz to something faster. A tick rate of 200Hz is a multiple of 18.20648Hz (the multiple is 11).

Arguments

`freq`   is the desired frequency of the ticker.

Returned Values

Notes/Warnings

1. You can only make the ticker faster than 18.20648Hz.
2. The higher the frequency, the more overhead you impose on the CPU.

Example

```
void  Task (void *pdata)
{
    .
    .
    OS_ENTER_CRITICAL();
    PC_VectSet(0x08, OSTickISR);
    PC_SetTickRate(400);        /* Reprogram PC's tick rate to 400 Hz */
    OS_EXIT_CRITICAL();
    .
    .
    for (;;) {
        .
        .
    }
}
```

PC_VectGet()

void *PC_VectGet(INT8U vect)

PC_VectGet() is used to obtain the address of the interrupt handler specified by the interrupt-vector number. An 80x86 processor supports up to 256 interrupt/exception handlers.

Arguments

vect   is the interrupt-vector number, a number between 0 and 255.

Returned Values

The address of the current interrupt/exception handler for the specified interrupt-vector number.

Notes/Warnings

1. Vector number 0 corresponds to the **reset** handler.
2. It is assumed that the 80x86 code is compiled using the large model option and thus all pointers returned are far pointers.
3. It is assumed that the 80x86 is running in real mode.

Example

```
void  Task (void *pdata)
{
    void (*p_tick_isr)(void);

    .
    .

    p_tick_isr = PC_VectGet(0x08);  /* Get tick handler address */
    .
    .

    for (;;) {
       .
       .
    }
}
```

PC_VectSet()

```
void PC_VectSet(INT8U vect, void *(pisr)(void))
```

PC_VectSet() is used to set the contents of an interrupt-vector-table location. An 80x86 processor supports up to 256 interrupt/exception handlers.

18

Arguments

vect   is the interrupt-vector number, a number between 0 and 255.

pisr   is the address of the interrupt/exception handler.

Returned Values

Notes/Warnings

1. You should be careful when setting interrupt vectors. Some interrupt vectors are used by the operating system (DOS and/or μC/OS-II).

2. It is assumed that the 80x86 code is compiled using the large model option and thus all pointers returned are far pointers..

Example

```
void  InterruptHandler (void)
{
}



void  Task (void *pdata)
{
    .

    .

    PC_VectSet(64, InterruptHandler);

    .

    .

    for (;;) {
        .

        .

    }
}
```

18.05 Bibliography

Chappell, Geoff
DOS Internals
Reading, Massachusetts
Addison-Wesley, 1994
ISBN 0-201-60835-9

Tischer, Michael
PC Internals, System Programming 5ᵗʰ Edition
Grand Rapids, Michigan
Abacus, 1995
ISBN 1-55755-282-7

Villani, Pat
FreeDOS Kernel
Lawrence, Kansas
CMP Books, 1996
ISBN 0-87930-436-7

A

C Coding Conventions

Conventions should be established early in a project. These conventions are necessary to maintain consistency throughout the project. Adopting conventions increases productivity and simplifies project maintenance.

Many ways exist to code a program in C (or any other language). The style you use is just as good as any other, as long as you strive to attain the following goals:

- Portability
- Consistency
- Neatness
- Easy maintenance
- Easy understanding
- Simplicity

Whichever style you use, I emphasize that it should be adopted consistently throughout all your projects. I further suggest that a single style be adopted by all team members in a large project. To this end, I recommend that a C programming style document be formalized for your organization. Adopting a common coding style reduces code maintenance headaches and costs. Adopting a common style helps avoid code rewrites. This section describes the C programming style I use. The main emphasis on the programming style presented here is to make the source code easy to follow and maintain.

I don't like to limit the width of my C source code to 80 characters. My limitation is actually how many characters can be printed on an 8.5" by 11" page, using an 8-point, fixed-width font. With an 8-point font, you can accommodate up to 132 characters and have enough room on the left of the page for holes for insertion in a three-ring binder. Allowing 132 characters per line prevents having to interleave source code with comments.

A.1 Header

The header of a C source file is shown below. Your company name and address can be on the first few lines, followed by a title describing the contents of the file. A copyright notice is included to give warning of the proprietary nature of the software.

```
/*
*****************************************************************************************
*                                    Company Name
*                                      Address
*
*                      (c) Copyright 20xx, Company Name, City, State
*                                   All Rights Reserved
*
*
* Filename    :
* Programmer(s):
* Description  :
*****************************************************************************************
*/

/*$PAGE*/
```

The name of the file is supplied and is followed by the name of the programmer(s). The name of the programmer who created the file is given first. The last item in the header is a description of the contents of the file.

I like to dictate when page breaks occur in my listings if my code doesn't fit on a printed page. In fact, I like to find a logical spot such as after a comment block if both the comment block and the actual code don't fit on one page. For historical reasons, I insert the special comment /*$PAGE*/ followed by a form feed character (0x0C). I like to use the /*$PAGE*/ because it tells the reader where the page break occurs.

A.2 Include Files

The header files needed for your project immediately follow the revision history section. You can either list only the header files required for the module or combine header files in a single header file as I do in a file called INCLUDES.H. I like to use an INCLUDES.H header file because it prevents you from having to remember which header file goes with which source file, especially when new modules are added. The only inconvenience is that it takes longer to compile each file.

```
/*
*****************************************************************************************
*                                    INCLUDE FILES
*****************************************************************************************
*/
```

```
#include "INCLUDES.H"


/*$PAGE*/
```

A.3 Naming Identifiers

C compilers, which conform to the ANSI C standard (most C compilers do by now), allow up to 32 characters for identifier names. Identifiers are variables, structure/union members, functions, macros, #defines, and so on. Descriptive identifiers can be formulated using this 32-character feature and use acronyms, abbreviations, and mnemonics (see Section Section A.4 , "Acronyms, Abbreviations, and Mnemonics"). Identifier names should reflect the use of the element. I like to use a hierarchical method when creating an identifier. For instance, the function OSSemPend() indicates that it is part of the operating system (OS), it is a semaphore (Sem), and the operation being performed is to wait (Pend) for the semaphore. This method allows me to group all functions related to semaphores together. You should notice that some of the functions in μC/OS-II start with OS_ instead of OS. This is done to show you that the OS_ functions are internal to μC/OS-II even, though they are global functions.

Variable names should be declared on separate lines rather than combining them on a single line. Separate lines make it easy to provide a descriptive comment for each variable.

I use the file name as a prefix for variables that are either local (static) or global to the file. This process makes it clear that the variables are being used locally and globally. For example, local and global variables of a file named KEY.C are declared as follows

```
static  INT16U KeyCharCnt;          /* Number of keys pressed        */
static  char   KeyInBuf[100];       /* Storage buffer to hold chars  */
        char   KeyInChar;           /* Character typed               */


/*$PAGE*/
```

Uppercase characters are used to separate words in an identifier. I prefer to use this technique rather than making use of the underscore character (_) because underscores do not add meaning to names and also use up character spaces.

Global variables (external to the file) can use any name, as long as they contain a mixture of uppercase and lowercase characters and are prefixed with the module/file name (i.e., all global keyboard–related variable names are prefixed with the word Key).

Formal arguments to a function and local variables within a function are declared in lowercase. The lowercase makes it obvious that such variables are local to a function; global variables contain a mixture of upper and lowercase characters. To make variables readable, you can use the underscore character (_).

Within functions, certain variable names can be reserved to always have the same meaning. Some examples are given below, but others can be used as long as consistency is maintained.

i, j, and k	for loop counters
p1, p2, ... pn	for pointers
c, c1, ... cn	for characters
s, s1, ... sn	for strings

ix, iy, and iz	for intermediate integer variables
fx, fy, and fz	for intermediate floating-point variables

To summarize, use

formal parameters in a function declaration should only contain lowercase characters.

auto variable names should only contain lowercase characters.

static variables and **functions** should use the file/module name (or a portion of it) as a prefix and should use of upper/lowercase characters.

extern variables and **functions** should use the file/module name (or a portion of it) as a prefix and should use of upper/lowercase characters.

A.4 *Acronyms, Abbreviations, and Mnemonics*

When creating names for variables and functions (identifiers), use acronyms (e.g., OS, ISR, and TCB), abbreviations (e.g., buf & doc), and mnemonics (e.g., clr, and cmp). The use of acronyms, abbreviations, and mnemonics allows an identifier to be descriptive while requiring fewer characters. Unfortunately, if acronyms, abbreviations, and mnemonics are not used consistently, they can add confusion. To ensure consistency, I have opted to create a list of acronyms, abbreviations, and mnemonics that I use in all my projects. The same acronym, abbreviation, or mnemonic is used throughout, after it is assigned. I call this list the *Acronym, Abbreviation, and Mnemonic Dictionary,* and the list for μC/OS-II is shown in Table A.1. As I need more acronyms, abbreviations, or mnemonics, I simply add them to the list.

Table A.1   Acronyms, abbreviations, and mnemonics used in this book.

Acronym, Abbreviation, or Mnemonic	Meaning
Addr	Address
Blk	Block
Chk	Check
Clr	Clear
Cnt	Count
CPU	Central Processing Unit
Ctr	Counter
Ctx	Context
Cur	Current
Del	Delete
Dly	Delay

Table A.1   Acronyms, abbreviations, and mnemonics used in this book. *(Continued)*

Acronym, Abbreviation, or Mnemonic	Meaning
Err	Error
Ext	Extension
FP	Floating Point
Grp	Group
HMSM	Hours Minutes Seconds Milliseconds
ID	Identifier
Init	Initialize
Int	Interrupt
ISR	Interrupt Service Routine
Max	Maximum
Mbox	Mailbox
Mem	Memory
Msg	Message
N	Number of
Opt	Option
OS	Operating System
Ovf	Overflow
Prio	Priority
Ptr	Pointer
Q	Queue
Rdy	Ready
Req	Request
Sched	Scheduler
Sem	Semaphore
Stat	Status or Statistic
Stk	Stack
Sw	Switch

A

Table A.1   *Acronyms, abbreviations, and mnemonics used in this book. (Continued)*

Acronym, Abbreviation, or Mnemonic	Meaning
Sys	System
Tbl	Table
TCB	Task Control Block
TO	Timeout

There might be instances where one list for all products doesn't make sense. For instance, if you are an engineering firm working on a project for different clients and the products that you develop are totally unrelated, then a different list for each project is more appropriate. The vocabulary for the farming industry is not the same as the vocabulary for the defense industry. I use the rule that if all products are similar, they use the same dictionary.

A common dictionary to a project team also increases the team's productivity. It is important that consistency be maintained throughout a project, irrespective of the individual programmer(s). After buf has been agreed to mean *buffer* it should be used by all project members instead of having some individuals use buffer and others use bfr. To further this concept, you should always use buf even if your identifier can accommodate the full name; stick to buf even if you can fully write the word *buffer*.

A.5 Comments

I find it very difficult to mentally separate code from comments when code and comments are interleaved. Because of this, I never interleave code with comments. Comments are written to the right of the actual C code. When large comments are necessary, they are written in the function description header.

Comments are lined up as shown in the following example. The comment terminators (* /) do not need to be lined up, but for neatness I prefer to do so. It is not necessary to have one comment per line because a comment can apply to a few lines.

```
/*
*********************************************************************************
*                                   atoi()
*
* Description : Function to convert string 's' to an integer.
* Arguments   : ASCII string to convert to integer.
*               (All characters in the string must be decimal digits (0..9))
* Returns     : String converted to an 'int'
*********************************************************************************
*/
```

```
int atoi (char *s)
{
    int n;                          /* Partial result of conversion              */


    n = 0;                          /* Initialize result                         */
    while (*s >= '0' && *s <= '9' && *s) {  /* For all valid characters and not end of string */
        n = 10 * n + *s - '0';      /* Convert char to int and add to partial result */
        s++;                        /* Position on next character to convert     */
    }
    return (n);                     /* Return the result of the converted string */
}


/*$PAGE*/
```

A.6 #defines

Header files (.H) and C source files (.C) might require that constants and macros be defined. Constants and macros are always written in uppercase with the underscore character used to separate words. Note that hexadecimal numbers are always written with a lowercase *x* and all uppercase letters for hexadecimal *A* through *F*. Also, you should note that the contant names are all lined up, as well as their values.

```
/*
*********************************************************************************************
*                                   CONSTANTS & MACROS
*********************************************************************************************
*/

#define  KEY_FF           0x0F
#define  KEY_CR           0x0D
#define  KEY_BUF_FULL()   (KeyNRd > 0)


/*$PAGE*/
```

A.7 Data Types

C allows you to create new data types using the typedef keyword. I declare all data types using uppercase characters and follow the same rule used for constants and macros. Because of the context in which constants, macros, and data types are used, confusion between the elements does not occur. Because different microprocessors have different word lengths, I like to declare the following data types (assuming Borland C++ v4.51)

```
/*
********************************************************************************
*                                 DATA TYPES
********************************************************************************
*/

typedef  unsigned char  BOOLEAN;            /* Boolean              */
typedef  unsigned char  INT8U;              /*  8 bit unsigned      */
typedef  char           INT8S;              /*  8 bit signed        */
typedef  unsigned int   INT16U;             /* 16 bit unsigned      */
typedef  int            INT16S;             /* 16 bit signed        */
typedef  unsigned long  INT32U;             /* 32 bit unsigned      */
typedef  long           INT32S;             /* 32 bit signed        */
typedef  float          FP;                 /* Floating Point       */

/*$PAGE*/
```

Using these #defines, you always know the size of each data type.

A.8 *Local Variables*

Some source modules require that local variables be available. These variables are only needed for the source file (file scope) and should be hidden from the other modules. Hiding these variables is accomplished in C by using the static keyword. Variables can either be listed in alphabetical order or in functional order.

```
/*
********************************************************************************
*                              LOCAL VARIABLES
********************************************************************************
*/

static  char    KeyBuf[100];
static  INT16S  KeyNRd;

/*$PAGE*/
```

A.9 Function Prototypes

This section contains the prototypes (or calling conventions) used by the functions declared in the file. The order in which functions are prototyped should be the order in which the functions are declared in the file. This order allows you to quickly locate the position of a function when the file is printed.

```
/*
*********************************************************************************
*                            FUNCTION PROTOTYPES
*********************************************************************************
*/


        void      KeyClrBuf(void);
static  BOOLEAN   KeyChkStat(void);
static  INT16S    KeyGetCnt(int ch);


/*$PAGE*/
```

Also note that the `static` keyword, the returned data type, and the function names are all aligned.

A.10 Function Declarations

As much as possible, there should only be one function per page when code listings are printed on a printer. A comment block should precede each function. All comment blocks should look as shown below. A description of the function should be given and include as much information as necessary. If the combination of the comment block and the source code extends past a printed page, a page break should be forced (preferably between the end of the comment block and the start of the function). This break allows the function to be on a page by itself and prevents having a page break in the middle of the function. If the function itself is longer than a printed page, then it should be broken by a page break comment (`/*$PAGE*/`) in a logical location (i.e., at the end of an `if` statement, instead of in the middle of one).

More than one small function can be declared on a single page. They should all, however, contain the comment block describing the function. The beginning of a function should start at least two lines after the end of the previous function.

```
/*
*********************************************************************************
*                            CLEAR KEYBOARD BUFFER
*
* Description : Flush keyboard buffer
* Arguments   : none
* Returns     : none
* Notes       : none
*********************************************************************************
*/
```

```
void KeyClrBuf (void)
{



}
/*$PAGE*/
```

Functions that are only used within the file should be declared `static` to hide them from other functions in different files.

By convention, I always call all invocations of the function without a space between the function name and the open parenthesis of the argument list. Because of this, I place a space between the name of the function and the opening parenthesis of the argument list in the function declaration, as shown above. This way I can quickly find the function definition using a `grep` utility.

Function names should make use of the file name as a prefix. This prefix makes it easy to locate function declarations in medium to large projects. It also makes it very easy to know where these functions are declared. For example, all functions in a file named `KEY.C` and functions in a file named `VIDEO.C` could be declared as follows

```
KEY.C
        KeyGetChar()
        KeyGetLine()
        KeyGetFnctKey()
VIDEO.C
        VideoGetAttr()
        VideoPutChar()
        VideoPutStr()
        VideoSetAttr()
```

It's not necessary to use the whole file/module name as a prefix. For example, a file called `KEYBOARD.C` could have functions starting with `Key` instead of `Keyboard`. It is also preferable to use uppercase characters to separate words in a function name instead of using underscores. Again, underscores don't add meaning to names, and they use up character spaces. As mentioned previously, formal parameters and local variables should be in lowercase, which makes it clear that such variables have a scope limited to the function.

Each local variable name **must** be declared on its own line, which allows the programmer to comment each one as needed. Local variables are indented four spaces. The statements for the function are separated from the local variables by three spaces. Declarations of local variables should be physically separated from the statements because they are different.

A.11 Indentation

Indentation is important to show the flow of the function. The question is, how many spaces are needed for indentation? One space is obviously not enough, while eight spaces is too much. The compromise I use is four spaces. I also never use tabs, because various printers interpret tabs differently; your code might not look as you want. Avoiding tabs does not mean that you can't use the Tab key on your keyboard. A good editor gives you the option to replace tabs with spaces (in this case, 4 spaces).

A space follows the keywords `if`, `for`, `while`, and `do`. The keyword `else` has the privilege of having one before and one after it if curly braces are used. I write `if (condition)` on its own line and the statement(s) to execute on the next following line(s) as follows

```
if (x < 0)
    z = 25;

if (y > 2) {
    z = 10;
    x = 100;
    p++;
}
```

instead of the following method

```
if (x < 0) z = 25;
if (y > 2) {z = 10; x = 100; p++;}
```

There are two reasons for this method. The first is that I like to keep the decision portion separate from the execution statement(s). The second reason is consistency with the method I use for `while`, `for`, and `do` statements.

`switch` statements are treated as any other conditional statement. Note that the case statements are lined up with the case label. The important point here is that `switch` statements must be easy to follow. `cases` should also be separated from one another.

```
if (x > 0) {
    y = 10;
    z =  5;
}
```

```
if (z < LIM) {
    x = y + z;
    z = 10;
} else {
    x = y - z;
    z = -25;
}
```

```
for (i = 0; i < MAX_ITER; i++) {
    *p2++ = *p1++;
    xx[i] = 0;
}
```

```
while (*p1) {
    *p2++ = *p1++;
    cnt++;
}
```

```
do {
    cnt--;
    *p2++ = *p1++;
} while (cnt > 0);
```

```
switch (key) {
    case KEY_BS :
        if (cnt > 0) {
            p--;
            cnt--;
        }
        break;

    case KEY_CR :
        *p = NUL;
        break;

    case KEY_LINE_FEED :
        p++;
        break;

    default:
        *p++ = key;
        cnt++;
        break;
}
```

A.12 Statements and Expressions

All statements and expressions should be made to fit on a single source line. I never use more than one assignment per line, such as

```
x = y = z = 1;
```

Even though this version is correct in C, when the variable names get more complicated, the intent might not be as obvious.

The following operators are written with no space around them:

`->`	Structure-pointer operator	`p->m`
`.`	Structure-member operator	`s.m`
`[]`	Array subscripting	`a[i]`

Parentheses after function names have no space(s) before them. A space should be introduced after each comma to separate each actual argument in a function. Expressions within parentheses are written with no space after the opening parenthesis and no space before the closing parenthesis. Commas and semicolons should have one space after them.

```
strncat(t, s, n);
for (i = 0; i < n; i++)
```

The unary operators are written with no space between them and their operands:

```
!p    ~b    ++i    --j    (long)m    *p    &x    sizeof(k)
```

The binary operators are preceded and followed by one or more spaces, as is the ternary operator:

```
c1 = c2    x + y    i += 2    n > 0 ? n : -n;
```

The keywords `if`, `while`, `for`, `switch`, and `return` are followed by one space.

For assignments, numbers are lined up in columns, as if you were to add them. The equal signs are also lined up.

```
x        = 100.567;
temp     =  12.700;
var5     =   0.768;
variable =  12;
storage  = &array[0];
```

A.13 Structures and Unions

Structures are typedef, where allows a single name to represent the structure. The structure type is declared using all uppercase characters with underscore characters used to separate words.

```
typedef struct line {          /* Structure that defines a LINE           */
    int  LineStartX;           /* 'X' & 'Y' starting coordinate           */
    int  LineStartY;
    int  LineEndX;             /* 'X' & 'Y' ending  coordinate            */
    int  LineEndY;
    int  LineColor;            /* Color of line to draw                   */
} LINE;
```

```
typedef struct point {         /* Structure that defines a POINT          */
    int  PointPosX;            /* 'X' & 'Y' coordinate of point           */
    int  PointPosY;
    int  PointColor;           /* Color of point                          */
} POINT;
```

Structure members start with the same prefix (as shown in the examples above). Member names should start with the name of the structure type (or a portion of it), which makes it clear when pointers are used to reference members of a structure, such as

```
p->LineColor;   /* We know that 'p' is a pointer to LINE */
```

A.14 Bibliography

Babich, Wayne A.
 Software Configuration Management
 Reading, Massachusetts
 Addison-Wesley Publishing Company, 1986
 ISBN 0-201-10161-0

Long, David W. and Christopher P. Duff
 *A Survey of Processes Used in the Development of Firmware for a
 Multiprocessor Embedded System*
 Hewlett-Packard Journal, October 1993, p.59-65

McConnell, Steve
 Code Complete
 Redmond, Washington
 Microsoft Press, 1993
 ISBN 1-55615-484-4

Merant, Inc.
   PVCS Version Manager
   735 SW 158th Avenue
   Beaverton, OR 97006
   (503) 645-1150

Merant, Inc.
   PVCS Configuration Builder
   735 SW 158th Avenue
   Beaverton, OR 97006
   (503) 645-1150

A

Licensing Policy for μC/OS-II

Even though μC/OS-II is provided in source form, μC/OS-II is **not** freeware nor is it Open Source software.

B.1 Colleges and Universities

μC/OS-II source and object code can be freely distributed (to students) by accredited colleges and universities without requiring a license, as long as no commercial application is involved. In other words, no licensing is required if μC/OS-II is used for educational use. Colleges and universities should register their courses by sending a class syllabus and providing a Web link so the class can be added to the Micrium Web site. Please send this information to:

    Universities@Micrium.com

B.2 Commercial Use

You must obtain an Object Code Distribution License to embed μC/OS-II in a commercial product. This is a license to put μC/OS-II in a product that is sold with the intent to make a profit. A license fee is required for such situations, and you need to contact Micrium, Inc., (see below) for pricing.

You must obtain a Source Code Distribution License to distribute μC/OS-II source code. Again, there is a fee for such a license, and you need to contact Micrium, Inc., for pricing.

    Licensing@Micrium.com

    or

Micrium, Inc.
949 Crestview Circle
Weston, FL 33327-1848
U.S.A.
1-954-217-2036 (Phone)
1-954-217-2037 (Fax)
http://www.Micrium.com

Appendix C

C

µC/OS-II Quick Reference

This appendix provides a summary of the services provided by µC/OS-II, assuming that you enabled everything (I didn't want to clutter this reference with conditional compilation statements). Of course, some of the services might not be included in your application, depending on the contents of OS_CFG.H.

The services are listed in the same order as they appear in the chapters:

- Miscellaneous (Kernel Structure)
- Task Management
- Time Management
- Semaphore Management
- Mutual Exclusion Semaphore Management
- Event Flag Management
- Message Mailbox Management
- Message Queue Management
- Memory Management

I also included a Task Assignment Worksheet, which allows you to plan your application by listing your application tasks.

Miscellaneous

(Chapter 3)

Function Prototypes

```
void        OSInit(void);

void        OSIntEnter(void);

void        OSIntExit(void);

void        OSSchedLock(void);

void        OSSchedUnlock(void);

void        OSStart(void);

void        OSStatInit(void);

INT16U      OSVersion(void);
```

Macros

```
OS_ENTER_CRITICAL()
OS_EXIT_CRITICAL()
```

Global Variables

```
INT8S      OSCPUUsage            // CPU usage in percent (%)
INT8U      OSIntNesting          // Interrupt nesting level (0..255)
INT8U      OSLockNesting         // OSSchedLock() nesting level.
BOOLEAN    OSRunning             // Flag indicating multitasking running
INT8U      OSTaskCtr             // Number of tasks created
OS_TCB     *OSTCBCur             // Pointer to current task's TCB
OS_TCB     *OSTCBHighRdy         // Pointer to highest priority task's TCB
INT8U      OSTaskCtr             // Number of tasks created
```

Task Management

(Chapter 4)
Function Prototypes

```
INT8U        OSTaskChangePrio(INT8U oldprio, INT8U newprio);

INT8U        OSTaskCreate(void   (*task)(void *pd),
                     void    *pdata,
                     OS_STK  *ptos,
                     INT8U   prio);

INT8U        OSTaskCreateExt(void  (*task)(void *pd),
                     void    *pdata,
                     OS_STK  *ptos,
                     INT8U   prio,
                     INT16U  id,
                     OS_STK  *pbos,
                     INT32U  stk_size,
                     void    *pext,
                     INT16U  opt);

INT8U        OSTaskDel(INT8U prio);

INT8U        OSTaskDelReq(INT8U prio);

INT8U        OSTaskResume(INT8U prio);

INT8U        OSTaskSuspend(INT8U prio);

INT8U        OSTaskStkChk(INT8U prio, OS_STK_DATA *pdata);

INT8U        OSTaskQuery(INT8U prio, OS_TCB *pdata);
```

OSTaskCreateExt() opt **Argument**

```
OS_TASK_OPT_STK_CHK           // Enable stack checking for the task
OS_TASK_OPT_STK_CLR           // Clear the stack when the task is create
OS_TASK_OPT_SAVE_FP           // Save Floating-Point registers
```

OSTaskDelReq() **Return Values**

```
OS_NO_ERR                     // The request has been registered
OS_TASK_NOT_EXIST             // The task has been deleted
OS_TASK_DEL_IDLE              // Can't delete the Idle task!
OS_PRIO_INVALID               // Invalid priority
```

OSTaskStkChk() **Data Structure**

```
typedef struct {
    INT32U  OSFree;            // # of free bytes on the stack
    INT32U  OSUsed;            // # of bytes used on the stack
} OS_STK_DATA;
```

OSTaskQuery() **Data Structure**

```
typedef struct os_tcb {
    OS_STK        *OSTCBStkPtr;        // Stack Pointer

    void          *OSTCBExtPtr;        // TCB extension pointer

    OS_STK        *OSTCBStkBottom;     // Ptr to bottom of stack
    INT32U         OSTCBStkSize;       // Size of task stack (#elements)

    INT16U         OSTCBOpt;           // Task options

    INT16U         OSTCBId;            // Task ID (0..65535)

    struct os_tcb *OSTCBNext;          // Pointer to next    TCB
    struct os_tcb *OSTCBPrev;          // Pointer to previous TCB

    OS_EVENT      *OSTCBEventPtr;      // Pointer to ECB

    void          *OSTCBMsg;           // Message received

    OS_FLAG_NODE  *OSTCBFlagNode;      // Pointer to event flag node
    OS_FLAGS       OSTCBFlagsRdy;      // Event flags that made task ready

    INT16U         OSTCBDly;           // Nbr ticks to delay task or, timeout
    INT8U          OSTCBStat;          // Task status
    INT8U          OSTCBPrio;          // Task priority (0 = highest)

    INT8U          OSTCBX;
    INT8U          OSTCBY;
    INT8U          OSTCBBitX;
    INT8U          OSTCBBitY;

    BOOLEAN        OSTCBDelReq;        // Flag to tell task to delete itself
} OS_TCB;
```

Time Management

(Chapter 5)
Function Prototypes

```
void        OSTimeDly(INT16U ticks);

INT8U       OSTimeDlyHMSM(INT8U  hours,
                          INT8U  minutes,
                          INT8U  seconds,
                          INT16U milli);

INT8U       OSTimeDlyResume(INT8U prio);

INT32U      OSTimeGet(void);

void        OSTimeSet(INT32U ticks);

void        OSTimeTick(void);
```

C

Semaphore Management

(Chapter 7)

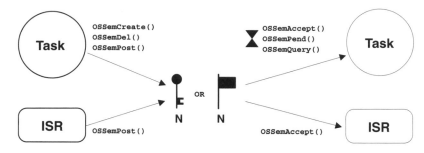

Function Prototypes

```
INT16U       OSSemAccept(OS_EVENT *pevent);

OS_EVENT    *OSSemCreate(INT16U cnt);

OS_EVENT    *OSSemDel(OS_EVENT *pevent, INT8U opt, INT8U *err);

void         OSSemPend(OS_EVENT *pevent, INT16U timeout, INT8U *err);

INT8U        OSSemPost(OS_EVENT *pevent);

INT8U        OSSemQuery(OS_EVENT *pevent, OS_SEM_DATA *pdata);
```

OSSemDel() opt **Argument**

```
OS_DEL_NO_PEND                              // Delete only if no task pending
OS_DEL_ALWAYS                              // Always delete
```

OSSemQuery()**Data Structure**

```
typedef struct {
    INT16U  OSCnt;                          // Semaphore count
    INT8U   OSEventTbl[OS_EVENT_TBL_SIZE];  // Wait list
    INT8U   OSEventGrp;
} OS_SEM_DATA;
```

Mutual Exclusion Semaphore Management

(Chapter 8)

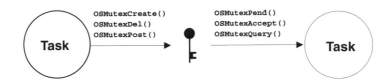

Function Prototypes

```
INT8U       OSMutexAccept(OS_EVENT *pevent, INT8U *err);

OS_EVENT    *OSMutexCreate(INT8U prio, INT8U *err);

OS_EVENT    *OSMutexDel(OS_EVENT *pevent, INT8U opt, INT8U *err);

void        OSMutexPend(OS_EVENT *pevent, INT16U timeout, INT8U *err);

INT8U       OSMutexPost(OS_EVENT *pevent);

INT8U       OSMutexQuery(OS_EVENT *pevent, OS_MUTEX_DATA *pdata);
```

OSMutexDel() opt **Argument**

```
OS_DEL_NO_PEND                          // Delete only if no task pending
OS_DEL_ALWAYS                           // Always delete
```

OSMutexQuery() **Data Structure**

```
typedef struct {
    INT8U   OSEventTbl[OS_EVENT_TBL_SIZE]; // Wait List
    INT8U   OSEventGrp;
    INT8U   OSValue;                    // Mutex value
                                        //      (0=used, 1=available)
    INT8U   OSOwnerPrio;                // Mutex owner's task priority
    INT8U   OSMutexPIP;                 // Priority Inheritance Priority or
                                        //      0xFF if no owner
} OS_MUTEX_DATA;
```

Event Flag Management

(Chapter 9)

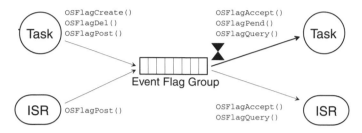

Function Prototypes

```
OS_FLAGS        OSFlagAccept(OS_FLAG_GRP *pgrp,
                             OS_FLAGS    flags,
                             INT8U       wait_type,
                             INT8U       *err);


OS_FLAG_GRP  *OSFlagCreate(OS_FLAGS    flags,
                           INT8U       *err);


OS_FLAG_GRP  *OSFlagDel(OS_FLAG_GRP  *pgrp,
                        INT8U         opt,
                        INT8U         *err);


OS_FLAGS        OSFlagPend(OS_FLAG_GRP *pgrp,
                           OS_FLAGS     flags,
                           INT8U        wait_type,
                           INT16U       timeout,
                           INT8U        *err);


OS_FLAGS        OSFlagPost(OS_FLAG_GRP *pgrp,
                           OS_FLAGS     flags,
                           INT8U        operation,
                           INT8U        *err);


OS_FLAGS        OSFlagQuery(OS_FLAG_GRP *pgrp,
                            INT8U        *err);
```

OSFlagDel() opt **Argument**

```
OS_DEL_NO_PEND                          // Delete only if no task pending
OS_DEL_ALWAYS                           // Always delete
```

Message Mailbox Management

(Chapter 10)

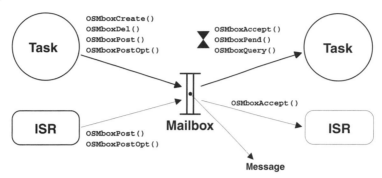

Function Prototypes

```
void        *OSMboxAccept(OS_EVENT *pevent);

OS_EVENT    *OSMboxCreate(void *msg);

OS_EVENT    *OSMboxDel(OS_EVENT *pevent, INT8U opt, INT8U *err);

void        *OSMboxPend(OS_EVENT *pevent, INT16U timeout, INT8U *err);

INT8U        OSMboxPost(OS_FVENT *pevent, void *msg);

INT8U        OSMboxPostOpt(OS_EVENT *pevent, void *msg, INT8U opt);

INT8U        OSMboxQuery(OS_EVENT *pevent, OS_MBOX_DATA *pdata);
```

OSMboxDel() opt **Argument**

```
OS_DEL_NO_PEND                          // Delete only if no task pending
OS_DEL_ALWAYS                           // Always delete
```

OSMboxPostOpt() opt **Argument**

```
OS_POST_OPT_NONE                        // POST to a single waiting task
                                        //    (Identical to OSMboxPost())
OS_POST_OPT_BROADCAST                   // POST to ALL waiting on mailbox
```

OSMboxQuery() **Data Structure**

```
typedef struct {
    void    *OSMsg;                         // Pointer to message in mailbox
    INT8U   OSEventTbl[OS_EVENT_TBL_SIZE]; // Waiting List
    INT8U   OSEventGrp;
} OS_MBOX_DATA;
```

Message Queue Management

(Chapter 11)

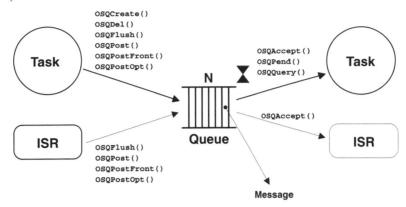

Function Prototypes

```
void        *OSQAccept(OS_EVENT *pevent);

OS_EVENT    *OSQCreate(void **start, INT16U size);

OS_EVENT    *OSQDel(OS_EVENT *pevent, INT8U opt, INT8U *err);

INT8U        OSQFlush(OS_EVENT *pevent);

void        *OSQPend(OS_EVENT *pevent, INT16U timeout, INT8U *err);

INT8U        OSQPost(OS_EVENT *pevent, void *msg);

INT8U        OSQPostFront(OS_EVENT *pevent, void *msg);

INT8U        OSQPostOpt(OS_EVENT *pevent, void *msg, INT8U opt);

INT8U        OSQQuery(OS_EVENT *pevent, OS_Q_DATA *pdata);
```

OSQDel() opt **Argument**

```
OS_DEL_NO_PEND                          // Delete only if no task pending
OS_DEL_ALWAYS                           // Always delete
OS_POST_OPT_FRONT                       // Simulate OSQPostFront()
```

OSQPostOpt() opt **Argument**

```
OS_POST_OPT_NONE                                // POST to a single waiting task
                                                //    (Identical to OSMboxPost())
OS_POST_OPT_BROADCAST                           // POST to ALL waiting on mailbox
```

OSQQuery() **Data Structure**

```
typedef struct {
    void        *OSMsg;                          // Pointer to next message
    INT16U      OSNMsgs;                         // # messages in queue
    INT16U      OSQSize;                         // Size of message queue
    INT8U       OSEventTbl[OS_EVENT_TBL_SIZE];   // Waiting List
    INT8U       OSEventGrp;
} OS_Q_DATA;
```

Memory Management

(Chapter 12)
Function Prototypes

```
OS_MEM       *OSMemCreate(void   *addr,
                          INT32U  nblks,
                          INT32U  blksize,
                          INT8U  *err);


void         *OSMemGet(OS_MEM *pmem, INT8U *err);


INT8U         OSMemPut(OS_MEM *pmem, void *pblk);


INT8U         OSMemQuery(OS_MEM *pmem, OS_MEM_DATA *pdata);
```

OSMemQuery() **Data Structure**

```
typedef struct {
    void   *OSAddr;             // Ptr to start of memory partition
    void   *OSFreeList;         // Ptr to start free list of memory blocks
    INT32U  OSBlkSize;          // Size (in bytes) of each memory block
    INT32U  OSNBlks;            // # blocks in the Partition
    INT32U  OSNFree;            // # free blocks
    INT32U  OSNUsed;            // # blocks used
} OS_MEM_DATA;
```

μC/OS-II, The Real-Time Kernel
Task Assignment Worksheet

Priority	Task Name	Stack Size (Bytes)	Description	Mutex PIP?
0				
1				
2				
3				
4				
5				
6				
7				
8				
9				
10				
11				
12				
13				
14				
15				
16				
17				
18				
19				
20				
21				
22				
23				
24				
25				
26				
27				
28				
29				
30				
31				
32				
33				
34				
35				
36				
37				
38				
39				
40				
41				
42				
43				
44				
45				
46				
47				
48				
49				
50				
51				
52				
53				
54				
55				
56				
57				
58				
59				
60				
61				
62				
63	μC/OS-II Idle Task			N/A

TO **Utility**

TO is a DOS utility that allows you to go to a directory without typing

    CD *path*

or

    CD ..*path*

TO is probably the DOS utility I use most because it allows me to move between directories very quickly. At the DOS prompt, simply type TO followed by the name you associated with a directory, then press the Enter key

    TO *name*

where *name* is a name you associated with a path. The names and paths are placed in an ASCII file called TO.TBL, which resides in the root directory of the current drive. TO scans TO.TBL for the name you specified on the command line. If the name exists in TO.TBL, the directory is changed to the path specified with the name. If the name is not found in TO.TBL, the message Invalid *NAME*. is displayed.

The DOS executable is in \SOFTWARE\TO\EXE\TO.EXE, an example of the names and paths is in \SOFTWARE\TO\EXE\TO.TBL, and the source code is in \SOFTWARE\TO\SOURCE\TO.C.

An example of TO.TBL and its format is shown in Listing D.1. Note that the name must be separated from the path by a comma.

Listing D.1   Example of TO.TBL

```
A,          ..\SOURCE
C,          ..\SOURCE
D,          ..\DOC
L,          ..\LST
O,          ..\OBJ
P,          ..\PROD
W,          ..\WORK
```

Listing D.1   Example of TO.TBL (Continued)

```
EX1L,      \SOFTWARE\uCOS-II\EX1_x86L\BC45\TEST                        (1)
EX2L,      \SOFTWARE\uCOS-II\EX2_x86L\BC45\TEST
EX3L,      \SOFTWARE\uCOS-II\EX3_x86L\BC45\TEST
Ix86L,     \SOFTWARE\uCOS-II\Ix86L\BC45
TO,        \SOFTWARE\TO\SOURCE
uCOS-II,   \SOFTWARE\uCOS-II\SOURCE
```

You can add an entry to TO.TBL by typing the path associated with a name on the command line, as follows

TO *name path*

TO appends this new entry to the end of TO.TBL, which avoids having to use a text editor to add a new entry. If you type

TO EX1L

TO changes the directory to \SOFTWARE\uCOS-II\EX1_x86L\BC45\TEST [LD.1(1)].

TO.TBL can be as long as needed, but each name must be unique. Note that two names can be associated with the same directory. If you add entries in TO.TBL using a text editor, all entries must be entered in uppercase. When you invoke TO at the DOS prompt, the name you specify is converted to uppercase before the program searches through the table. TO searches TO.TBL linearly from the first entry to the last. For faster response, you might want to place your most frequently used directories at the beginning of the file, although this action might not be necessary with today's fast computers.

Bibliography

Allworth, Steve T. 1981. *Introduction To Real-Time Software Design.* New York: Springer-Verlag. ISBN 0-387-91175-8.

Bal Sathe, Dhananjay. 1988. Fast Algorithm Determines Priority. *EDN* (India), September, p. 237.

Comer, Douglas. 1984.*Operating System Design, The XINU Approach.* Englewood Cliffs, New Jersey: Prentice-Hall. ISBN 0-13-637539-1.

Deitel, Harvey M. and Michael S. Kogan. 1992. *The Design Of OS/2.* Reading, Massachusetts: Addison-Wesley. ISBN 0-201-54889-5.

Ganssle, Jack G. 1992. *The Art of Programming Embedded Systems.* San Diego: Academic Press. ISBN 0-122-748808.

Gareau, Jean L. 1998. Embedded x86 Programming: Protected Mode. *Embedded Systems Programming*, April, p. 80–93.

Halang, Wolfgang A. and Alexander D. Stoyenko. 1991. *Constructing Predictable Real Time Systems.* Norwell, Massachusetts: Kluwer Academic Publishers Group. ISBN 0-7923-9202-7.

Hunter & Ready. 1986. *VRTX Technical Tips.* Palo Alto, California: Hunter & Ready.

Hunter & Ready. 1983. *Dijkstra Semaphores, Application Note.* Palo Alto, California: Hunter & Ready.

Hunter & Ready. 1986. *VRTX and Event Flags.* Palo Alto, California: Hunter & Ready.

Intel Corporation. 1986. *iAPX 86/88, 186/188 User's Manual: Programmer's Reference.* Santa Clara, California: Intel Corporation.

Kernighan, Brian W. and Dennis M. Ritchie. 1988. *The C Programming Language,* 2nd edition. Englewood Cliffs, New Jersey: Prentice Hall. ISBN 0-13-110362-8.

E

Klein, Mark H., Thomas Ralya, Bill Pollak, Ray Harbour Obenza, and Michael Gonzlez. 1993. *A Practioner's Handbook for Real-Time Analysis: Guide to Rate Monotonic Analysis for Real-Time Systems.* Norwell, Massachusetts: Kluwer Academic Publishers Group. ISBN 0-7923-9361-9.

Laplante, Phillip A. 1992. *Real-Time Systems Design and Analysis, An Engineer's Handbook.* Piscataway, New Jersey: IEEE Computer Society Press. ISBN 0-780-334000.

Lehoczky, John, Lui Sha, and Ye Ding. 1989. The Rate Monotonic Scheduling Algorithm: Exact Characterization and Average Case Behavior. In: *Proceedings of the IEEE Real-Time Systems Symposium.*, Los Alamitos, California. Piscataway, New Jersey: IEEE Computer Society, p. 166–171.

Madnick, E. Stuart and John J. Donovan. 1974. *Operating Systems.* New York: McGraw-Hill. ISBN 0-07-039455-5.

Ripps, David L. 1989. *An Implementation Guide To Real-Time Programming.* Englewood Cliffs, New Jersey: Yourdon Press. ISBN 0-13-451873-X.

Savitzky, Stephen R. 1985. *Real-Time Microprocessor Systems.* New York: Van Nostrand Reinhold. ISBN 0-442-28048-3.

Wood, Mike and Tom Barrett. 1990. A Real-Time Primer. *Embedded Systems Programming*, February, p. 20–28.

Companion CD

This book includes a companion CD and contains a self-extracting executable called uCOSV252.EXE. Because so much room is left on the CD, I decided to also include all the files so that you can browse the CD without having to install anything on your computer.

It is assumed that you have a Microsoft Windows 95, 98, NT, 2000, or XP computer system, running on an 80x86, and Pentium-class, or AMD, processor. You should have at least 10MB of free disk space to install µC/OS-II and its source files on your system.

Insert the companion CD into your CD-ROM drive, and execute the file uCOSV252.EXE, which should be found on the root directory of the CD. The splash screen, shown in Figure F.1, is displayed in the center of your screen.

Figure F.1 uCOSV252.EXE *splash screen.*

When you click OK, uCOSV252.EXE displays the screen shown in Figure F.2. Here you are asked to specify the folder (i.e., directory) where you want to install all the files for µC/OS-II. The default is to place the source tree on to your C:\ drive. You can specify other locations.

After making your selection (or if you accept the default location), press the Unzip button. After the file is unzipped, the message shown in Figure F.3 is displayed.

Figure F.2 Specify which folder.

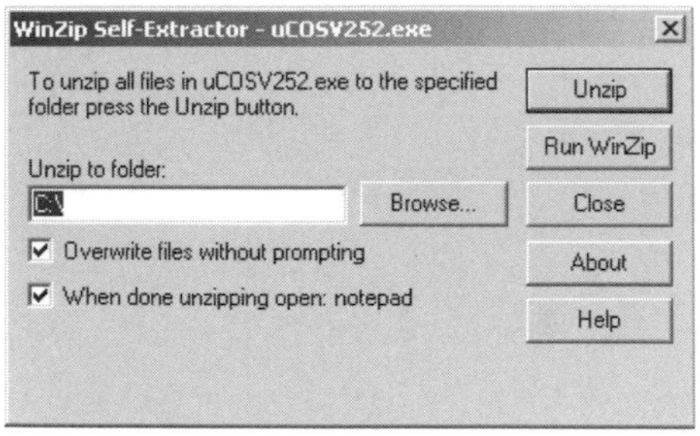

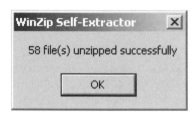

Figure F.3 Files unzipped message.

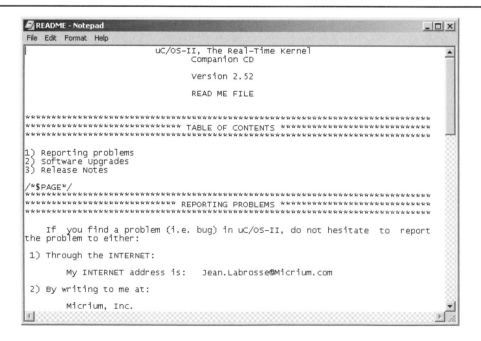

Press the OK button. Microsoft Notepad opens and shows you the contents of the `README.TXT` file, as shown in Figure F.4. From the File menu, choose close when you are done reading this file.

Figure F.4 `README.TXT`.

```
README - Notepad
File  Edit  Format  Help
                          uC/OS-II, The Real-Time Kernel
                                 Companion CD

                                 Version 2.52

                                 READ ME FILE

*****************************************************************************
****************************** TABLE OF CONTENTS ****************************
*****************************************************************************

1) Reporting problems
2) Software Upgrades
3) Release Notes

/*$PAGE*/
*****************************************************************************
***************************** REPORTING PROBLEMS ****************************
*****************************************************************************

    If  you find a problem (i.e. bug) in uC/OS-II, do not hesitate  to  report
the problem to either:

 1) Through the INTERNET:

        My INTERNET address is:   Jean.Labrosse@Micrium.com

 2) By writing to me at:

        Micrium, Inc.
```

F.1 *Files and Directories*

After the files are installed, your destination hard disk should contain the directories (folders) shown below. In fact, the CD also contains these folders and files.

\SOFTWARE — The main directory from the root where all µC/OS-II-related files are placed.

\SOFTWARE\TO — This directory contains the files for the TO utility (see Appendix D). The source file is TO.C, found in the \SOFTWARE\TO\SOURCE directory. The DOS executable file (TO.EXE) is in the \SOFTWARE\TO\EXE directory. Note that TO requires a file called TO.TBL, which must reside on your root directory. An example of TO.TBL is also found in the \SOFTWARE\TO\EXE directory. You need to move TO.TBL to the root directory to use TO.EXE.

\SOFTWARE\BLOCKS — The main directory where all building blocks are located. With µC/OS-II, I include a building block that handles PC-related functions used by the example code. The source files are PC.C and PC.H, found in the \SOFTWARE\BLOCKS\PC\BC45 directory.

\SOFTWARE\uCOS-II — The main directory where all µC/OS-II files are located.

\SOFTWARE\uCOS-II\DOC — This directory contains documentation files. Specifically, you will find:

README.TXT — This file is the README file for this release. When you first install µC/OS-II, you should see the contents of this file.

RevV252.PDF — This file contains the release notes for this release. You will need Adobe Acrobat Reader to view this file.

NewV252.PDF — This file contains the list of changes to µC/OS-II since the initial release of µC/OS-II (i.e., v2.00). Again, you will need to use Adobe Acrobat Reader.

QuickRefChartV252-Color.PDF — This file contains a quick reference chart for all the services provided by µC/OS-II. Again, you need to use Adobe Acrobat Reader. After the document is printed, you can either laminate it full size or fold the page in half and have a more compact reference chart.

TaskAssignmentWorksheet.PDF

TaskAssignmentWorksheet.XLS — These files allow you to list and organize your tasks. Again, you need to use Adobe Acrobat Reader. The .XLS file is a Microsoft Excel spreadsheet and can be used to create documentation for your application.

\SOFTWARE\uCOS-II\EX1_x86L\BC45 — This directory contains the source code for Example #1 (see Chapter 1), which is intended to run under DOS (or a DOS window under Microsoft Windows). The BC45 directory means that these files assume you have the Borland C/C++ compiler v4.5x. Of course, you could modify these files to use a different compiler if needed. You should find additional sub-directories under the BC45 directory. Each of the following directories contains four files as described below.

\SOURCE — INCLUDES.H — This file is the master include file used by µC/OS-II and the test code.

OS_CFG.H — This file is the µC/OS-II configuration file, which specifies which services you want to enable, how many tasks your application can have, and more.

TEST.C — This file is the test code for Example #1.

TEST.LNK — This file is the Turbo Assembler linker-command file and specifies which object files and libraries are used to make the final executable, TEST.EXE.

\TEST — MAKETEST.BAT is a DOS batch file that you need to execute to build the code for Example #1. MAKETEST.BAT assumes that you have the Borland MAKE utility present on your C: drive and in the C:\BC45\BIN directory. If your compiler is located in a different directory, you need to edit MAKETEST.BAT accordingly.

TEST.MAK — This file is a makefile that allows you to build the DOS executable TEST.EXE. TEST.MAK contains all the compiler, assembler, and linker commands to build TEST.EXE.

TEST.EXE — This file is the DOS executable for Example #1 that I built using my tools. You can execute this file in a DOS window under Microsoft Windows 95, 98, ME, NT, 2000, or XP.

TEST.MAP — This file is the linker MAP file.

\SOFTWARE\uCOS-II\EX2_x86L\BC45 — This directory contains the source code for Example #2 (see Chapter 1), which is intended to run under DOS (or a DOS window under Microsoft Windows). This directory is laid out exactly the same as EX1_x86L described previously. In other words, it contains files with identical names except that their contents are different.

\SOFTWARE\uCOS-II\EX3_x86L\BC45 — This directory contains the source code for Example #3 (see Chapter 1), which is intended to run under DOS (or a DOS window under Microsoft Windows). This directory is laid out exactly the same as EX1_x86L described previously. In other words, it contains files with identical names except that their contents are different.

\SOFTWARE\uCOS-II\EX4_x86L.FP\BC45 — This directory contains the source code for Example #4 (see Chapter 1), which is intended to run under DOS (or a DOS window under Microsoft Windows). This directory is laid out exactly the same as EX1_x86L described previously. In other words, it contains files with identical names except that their contents are different.

\SOFTWARE\uCOS-II\Ix86L\BC45 — This directory contains the source code for the processor-dependent code (also known as the port) of µC/OS-II for an 80x86 processor running in real-mode and compiled for the large model using the Borland C/C++ v4.5x compiler. This port also contains code to allow you to reentrantly use the floating-point emulation library provided with the Borland tools.

OS_CPU_A.ASM — This file contains the assembly language functions for the port. Specifically, this file contains OSStartHighRdy(), OSCtxSw(), OSIntCtxSw(), and OSTickISR().

OS_CPU_C.C — This file contains the C functions for the port.

OS_CPU.H — This file contains the C header for the port.

\SOFTWARE\uCOS-II\Ix86L-FP\BC45 — This directory contains the source code for the processor-dependent code (also known as the port) of µC/OS-II for an 80x86 processor running in real-mode and compiled for the large model using the Borland C/C++ v4.5x compiler. This port also makes use of the 80x86 processors that are equipped with a floating-point unit (FPU). In other words, tasks are able to use the FPU, and µC/OS-II saves the FPU registers during a context switch.

OS_CPU_A.ASM — This file contains the assembly language functions for the port. Specifically, this file contains OSStartHighRdy(), OSCtxSw(), OSIntCtxSw(), and OSTickISR().

OS_CPU_C.C — This file contains the C functions for the port.

OS_CPU.H — This file contains the C header for the port.

\SOFTWARE\uCOS-II\SOURCE — This directory contains the source code for the processor-independent portion of μC/OS-II. This code is fully portable to other processor architectures. This directory contains the following files:

OS_CORE.C	OS_FLAG.C
OS_MBOX.C	OS_MEM.C
OS_MUTEX.C	OS_Q.C
OS_SEM.C	OS_TASK.C
OS_TIME.C	uCOS_II.C
uCOS_II.H	

F

Index

Symbols

P

Z

EmbeddedSystems
P R O G R A M M I N G

Why Do Serious Embedded
Developers Read *Dr. Dobb's Journal?*

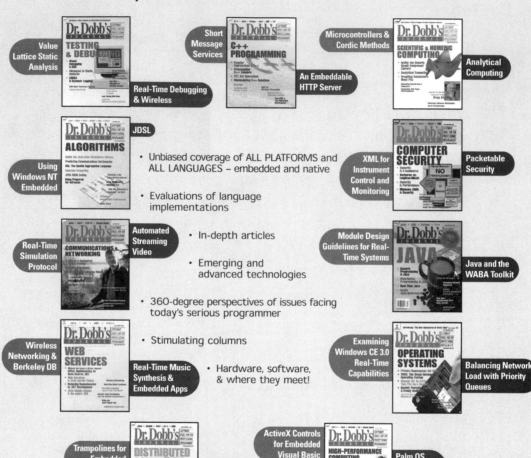

In each issue, serious developers depend on Dr. Dobb's Journal for an environment that is relevant, exciting and helpful to their jobs of creating unique and powerful software programs.

If your job demands a knowledge of emerging or advanced software technologies and tools, regardless of language or platform, embedded or native, you need to add Dr. Dobb's Journal to your toolbox.

To subscribe online using your
special embedded rate, go to:

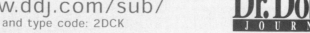

www.ddj.com/sub/

and type code: 2DCK

CMP
United Business Media

Dr. Dobb's
JOURNAL

SOFTWARE
TOOLS FOR THE
PROFESSIONAL
PROGRAMMER

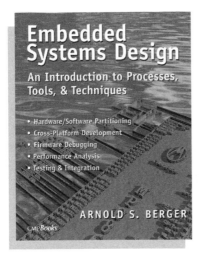

TCP/IP Lean
Web Servers for Embedded Systems
Second Edition

by Jeremy Bentham

Implement dynamic Web programming techniques with this hands-on guide to TCP/IP networking. You get source code and fully functional utilities for a simple TCP/IP stack that's efficient to use in embedded applications. This edition shows the Web server porting to the PIC16F877 chip as well as over an ethernet connection. Includes a demonstration port running on Microchip's PICDEM.net demonstration board. CD-ROM included, 559pp, ISBN 1-57820-108-X, $59.95

Practical Statecharts in C/C++
Quantum Programming for Embedded Systems

by Miro Samek

In the spirit of eXtreme programming, the author's quantum programming is a lightweight method that allows programmers to quickly hand-code working, real-time systems in C and C++ directly from UML statecharts. You get a cookbook with step-by-step instructions and complete source code to the state-oriented framework. CD-ROM included, 388pp, ISBN 1-57820-110-1, $44.95

What's on the CD-ROM?

The companion CD-ROM for *MicroC/OS-II, Second Edition,* contains all the source code for μC/OS-II and ports for the Intel 80x86 processor running in *real mode* and for the *large model.* The code was developed and executed on a PC running Microsoft Windows 2000, therefore it is assumed that you have a Microsoft Windows 95, 98, NT, 2000, or XP computer system, running on an 80x86, and Pentium-class, or AMD, processor. You should have at least 10MB of free disk space to install μC/OS-II and its source files on your system. Examples run in a DOS-compatible box under these environments. Development was done using the Borland International C/C++ compiler v4.51. Although μC/OS-II was developed and tested on a PC, μC/OS-II was actually targeted for embedded systems and can be ported easily to many different processor architectures.

The CD-ROM contains a self-extracting executable called `uCOSV252.EXE` as well as all files so that you can browse the CD without having to install anything on your computer.

**For more information on installation or specific files and directories on the CD,
see Appendix F.**